T0091857

SAP PRESS e-books

Print or e-book, Kindle or iPad, workplace or airplane: Choose
where and how to read your SAP PRESS books! You can now
get all our titles as e-books, too:

- By download and online access
- For all popular devices
- And, of course, DRM-free

Convinced? Then go to www.sap-press.com and get your
e-book today.

Financial Accounting with SAP S/4HANA®: Business User Guide

 **PRESS**

SAP PRESS is a joint initiative of SAP and Rheinwerk Publishing. The know-how offered by SAP specialists combined with the expertise of Rheinwerk Publishing offers the reader expert books in the field. SAP PRESS features first-hand information and expert advice, and provides useful skills for professional decision-making.

SAP PRESS offers a variety of books on technical and business-related topics for the SAP user. For further information, please visit our website: *www.sap-press.com*.

Janet Salmon, Stefan Walz
Controlling with SAP S/4HANA: Business User Guide
2021, 593 pages, hardcover and e-book
www.sap-press.com/5282

Mehta, Aijaz, Parikh, Chattopadhyay
SAP S/4HANA Finance: An Introduction (2nd Edition)
2023, 394 pages, hardcover and e-book
www.sap-press.com/5606

Anand Seetharaju, Mayank Sharma
General Ledger Accounting with SAP S/4HANA
2023, 886 pages, hardcover and e-book
www.sap-press.com/5630

Stoil Jotev
Asset Accounting with SAP S/4HANA
2020, 337 pages, hardcover and e-book
www.sap-press.com/5028

Stoil Jotev
Configuring SAP S/4HANA Finance (2nd Edition)
2021, 738 pages, hardcover and e-book
www.sap-press.com/5361

Jonas Tritschler, Stefan Walz, Reinhard Rupp, Nertila Mucka

Financial Accounting with SAP S/4HANA®: Business User Guide

Rheinwerk
Publishing

Editor Megan Fuerst
Copyeditor Julie McNamee
Cover Design Graham Geary
Photo Credit iStockphoto: 635978124/© Cecilie_Arcurs; 850496336/© MicroStockHub
Layout Design Vera Brauner
Production Hannah Lane
Typesetting III-satz, Germany
Printed and bound in Canada, on paper from sustainable sources

ISBN 978-1-4932-2431-9
© 2023 by Rheinwerk Publishing, Inc., Boston (MA)
2nd edition 2023

Library of Congress Cataloging-in-Publication Data
Names: Tritschler, Jonas, author. | Walz, Stefan, author. | Rupp, Reinhard,
  1953- author. | Mucka, Nertila, author.
Title: Financial accounting with SAP S/4HANA : business user guide / by
  Jonas Tritschler, Stefan Walz, Reinhard Rupp, Nertila Mucka.
Description: 2nd edition. | Bonn ; Boston : Rheinwerk Publishing, 2023.
Identifiers: LCCN 2023024406 | ISBN 9781493224319 (hardcover) | ISBN
  9781493224326 (ebook)
Subjects: LCSH: SAP HANA (Electronic resource) | Accounting--Computer
  programs.
Classification: LCC HF5679 .T75 2023 | DDC 657.0285/536--dc23/eng/20230627
LC record available at https://lccn.loc.gov/2023024406

Contents at a Glance

Dear Reader,

If you're relying on a map, it needs to be up to date.

My friend and I recently went on a hike at a remote preserve with gorgeous pine trees, challenging hills, and an unsurprising lack of cell service. We had a general familiarity with the area, having hiked there several years back, so we were feeling confident as we arrived. Snapping a photo of the map at the head of the trail, we began our hike toward a popular lookout point.

One hour later, and we were stopped in our tracks—the trail was blocked off. Two branching paths were available to us, neither of which were reflected on the map. After tossing the dice and choosing a direction, it took some time to realize we weren't making progress toward the lookout point. Another hour, and we threw in the towel. It was time to retrace our steps back to the start.

When you're navigating the branching pathways of your ERP system, having up-to-date guidance is just as important. In the SAP S/4HANA world, accountants need to know the best routes to complete their daily tasks. In this business user guide, you'll follow step-by-step instructions from the experts and explore all important transactions, apps, and reports that are featured in your daily work. Avoid the roadblocks and enjoy the view of the (system) landscape!

What did you think about *Financial Accounting with SAP S/4HANA: Business User Guide*? Your comments and suggestions are the most useful tools to help us make our books the best they can be. Please feel free to contact me and share any praise or criticism you may have.

Thank you for purchasing a book from SAP PRESS!

Megan Fuerst
Editor, SAP PRESS

meganf@rheinwerk-publishing.com
www.sap-press.com
Rheinwerk Publishing · Boston, MA

Contents

3   General Ledger Accounting   89

4 Accounts Payable

5   Accounts Receivable

6   Fixed Asset Accounting   389

7 Customer Project Accounting and Event-Based Revenue Recognition

Foreword

Digital transformation impacts all industries, and finance is the key enabler to support new business models in an intelligent ERP. Our customers want to get rid of painful, manual steps, and to do so, business processes must be fully integrated across the whole enterprise. Automation supported by intelligent technologies is key. For many of our customers, SAP S/4HANA is the gateway to digital transformation. As head of the SAP S/4HANA Finance development team, I am particularly pleased that, with this book, we get the opportunity to present the innovations and advantages of SAP S/4HANA financial and management accounting.

Always listening to our customers and partners, we leveraged the potential of the SAP HANA database to drive application innovations towards an intelligent enterprise. SAP HANA enabled us to rethink and redesign the finance application's architecture and business processes.

Also, we built the Universal Journal as the foundation for the new finance business architecture. Based on the Universal Journal, we redesigned business processes, built intelligent applications, enhanced functionality, simplified processes, and extended analysis capabilities.

By providing a single source of truth for financial and management accounting, the Universal Journal makes reconciliation between the general ledger and subledgers obsolete. It empowers us to replace period-end closing steps with true real-time and event-based valuation steps. This simplifies financial close and provides needed information in each process step. These innovations and the related business benefits are well illustrated in Chapter 7, which discusses the new project accounting in SAP S/4HANA Cloud.

In addition to insights into SAP S/4HANA Finance innovations, this book provides some background on how these innovations are embedded into SAP's cloud and on-premise strategy.

Finally, you receive a comprehensive step-by-step introduction to financial accounting, along with integrated business processes.

The book presented is the result of great teamwork. By bringing together expertise from SAP S/4HANA development with the perspective of end users and external auditors, this book provides a comprehensive view on innovations in the area of financial and management accounting. While Nertila Mucka and Jonas Tritschler provided their rich experience as auditors and end users, Reinhard Rupp added management and IT user perspective based on his many years of experience. To complete the team, Stefan Walz brought his rich finance experience gained in numerous customer engagements, always striving for real innovations alongside business processes.

This book helps you understand how SAP S/4HANA Finance improves your day-to-day processes and adds value to your overall business.

I congratulate the whole team for a great job!

Judith Pistor
Head of SAP S/4HANA Finance

Preface

Welcome to SAP S/4HANA financial accounting. With this book, we've provided step-by-step guidance for accounting professionals using SAP S/4HANA on a daily basis. We go through all the important ledgers—general ledger, accounts payable, accounts receivable, fixed assets—and give you insights on the new integration of management accounting and project accounting. Of course, we cover the new capabilities available for accounting through the Universal Journal, such as parallel ledgers, extension ledgers, multiple currencies, integrated market segment reporting, and integrated event-based revenue recognition (EBRR). With these innovations, we also want to draw your attention to where SAP S/4HANA financial accounting is heading. The deeper integration of financial applications simplifies accounting processes and enhances analysis options, but it certainly also has an impact on a company's organization. In addition, there is increased integration into business processes through innovations such as EBRR.

From a user perspective, we show both the SAP GUI way to display and process transactions as well as the SAP Fiori launchpad method.

The book covers the latest release for both on-premise SAP S/4HANA (2022) and SAP S/4HANA Cloud (2208).

Who This Book Is For

This book is for bookkeepers, accountants, and financial managers who are using SAP S/4HANA frequently to perform their work. With the new integration concept of financial accounting and management accounting, the book is also helpful for people working in management accounting and reporting. It's also recommended for people working hand in hand with accountants, such as those in sales, purchasing, or project management, to help them understand the full transactional end-to-end business process, including accounting and financial reporting. This information is particularly helpful in the case of an SAP S/4HANA implementation project.

How This Book Is Organized

This book is divided into seven chapters. After an introduction to SAP S/4HANA in Chapter 1, we dive into the accounting structure and innovations of SAP S/4HANA financial accounting in Chapter 2. Chapter 3 to Chapter 6 contains straightforward, step-by-step guidance for handling bookkeeping and accounting tasks within your organization. Chapter 7 is an excursion into the new project accounting in SAP S/4HANA Cloud, public edition and the innovation of EBRR.

Let's take a brief look at what is covered in each chapter of this book:

- **Chapter 1: Introduction to SAP S/4HANA**
  This chapter provides an introduction to SAP S/4HANA, starting with an explanation of the deployment models with a focus on the main differences between the on-premise and cloud solutions. In addition, the chapter gives insights into the Universal Journal, which is the common data basis for accounting as a single source of truth. Later, the chapter describes user simplifications and new functionalities in accounting thanks to the new technical architecture of SAP S/4HANA. The chapter closes by illustrating the available user interfaces (UIs) to work with the system.

- **Chapter 2: Organizational Structure and Integration**
  This chapter provides some financial accounting foundation information. It's important to recognize this information in the implementation phase because SAP S/4HANA accounting is integrated in almost all business scenarios, such as purchasing and sales. We explain the organizational elements of financial accounting and the assignment of the main organizational elements of logistics to accounting. We explain the central financial accounting settings and their innovations coming with the Universal Journal; for example, there are now new options for the ledger setup. Management accounting is now part of the Universal Journal and thus part of the general ledger. We cover how this is implemented in the system and how it impacts the accountant's work.

- **Chapter 3: General Ledger Accounting**
  This chapter is about general ledger accounting and marks the beginning of the step-by-step guidance of accounting in SAP S/4HANA. Before starting on processing transactions, we provide instructions on how master data is set up. You'll first become familiar with the general ledger accounts, charts of accounts, and financial statement structure standing and configurational data, before entering a journal entry. You'll also learn about processing bank statements, reconciling accounts, closing periods, and reporting from the general ledger. In this second edition, we'll provide deeper insight into the possibilities of parallel accounting based on the Universal Journal. In particular, we'll look at a new development, called universal parallel accounting. We've also added instructions for using the SAP Financial Closing cockpit for SAP S/4HANA to better manage the closing activities in chronological order.

- **Chapter 4: Accounts Payable**
  This chapter provides all the required knowledge to manage and process the accounts payable subledger in SAP S/4HANA as well as the integration of accounts payable into the purchase-to-pay process. We provide you with all the transactions you should know to create suppliers, process incoming invoices and credit notes, perform payments, and reconcile the accounts payable with the general ledger. Another important discussion covers the famous goods receipt/invoice receipt (GR/IR) clearing account. We end this chapter by explaining which period-closing activities

are required, and we show the most important reporting capabilities of this sub-ledger.

- **Chapter 5: Accounts Receivable**
This chapter focuses on the functions and activities of the accounts receivable sub-ledger as part of the order-to-cash business process. Here we explain the most relevant transactions to create and change customer master data as well as the transactions to record documents and further process them. We show you how to post invoices, down payment notes, credit memos, and payments, and we show you how to clear open items. We also give insight into how the down payment process and the dunning process are conceived in SAP S/4HANA. Accounts receivable period-end closing and reporting activities are essential elements discussed at the end of this chapter.

- **Chapter 6: Fixed Asset Accounting**
In this chapter, we present the concept of fixed asset accounting. We explain all activities to manage the whole lifecycle of a fixed asset from an accounting perspective. The asset lifecycle embraces the acquisition, capitalization, depreciation, revaluation, and disposal steps. We also discuss how the fixed assets subledger is attached to the general ledger and how integration with the purchase-to-pay process works. In the end, we show the period-end closing steps and explain the most important reporting activities.

- **Chapter 7: Customer Project Accounting and Event-Based Revenue Recognition**
In this chapter, we demonstrate an end-to end customer project scenario. You'll see how applications described in the previous chapters play together. You'll get first-hand insight into SAP S/4HANA Cloud, public edition, with its new applications built on SAP Fiori UI technology. In this second edition, we'll also take a deeper look at the Universal Journal's integrated EBRR functionality, which has been continuously expanded in recent releases. We'll also show how the potential of the Universal Journal, with its innovations combined with the SAP HANA database, can be leveraged by accountants. Concrete examples for period-end simplification and fascinating new analytical insights round out the book.

SAP Fiori Apps

Throughout this book, our default instructions are via the SAP GUI interface. However, at the end of each section, you can find a text box explaining whether there is a corresponding SAP Fiori app. If so, you can find the instructions for using the SAP Fiori interface method there.

For each task that has a corresponding SAP Fiori app, we will also provide the SAP Fiori ID in parentheses. You can use this ID to find the app on the SAP Fiori apps reference library at *http://s-prs.co/v493800*.

Acknowledgments

We, the authors, would like to express our sincere gratitude to the SAP PRESS team in Boston/Quincy. In the first line, our thanks go to Emily Nicholls. She is the one who motivated us to write this book. The discussions with Emily had a big impact on the structure and the scope of this book. Another big thank you goes to Megan Fuerst. Megan accompanied us during the writing and editing phase of this work. Her excellent reviews and comments have increased the quality of this book noticeably. You both—Emily and Megan—did a fantastic job!

Last but not least, we are grateful to our families and friends, who understood the lack of free time during this venture. They kept our backs clear from troubles as much as possible. Thank you all again!

Conclusion

Reading this book will provide you with a comprehensive overview of SAP S/4HANA financial accounting. This hands-on, step-by-step guide will help you process the most common accounting transactions for your daily usage and serve as your foundational knowledge source. In addition, we'll highlight important innovations and the direction in which SAP S/4HANA accounting is moving, including key simplifications (especially for closing processes), deeper integration, and expanded reporting possibilities.

Jump into Chapter 1 now to get an informative overview of SAP S/4HANA.

Chapter 1

Introduction to SAP S/4HANA

*Before we dive into your financial accounting tasks, it's important to
look at the system in which you'll be working: SAP S/4HANA. Understanding its features, simplifications, and innovations, as well as how to
interact with the system, is key to making the most of the suite.*

This chapter introduces the SAP S/4HANA suite from the user's perspective, explaining
the deployment models, architecture, and simplifications of SAP S/4HANA compared
to SAP Business Suite (SAP ERP 6.0). The extensibility features for SAP customers and
SAP partners are also covered in this chapter to help you see what's possible for adopting
business-specific requirements. This chapter ends by showing the interfaces through
which users interact with SAP S/4HANA.

1.1 Deployment Models

SAP S/4HANA is offered in several deployment models, which can be operated in different ways by different providers. It's not always easy to distinguish these options, so
let's take some time to differentiate them.

Irrespective of whether the software is operated in a cloud or not, the basic difference is
whether the software is the SAP S/4HANA Cloud solution or the on-premise SAP S/4HANA
solution. However, all members of the SAP S/4HANA product family are based on the
same program code. Therefore, a combination—in the sense of parallel operation—of
both versions or with other cloud solutions is possible (*hybrid models*).

In the following sections, we'll take a closer look at these three possible solutions.

1.1.1 On-Premise SAP S/4HANA

With the on-premise edition, you can operate SAP S/4HANA in your own data center
and in your own system landscape. You're then responsible for purchasing the hardware, and installing, administering, and maintaining the software by importing the
software changes.

As with the SAP ERP solution, you can outsource on-premise SAP S/4HANA and operate it in a private cloud. The large providers (also called *hyperscalers*)—Amazon Web Services (AWS), Google Cloud, and Microsoft (Azure)—offer the following operating models:

- **Infrastructure as a service (IaaS)**
  This service contains the hardware, backup, storage, and database.

- **Platform as a service (PaaS)**
  This service contains IaaS, operating systems, application frameworks, and a deployment platform for software development. Thus, the customer can concentrate on the deployment of the application.

- **Software as a service (SaaS)**
  This service contains the running application, which is only used by the customer. Therefore, the provider performs updates and maintenance.

Note

With on-premise SAP S/4HANA, SAP follows an annual innovation cycle. At the time of writing (summer 2023), the latest release is 2022, which is what will be covered in this book.

Because you or a provider on your behalf always operates on-premise SAP S/4HANA, this solution also offers a certain degree of flexibility for a customer's individual process setup and the rhythm of applying the SAP release updates. This is the main difference from SAP S/4HANA Cloud and is described next.

1.1.2   SAP S/4HANA Cloud: Public and Private Edition

In SAP S/4HANA Cloud, the software is operated and maintained by SAP. The customer accesses their SAP S/4HANA Cloud application with a browser from any network via the Internet and a unique customer-specific URL.

The key features of this solution in comparison to on-premise SAP S/4HANA are as follows:

- **Licensing model**
  Subscription licensing is used.

- **Infrastructure and maintenance**
  SAP is responsible.

- **Customization**
  Although customization is possible to some extent, there is far less flexibility compared to on-premise SAP S/4HANA.

- **Implementation**
  Implementation is faster through a ready-made platform with guided configuration. There is no option to change SAP code to make it customer specific.

- **Upgrades and support packages**
  These are managed by SAP on a regular basis.

- **Scope**
  The customer is also restricted by the fact that the complete on-premise scope isn't available.

However, the total cost of ownership (TCO) and total cost of implementation (TCI) are reduced dramatically. After the customer has selected the scope, the best practice content is deployed, and the selected business scenarios are available out of the box. Automatic updates of legal changes are ensured by a quarterly software update, which also includes the latest innovations.

There are two options for using SAP S/4HANA Cloud:

- **SAP S/4HANA Cloud, public edition**
  In this option, you have the full cloud approach in a SaaS offering. The infrastructure in the public cloud is shared with other customers, hosted and operated by SAP only. The upgrades are fixed and mandatory, managed by SAP. The user interface (UI) is purely SAP Fiori. Configuration is done using SAP Central Business Configuration and not with the Implementation Guide (IMG). The functionality for the different business scenarios is predefined by best practice content. The public edition is mainly used in a greenfield scenario. New customers mainly choose this deployment model (GROW with SAP).

- **SAP S/4HANA Cloud, private edition**
  In this option, SAP operates a dedicated cloud infrastructure that runs via a hyperscaler (e.g., Microsoft Azure, AWS, Google Cloud). Here you have the advantage of the cloud with the scope and flexibility of the on-premise solution. The customer has to manage the upgrade process and may choose his own upgrade rhythm. SAP takes care of the specific technical aspects of the upgrade only. Existing SAP ERP customers can move to SAP S/4HANA Cloud using different transformation services (RISE with SAP).

Note

Rise with SAP and *Grow with SAP* are offerings that guide customers on their digital transformation journey and bring them to the cloud. Both offerings are based on SAP S/4HANA Cloud and SAP Business Technology Platform (SAP BTP). While Grow with SAP addresses customers with no enterprise resource planning (ERP) system implemented, Rise with SAP addresses customers who are already working with an ERP system and who want to expand. Grow with SAP focuses on SAP S/4HANA Cloud, public edition. Rise with SAP offers capabilities for both SAP S/4HANA Cloud, public edition and SAP S/4HANA Cloud, private edition.

1.1.3 Hybrid Models

Because on-premise SAP S/4HANA and SAP S/4HANA Cloud are on the same program code and the same development level, both solutions can work on parallel operations very well with each other. In a typical application scenario, subsidiaries, for example, can be connected via the cloud with the on-premise edition in the parent company's data center. Further deployment scenarios are possible if certain business units in a broadly based group have specific requirements. These requirements can be implemented in a separate application and at the same time be integrated into the group as a whole.

However, hybrid solutions are particularly suitable if further cloud applications are to be combined either with on-premise SAP S/4HANA or with SAP S/4HANA Cloud. This applies in particular to SAP's complementary cloud applications:

- SAP Ariba
- SAP Concur
- SAP Fieldglass
- SAP SuccessFactors

1.2 Universal Journal

The Universal Journal can undoubtedly be described as the heart of SAP S/4HANA—at least from an accountant's point of view. It offers the potential for a drastic simplification of processes in financial accounting and management accounting while simultaneously increasing the reporting functionality. A look at the historical evolution of the accounting application helps illustrate the dimensions of this significant enhancement of the SAP application landscape (see Figure 1.1).

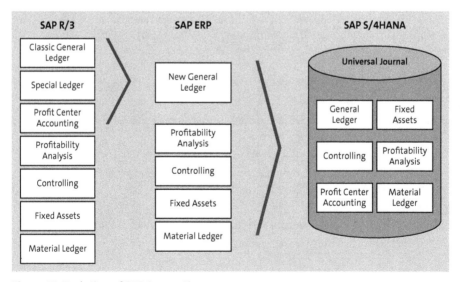

Figure 1.1 Evolution of SAP Accounting

While in SAP R/3, the various tasks in Management Accounting (CO) and Financial Accounting (FI) were handled by special modules with their respective data structures, the new general ledger in SAP ERP already provided a certain simplification and consolidation. SAP S/4HANA accounting takes the radical step of integrating all financial applications and their requirements into one common data model. We'll take a closer look at the key features of the Universal Journal in the following sections.

1.2.1   Single Source of Truth

Before we take a closer look at this topic, Figure 1.2 provides an overview of the various characteristics of the Universal Journal.

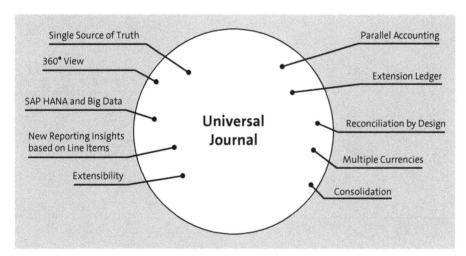

Figure 1.2 Key Characteristics of the Universal Journal

We'll discuss the individual characteristics in more detail throughout this chapter. For now, let's just look at the single source of truth, which we see in contrast to the often-quoted single *point* of truth.

In the past, the various data structures and applications required a great deal of reconciliation work, for example, to show identical sales revenues and operating results in CO and FI in SAP ERP. The goal was to achieve a single point of truth, which could only be accomplished through hard work. With the Universal Journal in SAP S/4HANA, this goal is already reached at the starting point, so that you actually have a single source of truth that makes the reconciliation work obsolete.

The features of the Universal Journal are summarized as follows:

- Data is presented in a common structure to make comparisons easier.
- All required currencies are provided.
- A 360-degree view is presented for objects of interest (profit and loss [P&L] + balance sheet + key performance indicators [KPIs]).

- Ad hoc group reporting is possible with views of unconsolidated and consolidated figures.

- With real-time reporting, up-to-date figures are available at every point in time.

- A full audit trail is provided.

- Legal requirements from a local and a group perspective are fulfilled.

- The basis for management reporting at every needed granularity is given and can be easily enhanced via extension fields and extension ledgers.

1.2.2 One Database and One Data Model for Accounting

As Figure 1.3 illustrates in another form, the previous data sets for the general ledger, profitability analysis, management accounting, asset accounting, and the material ledger are now integrated into one data model.

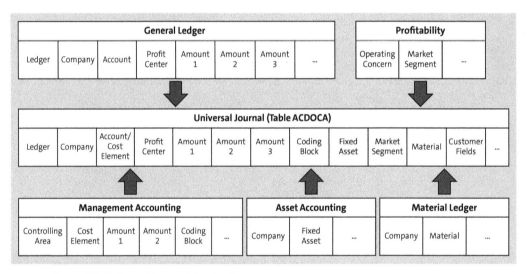

Figure 1.3 Universal Journal Application

This data model is then integrated into an extremely large database, as a single Universal Journal entry can have (technically) up to 999,999 line items with little or no need for summarization, depending on data volume.

This structure offers the following benefits:

- One journal entry line item is used with full details for all applications.

- Instant insight and easy extensibility are provided.

- Data is stored only once, reducing the memory footprint and resulting in no redundancy.

- No data transfer (e.g., settlement) between applications is required at period end.

- One data model is used for all applications. For example, now the general ledger account specifies the type of expense only—value field (profitability analysis) and revenue recognition secondary cost elements (results analysis) are no longer available. Secondary cost elements are now general ledger accounts.

- All universal entities are now potentially available for all applications. For example, the market segment attributes of the profitability analysis application are now available for other processes too, and the ledger is available in management accounting.

- Fast multidimensional reporting is available without replicating to SAP Business Warehouse (SAP BW).

1.2.3   Enhanced Reporting

The strength of SAP S/4HANA from the in-memory technology is clearly reflected in the fundamental shift in the reporting paradigm due to the Universal Journal. Let's look at the most important aspects here:

- **Journal entry item reporting**
  With the Universal Journal, SAP S/4HANA allows reporting based on single journal entry items. SAP S/4HANA can aggregate millions of lines very efficiently on the fly. Because the Universal Journal line items contain the full details, including customer extension fields, many of the detailed fields previously available in subsidiary ledger tables are now available in the single consolidated journal entry table ACDOCA.

  In addition to the still-available SAP ERP standard reports, there are new reports and SAP Fiori apps that query table ACDOCA to provide a much more flexible way of reporting data. It's not necessary to predefine the reports because they are now live, allowing users to include additional fields and drill down to the details.

  You can use any combination of filter criteria out of the Universal Journal to narrow down the results. Unlike in SAP ERP, it's no longer necessary to define and hit a database index or even aggregated data in your own database tables. In addition, with the new SAP Fiori accounting journal entry item UIs, you can select a specific line item from billions of records in table ACDOCA in less than one second.

- **Real-time data availability**
  With this real-time replication approach, there is no need to replicate data asynchronously to a data warehouse. As far as the data from SAP S/4HANA is concerned, business warehouses are obsolete.

- **Evaluation options**
  The Universal Journal also opens up improved evaluation options for external and internal auditors. The audit trail can start at the balance sheet item and go all the way down to the source document.

- **360-degree view for cost objects and market segments**
  The integration concept of the Universal Journal also opens up extended possibilities for financial reporting in accounting. Information that in SAP ERP could only be generated in conjunction with the CO module is now directly available in detail.

One example is the detailed work in progress (WIP) drilldown and the breakdown by market segment. A detailed description of these possibilities can be found in Chapter 7, Section 7.1.7. There, you'll also find a concrete example of the WIP drilldown by market segment.

- **Extensibility**

  In SAP ERP, the functionality and reporting were based on totals tables with the limitation of 16 key fields. That led to the necessity to install several special purpose ledgers (FI-SL) containing different sets of extension fields. With the line item–based architecture in SAP S/4HANA, all extension fields can be put in the central journal entry item table ACDOCA.

  As you can see in Figure 1.4, there are two options available for extensibility:

  - Coding block extension: Used for fields filled by users during document entry. Process integration transports the fields to the Universal Journal.
  - Extension inside table ACDOCA: Ideal for fields derived from other fields of table ACDOCA or from master data. Many table ACDOCA extension fields are possible. Technically, there are two solutions (business contexts) available: journal entry item and margin analysis extensibility.

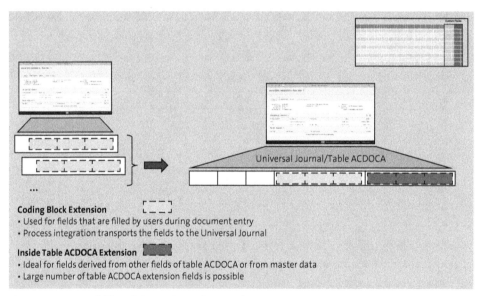

Figure 1.4 Extensibility of the Universal Journal

The dark-gray fields illustrate the possibility of defining additional fields directly in table ACDOCA and enable derivation logic to fill them for the relevant journal entries. Sources for derivation logic can be other table ACDOCA fields or master data fields, which are used in the journal entry document (e.g., sales order). The light-gray fields show the possibility that additional fields can be filled during document entry. All transactions supporting the coding block will allow the extensibility attribute to be maintained (e.g., supplier invoice, management accounting activity allocation).

All released extensibility fields automatically enhance core data services (CDS) views that are dependent on table ACDOCA (Universal Journal); thus, these fields automatically are available in new Universal Journal reporting.

1.3   Simplifications and Innovations

The introduction of the Universal Journal in the previous section already showed that this concept leads to a reduction of complexities in the system and thus to strong simplifications. On the other hand, it opens up the potential for innovations, which are continuously delivered.

In the following sections, these simplifications are outlined while showing that specific accounting requirements can still be met. The minimized reconciliation effort is a significant simplification; customer-specific requirements can be covered by extension ledgers and special ledgers without breaking up the integration concept of the Universal Journal. In addition, the year-end process has been greatly simplified and made more manageable. However, note that the data model for management accounting has now been integrated.

1.3.1   Minimized Reconciliations

As we discussed in Section 1.2.1 and referred to as the single source of truth, the integration concept of the Universal Journal minimizes the reconciliation work between the different ledgers. The process steps in period-close that performed the settlement between the applications are no longer necessary. All applications use the same entities and data structure, so they speak the same "language" in principle, which ensures that the values of the different applications are analyzable together.

This simplification can't be overestimated, but it does come at a cost. We show an example for the customer project scenario in Chapter 7. With the introduction of the Universal Journal and, for example, the switch from SAP ERP to SAP S/4HANA, the previous data structures and processes must be changed, which might require a big effort. If carefully planned and implemented with discipline, the advantages that accompany these new possibilities will soon justify the investment.

1.3.2   Extension Ledger versus Special Ledger

SAP S/4HANA accounting features a new extension ledger that stores only delta journal entries posted specifically to the extension ledger. Reporting on the extension ledger always includes the extension ledger reporting plus the data of the underlying standard ledger. In the overview of the special ledger and extension ledger principles shown in Figure 1.5, you can see that the special ledger in SAP Business Suite led to high data redundancy.

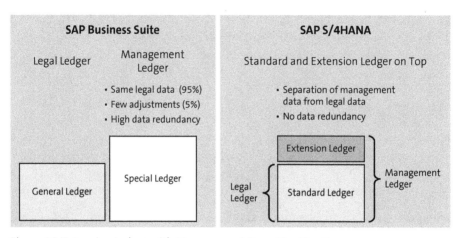

Figure 1.5 Extension Ledger with Management Reporting Use Case

In the extension ledger scenario, the common journal entry data is provided in the standard ledger. Only the adoption postings are done in the extension ledger, assuming that all postings in the underlying standard ledger are also available for reports of the extension ledger. Therefore, every extension ledger needs an assignment to a standard ledger. For more details, see our discussion of extension ledgers in Chapter 2, Section 2.2.3.

1.3.3   Simplified Period-End Close

As you know, day-to-day business keeps the accountant busy, but the critical days are the closing period, no matter whether it's a month-end, quarter-end, or year-end closing. Very tight schedules and high visibility for top management and the financial world characterize this process. SAP S/4HANA also brings decisive improvements here.

The architecture and the integration concept of SAP S/4HANA offer advantages that automatically affect the closing process. This concerns both the simplifications with the reconciliation work and the increased speed due to in-memory technology. Allocations, assessments, and other traditionally long-running batch jobs are much faster in SAP S/4HANA. For example, depreciations are now updated in real time. You also can see financial statements on the fly throughout the period.

In addition, transfers to SAP BW are also omitted. The effects of postings in period-end closing can be seen directly in reporting, as time-consuming iterations with SAP BW are no longer necessary.

Furthermore, there are now event-based closing postings—for example, event-based revenue recognition (EBRR; see Chapter 7, Section 7.2)—which brings parts of the period-end closing forward.

Now, let's explore SAP's main offerings for period-end close.

Financial Closing Cockpit

Another significant improvement affects the visibility and control of the whole process through a new dashboard, called the *SAP Financial Closing cockpit for SAP S/4HANA*.

The SAP Financial Closing cockpit is part of the SAP S/4HANA core system and is available in the on-premise edition. As shown in Figure 1.6, there has been a constant evolution of this application, from the plain Schedule Manager to a widely connected application.

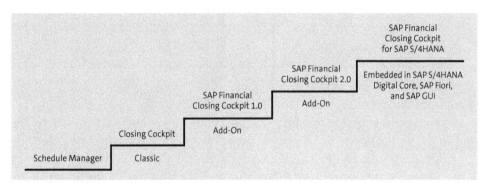

Figure 1.6 SAP Financial Closing Cockpit Evolution

You can access the SAP Financial Closing cockpit for SAP S/4HANA via **SAP Menu • Cross-Application Components • SAP S/4HANA Financial Closing Cockpit** (see Figure 1.7).

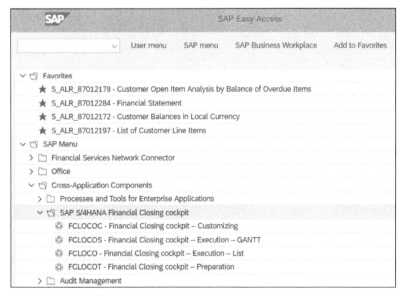

Figure 1.7 SAP S/4HANA Financial Closing Cockpit

Let's take a quick look at the key features of this cockpit. The SAP Financial Closing cockpit for SAP S/4HANA supports companies in planning, executing, monitoring, and analyzing financial closing tasks not only for a single company or legal entity but also for the entire group of companies. It offers error tracking, real-time status updates, automated processes, plan-to-actual comparison, process standardization, and easily accessible audit trails.

The functions and benefits of the tool depend on your respective role, as described here:

- **Member of the finance team**
  As a member of the finance team, you can execute tasks, marking the actual completion times and other issues. These tasks can be manual program tasks or batch job tasks. Regarding a manual task, you can drill down directly from the closing cockpit to the transaction (e.g., booking an accrual). After completion of the task, an email is sent to a colleague, who executes a dependent task. This accelerates the process and improves communication within the team.

- **Finance manager**
  As a finance manager, you have predefined templates for monthly, quarterly, and annual closing processes that you can use to list and plan all closing tasks. The cockpit also allows you to identify the critical path of the different tasks to monitor the completion of these tasks and to resolve issues. With the SAP Financial Closing cockpit for SAP S/4HANA, you can analyze the entire closing process and make changes to the plan for the next close. To control the process, the cockpit provides KPI analytical apps that provide progress updates for the process. These KPIs are also running on the group level, so you can analyze and compare different entities and identify best practices across the group.

In summary, the SAP Financial Closing cockpit for SAP S/4HANA offers a powerful tool to manage the closing cycle and provides visibility to the entire enterprise on the status and progress of the different activities during the closing period. In Figure 1.8, we give an example of task **29 Physical Inventory**. Note that the activity hasn't yet started and that a note is pending as a task.

There also some other new features:

- **Soft close**
  You can access a financial snapshot of the close process prior to the "official" close. Via SAP Fiori apps, you can pull a trial balance on the fly to get instant P&L insights.

- **Balance carryforward**
  After the close of the financial year, the ending balance must be carried forward to the beginning balance of the new fiscal year. Previously, no documents were created, but in SAP S/4HANA, an audit trail can be seen. Balance carryforward documents are stored within the Universal Journal with the document status **C** for carryforward.

The SAP Financial Closing cockpit for SAP S/4HANA is thus very well suited to support the closing process in plain corporate structures, which we'll describe in more detail in Chapter 3. Nevertheless, there's also a new application that is technologically positioned in a different way for supporting the closing process, which we'll discuss next.

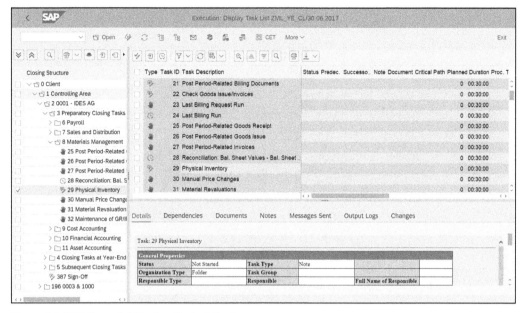

Figure 1.8 SAP Financial Closing Cockpit Tasks

Advanced Financial Closing

With SAP S/4HANA Cloud for advanced financial closing, SAP offers a cloud hub that orchestrates the entity close across a landscape of on-premise or cloud systems. The system is therefore suitable for effectively and efficiently supporting complex corporate and group structures in the closing process. Tasks from different application systems and from teams in different time zones can be organized in a standalone platform.

Figure 1.9 gives an idea of the data flow between SAP S/4HANA Cloud for advanced financial closing and different backend accounting systems.

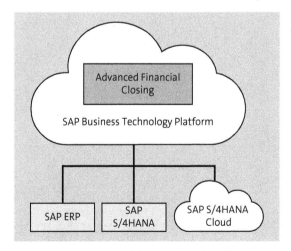

Figure 1.9 Data Flow with SAP S/4HANA Cloud for Advanced Financial Closing

In the Financial Close Overview app, a **Global Dashboard** provides an overview of the status of the closing process and the status of the various tasks. Key reporting metrics and drilldowns to the task level allow you to take immediate action.

The preceding brief descriptions of the SAP Financial Closing cockpit for SAP S/4HANA and SAP S/4HANA Cloud for advanced financial closing illustrate SAP's efforts with SAP S/4HANA to shift the benefit for users from processing operational transactions to controlling and monitoring reporting processes.

1.3.4   Management Accounting Integration

As already mentioned, the Universal Journal leads to a complete integration of management accounting with financial accounting. However, the management accounting processes are still running. Figure 1.10 shows the **SAP Menu** illustrating that the classic tasks of management accounting and controlling (e.g., cost element accounting, cost center accounting, product cost controlling, etc.) are still performed separately in the system.

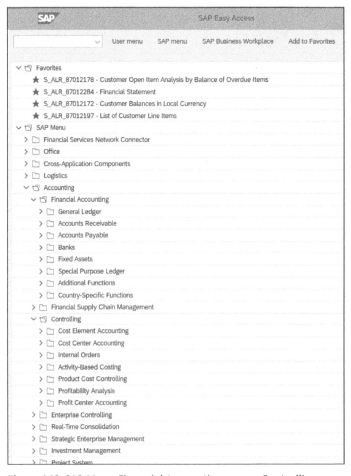

Figure 1.10 SAP Menu Financial Accounting versus Controlling

The integration concept rather refers to the fact that a consistent database has now been created with the Universal Journal, whereby this database serves as a common basis for financial accounting and management accounting.

You can see this best from the fact that the cost elements are now general ledger accounts, and this applies to the primary cost elements as well as to the secondary cost elements. All management accounting postings—such as cost center allocations—are now posted as journal entry items in the Universal Journal and subsequently are reflected in the general ledger. Therefore, reporting on secondary management accounting postings can be done with general ledger reporting.

As already mentioned, this integration concept of the Universal Journal is expanded by the extension fields and the extension ledgers. These enhancement options also provide additional flexibility in implementing special requirements in management accounting.

1.3.5   Parallel Accounting and Currencies

The Universal Journal allows multiple ledgers per company code, which enables parallel accounting. Parallel accounting allows businesses to maintain multiple accounting principles or standards for financial reporting, such as local Generally Accepted Accounting Principles (GAAP) and International Financial Reporting Standards (IFRS). Parallel accounting also allows posting of transactions in multiple ledgers, with each ledger representing a different accounting principle. It also ensures consistency and accuracy of financial data across all accounting principles. Finally, you can produce financial statements according to relevant accounting principles.

As a functional enhancement, universal parallel accounting is now available, which provides ledger-dependent valuation of all financial applications such as controlling and fixed assets, as discussed in Chapter 3.

SAP has further developed working with up to 10 different currencies in parallel. Companies can maintain several currencies in their system and post transactions in multiple currencies simultaneously. This allows for easy reporting and compliance with local accounting requirements.

1.3.6   Predictive Accounting

SAP S/4HANA includes a new function called predictive accounting, which uses the contract data of sales orders or purchase orders to provide information about expected costs and revenues and help companies make more informed decisions. One key feature, for example, is predictive forecasting. Companies can use predictive models to forecast future business performance, such as sales revenue, cash flow, or inventory levels. Through integration with other SAP modules, such as controlling and sales distribution, the system can provide a holistic view of business processes and performance.

1.3.7   Event-Based Revenue Recognition

Event-based revenue recognition (EBRR) enables companies to recognize revenue for goods and services based on specific events or milestones, rather than with billing. This means that revenue can be recognized as soon as specific events or milestones occur, such as delivery of a product or a cost-based percentage of completion. The function is particularly useful for companies in industries such as construction and professional services. Therefore, EBRR can help companies improve their financial reporting and compliance with accounting standards, while also providing greater visibility and control over their revenue recognition process. In addition to covering legal requirements, EBRR also provides a wide range of management accounting features. Of course, EBRR is based on the Universal Journal. It has been continuously expanded over the last releases and now also has a relevant functional footprint in on-premise SAP S/4HANA. We'll cover EBRR in more detail in Chapter 7, Section 7.2.

1.4   User Interfaces

SAP offers various UIs for SAP S/4HANA. However, a distinction must also be made between SAP S/4HANA Cloud and on-premise SAP S/4HANA. In the following sections, we'll give insights into the different possibilities.

1.4.1   SAP GUI

For on-premise SAP S/4HANA, SAP continues to offer classic access via SAP GUI, which must be installed locally on the computer. Figure 1.11 shows the access screen, where you enter your **User** ID and **Password**.

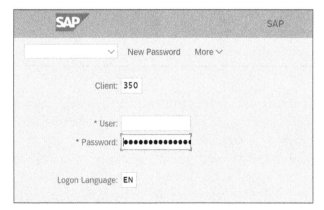

Figure 1.11 SAP GUI Login

After you're in the system, it's irrelevant whether the access was made with SAP GUI or with the web GUI. The old SAP GUI may be a bit more familiar and practical because you can start it directly from your PC. From a company's point of view, SAP GUI can also be advantageous because employees don't need access to the internet and can work only in the company network.

1.4.2   Web GUI

An easier and more convenient alternative is access via the web GUI. All you need here is a browser, the URL, and access authorization. This access is also possible via mobile devices.

The login screen for the web GUI is shown in Figure 1.12. Here, you enter your **User** name/**Password** and choose your **Language**.

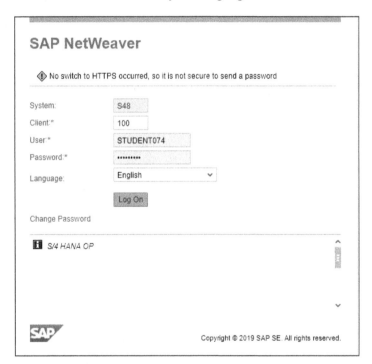

Figure 1.12 SAP Web GUI Login

After logging in, you'll see the **SAP Menu** in the traditional list form, as shown in Figure 1.13.

Figure 1.13 SAP Web GUI Menu

1.4.3 SAP Fiori

An important component of SAP S/4HANA is the completely redesigned user experience. This replaces the traditional transaction codes of the SAP GUI with a web-based UI.

The login page shown in Figure 1.14 immediately boosts the expectation that you're about to access a new SAP world. After the login, you're greeted by a visually designed UI that allows a very intuitive use of the various functions (see Figure 1.15).

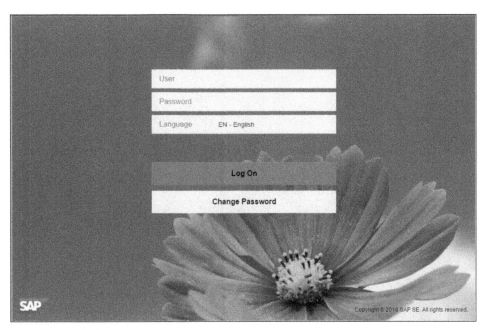

Figure 1.14 SAP Fiori Login

Figure 1.15 SAP Fiori Home Screen

The SAP Fiori **Home** screen, as shown in Figure 1.15, gives you an overview of all available apps grouped by categories (e.g., **Financial Accounting**) and with the possibility to work with the search function.

The **Edit Hompage** function enables you to design your individual workspace. This allows the concrete role and working environment of the respective user to be taken into account. The user will be assigned to business roles, such as general ledger accountant. To the business roles, specific apps are assigned. Tiles for apps that are specific to your business role appear when you access the system, as shown in Figure 1.16.

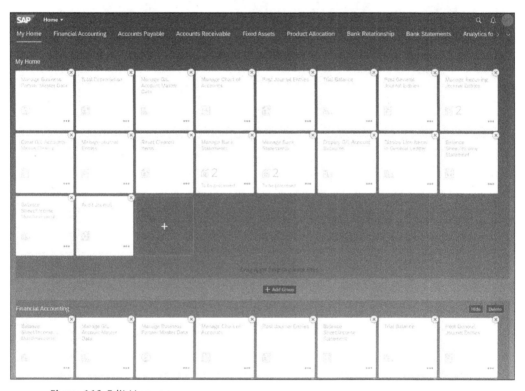

Figure 1.16 Edit Homepage

However, functionality is more important than visual design. With SAP Fiori, SAP offers ready-to-use apps that make your work easier and provide additional insights.

The SAP Fiori apps reference library provides information about and access to the constantly growing number of apps for different purposes and application environments. Thousands of apps are categorized by line of business, role, industry, application component, and technology/product version. You can access the SAP Fiori apps reference library at *http://s-prs.co/v493801*.

For users who work in the system, the **App Finder**, as shown in Figure 1.17, offers a practical way to find the apps available for their task area.

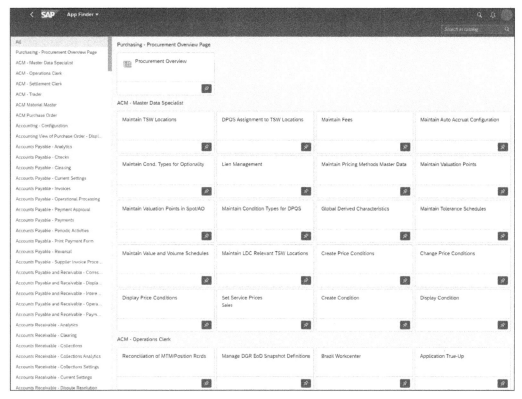

Figure 1.17 App Finder

Regarding the function of the apps, SAP offers the following three types:

- **Transactional apps**

  These apps are used to perform business process transactions or maintain master data. Example apps are Post General Journal Entry, Manage Supplier Invoice, Manage Cost Center, and Post Activity Allocation, which we'll discuss in later chapters.

  The master data transactional apps are especially important because they provide a more user-friendly way of reviewing, creating, and changing master data by downloading and uploading. Many approval apps are personalized to the specific user and offer the ability to review, confirm, or reject documents when the user has the approver role (e.g., the time sheet approval in the project manager role).

- **Analytical apps**

  These apps are used to display real-time analytics on actual and plan data, including KPIs. There are numerous examples for these useful apps. These apps provide a drag-and-drop method for pulling in general ledger dimensions for reporting on journal entry item or balance details. As mentioned, in principle, all Universal Journal fields are now available as reporting dimensions. Report results can be downloaded to Microsoft Excel and then converted to a graph for quick visual analysis. In addition, a report-to-report interface is available that allows further detail analysis with a different view.

SAP Smart Business drilldown apps are analytical apps that provide prebuilt KPI reporting. A good example is the Days Payable Outstanding app, which contains prebuilt analytics, including days payable outstanding by the past 12 months, by supplier, by company code, and by top 10 days payable outstanding.

- **Fact sheet apps**
  These apps are used to display key facts about master data and to navigate directly to associated master data or business transactions. Fact sheet apps allow you to drill down to display or edit associated master data and relevant business transactions.

  A good example is the Customer 360° View app, which contains customer master data and provides a direct link to key contacts, quotations, sales orders, contracts, customer returns, and fulfillment issues. This dashboard is a powerful tool for users who need a quick overview of the customer's status.

We'll explore many SAP Fiori apps that you'll use in your financial accounting tasks throughout this book.

1.5   Summary

Now you should have a basic understanding of the special features of SAP S/4HANA. Compared to the previous SAP ERP solution, SAP S/4HANA primarily offers a broader range of deployment scenarios. On one hand, this concerns the question of whether SAP S/4HANA Cloud should be used, which is fast and economically deployable but offers less room for individual solutions. On-premise SAP S/4HANA, on the other hand, offers more flexibility, and operating models in the cloud are also possible here.

The broader spectrum also includes the UI. As in the past, SAP S/4HANA still allows the traditional and familiar SAP GUI transactions. Significant progress, however, is achieved via SAP Fiori apps. This not only applies to the mobile and personalized use of SAP Fiori but also the analytical apps that provide a comprehensive overview of business issues much faster.

From the point of view of accountants, the biggest change is that the Universal Journal has created a uniform database for management accounting and financial accounting. We talked about the fundamental simplifications associated with this. Single source of truth instead of single point of truth is the slogan that sums up this aspect.

The Universal Journal is now the integrated and common source for management accounting and financial accounting and makes reconciliation work obsolete. At the same time, individual requirements of management accounting can be mapped by extension fields and extension ledgers.

Other important fundamental aspects of SAP S/4HANA are the huge opportunities for improved reporting, which affects speed, flexibility, and the real-time approach. This allows far-reaching analyses to be carried out on the fly.

These aspects are also reflected in the closing process. With the SAP Financial Closing cockpit for SAP S/4HANA, SAP S/4HANA offers a powerful tool that makes closing operations more efficient and transparent. We also gave a brief introduction to SAP S/4HANA Cloud for advanced financial closing, an architecture and technology platform to support large and complex international companies in the closing process.

After this general introduction to the system, it should now be easier for you to work through the next chapter, which deals with the fundamentals and basic understanding of the financial accounting activities in SAP S/4HANA. The next chapter starts with the business processes involved in financial accounting, continues with the organizational structures and key definitions, and closes with the integration concept of financial accounting and management accounting.

Chapter 2

Organizational Structure and Integration

Now, we'll move on to examine the financial accounting foundation, including key processes, building blocks that make up the organizational structure, and how it integrates with management accounting.

Financial accounting supports business processes and gives management a reliable view of the company's financial situation and its profitability. Almost all business transactions (e.g., sales, purchases, goods movements, manufacturing, and payroll) have touchpoints to financial accounting.

This chapter shows you the first step of the integration model of core business processes with accounting. Next and most importantly, we explain the basic organizational elements and financial central settings that you need to understand when setting up a system or dealing with an existing system. Finally, we explain the new integration concept of financial accounting and management accounting provided by SAP S/4HANA from an accounting perspective.

2.1 Standard Financial Accounting Processes

Financial accounting as a functional responsibility is involved in all the main business processes. However, the majority of bookings today no longer take place in accounting but in upstream process steps, so accounting is very dependent on the quality of the incoming information. If the incoming transaction data or referenced master data isn't complete and correct, accounting often acts as a repair shop for badly set up processes. Therefore, you should understand and influence the core processes in which accounting is involved. In the following sections, we'll describe the essential business processes for accounting.

2.1.1 Value Chain Overview

The entire value chain of a company consists of the design, build, sell, and support phases that can be broken down into different core processes, as shown in Figure 2.1. SAP differentiates between the following core processes:

- **Order-to-cash**
  This is the process from presales activities to cash collection with the main accounting part in accounts receivable.

- **Purchase-to-pay**
  This is the process from supplier selection to outgoing payments with the main accounting part in accounts payable.

- **Acquire-to-retire**
  This is the process of the lifecycle of assets with the main accounting part in asset management.

- **Record-to-report**
  This is the process from journal entry postings in the general ledger to data retrieval providing legal and management reporting.

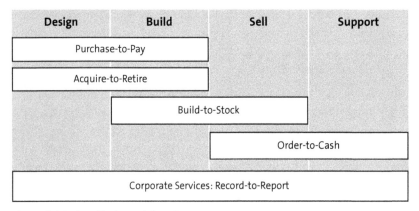

Figure 2.1 Value Chain and Core Processes

Figure 2.1 also illustrates that the accounting process as a support process is integrated in the entire value chain. However, on the other hand, you could argue that accounting itself is a process that leads to a result, namely the reports that provide information about the course of business.

We'll look in more detail at these core processes in the following sections. Before we do that, we should briefly consider the other processes involved in accounting:

- **Build-to-stock**
  This is the production process connected to the Material Ledger and product cost controlling.

- **Hire-to-retire**
  These are the human resource processes with touchpoints in payroll accounting.

- **Idea-to-market**
  This is the innovation process with connections to project accounting and intangible assets.

- **Plan-to-perform**

  This is the financial planning process with accounting as a starting point and comparison factor.

These processes are more strongly connected with other parts of the system, in particular with the different areas in logistics and human resources, but also with other parts in accounting, such as enterprise controlling.

Therefore, we'll focus on the core business processes whose related accounting activities (general ledger accounting, accounts payable, accounts receivable, and fixed asset accounting) are described in more detail in the next four chapters of this book.

2.1.2   Order-to-Cash and Accounts Receivable

It's certainly no exaggeration to describe the order-to-cash process as the lifeline of a company. This process is the link to the customers to whom the company must offer a value add with its services and products. In return, the customer provides the company with the liquidity it needs to continue as a business.

The order-to-cash process already starts with the first customer contacts in SAP Customer Relationship Management (SAP CRM). However, the process only becomes relevant for accounting when contract information is generated, which later arrives in accounting. This can be an inquiry or an offer where personal- and product-related information has already been exchanged. When this customer contact leads to a complete business transaction, the process goes through various functional areas in the SAP system, primarily sales, logistics, materials management, accounting, and treasury.

Figure 2.2 shows an overview of the following detailed process description. As you can see, the process runs through different areas of the system, starting in logistics/sales and distribution, going further to logistic execution, touching treasury, and finalizing in accounting when the payment and the journal entries are booked.

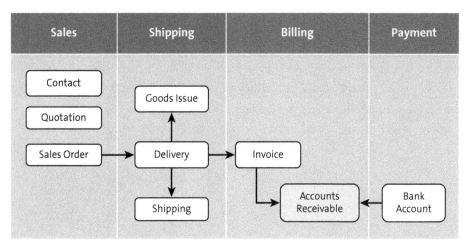

Figure 2.2 Order-to-Cash Process

For the success of the company, a functional and optimally designed order-to-cash process is enormously significant because it directly affects customer satisfaction. Measures of the performance of the order-to-cash process are throughput time, delivery quality, and payment behavior.

SAP Fiori offers a variety of apps that assist with managing and controlling the processes with actual data (e.g., the Sales Order Fulfillment app shown in Figure 2.3).

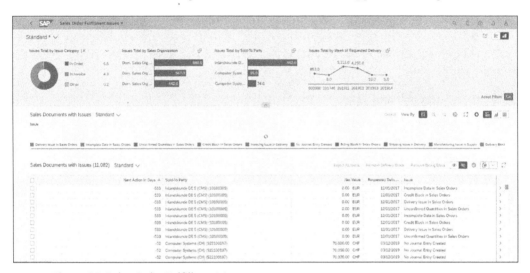

Figure 2.3 Sales Order Fulfillment Issues

Here, you get a good overview of an important part in the sales process. The orders are shown over time and segmented by processing status, data quality, and organizational units.

> **Further Resources**
>
> These apps are explained in detail in the SAP Fiori apps reference library at *http://s-prs.co/v493802*. In this constantly expanded collection, you can search for and view newly released apps for these tasks as well as for the other processes.

Figure 2.4 gives you an impression of the variety of topics with the search bar on the left. At the same time, the Sales Management Overview app is an impressive example of the support of sales management.

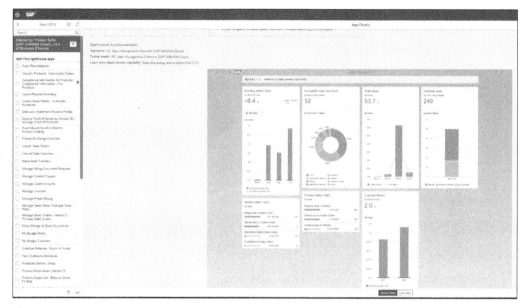

Figure 2.4 Sales Management Overview App

2.1.3 Purchase-to-Pay and Accounts Payable

Purchase-to-pay (also known as procurement-to-pay) is the other core process that represents the value chain of a company. Two aspects underline the importance of this process: (1) the saying "profit lies in purchasing" clearly indicates the close connection between purchasing and a company's success, and (2) this process is associated with spending money, so from an internal control point of view, it's paramount to ensure that the right amount of money goes to the right payee and that the expenses go to the correct cost.

In the brief overview of this process shown in Figure 2.5, you can see that the processes affect different functions and areas.

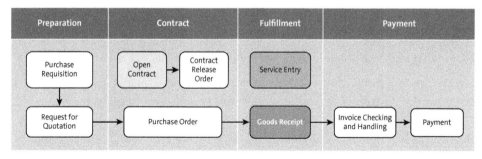

Figure 2.5 Purchase-to-Pay

The purchase requisition comes from different departments and arrives at the purchasing organization. The request for quotation and purchase order are the mainstays of purchasing. Fulfillment again affects different departments. With invoice checking, the information from purchasing (ordered quantity at a certain price) must now be compared with the information from fulfillment (correct quantity) and the data on the invoice (price and quantity), so that the payment can be released.

As shown in the order-to-cash process, SAP S/4HANA also provides a lot of support for management in the purchase-to-pay area by providing relevant information, as depicted in the Procurement Overview Page app shown in Figure 2.6. At a glance, you can see the most important information and tasks relevant for the management of the purchase-to-pay process.

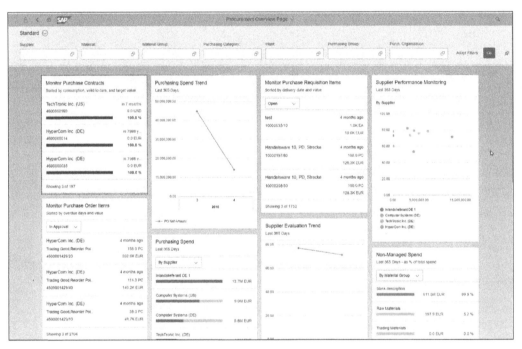

Figure 2.6 Procurement Overview Page App

2.1.4   Acquire-to-Retire and Fixed Asset Accounting

The acquire-to-retire process provides a company with fixed assets that could last several years. SAP provides the tools to support this process over this long period of time, as shown in Figure 2.7.

You can see that the process can be divided into four phases. Whereas the pre-acquisition and acquisition phases are mainly supported by the purchasing area, the monitoring phase is supported by the fixed assets department in accounting. Figure 2.7 shows the main functionalities in this process until the different forms of retirement, which are also supported within fixed assets.

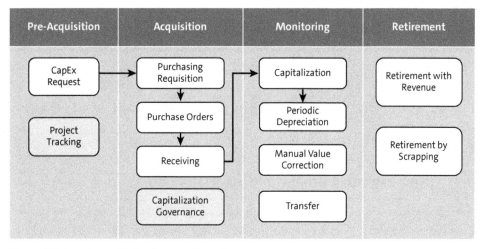

Figure 2.7 Acquire-to-Retire Process Overview

2.1.5   Record-to-Report and General Ledger

From an accounting perspective, the record-to-report process is the most important process because it involves accounting's responsibility for properly documenting business transactions and providing reliable information about the course of business. All accounting-related postings in the different areas ultimately converge in the general ledger, where they form the basis for financial reports.

Figure 2.8 shows the different phases of the process. The process is based on clear definitions of the company's structures and master data. Current postings and periodic closing are the operative activities in the general ledger. On this basis, reports can then be generated for various purposes.

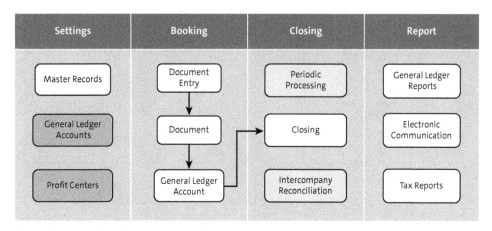

Figure 2.8 Record-to-Report Overview

Today, individual companies as legal entities are often part of a group of companies for which consolidated financial statements must be created. A very important task in accounting is therefore the identification and recording of intercompany transactions in preparation for consolidation. This is especially true for the general ledger, where the reconciliation and elimination of intercompany transactions must be supported.

Now let's go a little deeper into accounting and look at the central organizational elements and settings.

2.2   Organizational Elements of Financial Accounting

In this section, we describe the basic and fundamental specifications in the system. These specifications must be carefully considered during implementation because they have enormous consequences for other areas, impact operational processes, and can't be changed later so easily.

We'll discuss specifications both in mapping the entire corporate structure in its legal, business-related, and management-related dimensions and in fundamental definitions, which are felt more strongly by accounting but nevertheless have an impact on the entire company.

These necessary system settings can be found in the Implementation Guide (IMG) and can be accessed via Transaction SPRO.

2.2.1   Organizational Structures

The organizational structures that are relevant for financial accounting are defined in the IMG via menu path **Enterprise Structure • Definition • Financial Accounting**. You'll arrive at the screen shown in Figure 2.9. This is the area in the system where the main organizational structure elements are defined.

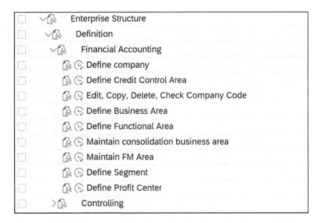

Figure 2.9 Enterprise Structure Definition in Financial Accounting

2

In the following sections, we'll explain the following organizational elements in more detail:

- Company
- Credit control area
- Company code
- Business area
- Functional area
- Segment
- Profit center
- Consolidation business area
- Financial management (FM) area

In addition to the preceding elements and to give you a better understanding of the overall context of the organizational structure, we also need to describe briefly the client element and the organizational context of the management accounting area with its basic controlling area elements.

Client

The *client* describes the technical framework of the system and is therefore the highest organizational element. For this reason, all the elements described in the following sections are located within a client. When implementing a system for a corporate group, from an accounting point of view, you should insist on mapping the entire corporate group within a client. This brings enormous advantages for master data management, the design of processes, and the representation of the group of companies in consolidation according to legal and business dimensions.

> **Note**
>
> All the organizational elements described in the following sections are located within a client. Ideally, an enterprise or group of companies should be installed in one client.

However, in the past, large corporations in particular have installed several clients over the course of time, and even within one company, different clients were sometimes installed in parallel. In this case, from an accounting point of view, it's therefore important for you to know how the coexistence of different clients can be organized in SAP.

Company

The organizational element *company* is intended by SAP in the system for a legal entity. It therefore describes a business organization for which accounting must be performed and a balance sheet must be drawn up for legal reasons.

However, legal independence in SAP isn't a mandatory prerequisite for setting up a company in the system. For example, a legally dependent branch or permanent establishment can also be created as a company to be addressed as a consolidation element.

Also similar to the client as a technical framework, the company conceptually represents a framework within which various organizational elements relevant to accounting can be defined. Therefore, basic elements for accounting, such as the chart of accounts, aren't defined on a company level. We'll see this in later sections.

Because the consolidated financial statements can primarily be understood as the consolidation of legally independent companies, it's logical that the company element is used for consolidation in SAP. It's also called *trading partner* in the reports (Section 2.3.4), which makes the meaning as legal entity a bit clearer.

To define a company, follow menu path **Enterprise Structure • Definition • Define Company**. First, you'll receive a list of companies, as shown in Figure 2.10.

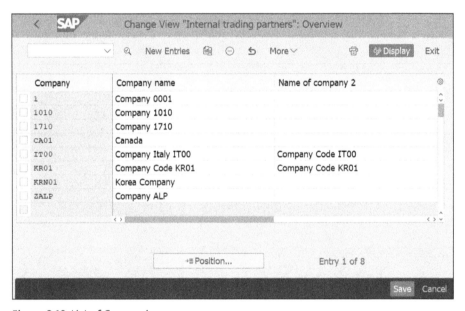

Figure 2.10 List of Companies

After selecting a company and clicking **Details**, you'll arrive at the screen shown in Figure 2.11.

The **Company** field represents the company ID (in this example, 1010), whereas the company ID may have six characters. The company IDs and the list of company IDs, usually provided by the parent company, have to be consistent across the group.

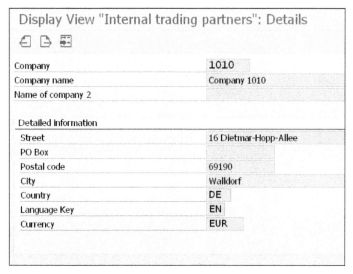

Figure 2.11 Company and Company Name

Company Code

The *company code* organizational element isn't equal to and doesn't have a 1:1 relationship with the *company* element. Rather, different company codes can be created within a single company. The purpose is to maintain a closed accounting system for each company code, with the option of generating a balance sheet and income statement for each company code. Therefore, all company codes within a company must use the same chart of accounts and fiscal year. However, you can have different currencies in use to maintain a cross-national corporation.

You can use company codes for a location, factory, business area, branch, or functional area, such as a development department, if you want a pro forma financial statement for these organizational elements.

To create a company code, follow menu path **Enterprise Structure • Definition • Financial Accounting • Edit, Copy, Delete, Check Company Code**. Select **Edit Company Code Data**. You'll arrive at a list with **Company Code** and **Company Name**. You can select a **Company Code** or click the **New Entries** icon to go to the screen shown in Figure 2.12, where you can enter a **Company Code** ID, **Company Name**, and **Additional data**, including **City**, **Country**, **Currency**, and **Language**.

The company code can also be used, for example, to record adjustment postings for tax balance sheet purposes, so that the combination of a commercial balance sheet company code with the tax adjustment postings results in a complete tax balance sheet.

> **Tip**
>
> You should therefore create a company code according to tax law, commercial law, and other financial accounting criteria.

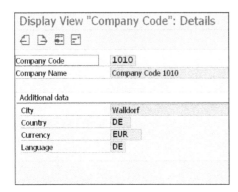

Figure 2.12 Definition of a Company Code

The advantage of the company code in, for example, comparison to a profit center, is that these units provide not only a result per unit but also a hard financial statement that includes all period-end closing steps and a legal company balance sheet.

For every company code, you need to control the financial postings, which is done mainly in the company code parameters. You can maintain these in Customizing by following IMG menu path **Financial Accounting • Financial Accounting Global Settings • Global Parameters for Company Code • Enter Global Parameters** (or use Transaction OBY6) to get a list of company codes. Double-click on a line to arrive at the screen shown in Figure 2.13.

Display View "Company Code Global Data": Details

Additional Data

Company Code	1010 Company Code 1010		Walldorf	
Country key	DE Currency	EUR	Language Key	DE

Accounting organization

Chart of Accts	YCOA	Country Chart/Accts	YIKR
Company	1010	FM Area	
Credit Control Area	1000	Fiscal Year Variant	K4
Ext. co. code	☐	Global CoCde	1010
Company code is productive	☐	VAT Registration No.	DE123456789
Hide Company Code in F4	☑		

Processing parameters

Document entry screen variant	2	☐ Business area fin. statements	
Field Status Variant	0010	☐ Propose fiscal year	
Pstng period variant	1010	☐ Define default value date	
Max. exchange rate deviation	10 %	☐ No forex rate diff. when clearing in LC	
Sample acct rules var.		☐ Tax base is net value	
Workflow variant	0001	☐ Discount base is net value	
Inflation Method		☑ Financial Assets Mgmt active	
Crcy transl. for tax		☐ Purchase acct proc.	
CoCd -> CO Area	2	☐ JV Accounting Active	
Cost of sales accounting actv.	2	☐ Hedge request active	
☑ Negative Postings Permitted		☐ Enable amount split	
		☑ Tax Reporting Date Active	
☐ Manage Postg Period			

Figure 2.13 Company Code: Central Parameters

As you can see in Figure 2.13, there are many processes whose parameters are defined on the company code level, and some of them are industry specific. Let's focus on some key parameters.

The company code is linked with other organizational elements of the accounting organization: **Company** and **Credit Control Area**. Additional important parameters are defined in the company code as well, such as **Chart of Accts** and **Fiscal Year Variant**, including some that are specific to your industry.

> **Note**
>
> The company code is the central organizational element of financial accounting in SAP S/4HANA. Each posting must be assigned to a company code. The company code can also be regarded as a building block in SAP S/4HANA. With this entity, accounting is connected to other applications.

This connection of the company code—as an element of financial accounting—to other functionalities also applies to management accounting. Therefore, we'll provide a brief description of the controlling area next.

Business Area

With the creation of a business area, you can represent a separate area of operations or responsibilities in a business organization—independent from the legal structure of a company or a group of companies. Within a client, you can define several business areas. You can create financial statements for business areas and use such statements for internal reporting purposes. With the **Maintain Consolidation Business Area** activity, you can create consolidations of two types of business areas:

- **Consolidation business area**
  A consolidation business area can be used for financial consolidation in group reporting. The function can be used to define a business area in an area other than group reporting. It can also be used to create a business area that has been specifically defined for exclusive use in group reporting.

- **Financial business area**
  In a financial business area, you can create your FM area. You structure the business organization from the perspective of cash budget management and management. You have to assign each company code that is relevant to cash budget management or funds management to an FM area. You can combine several company codes to a single FM area.

As you can see in Figure 2.14, each FM area has its own currency. The FM area currency must not be the same as the currency of the assigned company code.

FM Area	Name of FM Area	FM Area Currency
0001	FM area 0001	EUR
BC01	FM area 0001	EUR
BP01	FM area BP01	USD
ETPE	FM area 0001	EUR
F	FM Area for Company F	AUD
F1		EUR
HAG	HAG Management Consulting	EUR
OB10	FM area BP01	USD
SAPF	FM area 0001	EUR
WACM	FM area WACM	USD

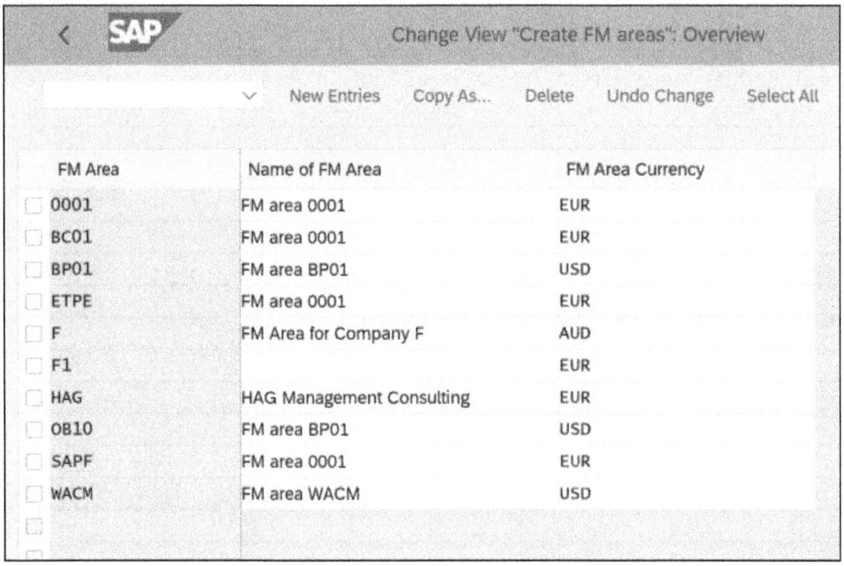

Figure 2.14 Create FM Areas

Controlling Area

Although the controlling area historically didn't belong to financial accounting with the Universal Journal, it has direct impact on the general ledger, so we introduce it here. This element is explained in more detail in Section 2.3.3, where the organizational units of management accounting are described.

The *controlling area* is an organizational unit within a company—although not limited to one company code—that is used for management accounting purposes. A controlling area may include one or more company codes, which may use different company code currencies. However, the assigned company codes have to use the same chart of accounts.

The purpose of the controlling area is to structure the business organization from a management accounting standpoint. Therefore, the definition of the controlling area isn't limited or dependent on legal limits or accounting regulations.

Because several company codes can be assigned to one controlling area, a group of companies can also organize management accounting across legal forms, even in different currencies. This also makes accounting much easier because intercompany cost charges can be carried out automatically.

Credit Control Area

The *credit control area* is an organizational unit that specifies and checks the credit limit for customers. This is a powerful tool for accounts receivable with a strong link to the sales organization—again via company code.

Figure 2.15 gives you an example of a credit control area defined in the IMG. To access, follow menu path **Enterprise Structure • Definition • Financial Accounting • Define Credit Control Area**.

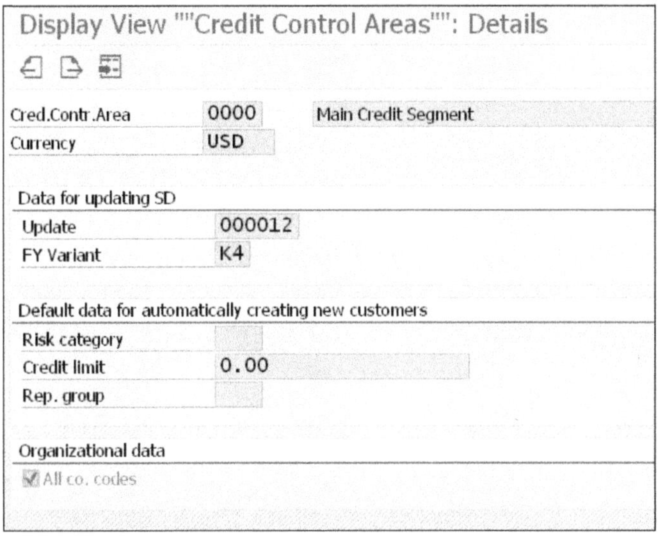

```
Display View ""Credit Control Areas"": Details

Cred.Contr.Area        0000        Main Credit Segment
Currency               USD


Data for updating SD
Update                 000012
FY Variant             K4


Default data for automatically creating new customers
Risk category
Credit limit           0.00
Rep. group


Organizational data
☑ All co. codes
```

Figure 2.15 Defining a Credit Control Area

A credit control area can be assigned to one or more company codes via IMG menu path **Enterprise Structure • Assignment • Financial Accounting – Assign Company Code to Credit Control Area**. You just add a credit control area (**Cred.Contr.Area**) to a company code in this view and click on **Save** (not shown). Similar to the controlling area used in management accounting, this allows a more centralized organization of accounts receivable management.

You can also link to the sales and distribution functionality under the **Data for updating SD** section. For example, with the **Update** parameter, you control when the amounts of open sales orders, deliveries, and billing documents are updated. For new customers, you can also set a **Risk category** and **Credit limit** to define default data.

When a customer is active in different company codes, the credit control area allows you to manage the customer's credit centrally. This also applies when different currencies are involved. As already mentioned, each company code may have a different currency. For the purpose of credit control, the system converts the relevant amounts (e.g., open sales orders, deliveries, and bills) in the defined currency of the credit control area.

Profit Centers

The *profit center* is an organizational unit of accounting that structures the enterprise in a management-oriented way. The purpose is to create a control unit that is independent of legal forms and may be defined group-wide, so subsequent profit centers can be used across companies.

For a profit center, you can generate results that are calculated according to cost-of-sales accounting and/or period accounting. The profit center is primarily oriented to the figures in the profit and loss (P&L) statement. However, by also reporting balance sheet numbers, you can support a control concept aiming for a return on capital employed (ROCE) or economic value added (EVA). ROCE compares earnings before interest and taxes (EBIT) with the capital invested in the company (e.g., fixed assets and working capital). To run this concept not only on the company level but also on the profit center level, you can derive the specific balance sheet numbers for the profit centers. EVA needs basically the same accounting numbers but compares the achieved ROCE with the capital costs for the company (e.g., weighted average costs of capital [WACC]).

You can create a profit center via Transaction KE51 or change a profit center via Transaction KE52 (see Figure 2.16).

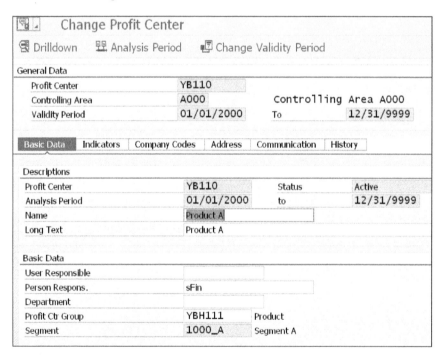

Figure 2.16 Defining a Profit Center

As you can see, each profit center is assigned to a **Controlling Area** and **Segment** (an organizational unit explained in the following section). You can also select the

Company Codes in which the profit center can be used; by default, all company codes assigned to the controlling area are active.

You can use the profit center to break down the legal accounting view according to internal company criteria. The activity and goods flow between profit centers can be reported. As an additional functionality, you can apply statistical transfer prices for this flow of goods across profit centers. However, in this case, the valuation of goods and services processed between profit centers can be different from the valuation approach in financial accounting.

Segment

Segments are used for segment reporting according to International Financial Reporting Standards (IFRS) and US Generally Accepted Accounting Principles (GAAP). In this context, segment reporting is an important tool for external accounting and consolidation to structure the entire company consistently into business segments. Usually, two different views have to be represented: breakdown by regions and breakdown by activity.

As shown earlier in Figure 2.16, when defining profit centers, you can enter an associated **Segment** in the master record of a profit center. The segment is then derived from the assigned profit center during posting.

Figure 2.17 shows the list of segments and their descriptions. To access this, follow IMG menu path **Enterprise Structure • Definition • Financial Accounting • Define Segment.**

Display View "Segments for Segment Reporting"

Segments for Segment Reporting

Segment	Description
1000_A	Segment A
1000_B	Segment B
1000_C	Segment C

Figure 2.17 Definition of Segments as the Basis for Segment Reporting

Functional Area

If you want to report according to the cost-of-sales format, you should use the functional area. A *functional area* is a financial accounting characteristic stored in the Universal Journal, which allows classifying expenses according to functions. To view the functional areas, follow IMG menu path **Enterprise Structure • Definition • Financial Accounting • Define Functional Area.** You'll arrive at the screen shown in Figure 2.18.

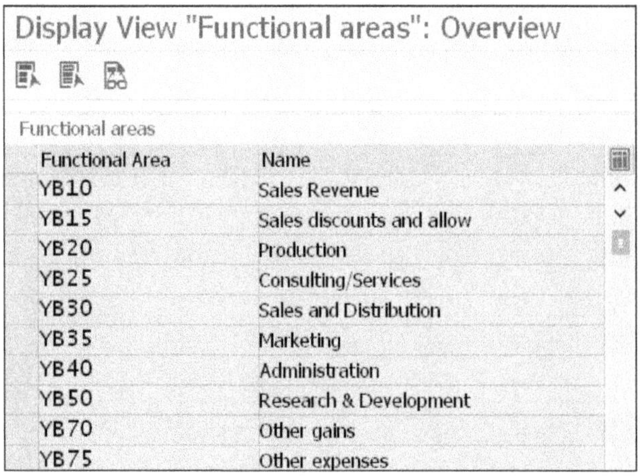

Display View "Functional areas": Overview

Functional areas

Functional Area	Name
YB10	Sales Revenue
YB15	Sales discounts and allow
YB20	Production
YB25	Consulting/Services
YB30	Sales and Distribution
YB35	Marketing
YB40	Administration
YB50	Research & Development
YB70	Other gains
YB75	Other expenses

Figure 2.18 Example of Functional Area Customizing

Enabling functional areas is a prerequisite for cost-of-sales accounting. The functional areas can be used as grouping criteria in the financial statement version, which is used for cost-of-sales reporting (see Chapter 3, Section 3.7.4).

The functional area is derived during the creation of the accounting document with the following access sequence:

1. The functional area is taken from the general ledger account, if one is assigned.
2. The functional area is taken from the account-assigned cost object. There are rules for every object to derive the functional area, for example, for projects defaulted by project profile, for cost centers by cost center category, and so on.

For manual postings, the functional area can be manually assigned.

Example

A professional services company needs to distinguish travel expenses posted on a customer project as cost of sales, and travel expenses caused by an employee of the accounting department and posted on the accounting department cost center as administration costs. To do so, we assign the **Administration** functional area to the cost center of the accounting department. This functional area can be defaulted by the cost center category. For the customer project, we assign the **Cost of Sales** functional area. This functional area can be defaulted by the project profile. When the travel expenses are recorded to these cost objects, the functional area is derived by the cost object master data and stored in the journal entry.

When implementing SAP S/4HANA, you first need to define the required functional areas. Then you need to ensure that they are process dependent and process derived by assigning them to various objects, such as projects, production orders, make-to-order sales orders, cost centers, and internal orders.

Now that we've looked at enterprise structure assignments within financial accounting, let's discuss some relationships between financial accounting and organizational structures in other functionalities.

2.2.2 Cross-Application Organizational Assignments

As already mentioned in Chapter 1, almost all business transactions have touchpoints with financial accounting. SAP's integration model therefore ensures that structural elements outside of accounting are meaningfully connected. In the following sections, the assignment and integration of such important elements will be explained. You can access all these assignments via IMG menu path **Enterprise Structure • Assignment.**

Plants

In logistics, the *plant* represents an organizational unit and a physical location where manufacturing takes place or goods and services are provided. The company is thus structured by the plant for production, procurement, maintenance, and material planning purposes.

The connection to accounting is made via the company code: each plant is assigned to a single company code, but a company code can be assigned to several plants. The assignment is made via IMG menu path **Enterprise Structure • Assignment • Logistics – General • Assign Plant to Company Code**. You'll arrive at the screen shown in Figure 2.19.

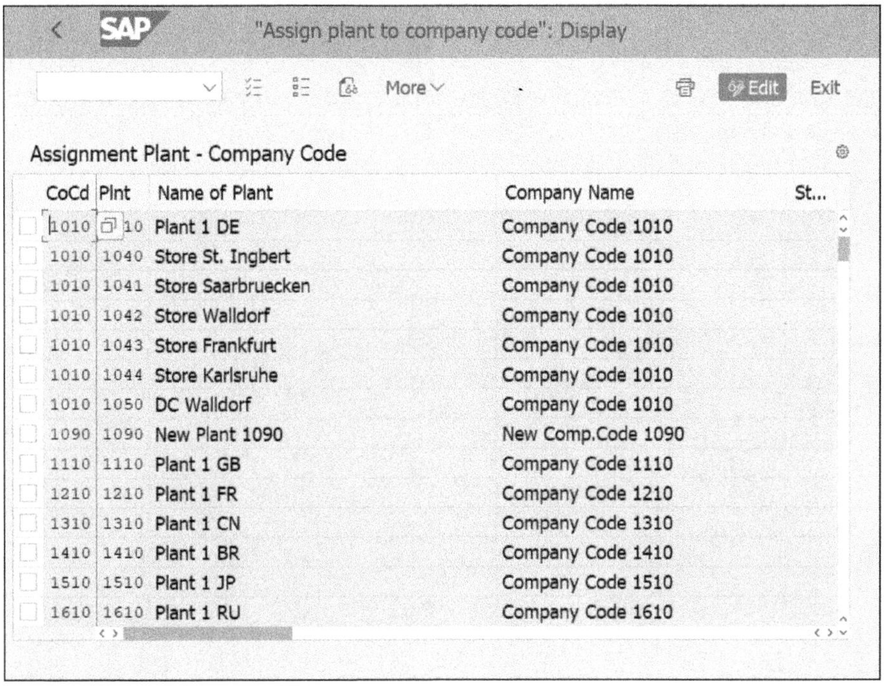
"Assign plant to company code": Display
More
Edit
Exit
Assignment Plant - Company Code
CoCd Plnt Name of Plant Company Name St...
1010 10 Plant 1 DE Company Code 1010
1010 1040 Store St. Ingbert Company Code 1010
1010 1041 Store Saarbruecken Company Code 1010
1010 1042 Store Walldorf Company Code 1010
1010 1043 Store Frankfurt Company Code 1010
1010 1044 Store Karlsruhe Company Code 1010
1010 1050 DC Walldorf Company Code 1010
1090 1090 New Plant 1090 New Comp.Code 1090
1110 1110 Plant 1 GB Company Code 1110
1210 1210 Plant 1 FR Company Code 1210
1310 1310 Plant 1 CN Company Code 1310
1410 1410 Plant 1 BR Company Code 1410
1510 1510 Plant 1 JP Company Code 1510
1610 1610 Plant 1 RU Company Code 1610

Figure 2.19 Assignment of a Plant to Company Code

To assign a new plant to a company code, you select the **New Entries** icon, add a **Company Code** and **Plant** on the following screen, and click **Save**.

Regarding accounting, the plant plays an important role in several areas:

- On the plant level, you can define the material prices and get your inventory valuation (only in exceptional cases for certain industries can you define the company code at the valuation level).
- The plant is an attribute in the Universal Journal to allow enhanced reporting.
- Each plant can have its own account determination.
- Inventory management and material stocks are managed within a plant.

Purchasing Organizations

Within the *purchasing organization*, you organize all business processes regarding purchasing. On this level, you control, for example, the purchase requests and orders, and you define price conditions and purchasing info records.

Responsibilities for purchasing processes can have either centralized or decentralized regulation. Depending on this decision, you define the integration into accounting and the relationship to the company code.

To create a group-wide, central purchasing organization, all or several company codes can be assigned to a purchasing organization. To create a more decentralized and company-specific purchasing organization, a one-to-one relationship between company code and purchasing organization is possible.

The assignment is done via IMG menu path **Enterprise Structure • Assignment • Materials Management • Assign Purchasing Organization to Company Code**. You'll arrive at the screen shown in Figure 2.20.

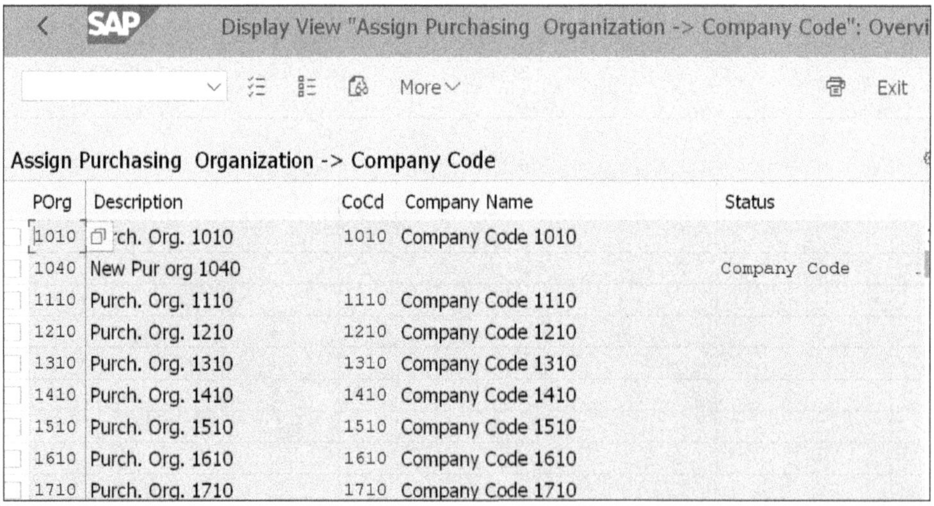
SAP
Display View "Assign Purchasing Organization -> Company Code": Overvi
More
Exit
Assign Purchasing Organization -> Company Code
POrg
Description
CoCd
Company Name
Status
1010 ch. Org. 1010 1010 Company Code 1010
1040 New Pur org 1040 Company Code
1110 Purch. Org. 1110 1110 Company Code 1110
1210 Purch. Org. 1210 1210 Company Code 1210
1310 Purch. Org. 1310 1310 Company Code 1310
1410 Purch. Org. 1410 1410 Company Code 1410
1510 Purch. Org. 1510 1510 Company Code 1510
1610 Purch. Org. 1610 1610 Company Code 1610
1710 Purch. Org. 1710 1710 Company Code 1710

Figure 2.20 Assignment of Purchase Organization to Company Code

To assign a purchase organization to a company code, you just add a company code (**CoCd**) to a purchase organization (**POrg**) in this view and click **Save**.

You also have the choice *not* to assign the purchasing organization directly to a company code (see the second line, purchase organization **1040**). As each purchasing organization must be assigned to one or more plants, and the plant is linked to a company code, this assignment path will be taken by derivation of the company code in the relevant purchasing business transaction.

Sales Organizations

With the *sales organization*, you organize your business processes for the sale of materials and services. Based on the sales organization, you can, for example, define master data (e.g., customer and product) and define prices and sales document types.

The integration into accounting is done via company code assignment: a sales organization is assigned to exactly one company code. You can assign the sales organization to the company code by following IMG menu path **Enterprise Structure • Assignment • Sales and Distribution • Assign Sales Organization to Company Code**. You'll arrive at the screen shown in Figure 2.21.

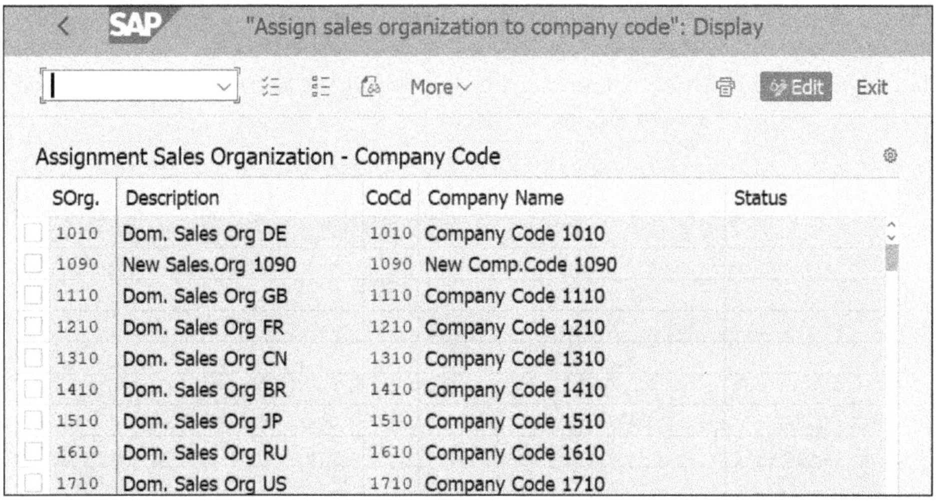

Figure 2.21 Assignment of Sales Organization to Company Code

To assign a sales organization to a company code, you just add a company code (**CoCd**) to a sales organization (**SOrg.**) in this view and click **Save**.

Personnel Area

The *personnel area* is an organizational unit in SAP that provides the functions required for personnel management, including time management and payroll functions.

A personnel area can be divided into several personnel subareas to follow the regional structure of a company with different locations.

Each personnel area is assigned to one company code, and all personnel subareas follow this assignment. To implement this assignment, follow IMG menu path **Enterprise Structure • Assignment • Human Resources Management • Assignment of Personnel Areas to Company Code**. You'll arrive at the screen shown in Figure 2.22.

Pers.area	Personnel Area Text	Company Code	Company Name	Ctry Grpg
1010	Region 1010 (DE)	1010	Company Code 1010	01
1110	Region 1110 (GB)	1110	Company Code 1110	08
1210	Region 1210 (FR)	1210	Company Code 1210	06
1310	Region 1310 (CN)	1310	Company Code 1310	28
1410	Region 1410 (BR)	1410	Company Code 1410	37
1510	Region 1510 (JP)	1510	Company Code 1510	22
1610	Region 1610 (RU)	1610	Company Code 1610	33
1710	Region 1710 (US)	1710	Company Code 1710	10

Figure 2.22 Assignment of Personnel Area to Company Code

To assign a personnel area to a company code, you just add a company code (**Company Code**) to a personnel area (**Pers.area**) in this view and click **Save**.

Now that you've learned how to apply your enterprise structure in the system, let's look at the main accounting settings and the required system implementation decisions.

2.2.3   Central Financial Accounting Settings and Decisions

After this necessary look beyond the borders, we now want to enter into the world of financial accounting and see what basic and permanent system settings must be made. Because these system settings can't be changed easily afterwards, careful analysis and well-founded decisions are required.

These specifications cover such crucial issues as the number and purpose of ledgers, applicable accounting principles, currencies, and defining the fiscal year and the number of periods. A special topic is the extension ledger, with which amounts that differ from those of a standard ledger can be displayed for accounting purposes.

Ledgers

In general ledger accounting, you can manage several parallel general ledgers, for example, to get financial statements according to different accounting principles, such as local GAAP and IFRS, and for tax accounting.

You define your ledgers and their parameters per company code in the following Customizing menu path: **Financial Accounting • Financial Accounting Global Settings • Ledgers • Ledger • Define Settings for Ledgers and Currency Types**. You'll arrive at the screen shown in Figure 2.23.

Ledger	Ledger Name	Leading	Ledger Type	Underlying Ledger	Subtype Val	Man.Pstgs Not Allwd	AcctgPrinc of Ledger
0L	Ledger 0L	☑	Standard Ledger ⌄			☐	
2L	Ledger 2L	☐	Standard Ledger ⌄			☐	IFRS
3L	Ledger 3L	☐	Standard Ledger ⌄			☐	USGP

Figure 2.23 Ledger Definition in IMG

There are two ledger types: leading and nonleading. The postings in the leading ledger are regarded as primary and are the default for postings in other ledgers if there is no custom valuation in these ledgers. All company codes are assigned to this leading ledger by default. The leading ledger allows you to provide group reporting, and it's used for consolidation.

You must designate one ledger—and only one—as the leading ledger. In the standard system, the leading ledger is 0L, so you can select the **Leading** checkbox for **Ledger 0L**.

Further parameters you define in the same IMG activity include selecting a **Ledger** and selecting **Company Code Settings for Ledger** (not shown) to arrive at the parameters screen shown in Figure 2.24.

Here you can specify the following:

- **Fiscal Year Variant**
  Value represents the number of posting periods in a given year (which we'll discuss later in this section).

- **Pstng period variant**
  Describes the posting period (e.g., beginning and end date of period).

- **Accounting Principle**
  Assigned on the ledger level or the ledger company code level. If you maintain it generally on the ledger level, you need not maintain it here. We'll discuss accounting principles further in the next section.

- **Functional Currency**
  Can be the company code or group currency.

- **Local Currency/Global Currency**
  Defined on the company code level. Additionally, you can activate eight freely defined currencies in parallel as well.

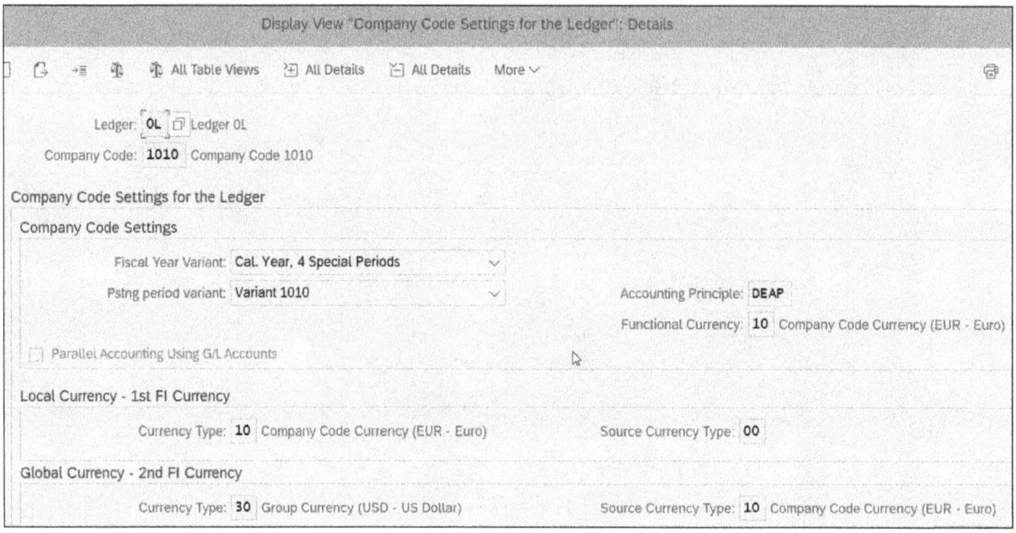

Figure 2.24 Company Code-Dependent and Ledger-Dependent Financials Parameters

When you create a ledger, the system automatically creates a ledger group with the same name. To simplify work in the individual functions and processes of general ledger accounting, you can group any number of ledgers together in a ledger group. With this, for example, you can enter a manual journal entry posting for several ledgers at the same time.

Accounting Principles

With the *accounting principle*, you control the valuation in several financial applications, for example, foreign currency valuation, asset deprecations, work in progress (WIP), and revenue recognition.

You first need to define the accounting principle by following IMG menu path **Financial Accounting • Financial Accounting Global Settings • Ledgers • Parallel Accounting • Define Accounting Principle**. You'll arrive at the screen shown in Figure 2.25.

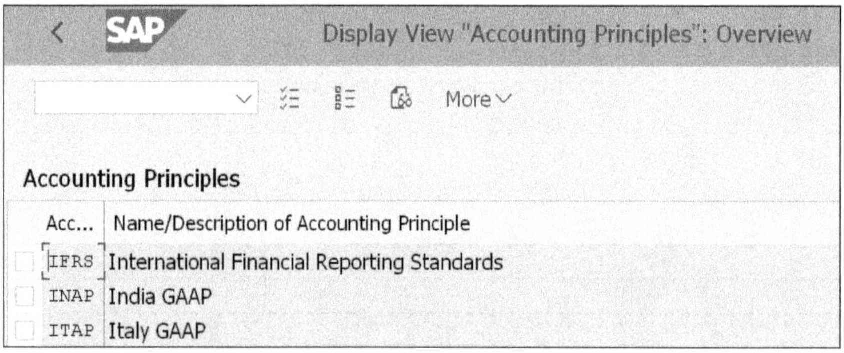

Figure 2.25 Definition of Accounting Principles

If the predelivered accounting principles aren't sufficient, you can create your own by selecting the **New Entries** icon. You can add a new accounting principle on the following screen, and click **Save**.

Then you assign the accounting principle to a ledger group in the same IMG node of parallel accounting with the **Assign Accounting Principle to Ledger Groups** activity. The screen shown in Figure 2.26 appears.

< **SAP**	Display View "Assignment of Accounting Principle to Target Ledger Grou	

[ ] ∨ ⠿ ⠿ ⨖ More∨

Assignment of Accounting Principle to Target Ledger Group

Accounting P...	Target Ledger Group	Description
IFRS	2L	Ledger 2L
INAP	OL	Ledger OL
ITAP	OL	Ledger OL

Figure 2.26 Assigning an Accounting Principle to a Ledger Group

You can assign an accounting principle to a target ledger group by first selecting the **New Entries** icon. Add the accounting principle and target ledger group on the new screen, and click **Save**.

Currencies and Currency Types

Currency setup plays an important role in financial accounting. You can configure currencies per the rules of the country defined in the company code. SAP S/4HANA provides currencies for every country. When you define a company code, currency is a basic piece of data that needs to be maintained.

In financial accounting, in addition to the transaction currency, the local currency (the company code currency) and the group currency are calculated and persisted in every journal entry by default. Additionally, there are eight freely defined currencies available.

For an example of how this looks for a company code, refer to Figure 2.24. The local currency—derived from the country Germany—is defined as **Euro**, and the global currency—derived from the controlling area—is **USD**.

To run the parallel currencies for all processes and functions in financial accounting, you need to maintain them in Customizing by following menu path **Financial Accounting • Financial Accounting Global Settings • Ledgers • Ledger • Define Settings for Ledgers and Currency Types**. Then select **Currency Types** in the dialog structure. You'll arrive at the screen shown in Figure 2.27. Here you define the **Currency Types** you want to manage in each ledger and company code.

Change View "Currency Types": Overview

More

Currency Types

Currency/Valuation...	Description	Short Description	Valuation View	Subtype Val	Plain Currency Type
00	Document Currency	Doc Crcy	Legal Valuation		
01	Document Currency in Group Valuation	Doc Crcy G	Group Valuation		00
02	Document Currency in Profit Center Valu...	Doc Crcy P	Profit Center Valua...		00
10	Company Code Currency	CCde Crcy	Legal Valuation		
11	Company Code Currency, Group Valuati...	CoCo, Grp	Group Valuation		10
12	Company Code Currency, Profit Center ...	CoCo, PrC	Profit Center Valua...		10
20	Controlling Area Currency	CArea Crcy	Legal Valuation		
30	Group Currency	Group Crcy	Legal Valuation		
31	Group Currency Profit Center Val	GC PCV	Group Valuation		30
32	Group Currency Group Val	GC GV	Profit Center Valua...		30
40	Hard Currency	Hard Crcy	Legal Valuation		
41	Hard Currency, Group Valuation	Hrd Crcy G	Group Valuation		40
42	Hard Currency, Profit Center Valuation	Hrd Crcy P	Profit Center Valua...		40
50	Index-Based Currency	Index Crcy	Legal Valuation		
51	Index-Based Currency, Group Valuation	Ind Crcy G	Group Valuation		50
52	Index-Based Currency, Profit Center Val...	Ind Crcy P	Profit Center Valua...		50
60	Global Company Currency	GloCo Crcy	Legal Valuation		

Figure 2.27 Currency Types

The currency type describes the usage and the role of the currency. For example, the **Valuation View** can be defined as **Legal Valuation**, **Group Valuation**, or **Profit Center Valuation**. Additionally, there is a **Settings Def. Level** column (not shown), which defines whether the currency conversion is **Global** or **Company Code-Specific**.

If you also activate one of the freely defined currencies, it will be calculated and stored for every journal entry. You can analyze it using the standard financial reports.

Fiscal Year Variants

With the *fiscal year variant*, you define the number of posting periods in a fiscal year, the number of special periods, and the determination of the posting period dependent on the posting date.

The fiscal year variant is defined on the company code and ledger levels. You maintain the fiscal year variants by following IMG menu path **Financial Accounting • Financial Accounting Global Settings • Ledgers • Fiscal Year and Posting Periods • Maintain Fiscal Year Variant**. You'll arrive at the screen shown in Figure 2.28.

First, you can check if the predelivered fiscal year variants work for you. You can create your own by selecting the **New Entries** icon. Add the new fiscal year variant ID and your required parameters such as number of posting periods and number of special periods, and click **Save**.

In our example, the standard delivered fiscal year variant **K4** shown in the **FV** column in Figure 2.28 means the posting period is equal to the calendar year (flag in first column) and four special periods (fourth column). Fiscal year variant **V6** means the posting period is shifted by six months, so July is equal to period 1, and June is period 12.

		Display View "Fiscal year variants": Overview							

More ∨

Fiscal year variants

FV	Description	Calend...	Year-d...	Number of po...	No.of special ...	Fiscal ...	Offset Bef...	Offset Afte...	Weekly...
K4	Cal. Year, 4 Special P...	✓	☐	12	4	☐	0	0	☐
M3	AA Apr-Mar, 24 Per.	☐	☐	24	0	☐	0	0	☐
M4	AA Cal. Year, 24 Per.	☐	☐	24	0	☐	0	0	☐
M6	AA Jul-Jun, 24 Per.	☐	☐	24	0	☐	0	0	☐
M9	AA Oct-Sep, 24 Per.	☐	☐	24	0	☐	0	0	☐
N3	AA Apr-Mar,24 P.,yr sh...	☐	☐	24	0	☐	0	0	☐
N6	AA Jul-Jun,24 P.,yr shi...	☐	☐	24	0	☐	0	0	☐
Q4	Quaterly2	☐	☐	4	0	☐	0	0	☐
QT	Quaterly	☐	☐	4	0	☐	0	0	☐
S3	Apr-Mar,4 Sp. Per,yr s...	☐	☐	12	4	☐	0	0	☐
S6	Jul-Jun,4 Sp. Per,yr sh...	☐	☐	12	4	☐	0	0	☐
SA	Configurable template ...	☐	☐	12	0	☐	0	0	☐
SZ	Configurable template ...	✓	☐	12	0	☐	0	0	☐
V3	Apr.- March, 4 special ...	☐	☐	12	4	☐	0	0	☐
V6	July - June, 4 special ...	☐	☐	12	4	☐	0	0	☐
V9	Oct.- Sept., 4 special p...	☐	☐	12	4	☐	0	0	☐

Figure 2.28 Definition of Fiscal Year Variants in IMG

Extension Ledger

Next to the standard ledger in SAP S/4HANA, a new type of ledger is now available: the *extension ledger*. We've already introduced this in an introductory way in Chapter 1, Section 1.3.2. Whereas the standard ledger contains a variety of different journal entries for all business transactions, you can post journal entries directly in an extension ledger, which is located on top of this standard ledger. As a result, the extension ledger only stores the delta entries that are posted specifically to the extension ledger. All postings in the underlying standard ledger are part of the extension ledger reporting. This setup avoids redundant data storage. When you run a report for an extension ledger, the journal entries of the extension ledger and the underlying standard ledger are always displayed aggregated.

You can create an extension ledger in the same way as in the ledger in Customizing by following menu path **Financial Accounting • Financial Accounting Global Settings • Ledgers • Ledger • Define Settings for Ledgers and Currency Types**. You'll arrive at the screen shown in Figure 2.29.

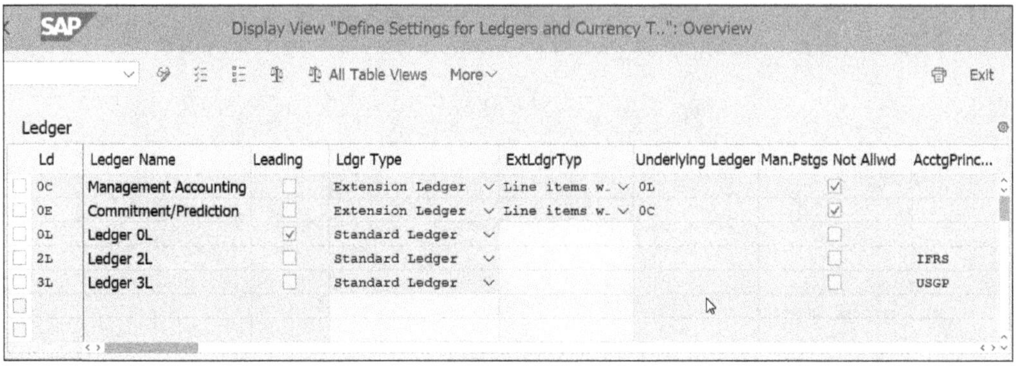

Figure 2.29 New Ledger Type: Extension Ledger

The first two ledgers are extension ledgers defined with the column **Ldgr Type**. For these two ledgers, you need to add one of the following **Ext.LdgrTyp**:

- **P**

  Line items with technical numbers for which deletion isn't possible. This type is used, for example, for prediction, commitments and statistical sales and distribution conditions.

- **S**

  Line items with technical numbers for which deletion is possible. This type is used for simulation data.

In our example, both extension ledgers are of type **P**.

In addition, it's mandatory to assign an **Underlying Ledger**, which must be a standard ledger or another extension ledger. In our example—public cloud scope—the two extension ledgers are both of type **P**, that is, deletion not possible. The management accounting ledger—ledger **OC**—is assigned to ledger **OL**. The second extension ledger—ledger **OE**—is assigned to the management accounting ledger.

You can assign multiple extension ledgers to a standard ledger. For the extension ledger, you can select whether manual postings are allowed.

> **Note**
>
> The following are possible use cases for extension ledgers:
>
> - You create an extension ledger that carries delta values for management accounting purposes (Section 2.3.2.). This can be additional values such as statistical costs, sales and distribution conditions, or manual management adjustments (e.g., profit center allocations).
> - You can create extension ledgers to capture commitment information, for example, coming from purchase orders.
> - You use the standard ledger for local GAAP. For IFRS reporting, you post the delta valuation in the assigned extension ledger.

2.3 Integration of Financial Accounting and Management Accounting

With the Universal Journal, financial accounting—more specifically, the general ledger—and management accounting are highly integrated and continuously reconciled. This means that a powerful and comprehensive data model is now available that can be used for process simplification and enhanced reporting insights. Due to the in-memory technology, the accounting reports can be drawn directly from the transactional data (the single journal entry item) without any prior aggregation—and this with breathtaking speed and easy-to-understand graphical evaluation tools.

In this section, we show you how this integration of management accounting is implemented in the system and how it affects the general ledger. We also show that the analyses that take place separately in the SAP ERP system in the Controlling (CO) module are now derived from the common Universal Journal database. This applies in particular to the market segment reporting.

> **Note**
>
> In this book, we can only give a few insights on controlling in SAP S/4HANA, but you can get more detailed coverage in *Controlling with SAP S/4HANA: Business User Guide* (SAP PRESS, 2021), which is available at *www.sap-press.com/5282*.

2.3.1 Management Accounting Postings in the General Ledger

With the introduction of the Universal Journal, the two-circuit system—having general ledger and management accounting separated—is obsolete. There is only one database, the Universal Journal, containing all relevant financial postings (see Chapter 1, Section 1.2). Management accounting is part of the general ledger, and reconciliation between CO and FI isn't necessary anymore. We now have a single source of truth, and efforts to reach the single point of truth are obsolete.

The management accounting business transactions now post in the general ledger. With this, for example, the following management accounting transactions are persisted in the Universal Journal:

- **Activity allocation**
  Quantity-based allocation (activity allocation or time sheet entry).
- **Cost center allocation**
  Amount-based allocation between cost centers, for example, posted with the universal allocation.
- **Overhead surcharge**
  Order cost object debited and cost center credited with the overhead general ledger account (e.g., material overheads on a production order).

- **Cost object settlement**
  Amount-based cost allocation of an order cost object to potential multiple receiver objects such as cost centers (e.g., settlement of internal project to cost center).

Figure 2.30 provides a general overview of management accounting postings based on t-account representations.

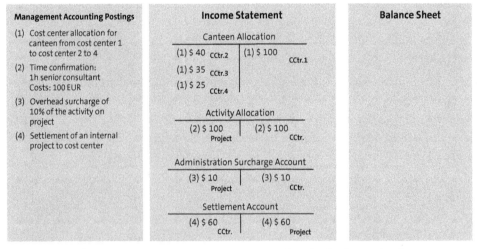

Figure 2.30 Reflection of Management Accounting Postings in the General Ledger

All these postings have in common that the same P&L general ledger account is used on the debit and credit lines, and the balance on the general ledger account for every posting is zero.

The direct integration of management accounting in the general ledger makes reconciliation between these applications and a manual transfer from management accounting postings in the general ledger obsolete. This simplifies the period-end close and enriches reporting. On the other hand, close coordination between these applications is required.

The management accounting postings don't touch the balance sheet. However, it must be recognized that postings on capitalizable cost objects or revenue-carrying cost objects lead to additional WIP or revenue recognition postings (see Chapter 7).

Let's look at how this works for the example of a time sheet entry. (This is a business process from the customer project scenario, which we discuss in more detail in Chapter 7.) Employees can access time sheet entry with the My Timesheet app (F0397). In Figure 2.31, you see an employee time recording of five hours on a customer project named **S/4HANA Implementation project.**

The time confirmation is processed as a quantity-based activity allocation crediting the employee cost center and debiting the customer project. It leads to the following journal entry in Figure 2.32. You can access this report with the SAP_BR_GL_Accountant role and the Display Line Items in General Ledger app. We select the ledger, the company code, and the journal entry of the time sheet posting.

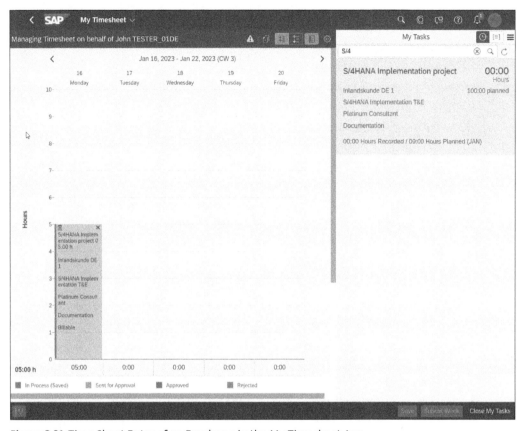

Figure 2.31 Time Sheet Entry of an Employee in the My Timesheet App

Figure 2.32 Time Sheet Journal Entry in the Display Line Items in General Ledger App

In Figure 2.32, you can analyze the created **Journal Entry 2300000054**, posted with the **Journal Entry Type CO (Secondary Cost)** (Section 2.3.3) and the management accounting business transaction type **RKL** (in the **Business** column), reflecting quantity-based allocation. The business transaction type is a field in the Universal Journal table that specifies the business transaction.

You can see that this document is created by a time sheet entry by the reference document type, which is shown in the **Reference Doc** column. Here the value is **CATS** (cross-application time sheet), which shows the reference to the time sheet.

The first line is the credit of the cost center; the second line is the debit of the project. In both lines, the same P&L general ledger account, **94308000 (Consulting)**, is used.

Now we'll show you that even though it's a management business transaction, it can have an impact on general ledger reporting, which underlines that there are good reasons to post them directly in the general ledger without waiting for period-end reconciliation.

In the far-right **Functional Area** column, **YB30** in the first journal entry item is derived from the cost center master, and in the second journal entry item, **YB25** is derived from the project master. Therefore, this posting influences the cost-of-sales reporting as we debit functional area **YB25** and credit **YB30**.

The **Profit Center** is different too: profit center **YB101** is derived from the cost center and **YB111** from the project. The **Segment** gets derived from the profit center. In this case, **1000_A** is derived for the first journal entry item segment and **1000_B** for the second; thus this allocation impacts the segment reporting.

2.3.2   Market Segment Reporting in the Universal Journal: The Margin Analysis Application

Depending on their business model, each customer defines a specific market segment. The market segment consists of attributes for which costs, revenues, and margins can be reported. Typical market segment attributes are customer and product sold, which can be taken from the operational data, such as the sales order item. Other attributes can be derived from these two attributes, such as industry and customer group from the customer master. With the provided extensibility capabilities (see Chapter 1, Section 1.2.3), the market segment can be enhanced with custom specific attributes. The resulting vector of attributes defines the market segment that will be inserted into the Universal Journal items.

The market segment is defined in the management accounting application profitability analysis by the organizational unit operating concern (see Figure 2.38 later in this chapter). By default, for example, customer, customer group, product, product group, sales organization, and industry are provided as attributes.

Note

There are two profitability solutions in place in on-premise SAP S/4HANA. We show here the Universal Journal–based margin analysis. This is the solution SAP focuses on in SAP S/4HANA and will be enhanced in the roadmap. In SAP S/4HANA Cloud, public edition, only margin analysis is available.

Costing-based profitability analysis, with its own database, is available (and will be in the future) in on-premise SAP S/4HANA as an additional solution.

If you activate margin analysis, all your configured market segment attributes are added as additional fields in the Universal Journal. In Figure 2.33, you can see how this is reflected in the time sheet posting introduced in the previous section.

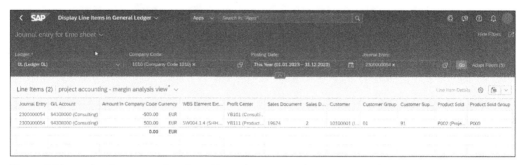

Figure 2.33 Market Segment View for a Time Sheet Journal Entry

Journal Entry 2300000054 is shown again but with different Universal Journal fields. We get the market segment view of the Universal Journal in the user-specific created **project accounting - margin analysis view.** In this app, you can define your own view variants by choosing your required fields out of the list of fields in the Universal Journal.

The second journal entry item reflects the posting on the customer project. Based on the customer project, the system is able to automatically derive market segment information from the project's assigned sales order item: **Customer, Customer Group, Product Sold, Product Sold Group, Customer Supplier Industry,** and **Sales Document** are automatically derived by the posting and stored in the Universal Journal for enhanced reporting functionality. More about this topic is discussed in Chapter 7.

If the Universal Journal's integrated profitability solution (that is, margin analysis) is activated (discussed in the next section), then additional management accounting business transactions post in the general ledger. These are all scenarios where the original general ledger posting lines are split up to obtain further information related to cost management.

Let's consider a few examples:

- The journal entries created by goods issues for sales order delivery are split up to get detailed information about the cost component split and to enable multilevel cross-margin reporting.

- The same is true for price differences coming from production orders. Here, additional information about production variances is provided by creating additional journal entry items with general ledger accounts for the different variance categories.

- The top-down allocation, in which you allocate costs and revenues to detailed market segments, creates journal entry items.

> **Note**
>
> As an accountant, you must be aware that additional documents are now posted in the general ledger triggered by management accounting business processes. A close alignment during the SAP S/4HANA implementation phase is required. This can also lead to changes in processes and structures between management accounting and financial accounting.

2.3.3   Interface Configuration

In this section, we'll show you how the interface is configured between financial accounting and management accounting, and how the two applications now work technically together. As mentioned, every management accounting transaction now posts in the general ledger. Therefore, you first need to define with which document type the management accounting business transactions are posted in the general ledger.

You find this Customizing in the following IMG menu path: **Financial Accounting • Financial Accounting Global Settings • Ledgers • Integration of Controlling with Financial Accounting • Define Document Type Mapping Variants for Postings in Controlling**. Mark the **DocType Mapping Var.**, and then select **Mapping of CO Bus. Transactions to Document Types** in the dialog structure. You'll arrive at the screen shown in Figure 2.34, which shows a selection of some controlling business transactions.

Display View "Mapping of CO Bus. Transactions to Document Types": Over

Dialog Structure	**DocType Mapping Var.** 000000A000
∨ Variant for Mapping CO Tran	
· Mapping of CO Bus. Trans	Mapping of CO Bus. Transactions to Document Types

CO Business Transaction	Text	Document type	Cross-Company Document Type
CPPA	ABC Actual process assessment	CO	CC
JRIU	JV-Seg.adjustm.assessment	CO	CC
JRIV	JV-Seg.adjustm.distribution	CO	CC
JVIU	JV Actual assessment	CO	CC
JVIV	JV Actual distribution	CO	CC
JVU1	JV Reposting costs	CO	CC
KAFD	External data transfer	CO	CC
KAMV	Manual cost allocation	CO	CC
KAZI	Actual cost center accrual	CO	CC
KAZO	Down payment	CO	CC
KFPI	Transfer price allocation	CO	CC
KGPD	Distribution acc. to peg	CO	CC
KOAL	Actual settlement of IAA	CO	CC
KOAO	Actual settlement	CO	CC
KOLI	Collective order delivery	CO	CC
KPIV	Actual cost distrib. cost obj.	CO	CC
KPIW	Act cost distrib. COB IAA	CO	CC
KSIO	Actual cost center split	CO	CC
KSI1	Actual split costs (primary)	CO	CC
KSI2	Actual split costs (secondary)	CO	CC
KSI3	Actual split costs IAA	CO	CC
KSII	Actual price calculation	CO	CC
KSPA	Assessment to CO-PA	CO	CC

Figure 2.34 Assignment of Controlling Business Transactions to General Ledger Document Type

Now let's take a quick look at the management accounting organizational units: controlling area and operating concern.

Organizational Units of Management Accounting

The controlling area is the organizational unit defining management accounting settings. It can be maintained in IMG by following menu path **Controlling • General Controlling • Organization • Maintain Controlling area. Select Activity Maintain Controlling Area**.

You'll arrive at the screen shown in Figure 2.35, where the basic settings for the controlling area are shown. From an accounting perspective, the definition of the group currency, the used chart of accounts, and the fiscal year variant are important. These attributes are defined in the company code too (refer to Section 2.2.1) and must match.

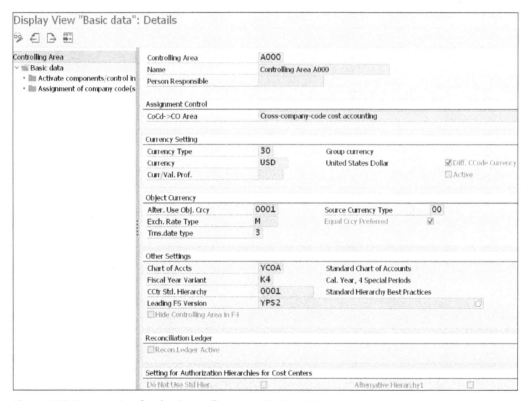

Figure 2.35 Customizing for the Controlling Area: Basic Settings

Additional settings and controls are defined on the controlling area level, such as the activation of cost objects, but we won't discuss these in further detail for the purposes of this book.

The controlling area can be assigned to one or more company codes. In this case, three settings need to be aligned. The fiscal year variant and the chart of account must be the same in the controlling area and in all assigned company codes, and the currency control must be aligned. The group currency for the assigned company codes is defined by the controlling area currency (refer to Section 2.2.1).

You need to take this into account when you assign the company codes to the controlling area in Customizing (see Figure 2.36). You get to this screen by selecting the **Controlling Area**; once there, select **Assignment of company code(s)** on the left.

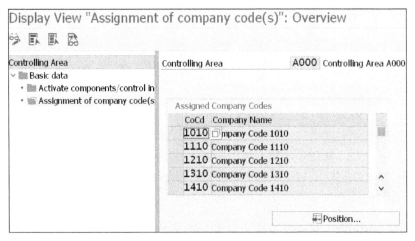

Figure 2.36 Customizing for Controlling Area: Company Code Assignment

Tip

To enable additional functionality, such as intercompany management accounting postings, to further align management accounting and financial accounting and to allow group reporting, we recommend using one cross-company code controlling area in SAP S/4HANA. In this case, all your company codes are assigned to one controlling area.

The next management accounting organizational unit is the operation concern. It's defined in Customizing by following IMG menu path **Controlling • Profitability Analysis • Structures • Define Operating Concern • Maintain Operating Concern**, which brings you to the screen shown in Figure 2.37.

With this organizational unit, you organize your market segment reporting. Based on the operating concern, you define your own market segment attributes (see Figure 2.38).

With the operating concern, you define the method (i.e., how you get your market segment data). As mentioned previously, there are two totally different profitability analysis solutions available in SAP S/4HANA. While **Costing-based** profitability analysis and the **Combined** solution share their own database, the **Margin Analysis** option is integrated in the Universal Journal.

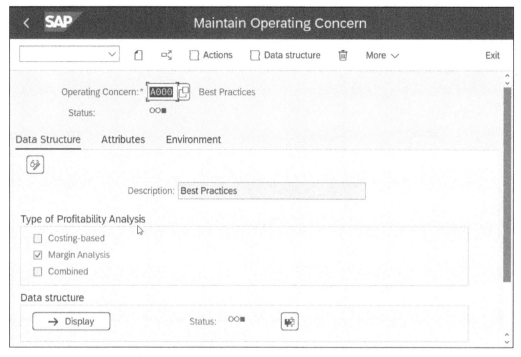

Figure 2.37 Customizing the Operating Concern

The examples of integrated market segment reporting shown in this book require margin analysis as a prerequisite.

> **Note**
>
> In the past, SAP customers mainly used costing-based profitability analysis. However, to use the additional reporting insights, activation of margin analysis, which is the Universal Journal's integrated profitability solution, is necessary.
>
> Migrating from SAP ERP using costing-based profitability analysis to SAP S/4HANA using margin analysis will lead to significant changes: the journal entries will be enhanced with additional fields, the data in costing-based profitability analysis data storage will need to be migrated to the Universal Journal, and the business processes will update margin analysis with different values, information, and points in time compared to costing-based profitability analysis.

For your market segment reporting, you need to define the relevant market segment attributes by following IMG menu path **Controlling • Profitability Analysis • Structures • Define Operating Concern • Maintain Characteristics**. Select **All Characteristics**, and click **Display** to arrive at the screen shown in Figure 2.38.

Display Characteristics: Overview						
Char.	Description	Short text	DTyp	Lgth.	Origin Table	Origin field d
ARTNRG	Generic Article	GenArticle	CHAR		40MARA	SATNR
AUART	Sales doc. type	SalesDocTy	CHAR		4VBAK	AUART
BONUS	Vol. Rebate Grp	Rebate Grp	CHAR		2MVKE	BONUS
BRSCH	Industry	Industry	CHAR		4KNA1	BRSCH
BZIRK	Sales District	District	CHAR		6KNVV	BZIRK
CHARG	Batch	Batch	CHAR		10VBAP	CHARG
COLLE	Collection	Collection	CHAR		10VBAP	FSH_COLLECTION
COPA_PRZNR	Business Proc.	BusProcess	CHAR		12	
CRMCSTY	CRM Cost Elmnt	CRM CstElm	CHAR		10	
CRMELEM	Marketing Element	Mrkt.Elem.	NUMC		8	
CRMFIGR	CRM Key Figure	CRM KF	CHAR		16	
EFORM	Form of manufacture	Manuf.form	CHAR		5	
EKGRP	Purch. Group	Purch. Grp	CHAR		3MARC	EKGRP
GEBIE	Area	Area	CHAR		4	
KDGRP	Customer Group	Cust.Group	CHAR		2KNVV	KDGRP

Figure 2.38 Market Segment Attribute Definition in Customizing

By default, you already get the customer, the sold product (**ARTNRG**), and the sales order as attributes. Then there are related attributes derived from the master data, such as the product group from the sold product or the industry (**BRSCH**) from the customer master. You can define your own attributes and define a derivation logic for how the attributes are derived.

> **Note**
>
> The market segment attributes you define in Customizing will be generated as Universal Journal fields. All these fields are part of the general ledger and are updated depending on the business process.

Connection between General Ledger Accounts and Cost Elements

As you've already seen in the examples in this chapter, cost elements are now general ledger accounts and part of the chart of accounts. The reporting of management accounting business transactions (mentioned in Section 2.3.1) now takes place in the general ledger reporting (see more in Chapter 3, Section 3.7).

In SAP S/4HANA, secondary cost elements—respectively, the general ledger accounts used by the management accounting business transactions—are part of the chart of accounts. Their master data is maintained using Transaction FS00.

Let's take a look at the maintenance of a secondary cost element by starting Transaction FS00 and selecting management accounting general ledger account **94308000 Consulting**. The general ledger accounts relevant for management accounting are controlled via the **G/L Account Type**, as shown in Figure 2.39. If **Secondary Costs** or **Primary costs or revenues** is selected, the general ledger account is relevant for management accounting. This means that an account assignment to a cost object, such as a cost center, is required.

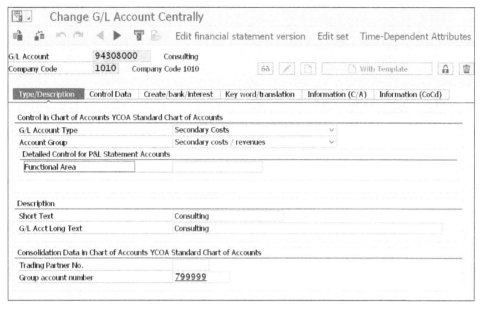

Figure 2.39 Maintenance of General Ledger Account: General View

Now we select the **Control Data** tab and get to the screen shown in Figure 2.40.

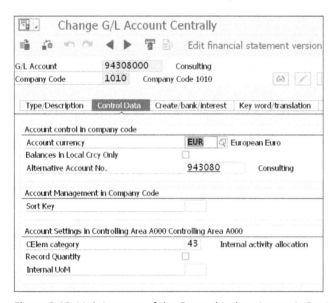

Figure 2.40 Maintenance of the General Ledger Account: Control Data

Here, the **CElem category** (cost element category) can be defined. Cost element categories are fixed values in SAP S/4HANA. They define the management accounting business transactions in which the general ledger accounts can be used. With the value help for the **CElem category** field, you get the available values on the screen shown in Figure 2.41.

Fixed	Short Descript.
21	Internal settlement
31	Order/project results analysis
41	Overhead Rates
42	Assessment
43	Internal activity allocation
50	Project-related incoming orders: Sales revenue
51	Project-related incoming orders: Other revenues
52	Project-related incoming orders: Costs
61	Earned value
66	Reporting Cost Element CO-PA

Figure 2.41 Cost Element Categories in SAP S/4HANA

Note

Secondary general ledger accounts—for example, with type **41 Overhead Rates** or **43 Internal activity allocation**—can't be used for primary postings such as Transaction FB50. They can only be used by the management accounting business transactions to which they are assigned.

Ledgers and Management Accounting

As mentioned in Section 2.2.3, there is an option to run the general ledger based on different parallel ledgers, which can be assigned to different accounting principles. This allows different valuations for the same operational transaction in parallel.

There are now two solutions for parallel valuation in cost management:

- Up to now, cost management has only worked with one valuation approach. The value from the leading ledger is adopted for all parallel standard ledgers.
- With on-premise SAP S/4HANA release 2022, universal parallel accounting is available, which allows parallel valuation in cost management, asset management, and materials management.

Example

You can operate with two standard ledgers, one following the IFRS accounting principle, which is the leading ledger, and another ledger following the local GAAP. In this case, the asset depreciation values—posted on a cost center—can be quite different in the two ledgers. Let's assume there is an amount of 1000 EUR in the IFRS ledger on the cost center and 800 EUR on the cost center in the local ledger. If you now start a cost center allocation with the rule to allocate all costs from the cost center to multiple receivers, there will be different results for the two valuation methods:

- If universal parallel accounting is active, the cost center will be credited in the IFRS ledger with 1000 EUR and in the local ledger with 800 EUR. The balance of the cost center in both ledgers will be zero.
- With the existing approach without active universal parallel accounting, the cost center will be credited in the IFRS ledger and local ledger with 1000 EUR, the value of the leading ledger. There will be a negative balance of −200 EUR in the local ledger on the cost center.

Note

Universal parallel accounting is the strategic orientation of SAP S/4HANA Finance for handling parallel valuations, for example, parallel group or profit center valuation. Its architecture is based on the use of parallel ledgers. Universal parallel accounting is active in SAP S/4HANA Cloud, public edition by default, and it's also available with initial functionality in on-premise SAP S/4HANA release 2022.

We'll discuss the activation and functionality of universal parallel accounting in Chapter 3. In this section, we'll explain how the solution used until now (without universal parallel accounting) is set up in the system.

To define this one value for processing and reporting, you need to assign one leading ledger to management accounting. You find this implementation activity by following IMG menu path **Financial Accounting • Global Settings • Ledgers • Integration of Controlling with Financial Accounting • Define Ledger for CO Version** to arrive at the screen shown in Figure 2.42.

Display View "Ledger From Which CO Reads Actual Data": Overview

Ledger From Which CO Reads Actual Data

CO Area	Version	Ledger (Compat.)	Controlling Area Name	Version Description	Ledger Name
A000	0	0L	Controlling Area A000	Plan/actual version	Ledger 0L

Figure 2.42 Ledger Assignment to the Controlling Area

With this, the valuation of the primary postings on cost objects—for example, asset depreciation or manual journal entries—is defined by ledger **0L**.

If you want to enter controlling-specific valuations in addition to the legal bookkeeping—other costs or additional costs—this can be done using an extension ledger (refer to Section 2.2.3). In the extension ledger, you can enter journal entries that are only available for management accounting reporting, but don't influence the legal reporting.

2.3.4   Intercompany Management Accounting Postings

With the integration of management accounting in the general ledger, there is now a new posting logic available for cross-company management accounting processes that provides real-time clearing and intercompany reconciliation. This section shows you what these postings look like and which additional functionality is available.

First, let's consider three examples where intercompany postings might be applicable:

- A consultant, who is an employee of a US company, records one hour of time spent directly on a customer project, which belongs to a company in Germany.

- For an intercompany shared IT service, you post a quantity-based activity allocation of 10 hours (Transaction KB21N) from the IT cost center in company code A to a receiver cost object, such as a cost center, in company code B.

- For intercompany shared service allocation of IT equipment, you post an amount-based cost allocation (Transaction KB11N or Transaction KB15N) from an IT cost center in company code A to a receiver cost center in company code B. Or, you post a cost center allocation with universal allocation.

Let's focus on the first example of intercompany time confirmation. This leads to the following posting shown with the Display Line Items in General Ledger app in Figure 2.43.

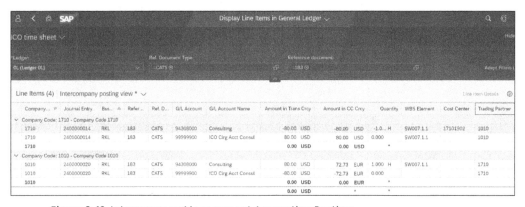

Figure 2.43 Intercompany Management Accounting Posting

As already shown in the example in Section 2.3.1, management accounting postings and, in particular, time confirmations, are reflected in the general ledger. With the time confirmation, the **Cost Center** of the employee is credited in US company code **1710** (see the first line). The customer project's **WBS Element** is debited in the German company code **1010** (see line 3). The transaction currency amount in USD is identical in the sending and receiving company code, that is, 80 USD (see the **Amount in Trans Crcy** column). Because two company codes are affected, two journal entry documents are created: **2400000014** in company code **1710** and **2400000020** in company code **1010** (see the **Journal Entry** column). To follow the double-entry bookkeeping standard, each journal entry must have a balance of zero, so offset line items are created using intercompany clearing accounts (here, general ledger account **99999900** in the **G/L Account** column).

All line items are referenced to the time sheet entry as shown in the reference document type (**Ref. D**) column and **183** in the reference document (**Refer**) column.

Because these documents are relevant for group consolidation, a **Trading Partner** is applied (see the far-right column). The journal entries in company code **1710** show the reference to company code **1010** and vice versa.

The intercompany clearing accounts are P&L accounts. You can define the used intercompany clearing accounts by following IMG menu path **Controlling • Cost Center Accounting • Actual Postings • Additional Transaction-Related Postings • Assign Intercompany Clearing Accounts**. You'll arrive at the screen shown in Figure 2.44.

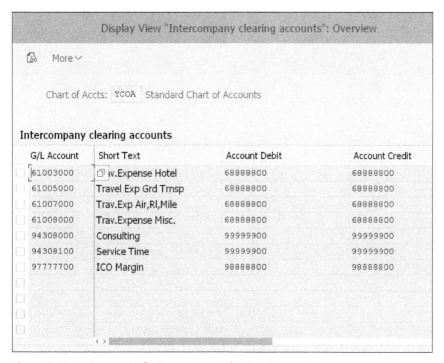

G/L Account	Short Text	Account Debit	Account Credit
61003000	v.Expense Hotel	68888800	68888800
61005000	Travel Exp Grd Trnsp	68888800	68888800
61007000	Trav.Exp Air,Rl,Mile	68888800	68888800
61008000	Trav.Expense Misc.	68888800	68888800
94308000	Consulting	99999900	99999900
94308100	Service Time	99999900	99999900
97777700	ICO Margin	98888800	98888800

Figure 2.44 Assignment of Intercompany Clearing Accounts

You can define the intercompany clearing account for your chart of accounts depending on the offset expense account. In this table, you need to add all expense accounts that you want to use for intercompany postings and assign an intercompany clearing account. As there is no cost object available for the clearing line item, the intercompany clearing account must not be a cost element. As mentioned, this means the general ledger account type in the general ledger account master must not be secondary costs, primary costs, or revenue.

This real-time consolidation posting based on the Universal Journal simplifies the period-end work and makes the reconciliation ledger used in SAP ERP obsolete.

In an additional—periodic—step, you can use all of these cross-company code management accounting postings that occurred in a period as the basis for creating an intercompany billing document (Transaction DP93). Based on the billing document in the sending company code, an accounts payable document in the receiving company code is generated. With these two documents, journal entry items for the affiliated revenue—affiliated and taxes—are generated.

Furthermore, a new functionality is now available in which an additional document containing an intercompany margin is generated for each intercompany activity allocation.

> **Note**
>
> For more information about this functionality of intercompany cost management allocations, read *Controlling with SAP S/4HANA: Business User Guide* (SAP PRESS, 2021), which is available at *www.sap-press.com/5282* or check out the blog at *http://s-prs.co/v569800*.

2.4 Summary

In this chapter, we've presented the most important SAP S/4HANA business processes and how they are mapped in general ledger accounting. You learned about the organizational elements relevant for general ledger accounting and their mapping to the logistical organizational units. In addition, you saw the main settings and decisions for the general ledger, which are the foundational elements to cover your reporting requirements.

You learned that it's a necessity to coordinate the setup with the other applications so that the business processes are mapped correctly in the general ledger. With the introduction of the Universal Journal, the level of integration has increased even further, along with the need to align the design of the business processes by system setup.

On the other hand, the effort for closing can be greatly reduced. This applies in particular to the reconciliation between the internal and external income statements. To obtain an identical result in all accounting applications and thus this single point of truth, extensive reconciliation work was previously necessary between FI and CO in SAP ERP. The Universal Journal now ensures this identity at the document level. The single point of truth thus becomes the single source of truth.

You've received a first insight into the financial accounting organizational structure and its integration with other applications, which will be further explored in the following chapters. We'll move on to discuss the general ledger core functionality in the next chapter. Understanding the role of the general ledger in SAP S/4HANA is important because there are many key business processes involved.

Chapter 3
General Ledger Accounting

The general ledger is the ultimate collecting pot of all financial information. After all information has been recorded and the books have been closed, reporting can begin. This chapter covers all standard activities in the general ledger, including the master data, daily accounting transactions, bank accounting, closing, and reporting.

In this chapter, we'll get started with the general ledger accounting process itself. This process is often referred to as record-to-report as transactional data has first been recorded and reconciled before financial information can be reported completely and accurately.

On our journey through the general ledger, you'll first learn about the general ledger master data. We discuss how to set up accounts, chart of accounts, and balance sheet structures before turning to how to process transactional data on accounts. We also cover a couple of things to consider when entering a journal document. We then dive deeper into bank accounts and bank accounting because a big portion of general ledger entries is made up of payment transactions coming from bank statements. We end the chapter by explaining two period-end activities: closing the period and reporting financial information. In this context, we cover the financial reporting capabilities of SAP S/4HANA, in particular, some new reporting features using SAP Fiori apps instead of SAP GUI.

3.1 Record-to-Report

From a legal perspective, financial accounting is a compulsory function for businesses because every company—even if it's a very small one—needs to record financial transactions, fulfill tax reporting requirements, and meet statutory obligations. Timely, complete, and accurate financial accounting also assists management in building better business controls, monitoring the financial situation, measuring profitability, and supporting management for better decision-making.

Record-to-report is a financial and accounting management process which ensures that all business transactions (e.g., sales, purchases, payments, etc.) are recorded completely and accurately within an accounting system and its (sub-)ledgers and that all entered transactions are ultimately collected and recorded in the general ledger.

Our focus in this section will be on the SAP record-to-report processes, which include the activities of subledger closing, reconciliation, periods processing, recording and adjusting journal entries, and financial reporting. Let's start by discussing the subledger closing concept in SAP S/4HANA.

3.1.1   Subledger Closing

A *subledger* is a ledger that contains all the detailed information from a subset of transactions. Regularly, all transactions or balances of subledger accounts are rolled up into the general ledger. Typical subledgers in financial accounting are accounts receivable, accounts payable, and fixed assets ledgers. In the *accounts receivable subledger*, customer invoices and customer payments are stored as well as detailed information about the transaction dates, billing information, services provided, goods shipped, payment type, and so on.

In a broader sense, materials management (more specifically, the Material Ledger) is also a subledger to the general ledger because inventory movements will also be rolled up into the general ledger. Traditionally, subledger transactions are aggregately reflected in the general ledger on a periodical basis. Therefore, if you're looking for some general ledger information in an account that contains this aggregated level of information, you must then access the subledger to get the full information regarding the relevant transactions.

With SAP R/3 in the early 1990s, all mentioned subledgers had been integrated in real time in the general ledger. Now, with SAP S/4HANA, subledger transaction details also can be shown through general ledger reporting functionalities because the database for all ledgers—subledgers and general ledgers—is one big table called table ACDOCA. You learned about this concept in Chapter 1, Section 1.2, when we introduced the Universal Journal.

However, the concept of a fully integrated accounting system only works without trouble if the system is set up correctly and if users enter and maintain master data accurately. To get a better understanding of what this means, let's look at the accounts payable subledger and the vendor account master data.

As you know, a vendor is a company supplier from whom you purchase goods or services. Every vendor master record belongs to a subledger account. All the vendor transaction details are maintained in the accounts payable subledger, which then rolls up into a general ledger account. In this case, this roll-up account is called the *accounts payable reconciliation account*. You can find this reconciliation account in the master record of a vendor account, as shown in Figure 3.1.

SAP Fiori App

The corresponding SAP Fiori app is called Manage Business Partner Master Data (F3163). It's visually and functionally the same as SAP GUI.

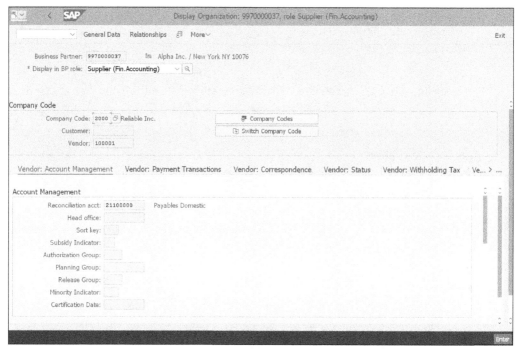

Figure 3.1 Reconciliation Account 21100000 for Business Partner/Supplier 9970000037

As a prerequisite of the subledger closing, all subledger transactions should be recorded completely. Depending on the subledger type, there are clearing accounts to be considered (e.g., fixed assets clearing, bank account clearing, and goods receipt/invoice receipt [GR/IR] clearing account) and valuation runs (foreign currency valuation, inventory valuations, assets depreciations, etc.) to be performed. After that, especially in fixed assets and the Material Ledger, subledger periods have to be closed. A reconciliation process with the general ledger is only possible after performing these closing activities in the subledgers.

3.1.2   Reconciliations

As explained in the previous section, financial accounting contains several subledgers, including accounts payable, accounts receivable, and fixed asset accounts. Each customer, vendor, and asset is created in a separate account in a subledger that is linked with a certain reconciliation account. When you create a vendor account, for example, the system prompts you to enter a reconciliation account. A *reconciliation account* is considered a control account to perform the reconciliation between the subledgers and the general ledger. For each entry posted in the subledger, the same amount is automatically updated to the related reconciliation account.

To create a reconciliation account in SAP S/4HANA, you must follow the same method used for all other general ledger accounts with some additional attributes that need to be configured.

Follow application menu path **Accounting • Financial Accounting • General Ledger • Master Records • G/L Accounts • Individual Processing • Centrally**, or use Transaction FS00. You'll arrive at the **Edit G/L Account Centrally** screen.

Click on **More** to switch to the **Create G/L Account Centrally** screen, as shown in Figure 3.2, where you must enter the company code and the general ledger account number, which you're going to create. Fill out the following tabs:

- **Type/Description**
  In the **Type/Description** tab, select **Balance Sheet Account** in the **G/L Account Type** dropdown, and select **Recon.account AP/AR** in the **Account Group** dropdown. Under **Consolidation Data in Chart of Accounts YCOA Standard Chart of Accounts**, enter the **Group Account Number**.

- **Control Data**
  In the **Control Data** tab, choose **Vendors** for **Recon. Account for Acct Type**. As a result, you're creating a reconciliation account for vendors' subledger accounts.

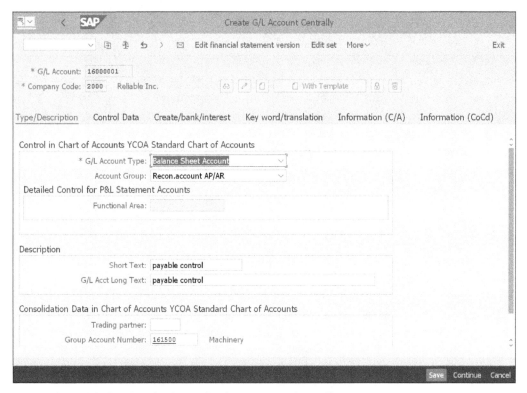

Figure 3.2 Creating the General Ledger Account Centrally

It's recommended to enter **Sort key** "001" under **Account Management in Company Code**, if you want the transactions posted to this account presorted by posting date, as shown in Figure 3.3. Alternatively, entering **Sort key** "002" will presort account entries by document number.

- **Create/bank/interest**
  In the **Create/bank/interest** tab, select the **Field status group** corresponding to the reconciliation accounts, as shown in Figure 3.4.

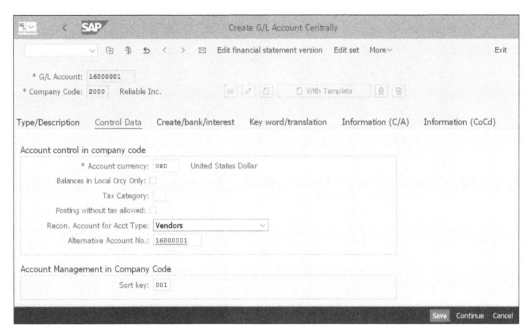

Figure 3.3 Selecting the Reconciliation Account Type

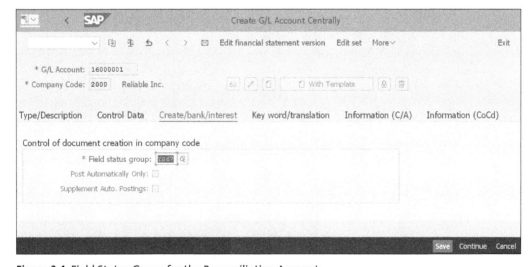

Figure 3.4 Field Status Group for the Reconciliation Account

After you've entered the required data, click the **Save** button, and a **Data Saved** message will appear at the bottom of the screen.

Now, if you need to display the reconciliation account that you've just created or any other account, you must follow the same application menu path mentioned at the beginning of the section and enter the account number you need to show in the **G/L Account** field. For example, enter the reconciliation account "16000001" in the **G/L Account** field, and then click the display icon 🔍, as shown in Figure 3.5. To show other attributes of this account, you can click on other tabs, such as **Control Data** and **Create/bank/interest**.

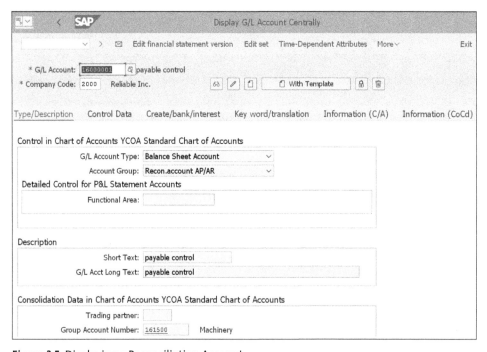

Figure 3.5 Displaying a Reconciliation Account

With proper reconciliation accounts set up for all subledgers and the reconciliation account correctly entered in each customer and supplier master data (we'll show how this is done later in this chapter and in Chapter 4), the subledger to general ledger reconciliation will never cause any trouble because it's technically impossible to have deviations between the balance of the general ledger account and the sum of the corresponding subledger items. However, accountants like to reconcile balances. For this reason, there are a couple of reconciliation reports that show the accumulated values of the subledgers and compare these values (either balances of subledger accounts or the sum of subledger posting document amounts) with balances of the general ledger reconciliation accounts. For each of the subledgers, we'll show this in their respective subledger chapters: Chapter 4 (accounts payable), Chapter 5 (accounts receivable), and Chapter 6 (fixed assets).

3.1.3 Record and Adjust

After subledgers have been reconciled and closed for a specific period, general ledger document entries and adjustments can be posted. Some accounting processes may be still manual, although they can be automated. There might be an external payroll system, where personnel expenses and payments to employees are posted manually on a monthly basis. Additionally, some provisions, reserves, and accruals will be posted manually through a journal entry document.

Moreover, some valuations, for instance, for inventory deprecations, may be posted manually on value adjustment accounts. You'll learn how manual documents can be entered in the general ledger in Section 3.3.

After all manual journal entries are posted (in addition to the subledger postings) and all value adjustments are posted on correction accounts, financial accounting for a specific period is complete and periods can be closed (Section 3.6.1).

3.1.4 Period Control

In this section, we'll describe the system logic and the main requirements for period control. *Period control* is a procedure that calculates and determines the time portions of start and end dates for asset transactions. Period control can be set, for example, for acquisitions, retirements, intercompany transfers, revaluations, and so on.

You can define posting periods in the fiscal year variants and can open or close these posting periods for posting. Although you can open some periods in the same time, usually only the current posting period is open for posting.

You can define a posting period by following path **Accounting • Financial Accounting • General Ledger • Environment • Current Settings • Open and Close Posting Periods**, or by using Transaction FAGL_EHP4_T001B_COFI. The complete steps for defining the posting period are discussed in Section 3.6.1.

3.1.5 Reporting and Analysis

SAP S/4HANA offers all the features you need for reporting. For statutory reporting, you'll find the following most important general ledger reports:

- **Financial statement**
  This report allows you to quickly retrieve any balance sheet and profit and loss (P&L) statement of any period for any company you held in SAP S/4HANA. It always includes the comparison to the prior year or any prior period you want to compare with.
- **Trial balance**
  This report shows you all account balances of a company for a certain period.
- **Compact document journal**
  This report provides you with a complete list of all financial accounting documents of the period selected.

Follow this application menu path to access all the reports you need: **Accounting • Financial Accounting • General Ledger • Information System • General Ledger Reports**.

SAP Fiori Apps

Following are the corresponding SAP Fiori apps for these reports:

- **Display Financial Statement (F0708)**
  The report generated from this app is much easier to read than the financial statement report from SAP GUI. Further, selecting fields and setting filters are easier than in the SAP GUI version.

- **Trial Balance (F0996A)**
  Thanks to a navigation panel, the Trial Balance app has easy-to-use drag-and-drop capabilities for selecting fields and dimensions. The filters applied are always shown at the top of the screen.

- **Audit Journal (F0997)**
  With this app, you can generate the document journal lists for any company and for any period. It's easier to select fields and to add filters than to use the compact document journal in SAP GUI.

The SAP Fiori apps have the advantage that you see the selected fields and the applied filters in the same screen with the results.

At this point, we just want to make you familiar with the SAP GUI menu path and the existence of corresponding SAP Fiori apps. All general ledger reports from SAP GUI and from SAP Fiori apps mentioned here are explained in Section 3.7.

To query and analyze accounts and documents, there are a couple of reports available that you can use to display single journal entry documents, or you can browse document entries on accounts:

- **Display Document**
  You can view and analyze any posted general ledger document. You just enter the **Document No.** and the relevant fiscal year, and you'll find it displayed.

- **Display Account Line Items**
  You can browse all line items posted to a selected general ledger account.

To display a single document, follow application menu path **Accounting • Financial Accounting • General Ledger • Document • Display**, or use Transaction FB03. To analyze line items on an account, go to **Accounting • Financial Accounting • General Ledger • Account • Display/Change Line Items or Line Item Browser**, or use Transaction FAGLL03 or Transaction FAGLL03H.

We'll explain how to analyze accounts and documents with examples in Section 3.7.

SAP Fiori Apps

The corresponding SAP Fiori app for displaying general ledger documents is Display Journal Entries in T-Account View (F3664). This app has the advantage that it visualizes the journal entry as t-accounts.

The corresponding SAP Fiori app to display general ledger account line items and balances is called Display Account Line Items in General Ledger (F0706). It's more convenient than the SAP GUI version because the selected fields and entered filters are always shown at the top of the screen.

For searching and analyzing any account or document entries in the general ledger, you can also use the Audit Journal app (F0997) mentioned earlier. The Audit Journal app is a very flexible tool that can be used for multiple purposes, including analyzing documents by date, creator, accounts, and so on.

So far, this has been a quick walk through the general ledger accounting record-to-report process. We now need to discuss general ledger accounting in a more detailed way. Let's start by diving into the general ledger master data.

3.2   General Ledger Master Data

Master data remains unchanged over a long period of time and contains information that is repeatedly required in the same way. In financial accounting, there are general ledger accounts, customer accounts, banks, and fixed assets. Each type of master data is necessary to operate specific business processes.

In the general ledger, the following master data is managed:

- General ledger accounts
- Chart of accounts
- Financial statement versions

General ledger account master data deals with accounting transactions, especially with how they are posted and how the posting is then processed. Before starting a posting to an account, master data of this account must already exist; otherwise, it isn't possible to perform this transaction. So, master data has an important role in SAP and all its business processes. It's only created once and is used over a long period of time for financial accounting and management.

Another attribute you have to know about master data is that although it can be created separately for each module, it can be assigned to and used in other modules as well. For example, if you've created an asset master record in asset accounting, you can also reference it in both purchase orders and financial accounting transactions.

Now that you have some basic understanding of master data, we'll explain and analyze the structuring and modeling of the financial accounting master data. Then, we'll walk through each of the three types of general ledger master data in detail.

3.2.1 Master Data Structure

Master data for general ledger accounts and profit centers in SAP GUI are found in the SAP user menu. Unfortunately, the maintenance of financial statement versions can only be accessed through the Customizing menu.

You can follow these paths for the SAP user menu and the Customizing menu:

- **SAP user menu**
  Accounting • Financial Accounting • General Ledger • Account • Master Records • G/L Accounts

- **Customizing menu**
  SAP Menu • Tool • Customizing • IMG • SPRO–Execute Project • SAP Reference IMG • Financial Accounting • General Ledger Accounting • Master Data • G/L Account • Define Financial Statement Version

---

SAP Fiori App

The corresponding SAP Fiori App is called Manage G/L Account Master Data (F0731).

In Figure 3.6, you can see how the Manage G/L Account Master Data app looks in SAP Fiori. With this app, you can search for the respective general ledger account you want to change by applying filters. If you want to create a new general ledger account, you click on the **Create** button. A new screen pops up where you can enter all the characteristics of the new account.

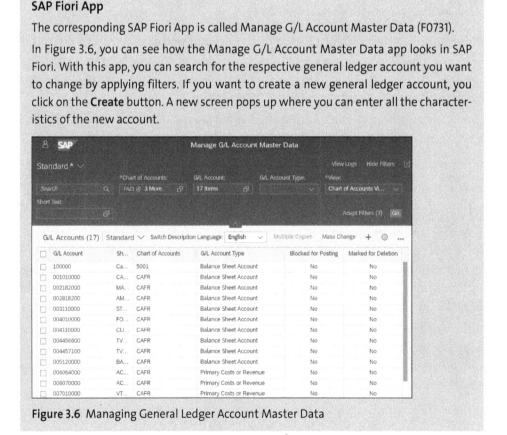

Figure 3.6 Managing General Ledger Account Master Data

Now that you've seen an overview of master data and know where to find it, let's discuss the master data in general ledger accounts.

3.2.2   General Ledger Accounts

General ledger accounting in SAP S/4HANA manages general ledger account master data, posts financial journal entries, and runs financial statements. It also contains and maintains internal management reporting requirements.

> **Note**
>
> A new feature of SAP S/4HANA is that cost element master data has merged with general ledger master data so that the cost element definition is now part of general ledger master data maintenance. The former transaction codes to create, change, or display cost elements (Transactions KA0*) now go directly to Transaction FS00.

From a financial accounting perspective, a *general ledger account* is the element where general ledger journals are posted by debit and credit entries. All accounting takes place on accounts. In school, you may have learned how to draw t-accounts where debit and credit amounts must be shown. In SAP S/4HANA, general ledger account master data is one of the most important kinds of master data because it plays a major role in the process and data integration model. Generally speaking, there are four types of general ledger accounts:

- **Balance sheet account**
  Balance sheet accounts are used for any kind of assets, liabilities, and equities.

- **Nonoperating expense and income**
  This type of expense or income isn't attached to sales as revenue or cost of sales account.

- **Primary costs or revenue**
  As mentioned in the preceding note, management accounting is integrated into financial accounting. They together build one common data basis. Primary costs include material costs, personnel costs, and energy costs. They come from a purchase with an external party. The same applies to primary revenue.

- **Secondary costs**
  Secondary costs are typically overhead costs that stem from cost allocation. They also stem from the accumulation of primary costs, which are allocated to other cost elements in management accounting, such as cost centers, projects, or other cost carriers.

By following the menu paths in the previous section, you'll arrive at the screen shown in Figure 3.7. Here, you can see the four general ledger account types in the **Edit G/L Account Centrally** screen by selecting the **G/L Account Type** dropdown.

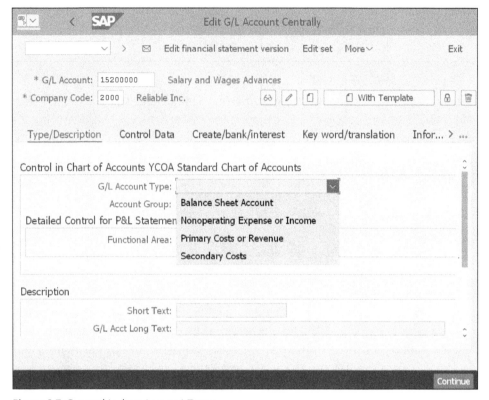

Figure 3.7 General Ledger Account Types

Next to the account type, the **Account Group** is also very relevant, as shown in Figure 3.8. The account group defines whether the account is conceived to be used for manual general ledger postings or whether it's part of the integration model in SAP S/4HANA. If the account group is a reconciliation account (**Recon.account AP/AR**, **Fixed assets accounts**, **Liquid funds accounts**, or **Materials management accounts**), manual general ledger postings are denied by the system. The general ledger posting is done as soon as a subledger transaction is entered. If the account group comprises **G/L accounts** or **Income statement accounts**, manual general ledger entries can be posted.

You can post almost every type of transaction on general ledger accounts manually, which is how general ledger accounts can end up being used in a very work-intensive and inefficient way. When deploying the full scope of functionalities of SAP S/4HANA, manual postings are becoming less necessary and therefore occur less frequently. In the best case, you automate almost all accounting postings through processing business transactions in subledgers (e.g., transactions in the materials management subledger or sales subledger). For instance, a material movement such as a goods receipt posting in the Material Ledger will trigger an automated posting in general ledger inventory and goods receipt accounts. This is realized through a setup of *account determination rules*.

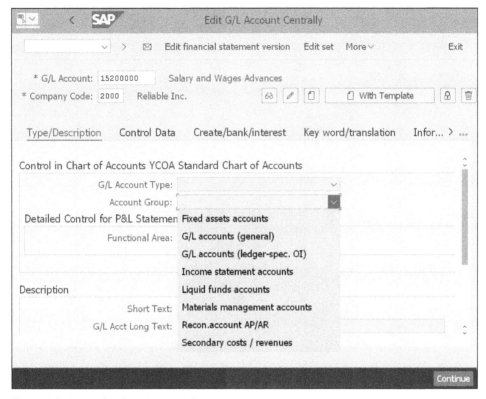

Figure 3.8 General Ledger Account Groups

Prior to performing a posting to general ledger accounts, it's necessary to assign an operative chart of account to the company code in the system configuration (Customizing). You can add, merge, and block as many general ledger accounts as you like, and their basic structure in the chart of accounts remains slightly stable during a certain fiscal year.

The chart of accounts represents the inventory of all the assembled general ledger accounts, which are assigned to a company code. The first step you need to follow after you set up the financial accounting is to define the structure of the chart of accounts with a solid and static ground basis for financial reporting. Considering that there could be a large number of general ledger accounts, SAP S/4HANA enables you to fragment them into groups.

To view and define account groups and their ranges in a general ledger account, use path **Tools • Customizing • IMG • SPRO – Execute Project • SAP Reference IMG • Financial Accounting • General Ledger Accounting • Master Data • G/L Account • Preparations • Define Account Group**, or use Transaction OBD4.

The **Change View "G/L Account Groups": Overview** screen appears (see Figure 3.9). In this screen, you can see the chart of accounts number, account group, names, and ranges of account numbers.

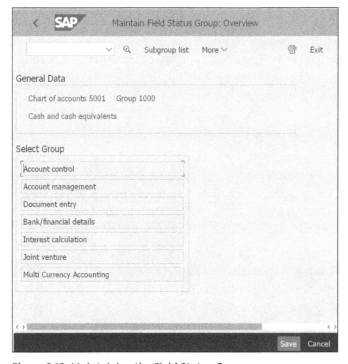

Figure 3.9 Defining the Account Group

Select any of these records, and the **Maintain Field Status Group: Overview** screen appears, in which you can change any attribute of the chart of accounts and account group, as shown in Figure 3.10:

- **Account control**
  Here you can decide whether the master data fields **Currency**, **Tax Category**, **Reconciliation Account**, and **Exchange Rate Difference** are suppressed or displayed in the master data and whether they are optional or required fields.

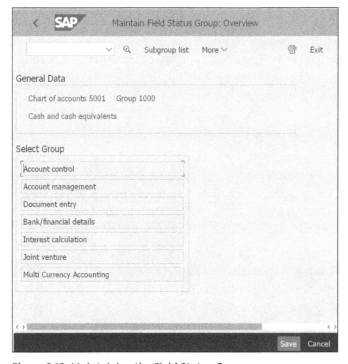

Figure 3.10 Maintaining the Field Status Group

- **Account management**
  Here you can decide whether the master data fields **Open Item Management, Sort Key, Authorization Group**, and **Administrator** are suppressed or displayed in the master data and whether they are optional or required fields.

- **Document entry**
  Here you can decide whether the master data fields **Reconcil.acct Ready for Input, Field Status Group, Post Automatically Only**, and **Supplement Automatic Postings** are suppressed or displayed in the master data and whether they are optional or required fields.

- **Bank/financial details**
  Here you can decide whether the master data fields **Planning Level, Commitment Item, Relevant to Cash Flow**, and **House Bank** are suppressed or displayed in the master data and whether they are optional or required fields.

- **Interest calculation**
  Here you can decide whether the master data field **Interest Calculation** is suppressed or displayed in the master data and whether it's an optional or a required field.

- **Joint venture**
  Here you can decide whether the master data field **Recovery Indicator** is suppressed or displayed in the master data and whether it's an optional or a required field.

- **Multi Currency Accounting**
  Here you can decide whether the master data field **Multi Currency Accounting** is suppressed or displayed in the master data and whether it's an optional or a required field.

SAP Fiori App

There is no corresponding SAP Fiori app as of SAP S/4HANA release 2022. Generally speaking, apps for configuration tasks will be developed in upcoming releases.

Now that you have a better understanding of the overall structure and importance of general ledger accounts, let's take a closer look at the chart of accounts.

3.2.3   Chart of Accounts

The *chart of accounts* is a list of general ledger accounts that contains information on all general ledger accounts, such as the account number, account name, general ledger account type, how an account functions, and how a general ledger account is created in a company code. It's always important to keep in mind that financial reporting is based on general ledger account transaction details and balances.

When a chart of accounts is assigned to the company code, the general ledger is updated according to this chart of accounts. This chart of accounts becomes the operating chart of accounts, which is used for the daily postings in this company code.

If there are multiple company codes and you want to harmonize the general ledger reporting, you have the following options:

- You can use the same chart of accounts for all company codes if the company codes all have the same requirements for the chart of accounts setup. This could be the case if all company codes are in the same country.
- You can assign up to two additional charts of accounts if the individual company codes need different charts of accounts. This could be the case if company codes exist in multiple countries.

In SAP S/4HANA, charts of accounts function in three different ways:

- **Operating chart of accounts**
  This type contains the general ledger accounts that you use for posting accounting entries during daily operations. It's assigned to a company code through Transaction OBY6 and is used for both financial accounting and controlling. The operating chart of accounts contains the expense and revenue accounts that are also components of controlling.

- **Group chart of accounts**
  This type contains the general ledger accounts of the entire company group and is used for consolidation purposes.

- **Country-specific chart of accounts**
  This type contains the general ledger accounts needed to meet a country's specific legal and tax requirements in case of multinational companies where a separate company code is assigned for each country. The same Transaction OBY6 is used to assign to a company code.

To see the charts of accounts assigned for your company, use the following path: **Tools • Customizing • IMG • SPRO – Execute Project • SAP Reference IMG • Financial Accounting • General Ledger Accounting • Master Data • G/L Account • Preparations • Edit Chart of Accounts List**. Double-click this transaction, and the screen shown in Figure 3.11 appears.

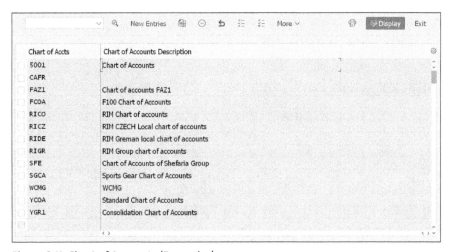

Figure 3.11 Chart of Accounts (Examples)

SAP Fiori App

The corresponding SAP Fiori app is called Manage Chart of Accounts (F0763A). After you open the app, you'll arrive at a list of charts of accounts and their descriptions from which you can select the desired chart of accounts to continue in the previous function of master data maintenance. In Figure 3.12, you can select the chart of accounts that you need to consider, and then click the > arrow. In Figure 3.13, you can see the results for the selected criteria.

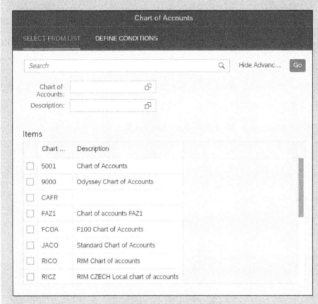

Figure 3.12 Chart of Accounts in SAP Fiori

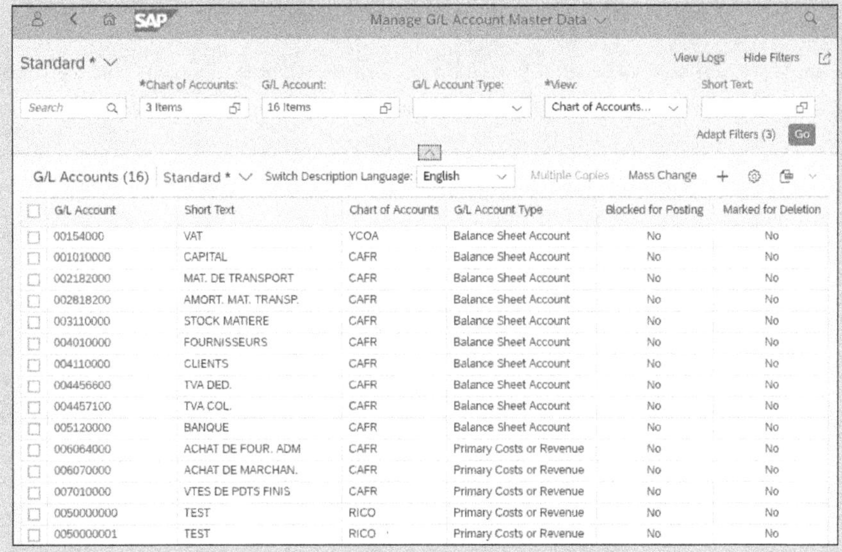

G/L Account	Short Text	Chart of Accounts	G/L Account Type	Blocked for Posting	Marked for Deletion
00154000	VAT	YCOA	Balance Sheet Account	No	No
001010000	CAPITAL	CAFR	Balance Sheet Account	No	No
002182000	MAT. DE TRANSPORT	CAFR	Balance Sheet Account	No	No
002818200	AMORT. MAT. TRANSP.	CAFR	Balance Sheet Account	No	No
003110000	STOCK MATIERE	CAFR	Balance Sheet Account	No	No
004010000	FOURNISSEURS	CAFR	Balance Sheet Account	No	No
004110000	CLIENTS	CAFR	Balance Sheet Account	No	No
004456600	TVA DED.	CAFR	Balance Sheet Account	No	No
004457100	TVA COL.	CAFR	Balance Sheet Account	No	No
005120000	BANQUE	CAFR	Balance Sheet Account	No	No
006064000	ACHAT DE FOUR. ADM	CAFR	Primary Costs or Revenue	No	No
006070000	ACHAT DE MARCHAN.	CAFR	Primary Costs or Revenue	No	No
007010000	VTES DE PDTS FINIS	CAFR	Primary Costs or Revenue	No	No
0050000000	TEST	RICO	Primary Costs or Revenue	No	No
0050000001	TEST	RICO	Primary Costs or Revenue	No	No

Figure 3.13 Managing General Ledger Account Master Data

3.2.4 Financial Statements

In this section, we'll describe an overview of the *financial statement version*, which is a tree designed specifically to organize and group general ledger accounts to get the balance sheet and income statement for the purpose of statutory reporting. SAP S/4HANA enables you to define multiple financial statement versions to generate financial statements in different formats. The financial statement version is maintained per organization requirements.

To define the financial statement version in the systems, use the following path: **Tools • Customizing • IMG • SPRO – Execute Project • SAP Reference IMG • Financial Accounting • General Ledger Accounting • Master Data • G/L Accounts • Define Financial Statement Version**.

After you double-click **Define Financial Statement Version**, another screen called **Change View "Financial Statement Versions": Overview**, as shown in Figure 3.14.

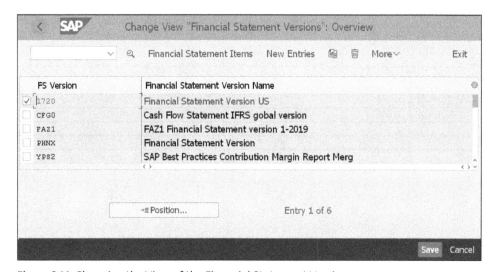

Figure 3.14 Changing the View of the Financial Statement Version

You can define a new financial statement version for a specific chart of accounts by making a selection in the **Chart of Accounts** field, by checking the **Group Account Number** checkbox for a group chart of accounts, or by assigning none of the general specifications (see Figure 3.15). Click the **Save** button to save your new financial statement version.

To edit a financial statement version, a shortcut has been provided that is much more convenient. Go to the general ledger to view any general ledger account by following path **Accounting • Financial Accounting • General Ledger • Master Records • G/L Accounts • Individual Processing • Centrally**.

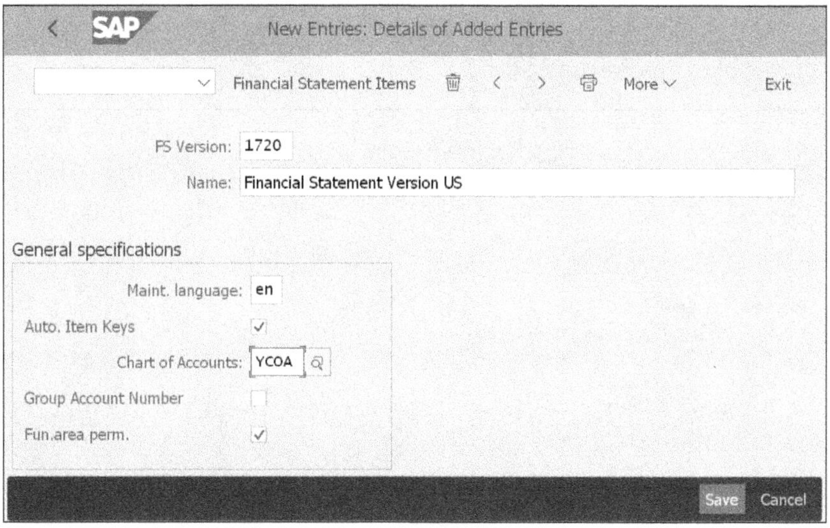

Figure 3.15 Defining a New Financial Statement Version

Click on **Edit financial statement version** at the top of the screen shown in Figure 3.16, and select the **FS Version** code that you're going to edit from the popup that appears, as shown in Figure 3.17.

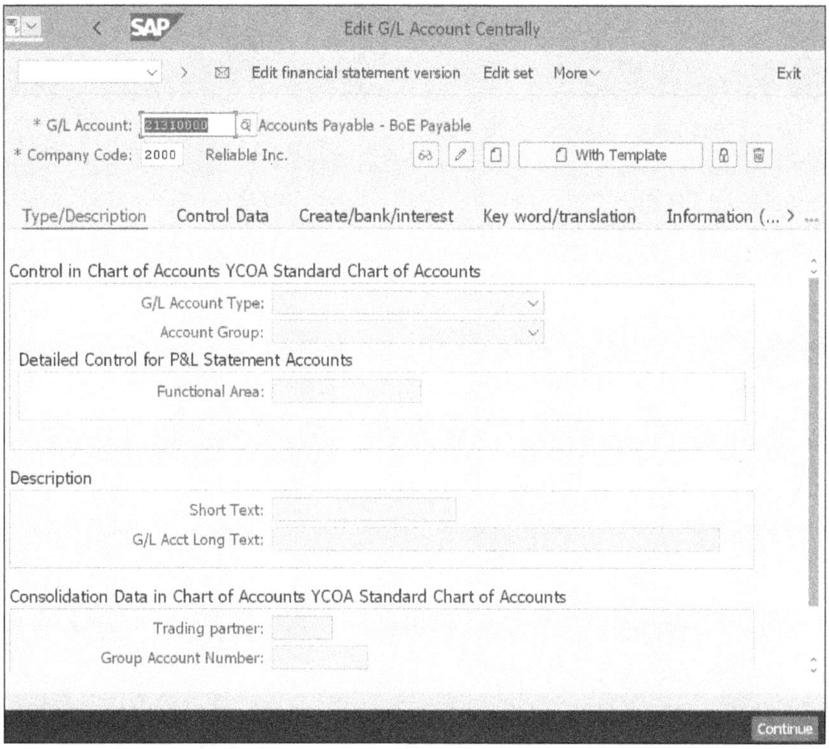

Figure 3.16 Editing the Financial Statement Version

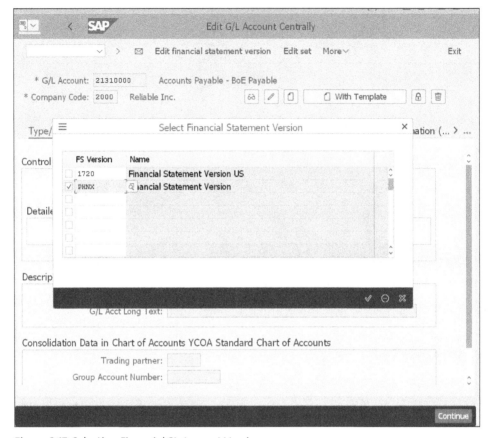

Figure 3.17 Selecting Financial Statement Version

After you've selected the financial statement version and clicked the green checkmark, you reach the **Change Financial Statement Version** screen, as shown in Figure 3.18. In this screen, you can edit the assignment of general ledger accounts to a financial statement line item. In this case, let's edit the financial statement line item **Trade Receivables – Domestic.** You can assign single accounts or account ranges **From Acct** to **To Account**. In this example, assign the account number **12119200** to the financial statement line item **Trade Receivables – Domestic**. The account always will be shown in this financial statement line item regardless of whether it has a debit or credit balance because both the **D** (debit) and **C** (credit) checkboxes are selected.

After you've entered a specific account or an interval of accounts, click the continue icon, and then click the **Save** button at the bottom-right corner of the main screen.

SAP Fiori App

The corresponding SAP Fiori app is called Maintain Financial Statement Versions (OB58). This app is visually and functionally the same as the SAP GUI transaction.

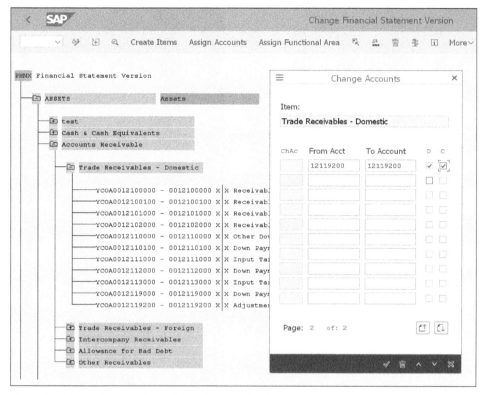

Figure 3.18 Changing the Financial Statement Version

Now that you understand how to set up and change the general ledger master data, you're ready to enter transactional data in the general ledger. The next section explains thoroughly how documents can be preliminarily entered, posted, and reversed in the general ledger.

3.3   General Ledger Posting Documents

A manual posting in the general ledger will create a journal entry document without any connections to subledgers or any business transactions entered in SAP S/4HANA. Some accounting processes generally aren't fully supported with automated functions, such as provisions, accruals, or valuation adjustments for certain assets and liabilities. For these purposes, manual general ledger postings are usually required.

The creation of a manual journal entry is subject to many restrictions. Not all general ledger accounts can be used for manual postings because there are some technical accounts, such as reconciliation accounts, that are blocked for manual postings. Further, a couple of other conditions need to be met before a general ledger document is recorded accurately. During the creation of a journal entry document, SAP S/4HANA checks whether debits and credits are balanced (according to the accounting balancing principal, any posting document should net to a balance of zero) and whether all accounting-relevant and required attributes are entered completely.

In this section, you'll learn how to post journal entry documents, how to park and to hold them, and how to reverse posting documents. We'll also explain how parallel accounting works and how you can use the SAP Financial Closing cockpit for SAP S/4HANA to better manage closing activities.

3.3.1 Journal Document Entry

A *journal entry* document—like any type of transactions entered in SAP—consists of document header information (e.g., company code, transaction currency, posting date, document date, document type, and description) and document body information (e.g., debit and credit accounts and amounts, tax codes, and other accounting information, including profit center, cost center, posting line description, etc.).

To create a journal entry document (referred to as a general ledger account document in the system), you can either use Transaction FB50 or follow SAP GUI menu path **Accounting • Financial Accounting • General Ledger • Document Entry • Enter G/L Account Document**.

The **Enter G/L Account Document** entry screen appears, as shown in Figure 3.19. The fields that appear on the document details may vary depending on your system configuration and editing options. The document is divided into a document header and line items. The document header contains information that applies to the entire document, such as **Posting Date**, **Document Date**, or information in the **Reference** field. There can be between 2 and 999 line items that contain information referring to the individual items, such as the posting key or account number.

Document type SA is the default document type for Transaction FB50.

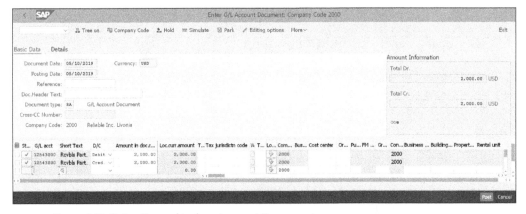

Figure 3.19 Enter General Ledger Account Document

In this screen, you can see all available fields to be filled. There are two tabs: **Basic Data** and **Details**. In the **Basic Data** tab, enter the **Document Date**, **Posting Date**, and document **Currency**. In the **Reference** field, for example, you enter the document number of an original document, which is external to your system, or a contract number to which the transaction refers. In the **Doc.Header Text** field, it's recommended to enter informative text related to the transaction. SAP S/4HANA proposes the company code currency in the **Currency** field. If you want to post the document in a different currency, you can change this default value using the input help by pressing the F4 key in this field.

In the **Details** tab, you can enter some additional information in relation to the basic data entered. For example, you can obtain the exchange rate for the amounts posted in a foreign currency.

Some fields are already prepopulated with the default values, such as the **Posting Date**, which takes the current date by default. You can define certain values as default values by clicking the **Editing options** button in the menu bar of the **Enter G/L Account Document** entry screen to open the screen shown in Figure 3.20.

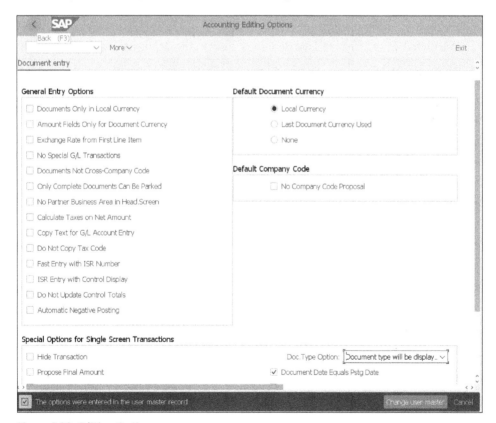

Figure 3.20 Editing Options

In this screen, the posting date is set as the default value for the document date. You can also define a specified option for the document type in the **Doc.Type Option** drop-down, such as displaying the document type, defining it as an input field, displaying it with a short name, and other available options. To apply the relevant changes, click on the **Change user master** button in the bottom right of the **Accounting Editing Options** screen. A message will appear informing you that the options were entered in the user master record.

After you've entered the basic data, you need to continue with the document items where at least two line items that net to a balance of zero must be created. In the bottom part of the entry screen shown previously in Figure 3.19, you can enter the general ledger account number for each item, indicate whether it's a debit or credit posting, and enter the amount per item.

Keep in mind that you must have entered at least two items with cleared debit and credit amounts to turn the traffic light green and post the transaction successfully. You can check the traffic light signal under the **Amount Information** area in the entry screen (you'll see that it's green, in our example). If you have some posting transactions that require different fields/dimension (profit center, cost center, tax code, etc.) in the posting lines, you can look for an appropriate predefined screen variant. To select an appropriate screen variant, click the **Tree on** button next to the command field in the upper-left corner of the screen (refer to Figure 3.19). Another area with working templates will appear in which you can select a screen variant in the relevant list (shown in Figure 3.21). The **Items** area at the bottom of the screen is then updated with the corresponding fields according to the selected screen variant.

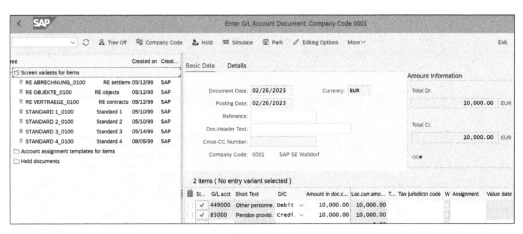

Figure 3.21 Selecting Screen Variants for Items

After you've selected a screen variant, you can close the area by clicking the **Tree off** button. You'll go back again to the entry screen where you can continue to prepare and obtain values in the individual line items.

If you double-click on a line item, a detail screen of the item appears where you can see additional input fields, as shown in Figure 3.22 for debit entry and Figure 3.23 for credit entry.

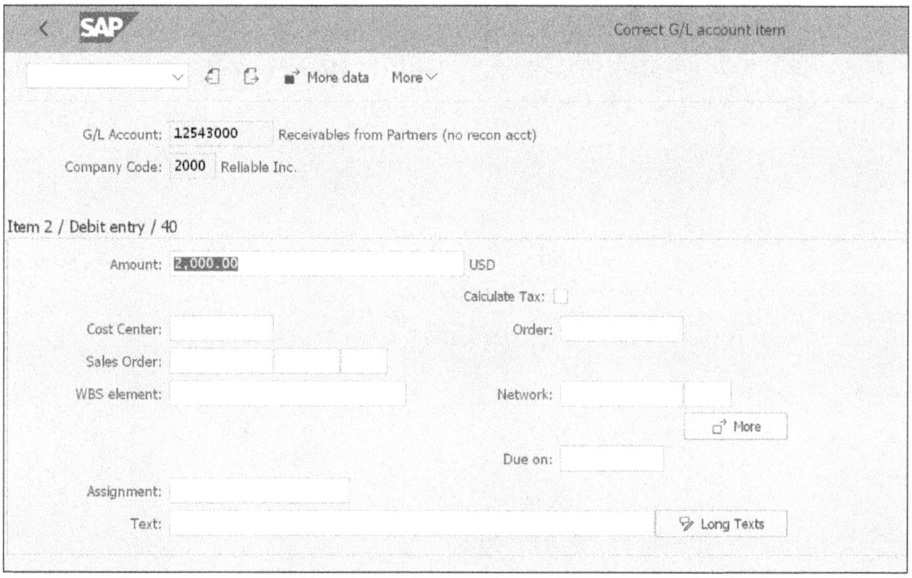

Figure 3.22 Detail Screen of an Individual Line Item in a Debit Entry

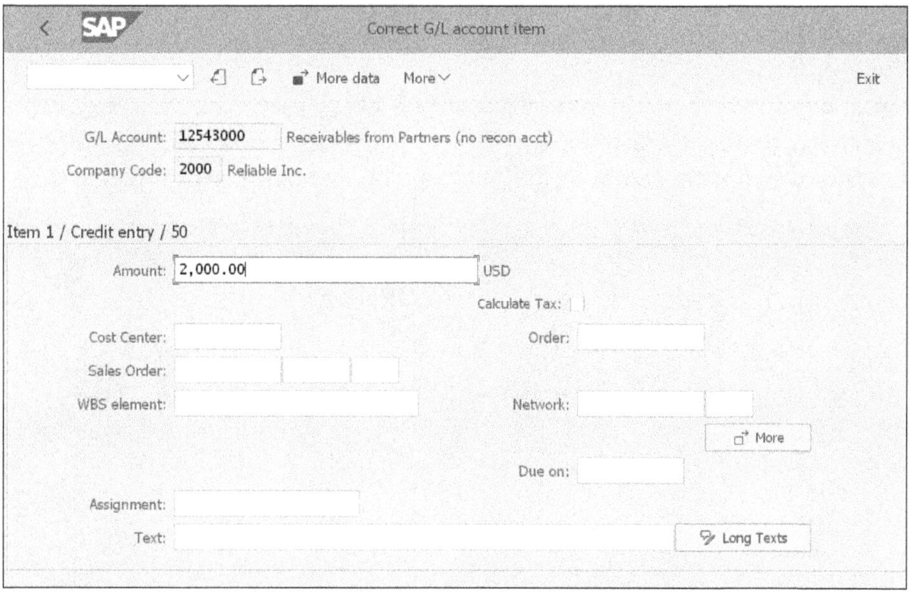

Figure 3.23 Detail Screen of an Individual Line Item in a Credit Entry

Typically, you enter a **Cost Center**, a **Sales Order**, and a work breakdown structure (**WBS**) **element**, if applicable. A WBS is a project or a part of a project. In every case, you should enter a description in the **Text** field.

After you've entered all the data in the document line items, you can post the document or simulate it to preview whether the posting is accurate or further changes are needed. To start the simulation of the general ledger document posting, click on the **Simulate** button in the top center of the entry screen (refer to Figure 3.19). If the simulation is unsuccessful, an error message appears. If it's successful, a screen showing the document overview appears, as shown in Figure 3.24.

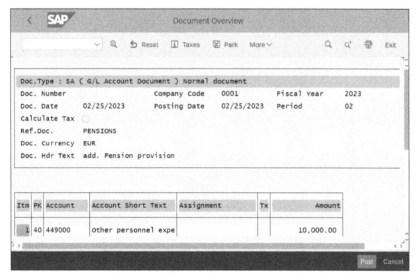

Figure 3.24 Document Overview of Successful Simulation

The next step after the simulation process is posting the journal voucher. You can click the **Post** button in the bottom-right corner of the screen. After a successful posting, a message with a document number appears in the bottom of the screen, as shown in Figure 3.25.

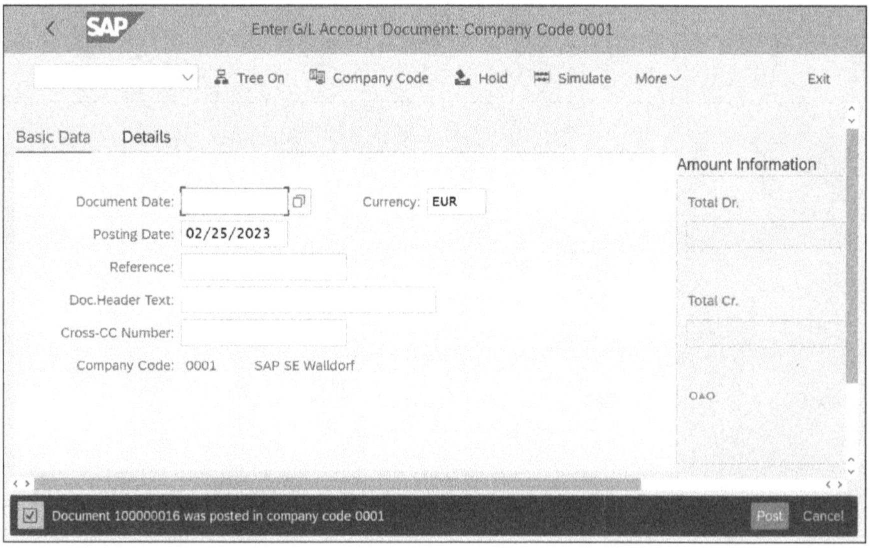

Figure 3.25 Document Posting Message

Each posted document contains data that uniquely identifies it:

- Document number
- Company code
- Fiscal year

> **SAP Fiori App**
>
> The corresponding SAP Fiori app is called Post General Journal Entries (F0718). The home screen is shown in Figure 3.26. This app is visually quite different, but the functionally is pretty similar to the SAP GUI version. As in SAP GUI, you have to enter the document header fields and then the line-item fields. If you follow the tabs, you can attach any external document and enter some verbal description. The journal entry can be posted only if the balances offset to zero.

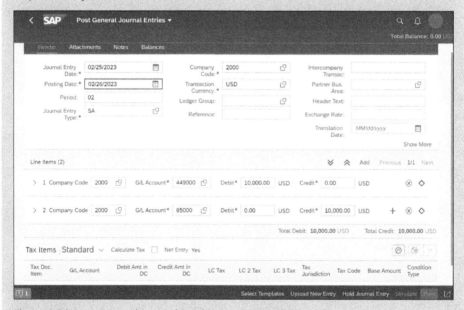

Figure 3.26 Post General Journal Entries App in SAP Fiori

3.3.2   Post, Park, and Hold

In this section, we'll demonstrate the steps to create general ledger accounting documents in different ways—post, park, and hold—and clearly distinguish the purpose of each method. When creating and posting documents, these features allow you to initiate a job and continue to work on it from the point where it was interrupted. We'll walk through each step in the following sections.

Posting

The *posting* function has been explained previously in the process of journal document entry where you learned that for general ledger account postings, you have to enter document header data (document date, document type, company code, posting date, and currency) and data for the individual line items (see the previous section). Postings are always deposited as documents in the system, which represent proof of a relevant business transaction. Each document has its own unique number. The process of posting occurs in this sequence: a posted document (i.e., a completed general ledger document) generates a general ledger accounting document number and accordingly updates the general ledger account balances.

SAP Fiori App

The corresponding SAP Fiori app is called Post General Journal Entries, which we discussed in the previous section.

Parking

Parking is a function you can use when a document is incomplete, and you need to make further changes, verifications, and approvals before the general ledger document posting. In addition, when you're entering data, you may be interrupted or may not have all the necessary data (e.g., bank charges or the appropriate cost center), so you can park the document to temporarily save it without updating the transaction's figures or general ledger account balances. However, parked document data can be used for system evaluations; for example, parked invoice amounts can be used as a reference to calculate the advance return for tax on sales and purchases. You can make the appropriate changes or delete the parked document for as long as it's in the parked position.

To enter and park a general ledger accounting document, you can use Transaction FV50 in the command field or follow application menu path **Accounting • Financial Accounting • General Ledger • Document Entry • Edit or Park G/L Document**.

The **Park G/L Account Document** entry screen appears, as shown in Figure 3.27. The fields that appear in the **Basic Data** tab may be manually or automatically populated depending on the system configuration. In Figure 3.27, the **Document Date** field was manually chosen while the other fields (**Posting Date**, **Currency**, and **Company Code**) were populated by their default values. This was already explained in Section 3.3.1.

Figure 3.27 General Ledger Account Document Parking

After you've entered the basic data, you need to populate at least two line items that net to a balance of zero, as shown in Figure 3.28. For each line item, you can enter the general ledger account number, indicate whether it's a debit or credit posting, and enter the amount.

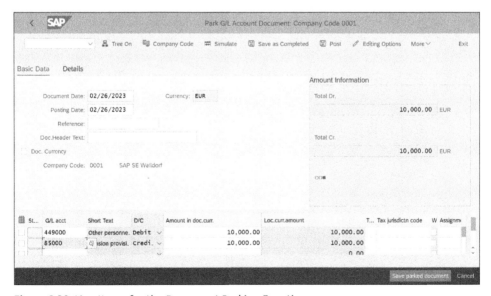

Figure 3.28 Line Items for the Document Parking Function

In the bottom-right corner, click the **Save parked document** button, and a message with the new parked document number will appear, as shown in Figure 3.29.

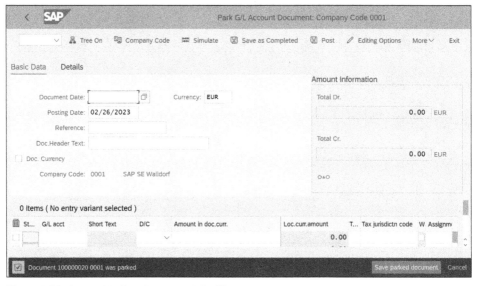

Figure 3.29 General Ledger Document Parking Message

Another similar function you need to know about is the **Save as Completed** option. Unlike the document parking function, however, it should be used when you're sure that the document is finalized and confirmed for its accuracy. This function is used as a last step for final approval prior to posting. Both parked documents and documents that are saved as completed can be modified before being posted.

To save a general ledger accounting document as completed, you must follow the same steps as for document parking. However, this time, click the **Save as Completed** button in the menu bar, and a message with the new parked document number will appear in the bottom-left corner, as shown in Figure 3.30.

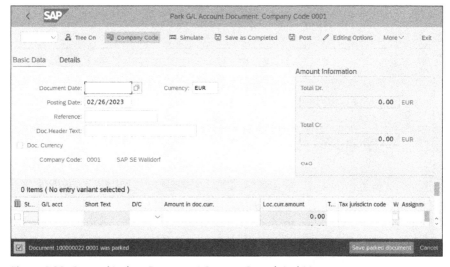

Figure 3.30 General Ledger Document Save as Completed Message

SAP Fiori App

The corresponding SAP Fiori app is Park General Journal Entries (FV50). This SAP Fiori app is visually and functionally the same as the SAP GUI transaction. The preceding instructions can be used with both.

Holding

Holding is a function that temporarily keeps data saved. You can use it if you have some incomplete data or are interrupted while creating the document. In this condition, as in the parking function, you can temporarily save the general ledger document without updating the transaction's figures or general ledger account balances. Consequently, no number is assigned to the document. In this stage, the held documents can be modified, deleted, parked, or posted.

To hold a general ledger accounting document, you can either use Transaction FB50 in the command field or follow application menu path **Accounting • Financial Accounting • General Ledger • Document Entry • Enter G/L Account Document**. The **Enter G/L Account Document** entry screen appears, as shown in Figure 3.31.

The data completeness isn't relevant in the case of the **Hold** function because there are no system checks implemented in that phase. You can hold a document even with only one completed line item, as shown in Figure 3.31.

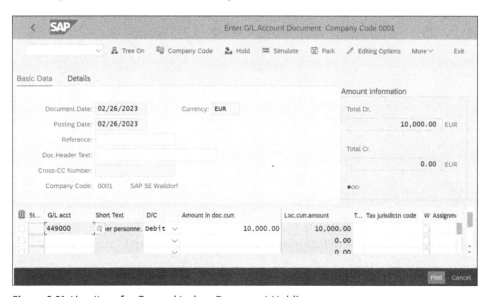

Figure 3.31 Line Item for General Ledger Document Holding

To continue with the holding process, press the F5 key, or click on the **Hold** button on the menu bar. Another screen pops up requiring you to enter a **Temporary Document Number**, as shown in Figure 3.32.

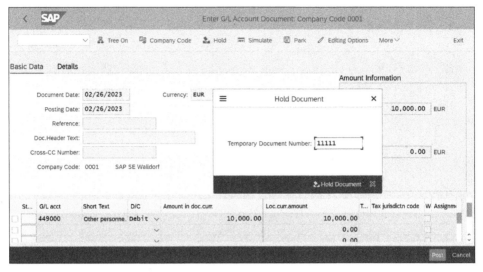

Figure 3.32 Temporary Document Number Popup Message

To continue, press the ⌨Enter⌨ key, or click the **Hold Document** button in the **Hold Document** popup window. A temporary accounting document has been created, demonstrated by the held document number message in the bottom-left corner, as shown in Figure 3.33.

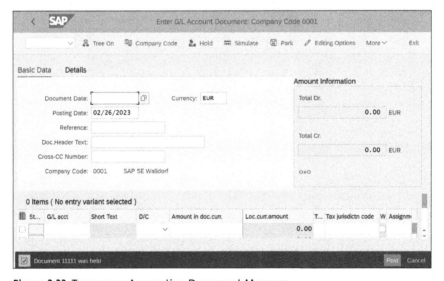

Figure 3.33 Temporary Accounting Document Message

SAP Fiori App

The corresponding SAP Fiori app to hold documents is the Post General Journal Entries app, as discussed previously.

Holding documents with this app is very similar to the SAP GUI version. The only difference is that the **Hold Journal Entry** button is at the bottom of the screen (see Figure 3.34).

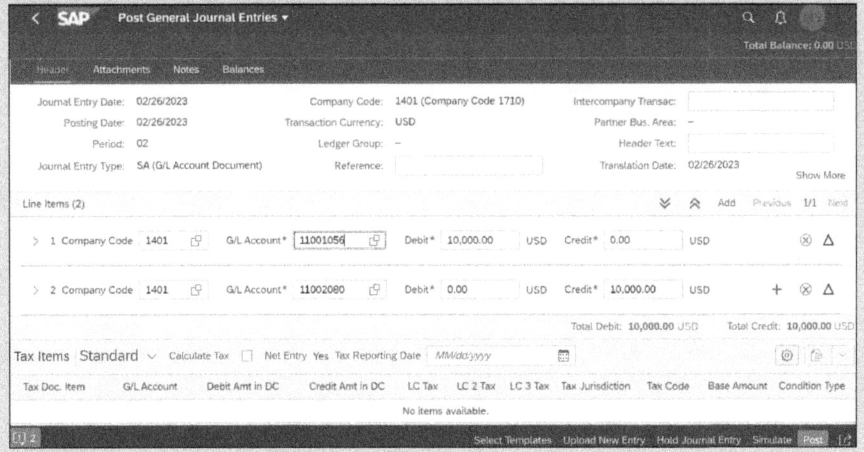

Figure 3.34 Hold Journal Entry in SAP Fiori

3.3.3   Recurring Documents

In this section, we'll frame the system logic and requirements regarding the recurring documents function. *Recurring documents* are accounting transactions that are periodically repeated, such as monthly, quarterly, and yearly. Examples of recurring transactions include rental payments or insurance payments. They can be configured to run with a fixed run schedule, such as a standing order that everyone can maintain in the banking account for rental payment, loan installment, and monthly fees. The initial recurring entry document contains all the details and data required to be included in the frequent posting accounting documents. This document doesn't affect the financial figures and account balances, but it's used as a master document entry on which the accounting documents are created after the scheduled program is executed.

Create Recurring Document

To create the initial recurring entry document, you can either use Transaction FBD1 in the command field or follow application menu path **Accounting • Financial Accounting • General Ledger • Document Entry • Reference Documents • Recurring Document**.

The **Enter Recurring Entry: Header Data** screen appears, as shown in Figure 3.35. In this screen, you first have to select the relevant company code for the recurring document. Then, fill in the fields in the following areas:

- **Recurring entry run**
  After you enter a company code, focus on the **Recurring entry run** area, where you must specify the parameters for the recurring entry. **First Run On** refers to the first

date when the accounting document will be carried out. **Last Run On** refers to the last date when the accounting document will be carried out. **Interval in Months** specifies the frequency of the run; for example, for a monthly frequency, you must enter "1". **Run Date** specifies in which date of the month the recurring entry will be posted. **Run Schedule** can be specified if there is some variability in the posting date.

- **Document header information**
  Information entered in **Document header information** is reflected in each accounting document that is created. Here, enter the **Document Type**, **Currency/Rate**, **Translation dte** (translation date) of the currency conversion, **Reference**, **Document Header Text**, and, in case of an intercompany transaction with your organization, trading partner's business area (**Trading Part.BA**).

- **First line item**
  At the bottom of the screen, you enter the data for the first line item, depending on whether it's relevant:
  - **PstKy** (posting key): Indicates whether the posting line is a debit or credit item. The standard posting key for a debit is 40, and the standard posting key for a credit is 50.
  - **Account:** Number of the account.
  - **SGL Ind** (general ledger indicator): Typically used when you post a down payment request instead of a customer invoice.
  - **TType** (transaction type): Helps to distinguish between transactions such as acquisitions, credit memos, good receipts, or asset retirements.

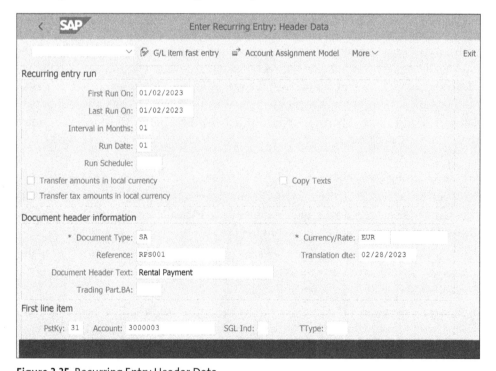

Figure 3.35 Recurring Entry Header Data

After you've entered the required data, press the ⌈Enter⌋ key, and another screen appears to add vendor details in the first line item, as shown in Figure 3.36. You may choose a vendor if applicable for the recurring transaction. If you've chosen posting key **31**, you must enter a vendor because posting key **31** is used for supplier invoices, which require a vendor. In this example, **Vendor 3000003** has been selected as an inter-company supplier for **Company Code 0001**.

In the bottom portion of the screen (**Next line item**), you can add a posting key (**PstKy**) and **Account** for the second line item. After entering all the data, click the **Post** button at the bottom right of the screen.

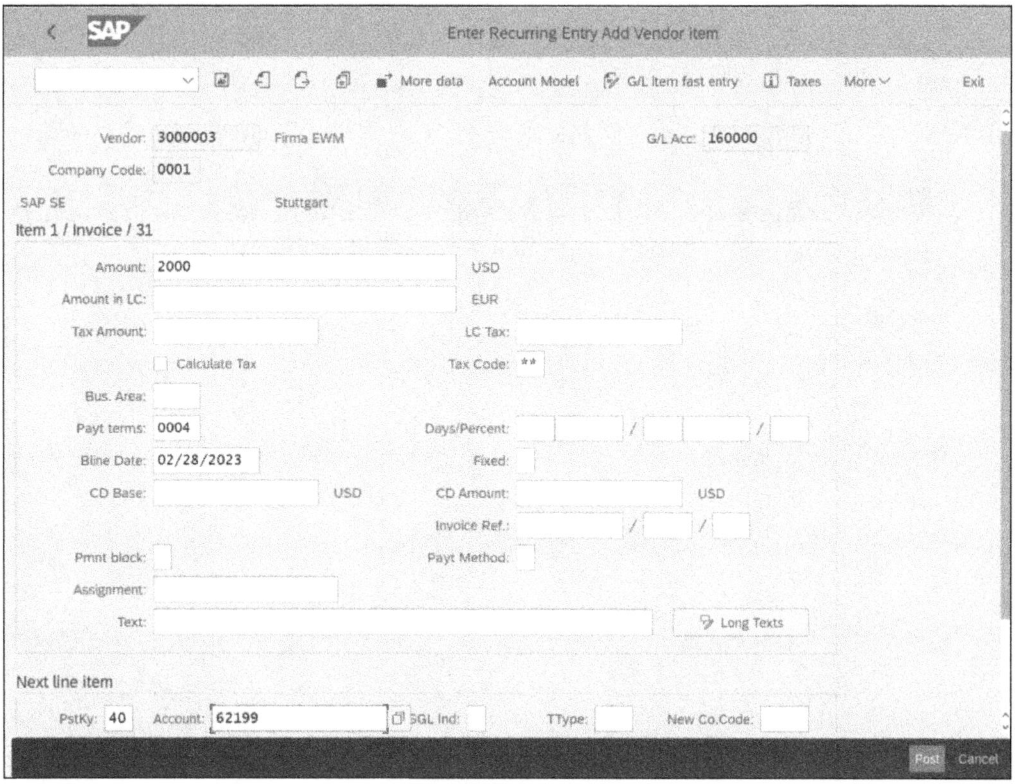

Figure 3.36 Adding Vendor Data in the First Line Item

The **Enter Recurring Entry Add G/L account item** screen appears, as shown in Figure 3.37. You can enter the **Amount**, fill in other fields as needed, and enter a meaningful description in the **Text** field.

After you complete the second line item, click the **Post** button at the bottom right of the screen, and a message pops up saying that the document has been stored in the specified company code, as shown in Figure 3.38.

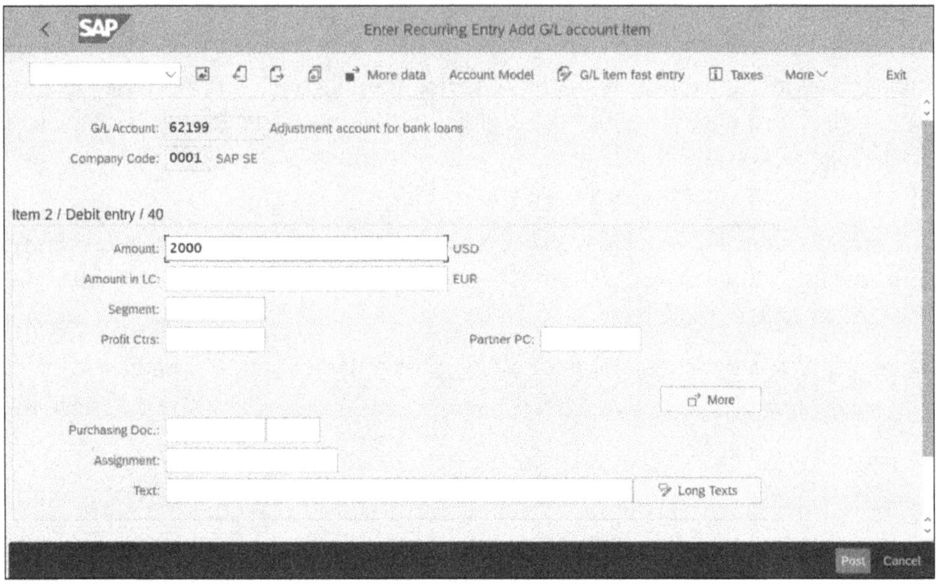

Figure 3.37 Adding the General Ledger Account in the Second Line Item

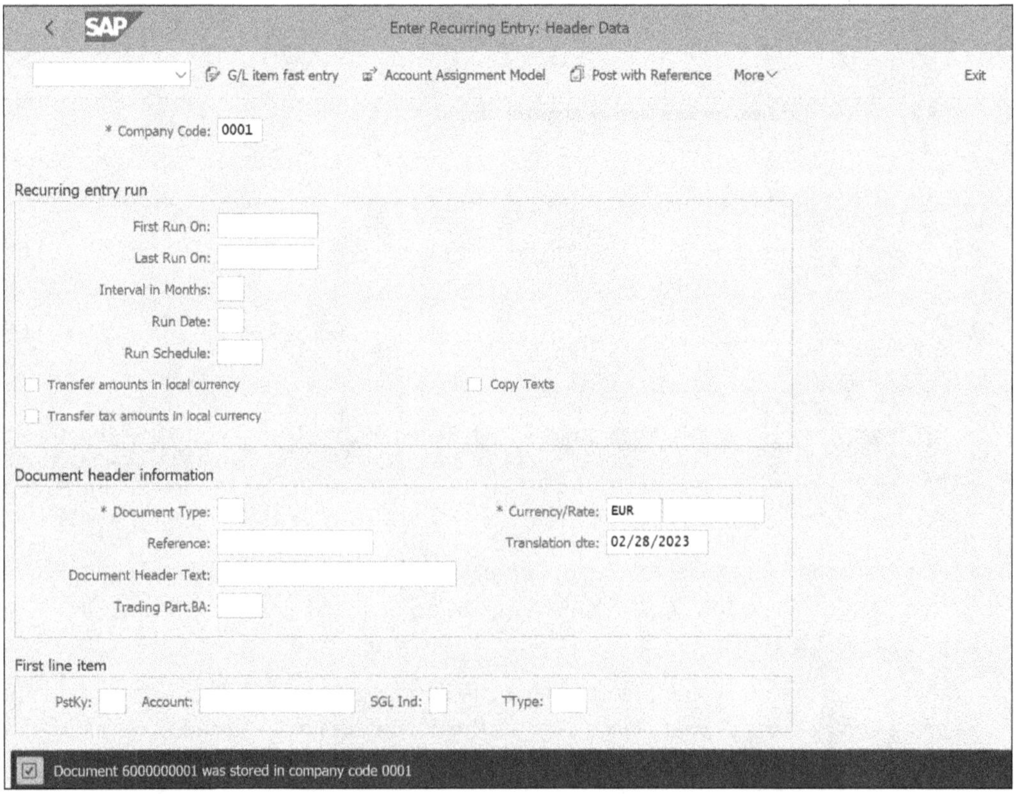

Figure 3.38 Recurring Document Entry Message

Display Recurring Document

Now that you've created a recurring document, you can display it using Transaction FBD3 in the command field. In the **Display Recurring Document: Initial Screen**, you must enter the document number that you just created, the company code, and the fiscal year, as shown in Figure 3.39. After entering the values, click the continue icon or press the Enter key. The **Display Recurring Document: Data Entry View** screen appears showing the detailed recurring document (see Figure 3.40).

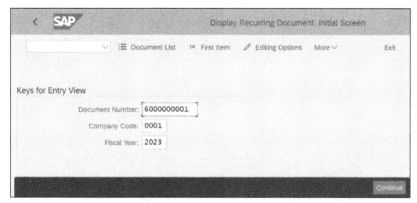

Figure 3.39 Displaying the Recurring Document Using Transaction FBD3

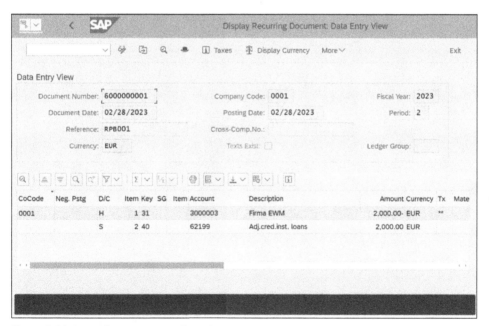

Figure 3.40 Recurring Document Overview

On this screen, you can press the F5 key or click the hat icon 🎩 in the menu bar to display the document header details, as shown in Figure 3.41. To display the recurring entry data, press the F7 key (see Figure 3.42).

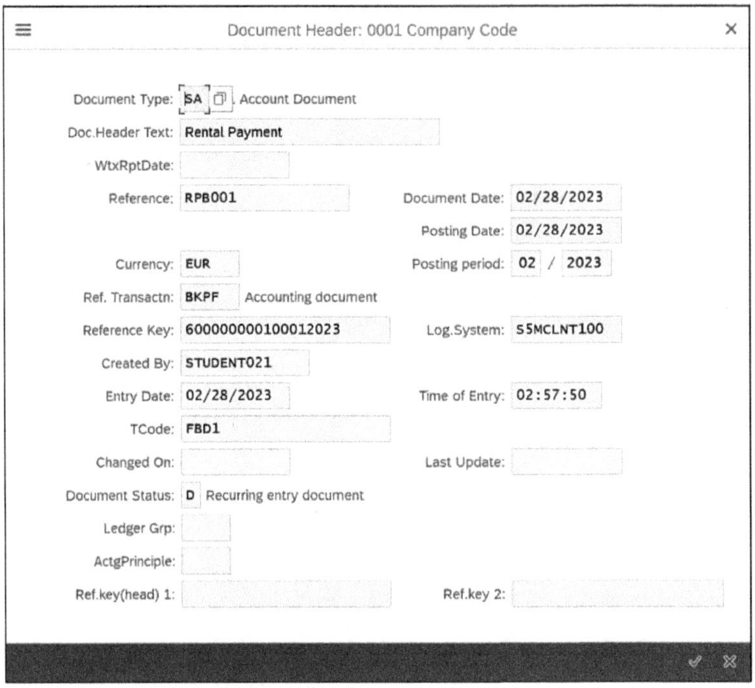

Figure 3.41 Recurring Document Header Details

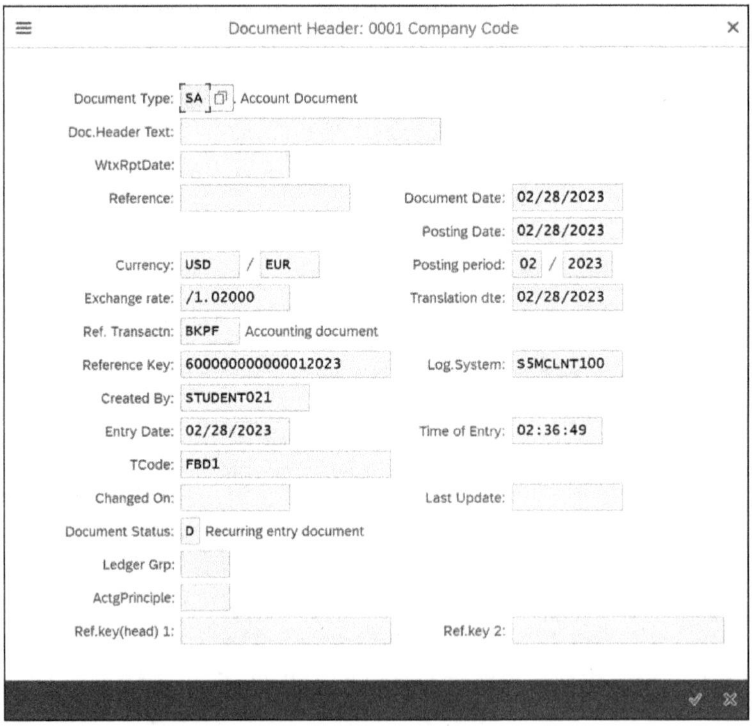

Figure 3.42 Recurring Document Entry Data

Now, going back to Figure 3.40, you can change the current display by clicking the icon in the menu bar. The **Change Recurring Document** screen appears. To display another recurring document, click the icon, and the **Other Document** window pops up, where you can input the document number you want to display, as shown in Figure 3.43. Click on the confirm (checkmark) button, and the new document number will be displayed in the **Display Recurring Document** screen.

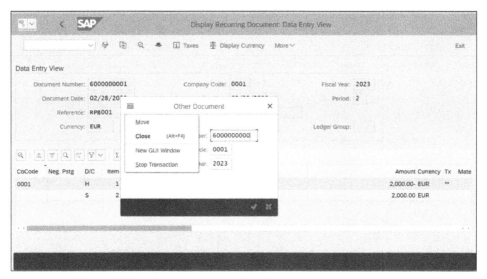

Figure 3.43 Changing the Recurring Document

SAP Fiori App

The corresponding SAP Fiori app is called Manage Recurring Journal Entries (F1598), as shown in Figure 3.44. With this app, you can do all that you can do with SAP GUI Transaction FBD1 (Create), Transaction FBD2 (Change), and Transaction FBD3 (Display) regarding recurring journal entries. This app is functionally similar to the SAP GUI processes we've described previously.

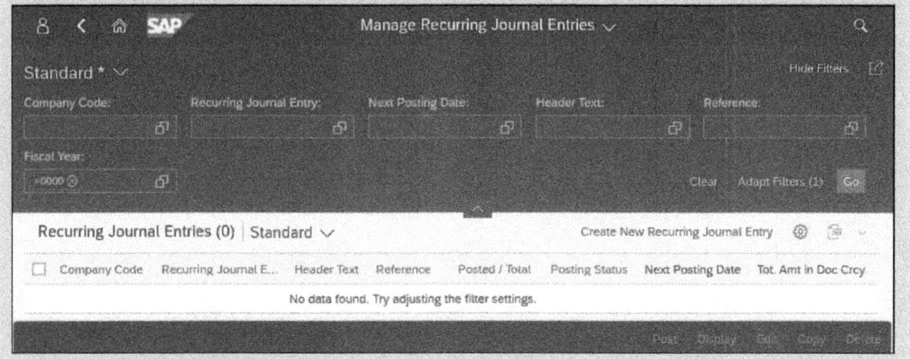

Figure 3.44 Managing Recurring Journal Entries in SAP Fiori

3.3.4   Post with References

Through this function, *post with references*, SAP S/4HANA allows you to easily create and post a document copying the accounting data from an existing posted document. You may need to make some additional changes through the several flow control indicators, depending on your current document specifications. For example, your new general ledger document consists of different amounts from the existing posted document. At this point, you can select **Do Not Propose Amounts** in the listed flow control indicators. This means that you must enter amounts manually in the document line item. If you want a faster entry screen for general ledger account line items, you can select another flow control: **Enter G/L Account Items**. This means that line items will be processed from one screen only instead of separate screens for each item. If you don't select any of the indicators, you can use the post with reference function to post a new document with the same details as the appointed existing document.

In this section, we'll walk through how the post with reference function works. We'll demonstrate with an example using these two flow controls.

To post a document using post with reference, you can either use Transaction FB50 in the command field or follow application menu path **Accounting • Financial Accounting • General Ledger • Document Entry • Enter G/L Account Document**.

Either way, you'll arrive at the **Enter G/L Account Document** entry screen shown in Figure 3.45. Choose **More • Goto • Post with Reference**. You can also use the shortcut (Shift)+(F9).

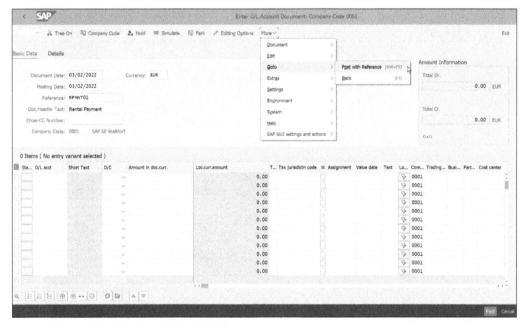

Figure 3.45 Selecting Post with Reference

The **Post Document: Header Data** screen appears, as shown in Figure 3.46, where, apart from the fields in the **Reference** area (**Document Number**, **Company Code**, and **Fiscal Year**), you can select the **Flow control** indicators. In this example, choose **Enter G/L Account Items** and **Do Not Propose Amounts**.

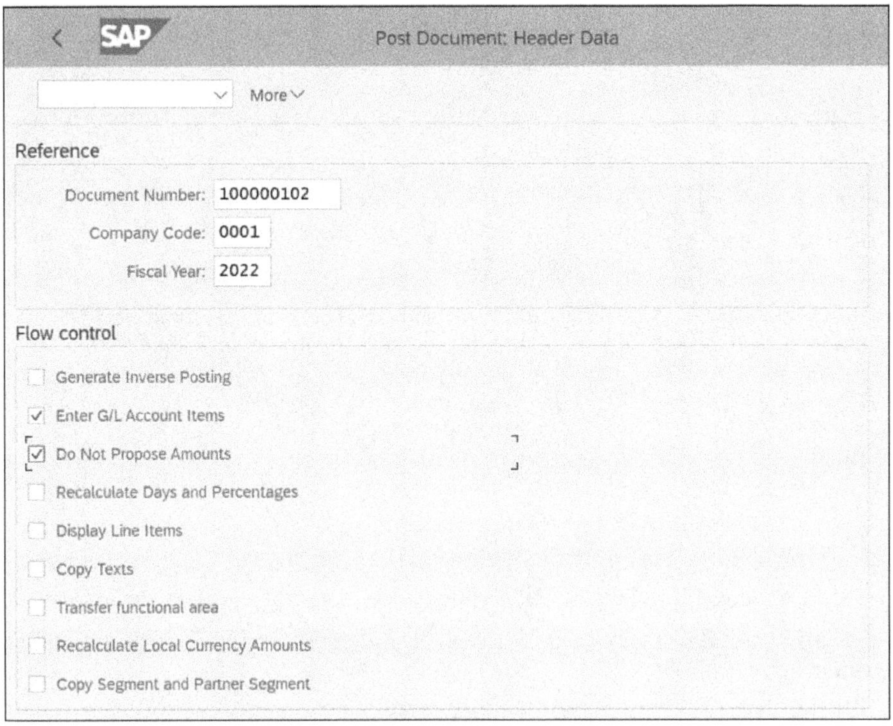

Figure 3.46 Post with Reference Selection Screen

Table 3.1 provides the complete list of flow controls you can use during the post with reference function.

Flow Chart Indicator	Description
Generate Inverse Posting	This is the easiest way to reverse all debit and credit line items with one click. As a result, the reference document and the reversal document offset each other completely. No manual intervention is required.
Enter G/L Account Items	The reference document is copied, and the line items are then transferred to the fast entry screen for general ledger accounts so that several line items can be processed on one screen.
Do Not Propose Amounts	The new document takes all the same line items, omitting the amounts. The amounts therefore have to be entered manually.

Table 3.1 Flow Control List to Post with Reference

Flow Chart Indicator	Description
Recalculate Days and Percentages	Payment terms from the reference document are copied into the new document. Days and percentages are recalculated taking the new dates into account.
Display Line Items	All the line items are copied from the reverence document in the new document individually.
Copy Texts	The text from the reference document is copied to the new document.
Transfer functional area	The functional area of the reference document is transferred to the new one. This isn't a standard process. Generally, the functional area is derived by cost-of-sales accounting substitution.
Recalculate Local Currency Amounts	The local currency amount is converted and recalculated if there are different currencies.
Copy Segment and Partner Segment	The segment and partner segments are transferred from the reference document to the new one (instead of deriving it via a defined rule).

Table 3.1 Flow Control List to Post with Reference (Cont.)

After you've reviewed the fields in the **Reference** section and the relevant indicators, press the Enter key to see the screen of the general ledger document creation process, as shown in Figure 3.47.

Figure 3.47 General Ledger Document Creation Using Post with Reference

The document header contains data such as document date, posting date, company code, and currency from the referring document. You can edit the prepopulated fields and enter data in the other fields, such as the **Document Number** of the reference transaction, **Doc.Header Text**, and **Reference**.

In the example shown in Figure 3.48, a prepopulated ready-to-post document has been generated from reference document 10000102. After you've edited the header information, press the [Enter] key, and another screen will appear.

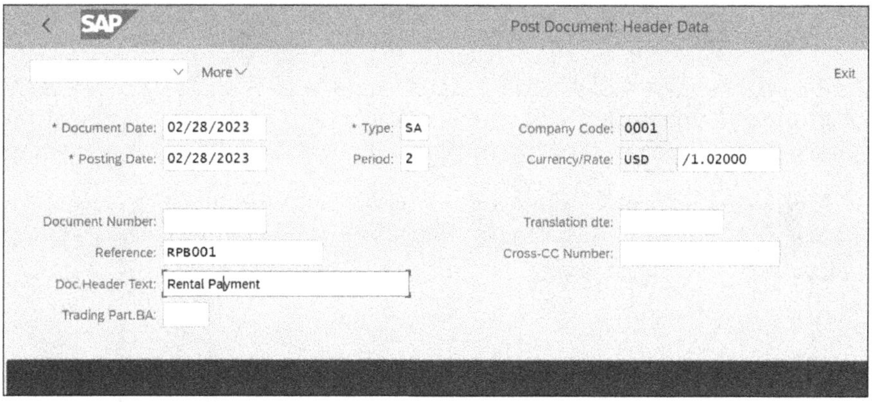

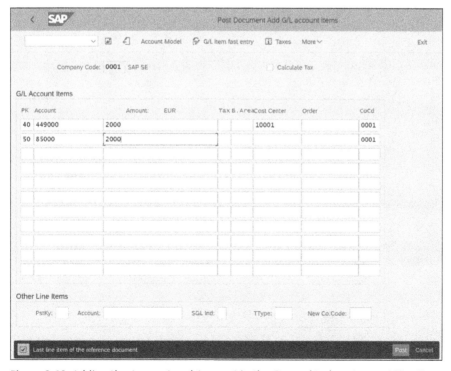

Figure 3.48 Post with Reference Header Data

As you can see in Figure 3.49, both line items are displayed and populated in the screen. This is because you've already selected the flow control **Enter G/L Account Items**.

Figure 3.49 Adding the Account and Amount in the General Ledger Account Line Items

You can now change the prepopulated debit and credit accounts as well as the amount. In this example, the debit account has been changed to **449000** and the credit account has been changed to **85000**. The amount is set at 2,000 USD.

After you've filled in the other relevant fields, such as **Tax** code or **Cost Center**, click the **Post** button in the bottom-right corner or press ⌈Ctrl⌉+⌈S⌉. A message appears with the document number posted and a document display overview screen with both line items containing new document data (see Figure 3.50).

By following just these few easy steps, you can create and post a general ledger document referring to an existing posted document, making some or no changes in the relevant data.

Figure 3.50 Post with Reference General Ledger Document Message

---

SAP Fiori App
There is no corresponding SAP Fiori app as of SAP S/4HANA 2022.

Now that you're more familiar with the general ledger document posting using quicker methods and post with reference, we'll jump into the next section where we've described another similar function: post with clearing.

3.3.5   Post with Clearing

In this section, we'll describe SAP's clearing function and the concept of open items in financial accounting by showing you how to perform clearing of open items in SAP S/4HANA. First, however, you need to understand the concept of open items.

Open items are considered incomplete transactions, for example, pending customer payments. The financial documents that contain open items won't get lost after being cleared but are stored in the system. When performing the clearing transactions, you enter a general ledger document line item and then select the open items to be cleared. In this step, a clearing document will be generated that consists of the item created manually and the offsetting entry created automatically to net the open item amount.

The *post with clearing* function is mostly used for the general ledger, accounts receivable, and accounts payable open items. In the accounts payable ledger, there is a standard automatic clearing program that performs clearing posting for several accounts with different currencies at the same time.

Let's assume you're dealing with the standard supplier invoice case. You have an open item that stems from an invoice posting against a vendor account (supplier invoice). This open item will be closed through a payment to the vendor. By releasing the payment with the use of the clearing function, the open item will be cleared by the payment resulting in zero. The same logic is also followed for the open items in accounts receivable and any other open item in the general ledger.

To perform a posting with clearing, you can use Transaction F-04 in the command field or follow application menu path **Accounting • Financial Accounting • General Ledger • Document Entry • Post with Clearing**.

The **Post with Clearing: Header Data** screen appears, as shown in Figure 3.51. On this screen, you can enter the required fields such as **Document Date, Posting Date, Company Code**, and **Currency/Rate**. In the **Transaction to be processed** panel, select **Transfer posting with clearing**. At the bottom of the screen, enter the values for the first line item of the general ledger documents: **PstKy** and general ledger **Account** number.

After you've filled in this data, press the Enter key to go to the **Post with Clearing Add G/L account item** screen, as shown in Figure 3.52.

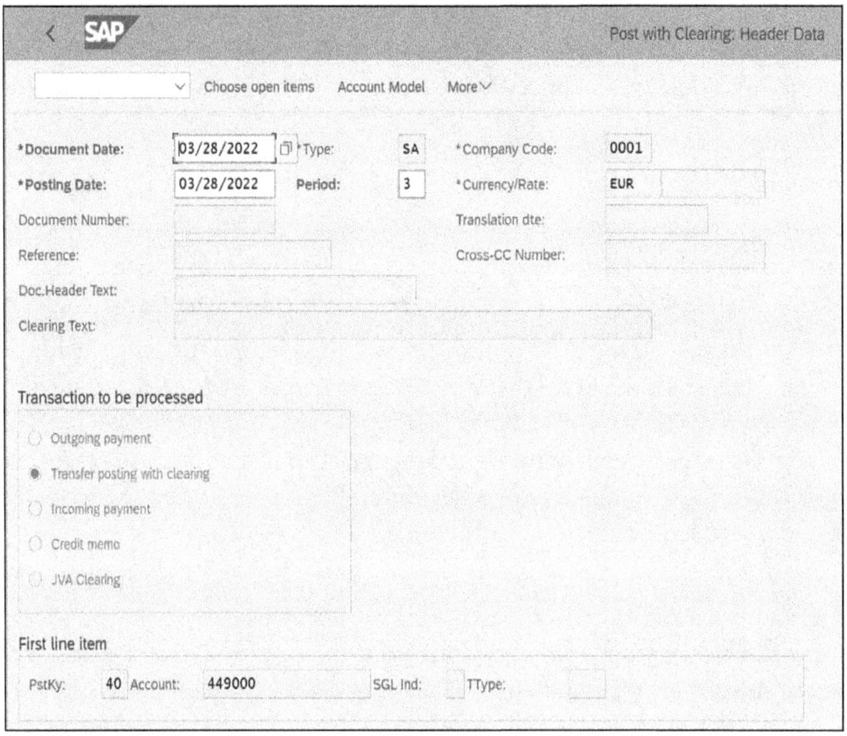

Figure 3.51 Post with Clearing: Header Data Screen

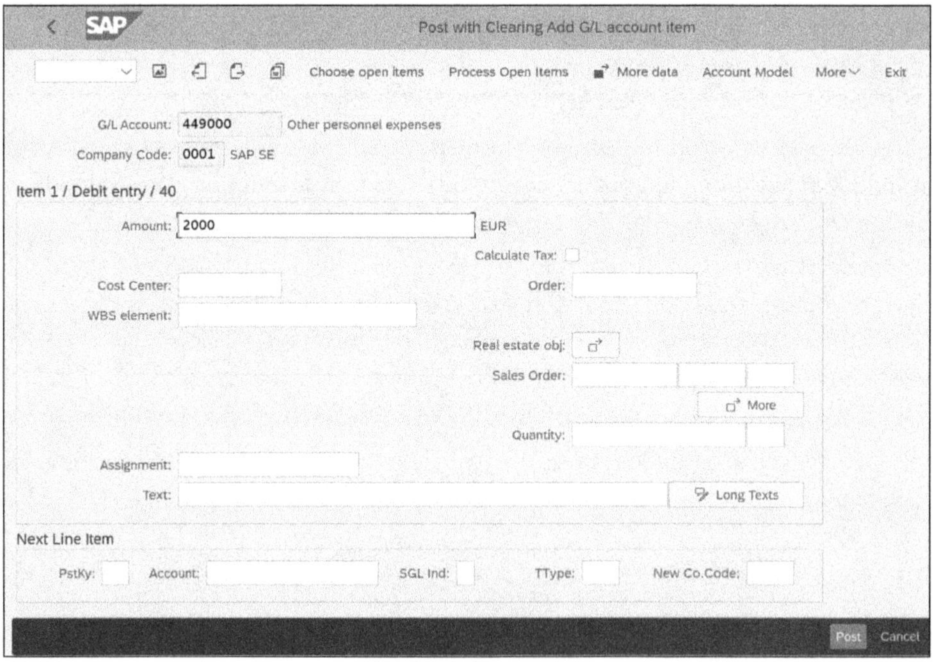

Figure 3.52 Post with Clearing Add G/L Account Item Screen

On this screen, you just enter the **Amount**, for example, USD "2000". Then, click the **Choose open items** button. The **Post with Clearing Select open items** screen appears, as shown in Figure 3.53.

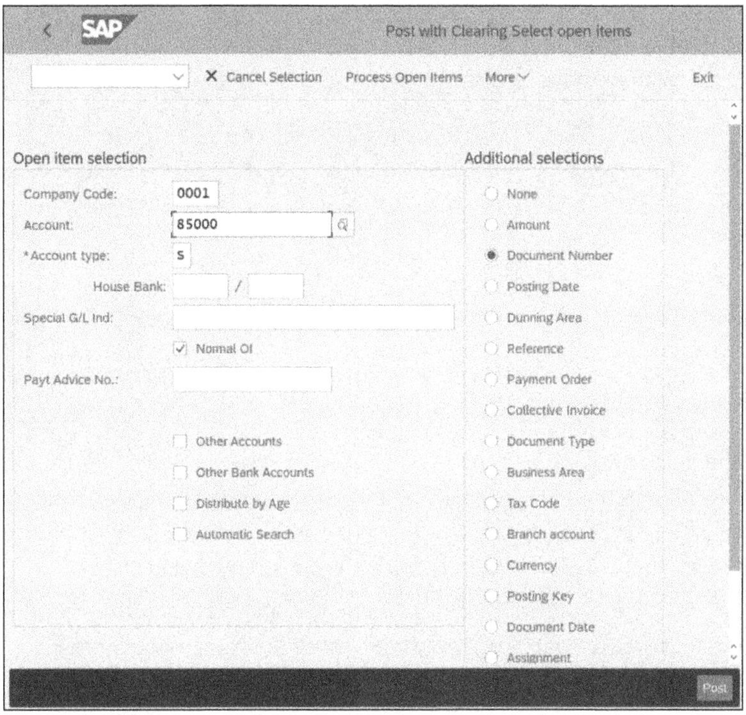

Figure 3.53 Post with Clearing Select Open Items Screen

The fields in the screen are already prepopulated by the company code and the account type. In the **Account** field, you enter the general ledger account containing the open item to be cleared. In the **Additional selections** area, you can select a field to find the open item easier. If you know the document number of the open item to be cleared, select **Document Number**, and click the **Process Open Items** button. Enter the **Document Number** in the screen that opens, and then click the **Process Open Items** button again. Ideally, you'll find the open item you want to clear. If so, the found open item will show up in a new screen, and you just have to click the **Post** button to clear the open item.

Once cleared, documents can't easily be reversed. They first have to be "uncleared" (reset) before they can be posted. We'll discuss this in the next section.

> **SAP Fiori App**
>
> The corresponding SAP Fiori app is called Clear G/L Accounts (F1579). With this app, you can manually clear general ledger account open items the same way you do with Transaction F-04.

In the start screen of the app, you can search for open items only by using three fields: **Company Code**, **G/L Account**, and **Posted By** (**Posting By** is a required field) (see Figure 3.54). If you want to use more fields to filter, go to **Adapt Filters**, where you can add up to five more filters: **Number of Open Items**, **Open Debit Amount**, **Open Credit Amount**, **Balance**, and **Alternative Account**.

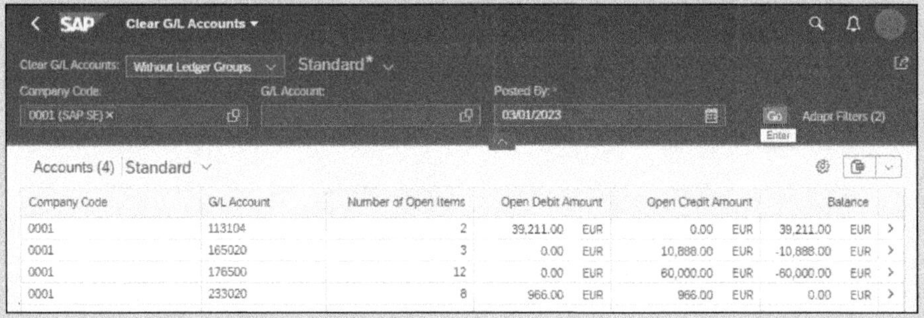

![SAP Clear G/L Accounts screen showing filter fields Company Code, G/L Account, Posted By, and a table of four accounts with Company Code, G/L Account, Number of Open Items, Open Debit Amount, Open Credit Amount, and Balance columns]

Figure 3.54 Clear General Ledger Accounts

In this example, the company code and the required posting date have been entered, resulting in four open items that can be cleared. The clearing process using SAP Fiori is easier. You click on the line where the open items are that you want to clear (e.g., the line with the 12 open items on account **176500**), and another screen appears (see Figure 3.55).

You select the items that you want to clear (e.g., items **2**, **3**, and **4** are selected here), and the items move into the **Items to Be Cleared** window on the bottom right (see Figure 3.56). Just click the **Post** button, and you're done.

Figure 3.55 Clearing Open Items in General Ledger Accounts (1)

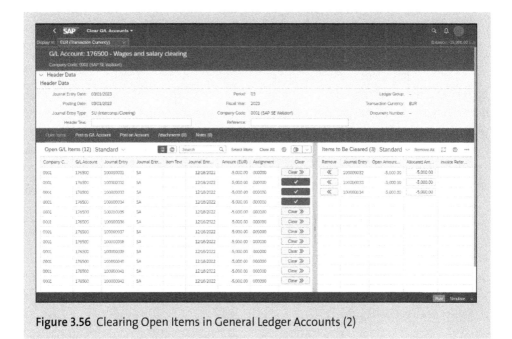

Figure 3.56 Clearing Open Items in General Ledger Accounts (2)

3.3.6 Parallel Accounting

In this section, we'll describe SAP's clearing function and the concept of open items in financial accounting by showing you how to perform clearing of open items in SAP S/4HANA. First, however, you need to understand the concept itself.

Parallel accounting in SAP refers to the ability to maintain multiple sets of accounting records simultaneously in a single SAP system. This functionality allows organizations to comply with different accounting standards, such as International Financial Reporting Standards (IFRS) and Generally Accepted Accounting Principles (GAAP), by maintaining separate ledgers for each set of accounting rules.

With parallel accounting, companies can manage multiple currencies, valuation methods, and reporting requirements, as well as ensure consistency in their financial reporting across different regulatory environments. This feature is particularly useful for global organizations with operations in different countries that have different accounting standards. In the past, SAP offered a couple of solutions to address this problem. Since SAP S/4HANA, the preferred solution has been the ledger method, where different ledgers are assigned to company codes. Each ledger represents a different set of accounting rules, and transactions are posted in all relevant ledgers simultaneously. This allows companies to easily generate financial statements and reports based on different accounting principles.

A prerequisite of using parallel accounting through ledgers is that there must be more than one ledger configured for your use. In SAP S/4HANA, there is always at least one ledger set up. If you don't need parallel accounting and you've set up only one ledger, each document entry exists only once. However, this is unrealistic because most companies—especially large ones—act globally.

Let's assume that a company group has to report on the group level (consolidated financial statements) according to US GAAP. Now let's further assume that the group not only has subsidiaries in the United States but also in Germany. Therefore, for the German entities, you need to report financial results according to German GAAP (called "HGB"). With this in mind, you set up set up one ledger, for instance, "L1," which serves US accounting purposes only, and you set up a second ledger—"L2"—which serves German GAAP accounting purposes only. However, manually posting every transaction twice doesn't make much sense because, in the majority of cases, identical transactions have to be recorded. This is the standard case. So, for this purpose, you can build a ledger group, for instance, "OL," where you post automatically in both ledgers. As this is the regular case, this ledger group is the default value for any posting. Therefore, it's called the leading ledger group OL. So, using OL as the ledger group while posting means that you post two identical journal entries in both ledger the US GAAP ledger and the German GAAP ledger.

From a theoretical perspective, you're almost set. Technically, SAP needs another element to be defined (and not only for documentation): the accounting principle. Every ledger group has to be assigned to an accounting principle. The assigned accounting principle finally documents the accounting principle used such as US GAAP, German GAAP, UK GAAP, and so on. It clarifies the usage of the ledger and helps in understanding the documents produced in the general ledger when using several parallel ledgers.

Note

A *ledger group* in SAP is a collection of ledgers that are assigned to a particular company code or multiple company codes. It provides a way to group together ledgers with similar characteristics, such as the same accounting principles, fiscal year variant, or chart of accounts. Ledger groups are used to manage financial accounting and reporting in SAP systems. They allow for the consolidation of financial data from multiple ledgers into a single report, making it easier to compare and analyze financial information across different organizational units or legal entities.

SAP supports two types of ledger groups: nonleading ledger groups and leading ledger groups. A nonleading ledger group is used to maintain accounting data for statutory purposes, such as tax reporting, while the leading ledger group is used for management reporting and is usually the primary ledger used for financial accounting.

Overall, the use of ledger groups in SAP enables organizations to streamline financial reporting and better manage their financial data across multiple ledgers and company codes.

Now that you have the theoretical background, let's see a real example of parallel accounting through parallel ledgers. To do so, recall Section 3.3.1 where you learned how to post a document in the general ledger using Transaction FB50. You'll now do the same with a slightly different first step: you can either use Transaction FB50L (instead of Transaction FB50) in the command field or follow application menu path **Accounting • Financial Accounting • General Ledger • Document Entry • Enter G/L Acct Document for Ledger Group**.

The **Enter G/L Acct Document for Ledger Group** entry screen appears, as shown in Figure 3.57. If you compare to Figure 3.19, you'll find only one slight difference: there is one field more to fill in, **Ledger Grp**.

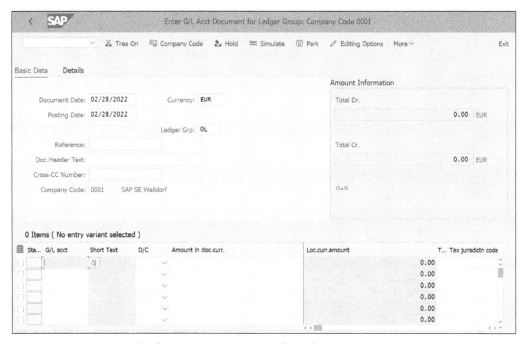

Figure 3.57 Enter General Ledger Account Document for Ledger Group

After having posted a document (10000004) using the leading ledger group OL to the company code (0001), which is assigned to two ledgers (OL and 3L), there are two journal entries generated. You can view both entries either by using Transaction FB03L in the command field or by following application menu path **Accounting • Financial Accounting • General Ledger • Document • Display in General Ledger View**.

In the screen in Figure 3.58, you enter the document number, company code, fiscal year, and leading ledger "OL", and then click the **Continue** button.

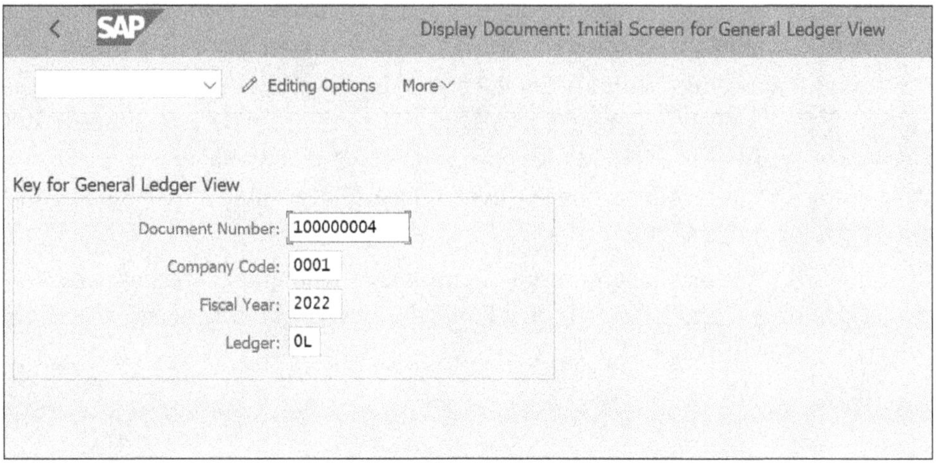

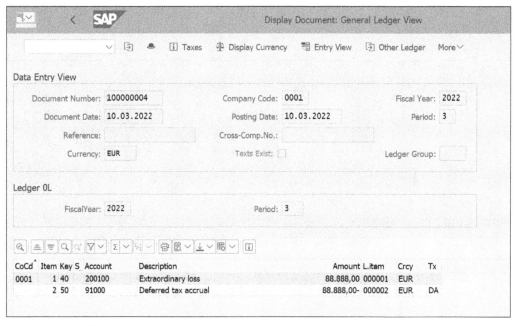

Figure 3.58 Display Document: Initial Screen for General Ledger View

In the following screen, **Display Document: General Ledger View**, you can see a complete journal entry. The middle of the screen shows **Ledger OL** followed by the **Fiscal-Year** and **Period** fields. Below that, you can see the respective posting in OL, as shown in Figure 3.59.

Figure 3.59 Display Document: General Ledger View (Ledger OL)

To see the posting in ledger L3 (local ledger for German GAAP), you have two possibilities. First, you just can go back to Transaction FBO3L and enter everything the same as you did in Figure 3.58, only with L3 instead of OL.

The second option is more elegant. You can use the **Other Ledger** button in the menu bar to select another ledger, in this case, **L3**, and the system displays the document **10000004** again but within **Ledger L3**, as shown in Figure 3.60.

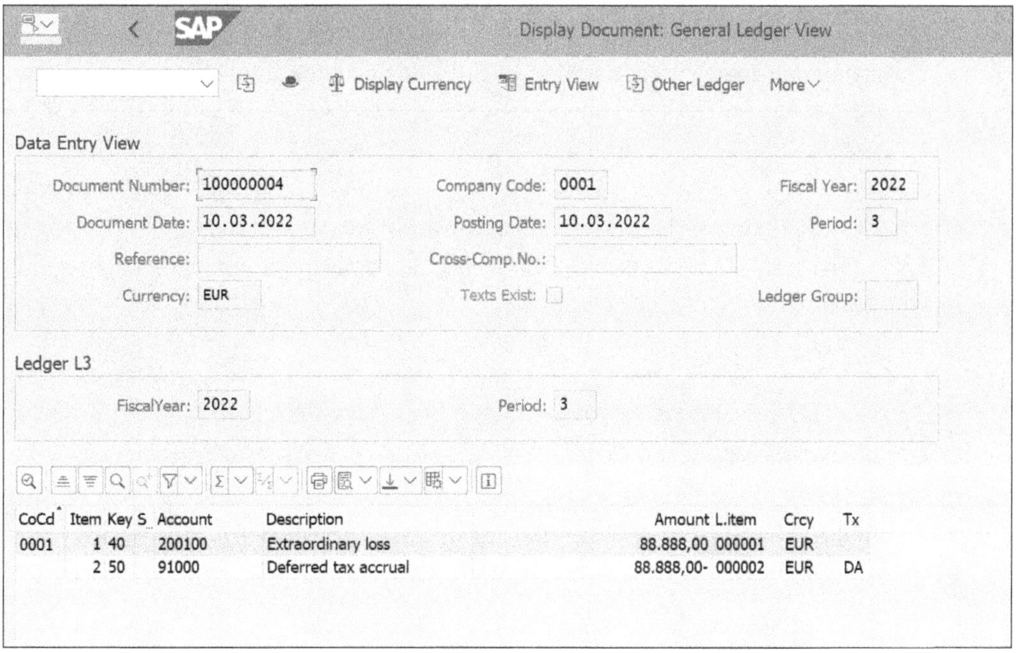

Figure 3.60 Display Document: General Ledger View (Ledger L3)

If you only want to post the document in L3, you just enter the document (shown earlier in Figure 3.57) by using L3 instead of OL. L3 isn't a leading ledger (group), so the posting will only concern the ledger (group) L3. For both ledgers, you can retrieve a complete set of reporting, which is the goal with the parallel accounting functionality.

3.3.7 Universal Parallel Accounting

Let's move on to a new chapter of parallel accounting. *Universal parallel accounting* provides enhanced functionality for ledgers and currencies based on the Universal Journal. It provides the basis for the calculation and posting of values per ledger and currency for all financials applications, creating a continuous parallel valuation along the end-to-end processes and making a ledger-dependent value chain analysis possible. Universal parallel accounting is a further step to merge controlling and accounting and to use the potential of the Universal Journal for controlling, the Material Ledger, and assets. Let's take a closer look at the use cases covered by universal parallel accounting.

Parallel Valuations

Universal parallel accounting supports parallel legal valuations through consistent calculation and posting of values for all standard ledgers, for example, IFRS and local GAAP.
This already works without universal parallel accounting in some financial processes as
you've seen in Chapter 2. Universal parallel accounting enables this parallel valuation
for further processes such as material valuation, asset deprecations, and especially controlling processes (e.g., settlement). For these scenarios without universal parallel
accounting, the leading ledger value is applied to all ledgers.

Let's take settlement as an example. You operate with two standard ledgers, one following the IFRS accounting principle, which is the leading ledger, and another ledger following the local GAAP. In our use case, costs are collected for a project that can be
handled differently in the two ledgers. Let's assume the costs can be 100% activated in
the leading IFRS ledger, costs can't be activated at all in the local ledger, and costs are
settled to a cost center. This can be achieved with active universal parallel accounting.
Here, you can apply ledger-dependent settlement rules (see Figure 3.61):

- The first line reflects the settlement to ledger **OL**. Here, we settle 100% of the costs to
  asset **40015-0**.

- The second line reflects the settlement to ledger **OD**. Here, the costs are settled to
  cost center **2000**.

> **Note**
>
> With the existing approach without active universal parallel accounting, you can only
> settle to one receiver. The receiver and the costs to be settled are taken from the lead-
> ing ledger.

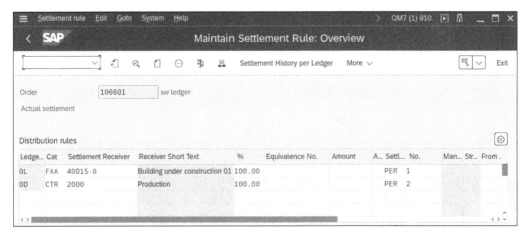

Figure 3.61 Ledger-Dependent Settlement Rule

Another example is that the settlement target in both ledgers is the same, that is, the fixed asset, but the costs are different in the two ledgers. With universal parallel accounting active, different values would be activated in the two ledgers; without universal parallel accounting active, the value on the leading ledger would be activated in both ledgers, which is another example for different values we provided in Chapter 2, Section 2.3.3.

With active universal parallel accounting, the cost rates are stored in the new table ACCOSTRATE, and no longer maintained with Transaction KP26. You get access to the table via Transaction FCO_COSTRATE_EDIT (see Figure 3.62). In the first column, you can enter the ledger, and see the dependent cost rates. In our example for activity type (**ActTyp**) **T001**, there is a rate of 110 EUR in ledger **2L** and a rate of 100 EUR in ledger **0L**.

Ld	Plan Categ	Cost Ctr	ActTyp	Cr	CoCd	BusT	From	Fro	Validity S	To F	To	Validity E	Crcy	Total Rate	Per	AU	I	Rece	SC	L	Pers.No.	WBS Element
	PLN	10101902	T001	00	1010	MSCR	2021	1	01.01.2021	9998	12	31.12.9998	EUR	100.00	1	H		1				
	PLN	10101902	T001	00	1010	MSCR	2021	1	01.01.2021	9998	12	31.12.9998	EUR	200.00	1	H		2				
	PLN	10101902	T001	00	1010	MSCR	2021	1	01.01.2021	9998	12	31.12.9998	EUR	50.00	1	H		0				
0L	PLN	10101902	T001	00	1010	MSCR	2021	1	01.01.2021	9998	12	31.12.9998	EUR	100.00	1	H						
2L	*	10101902	T001	00	1010	MSCR	2023	1	01.01.2021	9998	12	31.12.9998	EUR	110.00	1	H						
0L	*	10101902	T001	00	1010	MSCR	2023	1	01.01.2021	9998	12	31.12.9998	EUR	100.00	1	H						

Figure 3.62 Ledger-Dependent Cost Rates

Additionally, in the Material Ledger, you can maintain the ledger-dependent product valuation. Start Transaction MR21, and enter **Company Code** "1010" and **Plant** "1010" to get the screen shown in Figure 3.63.

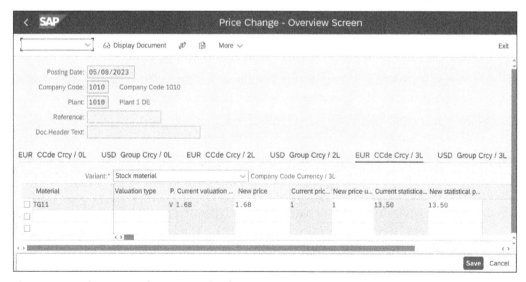

Figure 3.63 Ledger-Dependent Material Valuation

For **Material TG11**, a price of 1.68 EUR is maintained for ledger **3L**. In the tab bar, you see that there can be prices maintained for ledger **0L**, **2L**, and **3L**, which are all the ledgers active in company code **1010**.

With these new ledger-dependent valuation options, you can now provide a parallel value flow across end-to end processes (see Figure 3.64).

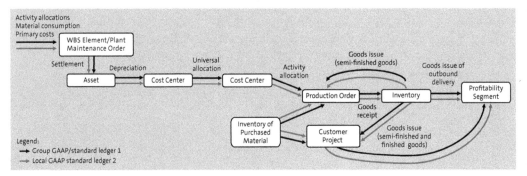

Figure 3.64 End-to-End Parallel Value Flow per Ledger/Accounting Principle

There can be multiple sources for valuation differences:

- Different capitalization rules for fixed assets and material valuation
- Ledger-dependent depreciation rules
- Ledger-specific general ledger postings
- Ledger-specific cost rates

This has an impact on the goods issue of material to production and projects, overheads on the WBS element and production order, and actual costing for products. This leads at the end to different margins in market segment reporting.

This continuous parallel evaluation allows for new functionalities on the roadmap. For example, a first version of the group ledger has already been released. The idea behind the group ledger is to eliminate intercompany profits during product transfers between company codes. This makes it possible to determine margins for the market segment from a group perspective.

Alternative Fiscal Years

International companies that have locations in several countries often want to map different fiscal year variants in those countries. For example, financial reporting at the corporate level may need to follow the calendar year in the leading ledger, while it may differ with a shifted fiscal year in the local ledgers.

The parallel use of fiscal year variants within one company code was only possible to a very limited extent in the fixed asset and controlling applications, causing many customers to use several controlling areas. These limitations have been addressed with universal parallel accounting, which now consistently supports alternative fiscal year variants as long as the period borders are the same in each fiscal year.

Enhanced Multicurrency Capabilities

With universal parallel accounting, up to 10 currencies are calculated and posted in parallel within the financial applications. Additionally, the currency handling changed within the controlling applications. In the past, the settlement or allocation was done in controlling based on the group/controlling area currency, and the other currencies were calculated with currency conversion. With universal parallel accounting, the allocations/settlements allocate each currency separately. This results in all currency amounts balancing to zero on the allocation sender side.

> **Note**
>
> Universal parallel accounting was delivered in SAP S/4HANA Cloud, public edition 2105 and is therefore active by default for all customers. A first version with several restrictions was delivered in on-premise SAP S/4HANA 2022 and SAP S/4HANA Cloud, private edition. Detailed and current information about the provided scope and restrictions is provided here: *https://launchpad.support.sap.com/#/notes/3191636.*

Now that we've discussed different actions and methods for posting documents, we'll move on to cover resetting and reversing documents in the next section.

3.4 Resetting and Reversing Documents

Reversing posting documents is another necessary function in SAP S/4HANA used occasionally during the working process. You can reverse a posting document if you recognize some errors after a successful posting. For example, you realize that the amount is posted incorrectly, you've selected the wrong date, or you've used the wrong currency. All these discrepancies can be easily solved if you know how to use the reversing function. Note that in the reversal process, you can reverse all documents for the corresponding posting run, but you can't reverse individual posting documents. The posting documents and reversal documents refer to the same posting run. Before reversing a posting document, you must know the type of the original posting document. Documents are classified into two categories, as clearing or nonclearing documents.

As described in Section 3.3.5, clearing documents are created with clearing Transaction F-04, which consists of two components: (1) the document header data and at least two-line items with both debit and credit entries that balance the document to a zero amount, and (2) the account clearing. In addition, as you read earlier, the clearing function allows you to change the status of open items into cleared items.

A nonclearing document is similar to a clearing document, but it doesn't clear the general ledger open items and doesn't turn the general ledger line from **Open** status to **Cleared** status. Our focus in this section will be on reversing both clearing and non-clearing documents. Let's start with reversing the nonclearing documents.

3.4.1   Reversing Nonclearing Documents

To reverse a nonclearing accounting document, you can follow one of the following application menu paths or use Transaction FBO8:

- **Accounting • Financial Accounting • General Ledger • Document • Reverse • Individual Reversal**
- **Accounting • Financial Accounting • Accounts Receivable • Document • Reverse • Individual Reversal**
- **Accounting • Financial Accounting • Accounts Payable • Document • Reverse • Individual Reversal**

After you double-click the **Individual Reversal** option from the menu path, the **Reverse Document: Header Data** screen appears, as shown in Figure 3.65. Fill in some required fields in the **Document Details** area as well as the **Reversal Reason** field.

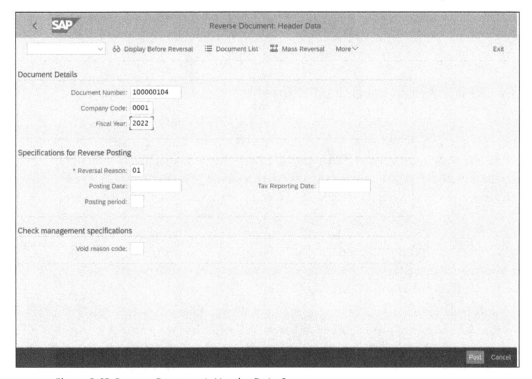

Figure 3.65 Reverse Document: Header Data Screen

In the **Reversal Reason** field, you can click on the input help next to the field (or press F4) to see the four possible values:

- 01 Wrong posting
- 02 Wrong period
- 03 Wrong prices and conditions
- 04 Return

In this example, **01 Wrong posting** has been selected. After you've filled in the required fields, click the **Post** button, and another screen appears showing the new general ledger document number (see Figure 3.66).

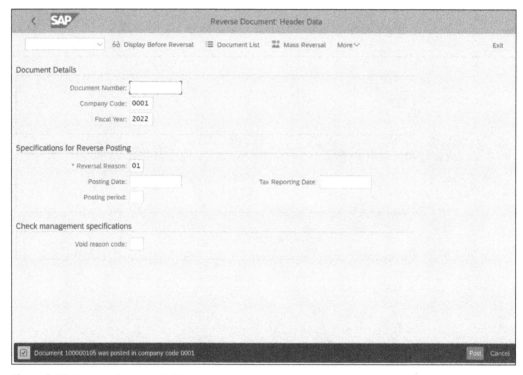

Figure 3.66 Reverse Document Message

In the application menu path, below **Individual Reversal**, you can double-click **Mass Reversal** or use Transaction F.80. This transaction can be used if you have more than one nonclearing document to reverse. In the **Mass Reversal of Documents: Initial Screen**, you can enter a range of document numbers. The **Ledger** field, which refers to your primary ledger, has been automatically populated, as shown in Figure 3.67. Under the **Reverse posting details** area, you can select the **Test Run** checkbox when you're performing a mass reversal of documents (see Figure 3.68).

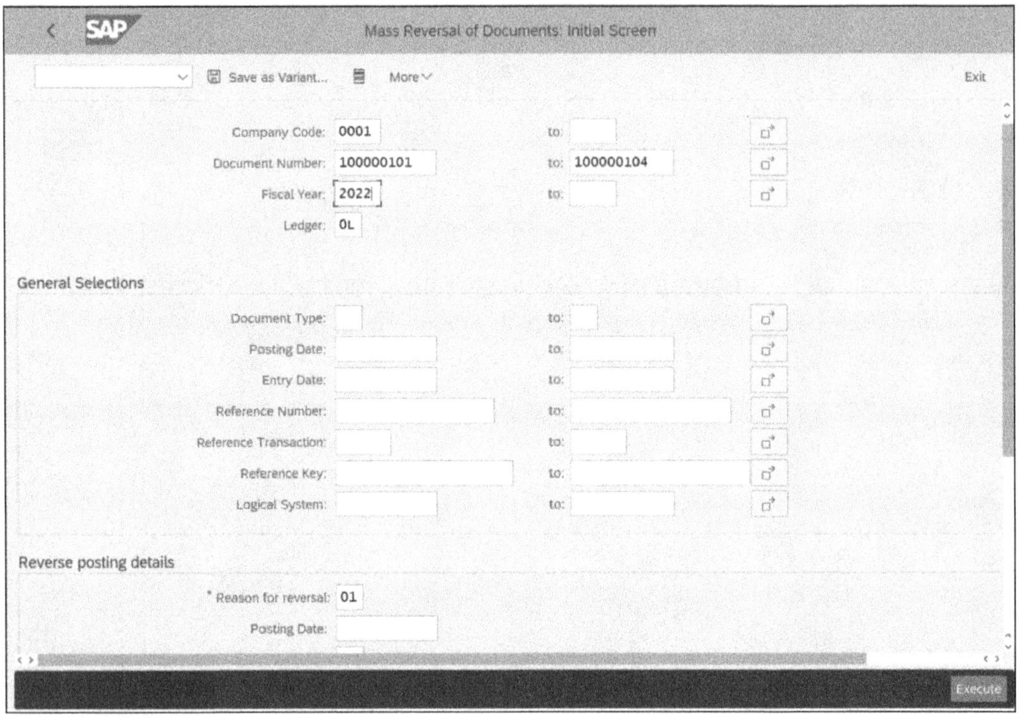

Figure 3.67 Mass Reversal of Documents: Initial Screen (1)

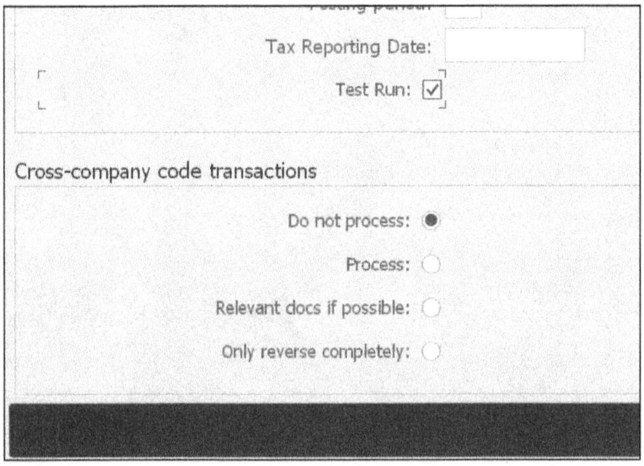

Figure 3.68 Mass Reversal of Documents Screen (2)

After you've entered the required elements, click the **Execute** button, and the reversal process starts to execute. The output is shown in the **Mass Reversal of Documents** screen with the detailed records for each reversed document, as shown in Figure 3.69.

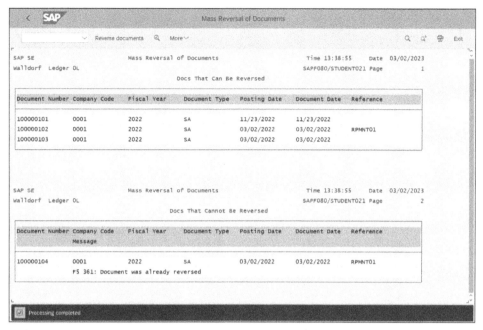

Figure 3.69 Mass Reversal Documents Message

SAP Fiori App

The corresponding SAP Fiori app is called Manage Journal Entries (F0717). With this app, you can easily search for the journal entry to be reversed and perform the reversal.

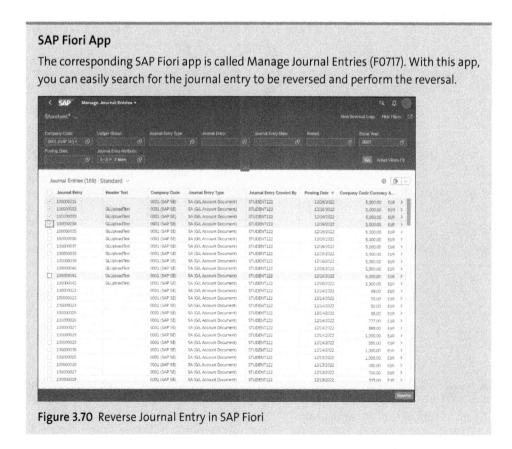

Figure 3.70 Reverse Journal Entry in SAP Fiori

To reverse a journal entry, you just need to select its checkbox and click the **Reverse** button (see Figure 3.70). After you click the **Reverse** button, the system asks you for the reversal reason (e.g., **Wrong Posting**), the posting date, tax reporting date, and the period, before you can post the reversal by just clicking **OK**.

3.4.2 Reversing Clearing Documents

Now that you understand the concept of reversing nonclearing documents, let's discuss the approach of reversing clearing documents. You may need to reverse a clearing of open items as well as all postings that were generated automatically during the clearing.

To reverse a clearing document, you can use one of the following application menu paths or use Transaction FBRA:

- Accounting • Financial Accounting • General Ledger • Document • Reset Cleared Items
- Accounting • Financial Accounting • Accounts Receivable • Document • Reset Cleared Items
- Accounting • Financial Accounting • Accounts Payable • Document • Reset Cleared Items

After you double-click on **Reset Cleared Items**, the **Reset Cleared Items** screen appears, where you can enter the required information, as shown in Figure 3.71.

Figure 3.71 Reset Cleared Items Screen

After you fill in the required fields (your **Clearing Document** number, **Company Code**, and **Fiscal Year**), press ⌈Enter⌋, or click on the **Reset cleared items** button. A prompting message box pops up showing three available selections, out of which you can choose only one, as shown in Figure 3.72.

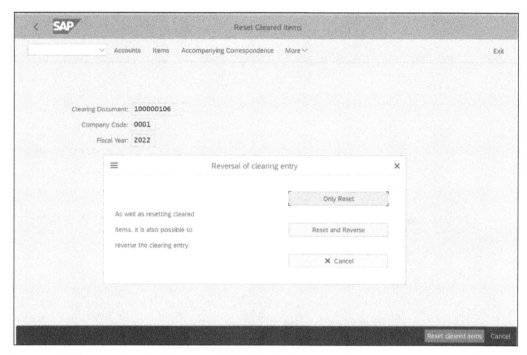

Figure 3.72 Three Options for the Reversal of a Clearing Document

As you can see, you can reverse the clearing document with a couple of functions:

- **Only Reset**
  This option doesn't reverse the cleared document, but it enables you to only reset the clearing information between a clearing document and the accounts receivable document or accounts payable document. You may have selected a wrong accounts receivable or accounts payable line item, and you can change the status of the accounts receivable item or accounts payable item from **Cleared** to **Open** with this function. The clearing document becomes an open item as well, and you can now link it with an appropriate accounts receivable item or accounts payable item.

- **Reset and Reverse**
  This option both resets and reverses the clearing document. For this example, select this option because it's more comprehensive. Another prompting message box appears asking you to define the **Reversal Reason**, as shown in Figure 3.73.

Figure 3.73 Reversal Cleared Document Message Box

Like the previous example, select the same reversal reason of **01 Wrong posting**, and press ⌜Enter⌝ or click the continue icon ☑. An information message box pops up showing that the clearing document has been reset, as shown in Figure 3.74. You'll receive a second message after you click the continue icon ☑ again in the information message box. In this message, you get the new document number posted in your company after reversing the clearing document, as shown in Figure 3.75.

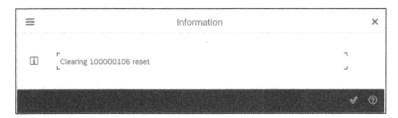

Figure 3.74 Resetting Cleared Document Information Message

Figure 3.75 Reversal Cleared Document Posted Message

After following and understanding these examples, you should be confident and able to perform a reversal of a noncleared/cleared document, accounts receivable document, accounts payable document, or even multiple documents.

SAP Fiori Apps

The corresponding SAP Fiori app is called Reset Cleared Items (FBRA). With this app, you can search for the list of clearing items (see Figure 3.76). To reset or reset and reverse an entry, you just need to select an item and click the **Reset** or **Reset and Reverse** button (see Figure 3.77).

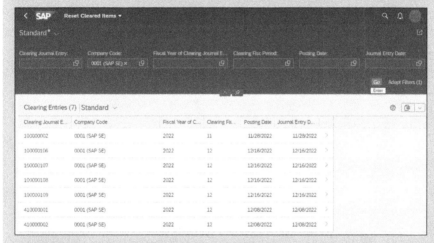

Figure 3.76 Reset Cleared Items Screen

Figure 3.77 Reset or Reset and Reverse Item

After the item has been reset or reversed a new message appears showing that a new document was posted in the company code.

There is also another SAP Fiori app that is also called Reset Cleared Items but has a different code (F2223). It's visually different but functionally very similar to Transaction FBRA, so we won't explain it here.

3.5   Bank Accounting

Bank accounting is an important part of financial accounting that deals with all accounting transactions relating to bank account movements. With the bank accounting functions in SAP S/4HANA, you can manage all incoming and outgoing payments, accounting balances, and bank master data.

In this section, we'll explain bank master data for the business partners, house banks, general ledger integration, relationship of house banks with the general ledger accounts, bank reconciliation, bank clearing, manual bank statements, and electronic bank statement (EBS) processing.

3.5.1   Bank Master Data

In Section 3.2, you learned that master data is data that remains unchanged over a long period of time and contains information that is continuously required in the same way. In this section, we'll focus on bank master records of business partners and house banks.

The difference between house banks and business partner banks is that *house banks* are the banks with which your company has a bank account and has settled a business relationship to perform any transactions. In these accounts, like usual bank accounts, it's possible to hold cash, execute outgoing and incoming payments, and deposit money. The bank accounts of your business partners form the extended master data of the business partner and belong to the business partner. If your business partner is a supplier, you need the bank account to transfer money to balance open items. If your business partner is a customer, you may have the right to direct debit the account of your customer.

Business Partner Bank Data

Business partners (e.g., vendors or customers) are the external parties with whom your company performs bank accounting transactions. These accounting transactions may refer to an outgoing transaction where you send money to your business partner (i.e., vendor) or receive an incoming payment from your business partner (i.e., customer). For every external bank account belonging to your customer or vendor, a bank account master record is set up and linked with the respective master record. Therefore, there is a connection bridge with the vendor and customer that allows you to perform the basic business processes, purchases, and sales as follows:

- Perform an outgoing payment to the vendor for the provided goods or services.
- Receive an incoming payment from a customer for the goods and service you've provided.

To open a bank master record transaction, follow application menu path **Accounting •**
Financial Accounting • Banks • Master Data • Bank Master Record.

Under **Bank Master Record**, you can find the most frequently used transactions: **Create –**
FI01, Change – FI02, Display – FI03, and **Display Changes – FI04.** There are also other transactions, such as **Create Internal Bank for SEPA – FISEPA, Transfer Bank Data – BAUP, Trans-**
fer BIC File – BIC2, Generate IBAN – IBANMD, and others. To create a bank account master
record, double-click on **FI01 – Create.** In the **Create Bank: Initial Screen,** enter the **Bank**
Country and bank number (**Bank Key**), as shown in Figure 3.78.

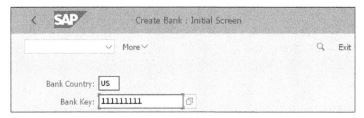

Figure 3.78 Create Bank: Initial Screen

Press Enter, and in the next **Create Bank: Detail Screen,** shown in Figure 3.79, enter
your **Bank name,** address, and **Bank number.** Click the **Save** button at the bottom right
of the screen. After the entered records are saved, you'll receive a message showing that
the bank has been created, as shown in Figure 3.80.

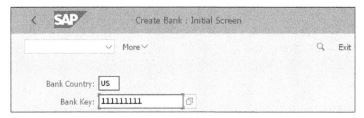

Figure 3.79 Create Bank Detail Screen

Figure 3.80 Create Bank Message

You must follow the same steps if you need to change or display a bank account master record. To display a bank, double-click **FI03 – Display** from the application menu path. In the **Display Bank: Initial Screen** that appears, as shown in Figure 3.81, enter the **Bank Country** and **Bank Key**, and then press Enter.

Figure 3.81 Display Bank: Initial Screen

The **Display Bank: Detail Screen** shows more detailed information for the bank master record, as shown in Figure 3.82.

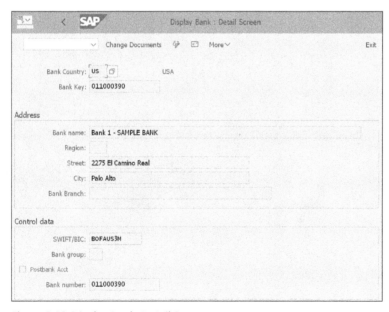

Figure 3.82 Display Bank: Detail Screen

Beneath the **Address** area is the very important bank **Control data** area. **SWIFT/BIC** is a unique string that identifies a bank. That bank number is then the individual bank account of a company or a business partner. Whether this bank will be a house bank or a business partner bank is determined either in Transaction FI12_HBANK or in the individual business partner master data. We'll see how this happens next.

To change a bank account master record, double-click on **FI02 – Change** in the application menu path. You follow the same procedure as for the two other transactions, and save the changes you perform in the **Change Bank: Detail Screen**.

Now that you've created a bank account master record, you must assign it to a vendor or customer master record. Let's consider an example of a bank linked to a customer master record. To see a customer master record, follow application menu path **Accounting • Financial Accounting • Accounts Receivable • Master Records • Display**. The **Customer Display: Initial Screen** appears, as shown in Figure 3.83.

Figure 3.83 Customer Display: Initial Screen

After you've defined the **Customer** and **Company Code** fields, click on the continue icon to open the screen in Figure 3.84, showing the information related to the business partner (vendor master data). If you want to check the general data of the vendor, you can double-click on the **General Data** tab on the top menu of the screen.

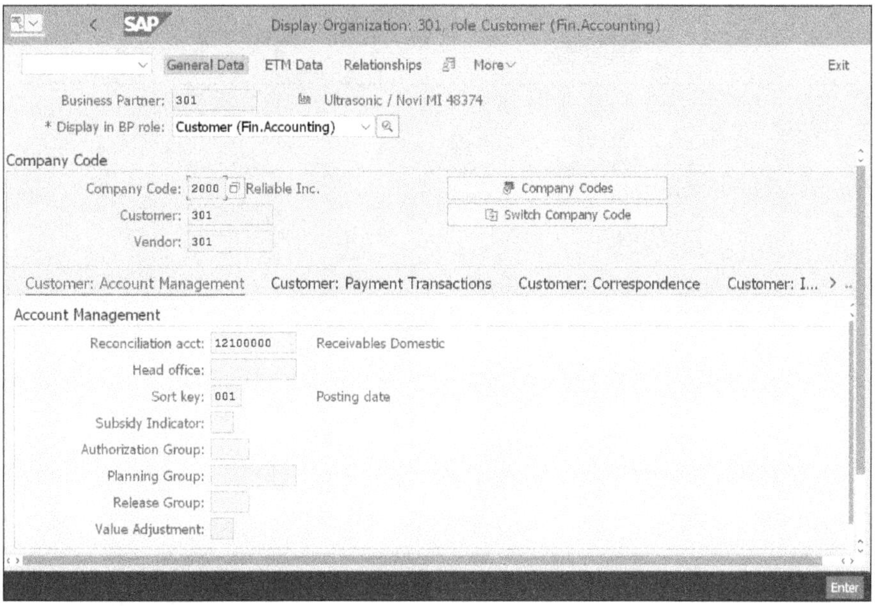

Figure 3.84 Display Vendor Master Data

House Bank

As we already mentioned in the previous section, the house bank is where the company has settled its bank accounts and is operating a business relationship. The frequently executed business processes include cash deposit, cash holding, and debiting or crediting transactions.

In the system, the house bank is identified with an account ID serving as a unique identifier. You need to create a separate general ledger account that serves for each house bank account. For reconciling the bank statement in SAP S/4HANA for each bank account, general ledger subaccounts are created. The linking between house bank and bank master data, which is centrally stored, is done by specifying the country and a country-specific key (e.g., the bank number). You can find the house bank in SAP S/4HANA by following application menu path **Accounting • Financial Accounting • Banks • Master Data • House Banks and House Bank Accounts**.

Let's consider the first transaction: **FI12_HBANK – Manage House Banks**. After you click this transaction, you first must select the **Company Code**, and then the **Change View "House Banks": Details** screen appears, as shown in Figure 3.85.

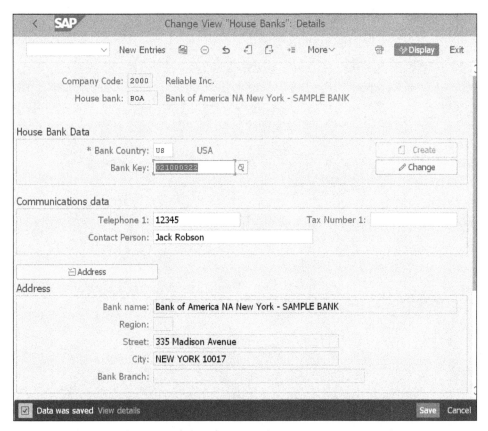

Figure 3.85 Managing House Bank Details

In this screen, you can make changes to the following:

- **House Bank Data**
  Maintain **Bank Country** and **Bank Key** from the user.

- **Communications data**
  Optionally, maintain the contact details of any person from the bank who takes care of your needs.

- **Address**
  Optionally, maintain the address of the bank. If you have more than one house bank, it makes sense to complete this data to better distinguish the different bank accounts.

Click the **Save** button.

Now that you know how to create bank master data, we'll move on to explain the general ledger integration and then how to process bank transactions in SAP S/4HANA.

SAP Fiori App

The corresponding SAP Fiori app is called Manage Banks (F1574). With this app, you can display, create, and change the data of the banks for your company (house banks), and you can display, create, and change the bank data of your customers and your suppliers (business partners' banks).

After you've started the app, you can display any bank account you've already created, or you can create a bank account using the **Create Bank** button on the bottom right (see Figure 3.86).

Although it looks a bit different, the creation steps are very similar to what you've seen in SAP GUI, so we won't repeat them here.

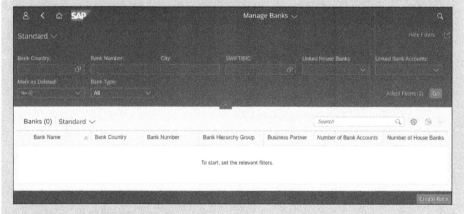

Figure 3.86 Manage Banks Screen

3.5.2 General Ledger Integration

In this section, we'll explain the integration of the company's bank accounts in the general ledger chart of accounts. You're already familiar with the concept of the general ledger account structure from Section 3.2. Now, you'll see in more detail how a particular bank account is reflected and reconciled in terms of general ledger accounts. Ideally, each bank account is represented by one general ledger account of a specific company. Using the relevant functionality, you have to assign the bank accounts to house bank and general ledger accounts and assign that particular bank account as well.

In financial accounting, there are two types of general ledger bank accounts (i.e., balance sheet accounts): *main bank accounts*, which are individually linked with a house bank account, and *bank clearing accounts*, whose main purpose is for bank reconciliation. The next sections will show the differences between these accounts and how to maintain them.

Bank General Ledger Account

As mentioned, each main general ledger bank account is specified in the house bank account, and each house bank account is specified in the general ledger bank account. They proceed in a bidirectional connection.

To manage house bank accounts, follow menu path **Accounting • Financial Accounting • Banks • Master Data • House Banks and House Bank Accounts**, or use Transaction FI12. In the screen that appears (see Figure 3.87), you select the relevant company code (**CoCd** column) (in this example, company code **2000**) and then click on **Bank Accounts**.

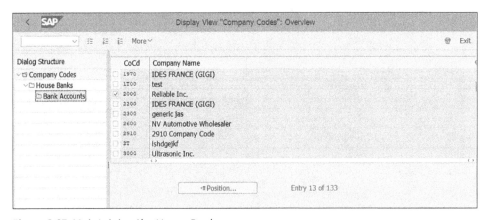

Figure 3.87 Maintaining the House Bank

After entering the bank key in the **House bank** field (in this example, "BOA"), the complete master data of the house bank for company code **2000** is displayed, as shown in Figure 3.88. In the **Bank Account Data** area, you also see the assigned general ledger account for the house bank. In this case, it's **G/L** account **64060000**. All other fields should be self-explanatory. If you want to edit the house bank master record, you just need to select the **Maintain Bank Account** button in the menu bar.

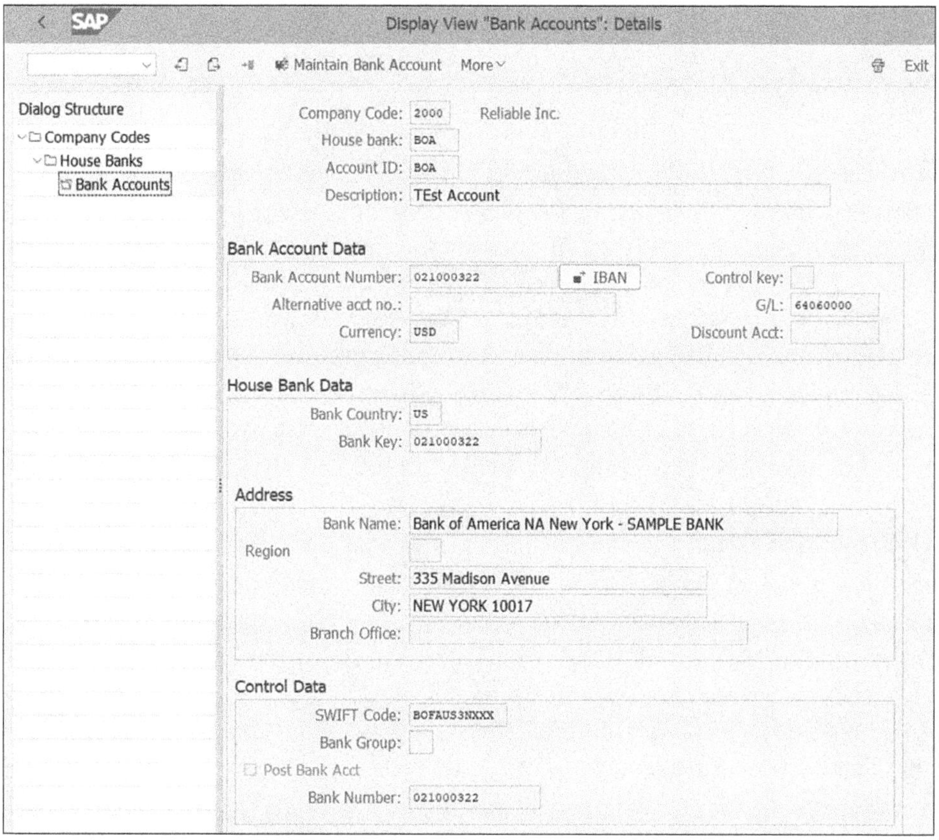

Figure 3.88 Display House Bank Master Data "BOA"

To create a new bank account, just click on the back arrow in the top-left corner of the screen, and the **Maintain Bank Account** button changes to the **Create Bank Account** button. Click on that button, and you can set up a new house bank master record.

Now that you have a clear idea of the bank account and its connectivity with the general ledger account, let's move on to the reconciliation process using the bank general ledger clearing account.

Bank General Ledger Clearing Account

As mentioned in the previous section, the purpose of the bank general ledger clearing account is for the reconciliation process. These accounts are used to hold transactions posted in financial accounting that aren't reconciled with an incoming bank transaction. The bank general ledger clearing account is much like a general ledger account used to manage the open items from the posted transactions with an **Open** status, which will be cleared and offset from another general ledger entry. At that moment, the item will change the status from **Open** to **Cleared**. For each bank account, a bank clearing account has to be created to post the bank transactions in transition and to ensure that the primary general ledger bank account always reconciles with the bank statements.

3.5.3   Bank Reconciliation

The *bank reconciliation* function is the process during which all the bank statement transactions are settled with all the transactions posted in the general ledger account. It's easy to understand how this process works. All the open items in the general ledger bank clearing accounts are cleared, and then offsetting entries are posted in the main bank accounts. In the SAP S/4HANA system, the reconciliation process is performed under two approaches: automatic and manual. The first approach is called electronic bank statement (EBS), where all the electronic statements are automatically imported into SAP S/4HANA and then reconciled and matched. The second approach is called manual bank statement (MBS), which has the same logic, but everything is manually performed by the SAP S/4HANA user. In the next two sections, we'll explain both methods in detail.

Electronic Bank Statement

EBS is the automatic method of the bank reconciliation process for which a predefined format is required. Banks worldwide normally use one of the most common standards for exchanging EBS (e.g., SWIFT, MT940, BAI, MultiCash, or any other bank-specific XML format). The received bank statements are uploaded in one of these formats through Transaction FF_5. This uploading or importing process is automatically performed through the scheduled jobs running on a daily basis.

To upload an EBS, you can follow menu path **Accounting • Financial Accounting • Banks • Input • Bank Statement • Import** or use Transaction FF_5.

Double-click in this transaction, and the **Bank Statement: Various Formats (SWIFT, MultiCash, BAI…)** screen appears, as shown in Figure 3.89. In this screen, you fill in some of the fields in the specified areas, such as the following:

- **File specifications**
  Specify the file format and file location, and then select **Import data**. Select **Workstation upload** if you want to upload the EBS locally from your PC. The **Zero Revenue Permitted (Swift)** checkbox is only relevant for SWIFT formats. Sometimes, there is more information on bank statements than transactions. To also allow comments and text additions from the bank to be imported, the **Zero Revenue Permitted (Swift)** checkbox needs to be ticked.

- **Posting parameters**
  Select one of the available options, such as **Post Immediately**, **Generate batch input**, or **Do Not Post**. Generating a batch input instead of an immediate posting will generate a batch input file, which can be later processed through the batch input file interface (Transaction SM35). If you select the **Only Bank Accounting** checkbox, the

statement will post to the general ledger bank accounts and won't allow posting to subledgers.

- **Cash management**
  Only use these options when you've set up and implemented the cash management application in SAP. If you don't use it, you can ignore these options.

- **Algorithms**
  Specify the document **BELNR number interval** and the document reference **XBLNR number interval**. Bank statement transactions outside of these intervals will be ignored by that automatic bank statement processing. Further, the processed transactions can be grouped in different bundles.

- **Output Control**
  Select your output preference, such as **Execute as background job**, **Print bank statement**, **Print posting log**, and so on.

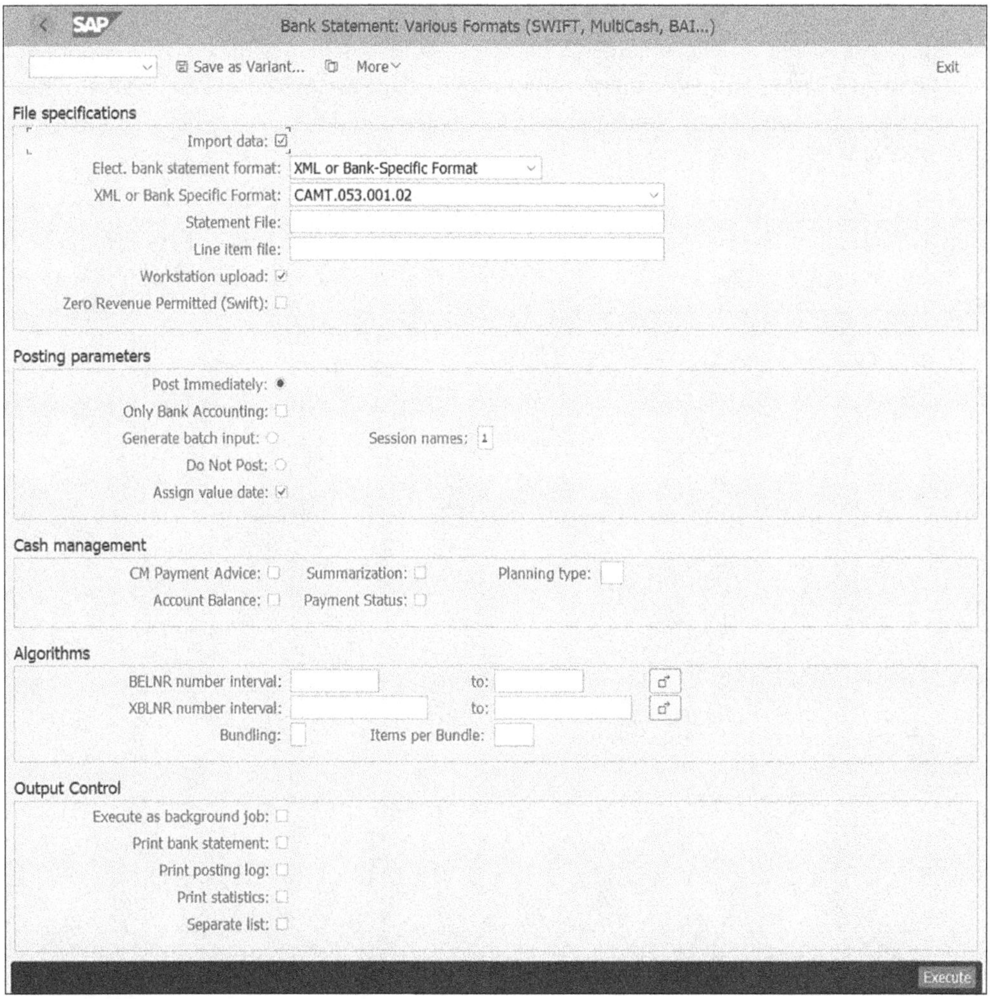

Figure 3.89 Electronic Bank Statement

After you've selected and entered the required data but before you click the **Execute** button, you can click the **Save as Variant** button at the top of the screen. By doing so, you can open the saved variant next time, and you don't have to fill in the same fields again. After the import process is executed, the bank posting logs showing all the details will appear.

The next step after the importing process of an EBS is the postprocessing of the bank statement transactions, which aren't cleared and reconciled automatically. We'll discuss this in the next section.

Postprocessing of Electronic Bank Statements

As explained in the previous section, for EBS, all the transactions on the bank statements are reconciled with general ledger line items in bank clearing accounts. In the SAP S/4HANA system, you can automatically import and forward the EBS and then postprocess those bank statements that haven't been posted and reconciled in the system.

Postprocessing of bank statements is performed in a screen transaction managing the daily processing of open bank statement items. This process checks the status of bank statements and then manually clears the bank statements that weren't automatically cleared.

In the system, you can perform a postprocess of an EBS by following application menu path **Accounting • Financial Accounting • Banks • Input • Bank Statement • Reprocess**, or use Transaction FEBA_BANK_STATEMENT. The **Selection of Bank Statement Items** screen appears, as shown in Figure 3.90.

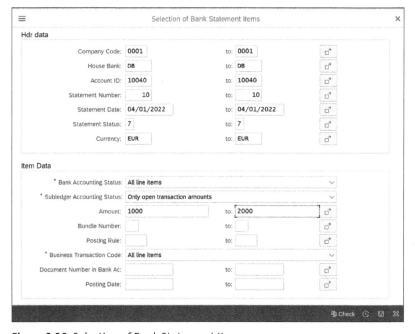

Figure 3.90 Selection of Bank Statement Items

In the **Hdr data** area, you identify the bank statement that you want to reprocess. To do so, specify the **Company Code**, **House Bank**, **Account ID**, and **Statement Number** fields of the EBS you want to reprocess.

In the **Item Data** section, you can limit the reprocessing to certain items of the EBS. For instance, you can enter a certain status, an account range, bundle number, document, and so on. These fields help you narrow the reprocessing to a subset of items of an EBS. Before executing the screen, you can save it as a variant to use it later.

The automatic processing should be the standard case. If it isn't yet configured in your system, you need to process each transaction of a bank statement manually, which we'll discuss next.

Manual Bank Statements

As we explained in the previous section, there is a predefined format of the bank statements to be processed. If you don't find any available format of the bank statement, or the account has a small number of transactions for which it isn't suitable to be processed via EBS, then you can create and upload an MBS.

To create and upload the MBS, follow application menu path **Accounting • Financial Accounting • Banks • Input • Bank Statement • Manual Entry**, or use Transaction FF67.

If you start Transaction FF67 for the first time in your system, it will ask you for some general specifications. After they are entered, the system won't ask you again. In the **Specifications** screen, as shown in Figure 3.91, you set up the following parameters:

- **Int. Bank Determin.**
  Here you can control whether the bank account is determined using the internal ID or the external account number. If this parameter is selected, the system searches for bank accounts via the internal house bank ID as well as the account details. The ID is maintained within the system configuration.

  If this parameter isn't selected, the system searches for bank accounts via the external bank account number and the external bank key (generally the bank number).

- **Import Advices**
  If you select this checkbox, cash management advices can be selected and automatically archived when a bank statement is created.

- **Start Variant**
  The variant name you enter here specifies which account assignment variant the system is to begin with during memo record processing. You can change the variants at any time during memo record processing.

- **Cust. Matchcode ID**
  This field is prefilled with a **D** for debtors (customers).

- **Vendor Matchcode ID**
  This field is prefilled with a **K** for creditors (suppliers).

- **Processing Type**
  Use this field to control whether postings via batch input are carried out online or as a background job.

- **Transfer Value Date**
  If you select this checkbox, then the system transfers the value date when posting the documents in financial accounting.

Figure 3.91 Specifications for Manual Bank Statements

SAP Fiori App

The corresponding SAP Fiori app for creating an MBS is called Manage Bank Statements (F1564), as shown in Figure 3.92. Although the screen of this app looks quite different, you have to fill in the same fields and process the bank statement the same way as with Transaction FF67.

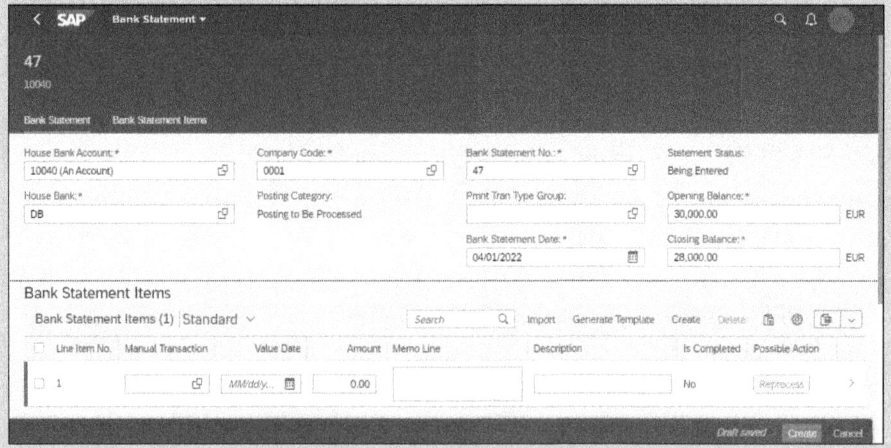

Figure 3.92 Process Manual Bank Statement Screen

You can click the continue ✅ icon to arrive at the next screen, **Process Manual Bank Statement**, as shown in Figure 3.93. You must fill in the required entry fields such as **Bank Account**, (bank) **Statement Number**, and (bank) **Statement Date,** as well as an **Opening Balance**, **Closing Balance**, and **Posting Date**. After that, click on **Continue** to enter the items one by one. After you've entered all bank statement items, click on the **Post statement** button, and you're done.

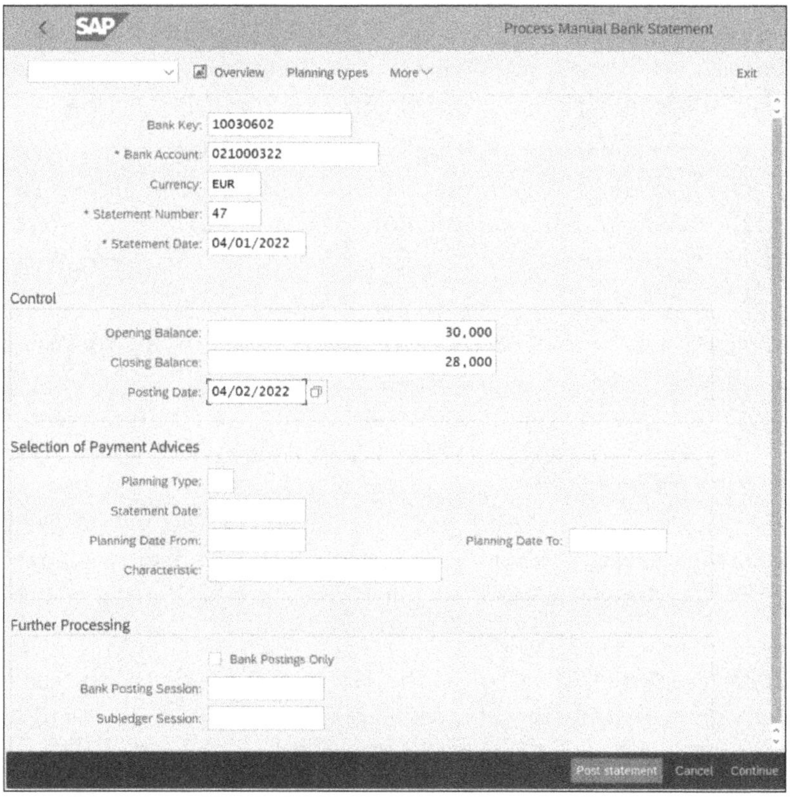

Figure 3.93 Process Manual Bank Statement Screen

Now you can process any kind of transaction in the general ledger. Next, you'll learn how to close the general ledger at period end.

3.6 General Ledger Period-End Closing

The financial closing cycle is the most critical period for financial accounting. In this section, we'll walk through financial end of month and end of year period-end closing processes alongside the opening and closing periods, balance carryforward, subledger reconciliation, foreign currency valuation, and GR/IR clearing.

SAP S/4HANA provides many possibilities for a company to improve the financial closing process. Regarding the standard closing procedure, SAP S/4HANA provides the *SAP
Financial Closing cockpit for SAP S/4HANA* as discussed in Chapter 1, Section 1.3.3. Many
companies track, monitor, and control their closing steps according to a period-end
closing schedule in a spreadsheet. Instead of a spreadsheet, you may use the SAP Financial Closing cockpit for SAP S/4HANA. Before you can use it efficiently, you should get
to know its functionality and configure it to your needs. We'll give a structured intro-
duction/guidance into the SAP Financial Closing cockpit for SAP S/4HANA later in Section 3.6.6. Before we do so, to help you understand the basic principles and closing
procedures in SAP, let's go through the required steps for closing the general ledger.

We begin the close in SAP by understanding the period control mechanism to open and
close specific accounting periods for defined accounts, followed by the subledger reconciliations and the foreign currency valuation run, as well as some other required
closing steps, such as settlement of clearing accounts and balance carryforward activities.

Let's begin the financial close process with the period control mechanism to open and
close specific accounting periods for defined accounts.

3.6.1   Opening and Closing Periods

In SAP S/4HANA, you can open and close periods in financial accounting by using
menu path **Accounting • Financial Accounting • General Ledger • Environment • Current
Settings • Open and Close Posting Periods**, or by using Transaction FAGL_EHP4_T001B_
COFI.

After you click **Open and Close Posting Periods**, the **Determine Work Area: Entry** screen
appears, in which you need to enter the **Pstng period variant** (posting period variant). In
this example, the variant **1710** is used, as shown in Figure 3.94.

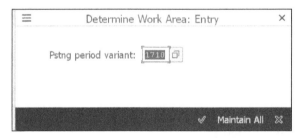

Figure 3.94 Defining the Posting Period Variant

Click the continue ✓ icon, and in the **Specify Time Interval: Overview** screen, click the
New Entries button to arrive at the screen shown in Figure 3.95.

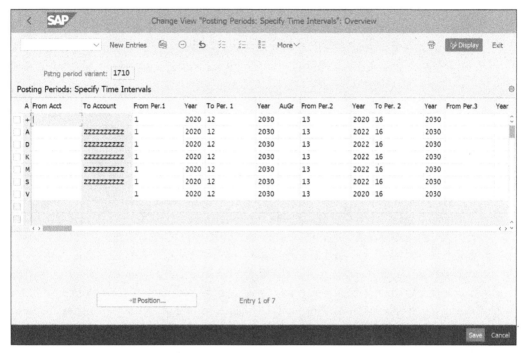

Figure 3.95 Controlling Posting Periods

Here, you can fill in the following important fields, as explained in Table 3.2.

#	Description
A	This is the account type where you can find these possible values: **+** (valid for all account types), **A** (assets), **D** (customers), **K** (vendors), **M** (materials), **S** (general ledger accounts), and **V** (contract accounts).
From Acct	Enter the account number range for which you want to change the periods.
To Account	Define a range of account numbers starting with the from account number and ending with the to account number.
From Per.1	Enter a posting period from which you want to open the posting period.
Year	Enter the fiscal year for which you want to open the posting period.
To Per. 1	Define a range of posting periods for which you want to enter posting periods.
Year	Define a range of years for which you want to open posting periods.

Table 3.2 Important Fields in Controlling Posting Periods

After you fill in these fields, click the **Save** button.

> **SAP Fiori App**
>
> The corresponding SAP Fiori app is called Manage Posting Periods (F2293). Although the visualization is different, the use and the functionality are very similar to what you've seen with Transaction FAGL_EHP4_T001B_COFI.

3.6.2   Subledger Reconciliation

In this section, we'll provide step-by-step instructions for reconciliation of the general ledger to subledger. To get started, let's refresh the concept of the general ledger as an amassing of all balance sheet and income statement accounts. It contains all journal entries posted to accounts as well. On the other hand, a *subledger* refers to a detailed record of transactions of an individual account, which, after being cumulated over time, are posted to the general ledger. For example, the accounts receivable subledger contains information related to all the issued invoices and payments received from the customer. At the end of the day, all the issued invoices and cash receipts entries are summarized and posted to the general ledger in two separate journal entries. The general ledger contains only the accumulated data so you can't find details for each individual transaction.

As this is a manual process in SAP S/4HANA, there is always the possibility of human errors. To discover and fix these errors, it's extremely important to perform reconciliation of the general ledger and the subledger balances on a periodic basis. If no error is found during reconciliation, it means that both balances match; however, if there are differences, then items need to be reconciled after analyzing and correcting if necessary. Some of the discrepancies found during the reconciliation could be, for example, because some items are included in the subledger but not in the general ledger or vice versa, and some items may be posted in the general ledger through a journal entry and aren't recorded in the subledger. Accounts receivable and accounts payable are two of the most important accounts that need to be reconciled on a monthly basis.

In the following, we've listed the steps you can follow to perform an accounts receivable or accounts payable reconciliation (for more details, see Chapter 5, Section 5.8.4, and Chapter 4, Section 4.6.6, respectively):

1. **Compare the balances of the general ledger account and subledger account**
   Analyze the general ledger and subledger balances to identify any differences. While analyzing, you should also check for transactions of an unusual nature, such as non-recurring transactions, which may have a higher risk of errors than recurring transactions performed on a regular basis. You need to check the sales journal (receivables) and purchases journal (payables) to detect entries posted to the wrong accounts, double-posted entries, transposition errors, and so on. After that, you should look at the cash receipts and cash payment journals for receivables and payables and then perform the relevant reconciliations.

2. **Investigate and evaluate the root cause for the difference**

   If you find some differences between the general ledger and subledger balances, the next step is to determine the reason for these discrepancies. The most common reasons include the following:

   - Items are posted to the general ledger, but not to the subledger.
   - Items are posted to the subledger, but not to the general ledger.

   Depending on the situation, adjustments may need to be made to the general ledger or to the subledger. Table 3.3 provides some examples to show where the adjustment should be made, depending on the root cause of the difference.

Difference Root Cause	Illustration	Adjustment
Adding up error	In the sales/purchase daybook, overstating/understating has occurred due to incorrect summarizing of totals.	Adjustment of the general ledger
Omission	A debit/credit balance has been omitted from the list of customer/supplier accounts.	Adjustment of the subledger
Duplication	The same transaction has been posted twice in a customer/supplier account.	Adjustment of the subledger
Transposition error	A sales/purchase invoice has been wrongly recorded in the individual account, for example, $87 instead of $78.	Adjustment of subledger
Wrong setoffs in individual accounts	A debit balance on the customer's ledger has been set off against a supplier's ledger credit balance.	Adjustment of the general ledger

Table 3.3 Reasons for Differences and Relevant Adjustments

3. **Make the necessary adjustments on the general ledger, subledger, or both**

   After you've figured out the reason for the difference, make the appropriate adjustments to the general ledger account or to the subledgers, depending on the reason and based on the reconciliation, to correct any errors, omissions, transposition errors, and so on. Table 3.3 can help you understand what kind of adjustment you need to apply.

4. **Make the relevant checks to compare and confirm the adjusted balances**

   Compare the general ledger balance to the subledger balance. If the balances are reconciled, then the reconciliation process is considered successfully completed. If any differences remain, continue to check again the subledger and journals that are part of the revenue and expenditure cycles to identify the reason for the difference and adjust it.

Let's walk through an example of subledger to general ledger reconciliation by reconciling the general ledger account **Trade Receivable – Foreign** from the company code 1710 with the accounts receivable subledger. Follow these steps:

1. Generate a general ledger report where you can see the period-ending balances quickly. The best report for this is the trial balance or the financial statement (which we'll discuss in Section 3.7.2 and Section 3.7.4, respectively). To generate the financial statement for company 1710 for 2022, use menu path **Accounting • Financial Accounting • General Ledger • Information System • General Ledger Reports • Financial Statement/Cash Flow • General • Actual/Actual Comparison • Financial Statement**, or use Transaction F.01.

2. In the screen that appears, fill in the **Company Code, Financial Statement Version, Reporting Year, Comparison Year**, and **Reporting Periods**, ideally from "1" to "16".

3. Choose any option for the list output (for this example, **ALV Tree Control** is selected).

4. Click the **Execute** button to see the financial statement shown in Figure 3.96. The account **12100000 Receivables Domestic** has a balance of USD **6,580.00**, which is to be reconciled.

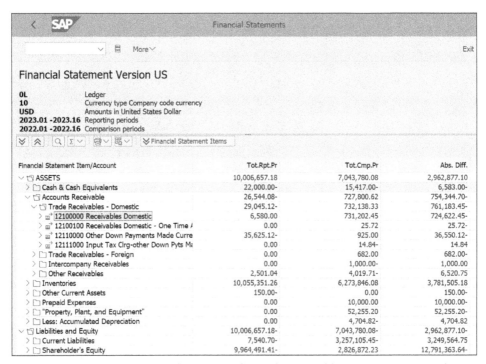

Figure 3.96 Extract from Financial Statement for Trade Receivables – Domestic Reconciliation

5. Generate the customer balances for domestic trade receivables from the accounts receivable subledger by following menu path **Accounting • Financial Accounting • Accounts Receivable • Information System • Reports for Accounts Receivable Accounting • Customer Balances • Customer Balances in Local Currency** or by using Transaction S_ALR_87012172.

6. In the **Customer Balances in Local Currency** screen, as shown in Figure 3.97, fill in the **Company code**, **Fiscal Year**, **Reporting Periods** from "1" to "16", and the **Reconciliation Account** as "12100000".

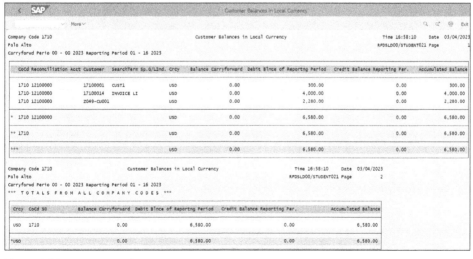

Figure 3.97 Customer Balances Selection

7. Click **Execute** to see the customer balances report, as shown in Figure 3.98. This report displays customer balances summing up to **6,580.00** USD, and the reconciliation of the general ledger account is done.

CoCd Reconciliation Acct	Customer	SearchTerm	Sp.G/Lind.	Crcy	Balance Carryforward	Debit Since of Reportng Period	Credit Balance Reporting Per.	Accumulated Balance
1710 12100000	17100001	CUST1		USD	0.00	300.00	0.00	300.00
1710 12100000	17100014	INVOICE LI		USD	0.00	4,000.00	0.00	4,000.00
1710 12100000	Z049-CU001			USD	0.00	2,280.00	0.00	2,280.00
* 1710 12100000				USD	0.00	6,580.00	0.00	6,580.00
** 1710				USD	0.00	6,580.00	0.00	6,580.00
***				USD	0.00	6,580.00	0.00	6,580.00

Company Code 1710   Customer Balances in Local Currency   Time 16:58:10   Date 03/04/2023
Palo Alto   RFDSLD00/STUDENT021 Page   2
Carryforwd Perio 00 - 00 2023 Reporting Period 01 - 16 2023
*** T O T A L S   F R O M   A L L   C O M P A N Y   C O D E S ***

Crcy	CoCd 50	Balance Carryforward	Debit Since of Reportng Period	Credit Balance Reporting Per.	Accumulated Balance
USD	1710	0.00	6,580.00	0.00	6,580.00
*USD		0.00	6,580.00	0.00	6,580.00

Figure 3.98 Customer Balances Report

3.6.3   Foreign Currency Valuation

If you want to create your financial statement, first you have to perform foreign currency valuation with all the necessary configurations, which makes it possible to valuate account balances in the reporting currency.

To access the foreign currency valuation, follow application menu path **Accounting • Financial Accounting • General Ledger • Periodic Processing • Closing • Valuate • Foreign Currency Valuation**, or use Transaction FAGL_FCV. You'll arrive at the screen shown in Figure 3.99.

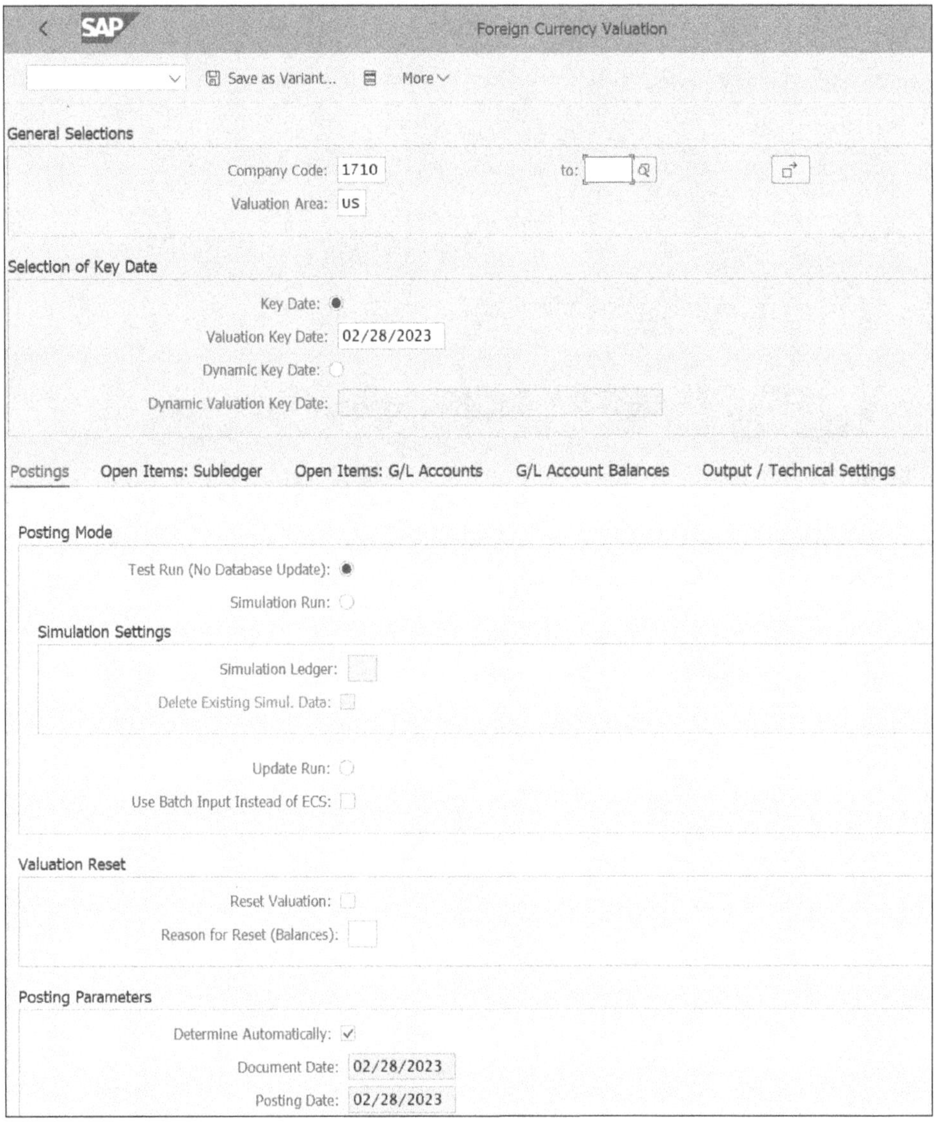

Figure 3.99 Foreign Currency Valuation Screen

The items and accounts included in the **Foreign Currency Valuation** screen are as follows:

- **General Selections**
  Enter the **Company Code**, **Valuation Key Date** (should be similar to the reporting date), and the respective **Valuation Area**.

- **Postings**
  If you don't want to do a test run (selected in this example), select **Update Run** to have the valuation posted. Posting parameters can be determined automatically. The system proposes the latest possible month-end as the valuation and posting date.

- **Open Items: Subledger**
  Here you can select the open items from the vendor and customer accounts, which are subject to translation into the local currency.

- **Open Items: G/L Accounts**
  Here you can select the open items posted directly to a general ledger account. Items posted in foreign currencies can then be revaluated to the valuation date.

- **G/L Account Balances**
  If there are general ledger account balances that are treated in a foreign currency (e.g., bank accounts in a foreign country), you can revaluate them on a specific reporting date.

- **Output / Technical Settings**
  Here you can specify some output control options, such as generating a log file, name of log file, and so on.

To start the foreign currency valuation run, click the **Execute** button, and the system will post the valuations.

3.6.4 Goods Receipt/Invoice Receipt Clearing

The GR/IR clearing process involves calculating the price variances between the goods receipt and invoice receipt, which then are allocated to inventory, price differences, or the assignment object based on the valuation procedure in the material master and the settings in the purchase order line item. The values are stored in the general ledger and GR/IR clearing account and are periodically settled using the GR/IR clearing function.

The GR/IR account should be maintained and analyzed on a regular basis where the system makes the match between goods receipts and invoice receipts based on the purchase order number, purchase order item, purchase order type, indicator of invoice verification, and material/delivery costs.

For the GR/IR clearing function, you can follow application menu path **Accounting • Financial Accounting • General Ledger • Periodic Processing • Closing • Reclassify • GR/IR Clearing**, or use Transaction F.19. The **Analyze GR/IR Clearing Accounts and Display Acquisition Tax** screen appears, as shown in Figure 3.100.

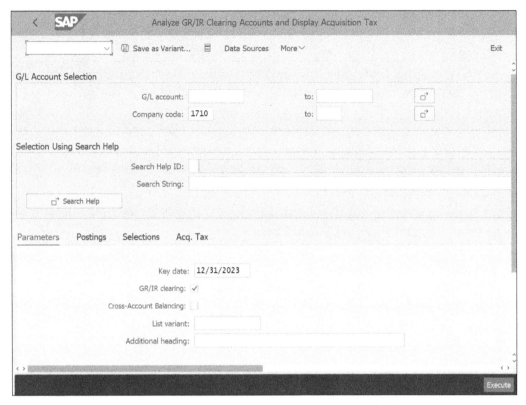

Figure 3.100 Analyze GR/IR Clearing Accounts and Display Acquisition Tax Screen

This transaction serves to analyze the GR/IR clearing accounts for a defined key date. The GR/IR clearing report shows cleared goods receipt postings on an item basis with supplier invoices on an item basis. Further, with this transaction, the remaining open items (not cleared goods receipt items and not cleared supplier invoice receipt items) can be posted to separate accounts (accounts that are delivered but not yet invoiced or invoiced but not yet delivered). The counter account for these postings is the GR/IR correction account. The GR/IR clearing account and the GR/IR correction account will sum up to zero at the entered key date. Only the two separate accounts (goods receipt not paid and invoice receipt no goods delivered) will have balances at the key date.

For this example, December 31, 2023, has been entered as a **Key date**. You also need to fill in the **Postings** tab fields shown in Figure 3.101. Enter the **Document date** and the **Posting date**. In the **Selections** tab, you can limit the performance of this report to certain vendors, reconciliation accounts, and so on. The fields in the **Acq. Tax** tab are only relevant in very special cases where you can deduct input tax in a value-added tax (VAT) regime, such as France.

During the execution process, for the specified key in GR/IR clearing accounts, all open items are selected at this date. The clearing program is also used for adjustment posting, which displays the business transactions in the balance sheet (e.g., not invoiced delivered goods or not delivered invoiced goods). Therefore, if the open items per purchase order and items in local currency don't summarize to a net balance zero, then the adjustment postings are generated. In other words, a credit balance in the GR/IR accounts refers to the delivered but not invoiced items. Likewise, a debit balance in GR/IR accounts refers to the items that are invoiced but not delivered.

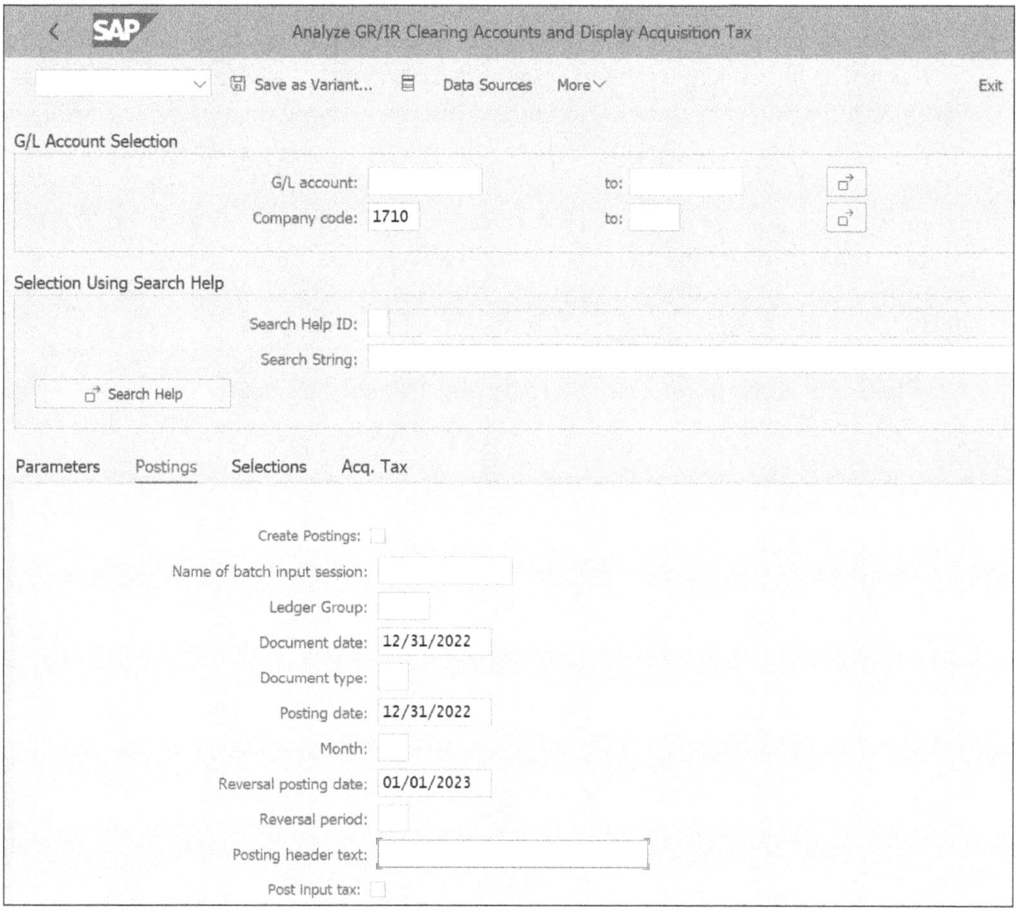

Figure 3.101 Adjustment Posting When Analyzing GR/IR Accounts Clearing

Notice that the adjustments to GR/IR are crucial for reporting to get an accurate period cutoff of assets and liabilities. However, these period-end adjustments have to be reversed at the beginning of the new period. This is required because subsequent purchasing activity may take place and net GR/IR line items to zero. Therefore, you can enter a specific reverse posting date (**Reversal posting date** field) on the **Postings** tab (see Figure 3.101). If you don't enter a date, the program reverses the postings on the next day following the key date.

SAP Fiori App

The corresponding SAP Fiori app is called Repost GR/IR Clearing (F.19). It's visually and functionally the same as the SAP GUI transaction.

3.6.5   Balance Carryforward

Balance carryforward postings in the general ledger is the last step in the closing process before you usually start financial reporting steps. This balance carryforward transaction transfers the balance of the general ledger account, including subledgers, local ledgers, and special ledgers, to the new fiscal year. After this procedure is executed, it automatically transfers postings from the previous fiscal year to the new fiscal year. This ensures that net profit/loss is accurately reported in the balance sheet. The program can be run multiple times, but usually it's executed only once at year-end close.

The system performs balance carryforward as follows:

- Balance sheet accounts along with additional account assignments are transferred to the same accounts in the new fiscal year. This ensures that the closing balance of the balance sheet in the old fiscal year is the same as the opening balance in the new fiscal year.

- P&L accounts are accumulated and carried forward to the retained earnings account, which must be maintained for all the summarized P&L accounts. This ensures that closing balances and opening balances of the P&L accounts are zero. Before transferring P&L, you have to be sure that the P&L account type is specified in the master record. In this way, you can set a retained earnings account for each chart of account.

The carryforward process performs the transactions in local currency, so don't expect that transaction currencies to be transferred in the new fiscal year.

The application menu path to execute the carryforward of the general ledger balance is as follows: **Accounting • Financial Accounting • General Ledger • Periodic Processing • Closing • Carrying Forward • Balance Carryforward**. Alternatively, you can use Transaction FAGLGVTR.

The **Balance Carryforward** screen appears, as shown in Figure 3.102. Here, you enter values in the **Ledger**, **Company Code**, and **Carry Forward to Fiscal Year** fields. You also can enter range values in the **Ledger** and **Company Code** fields. In the **Options** area of the screen, it's recommended to mark the **Test Run** checkbox so the program will be executed in test mode. Select the **Detailed** radio button for **Test Run** to ensure that you can see all accounts subject to balance carryforward in the test result.

After you've entered the necessary values, click the **Execute** button at the bottom right of the screen.

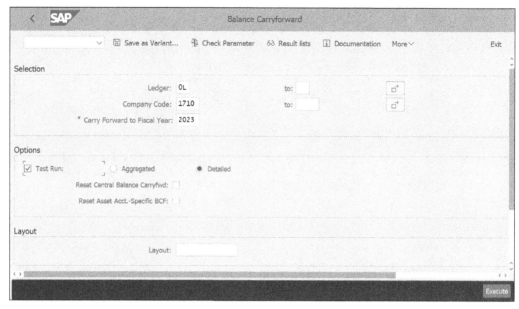

Figure 3.102 Balance Carryforward Screen

Next, the **Balance Carryforward: Result List** screen appears, as shown in Figure 3.103, with all of your generated carryforward balances.

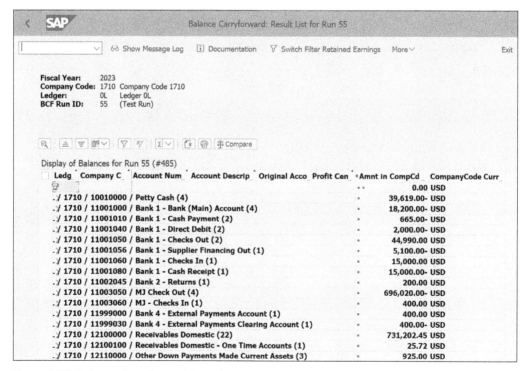

Figure 3.103 Balance Carryforward Overview

If you click on the **Show Message Log** button, it will lead you to a detailed message log screen where you can see detailed information about system warnings, successful steps taken, and the numbers of entries produced (in this case, **370** entries for the balance sheet and **115** for P&L, as shown in Figure 3.104).

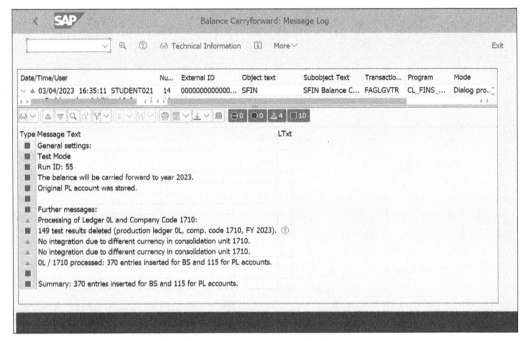

Figure 3.104 Balance Sheet Accounts Display: Details Screen

Now that you can run closing activities, let's take a look at tracking the closing activities in a structured manner using the SAP Financial Closing cockpit for SAP S/4HANA.

3.6.6   Financial Closing Cockpit

The SAP Financial Closing cockpit for SAP S/4HANA provides a structured and efficient approach to manage financial closing activities. It's designed to help organizations perform period-end activities and create financial statements accurately and on time.

With the SAP Financial Closing cockpit for SAP S/4HANA, users can monitor the progress of each closing task, track deadlines, and identify potential bottlenecks, all from a central location. It also provides predefined checklists, workflows, and reports to help users streamline the closing process and ensure that all tasks are completed according to the schedule.

The SAP Financial Closing cockpit for SAP S/4HANA includes several components such as the task list, document splitter, mass reversal, and reporting. Together, these tools help organizations automate the financial closing process, reduce errors, and increase efficiency.

> **Note**
>
> The SAP Financial Closing cockpit for SAP S/4HANA isn't only about general ledger closing activities. It's also a central location where you can manage and monitor all activities subject to financial closing through all subledgers, materials management, and sales.

Let's now dive into the system to see where you can find it and how it's structured.

Because the financial close is a task crossing the entire organization and because it isn't assigned to any module, you find it in the main section of cross-application components in the SAP menu: **Cross-Application Components • SAP S/4HANA Financial Closing Cockpit • Financial Closing Cockpit**.

When you reach there, you see a complete set of transactions for setting up and running the SAP Financial Closing cockpit for SAP S/4HANA:

- **Financial Closing Cockpit – Customizing**
- **Financial Closing Cockpit – Preparation**
- **Financial Closing Cockpit – Execution (List)**
- **Financial Closing Cockpit – Execution (GANTT)**

We'll walk through the usage of the SAP Financial Closing cockpit for SAP S/4HANA by creating a template with three closing steps as an example. From this closing template, we'll prepare a specific month-closing activity list, and then execute it via the steps in the closing activity list.

We start with the **Financial Closing Cockpit – Customizing** transaction (Transaction FLOCOC). The term "Customizing" translated in SAP language may be misleading in this context. It's better described as a setup step—a mandatory prerequisite to use the SAP Financial Closing cockpit for SAP S/4HANA—usually done by an accounting professional. An SAP consultant working in the pure core configuration of SAP (Customizing – SAP Implementation Guide) isn't required. With the use of the Transaction FLOCOC, you simply create templates for any closing activities you want to perform, document, and monitor within the SAP application (and not in a spreadsheet, e.g., month-end closes, quarterly closes, or year-end close).

The first screen in the SAP Financial Closing cockpit for SAP S/4HANA is shown in Figure 3.105.

You first have to create a task group, which later serves as a template for specific closing periods, through the **Create Task Group** button in the menu bar. The task group is the highest node in your closing structure displayed after being created in the left frame of your screen. Before you click the green checkmark at the bottom of the window, you have to name the **Task Group** and assign it to a responsible user, user group, role, or any organizational unit, as shown in Figure 3.106. Optionally, you can protect it by using an authorization group.

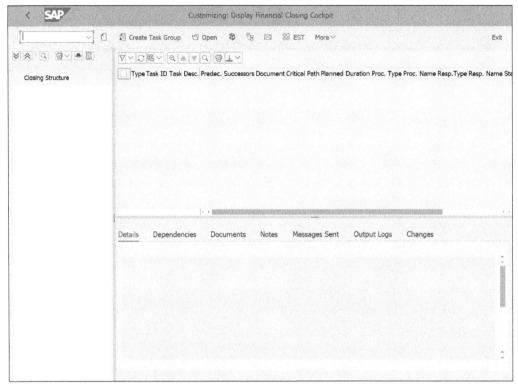

Figure 3.105 SAP Financial Closing Cockpit for SAP S/4HANA: Customizing

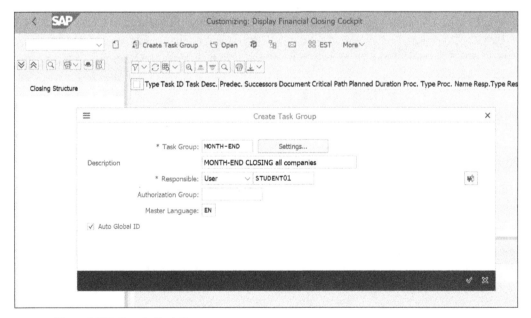

Figure 3.106 Create Task Group

> **Note**
>
> In this section and in all other sections of this book, we skip all authorization and user rights topics because it's a topic that would fill a book itself.

If you want the system to generate an ID for the task group automatically, select the **Auto Global ID** checkbox.

Having done this, it's recommended to group your closing activities by organizational elements such as company codes. To do so, go to your newly created **MONTH-END Task Group** on the right side of the screen and right-click to open the context menu. Select **Create Subfolder**, as shown in Figure 3.107.

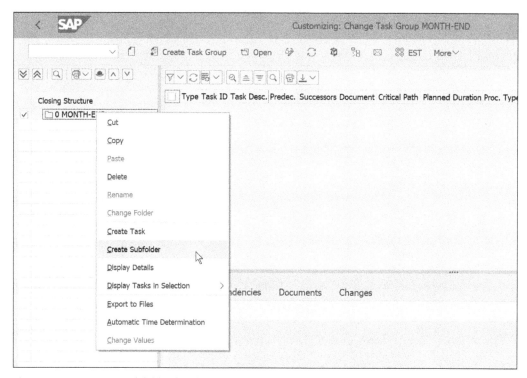

Figure 3.107 Create a Subfolder for Grouping the Activities in an Organization

The subfolder needs only a description for a responsible user (or user group) to be created. After that, you can set up a task. Hover on the subfolder, right-click, and select **Create Task**. The following screen opens, where you can see that there are plenty of task types to be used, as shown in Figure 3.108.

In the SAP Financial Closing cockpit for SAP S/4HANA, the **Task Type** refers to a specific type of activity or task that needs to be performed during the financial closing process.

Task types are used to group related tasks together and to define the sequence in which they should be executed.

Figure 3.108 SAP Financial Closing Cockpit for SAP S/4HANA: Display/Create/Change Task

We'll explain the top four that are most frequently used:

- **Note**
  The task type **Note** is used to create notes or comments related to the financial closing process. Notes can be used to provide additional information or context about a task or to communicate important details to other team members involved in the closing process. This task type is often used to document issues, concerns, or decisions that arise during the closing process. For example, if an account reconciliation is incomplete or there is a discrepancy in the financial statements, a note can be created to document the issue and communicate it to other team members.

- **Transaction**
  The task type **Transaction** allows users to access and execute transactions directly from the SAP Financial Closing cockpit for SAP S/4HANA, without having to navigate

to other areas of the SAP system. This can help streamline the closing process and improve efficiency by reducing the time and effort required to perform these tasks manually.

- **Program**

  The task type **Program** is used to execute programs or reports as part of the financial closing process. This task type allows users to access and execute programs directly from the SAP Financial Closing cockpit for SAP S/4HANA, without having to navigate to other areas of the SAP system. To do so, you need to have variants saved for each of the programs. Variants are predefined sets of parameters or options that can be used to execute a program or report.

- **Job**

  The task type **Job** in is used to schedule and execute batch jobs as part of the financial closing process. Batch jobs are typically used to perform tasks such as posting journal entries, updating account balances, printing lists, and running reports required for the closing process. This task type allows users to schedule and monitor batch jobs directly from the SAP Financial Closing cockpit for SAP S/4HANA, without having to navigate to other areas of the SAP system.

In our case, we've set up now three closing activities: the **email to inform about starting the month close** note, the **Foreign Currency Valuation** transaction, and the **Produce Balance Sheet** program. You can see that all these tasks have different symbols because they all are different in task type, as shown in Figure 3.109. You can also see that in the closing structure, every step receives a subsequent number—called **Task ID**. Note the frame in the lower area of the screen. It shows details for a selected task (in our case, for **Task ID 2, email to inform about starting the month close**).

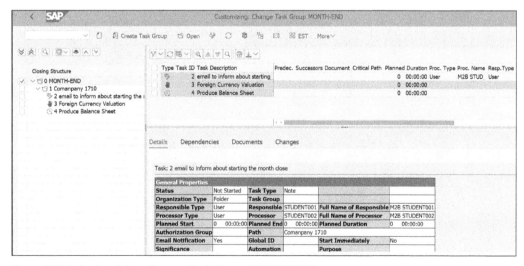

Figure 3.109 Customizing: Change Task Group MONTH-END

Each task can be enriched with more information if required. In terms of optimization for speed and continuous improvement of the financial close process, you can maintain dependencies (predecessors, successors), the planned time to run the task, and whether it's part of the critical path. We won't do that in this example in order to keep the close activities as simple as possible, so you can follow along and better understand the concept itself.

Assuming that the template for a typical month-end close is now complete, you can now generate a specific periodic task list from it using the **Financial Closing Cockpit – Preparation** transaction (Transaction FCLOCOT). To have a more realistic month-end closing activity list, you can open a standard month-end closing template called **1-FC-MONTH**, which is predefined by SAP as a common template for all SAP S/4HANA users. This template covers 19 folders and 119 task IDs, as shown in Figure 3.110.

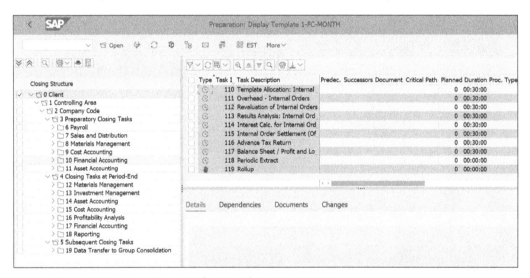

Figure 3.110 Preparation: Display Template 1-FC-MONTH

To generate a specific month activity list for a close in February 2022, go to menu path **More • Template/Task List • Create Periodic Task List** or just press F2.

A new window appears in which you must specify the **Key Date**, **Closing Type**, **Posting Period**, **Fiscal Year**, **Status**, **Responsible User** (or user group), and **Description** (see Figure 3.111).

After saving, either run the **Financial Closing Cockpit – Execution – List** transaction (Transaction FCLOCO) or the **Financial Closing Cockpit – Execution GANTT** transaction (Transaction FCLOCOS). Both are pretty much the same. We couldn't detect any differences between the transactions, and even though you might expect one to produce a list and the other to produce a Gantt chart, both actually show the activities as a list.

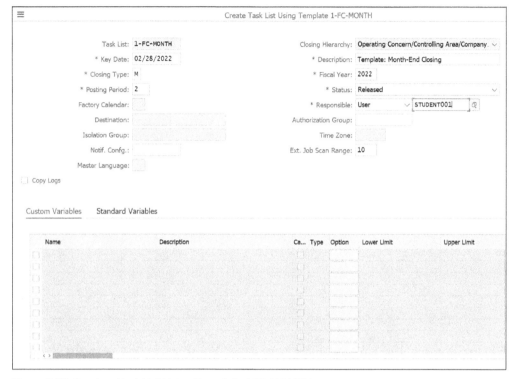

Figure 3.111 Create a Task List Using Template 1-FC-MONTH

In the menu bar, click the **Open** button (next to the transaction code field, see Figure 3.112), and select the generated specific month-end closing activity list—in this case, the one just generated for February 2022.

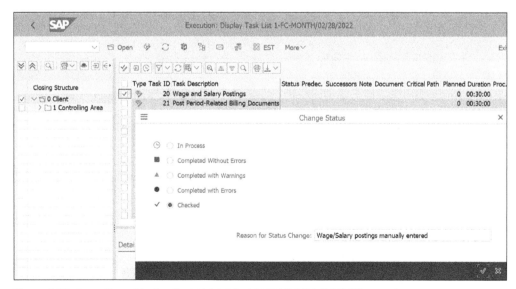

Figure 3.112 Execution: Display Task List 1-FC-MONTH/02/28/2022/Change Status

The responsible user for executing the task can now run all the closing steps one by one. Automated ones can be scheduled and executed; manual ones need just documentation in terms of a change of status. We'll show how this works with an example using a note, which is a manual user task. For this example, select **Task ID 20: Wage and Salary Postings**. Because it's a manual closing step, click on the 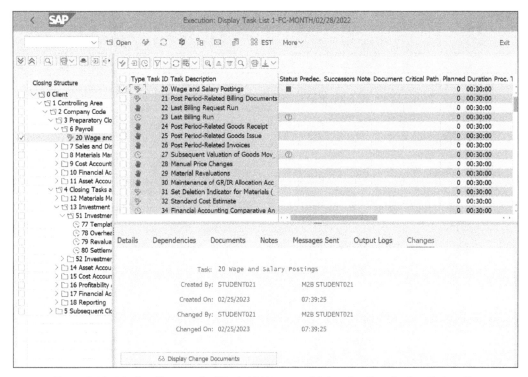 icon to access a popup where you can set the status to **Checked** and document its performance as "Wage/Salary postings manually entered" in the **Reason for Status Change** field.

After having performed these tasks, you can see detailed information in the lower part of the screen. The system records all relevant details and changes to closing step activities, which can be retraced by clicking on **Display Change Documents** at the bottom of the screen shown in Figure 3.113.

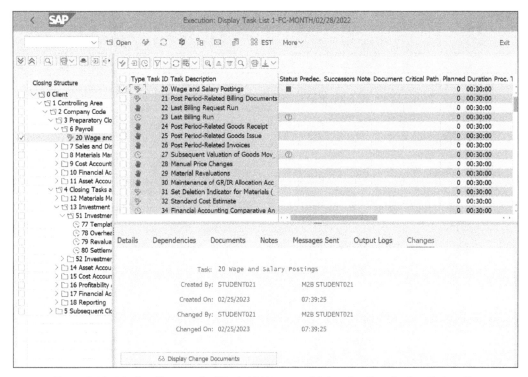

Figure 3.113 Display Changes for "Task 20 Wage and Salary Postings" after Status Change

If the closing steps are automated (task type **Program** or **Job**), you can see the output logs after having performed them in the **Output Logs** tab in the lower frame of screen.

You now have acquired the skills to work with the SAP Financial Closing cockpit for SAP S/4HANA on your own. You should now be able to generate your own month-end closing schedule within the SAP application.

Note

Additionally, SAP provides a cloud solution with SAP S/4HANA Cloud for advanced financial closing. It's available as an add-on scope item that can be subscribed to (not in SAP S/4HANA Cloud standard) consisting of five SAP Fiori apps, as shown in Figure 3.114. As a cloud solution, it can be connected to SAP ERP and SAP S/4HANA, public cloud and on-premise. Although we won't explain it here, note that the procedure is very similar to the one in on-premise SAP S/4HANA with an SAP GUI interface.

SAP S/4HANA Cloud for advanced financial closing is particularly interesting for large enterprise customers with complex system landscapes and often multiple ERP instances because SAP S/4HANA Cloud for advanced financial closing can fully demonstrate its strength as a cloud hub in these scenarios. But there are also small SAP S/4HANA Cloud customers who are successfully using SAP S/4HANA Cloud for advanced financial closing. Of course, the SAP Financial Closing cockpit for SAP S/4HANA continues to be offered, especially in cases where local data storage is required by law (China, Saudi Arabia, etc.).

SAP S/4HANA Cloud for advanced financial closing can especially show its strength in the context of parallel accounting (refer to Section 3.3.6 and Section 3.3.7) because all closing jobs that are executed multiple times can be automated very well.

Figure 3.114 SAP Fiori Apps for SAP S/4HANA Cloud for Advanced Financial Closing

You can learn more about SAP S/4HANA Cloud for advanced financial closing at *https://help.sap.com/docs/advanced-financial-closing* and read the SAP PRESS E-bite *Introducing SAP S/4HANA Cloud for Advanced Financial Closing (AFC)* (SAP PRESS, 2022), which is available at *www.sap-press.com/5528*.

Now that you've performed the closing activities using the SAP Financial Closing cockpit for SAP S/4HANA or a spreadsheet to monitor the progress, your financial information is complete, accurate, and ready to be reported.

3.7   General Ledger Reporting

Another feature of SAP S/4HANA is the reporting of general ledger accounts in real time in different format types, such as XML, PDF, TXT, and XBLR. General ledger reporting helps companies, and especially management, check and review all account movements within a defined period. The trial balance report, for example, at month-end closing, can show the opening balance, accumulated debit and credit amounts, and year-to-date accumulated debit and credit amounts.

To access the general ledger reporting function in SAP S/4HANA, follow application menu path **Accounting • Financial Accounting • General Ledger • Information System • General Ledger Reports**, as discussed in Section 3.1.5. Here you can see various general ledger reports that can be generated from this menu path. In the following sections, we'll discuss accounts inquiry, trial balance, financial statement line items, and document journal reports.

3.7.1   Accounts Inquiry

To review transactions posted on a general ledger account, you can follow application path **Accounting • Financial Accounting • General Ledger • Account • Display Balances**, or use Transaction FAGLB03.

You'll access the screen shown in Figure 3.115. Here, we selected the account **11001000** (Bank1 Main Account) in **Company 1710** for **Fiscal Year 2022**.

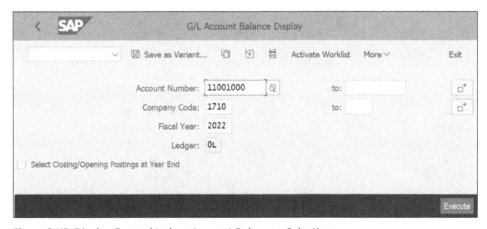

Figure 3.115 Display General Ledger Account Balances: Selection

Then, click the **Execute** button at the bottom right of the screen to see the account balances evolution through the fiscal year, as shown in Figure 3.116.

For every reporting **Period** from **1** to **16**, you can see the **Debit** and **Credit** balances, the **Balance** for the individual period, and a year-to-date **Cumulative Balance**. For further investigation, you can easily click any number, and the system shows you the items from which the balance is made.

If you click on the month balance of the reporting period **8**, **12,000.00** USD, for example, the screen shown in Figure 3.117 appears. You see the item entries on the account in period **8**. If you want to see all line items posted within fiscal year 2022, just click on **Cumulative Balance** at reporting period **16**.

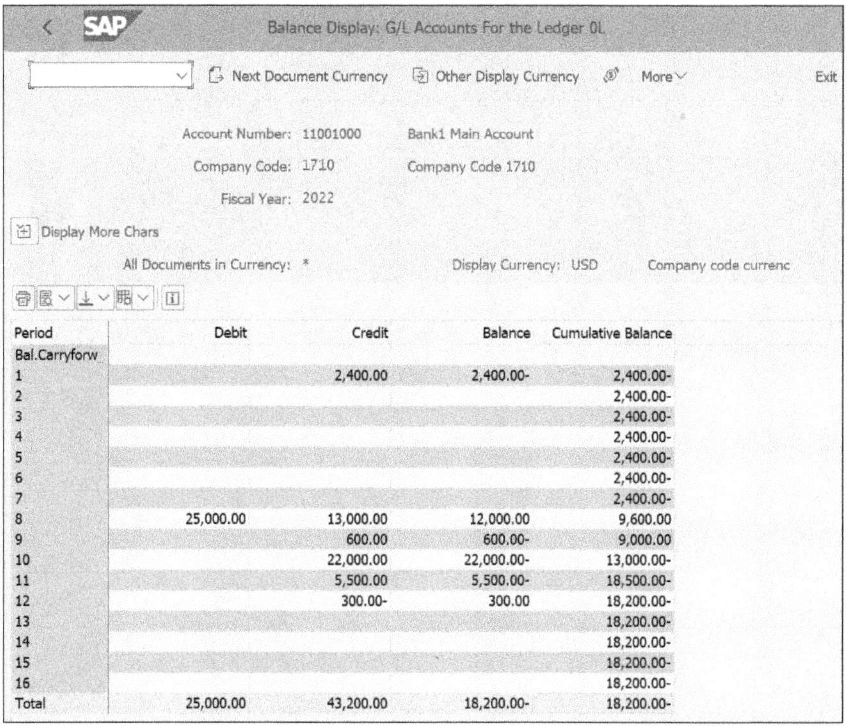

Period	Debit	Credit	Balance	Cumulative Balance
Bal.Carryforw				
1		2,400.00	2,400.00-	2,400.00-
2				2,400.00-
3				2,400.00-
4				2,400.00-
5				2,400.00-
6				2,400.00-
7				2,400.00-
8	25,000.00	13,000.00	12,000.00	9,600.00
9		600.00	600.00-	9,000.00
10		22,000.00	22,000.00-	13,000.00-
11		5,500.00	5,500.00-	18,500.00-
12		300.00-	300.00	18,200.00-
13				18,200.00-
14				18,200.00-
15				18,200.00-
16				18,200.00-
Total	25,000.00	43,200.00	18,200.00-	18,200.00-

Figure 3.116 Display General Ledger Account Balances

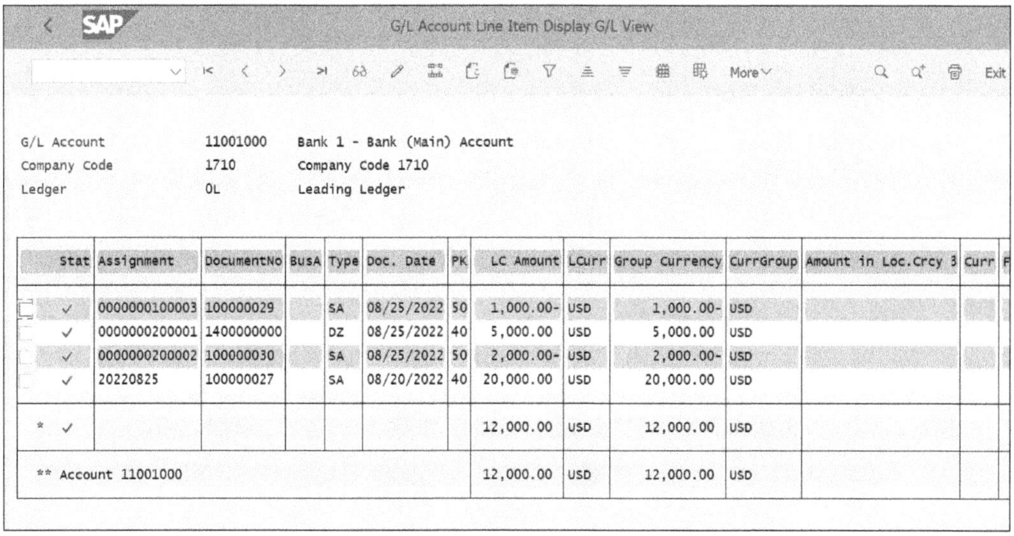

Stat	Assignment	DocumentNo	BusA	Type	Doc. Date	PK	LC Amount	LCurr	Group Currency	CurrGroup	Amount in Loc.Crcy 3	Curr
✓	0000000100003	100000029		SA	08/25/2022	50	1,000.00-	USD	1,000.00-	USD		
✓	0000000200001	1400000000		DZ	08/25/2022	40	5,000.00	USD	5,000.00	USD		
✓	0000000200002	100000030		SA	08/25/2022	50	2,000.00-	USD	2,000.00-	USD		
✓	20220825	100000027		SA	08/20/2022	40	20,000.00	USD	20,000.00	USD		
* ✓							12,000.00	USD	12,000.00	USD		
** Account 11001000							12,000.00	USD	12,000.00	USD		

Figure 3.117 General Ledger Line Items for Period 8

SAP Fiori App

The corresponding SAP Fiori app is called Display G/L Account Balances (F0707). It's visually very similar to what you've seen in this section (compare Figure 3.117 with Figure 3.118). You can use this app to check and compare the balances and the credit and debit amounts of a ledger in a company code for each period of a fiscal year.

Figure 3.118 General Ledger Account Balances in SAP Fiori

3.7.2   Trial Balance

In the trial balance report, all debit and credit balances over a specified period of time are displayed, including the calculation of opening and closing balances in the Universal Journal table ACDOCA. In other words, a trial balance represents a list of general ledger account balances. You can execute this report for each ledger and all company codes you've recorded in SAP S/4HANA. It provides you with an overview that takes into consideration various parameters, such as profit center, account type, segment, function area, business area, supplier, and so on. In addition, the report enables you to make a comparison on a yearly basis, for example, from the previous year to the current year. The end trial balance shows that you've done all your journals and ledgers correctly.

There are two transactions to discuss in this section: Transaction S_ALR_87012277 (G/L Account Balances) gives you an overview of the general ledger accounts. Alternatively, you can access Transaction S_ALR_87012301 (Totals and Balances) in the IMG, where you can get an overall result of the trial balance showing the subtotal amount for the general ledger account and subledger accounts.

General Ledger Account Balances

To get the trial balance report, follow menu path **Accounting • Financial Accounting • General Ledger • Information System • General Ledger Reports • Account Balances • General • G/L Account Balances**. Selecting **G/L Account Balances** (Transaction S_ALR_87012277) gives you an overview of the general ledger accounts.

Let's start with the trial balance for a range of general ledger accounts. For that, you need to click on **G/L Account Balances** to arrive at the **G/L Account Balances** screen, as shown in Figure 3.119.

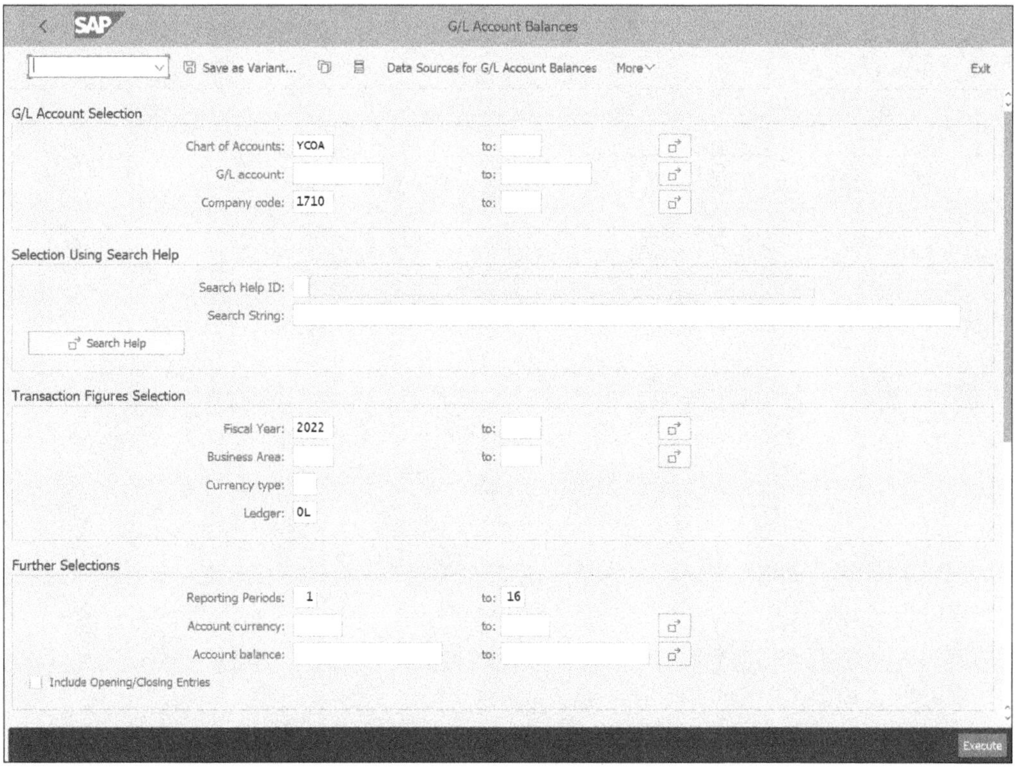

Figure 3.119 Trial Balance on General Ledger Account Selections

In the first area, **G/L Account Selection**, you can define the range of **Chart of Accounts**, **G/L account**, and **Company code**. You can also define other criteria depending on your selection, such as **Fiscal Year**, **Business Area**, **Reporting Periods**, and so on in the other areas of the screen.

After you fill in all the necessary data, you can click the **Execute** button at the bottom right of the screen. In the **G/L Account Balances** screen that appears, as shown in Figure 3.120 and Figure 3.121, you can see an overview of balance records related to the specified criteria in the previous step.

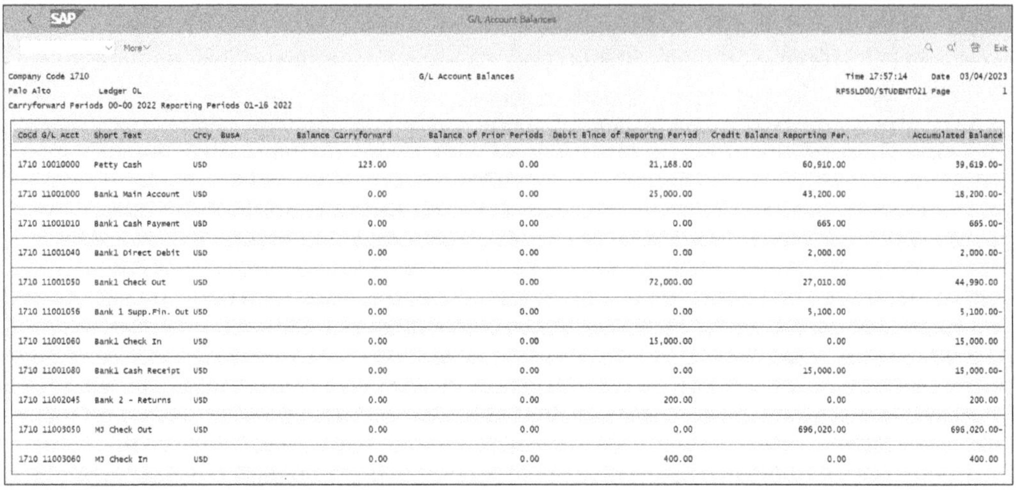

Company Code 1710 G/L Account Balances Time 17:57:14 Date 03/04/2023
Palo Alto Ledger 0L RFSSLD00/STUDENT021 Page 1
Carryforward Periods 00-00 2022 Reporting Periods 01-16 2022

CoCd	G/L Acct	Short Text	Crcy	BusA	Balance Carryforward	Balance of Prior Periods	Debit Blnce of Reportng Period	Credit Balance Reporting Per.	Accumulated Balance
1710	10010000	Petty Cash	USD		123.00	0.00	21,168.00	60,910.00	39,619.00-
1710	11001000	Bank1 Main Account	USD		0.00	0.00	25,000.00	43,200.00	18,200.00-
1710	11001010	Bank1 Cash Payment	USD		0.00	0.00	0.00	665.00	665.00-
1710	11001040	Bank1 Direct Debit	USD		0.00	0.00	0.00	2,000.00	2,000.00-
1710	11001050	Bank1 Check Out	USD		0.00	0.00	72,000.00	27,010.00	44,990.00
1710	11001056	Bank 1 Supp.Fin. Out	USD		0.00	0.00	0.00	5,100.00	5,100.00-
1710	11001060	Bank1 Check In	USD		0.00	0.00	15,000.00	0.00	15,000.00
1710	11001080	Bank1 Cash Receipt	USD		0.00	0.00	0.00	15,000.00	15,000.00-
1710	11002045	Bank 2 - Returns	USD		0.00	0.00	200.00	0.00	200.00
1710	11003050	MJ Check Out	USD		0.00	0.00	0.00	696,020.00	696,020.00-
1710	11003060	MJ Check In	USD		0.00	0.00	400.00	0.00	400.00

Figure 3.120 Trial Balance Result for the Selected General Ledger Accounts (1)

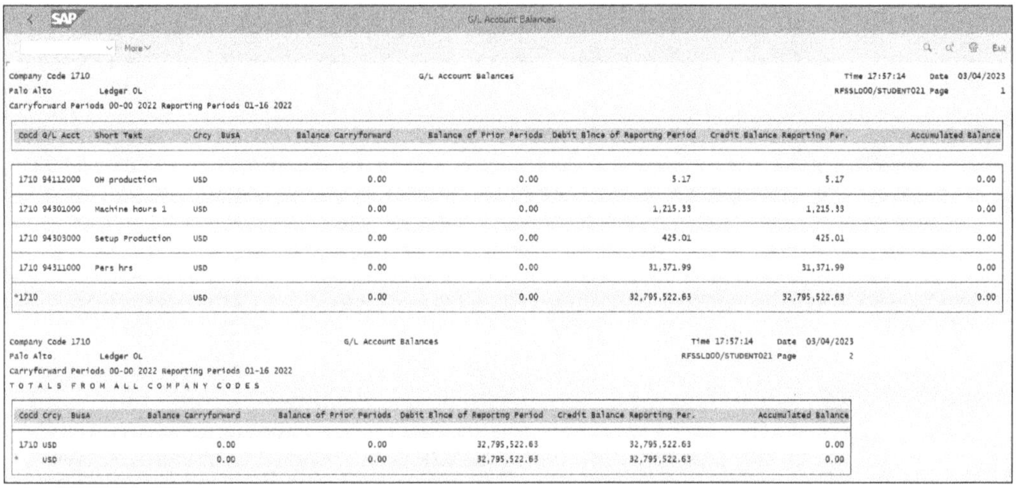

Company Code 1710 G/L Account Balances Time 17:57:14 Date 03/04/2023
Palo Alto Ledger 0L RFSSLD00/STUDENT021 Page 1
Carryforward Periods 00-00 2022 Reporting Periods 01-16 2022

CoCd	G/L Acct	Short Text	Crcy	BusA	Balance Carryforward	Balance of Prior Periods	Debit Blnce of Reportng Period	Credit Balance Reporting Per.	Accumulated Balance
1710	94112000	OH production	USD		0.00	0.00	5.17	5.17	0.00
1710	94301000	Machine hours 1	USD		0.00	0.00	1,215.33	1,215.33	0.00
1710	94303000	Setup Production	USD		0.00	0.00	425.01	425.01	0.00
1710	94311000	Pers hrs	USD		0.00	0.00	31,371.99	31,371.99	0.00
*1710			USD		0.00	0.00	32,795,522.63	32,795,522.63	0.00

Company Code 1710 G/L Account Balances Time 17:57:14 Date 03/04/2023
Palo Alto Ledger 0L RFSSLD00/STUDENT021 Page 2
Carryforward Periods 00-00 2022 Reporting Periods 01-16 2022
T O T A L S F R O M A L L C O M P A N Y C O D E S

CoCd	Crcy	BusA	Balance Carryforward	Balance of Prior Periods	Debit Blnce of Reportng Period	Credit Balance Reporting Per.	Accumulated Balance
1710	USD		0.00	0.00	32,795,522.63	32,795,522.63	0.00
*	USD		0.00	0.00	32,795,522.63	32,795,522.63	0.00

Figure 3.121 Trial Balance Result for the Selected General Ledger Accounts (2)

Totals and Balances

Now let's check what Transaction S_ALR_87012301 under **Totals and Balances** will bring out. Follow menu path **Accounting • Financial Accounting • General Ledger • Information System • General Ledger Reports • Account Balances • General • Totals and Balances.**

In the first area of the **G/L Account Selection** screen, you can define the range of **Chart of Accounts**, **G/L account**, and **Company code**. You can also define other criteria depending on your selection, such as **Fiscal Year**, **Business Area**, **Reporting Periods**, and so on in the other areas of the screen. Let's use the same input data as in the previous example.

Now you can click the **Execute** button at the bottom right of the screen, and the **G/L Account Balances** screen appears, as shown in Figure 3.122 and Figure 3.123. In this screen, you can see an overview of total balance records related to the predefined selection criteria. As you can see, the **G/L Account Balances** area is presented as a summarized amount of general ledger accounts and subledger accounts.

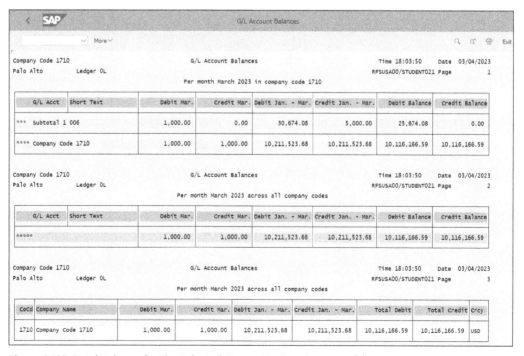

Figure 3.122 Total Balance for the Selected General Ledger Accounts (1)

Figure 3.123 Total Balance for the Selected General Ledger Accounts (2)

3.7.3   Display General Ledger Account Line Items

In SAP S/4HANA, you can display the general ledger account line items using Transaction FAGLL03. For the line item browser, you can use Transaction FAGLL03H or follow these application menu paths:

- **Accounting • Financial Accounting • General Ledger • Account • Display/Change Line Items**

- **Accounting • Financial Accounting • General Ledger • Account • Line Item Browser**

If you double-click **Line Item Browser**, the **G/L Account Line Item Browser (G/L View)** screen appears, as shown in Figure 3.124 and Figure 3.125.

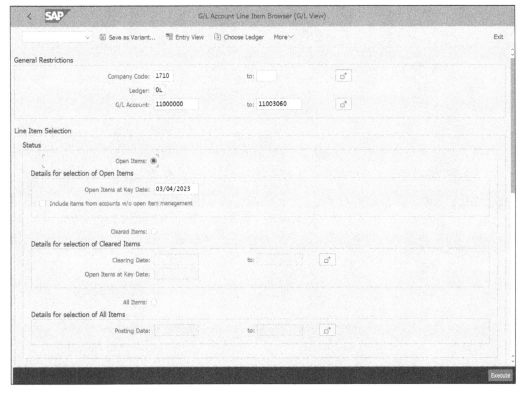

Figure 3.124 G/L Account Line Item Browser (G/L View) Screen (1)

Here, you can fill in the required data, such as **G/L Account, Company Code, Posting Date, Ledger,** and so on. If you want to see only open items on the general ledger account, just select **Open Items.** When selecting open items, you need to enter a key date. Otherwise, you can also select **All Items** or **Cleared Items** if this is related to your inquiry.

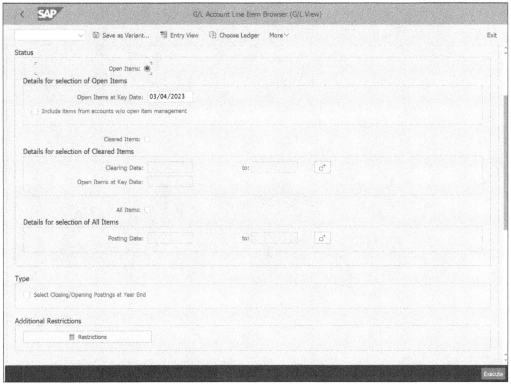

Figure 3.125 G/L Account Line Item Browser (G/L View) Screen (2)

SAP Fiori App

In SAP Fiori, you can check general ledger account line items using the Display Line Items in General Ledger app (F2217), as shown in Figure 3.126. In this SAP Fiori app, you can check general ledger account line items very conveniently. You can easily switch between the general ledger view and the journal entry view. In both views, you can display open and cleared items for accounts managed by open items, or you can display all the items for an account. In addition, you can select items based on the posting date, and you can choose whether the app displays normal items, noted items (items to remind you of outstanding payments), parked items (incomplete and not yet posted journal entries) only, or all items.

In the results list, which you receive after clicking the **Go** button, you can group, sort, and filter the general ledger account line items using characteristics such as general ledger account, profit center, or any other criterion, as shown in Figure 3.127.

Additionally, you can easily export the result list to a Microsoft Excel spreadsheet by clicking the spreadsheet icon next to the settings wheel.

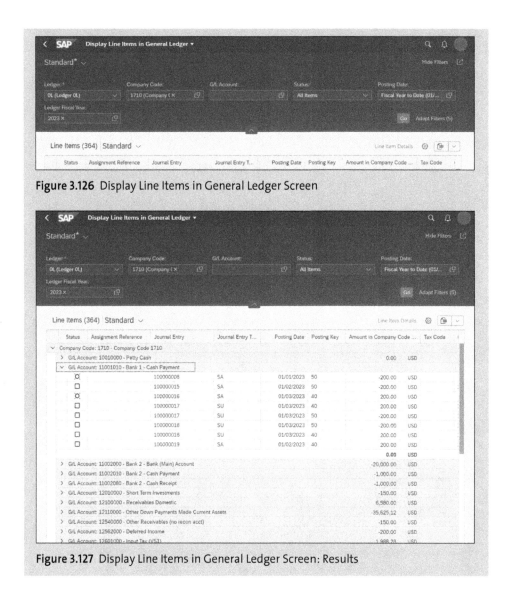

Figure 3.126 Display Line Items in General Ledger Screen

Figure 3.127 Display Line Items in General Ledger Screen: Results

3.7.4   Financial Statement

Now, we'll explain how to display financial statements, so you'll be able to generate reports displaying balance sheets and statements referring to P&L for a specific company. You can find financial statements by following application menu path **Accounting • Financial Accounting • General Ledger • Periodic Processing • Closing • Report • Financial Statement/Cash Flow • General • Actual/Actual Comparison • Financial Statement**, or by using Transaction F.01.

The **Financial Statements** screen appears, as shown in Figure 3.128 and Figure 3.129.

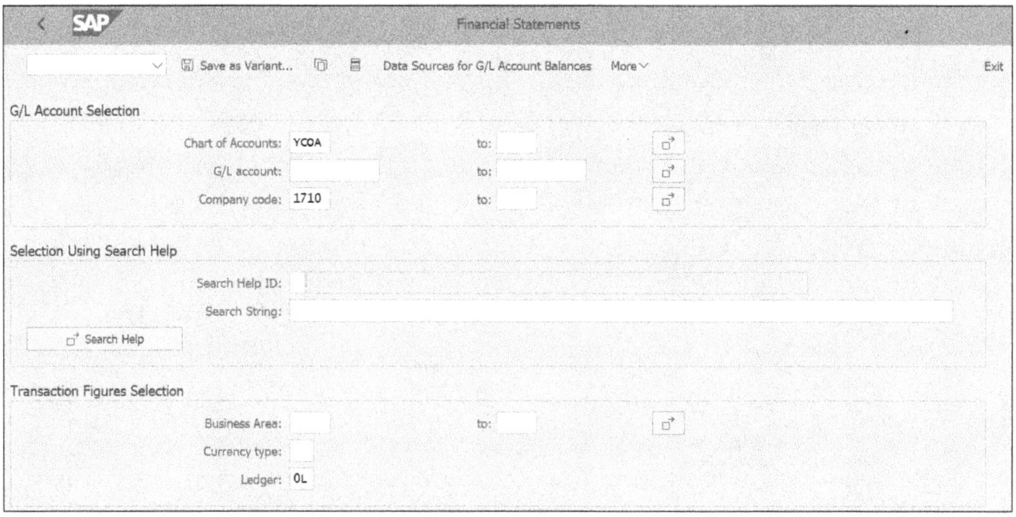

Figure 3.128 Financial Statements Screen (1)

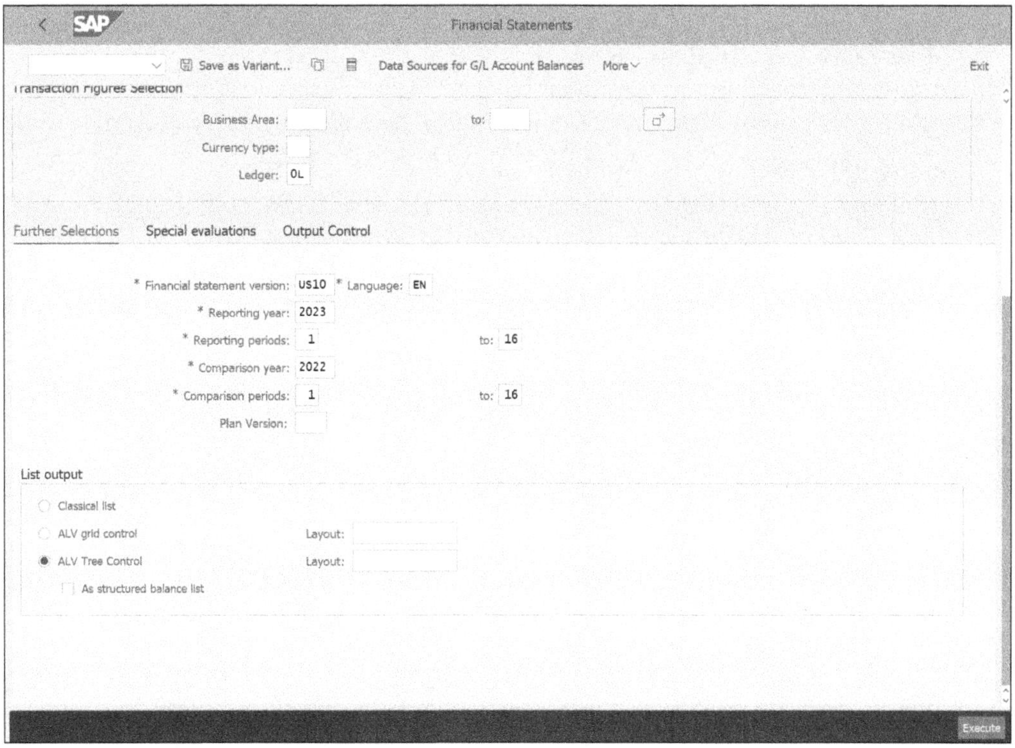

Figure 3.129 Financial Statements Screen (2)

Fill in the **Company code, Financial statement version, Reporting year, Comparison year,** and **Comparison periods,** and select a **List output** option (we recommend **ALV Tree Control**) before you click the **Execute** button. The result is shown in Figure 3.130.

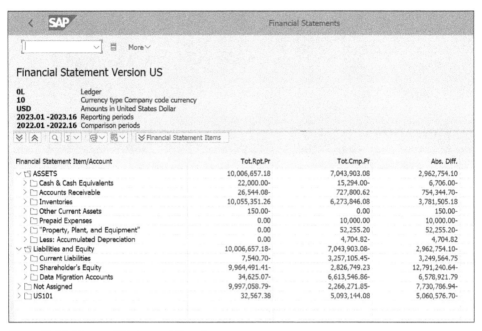

Figure 3.130 Financial Statement Result

SAP Fiori App

The corresponding SAP Fiori app is called Display Financial Statement (F0708). It's easier to read and to drill down than in the SAP GUI version.

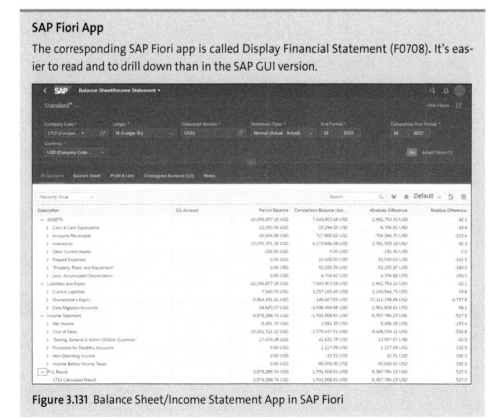

Figure 3.131 Balance Sheet/Income Statement App in SAP Fiori

3

You just need to enter a company code, the respective financial statement version, and the periods, and then click **Go** to get to the screen shown in Figure 3.131.

3.7.5 Compact Document Journal

In this section, we'll discuss the compact document journal in SAP S/4HANA. This function is used right after you've finished the closing posting, and you need to select a couple of reports to document the entries created during a specific period. This function provides you with a list of all financial accounting documents that were in play during the selected period. You can access this function by following application menu path **Accounting • Financial Accounting • General Ledger • Information System • General Ledger Reports • Document • General • Compact Document Journal** or using Transaction S_ALR_87012289.

You can double-click on **Compact Document Journal** to open the **Compact Document Journal** screen, as shown in Figure 3.132 and Figure 3.133. Enter the **Company Code, Document Number, Fiscal Year, Ledger, Ledger Group**, and so on. After you've filled in the required data, click the **Execute** button.

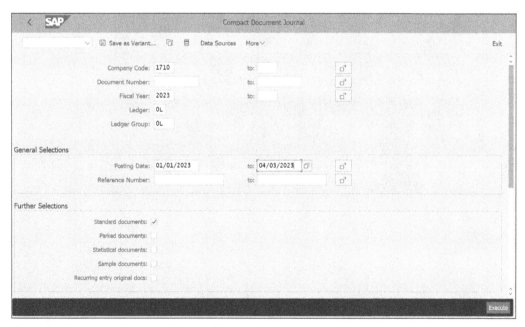

Figure 3.132 Compact Document Journal Screen (1)

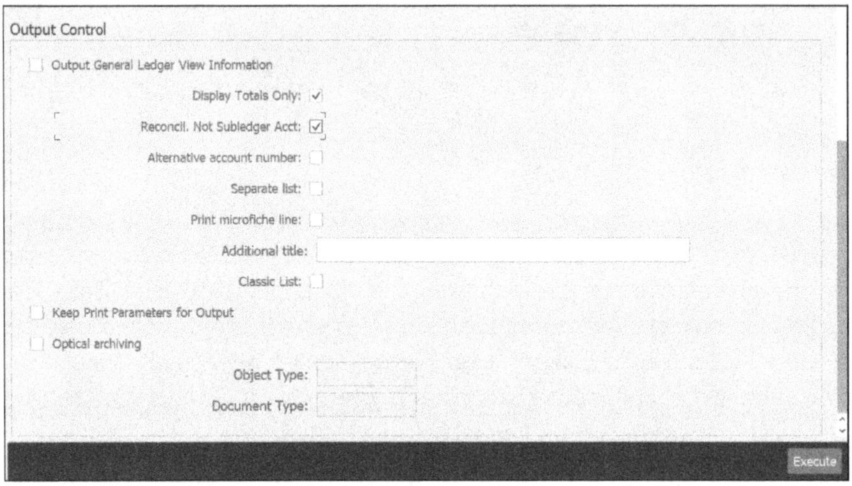

Figure 3.133 Compact Document Journal Screen (2)

SAP Fiori App

The corresponding SAP Fiori app is called Audit Journal (F0997). It's more flexible than the compact document journal in SAP GUI.

With this report, as shown in Figure 3.134, you can generate any general ledger journal entry list you want. You have 15 fields to use for filtering any documents you need.

Figure 3.134 Audit Journal App in SAP Fiori

3.8 Summary

In this chapter, you learned about the general ledger accounting process from record to report. You're now able to set up and change general ledger master data and process any kind of transaction in the general ledger, especially journal entries. You also learned how to perform a reverse posting in different ways. In addition, you can distinguish regular postings from open items postings, and you've seen how to clear open items and reset wrong clearings.

You also got some deeper insights into bank accounting, its integration into the general ledger, and the processing of bank statements. You finished this chapter by practicing financial closing activities such as period control, subledger reconciliation, and balance carryforward processing. Finally, we covered the important general ledger reports both in SAP GUI and in SAP Fiori.

Overall, you've acquired the skills to dive deeper into the accounts payable, accounts receivable, and fixed assets subledgers. We'll begin with accounts payable in the next chapter.

Chapter 4

Accounts Payable

Accounts payable is the accounting part of the purchase-to-pay process. Ideally, every acquisition results in a vendor invoice and a payment. The accounts payable ledger in SAP S/4HANA is where all vendor accounts are managed. In this chapter, we'll cover the most important areas of accounts payable, from the purchase-to-pay process through reporting.

Accounts payable in SAP S/4HANA is where you manage and record accounting data for all the vendors with whom your company procures goods and services. From the basis of a purchase order and a goods receipt, you record supplier invoices, perform and approve payment for any purchases, clear the open items in the payable accounts, and process any kind of correction, valuation, and adjustment postings. As you've already learned in Chapter 3, transactions performed in accounts payable are directly reflected in the general ledger. Every posting performed in accounts payable generates an entry in this way on the respective general ledger accounts, which ensures that accounts payable reconciles with general ledger at all times. This real-time updating is possible through the settings in accounts payable and general ledger account master data when the accounts are created. Furthermore, the system provides you with balances and open items reports in accounts payable to track the outstanding payments and balances of all vendors.

Starting from the master data setup of vendor accounts, this chapter shows you how to record vendor invoices and trigger payments, as well as deal with special cases such as credit memos and down payment processing. The chapter ends by discussing the closing process followed by reporting functionalities.

Let's start by discussing the procure-to-pay process in the business context before diving deeper into accounts payable.

4.1 Purchase-to-Pay

The procurement process in SAP S/4HANA is triggered when the company needs to purchase goods or services from a vendor of your company. Accounts payable in the purchase-to-pay process is touched by the end of the process when it comes to recording invoices and paying bills.

In SAP S/4HANA, the purchase-to-pay process comprises all the business tasks, starting from a purchase requisition and ending with the payment to the vendor. Following are the basic process activities:

1. Prepare a purchase requisition.
2. Prepare a purchase order.
3. Receive goods delivery and perform inventory management.
4. Post a goods receipt.
5. Perform invoice verification for the acceptance of goods inspection.
6. Enable and issue the payment.

You'll learn how to process each of these steps in SAP S/4HANA in the following sections.

4.1.1   Purchase Requisition

The purchase-to-pay business process begins with the creation of a purchase requisition. Generally, every procurement in any organization has requirements gathering as a starting point. As soon as the requirements are collected, the next step is to inform the purchasing organization.

> **Note**
>
> The purchasing organization is an SAP technical term. From a business perspective, it's the purchasing department at the headquarters, subsidiary, branch office, or plant.

The vehicle to document the collected requirements and needs for any department of your company is a *purchase requisition*. Therefore, a purchase requisition is an internal request for purchasing activities in the form of a document listing the specific requirements for materials or services. Don't consider purchase requisitions as orders to directly buy goods, materials, or services from a vendor; instead, this is an internal request that remains within your company.

When a purchasing requisition is created, it needs approval from the purchasing organization. After approval, purchase requisitions can only be modified to a limited extent.

Depending on the company's procurement process, there are certain types of procurement for which a purchase requisition can be created:

- **S: Standard**
  The company gets the finished materials from the vendor.
- **L: Subcontracting**
  The company provides the raw material to the vendor and gets the finished material.

- **K: Consignment**
  The company procures the materials, which are then stored in its warehouse, and pays the vendor for that.
- **U: Stock transfer**
  The material is taken from the organization internally.
- **S: Third party**
  The company pays an external third party for the service it provides.

Now that you have an overview of the purchase requisition document, you can follow application menu path **Logistics • Materials Management • Purchasing • Purchasing Requisition • Create**, or use Transaction ME51N.

On the SAP menu screen, you can execute one of the listed functions: **Create**, **Edit**, or **Display** purchase requisition. You're creating a purchase requisition in this example, so click the **Create** button to open the **Create Purchase Requisition** screen, as shown in Figure 4.1.

Fill in all the required fields, such as **Item** number, **Material** number (from the material master), material **Quantity**, **Delivery Date**, and **Plant**. The **Material Data** tab gets filled in automatically as soon as you enter a valid and existing material number in the **Material** field.

To complete the purchase requisition, enter a valuation price in the **Valuation** tab. This valuation price reflects the estimated purchase price. For an accountant, it's important to know that SAP S/4HANA will post the goods receipt to an inventory account based on the entered purchase price.

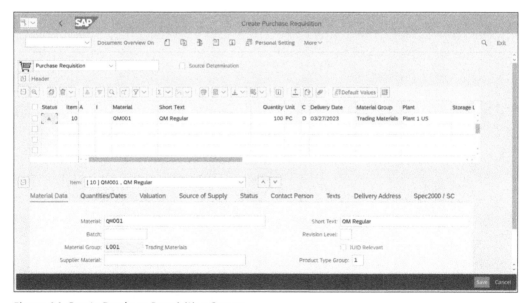

Figure 4.1 Create Purchase Requisition Screen

After you've entered the required details, click the **Save** button. You'll receive the **A new Purchase Requisition has been created** message notification.

To view a purchase requisition, click on **Display** from the application menu path, or use Transaction ME53N. The **Display Purchase Req** screen shows you the latest opened purchase requisition.

To see any other purchase requisition, click **More • Purchase Requisition • Other Requisition** from the menu bar, or use the ⌈Shift⌉+⌈F5⌉ shortcut keys. In the **Select Document** popup window that appears, enter the purchase requisition number, and click the **Other Document** button.

In Figure 4.2, you can see all the details of the purchase requisition you're looking for. You can go through different tabs as well, such as **Material Data**, **Quantities/Dates**, **Valuation**, **Account Assignment**, and so on.

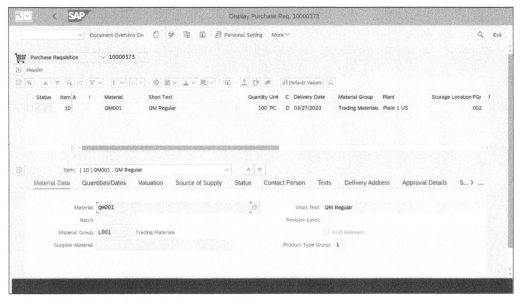

Figure 4.2 Displaying Purchase Requisitions

SAP Fiori App

The corresponding SAP Fiori app is called Create Purchase Requisition (F1643). In Figure 4.3, you can see the screen of the purchase requisition in SAP Fiori. You need to click on the **Create Item** button, and another screen with the same name appears, as shown in Figure 4.4.

After you fill in the required fields (**Material**, **Valuation Price**, **Price Unit**, **Quantity Requested**, and **Delivery Date**), you can click on **Add to Cart** to save the newly created item.

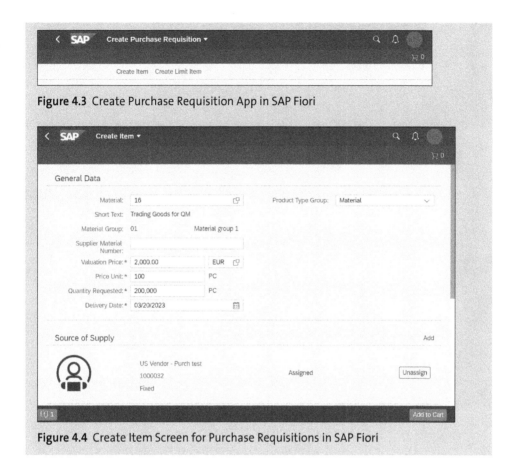

Figure 4.3 Create Purchase Requisition App in SAP Fiori

Figure 4.4 Create Item Screen for Purchase Requisitions in SAP Fiori

4.1.2 Purchase Order

Unlike purchase requisitions, which are internal requests in your company, the *purchase order* is a document addressed to a vendor. This request form is delivered from the purchasing company to a defined vendor to provide certain products, goods, or services in a specified quantity and on a specific delivery date. When you initiate the creation of a purchase order, you can refer to the previously created purchase requisition.

In this section, we'll walk through both creating and displaying a purchase order.

Create a Purchase Order

To create a purchase order, you can follow application menu path **Logistics • Materials Management • Purchasing • Purchase Order • Create**. In this menu path, you can select one of the following possible options to create a purchase order:

- **Vendor/Supplying Plant Known (Transaction ME21N)**
  If you know both the vendor from whom you're buying the material and the plant for which you're performing the goods provisioning, you use this transaction.

- **Via Requisition Assignment List (Transaction ME58)**
  If a purchase requisition exits, you can derive your purchase order from an existing purchase requisition.

- **Automatically via Purchase Requisitions (Transaction ME59N)**
  In the best case, the purchase requisition already contains all the necessary information, so you can convert the purchase requisition into a purchase order automatically via this transaction.

There's also another option to create or display an extended purchase order. Let's consider an example of how to create a purchase order when using the **Vendor/Supplying Plant Known** option. Double-click Transaction ME21N to open the **Create Purchase Order** screen, as shown in Figure 4.5.

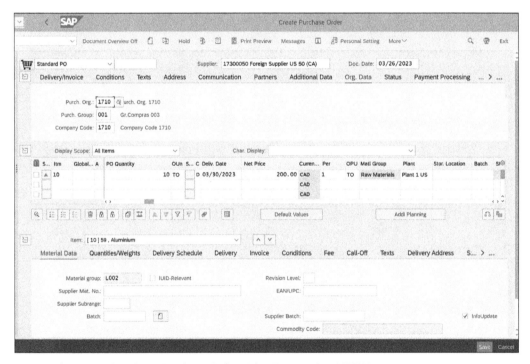

Figure 4.5 Creating a Purchase Order Using Transaction ME21N

Enter the vendor (supplier) number of the **Supplier** from which you want to order the items shown in the lines at the bottom of the screen. The **Doc. Date** is prepopulated by the current date.

On the **Org. Data** tab, choose the plant to be provisioned (**Purch. Org**), **Purch. Group**, and **Company Code**. The other fields aren't required but should be filled in as well, if applicable.

At the bottom of the screen, enter the **Itm** (item) number, **Material**, **PO Quantity**, and **Net Price**. After you've filled in all the required entry fields, click **Save**. The **Material** group, purchase order unit of measure (**OUn**), and order price unit (**OPU**) fields will be populated automatically after you save the purchase order.

Display a Purchase Order

To see a purchase order, click on **ME23N – Display** from the application menu path. In the **Standard PO** screen that appears, as in the purchase requisition example, choose **More • Purchase Order • Other Purchase Order** from the menu bar, or use the $\boxed{\text{Shift}}$+$\boxed{\text{F5}}$ shortcut. In the **Select Document** screen, enter the purchase order number, and then click **Other Document**.

In the lower part of Figure 4.6, you can see all the details of a purchase order by going through different tabs such as **Material Data**, **Quantities/Weights**, **Delivery Schedule**, **Invoice**, **Delivery Address**, and so on.

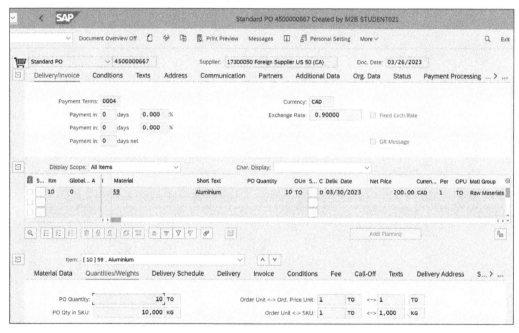

Figure 4.6 Displaying a Purchase Order

> **SAP Fiori App**
>
> The corresponding SAP Fiori app is called Create Purchase Order Advanced (ME21N). It's visually and functionally the same as the SAP GUI transaction.

Now that you understand how to create and proceed with a purchase order, let's follow the workflow with the goods receipt process.

4.1.3   Goods Receipt

In the purchasing process, the next step after you've created a purchase order is to receive the goods or the services you've already ordered. A *goods receipt* refers to receiving the goods or materials physically from the external vendor or supplier to the warehouse of the purchaser. In SAP S/4HANA, there are four different types of goods receipts:

- **Goods receipt with reference to a purchase order**
  You've already generated a purchase order in the system. The goods receipt can then be matched with the data of the purchase order.

- **Goods receipt with reference to a production order**
  A production order is open that requires a goods receipt.

- **Goods receipt with reference to a delivery**
  This type of goods receipt is often used with an intercompany stock transfer.

- **Goods receipt without reference**
  Goods can be received without a reference. This may happen if SAP isn't used as the order system, or orders are made through emails, external portals, or even through calls.

To create a goods receipt, you need to execute Transaction MIGO or follow application menu path **Logistics • Materials Management • Inventory Management • Material Document • Display, Change, Copy, Cancel, Subsequent Delivery**. You'll arrive at the screen shown in Figure 4.7.

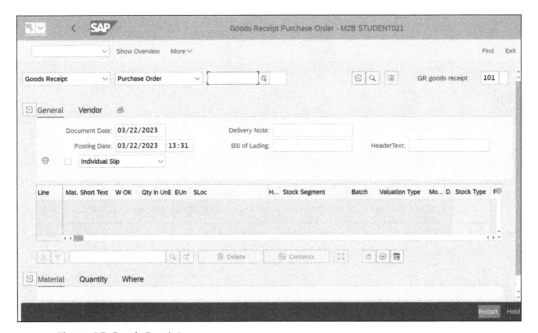

Figure 4.7 Goods Receipt

You just have to enter a purchase order number, which hasn't yet been delivered, next to the **Purchase Order** field (for this example, "4500000668"), and press `Enter`. All fields will be automatically filled in with information from the purchase order, as shown in Figure 4.8.

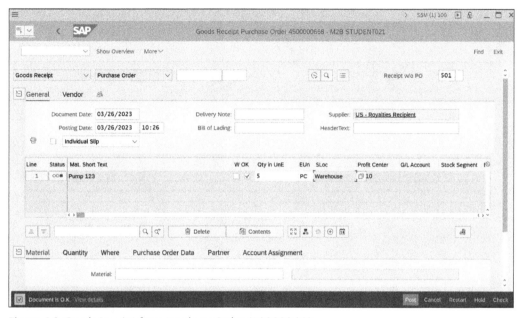

Figure 4.8 Goods Receipt from Purchase Order 4500000668

After reviewing all the entries and double-checking the received quantities, you just need to select the checkbox in the **OK** column and click the **Post** button to post the goods receipt.

SAP Fiori App

The corresponding SAP Fiori app is called Post Goods Receipt for Purchase Order (F0843). In Figure 4.9, you can see the mentioned app in SAP Fiori. You're asked to enter the purchase order number, supplier, plant or a plant name, and then press the `Enter` key.

In the **Purchase Order** field, enter the purchase order number for which you want to confirm and post the goods receipt. In the screen that appears, all fields are filled in from the purchase order you refer to (see Figure 4.10). Click the **Post** button at the bottom of the screen to finish the transaction.

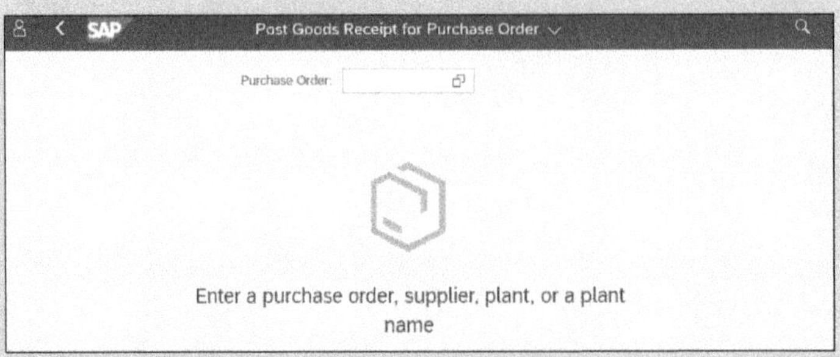

Figure 4.9 Post Goods Receipt for Purchase Order App in SAP Fiori

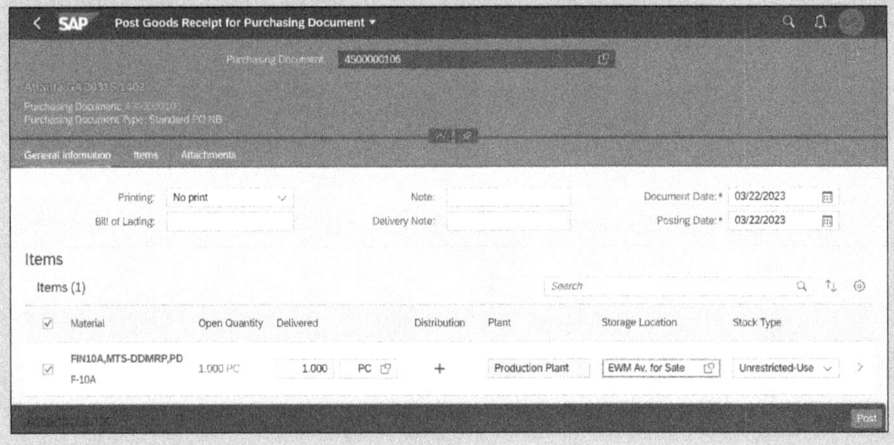

Figure 4.10 Posting Goods Receipt in SAP Fiori

This posting is the first one in the purchase-to-pay process that touches the general ledger. The goods receipt is usually posted on an inventory account. The counter account according to the standard SAP process is the goods receipt/invoice receipt account (GR/IR). The accounting entry is "debit inventory account credit GR/IR account."

In the next section, we'll explain how to process an invoice receipt subsequently to a goods receipt.

4.1.4   Invoice Receipt

Regularly, a supplier invoice (*invoice receipt*) follows a goods receipt and is therefore a subsequent document in the purchase-to-pay process. However, sometimes you first receive the supplier invoice before you receive the ordered material. This may happen, for example, when the shipping of goods takes a long journey by ship across the globe. Regardless, as long as you have a corresponding purchase order in the system, you'll have a unique reference through the process flow.

A supplier invoice is posted as follows: debit GR/IR account, credit supplier account. After performing this accounting entry, the GR/IR account relating to this purchase is balanced to zero. The GR/IR account therefore is a clearing account. On the debit side of the GR/IR account, all goods receipts are posted; on the credit side, invoices are posted. Ideally, an invoice (more specifically, invoice item lines) matches a goods receipt (more specifically, goods receipt item lines), and they can be cleared against each other. Uncleared items (e.g., a goods receipt without an invoice or vice versa) will remain sitting uncleared on the GR/IR account. A view into the GR/IR account will show all uncleared items. Clearing problems can also derive from differences in prices and quantities between goods receipts and invoice receipts. Therefore, someone has to review this account on a regular basis, which would be a very good internal control in the purchase process.

Now, let's walk through how to create an invoice receipt and perform recurring checks on a specific invoice receipt.

Create an Invoice Receipt

To create an invoice receipt in the system, you can use Transaction MIRO, or you can follow application menu path **Logistics • Materials Management • Logistic Invoice Verification • Document Entry • Enter Invoice**. In the **Enter Incoming Invoice** screen, as shown in Figure 4.11, fill in the required data, such as **Invoice date**, **Posting Date**, and **Reference** (usually the document number of the supplier invoice).

Enter the purchase order number next to the **Purchase Order/Scheduling Agreement** field, and press Enter. The system retrieves the information from the purchase order and the goods receipt, and the line in the **PO Reference** tab is filled, as shown in Figure 4.11.

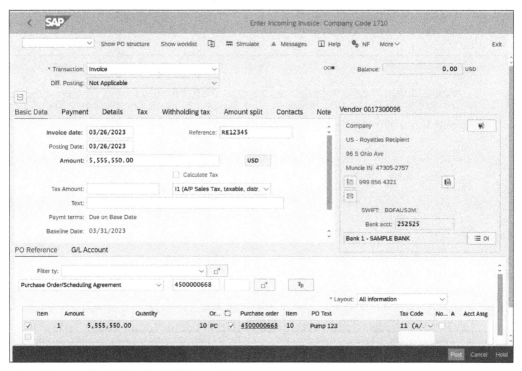

Figure 4.11 Invoice Verification before Posting

Now you can verify the amount and compare it with the supplier invoice. If the amount on the supplier invoice is the same, just enter the amount in the **Amount** field in the **Basic Data** tab, check the **OK** box (next to the **PC** value) in the purchase order line, and press ⎡Enter⎤. The traffic light next to the balance will turn green, and the invoice is ready to post.

Click the **Post** button to do so (see Figure 4.12).

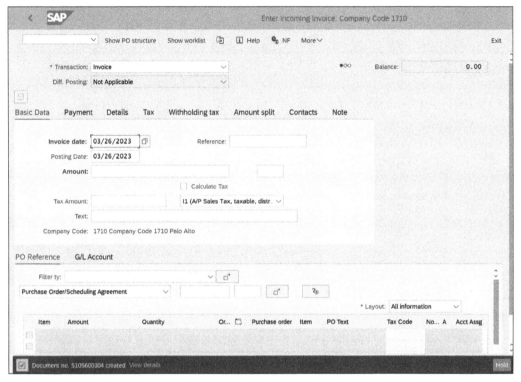

Figure 4.12 Supplier Invoice: Ready to Post

SAP Fiori App

The corresponding SAP Fiori app is called Create Supplier Invoice/Create Supplier Invoice Advanced (MIRO). It's visually and functionally the same as the SAP GUI transaction.

Now if you want to see the document flow from the purchase order to the goods receipt to the supplier invoice, you can, for instance, display the generated invoice by following application menu path **Logistics • Materials Management • Logistic Invoice Verification • Further Processing • Display Invoice Document** or by using Transaction MIR4.

You'll arrive at the **Display Invoice Document** screen, as shown in Figure 4.13, where you define the **Invoice Document No.** and the **Fiscal Year**.

Figure 4.13 Display Invoice Screen

After pressing the [Enter] key, you'll arrive at the next screen, as shown in Figure 4.14. On the left part of the screen, you see the complete document flow under **Display - PO structure**.

You can see the source document is purchase order **4500000650**. The follow-on document is goods receipt **5105600302**, posted as of March 21, 2023. Subsequently, there is supplier invoice **5105600168**.

Here, there are no differences between these documents relating to price and quantity. However, if there are differences or missing follow-on documents, recurring checks are needed, which we'll discuss in the next section.

Figure 4.14 Displaying the Purchase Order Structure

Perform Recurring Checks

In SAP S/4HANA, you can check for a specific purchase order if there are differences in terms of quantity and price between goods receipts and received supplier invoices. We mentioned the importance and the necessity of checking the GR/IR clearing account on a regular basis.

To perform recurring checks on at least a monthly basis, you can use a standard list of GR/IR balances report by either starting Transaction MB5S or by following application menu path **Logistics • Materials Management • Inventory Management • Environment • Balances Display • List of GR/IR Balances**.

In the **List of GR/IR Balances** screen that appears, as shown in Figure 4.15, you can query for your specified purchase order and fill in other criteria as well. For this example, enter the purchase order number, "4500000232". If you've given a unique purchase order number, you don't need to fill in more fields. If you're not sure about that, enter at least the respective **Purch. organization**. To get the full information with this report, select the **Cleared Items too** checkbox, and then click the **Execute** button.

The output report shows you the purchase order, item number, **Quantity Received (12)**, **Invoice Quantity (24)**, **GR value** (USD **12**), and **Invoice amount (24)** from left to right, as shown in Figure 4.16.

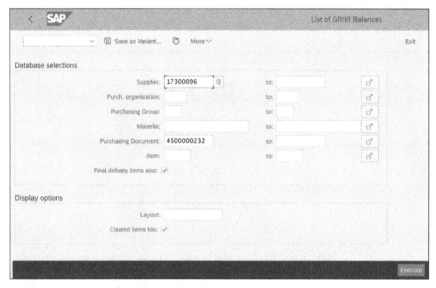

Figure 4.15 List of GR/IR Balances for a Purchase Order: Selection Screen

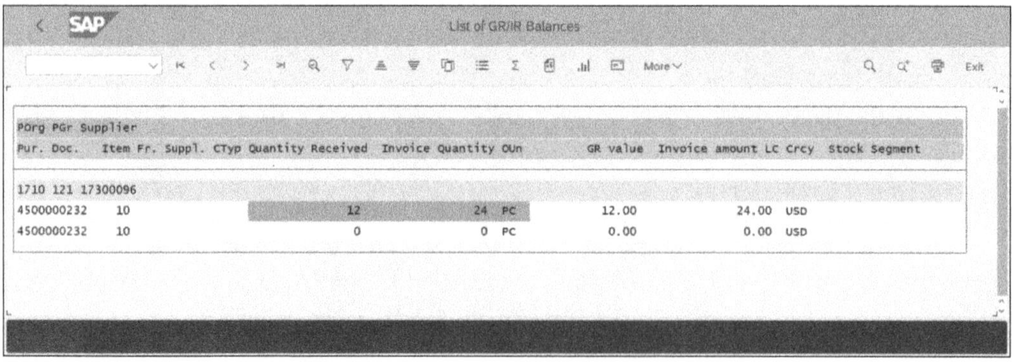

Figure 4.16 List of GR/IR Balances for a Purchase Order: Results

You can double-click on the purchase order record, and another screen appears that shows the history of purchase order **4500000232** for GR/IR, as shown in Figure 4.17.

Here, you can switch between goods receipt (**5000000370**) and invoice receipts (**5105600172, 5105600169**) and vice versa by clicking in the respective line. You can also see all the related details for this purchase order, such as vendor data, payment information, bank information, tax details, material document number, amount, accounting document, Material Ledger, and so on. You can click on each of these to check that everything matches between the goods receipt and the invoice receipt.

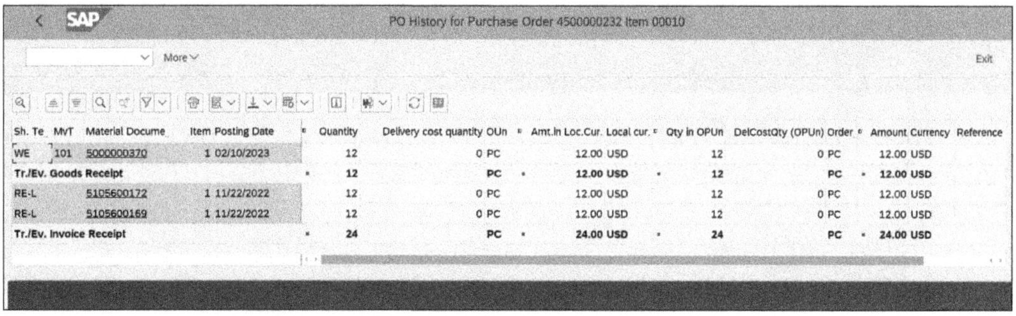

Figure 4.17 History for Purchase Order 4500000232

Now, in the next section, let's discuss the final step of the purchase-to-pay process: invoice payment.

4.1.5   Invoice Payment and Vendor Checking Balances

After the accounts payable invoice is created, as explained in the previous section, the final step in the purchase-to-pay process is to perform the payment transfer to the vendor/supplier. In this section, we'll discuss the vendor account balances before and after the payment transfer. You'll find a more detailed description in Section 4.4 in the discussion about outgoing payments.

Now you can refresh your knowledge regarding the open items discussed in Chapter 3. As we've explained, open items are considered incomplete transactions because a final posting in their lifecycle is missing. The open item in terms of an unpaid supplier invoice will be closed through a payment to the supplier. By releasing the payment, the open item will be cleared by the payment, resulting in a zero closing balance.

To see the vendor account balances, you can use Transaction FK10N or follow application menu path **Accounting • Financial Accounting • Accounts Payable • Account • Display Balances**.

You'll arrive at the **Vendor Balance Display** screen, as shown in Figure 4.18. Here, you need to define the **Supplier** account for which you need to perform an outgoing payment, the **Company Code**, and the **Fiscal Year**. Then click the **Execute** button. Notice that there are three open items on the vendor account in this example. The open item with the amount **112,000** USD is from invoice 5100000001.

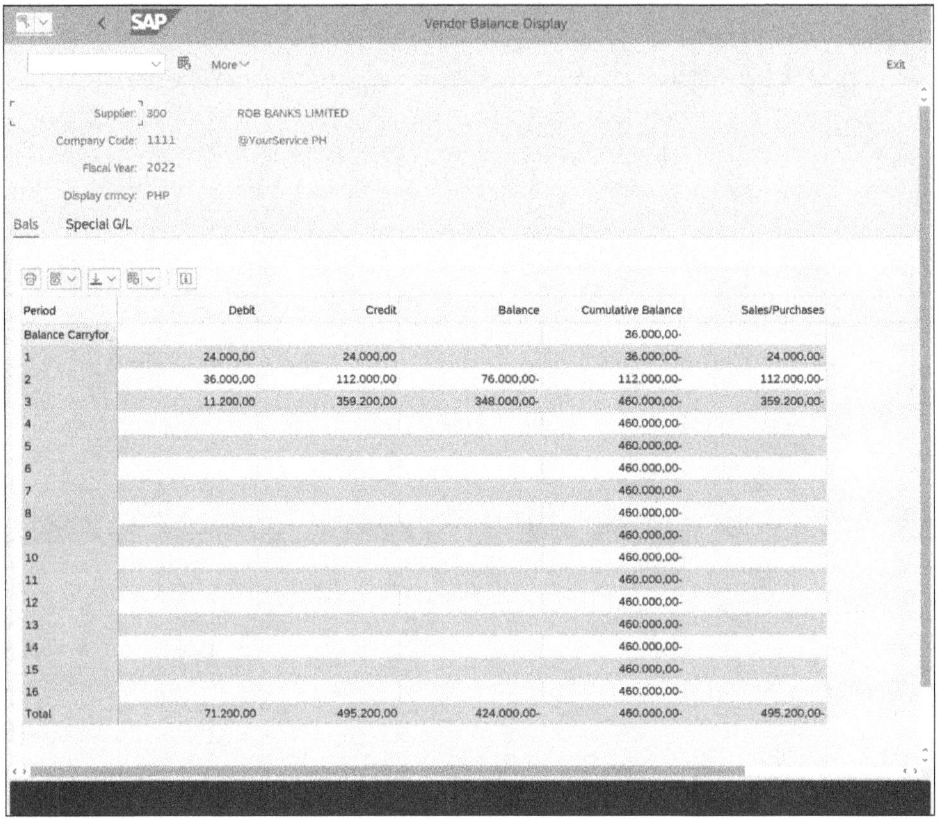

Figure 4.18 Displaying the Vendor Account Balance

Double-click on your relevant line item, and a detailed overview of this open item will open, as shown in Figure 4.19.

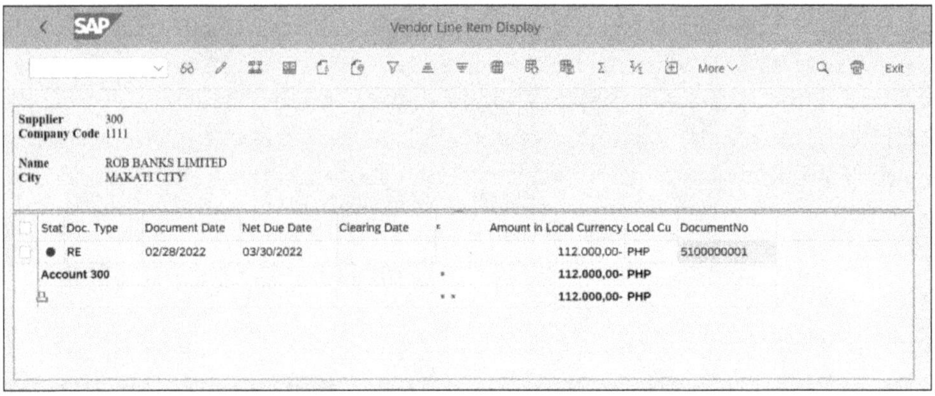

Figure 4.19 Vendor Open Line Item

To clear this item, you need to send the payment to the vendor, which is done using either a periodic payment run for settling open supplier invoices using Transaction F110 or an individual payment using Transaction F-53 (manual payment). Let's skip the payment process here as we'll discuss it further in Section 4.4.

After you've performed all the steps in the outgoing payment process, you can check the balance account again to see how it's presented after the selected open item has been cleared, as shown in Figure 4.20. It's important to mention that the payment was received in 2023.

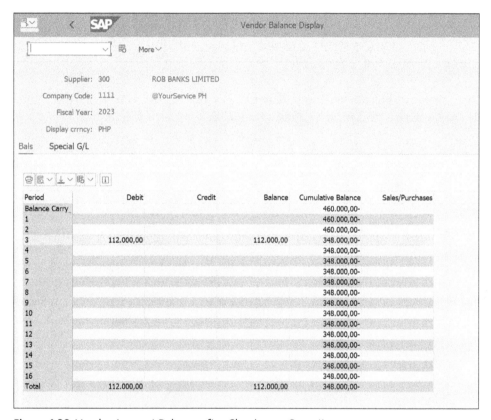

Figure 4.20 Vendor Account Balance after Clearing an Open Item

As you can see, the **Debit** column shows the amount **112,000** (PHP), which is the payment. If you click on the relevant line item, then you'll see that the **Status** has turned to green, which means that it's already a cleared item, as shown in Figure 4.21.

SAP Fiori App

The corresponding SAP Fiori app is called Display Supplier Balances (FK10N). It's visually and functionally the same as the SAP GUI transaction.

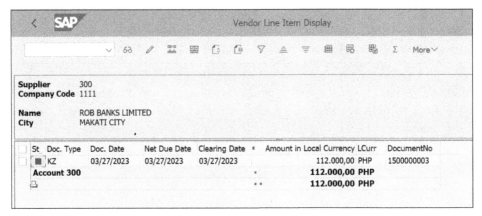

Figure 4.21 Vendor Cleared Line Item

Now that you understand the purchase-to-pay process, we'll focus on the vendor accounts, master data, vendor invoices, and so on in the next section.

4.2   Vendor Accounts

A *vendor account* (or supplier) is a master record in accounts payable that is created once for each supplier. The vendor master database contains all the information about the vendors, such as name, address, currency, payment conditions, contact person, and so on. It also includes accounting information, such as the reconciliation account in the general ledger. In large entities, the vendor master record is managed by two departments: accounting and purchasing. Every vendor master record is considered a subledger account, and the accumulative balance of all vendor master records is reflected in a single general ledger account—the accounts payable reconciliation account.

A vendor account has three segments:

- **General data at the client level**
  This segment contains the general data of a vendor account, such as vendor name, vendor number, vendor address, and so on.

- **Company code segment**
  This segment contains specific data of the company code. If it's settled, a business relationship with a specific vendor is also required to be created in the company code segment for that vendor.

- **Purchasing area segment**
  This segment contains all the specific data of the vendor in the purchasing organization.

> **Note**
> As our focus in this book lies on financial accounting, we won't cover the purchasing area segment because this is part of the materials management and purchasing functionalities.

To create or maintain a vendor master record, you can use Transaction BP to **Create**, **Change** and **Display** a vendor. Although application menu path **Accounting • Financial Accounting • Accounts Payable • Master Records** still leads you to obsolete Transactions FK01 (**Create**), FK02 (**Change**), and FK03 (**Edit**), those aren't valid anymore, and you'll be redirected to Transaction BP instead.

We'll explore how to create and display vendor master records in the following sections.

4.2.1   Vendor General Data

Vendor general data applies to each company code in your organization without exception. In this section, we'll walk through both creating a vendor master record with a supplier business partner and displaying the vendor general data.

Create a Business Partner

To create a vendor master record, you need to use Transaction BP in the transaction input field. You'll arrive first at the **Maintain Business Partner** screen, where you have to choose **More** in the menu header followed by **Business Partner** and **Create**. You can now choose between the creation of **Business Partner** as **Person**, **Organization**, or **Group** (in this example, **Organization** was selected), which takes you to the **Create Organization** screen shown in Figure 4.22. Here, you can see how to create a business partner with a supplier role.

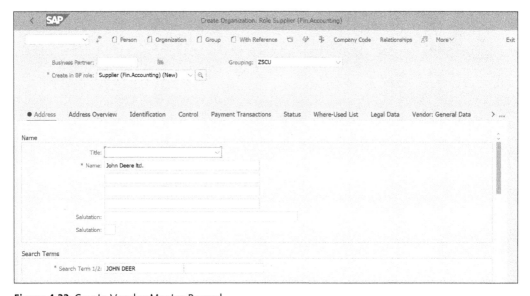

Figure 4.22 Create Vendor Master Record

To create the business partner with a supplier role, select the **Supplier (Fin.Accounting) (New)** role for your business partner in the **Create in BP role** field. Fill out the following tabs:

- **Address**

  In the **Address** tab, enter at least the last name of your supplier in the **Name** field and the match code in the **Search Term 1/2** field.

- **Address Overview**

  Enter the complete address in the **Address Overview** tab.

- **Control**

  Go to the **Control** tab and select a **Business Partner Type**.

Click on **Company Code** in the menu bar to go from the **General Data** view to the **Company Code** data view, as shown in Figure 4.23. You can also toggle back and forth between both views by clicking on **General Data** or **Company Code**, depending on where you are at that time.

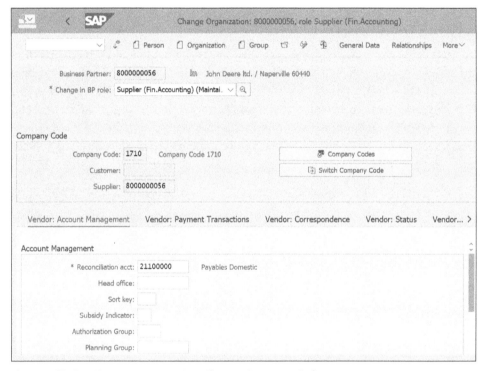

Figure 4.23 Creating Master Data Specific to a Company Code

Select a company code in the **Company Code** field, and press ⌈Enter⌋. Enter the reconciliation account in the **Vendor: Account Management** tab and a payment term in the **Vendor: Payment Transactions** tab. After you've filled in all the required data, click the **Save** button.

Display a Vendor

Next, to display a vendor, enter Transaction BP. The **Maintain Business Partner** screen appears, as shown in Figure 4.24, where you select **Business Partner** from the **Find** field and

Supplier Number from the **By** field, followed by the supplier number you enter. Press Enter , and in the window below the selection fields, the business partner appears in one line.

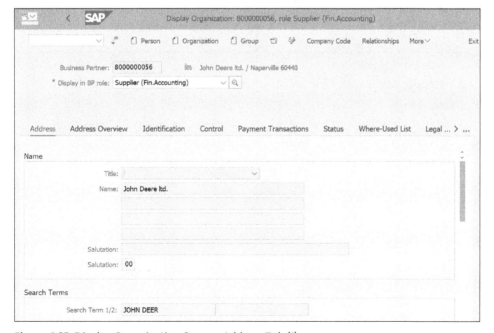

Figure 4.24 Maintain Business Partner

By double-clicking on the **Partner** number that appeared, you'll be directed to the **Display Organization Screen**, as shown in Figure 4.25 and Figure 4.26. Here, you can see all the general data of the supplier such as address, address overview, identification, control, and so on.

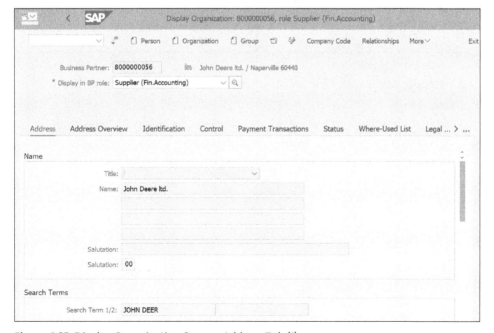

Figure 4.25 Display Organization Screen: Address Tab (1)

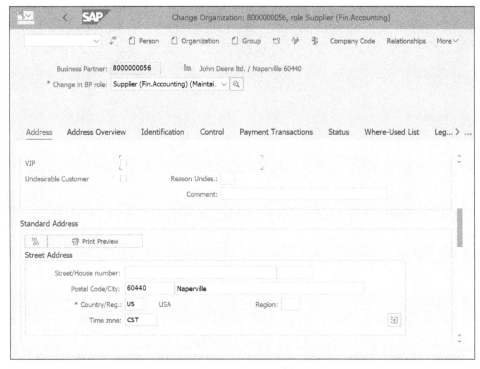

Figure 4.26 Display Organization Screen: Address Tab (2)

Click on the **Identification** tab to see the following key sections, as shown in Figure 4.27 and Figure 4.28:

- **Organizational Data**
  The fields in this box aren't required, but they help to specify your supplier in terms of the legal form and legal entity type.

- **Identification Numbers**
  If your supplier has any external identifiers, you can enter them here.

- **Tax Numbers**
  The tax numbers are critical for any tax reporting purposes and should be maintained in this box. If the supplier is a natural person, check the **Natural Person** box.

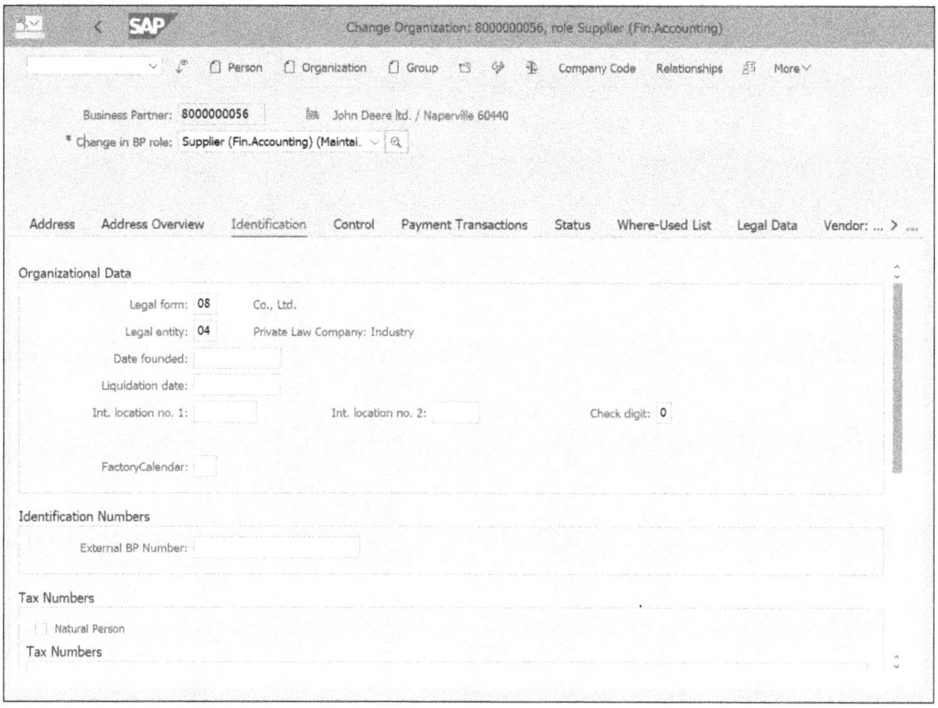

Figure 4.27 Display Organization Screen: Identification Tab (1)

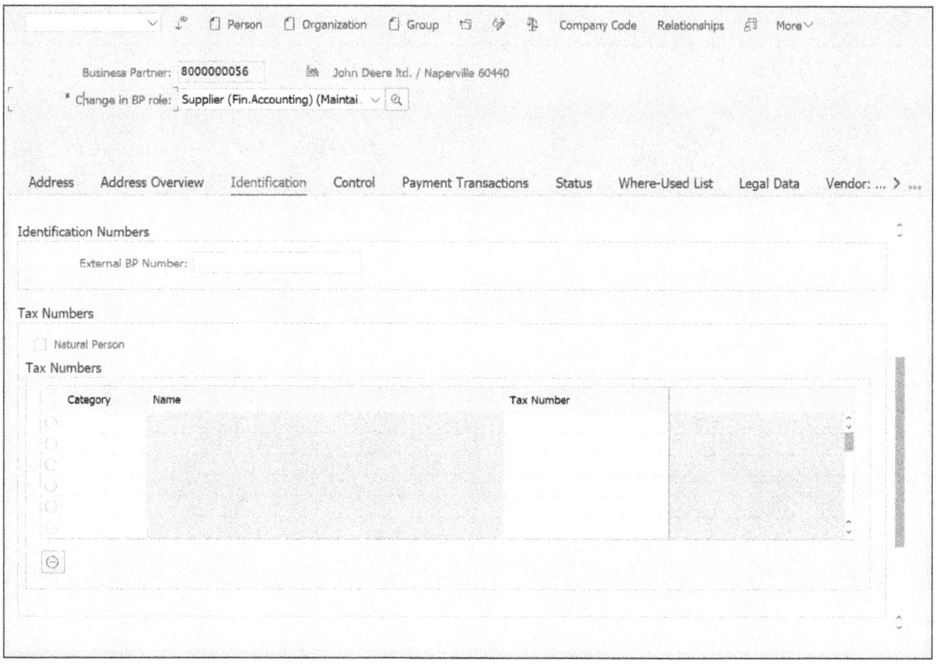

Figure 4.28 Display Organization Screen: Identification Tab (2)

SAP Fiori App

The corresponding SAP Fiori app is called **Manage Supplier Master Data (F1053A)**. In Figure 4.29, you can see how the mentioned app looks in SAP Fiori. All existing vendors are listed from which you can select one to see all of its data.

From this screen, you can click the **Create** button to begin setting up new vendor master data for a **Person** or **Organization**. In Figure 4.30, you can see the fields you need to fill in to create a new vendor for your organization. You enter the same fields as mentioned before (i.e., **Business Partner Role**, **Name**, **Standard Address**, **Company Code**, and **Reconciliation Account**). Click the **OK** button to create your new vendor.

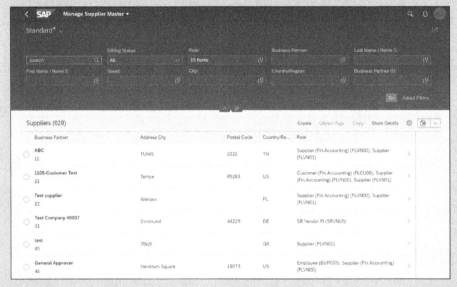

Figure 4.29 Manage Supplier Master Data in SAP Fiori

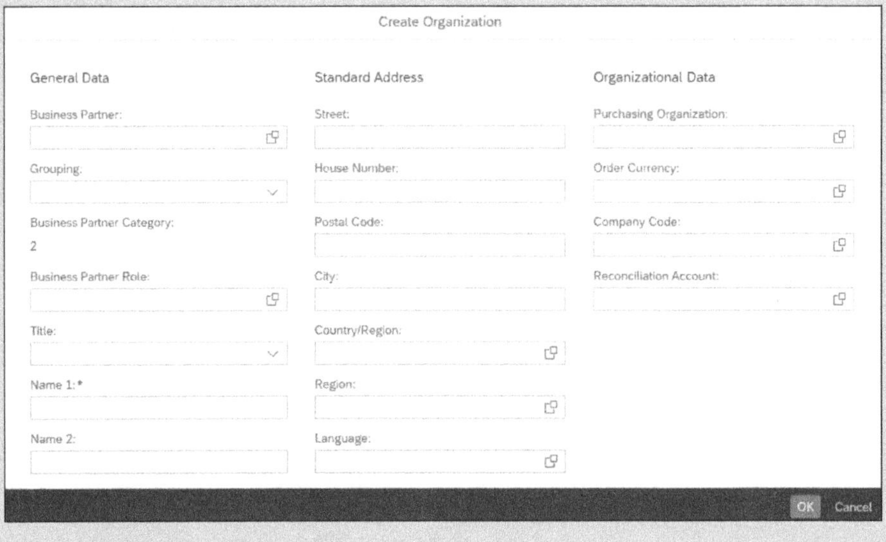

Figure 4.30 Create Vendor Organization Type in SAP Fiori

4.2.2   Vendor Company Code Data

You can check vendor company code data using the same Transaction BP (Display), as you did for the general data. Select **Business Partner** in the **Find** field and **Supplier Number** in the **By** field, enter the supplier number, and then press ⌷Enter⌷ to continue. You then see the selected business partner in a line as shown in Figure 4.31.

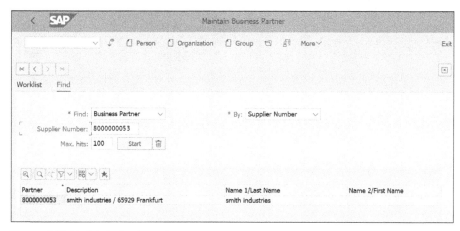

Figure 4.31 Maintain Business Partner

Now double-click on the **Partner** number to go to the general data view, as shown in Figure 4.32 (compare also to the prior section).

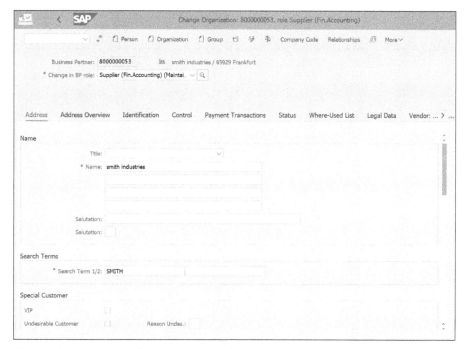

Figure 4.32 Display Supplier Accounting Information

Click now on **Company Code** in the menu to explore the company-specific supplier master data. You immediately will see the **Reconciliation acct** of the organization in the **Vendor: Account Management** tab (see Figure 4.33) and all other accounting- and payment-relevant information specific to the company code **4900**. In our example, the reconciliation account in the general ledger for company code **4900** for supplier **8000000053** is **21100000 Payables Domestic**.

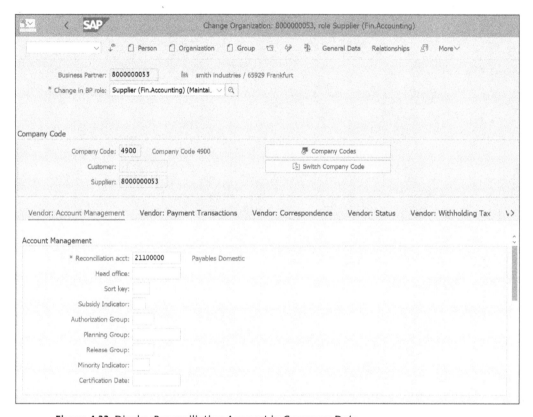

Figure 4.33 Display Reconciliation Account in Company Data

Go to the **Vendor: Payment Transactions** tab next to check the bank details, such as **Bank Key**, **Bank Account**, **Country**, **IBAN**, and so on.

To switch back to the **General Data** view, just click on **General Data** in the menu bar. As mentioned earlier, you can toggle between the **General Data** and **Company Code** views.

SAP S/4HANA separates general data from accounting-relevant master data in a vendor master record because there is a big advantage in doing so. From a group perspective, you need to set up the vendor only once (general data). So that one and the same vendor can be used as a business partner to several companies within your group, you can individually set up and maintain the accounting-relevant information for each of the companies doing business with the vendor. This makes sense because for one company in your group, the vendor is a domestic supplier (and therefore needs a reconciliation account for domestic payables), but for another company in your group, the vendor may be a cross-border supplier (and therefore needs another reconciliation account). Many more properties (payment terms, shipping information, etc.) can deviate from company to company in your group. Therefore, separating general data from accounting-relevant master data helps to not set up a full vendor master data record of one and the same vendor for several companies in your group. Instead, you create the vendor only once and maintain company code–specific properties in the accounting master data of the vendor. There are plenty of other advantages from a logistics and supply chain perspective, although we won't address those here because they go far beyond the scope of the book.

Now that you've learned about vendor account master data, including general data and company code data, we'll discuss how to create vendor invoices and GR/IR matching in the next section.

4.3   Vendor Invoices

Each company needs to pay its suppliers for the goods, materials, or services provided. When you enter the invoice to be paid directly in financial accounting without matching to the respective purchase order, you're recording vendor invoices. This may be the option if your company hasn't placed an order to the supplier through SAP S/4HANA. If there is a purchase order and even a goods receipt, you'll process the invoice through the purchase-to-pay process using the function in logistics where you enter the invoice to be paid in the system that matches the respective purchase order. In this case, when creating the invoice, the system will fill in all the fields automatically. Assuming that there is no difference between purchase order, goods receipt, and supplier invoice, no human intervention is needed. Let's see now how both cases of vendor invoice processing are treated in the system.

4.3.1   Automatic Creation of Vendor Invoices (from Logistics)

Creation of *automatic vendor invoices* is only available for purchase order invoices. This process allows you to automatically process invoices initiated from a defined vendor without any human intervention, considering that the automatically extracted data is correct. As mentioned in Section 4.1.4, you can use Transaction MIRO to create an invoice receipt referring to the purchase order. Therefore, the invoice details are populated based on the purchase order details, and when you post the documents, two documents are created: a material document called the *logistics invoice* in materials management and the accounts payable invoice posted in financial accounting.

Let's consider the following illustrative example. You can take any of the fulfilled and billed purchase orders in the system to trace the document flow.

Go to SAP menu path **Logistics • Materials Management • Purchasing • Purchase Order • Display**, or use Transaction ME23N to display a document flow in logistics, as shown in Figure 4.34.

Click on the **Purchase Order History** tab in the **Item** area of the screen. In Figure 4.34, you see the goods receipt and the invoice receipt for purchase order **4500001518**.

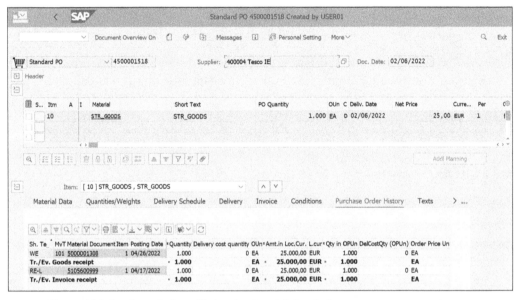

Figure 4.34 Purchase Order with Invoice Receipt Created

Click on the invoice document number **5105600999**, which leads you to the screen **Display Invoice Document**, as shown in Figure 4.35.

Remember that there are two available invoice documents in the system: the material document in materials management and the accounts payable document. In the current view, the material document of a supplier invoice is shown. If you click on the **Follow-On Documents** button on the upper menu, you can also see the financial accounting document in accounts payable, as shown in Figure 4.36.

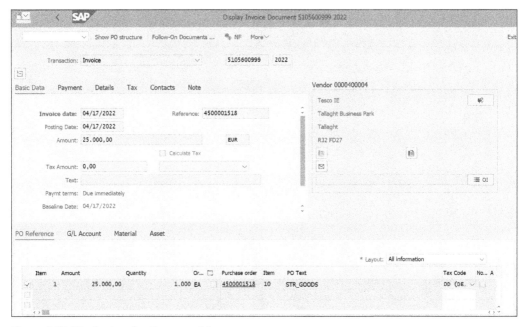

Figure 4.35 Display Invoice Document Screen

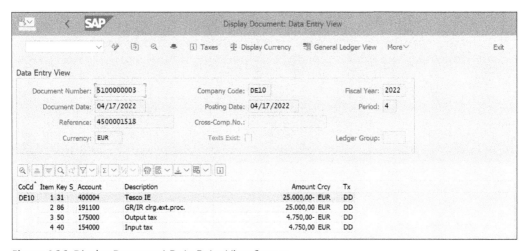

Figure 4.36 Display Document Data Entry View Screen

Click on **General Ledger View** in the menu bar, and the **Display Document: General Ledger View** screen appears, as shown in Figure 4.37.

Figure 4.37 Display Document: General Ledger View

Here you see the general ledger accounting entry, which is directly connected to the accounts payable ledger through the supplier account number **400004** (Figure 4.36) and the linked reconciliation account **160000 AP-domestic** (Figure 4.37).

Now, let's jump into the next section where you'll learn how to create a "direct" invoice without connecting to logistics in accounts payable of financial accounting.

4.3.2   Direct Invoices

Unlike automatic invoices, direct invoices aren't created by referring to a purchase order. They don't have a respective material invoice number as in the case of automatic invoices. For accounts payable invoices, the standard document type is KR, whereas for the invoices created from logistics, the standard document type is RE. Let's walk through the process to find open items and create direct invoices for them.

Find Open Items

To display and search for direct invoices, you can use the vendor line-item report by following application menu path **Accounting • Financial Accounting • Accounts Payable • Account • Display/Change Line Items** or using Transaction FBL1N. The **Vendor Line Item Display** screen will appear, as shown in Figure 4.38.

Here, you can define the range of vendor accounts, company code, and line items (open items, cleared items, all items), depending on your needs.

Figure 4.38 Vendor Line Item Display Screen

After you've defined all the criteria, click the **Execute** button to go to the screen shown in Figure 4.39. Here, you can see the line items of the selected vendor. The red status means that the items are still open.

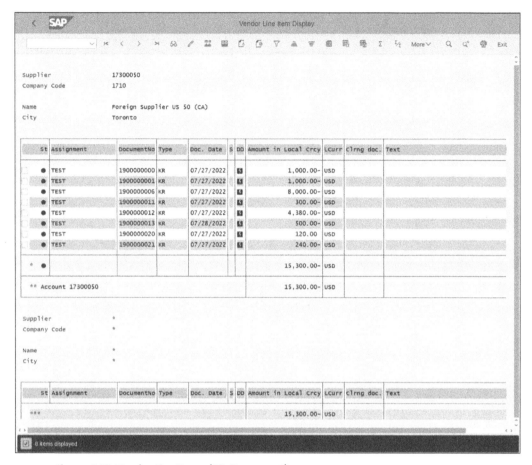

Figure 4.39 Vendor Line Items (KR: Document)

> **SAP Fiori App**
>
> The corresponding SAP Fiori app is called Display Supplier Invoice (MIR4/MIR5). It's visually and functionally the same as the SAP GUI transaction.

Create Direct Invoices

Now that you know how to find direct invoices, let's discuss how to create an accounts payable direct invoice in the first place. Follow application menu path **Accounting • Financial Accounting • Accounts Payable • Document Entry • Invoice**, or use Transaction FB60.

The **Enter Vendor Invoice** screen appears, as shown in Figure 4.40. The screen is divided into two main parts: (1) the header information of the transaction with the **Basic data**, **Payment**, **Details**, **Tax**, **Withholding tax**, **Amount split**, and **Notes** tabs, and (2) the line items, where the debit and credit entries are done. Fill out the following tabs:

- **Basic data**
  In the **Basic data** tab, enter the **Vendor** number, **Invoice date, Posting Date, Document type** (select **Vendor Invoice**), **Amount, Reference**, and **Text**.

- **Payment**
  Enter payment terms in the **Payment** tab to finish the header data entry.

- **Details**
  In the **Details** tab, enter the header text for the invoice you want to post.

Now you can move on to the line items by selecting the counter account for the vendor **G/L acct**. At least one line has to be filled with a **Debit** entry. Then, if the balance is zero, you can post the transaction by clicking the **Post** button.

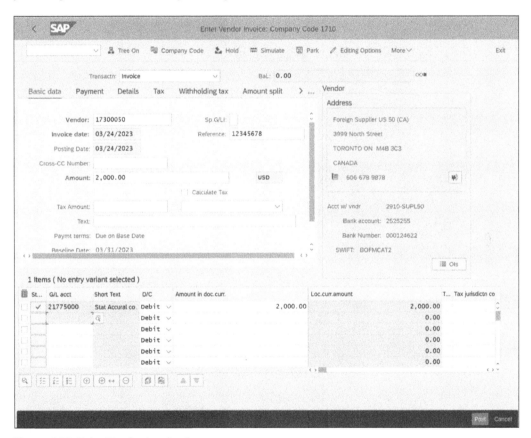

Figure 4.40 Enter Vendor Invoice Screen

Click the **Simulate** button to check if there are any errors before you post the document. If the document simulation is successful, an overview screen will appear with overall information as shown in Figure 4.41.

Finally, click the **Post** button to post the vendor invoice document. You'll receive a message with the new document number at the bottom of the screen.

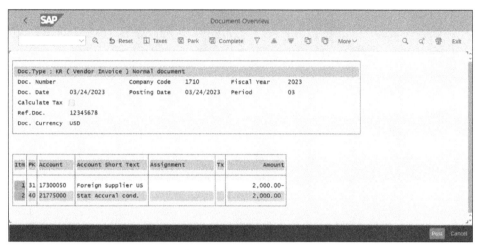

Figure 4.41 Document Overview before Posting

SAP Fiori App

The corresponding SAP Fiori app is called Create Supplier Invoice (F0346A). In Figure 4.42 and Figure 4.43, you can see what this app looks like in SAP Fiori.

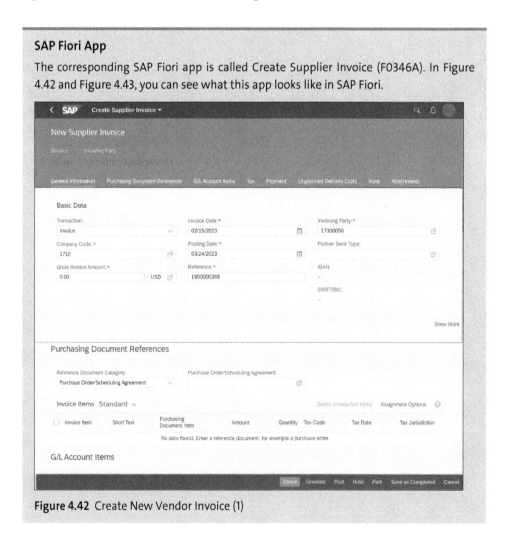

Figure 4.42 Create New Vendor Invoice (1)

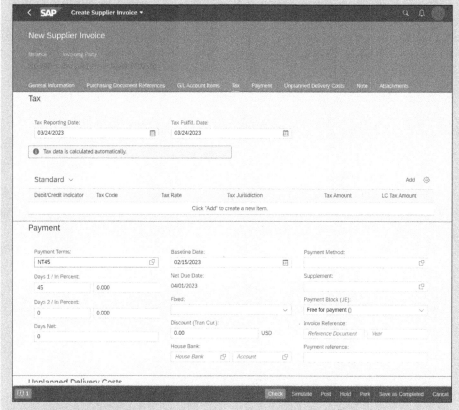

Figure 4.43 Create New Vendor Invoice (2)

Like in SAP GUI, you need to enter the required data in the header and at least one line item in the **Items** area. Then you can click the **Simulate** button to check if there is an error before you post the document. If the simulation process is successfully completed, click the **Post** button to post the vendor invoice.

Now that you've learned how invoices are created, let's see how they are paid.

4.4   Outgoing Payments

The outgoing payment process is also important in financial accounting in SAP S/4HANA. After the supplier invoice is recorded, the next step is to settle it when it's due via payment. This is the last step in the procure-to-pay process. However, from an accounting perspective, there may be a few little tasks to be performed such as processing the bank statement and cleanup work if foreign currencies are involved. Today, the most common payment method in business-to-business industries is a transfer of money from bank to bank through a bank transfer. Ideally, supplier accounts are settled on a regular basis, such as weekly or biweekly, or even daily in large companies. Most of the periodic payments against standard vendors are scheduled to be executed automatically on specific days. However, in urgent situations, you may need to perform manual individual payments as well to avoid any penalties or fines from a business or tax perspective or to account for bank accounts that aren't configured correctly from a system's technical perspective.

Vendor payments can be made via cash, check, letter of credit, manual transfer, payment order, and so on. In this section, we'll talk about two types of payments: direct (manual) invoice payment, where the invoice is directly created, and automatic payment.

The standard is to make an automatic payment through the payment run using Transaction F110. This can be done if all your suppliers have bank accounts, and you can settle the open items by transferring money from your bank account to theirs. The manual payment is normally an exception. Let's assume you paid the supplier by cash. Or, in the other case, you don't want to wait until the next automatic payment run because of a due date you want to hold. Then, the only option you have is to use the manual payment function in SAP S/4HANA.

Let's now see how both transactions work.

4.4.1   Manual Payment

Manual payments can be issued using two different transactions: Transaction F-53 (Post) or Transaction F-58 (Post + Print). The difference between these two transactions is that Transaction F-58 generates a printed payment output form, unlike Transaction F-53. Both transactions create a payment document in the system, which clears open invoices and accordingly updates the general ledger.

The manual payment can be performed with two options:

- **Partial payment**
  This type of payment is used when you perform a partial payment for a defined open item. The system will show the payment still in **Unpaid** status until the total amount is settled.

- **Residual payment**
  This payment is similar to partial payments, but the open invoice is cleared with the residual payment, and the system will create a new outstanding document.

To issue a manual outgoing payment, use Transaction F-53, or follow application menu path **Accounting • Financial Accounting • Accounts Payable • Document Entry • Outgoing Payment • Post**. The **Post Outgoing Payments: Header Data** screen appears, as shown in Figure 4.44.

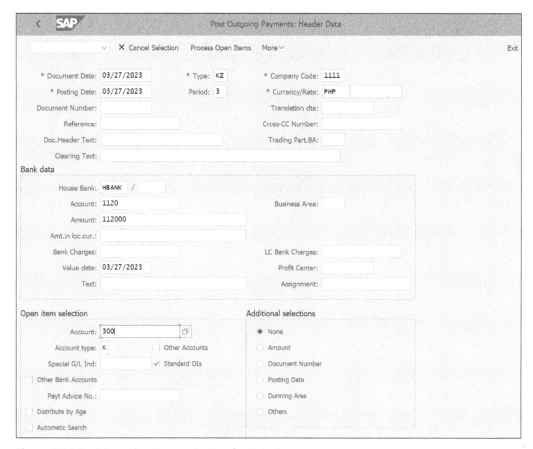

Figure 4.44 Post Outgoing Payments: Header Data Screen

Enter the fields that appear on the header: **Document Date**, **Posting Date**, **Currency/ Rate**, **Company Code**, **Reference** number, and so on. Then, fill in the following areas:

- **Bank data**
  In the **Bank data** area, enter the bank general ledger **Account** number of the bank from which the payment is triggered and the **Amount** you need to pay the vendor. This amount is populated with the purchase invoice amount.

- **Open item selection**
  In the **Open item selection** area, enter the vendor number in the **Account type** field (**K** stands for creditor).

- **Additional selections**
  In the **Additional selections** area, specify more details to find the invoice that will be settled by the manual payment you're going to post. For example, if you know the document number of the invoice, which is paid, select the **Document Number** radio button from the list, and the system will ask for the number. You can also find the

open item (invoice to be paid) quickly if you just know the amount by choosing the **Amount** radio button.

In this example, **None** is selected, so all open items will be shown on the selected vendor account **300**.

After you've filled in the fields on the initial screen, click the **Process Open Items** button at the top of the screen to display the list of open items, as shown in Figure 4.45.

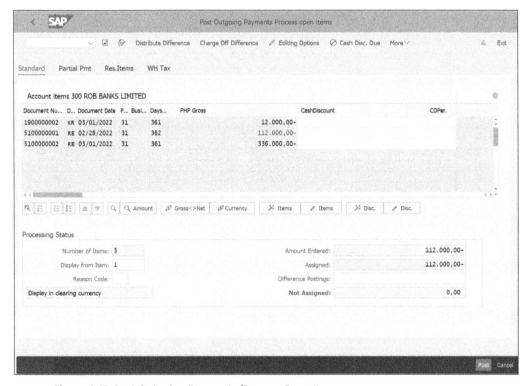

Figure 4.45 Post Outgoing Payments/Process Open Items

If you click on one of the document numbers of the open items, for example, **PHP 112,000**, it will appear on an overview screen of this open item, as shown in Figure 4.46.

Go back to the **Post Outgoing Payments Process open items** screen shown in Figure 4.45, and continue with the post outgoing payment process. After you check the details of this open invoice, click the **Post** button. The system will create a clearing document that changes the status of the invoice from **Open** to **Clear**.

To reach the screen showing that the selected open item to be paid, **PHP 112,000**, now appears as a cleared item (see Figure 4.47), follow application menu path **Accounting • Financial Accounting • Accounts Payable • Account • Display/Change Line Items**, or use Transaction FBL1N. Enter the respective **Vendor**, and select all items.

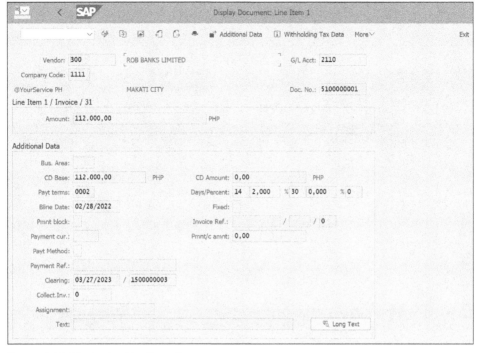

Figure 4.46 Displaying the Open Item

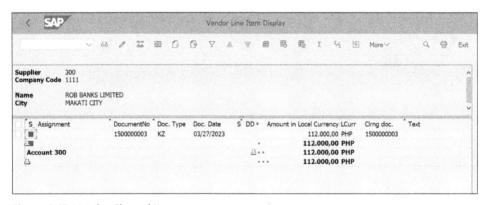

Figure 4.47 Vendor Cleared Item

SAP Fiori App

The corresponding SAP Fiori app is called Post Outgoing Payment (F1612). It's more intuitive and user friendly than Transaction F-53 in SAP GUI. The screen is divided into two parts: the upper part, where you have to specify where the money is paid from, and the lower part, where the payment goes to, as shown in Figure 4.48.

First, enter the **General Information** (**Company Code**, **Posting Date**, and **Journal Entry Date**), and second, select the bank account from which the money comes (or a petty cash account if you've paid the supplier in cash), and determine the **Amount** of payment. The **Journal Entry Type** is prefilled with **KZ** (vendor payment), and the **Posting Date** is the current day by default.

If you then enter a specific supplier and click the **Show Items** button, the lower half of the screen will show all open items of the selected supplier, as shown in Figure 4.49. The balance, which is red, is also shown in the upper-right corner of the screen.

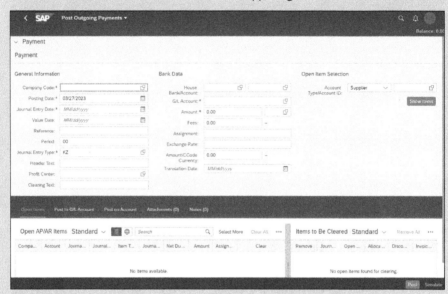

Figure 4.48 Post Outgoing Payment App in SAP Fiori

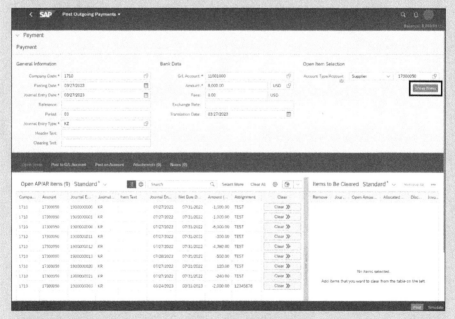

Figure 4.49 Post Payment to Supplier Account/Open Item

Now you just have to select the open item, which should be cleared through the payment. You do this by clicking on the **Clear** button, which sends the item to be cleared to the **Items to Be Cleared** area to the right of the screen, as shown in Figure 4.50.

Figure 4.50 Post Outgoing Payment/Clear Open Item

Now the balance in the upper-right corner of the screen has turned green and is zero, meaning that you've completely cleared the open item by clicking the **Post** button.

Now that you've learned how to create a manual outgoing payment, let's discuss the automatic payment process.

4.4.2   Automatic Payment Program

The financial accounting *automatic payment program* in SAP S/4HANA is the process of posting accounts payables automatically, such as the payment to a vendor, based on vendor invoices. This program finds the pending invoices and reviews the due date payments, which are then approved and paid. The process of the automated payment program passes through some steps, such as maintaining the program parameters, creating the payment proposal, and then executing the payment order.

Before executing the payment program, you need to configure some settings for the payment process. Next, we'll show you the steps to follow to configure the automated payment program, and then we'll move on to running it.

Setup

To execute the automated payment program, use Transaction F110, or follow application menu path **Accounting • Financial Accounting • Accounts Payable • Periodic Processing • Payments**. The **Automatic Payment Transactions: Status** screen appears, as shown in Figure 4.51.

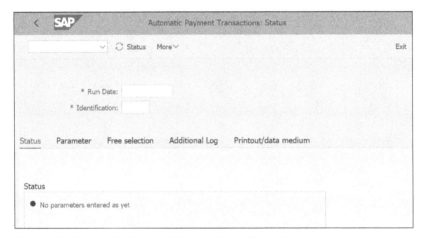

Figure 4.51 Automatic Payment Transactions: Status Screen

Enter the required fields **Run Date** (usually the current date) and **Identification** (any character string with five characters). You can later search for this string to find the performed payment run quicker.

Fill in the parameters for your payment run on the **Parameter** tab, as shown in Figure 4.52. The **Posting Date** and the **Docs Entered up to** are prepopulated by the current date.

In the **Payments Control** box, the company code, the payment method, and the date for your payment run are populated because you defined the payment run on the **Parameter** tab. The payment methods (**Pmt Meths**) have the preconfigured values **B** for bank transfer (general), **C** for check, **D** for domestic bank transfer, or **N** for card payment. In the **Next PstDate** field, you can see the next date when the next automatic payment program is expected to run. Until this date, the program finds all the due date invoices after the last run date and schedules them to be paid in this payment run.

In the **Accounts** box, select the range of **Supplier** accounts you want to settle. If you owe money to some of your customers or have the right to direct debit your customers' bank accounts, you can also enter a range of **Customer** accounts.

Save the entries you've made so far by clicking the **Save Parameters** button. You'll receive a message that the details have been saved.

In the **Free selection** tab, define your exception to exclude certain open items that you don't want to pay. Then, in the **Additional Log** tab, define what details should be logged in the payment log. Finally, to print the payment transaction, select the printer and media in the **Printout/data medium** tab.

Figure 4.52 Automatic Payment Run: Parameters

Go back to the **Status** tab, and you can see that it has turned green, as shown in Figure 4.53.

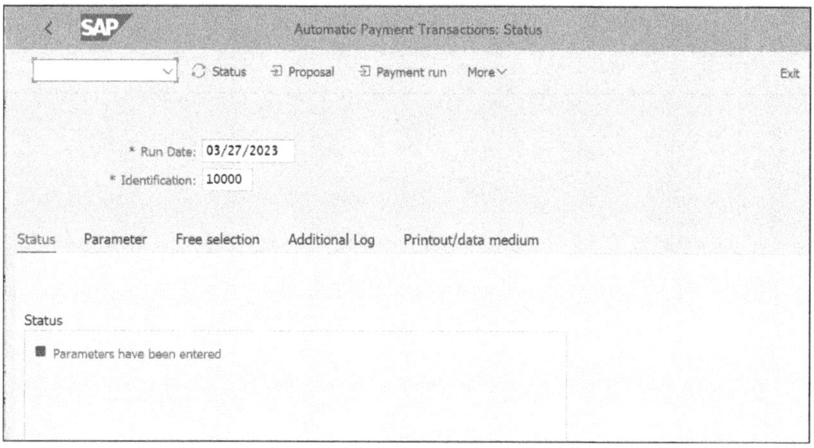

Figure 4.53 Automatic Payment Run: Green Status

Generate a payment proposal run by clicking on the **Proposal** menu bar item or directly start the payment run with the **Payment run** menu bar item. Before executing the payment program, it's recommended to double-check the settings configuration.

You can configure the payment program by choosing **More • Environment • Maintain Configuration** from the menu bar. In the screen that opens (see Figure 4.54), settings for the automatic payment program are categorized into several groups from which you can configure the relevant settings and options:

- **All company codes**
  Click **All company codes**, and you'll arrive at the screen shown in Figure 4.55, where you can select one of the company codes and double-click on it.

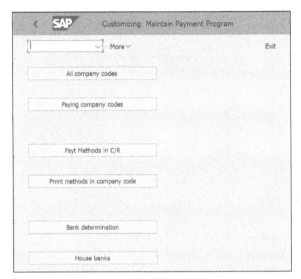

Figure 4.54 Customizing: Maintain Payment Program Screen

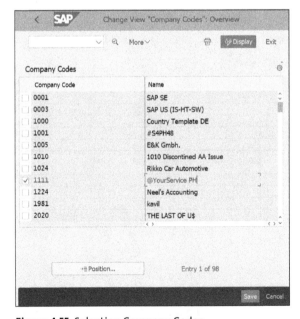

Figure 4.55 Selecting Company Codes

Another screen will appear, as shown in Figure 4.56 and Figure 4.57, where you can define the relevant settings for the selected company code, such as the paying company, which is normally identical with the company code in the header of the screen, as well as cash discounts and tolerances for payments relevant to early payment discounts. After you've entered all the required fields, click **Save** to save the data.

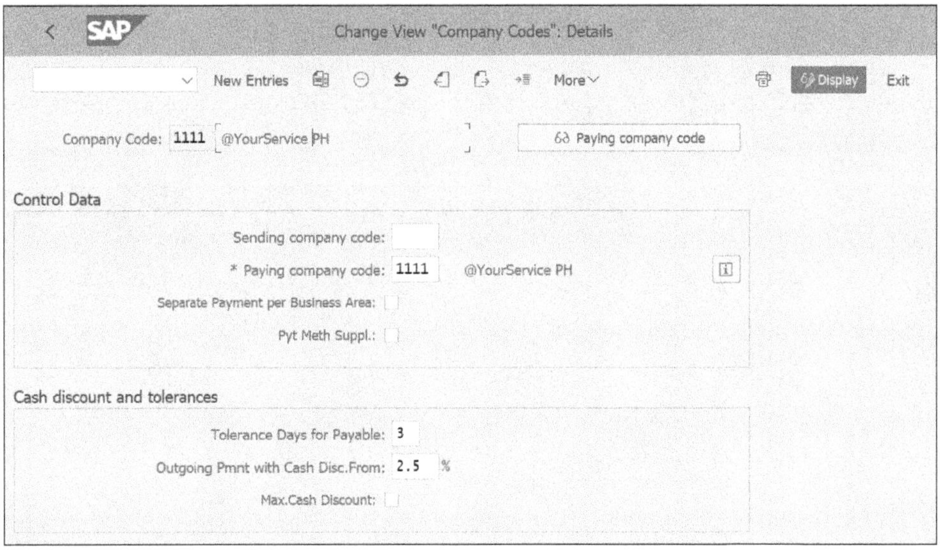

Figure 4.56 Company Codes Settings (1)

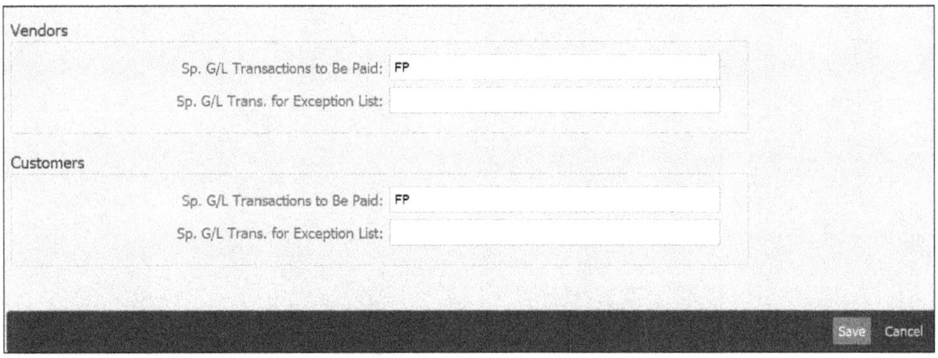

Figure 4.57 Company Codes Settings (2)

- **Paying company codes**
  Here, you perform the following settings:
  - **Control Data**: Minimum amounts for incoming and outgoing payment.
  - **Bill of Exchange**: Bill of exchange parameters.
  - **Forms**: Forms for payment advice and Electronic Data Interchange (EDI).

Let's start with the **Control Data** section, as shown in Figure 4.58. Here, you can enter a **Minimum Amount for Outgoing Payment** (because you don't want to pay cent amounts, the transactions cost would be higher) and a **Minimum Amount for Incoming Payment** for your customer. Further, if you don't want to have any automatic postings of exchange rate differences, select the box next to **No Exchange Rate Differences**. The **Separate Payment for Each Ref.** checkbox may be selected if you don't want to have a netting of incoming and outgoing payments with the same reference. You should select the **Bill/Exch Pymt** checkbox if you want to use bills of exchange, bill of exchange payment requests, or the check/bill of exchange procedure in the paying company code.

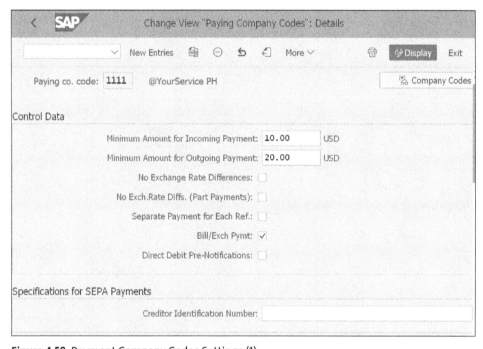

Figure 4.58 Payment Company Codes Settings (1)

In the **Bill of Exchange Data** section, you can configure how the bill of exchange looks. Although bills of exchange were very common in the 1980s and 1990s, they are disappearing because they are no longer relevant today, so we won't explain them here.

Finally, in the **Forms** section (see Figure 4.59), you define the format of the payment advice you generate with the payment run. In addition, if you generate an EDI file, you can select the specific data format. SAP has its own format called SAPscript. An SAP consultant can customize this format and add and change **Letter Header**, **Footer**, **Signature Text**, and **Sender** details to it.

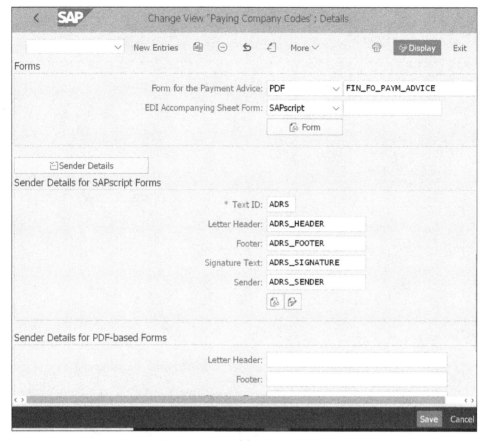

Figure 4.59 Paying Company Codes Settings (2)

After you've filled in the required fields, click the **Save** button, and you receive the message that the data is saved.

- **Payt Methods in C/R**
Here, you configure the methods of payment, settings for individual payment methods, document types for posting, print programs, and permitted currencies for each country relevant for your organization.

Figure 4.60 shows how the payment method **B** (bank transfers for outgoing payments) for **Country US** is configured.

Scroll down to see further settings for payment type **B – Bank Transfer** (see Figure 4.61). This configuration is country-specific, and the settings are normally preconfigured in so-called country templates when SAP S/4HANA is implemented. To explain all the fields and implications would go far beyond the scope of this book. Any changes would require country-specific expertise by a local SAP consultant.

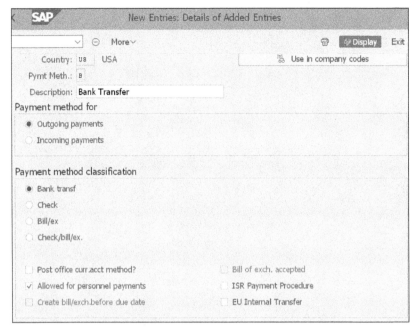

Figure 4.60 Payment Methods in Country (1)

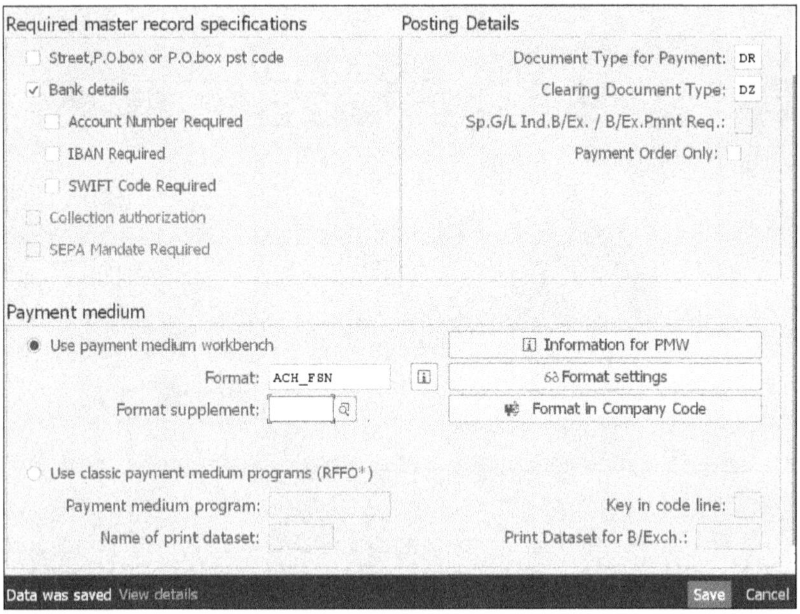

Figure 4.61 Payment Methods in Country (2)

- **Pmnt methods in company code**
  Here, you perform settings such as minimum and maximum payment amounts, grouping possibilities, bank optimization, forms for payment media, and so on.

  Figure 4.62 shows the configuration of payment method **T – Bank Transfer** for company code **1111**. The payment program will select this payment method for any payments above the minimum amount and below the maximum amount. The payment items can be grouped per day or shown individually. You can further configure whether foreign business partners, foreign currencies, or foreign bank accounts are allowed through the payment method assigned to the specific company code.

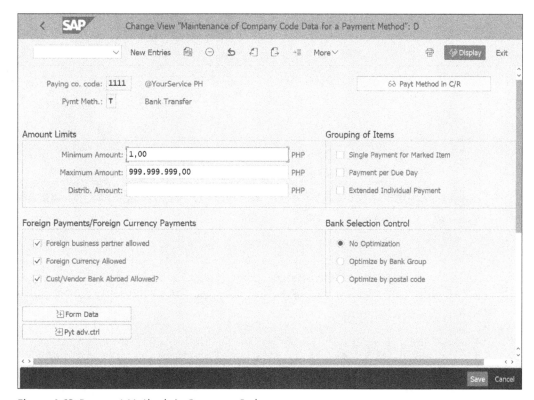

Figure 4.62 Payment Methods in Company Code

- **Bank determination**
  Here, you preconfigure your bank preferences by choosing which bank account is used for the defined payment methods. In our example, as shown in Figure 4.63, payment method **C** (check) is done in **USD** with house bank **USBK1**. On the second rank for the same payment method, you find house bank **USBK2**.

- **House banks**
  Here, you check the assignment of house banks to company codes.

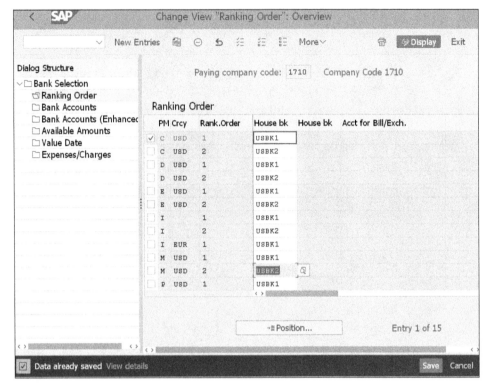

Figure 4.63 Ranking Order

Automatic Payment Run

After you've finished with the configuration steps for the payment process, then you can continue with the execution of the payment program. We'll start back at the **Status** screen shown in Figure 4.64.

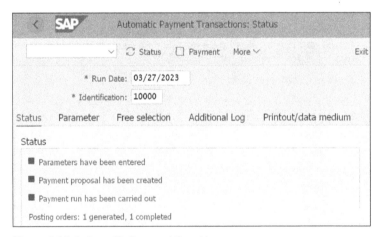

Figure 4.64 Automatic Payment Run Message

In the top menu, choose **More • Payment Run • Reorganization**. On the screen that appears, select the **Start immediately** checkbox to start the payment run immediately. Click the **Execute** icon, or press the ⌜Enter⌟ key.

After the payment has been performed successfully, a message with green indicators appears in the **Status** tab showing that the payment run has been carried out, the parameters have been entered, and so on (see Figure 4.64).

SAP Fiori Apps

The corresponding SAP Fiori apps are called Schedule Automatic Payment (F110) and Schedule Automatic Payment Periodically (F110S). They are visually and functionally the same as SAP GUI.

However, there is also another SAP Fiori app called Manage Automatic Payments (F0770). Figure 4.65 shows the screen where you can configure automated payment in SAP Fiori.

The functions are completely the same even if the visualization is different. First, click on the **Create Parameter** button to create a new payment run. Then, add parameters as you did earlier in SAP GUI with Transaction F110, and schedule the payment run by clicking on **Schedule Payment**, where you can decide whether you want to first run a proposal run before you run the "real" payment. With the **Parameters Created**, **Proposals Processed**, and **Payments Processed** tabs, switch between the parameters, the processed proposals, and the processed payments.

Knowing the traditional Transaction F110, you'll be able run a payment similarly.

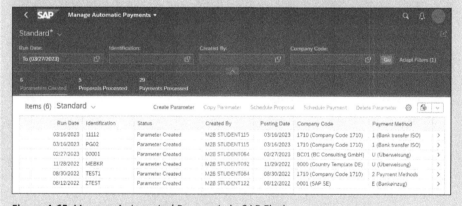

Figure 4.65 Manage Automated Payments in SAP Fiori

4.5 Process Exceptions

Some exceptions can appear during the process-to-pay process. We'll start with creating vendor credit memos (credit notes) and then explain the treatment for down payments.

4.5.1   Credit Memos

As you've already learned, for each good or service received from the vendor, the company issues outgoing payments. In some exceptions, the vendor or seller company may need to make some adjustments in terms of the paid amount in its account. In this case, a *credit memo* document is issued by the vendor. A credit memo (aka *credit memorandum* or *credit note*) is a document issued by the vendor, crediting the vendor account with an amount that is paid back from the vendor to the buyer in terms of an earlier invoice. The credit memo may contain details and explanations for the amount credited on the memo that has been issued. A credit memo can be issued for several reasons:

- Returned goods from the buyer to the vendor
- Pricing dispute/disagreement
- Marketing allowance
- Other reasons the buyer wouldn't pay the full invoice amount

In accounting, a credit memo is considered a reduction of the accounts receivable balance from the seller (vendor) side or a reduction of the accounts payable balance from the buyer (customer) side.

In SAP S/4HANA, you can post a credit memo by entering Transaction FB65 or by following application menu path **Accounting • Financial Accounting • Accounts Payable • Document Entry • Credit Memo**. The **Enter Vendor Credit Memo** screen appears, as shown in Figure 4.66.

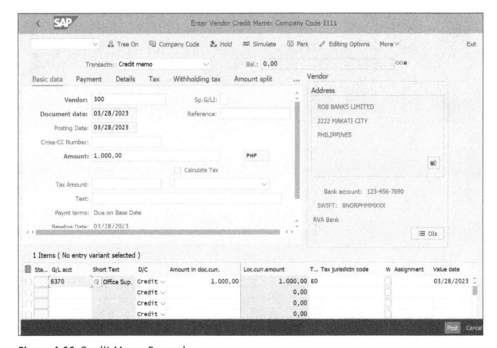

Figure 4.66 Credit Memo Example

In the **Basic data** tab, fill in the fields for the **Vendor**, **Document date**, **Posting Date**, **Amount**, **Tax Amount** (if applicable), and **Text**. For a credit memo, you usually don't have to fill in the fields of the other tabs.

After you've entered the required data in the respective fields, go to the line item, and enter at least one general ledger line item (**G/L acct**, debit/credit indicator (**D/C**), **Amount in doc.curr.**, etc.). This line item corresponds to an offset of an expense account.

Simulate the posting by clicking the **Simulate** button at the top of the screen. Based on the entered data, you'll receive an unsuccessful result with an error message or a successful result showing the document how it would be posted if you eventually do so. After running the simulation, click the **Post** button, and a message with the new document number will appear.

The vendor credit memo that you just posted is shown in Figure 4.67. Note that the posting key for the debit entry for the credit memo is **21**. The posting key **50** is standard for a general credit entry.

Figure 4.67 Display Credit Memo

SAP Fiori App

The corresponding SAP Fiori app is called Credit Memo Request (F1846). It's visually different but functionally very similar to what you've seen for SAP GUI Transaction FB65.

Now that you've learned what a vendor credit memo is and how to post one, let's focus on the vendor down payment transaction.

4.5.2   Down Payments Sent

Down payments are also considered advance payments because they are payments made in advance to the vendor before receiving goods or services. Down payments are first initiated by a payment request, which is a note from the supplier (noted item) that doesn't impact the balance sheet. Therefore, the general ledger account balances remain unchanged. These noted items enable the system to automatically post the vendor down payments using the payment program. After the company receives the goods/services or the receipt, the down payment starts the clearing process against the final invoice.

You can create a down payment request by entering Transaction F-47, or following application menu path **Accounting • Financial Accounting • Accounts Payable • Document Entry • Down Payment • Request.**

The **Down Payment Request: Header Data** screen appears, as shown in Figure 4.68. Enter data in the required fields, such as **Document Date, Posting Date, Company Code, Currency/Rate,** and **Document Number.**

In the **Vendor** area, you can specify a vendor account in the **Account** field and a special general ledger indicator in the target special general ledger indicator (**Trg.Sp.G/L Ind.**) field. With this field, you can post differently from how you post the standard accounts payable entry. A down payment request isn't recognized as an asset or a liability in the balance sheet nor in the profit and lost (P&L) statement. With the use of **Trg.Sp.G/L Ind.,** the posting becomes a shadow posting. There are different general ledger indicators, such as **A** for down payment on current assets, **C** for rent deposit, **D** for doubtful receivables, and so on.

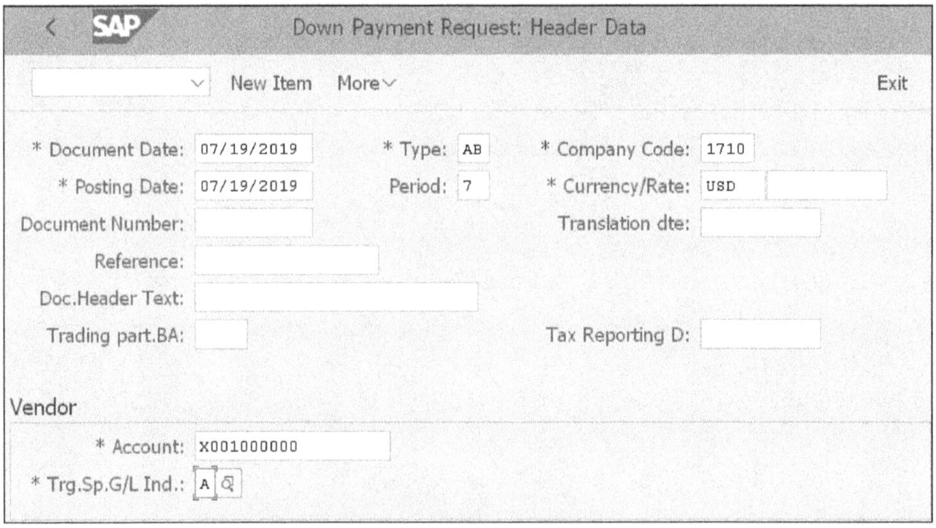

Figure 4.68 Down Payment Request: Header Data Screen

After the header data has been completed, click the **New Item** button at the top of the screen, which opens the **Down Payment Request Add Vendor item** screen, as shown in Figure 4.69.

Fill in the required **Amount** and **Due on** fields for the down payment. Depending on your requirements, you may also fill in the **Payt Method**, **Cost Center**, **Profit Ctr**, **Order**, and so on.

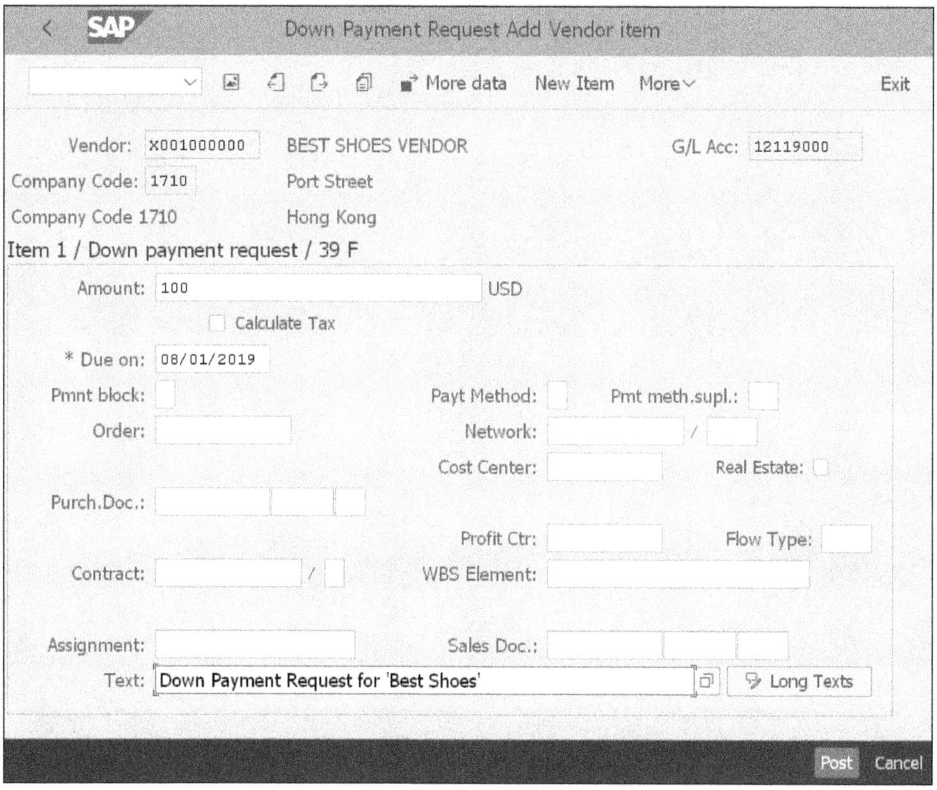

Figure 4.69 Adding the Vendor for the Down Payment Request

When you've completed the vendor item's fields, click the **Post** button. You'll receive a message with a new document number posted in your company. Now, this payment request is ready to be paid to the specified vendor following the instructions already explained in Section 4.4.2.

SAP Fiori Apps

The corresponding SAP Fiori app is called Manage Supplier Down Payment Requests (F1688), as shown in Figure 1.70. To create a down payment request, click on the **Create** button on the right side of the screen. Although it looks different, as shown in Figure

---

4.71, the same fields need to be filled, and then you can click the **Post** button to finish the creation step of a down payment request.

Figure 4.70 Down Payment Request in SAP Fiori (1)

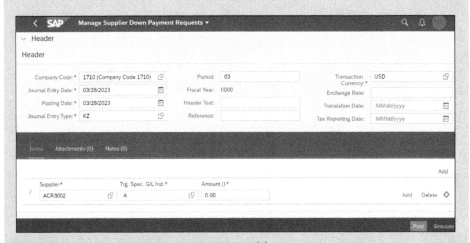

Figure 4.71 Down Payment Request in SAP Fiori (2)

In addition, SAP Fiori offers the helpful Monitor Purchase Order Down Payments app (F2877) to monitor all down payment requests relating to purchase orders in the system. When you start the app, you can choose a **Display Currency** (e.g., **USD**) and then click **Go** to get a graphical overview and list of the relevant purchase order and down payment documents grouped by suppliers, as shown in Figure 4.72. After marking a purchase order line (line is highlighted blue), as shown in Figure 4.73, you can create a down payment request for the marked purchase order. Just click on **Create Down Payment Request**, and you'll be redirected to the Manage Supplier Down Payment Requests app, explained at the beginning of this box. This procedure has the advantage that thanks to the link to the purchase order, all required fields are prefilled so that you just have to click the **Post** button to finish the transaction, as shown in Figure 4.74.

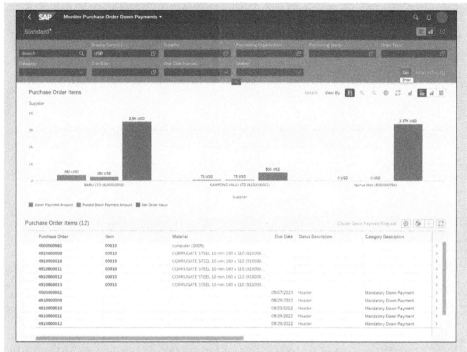

Figure 4.72 Monitor Purchase Order Down Payments (1)

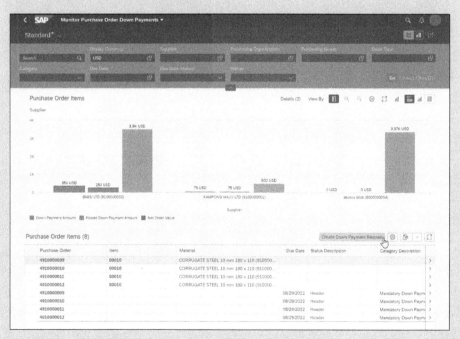

Figure 4.73 Monitor Purchase Order Down Payments (2)

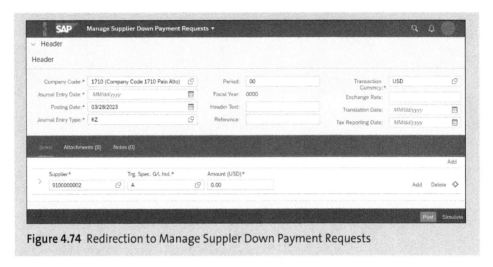

Figure 4.74 Redirection to Manage Suppler Down Payment Requests

In the upcoming section, we'll discuss the period-end closing of the accounts payable subledger, referring to the most important topics, such as accounts payable reconciliation, valuation of foreign currency, GR/IR accounts clearing process, and reporting.

4.6   Accounts Payable Period-End Closing

We took our first look at period-end closing for the general ledger in Chapter 3, Section 3.6. Before continuing with these closing operations in general ledger accounting, you first need to perform the closing process in the subledger accounting you're using—in this case, accounts payable. In this section, we'll describe accounts payable reconciliation, foreign currency valuation, reclassification runs, and GR/IR clearing.

4.6.1   Opening and Closing Periods

SAP S/4HANA provides many possibilities for a company to improve the financial closing process. In many companies, accounts payable is closed at the end of each period to ensure accuracy in the vendor files for the period-to-date and year-to-date totals. In the closing process, all information in the current period is transferred into the vendor history file. The completed transactions, such as paid invoices, are also discarded from the current period file, so you can control the amount of information contained in the current period transaction report. When there are a large number of transactions, the closing period could also occur on a daily basis. Therefore, when the period-end closing comes, there will be fewer transactions to be transferred and higher accuracy.

In SAP S/4HANA, you can open and close periods in accounts payable financial accounting by following application menu path **Accounting • Financial Accounting • Accounts Payable • Environment • Current Settings • Open and Close Posting Periods** or using Transaction FAGL_EHP4_T001B_COFI.

Double-click the selected transaction, and the **Determine Work Area: Entry** screen pops up where you have to enter the posting period variant, for example, "1710", as shown in Figure 4.75.

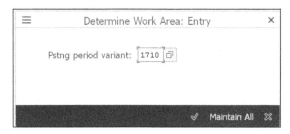

Figure 4.75 Accounts Payable Posting Period Variant

Click on the green checkmark to go to the **Specify Time Interval: Overview** screen. Click the **New Entries** button to arrive at the screen shown in Figure 4.76.

Fill in the key fields shown in Table 4.1 (as described in Chapter 3, Section 3.6.1). The only difference for accounts payable is the relevant account type (**A**), which is **K** in accounts payable.

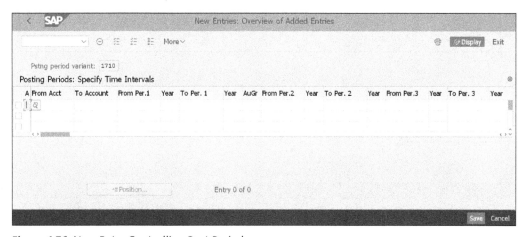

Figure 4.76 New Entry Controlling Post Period

#	Description
A	This is the account type where you can find these possible values: **+** (valid for all account types), **A** (assets), **D** (customers), **K** (vendors), **M** (materials), **S** (general ledger accounts), and **V** (contract accounts).
From Acct	Enter the account number range for which you want to change the periods.

Table 4.1 Important Fields in Controlling Posting Periods

#	Description
To Account	Define a range of account numbers starting with the from account number and ending with the to account number.
From Per.1	Enter a posting period from which you want to open the posting period.
Year	Enter the fiscal year for which you want to open the posting period.
To Per. 1	Define a range of posting periods for which you want to enter posting periods.
Year	Define a range of years for which you want to open posting periods.

Table 4.1 Important Fields in Controlling Posting Periods (Cont.)

Save all the entered data in Figure 4.76, and the result will be shown as in Figure 4.77.

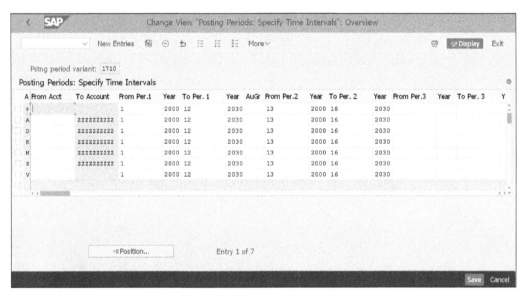

Figure 4.77 Accounts Payable Controlling Posting Periods

SAP Fiori App

The corresponding SAP Fiori app is called Manage Posting Periods (F2293). During period-end closing, the general ledger account should change the fiscal posting period so all financial postings are performed in the corresponding period. In this way, the correct financial operation result is ensured. This app helps to change, schedule, or monitor the periods easily.

In Figure 4.78, you can see how the mentioned app looks in SAP Fiori. You need to enter the **Posting Period Variant**, **Fiscal Year Variant**, and **Account Type** (e.g., **+** for all account types, **A** for assets, **D** for customers, **K** for vendors, etc.). Then click the **Go** button to show the results of this app.

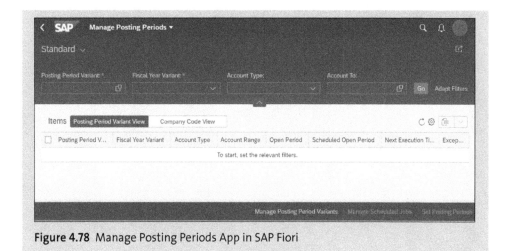

Figure 4.78 Manage Posting Periods App in SAP Fiori

4.6.2   Foreign Currency Valuation

In this section, we'll explain the foreign currency valuation and the necessary configurations you need to apply to run the valuation. If you want to create the financial statement of your company, you should carry out a foreign currency valuation so that the account balances are revaluated at the reporting date.

To access the foreign currency valuation in accounts payable, follow application menu path **Accounting • Financial Accounting • Accounts Payable • Periodic Processing • Closing • Valuate • Valuation of Open Items in Foreign Currency**, or use Transaction FAGL_FCV. You'll arrive at the screen shown in Figure 4.79.

Enter the required data in the **General Selections** and **Selection of Key Date** areas of the screen, such as **Company Code**, **Valuation Area**, and **Valuation Key Date**. Go through the following tabs and settings:

- **Postings**
  Select **Test Run (No Database Update)**, which controls whether the test run takes place or not, or **Simulation Run**, which enables you to simulate a foreign currency valuation run in the same valuation area as the production run, in posting mode. In the **Simulation Settings**, define the **Simulation Ledger** in which the simulation run results are stored. Choose whether or not to delete the existing simulation data. You can enter the other fields as well if necessary.

- **Open Items: Subledger**
  Define the vendor range to perform the valuation of open items for certain vendor accounts to specify the open items.

- **Open Items: G/L Accounts**
  Define the selection criteria to valuate open items for certain general ledger accounts.

- **G/L Account Balances**
  Specify that the balances of the selected general ledger accounts will be evaluated.

- **Output / Technical Settings**
  Enter information about the log storage (if the logs are saved in the database or not), name the result list, and configure some other settings if needed.

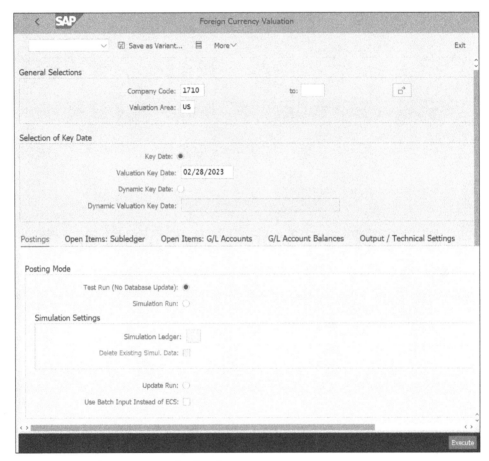

Figure 4.79 Foreign Currency Valuation Screen

After you've entered and selected all necessary data, click on the **Execute** button to generate the valuation document.

SAP Fiori App

The corresponding SAP Fiori app is called Perform Foreign Currency Valuation (FAGL_FCV), which is visually and functionally the same as the SAP GUI transaction. If you run SAP S/4HANA Cloud 2208 or 2302, there is a new app called Foreign Currency Valuation Run (F5985), which simplifies the procedure a bit and is more user friendly.

4.6.3   Goods Receipt/Invoice Receipt Clearing

As we discussed in Chapter 3, Section 3.6.4, the GR/IR clearing account itself is a program that investigates GR/IR clearing accounts at a defined key date and generates adjustment postings if needed. These are important to show the business transactions correctly in the balance sheet such as goods delivered but not invoiced or goods invoiced but not delivered.

The main purpose of this program for accounts payable is to clear the clearing accounts or the offset accounts involved and impacted during the GR/IR posting process. It selects all open items in GR/IR clearing accounts and then checks whether or not the open items per purchase order number and item in local currency balance to a zero amount. If they don't balance each other, the clearing run creates adjustment postings accordingly.

On a daily basis, it's very likely that discrepancies between the goods receipt and the quantity invoiced for a specific purchase order may arise. These discrepancies consequently could cause a fictitious positive (credit) or a negative (debit) balance. The GR/IR clearing run will do simple logic in this circumstance by performing a check between the quantity of received goods and those invoiced. Then, according to the results, a credit or a debit balance will be posted. This process should be executed periodically, for example, at the end of a month, quarter, or at least every fiscal year.

To execute GR/IR clearing, run Transaction F.19, or follow application menu path **Accounting • Financial Accounting • General Ledger • Periodic Processing • Closing • Reclassify • GR/IR Clearing**. The **Analyze GR/IR Clearing Accounts and Display Acquisition Tax** screen appears, as shown in Figure 4.80.

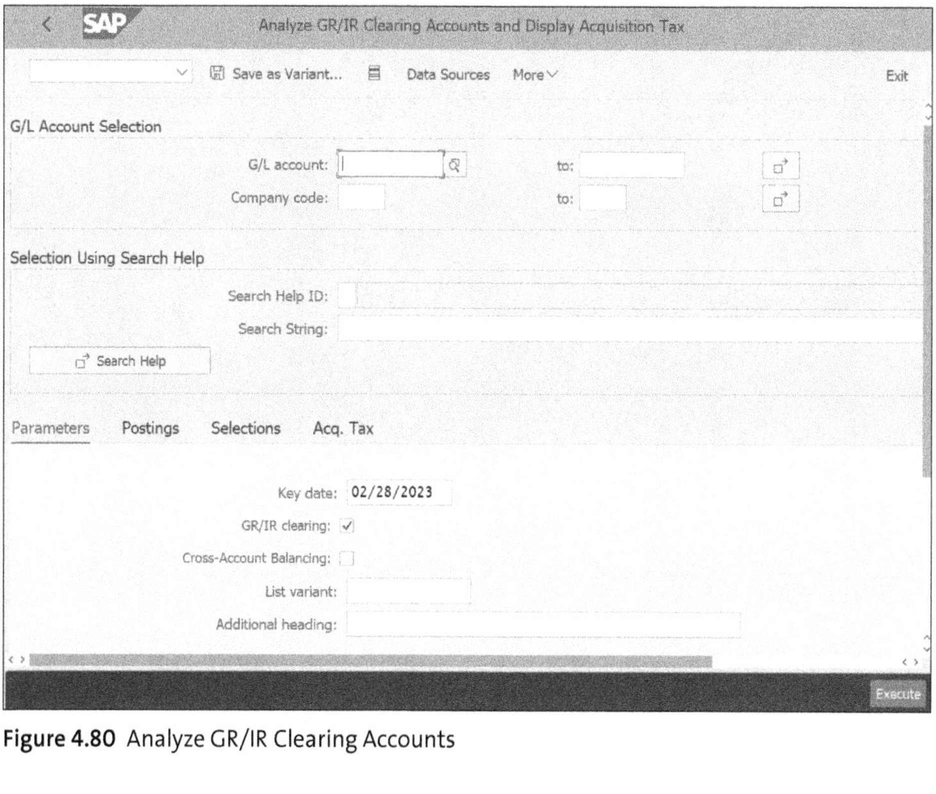

Figure 4.80 Analyze GR/IR Clearing Accounts

With this transaction, you can analyze different GR/IR clearing accounts for a specified key date. Enter the **Document date** and the **Posting date** in the **Postings** tab. In the **Selections** tab, restrict the searching to certain vendors, reconciliation accounts, and so on. Enter data in the **Acq. Tax** (acquisition tax) tab if necessary. It can be relevant in very special cases where you can deduct input tax in a value-added tax (VAT) regime, such as France.

As described in Chapter 3, Section 3.6.4, adjustments to GR/IR are crucial for reporting to get an accurate period cutoff of assets and liabilities. However, these period-end adjustments must reverse in the beginning of the new period because subsequent purchasing activity may occur and net GR/IR line items to zero. Therefore, you can enter a specific **Reversal posting date** on the **Postings** tab, as shown in Figure 4.81. If you don't enter a date, the program reverses the postings on the next day following the **Key date**.

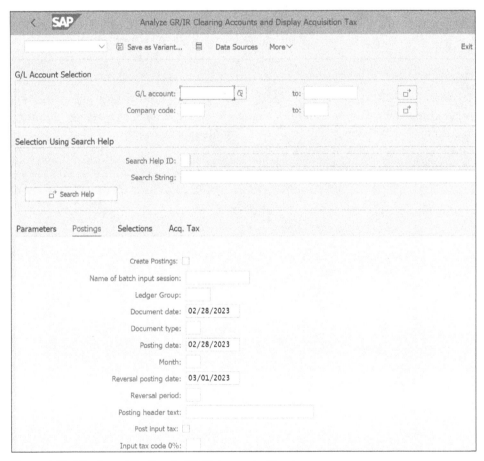

Figure 4.81 Adjustment Posting in GR/IR Accounts Clearing

Now that the GR/IR clearing run is complete, the accounts payable open item clearing has to be run too. We'll show how this works in the next section.

4.6.4   Automatic Open Item Clearing

To run the automatic open item clearing for accounts payable, you can use Transaction F.13 or follow application menu path **Accounting • Financial Accounting • Accounts Payable • Periodic Processing • Automatic Clearing • Automatic Clearing**.

This program performs the automatic clearing of the open items from specified vendors and selects all accounts specified in the value sets with debit and credit postings. In the **Automatic Clearing** screen that appears, as shown in Figure 4.82 and Figure 4.83, you can enter the following required data: **Company Code**, **Fiscal Year**, **Assignment** (as an additional information reference field of the open item [transaction] posted in the line item), **Document Number**, **Posting Date**, and so on.

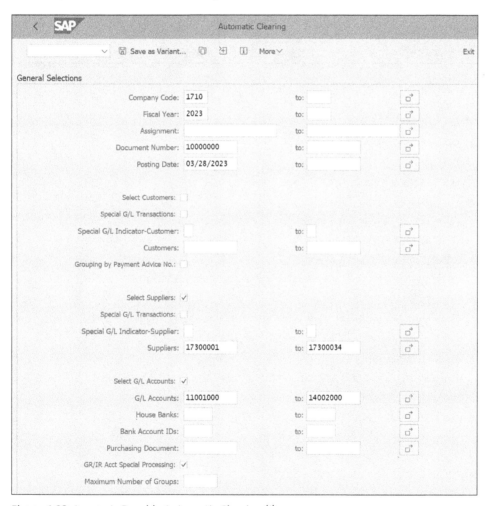

Figure 4.82 Accounts Payable Automatic Clearing (1)

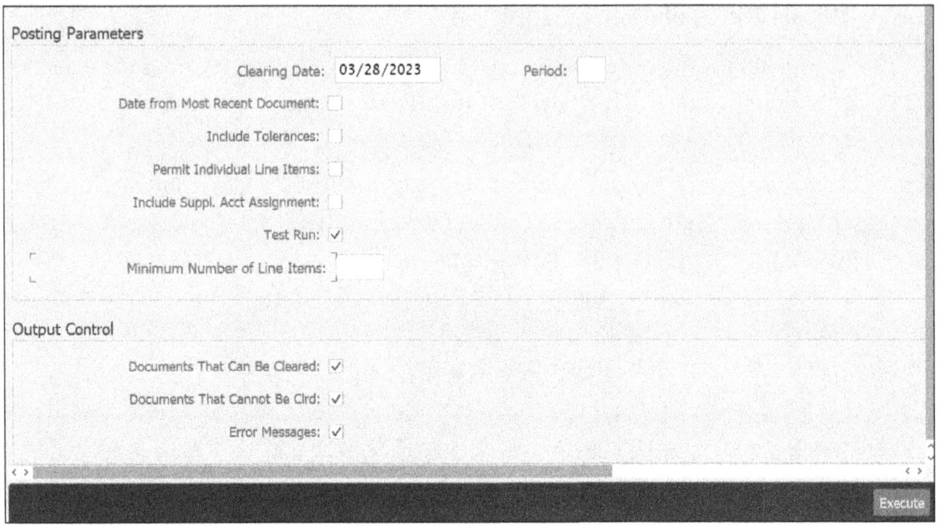

Figure 4.83 Accounts Payable Automatic Clearing (2)

Then, select the checkboxes that are relevant for the vendor:

- **Select Suppliers**
  By selecting this field, all vendor open items that aren't special general ledger transactions are selected.

- **Special G/L Transactions**
  By selecting this field, all open items on the credit side that are special general ledger transactions are selected.

- **Special G/L Indicator-Supplier**
  This indicator identifies a special general ledger transaction.

- **Suppliers**
  Here, you can define an alphanumeric key or range of keys that uniquely identifies the vendor in the SAP S/4HANA system.

- **Select G/L Accounts**
  By selecting this field, you can perform the valuation of open items for certain general ledger accounts.

- **G/L Accounts**
  Here, the general ledger account number is defined that identifies the general ledger account in a chart of accounts.

- **GR/IR Acct Special Processing**
  By selecting this field, documents are assigned to GR/IR accounts using the material document, in addition to the purchase order number and the purchase order item.

You can also fill in or check the other fields, but, in general, selecting the relevant fields is up to the specific case of your company.

For GR/IR accounts, the program logic performs a check of matching documents (goods receipts and invoice receipts) that can be cleared. Regarding the GR/IR matching and clearing process, the **Automatic Clearing** screen provides the **GR/IR Acct Special Processing** checkbox, which you can select if the assignment of goods receipts to the corresponding invoice receipts based on the purchase order number and purchase order item is insufficient. This indicator then not only matches GR/IR items by purchase order number and purchase order item but also by material document if a goods receipt–related invoice verification is defined in the purchase order item.

After you've filled in all the required data, you can click the **Execute** button. A detail list screen appears (see Figure 4.84), showing the details of the selected item to be cleared. After the test run was performed successfully, you can run the real transaction by unchecking the **Test Run** checkbox shown previously in Figure 4.83.

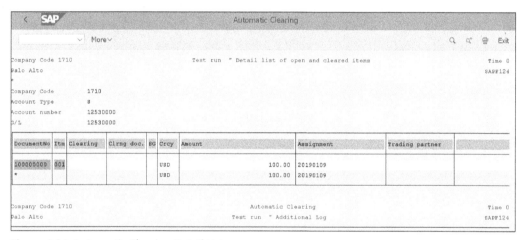

Figure 4.84 Automatic Clearing Detail List

SAP Fiori App

The corresponding SAP Fiori app is called Clear GR/IR Clearing Account (MR11). It's visually and functionally the same as the SAP GUI transaction.

In the next section, we'll discuss reclassification of accounts payable within the financial closing process.

4.6.5   Reclassification Run

While preparing financial statements, there are two requirements to be fulfilled for accounts payable:

- Display the debit balance on the vendor account as a receivable and the credit balance on the customer account as a payable in such cases.
- Sort items based on the remaining terms for balance sheet reporting.

In this section, we'll walk through the reclassification run process, starting with the necessary configuration and ending with performing the run itself.

Configure

For the *reclassification* process, also called the regrouping process, some basic configurations must be applied. You must define a sort method interval in Customizing as well as accounts determination for the reclassification. To do so, follow application menu path **Tools • Customizing • IMG • SPRO – Execute Project • SAP Reference IMG • Financial Accounting • General Ledger Accounting • Periodic Processing • Reclassify • Transfer and Sort Receivables and Payables • Define Sort Method and Adjustment Accts for Regrouping Receivables/Payables**. In the **Change View "Sort Methods": Overview** screen that appears (see Figure 4.85), view the existing intervals by double-clicking the **Payables** folder. The **Change View "Payables": Overview** screen opens (see Figure 4.86).

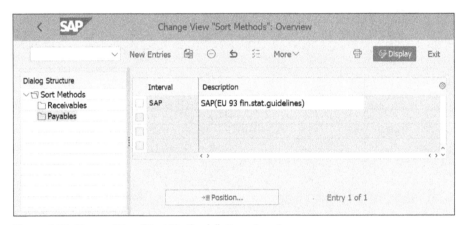

Figure 4.85 Change View "Sort Methods": Overview Screen

You can see that the configuration contains three account determination keys for this sort method in the **Accounts** column with the values **V02**, **V03**, and **V04**, respectively. These keys define accounts or posting keys to transfer posting of open items, indicate time intervals of the sort method, which type of posting will be used, the managing method, and so on. These keys are also linked to the particular general ledger accounts, which are taken into consideration during processing. The first column (**Descending**) specifies the remaining life for the sorting of open items. **Time unit** indicates the time dimension (days, months, years).

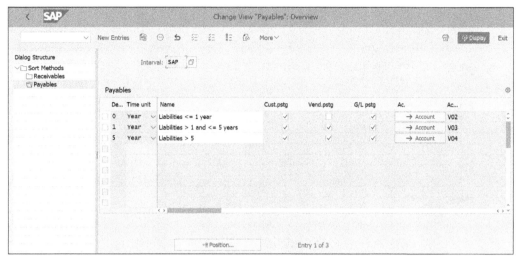

Figure 4.86 Change View "Payables": Overview Screen

In the **G/L pstg** column, select the checkbox to carry out transfer postings for this account type. In the **Accounts** column, define the chart of accounts you'll use.

Click on the **Account** button (under the **Ac.** column) in the first account determination key (**V02**), where you'll be asked to define the chart of accounts you're using in the following screen (see Figure 4.87). In this example, the standard chart of accounts **YCOA** is used. In the **Account assignment** area, you'll see the list of accounts defined to be used for the key.

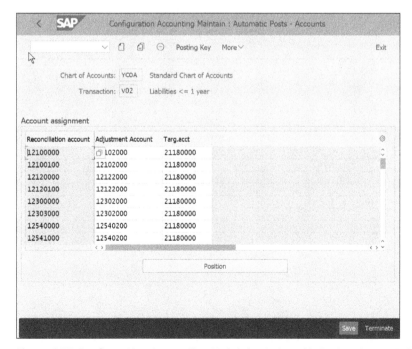

Figure 4.87 Configuration Accounting Maintain: Automatic Posts – Accounts Screen

The first column **Reconciliation account** contains the reconciliation accounts specified for the sorting and grouping program. The **Adjustment Account** column contains the adjustment accounts that will be posted to. The **Targ.acct** column is for the target account that will be used for the offset postings.

Process Open Items

Now that you've completed the configuration steps, let's focus on the processing of open items using the reclassification/regrouping report. To process open items, you can run Transaction FAGLF101 or follow application menu path **Accounting • Financial Accounting • Accounts Payable • Periodic Processing • Closing • Sorting/Reclassification (New)**.

The **Balance Sheet Supplement - OI - Analysis** screen appears, as shown in Figure 4.88. In the header area, enter the **Company Code** and **Balance Sheet Key Date**, as well as the **Sort Method**, which is a unique key used for sorting open items according to a method and valuation area. Then, in the **Selections** tab, enter the account type for vendor ("K") and the **Supplier** number. In the **Parameters** tab, you can select any options in the **Grouping** area, in **Other Parameters**, and in **List Output** to define the layout for the list format. In the **Output** tab, you can define the log storage criteria, such as displaying logs, saving logs, and entering the name under which the system stores the results list.

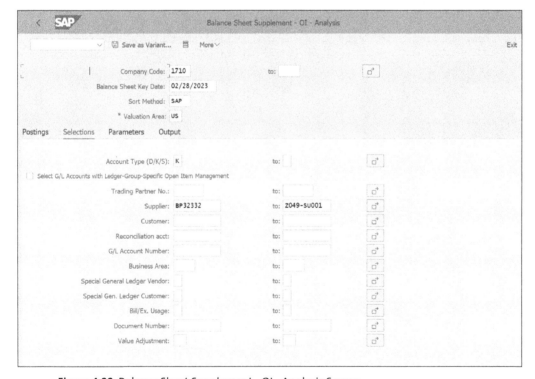

Figure 4.88 Balance Sheet Supplement - OI - Analysis Screen

Now, run the report by clicking the **Execute** button. The results will appear as shown in Figure 4.89. As you can see, the report in this example has been grouped by account and summed on valuated amount.

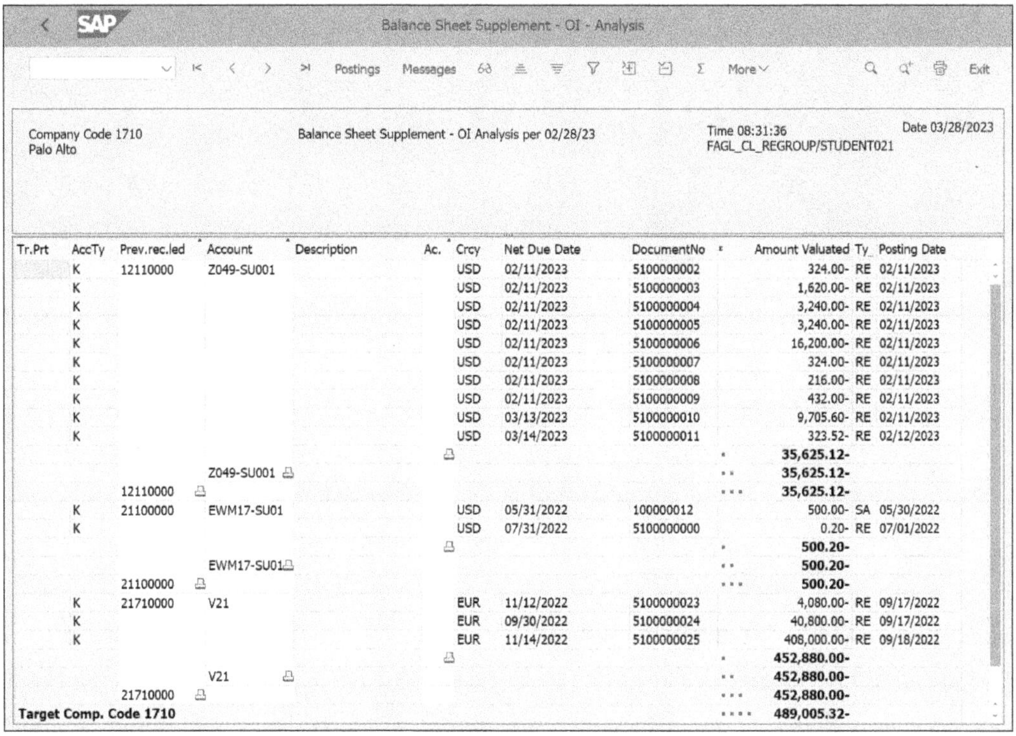

Tr.Prt	AccTy	Prev.rec.led	Account	Description	Ac.	Crcy	Net Due Date	DocumentNo		Amount Valuated	Ty	Posting Date
	K	12110000	Z049-SU001			USD	02/11/2023	5100000002		324.00-	RE	02/11/2023
	K					USD	02/11/2023	5100000003		1,620.00-	RE	02/11/2023
	K					USD	02/11/2023	5100000004		3,240.00-	RE	02/11/2023
	K					USD	02/11/2023	5100000005		3,240.00-	RE	02/11/2023
	K					USD	02/11/2023	5100000006		16,200.00-	RE	02/11/2023
	K					USD	02/11/2023	5100000007		324.00-	RE	02/11/2023
	K					USD	02/11/2023	5100000008		216.00-	RE	02/11/2023
	K					USD	02/11/2023	5100000009		432.00-	RE	02/11/2023
	K					USD	03/13/2023	5100000010		9,705.60-	RE	02/11/2023
	K					USD	03/14/2023	5100000011		323.52-	RE	02/12/2023
									•	**35,625.12-**		
			Z049-SU001						••	**35,625.12-**		
		12110000							•••	**35,625.12-**		
	K	21100000	EWM17-SU01			USD	05/31/2022	100000012		500.00-	SA	05/30/2022
	K					USD	07/31/2022	5100000000		0.20-	RE	07/01/2022
									•	**500.20-**		
			EWM17-SU01						••	**500.20-**		
		21100000							•••	**500.20-**		
	K	21710000	V21			EUR	11/12/2022	5100000023		4,080.00-	RE	09/17/2022
	K					EUR	09/30/2022	5100000024		40,800.00-	RE	09/17/2022
	K					EUR	11/14/2022	5100000025		408,000.00-	RE	09/18/2022
									•	**452,880.00-**		
			V21						••	**452,880.00-**		
		21710000							•••	**452,880.00-**		
Target Comp. Code 1710									••••	**489,005.32-**		

Figure 4.89 Balance Sheet Supplement Result

Now referring to the initial screen (refer to Figure 4.88), go to the **Postings** tab, and select the following checkboxes, as shown in Figure 4.90:

- **Generate Postings**
  The system starts to immediately execute the posting created during the report run.
- **Use Batch Input Instead of ECS**
  The system generates a default file named **FAGL_CL_REGR**, where the postings are stored. You can remove this value if you want to make the posting immediately.

In this way, you can view the posting records for the regrouped payables.

Click on the **Execute** button, and the postings start to be generated. You can review the batch input session using Transaction SM35, which also includes the mentioned batch input file.

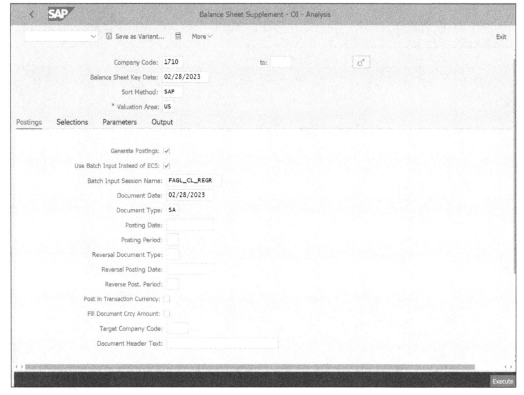

Figure 4.90 Balance Sheet Supplement: Postings Tab

SAP Fiori App

The corresponding SAP Fiori app is called Regroup Receivables/Payables (FAGLF101). It's visually and functionally the same as the SAP GUI transaction.

Now that you know how to run resorting and reclassification of accounts payable, let's continue with another important financial accounting process: accounts payable reconciliation.

4.6.6   Accounts Payable Reconciliations

Unlike in SAP ERP, now all information related to financial documents is stored in one single table in SAP S/4HANA instead of multiple tables. As Chapter 1 explained, table ACDOCA contains data that formerly had been stored in separated tables, such as ledger, asset accounting, controlling, Material Ledger, and so on. From a technical perspective, reconciliation of multiple tables or modules is now avoided. However, from an accounting content perspective, there may be some problems due to master data records that aren't maintained well, changes, failures in reconciliation account master data, or manual postings, which make it necessary to reconcile accounts payable with general ledger anyway.

In this section, we'll explain and perform an accounts payable reconciliation. At the end of each reporting period, before closing the books, it must be verified that the total in the accounts payable outstanding balance matches the accounts payable balance in the general ledger. In this way, the financial accounting department ensures the accuracy of the reported accounts payable figures in the balance sheet.

For each vendor, a separate account is created in the subledger that is linked with a certain SAP S/4HANA reconciliation account. When you create a vendor master record, the system will require you to enter the **Reconciliation acct** field, as you saw in Section 4.2.2. The reconciliation account is considered a control account to perform the reconciliation between the subledgers and the general ledger. You know that when you post an item to a vendor subledger account, the same amount is automatically posted to the general ledger, which is the related reconciliation account assigned to this vendor.

In Chapter 3, Section 3.1.2, you've already learned how to create and display a reconciliation account in a master record. In this section, we'll explain how to perform the reconciliation process in accounts payable.

During closing periods, no matter if it's month-end, quarter-end, or year-end, it's necessary to compare the transaction figures with the total balances of the posted items. The system will perform a comparative analysis as follows:

- Comparing the debit and credit balances/figures of the vendor accounts with the total balances (credit and debit) of posted items
- Comparing the debit and credit balances/figures with the application indexes/secondary indexes (secondary indexes used for accounts administered on an open item basis or for line-item display)

With reconciliation accounts for all subledgers, subledger to general ledger reconciliation is guaranteed by financial accounting in SAP S/4HANA and its integration model. However, accountants love to reconcile balances. For this reason, there are a couple of reconciliation reports that show the accumulated values of the subledgers and compare these values (either balances of subledger accounts or the sum of subledger posting document amounts) with balances of the general ledger reconciliation accounts. We'll walk through these in the following sections.

Note

You must close the posting period for which you're going to perform the reconciliation process/comparative analysis. In this way, you're sure that no adjustments are made to the transaction figures or items/documents during the reconciliation process. Changes performed during the reconciliation could cause problems.

Display Documents

Now, let's see what it looks like to assign the reconciliation account to a vendor after you perform a payment by going back to Section 4.1.5, where you performed a manual payment using Transaction F-53 to clear a vendor open item of PHP 112,000. The document number created after the payment is 1500000003. Using the display document transaction in accounts payable, Transaction FB03, you can show the document created for the cleared item (see Figure 4.91). You can access this transaction by following menu path **Accounting • Financial Accounting • General Ledger • Document • Display**.

Figure 4.91 Display Document Entry after Payment

Figure 4.92 General Ledger View

The financial entry posting the bank account and vendor account is shown in the **Data Entry View** area. If you click on the **General Ledger View** button, the screen will appear with the same entries but showing the reconciliation account assigned to the vendor master data, **AP Dom (Recon) V** (see Figure 4.92). The posting entry performed to the vendor account is automatically reflected to the reconciliation account as well.

Compare Balances and Open Items

To perform accounts payable reconciliation, it's recommended to compare general ledger account balances with accounts payable balances and accounts payable open items. Compare vendor balances by accessing the vendor balances report using Transaction S_ALR_87012082 menu path **Accounting • Financial Accounting • Accounts Payable • Information System • Reports for Accounts Payable Accounting • Vendor Balances • Vendor Balances in Local Currency**.

The screen shown in Figure 4.93 appears after you double-click on the report name. Here, you define the selection criteria, such as **Company code**, **Vendor account** (if you want to limit searching to a certain vendor), **Fiscal Year**, **Reporting periods**, **Reconciliation account**, and so on. You can also fill in other fields if required.

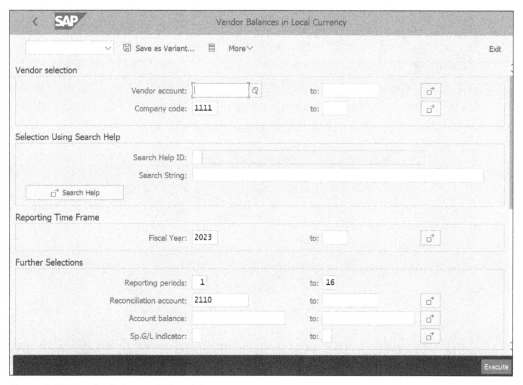

Figure 4.93 Vendor Balances in Local Currency

Click the **Execute** button, and the results will be shown as in Figure 4.94.

Vendor Balances in Local Currency

@YourService PH — Vendor Balances in Local Currency — Time 20:04:06 — Date 03/28/2023
Quezon City — RFKSLD00/USER65 — Page 1
Carryforwd Perio 00 - 00 2023 Reporting Period 01 - 16 2023

CoCd	Reconciliation Acct	Supplier	SearchTerm	Sp.G/LInd.	Crcy	Balance Carryforward	Debit Blnce of Reportng Period	Credit Balance Reporting Per.	Accumulated Balance
1111	2110	300	RONALDM		PHP	460.000,00-	113.000,00	0,00	347.000,00-
1111	2110	302	BACON		PHP	114.736,88-	0,00	0,00	114.736,88-
1111	2110	303	RONALDM		PHP	110.062,50-	0,00	51.500,00	161.562,50-
1111	2110	306	RR		PHP	134.400,00-	0,00	0,00	134.400,00-
1111	2110	307	RR		PHP	13.608.000,00-	0,00	0,00	13.608.000,00-
* 1111	2110				PHP	14.427.199,38-	113.000,00	51.500,00	14.365.699,38-
** 1111					PHP	14.427.199,38-	113.000,00	51.500,00	14.365.699,38-
***					PHP	14.427.199,38-	113.000,00	51.500,00	14.365.699,38-

@YourService PH — Vendor Balances in Local Currency — Time 20:04:06 — Date 03/28/2023
Quezon City — RFKSLD00/USER65 — Page 2
Carryforwd Perio 00 - 00 2023 Reporting Period 01 - 16 2023
T O T A L S F R O M A L L C O M P A N Y C O D E S

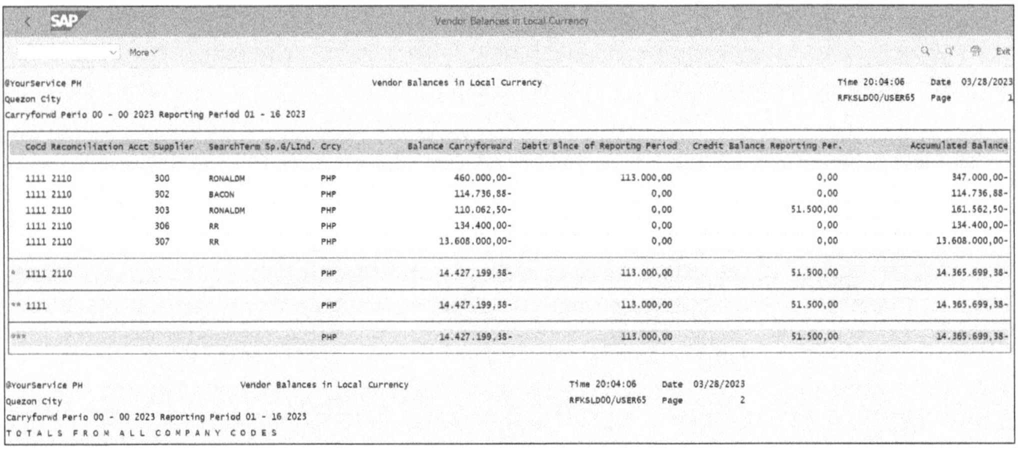

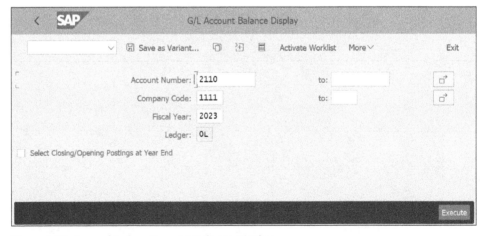

Figure 4.94 Vendor Balance in Local Currency Overview

From these results, you can see a list of all vendor account balances line by line, starting with the balance carryforward, debit entries balance, credit entries balance, and accumulated balance. It sums up all the columns and gives you a total on the general ledger reconciliation account level.

To compare accounts payable balances with general ledger balances, access the balance on reconciliation general ledger report via Transaction FAGLB03 or menu path **Accounting • Financial Accounting • General Ledger • Account • Display Balances**.

The screen shown in Figure 4.95 appears when you double-click on the transaction code. Enter the required data, such as **Account Number**, **Company Code**, and **Fiscal Year**, as well as **Ledger**, which defines a ledger in general ledger accounting.

Figure 4.95 General Ledger Account Balance Display

Click the **Execute** button, and the results will appear as in Figure 4.96, showing the account balance evolution through the fiscal year. For every reporting period from **1** to

16, you can see the debit and credit balances, the balance for the individual period, and a cumulative reporting year-to-date balance. For further investigation, you can easily drill down on any value to see the items from which the balance is made.

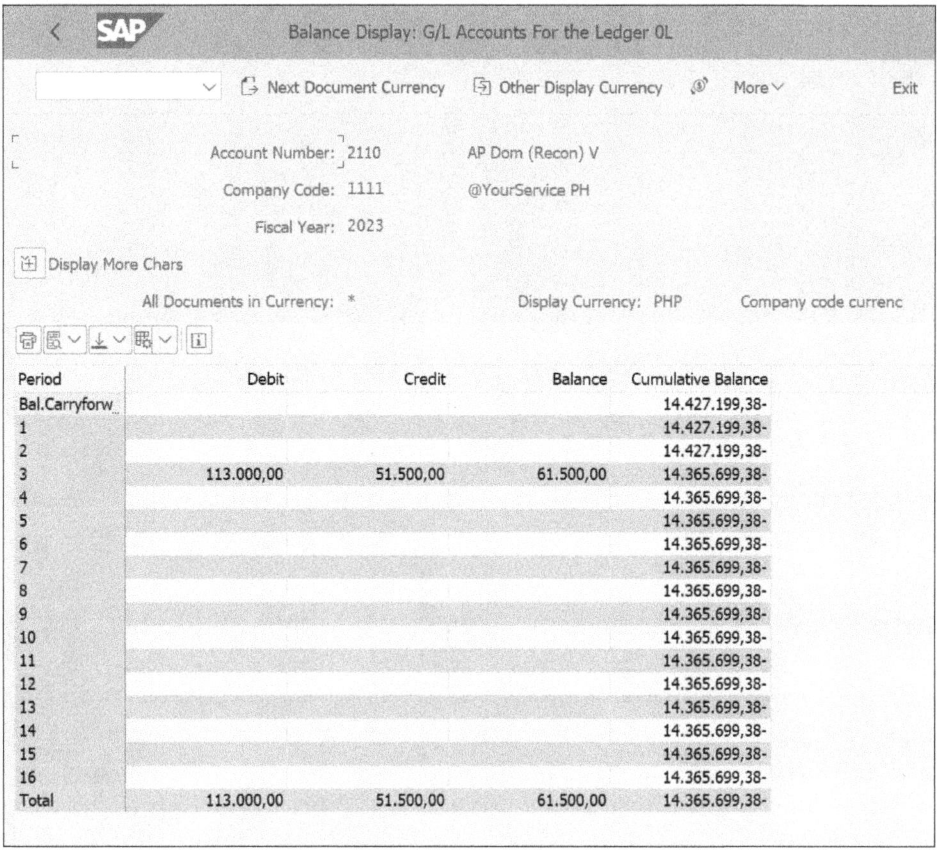

Figure 4.96 Display Balance Overview for Account 2110

To compare general ledger accounts with open accounts payable items, access the vendor open items report by using Transaction S_ALR_87012103 or by following menu path **Accounting • Financial Accounting • Accounts Payable • Information System • Reports for Accounts Payable Accounting • Vendor Items • List of Vendor Line Items.**

The screen shown in Figure 4.97 appears. Enter the required data, such as **Vendor account** (if you want to limit searching criteria on certain vendors) **Company code**, **Open Items** (if you want to show open items), **Cleared Items**, or **All Items**. Under the **Type** area, you can select any of the listed parameters, such as **Standard Documents** (determines that only documents relevant to the accounting department will be evaluated), **Parked documents** (the program also selects the documents from preliminary posting), and **Noted Items** (noted items are to be evaluated). In the **Further Selections** area (not shown), define the line-item reconciliation account number. If required, you can also fill in or check the other available fields.

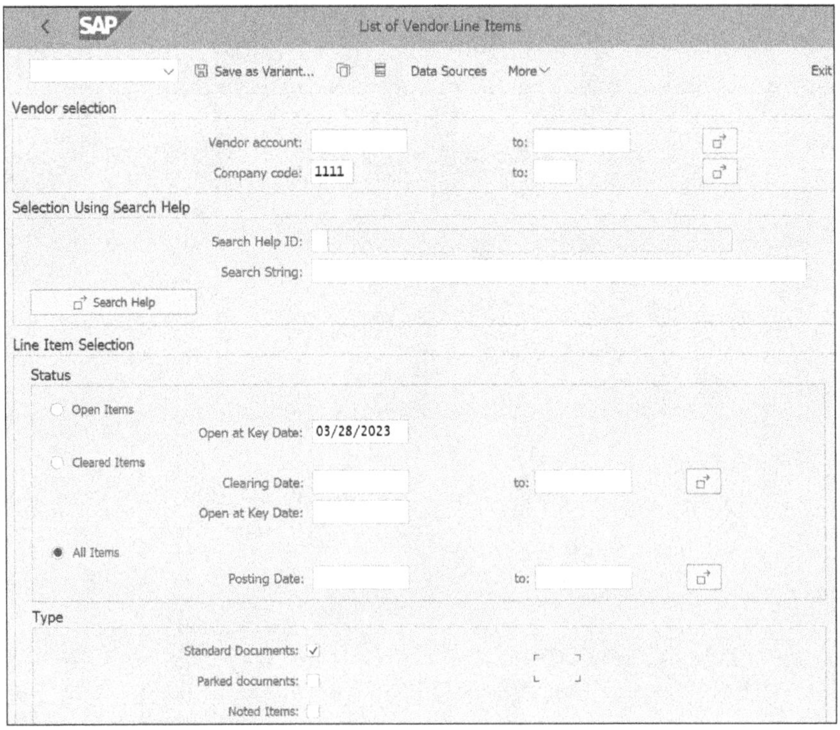

Figure 4.97 List of Vendor Line Items

Click the **Execute** button to execute the report. The result shows all the vendor items for company code 1710 and the complete names and addresses of the vendors (see Figure 4.98 and Figure 4.99). In the end of the report, you can compare the sum of all vendor items posted to account **2110** with Figure 4.96. They both result in the same **14,365,699.38**.

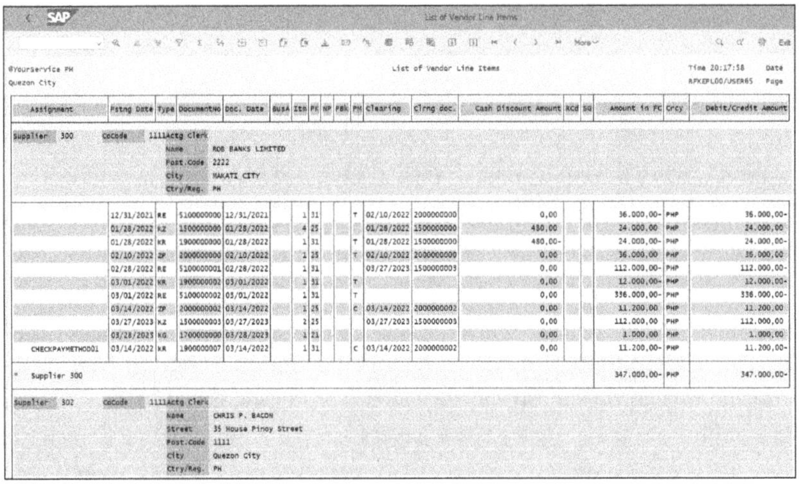

Figure 4.98 List of Vendor Line Items (1)

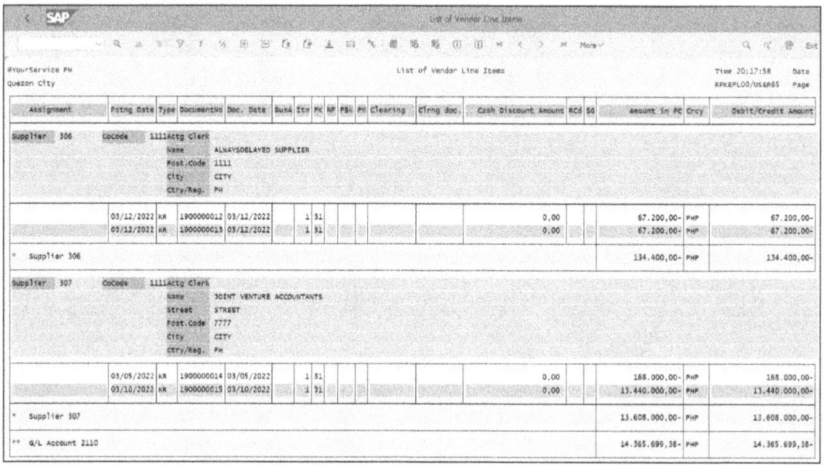

Figure 4.99 List of Vendor Line Items (2)

SAP Fiori App

In SAP Fiori, instead of running each report, you can use the Display Line Item in General Ledger app (F2217). In the screen that appears, enter **Ledger**, **Company Code**, **G/L Account**, item **Status**, **Open on Key Date**, and **Ledger Fiscal Year**, as shown in Figure 4.100.

You can add the supplier name column through the settings icon ⚙. In the search box, select the name of the supplier, and put it in front using drag and drop. Then, if the list of items is too long and belonging to a huge number of suppliers, you can group it by supplier name (right-click on the **Name of Supplier** column, and select **Group**), and the final result is shown in Figure 4.101. What you get is a simple vendor balances report. This is an example of a simplification using new SAP Fiori apps.

Figure 4.100 Display Line Items in the General Ledger

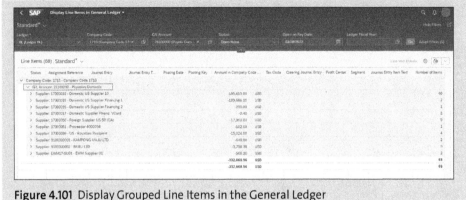

Figure 4.101 Display Grouped Line Items in the General Ledger

4.7   Accounts Payable Reporting

Accounts payable reporting and analyzing features enable companies to verify and track expenses and bill payment, assist with cash flow management, and more. Proper recording of accounts payable entries facilitates the production of timely and accurate reports to ensure that vendors are paid on time and the company credit rating isn't negatively affected. Using accounts payable reporting and analyzing features in SAP S/4HANA, you can produce a variety of reports that provide up-to-date information with drilldown capabilities to investigate source documents. In the following sections, we'll explain some reports and transactions that are recommended for use in the accounts payable ledger.

4.7.1   Accounts Inquiry

You can easily inquire about any vendor accounts to check for supplier invoices, open items, and accounts clearing issues; balance confirmations; and questions from the purchasing department or the vendor.

There are two transaction codes you can use:

- **Transaction FK10N – Display Balances**
  Using this report, you can show a specific supplier balance or a range of supplier balances.

- **Transaction FBL1H – Line Item Browser**
  Using this report, you can show all the supplier line items. The line item browser report displays a list of all aggregated line-item information based on the restrictions applied on the selection screen.

To inquire on an account, follow application path **Accounting • Financial Accounting • Accounts Payable • Account • Display Balances or Line Item Browser**, or use Transactions FK10N or FBL1H, respectively.

You can start with using the vendor account balances (Transaction FK10N – Display Balances). Figure 4.102 shows the account balances for the selected vendor **17300050**.

From there, you can easily drill down to transactions performed in any period. To see the details of all movements on a vendor account, just click on the total in the **Balance** column. You get the complete list of items processed in the fiscal year **2023**, as shown in Figure 4.103. If you would've clicked on **Cumulative Balance**, the system would generate a list of all transactions performed with the vendor—regardless of the year.

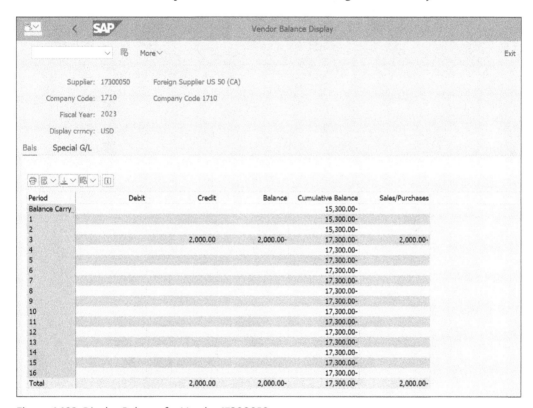

Figure 4.102 Display Balance for Vendor 17300050

By double-clicking on a balance in the **Vendor Balance Display** screen (shown in Figure 4.102), you jump into the vendor line-item display, which you could've also opened by entering Transaction FBL1H. The red status flag means that the items aren't cleared; in this case specifically, it means that the supplier invoices from vendor 17300050 aren't paid. After clearing against an outgoing payment, the status will turn green, which isn't shown in this view.

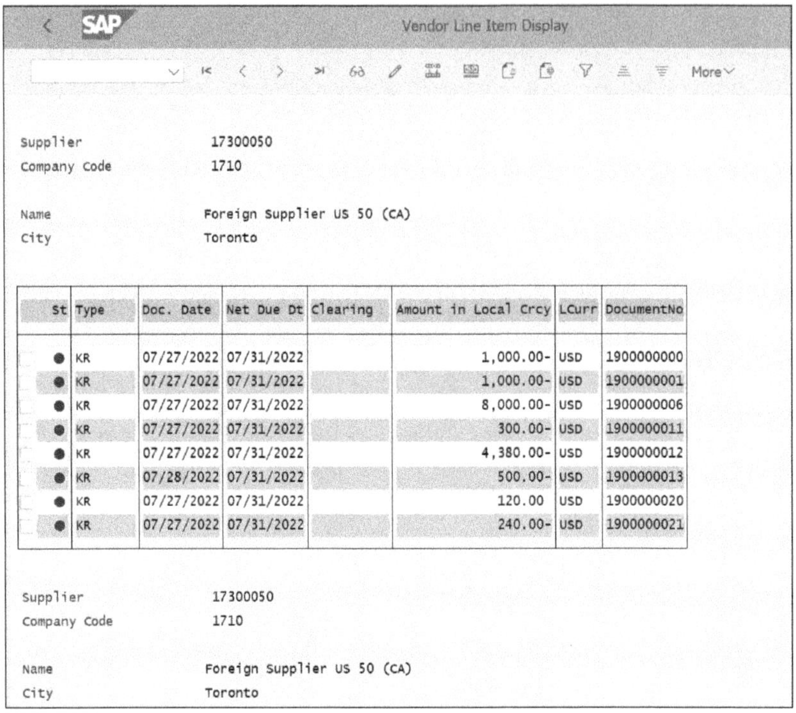

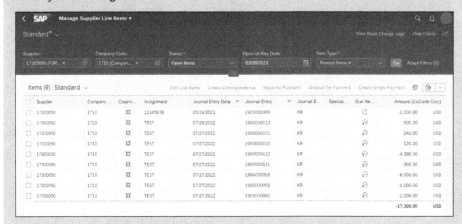

Figure 4.103 Detail Line-Item Report for Vendor Account 17300050

SAP Fiori App

The corresponding SAP Fiori app is called Display Supplier Balances (F0701). From the **Display Supplier Balances** screen, you directly jump to the Manage Supplier Line Items app (F0712) in SAP Fiori, which is also very similar to the screen of Transaction FBL1H, which you see in Figure 4.104.

Figure 4.104 Manage Supplier Line Items App in SAP Fiori

It's functionally and visually very close to Transaction FK10N, as shown in Figure 4.105.

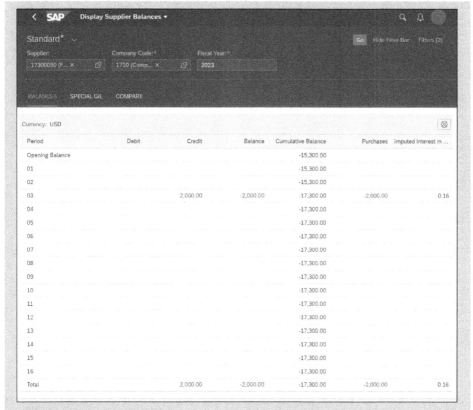

Figure 4.105 Display Supplier Balances App in SAP Fiori

4.7.2 Accounts Balance Report

The vendor account balances report is a helpful tool for accounts reconciliation when preparing the financial statement. Using this report, you can see the outstanding balances of the supplier accounts, and balances in debits and credits for a particular company code, key date, and supplier.

In SAP S/4HANA, you can use Transaction S_ALR_87012082 or follow application menu path **Accounting • Financial Accounting • Accounts Payable • Information System • Reports for Accounts Payable Accounting • Vendor Balances in Local Currency**.

When you start the transaction, you reach the **Vendor Balances in Local Currency** screen, as shown in Figure 4.106. Here, you enter the **Company Code**, **Fiscal Year**, and **Reporting periods**, as well as a **Reconciliation account**, if you want to focus on a certain type of vendor balance, such as domestic payables. In the **Output Control** area, you can select any of the listed options. In this example, the **Normal balances** indicator has been selected, which displays normal balances for the selected accounts. You can also select other indicators, such as **Special G/L balances** (shows the special general ledger account balances for each special general ledger transaction for the selected accounts),

Corporate group version (the balances for all company codes of each account are displayed together for that account), and so on.

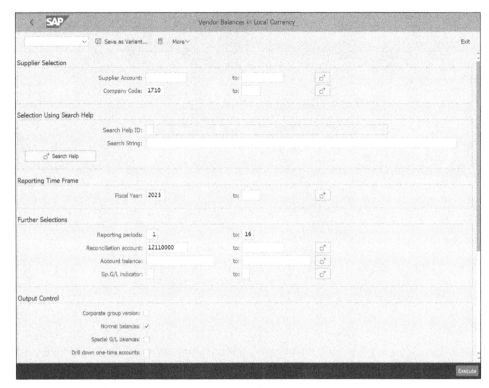

Figure 4.106 Vendor Balances in Local Currency Screen

CoCd	Reconciliation Acct	Supplier	SearchTerm	Sp.G/LInd.	Crcy	Balance Carryforward	Debit Bince of Reportng Period	Credit Balance Reporting Per.
1710	12110000	BP00010	FUNGHI		USD	0.00	40.00	80.00
1710	12110000	BP00011	RISO		USD	0.00	40.00	80.00
1710	12110000	BP00012	GRANA		USD	0.00	40.00	80.00
1710	12110000	BP0005	ACEA		USD	0.00	1,500.00	1,500.00
1710	12110000	BP0017	GENNNNY		USD	0.00	0.00	10,000.00
1710	12110000	BP0018	GENNNNNY		USD	0.00	0.00	3,000.00
1710	12110000	BP0028	VIVO FERRO		USD	0.00	3,000.00	6,000.00
1710	12110000	BP007	CID SPA		USD	0.00	0.00	110,000.00
1710	12110000	BP0071	PLASTICA		USD	0.00	0.00	6,000.00
1710	12110000	BP0076	VETRO&ALLU		USD	0.00	3,000.00	3,270.00
1710	12110000	BP0096	STELLA2 SR		USD	0.00	100.00	100.00
1710	12110000	BP0097	STELLA3 SR		USD	0.00	100.00	200.00
1710	12110000	BP0098	STELLA SRL		USD	0.00	100.00	100.00
1710	12110000	BP01	ACEA		USD	0.00	1,500.00	1,500.00
1710	12110000	BP0101	MERET		USD	0.00	5,000.00	5,000.00
1710	12110000	BP0128	PAGAMENTI		USD	0.00	0.00	40.00
1710	12110000	BP0167	PUBBLICITA		USD	0.00	2,100.00	2,100.00
1710	12110000	BP0168	STUDIO DG		USD	0.00	220.00	220.00
1710	12110000	BP0169	COLORI SRL		USD	0.00	1,215.00	1,215.00
1710	12110000	BP02	ENEL		USD	0.00	350.00	350.00
1710	12110000	BP0202	RONNIE COL		USD	0.00	20,200.00	20,200.00

Figure 4.107 Vendor Balances in Local Currency Result (1)

Click the **Execute** button. The results screen (see Figure 4.107 and Figure 4.108) shows you a list of all vendor account balances line by line, starting with the balance carryforward, debit entries balance, credit entries balance, and accumulated balance. It sums up all the columns to give you a total on the general ledger reconciliation account level.

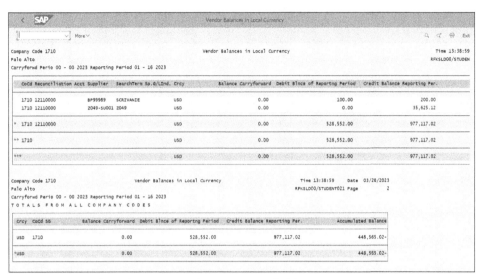

Figure 4.108 Vendor Balances in Local Currency Result (2)

SAP Fiori App

The corresponding SAP Fiori app is called Display Supplier Balances (F0701). In Figure 4.109, you can see how the mentioned app looks in SAP Fiori.

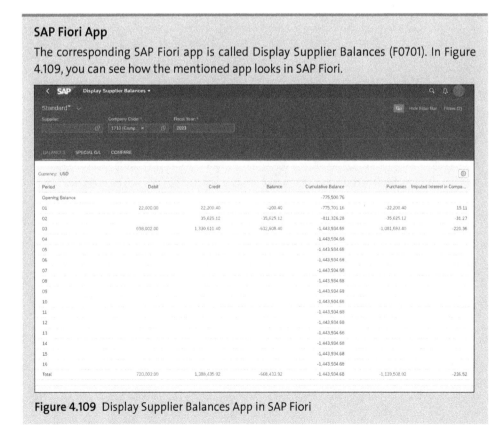

Figure 4.109 Display Supplier Balances App in SAP Fiori

In the header section, enter the selection criteria, such as **Supplier** (if you need to restrict for a specific supplier), **Company Code**, and **Fiscal Year**, and then click the **Go** button to show the balances sorted by **Period** (from **01** to **16**). This app can show the debit/credit balances by company code, fiscal year, and supplier.

You can drill down on a particular record of a period and further analyze the amounts by showing all related line items. In this case, you're automatically redirected to the Manage Supplier Line Items app (F0712). For example, if you double-click the credit balance in **Period 07**, the result will be as shown in Figure 4.110. By clicking the **COMPARE** button, you can compare purchases between two fiscal years, as shown in Figure 4.111.

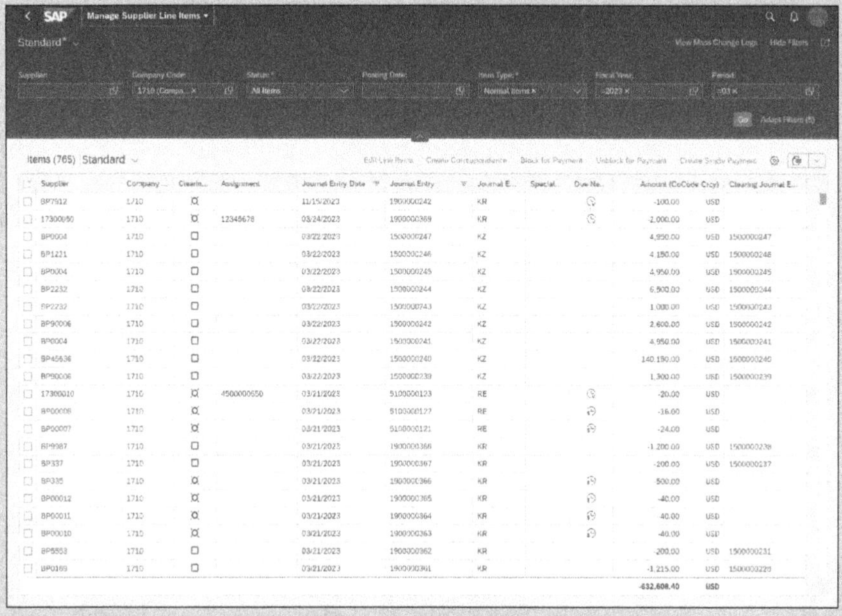

Figure 4.110 Detailed Analysis of Related Line Items for Period 03

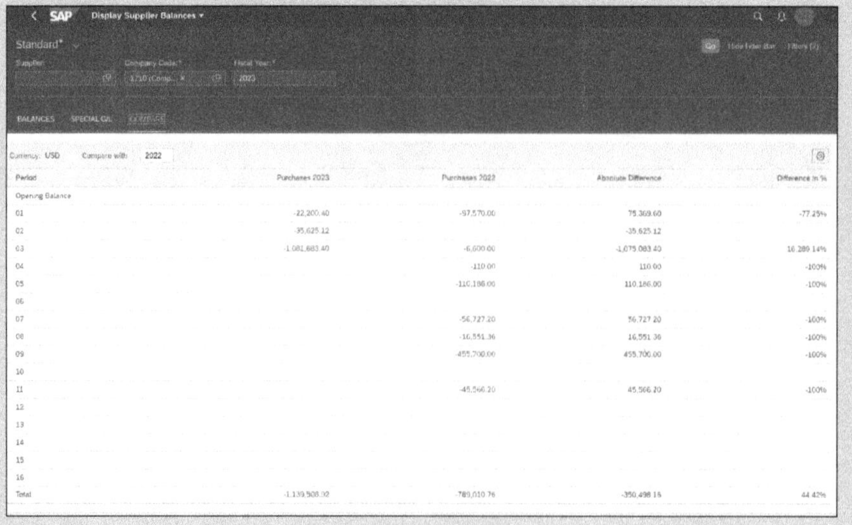

Figure 4.111 Comparing Supplier Balances

Very often, you'll need more information than the account balances of your vendors. To clarify and analyze all vendor accounts overall, you need a breakdown of each account balance into line items. For this reason, let's now discuss how you can generate accounts payable open item lists in SAP S/4HANA.

4.7.3 Open Item List

The accounts payable (or vendor) open item list is a report with which you can display all unpaid or uncleared invoices of all your vendors. The report shows the documents and accounting line items posted to a vendor account.

Use Transaction S_ALR_87012103 to start the accounts payable open item list screen, or follow application menu path **Accounting • Financial Accounting • Accounts Payable • Information System • Reports for Accounts Payable Accounting • Vendors: Items • List of Vendor Line Items**.

In the start screen of the vendor line items report, as shown in Figure 4.112, you can filter the information referring to **Supplier Account**, **Company Code**, item **Status**, and so on.

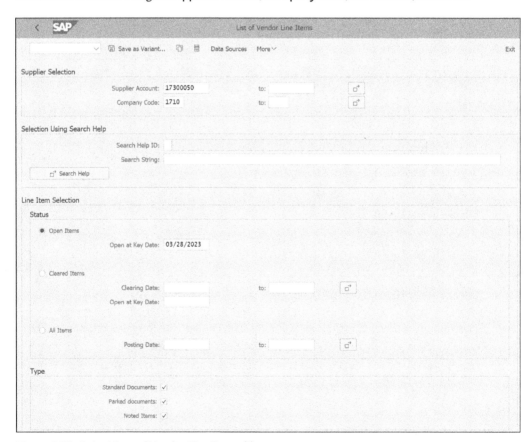

Figure 4.112 Entry View of Vendor Line Items (1)

Under the **Type** area, you can select any of the listed parameters, such as **Standard Documents** (determines that only documents relevant to the accounting department will be evaluated), **Parked documents** (the program also selects the documents from the preliminary posting), or **Noted Items** (noted items are to be evaluated).

In the **Further Selections** area, define the **Line Item Reconciliation Acct** number, as shown in Figure 4.113. If required, you can also fill in or check the other fields in both screens.

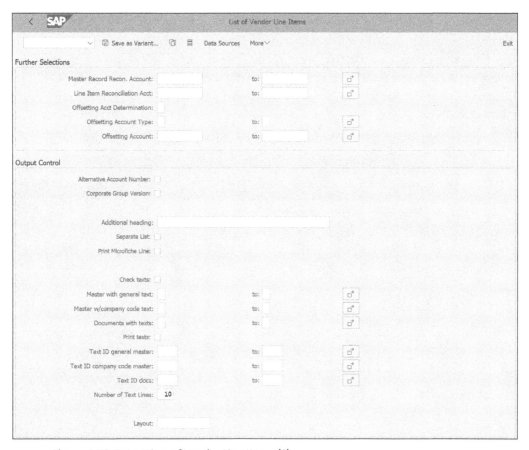

Figure 4.113 Entry View of Vendor Line Items (2)

To select only open items, you select **Open Items** in the **Line Item Selection/Status** area and enter a reporting date (**Open at Key Date**). Click the **Execute** button to execute the report, and all open items of all vendors for company code 1710 are listed. The report also shows complete names and addresses of the vendors (see Figure 4.114).

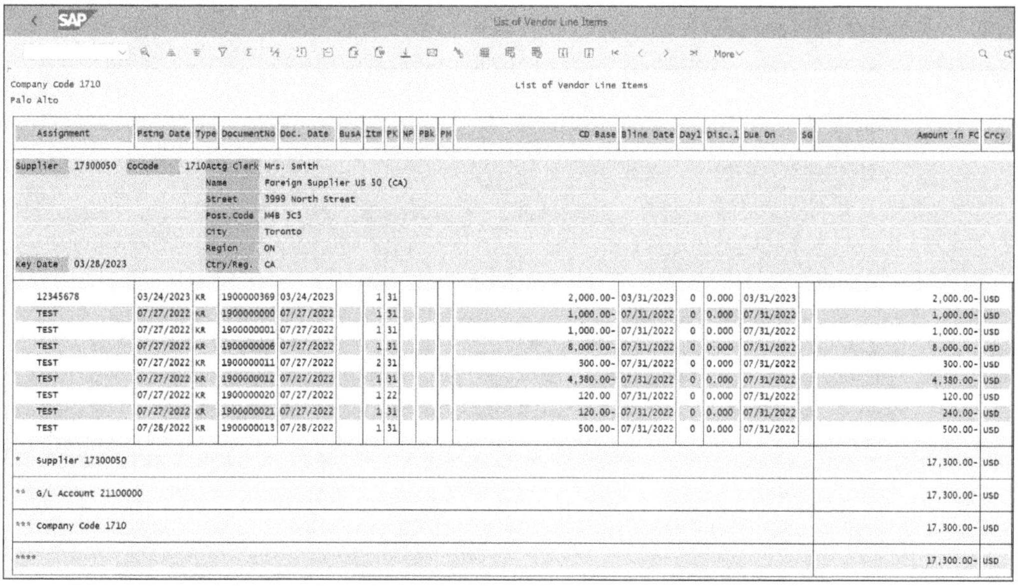

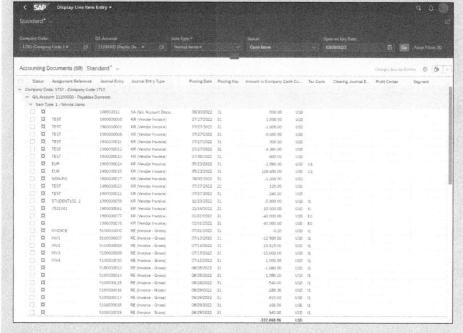

Figure 4.114 Overview of Open Vendor Line Items

SAP Fiori Apps

The corresponding SAP Fiori apps are called Display Line Item Entry (F2218), through which you can analyze general ledger account line items in deep detail, and Display Line Item in General Ledger Report (F2217), through which you can check general ledger account line items in the general ledger view.

Figure 4.115 Display Line Item Entry App in SAP Fiori

Figure 4.115 shows the Display Line Item Entry app, in which you can define the **Company Code**, **G/L Account**, **Item Type**, **Status**, and **Open on Key Date** (showing all open items until this specified date). The selection has been restricted to general ledger account **21100000** as in the preceding example in SAP GUI. Click the **Go** button, which leads you to the list of items shown at the bottom in Figure 4.115.

You can add the **Name of Supplier** column through the settings icon ⚙. In the search box, enter and select **Name of Supplier**, and click **OK**. Then you can put it in front with drag and drop. You'll get the view shown in Figure 4.116.

Figure 4.116 Display Line Item Entry, Including the Name of Supplier Column

4.8   Summary

In this chapter, you've seen how accounts payable accounting in SAP S/4HANA works in detail. You've learned about the integration of accounts payable in the purchase-to-pay process, starting with purchase requisitions, purchase orders, goods receipts, invoice receipts, and payment transactions. You've expanded your knowledge about vendor accounts and their master records. Moreover, you've learned how to post two types of vendor invoices (automatic or direct), followed by necessary configurations to perform a manual or automated outgoing payment. In addition to these essential components of accounts payable, you gained a deeper understanding of other parts of the accounts payable process, such as credit memos, down payments, period-end closing, and reporting. We finished this chapter by practicing some accounts payable inquiries, such as vendor account balances, vendor open and closed items, and so on. Overall, now that you understand these basic accounts payable steps, you can manage your way as an accounts payable clerk in the SAP S/4HANA environment.

In the next chapter, we'll move on to accounts receivable.

4

Chapter 5

Accounts Receivable

Selling products and services is the core activity of every business model. After customers have been acquired, sales orders are placed from which processing activities are derived, and documents such as delivery notes, customer invoices, payments, credit memos, and so on are generated. In accounting, customer accounts are managed in accounts receivable, which is the focus of this chapter.

Accounts receivable is the mirror image of the accounts payable ledger and has a very similar structure in data and functions to what you saw in Chapter 4. It's used for managing and recording accounting and payment data for all the customers to whom your company sells goods and services. In principle, the main activities are recording customer invoices, matching incoming payments to the respective customer invoices, and monitoring and dunning open items.

Usually, and, especially in business-to-business transactions, goods and services need not be paid before or at the time of receiving. Instead, companies agree on payment terms. In essence, the selling company grants the buying company a short-term loan. This is why the accounts receivables are shown in the balance sheet as current assets.

How many goods and services a customer is allowed to buy is determined by the customer's creditworthiness. Usually, a credit department makes background checks on the customer and determines a certain threshold of creditworthiness, resulting in a credit limit. If the customer exceeds this threshold, goods and services are normally no longer delivered.

That's the story of accounts receivable in a nutshell, following is how we break down this chapter to cover all the mentioned topics in more detail: We'll start with the order-to-cash process where you'll gain a pretty good overview of the transactions processed in SAP S/4HANA. After that, we cover the master data of customer accounts before discussing the transactional part of customer invoices, incoming payments, and credit memo processing. We'll then talk about customer down payments, which are treated specially in SAP S/4HANA. Next, the dunning process and the credit management functions are explained. We end this chapter with discussing the accounts receivable period-end closing and reporting capabilities.

Let's now get an overall understanding of the order-to-cash process and all its transactions performed in SAP S/4HANA.

5.1   Order-to-Cash Process

The *order-to-cash* business process is used for processing the sales order for the goods and services, managing the company receivables, and accumulating the relevant payments from its customers. This process is a mirror image of the purchase-to-pay process. Remember, the purchase-to-pay process starts with the purchase requisition and the purchase order. When the buyer company creates the purchase order, the selling company enters a sales order, and the interactions between seller and buyer goes ahead. The processing of a sale is part of the sales and distribution activities in SAP S/4HANA.

You can access the **Sales and Distribution** folder in the following IMG menu path: **Logistics • Sales and Distribution**. This folder contains all the activities from a logistics perspective, which are **Master Data**, **Sales**, **Shipping**, **Billing**, and **Credit Management**.

In the following sections, we'll discuss how sales orders are created and processed in the system.

5.1.1   Sales Order

A *sales order* is a document generated in the system based on a purchase order document received from the customer or buyer. Like the purchase order, a sales order document specifies some important details about the goods or services, quantity, price, customer information (e.g., shipping address and billing address), terms and conditions, and so on. A sales order is considered an agreement between the buyer and seller ensuring that the ordered product is delivered on an agreed-upon date and at an agreed-upon quantity and price.

Sales orders are an essential part of order management and inventory in a company. Orders provide information, for example, on whether a specific product is still in stock or not, the remaining quantity, and so on. In this way, the purchasing department is always alerted and able to make forecasts and perform additional orders from their vendors.

The sales order process is also very connected with the finance section of the company as it normally affects the business accounting part. Communication is always flowing between finance and sales departments in terms of revenue recognition, order management, and billing information.

You can create a sales order by following application menu path **Logistics • Sales and Distribution • Sales • Order • Create**. Instead of following the menu path, you can also execute the respective transactions for each function:

- Transaction VA01 to create a sales order
- Transaction VA02 to change a sale order
- Transaction VA03 to display a sales order

Let's walk through the steps to create a sales order. Execute Transaction VA01 or double-click on the relevant transaction name in the application menu path. The **Create Sales Documents** screen opens, as shown in Figure 5.1.

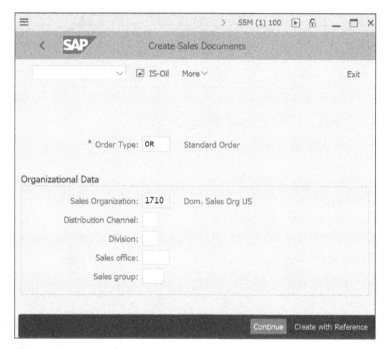

Figure 5.1 Create Sales Documents Screen

Here, you can enter the initial information, such as the **Order Type** you're going to create, and you can specify some organizational data, such as **Sales Organization**, **Distribution Channel**, **Division**, and so on.

Two buttons are available here: **Continue** as a normal way to enter all data from scratch, or **Create with Reference** to create sales orders with reference to an inquiry, quotation, contract, billing document, and so on. In this case, the **Create with Reference** popup appears, where you can see that the order can be created with reference to any of the available options (**Inquiry**, **Quotation**, **Order**, etc.), as shown in Figure 5.2. These are different functions set up in the system using the copy controls setup. Not all of these functions are available in all systems because it depends on how the system is set up and how the configurations are done.

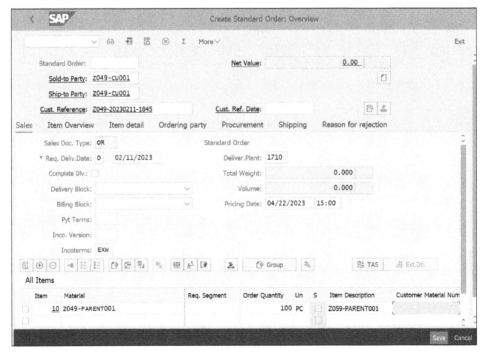

Figure 5.2 Create Sales Order with Reference

Both options lead to the same screen shown in Figure 5.3. The difference is that when the sales order is created with reference, all data from the existing document when you choose any of the available options is copied to the relevant fields in the sales order. For this example, use the **Continue** option. The **Create Standard Order: Overview** screen appears, as shown in Figure 5.3.

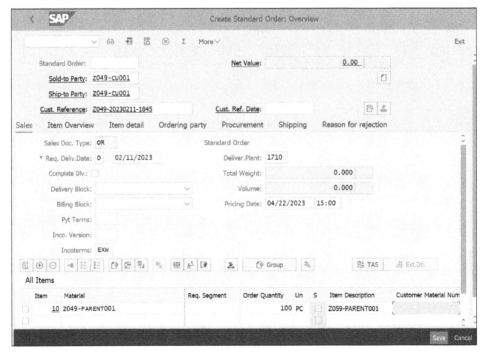

Figure 5.3 Create Standard Order: Overview Screen

Here, you need to enter the required data of the header information, such as **Sold-to Party** for the customer who makes the order, **Ship-to Party** for the party who receives the delivery of the goods, and **Cust. Reference**, which is the number the customer uses to identify a purchasing document (order or inquiry). You can also define items information in the required fields by going through the following tabs:

- **Sales**
  You can enter the **Req. Deliv.Date** as the requested delivery date of the document by which the customer should receive delivery of the goods, **Pyt Terms** as the terms of payment, and **Pricing Date** as an optional field that determines date-related pricing elements, such as conditions and foreign exchange rate.

- **Item Overview**
  You can enter the requested delivery date of the document and the delivering plant that represents the plant from which the goods should be delivered to the customer.

- **Item detail**
  Most of the fields are automatically updated by taking the values already entered in the previous tabs and in the **All Items** record. You can define the **Reason for rejection**, for example, when a customer request/credit memo is rejected because it isn't accepted by the company.

- **Ordering party**
  The **Req. Delivering date** and **Pricing Date** fields are automatically updated.

You can go through the other tabs to see the fields that are already populated and other fields that you can fill in, if necessary, per the specific case.

> **Note**
>
> On each screen, to get the concept of each field (either mandatory or optional), you can select the desired field and press the $\boxed{\text{F1}}$ key or right-click the **Help** function. A popup window will appear with the relevant explanation for each selected field.

Click the **Save** button, and you'll receive a message at the bottom of the screen with the new standard order number. Now, if you click on the display icon (glasses) at the top of the screen, you can see all the details of the standard order you've just created (see Figure 5.4).

Here, you can see the header information and several tabs as well as the line items with the sales order information at the bottom. Note that sales order documents don't update the accounting figures. The accounting starts to be affected after the billing document is generated in the system, producing an open receivable in the customer account in the accounts receivable functionality.

Figure 5.4 Display Standard Order

SAP Fiori App

The standard corresponding SAP Fiori app is called Create Sales Order (VA01). This app is visually and functionally identical to the SAP GUI transaction. However, since SAP S/4HANA 2021, there is a new more user-friendly app to create sales orders called Manage Sales Orders (F3893), as shown in Figure 5.5. You can use it to display **Sales Orders** for any customer and to create sales orders by clicking **Create** in the center of the screen. From there, it's just visually different, but if you follow the instructions explained for the SAP GUI version, you can easily process a sales order in SAP Fiori as well.

Figure 5.5 Manage Sales Orders and Create Sales Orders in SAP Fiori

In the next section, we'll explain the outbound deliveries as the subsequent step after the sales order document is created.

5.1.2   Outbound Delivery

The *outbound delivery* is a document created after execution of the sales order document. This document represents the goods or services to be delivered to the goods recipient. All information related to the shipping schedule, such as packing, transporting, picking, and goods issuing, is included in an outbound delivery.

You can create an outbound delivery by using Transaction VL01N or following application menu path **Logistics • Sales and Distribution • Sales • Order • Subsequent Function • Outbound Delivery**. This transaction is followed by another window (see Figure 5.6), where you need to enter the **Shipping Point** and **Order** number as mandatory fields. Here you see that the processing of an outbound delivery isn't possible without a sales order. This is a system-forced control.

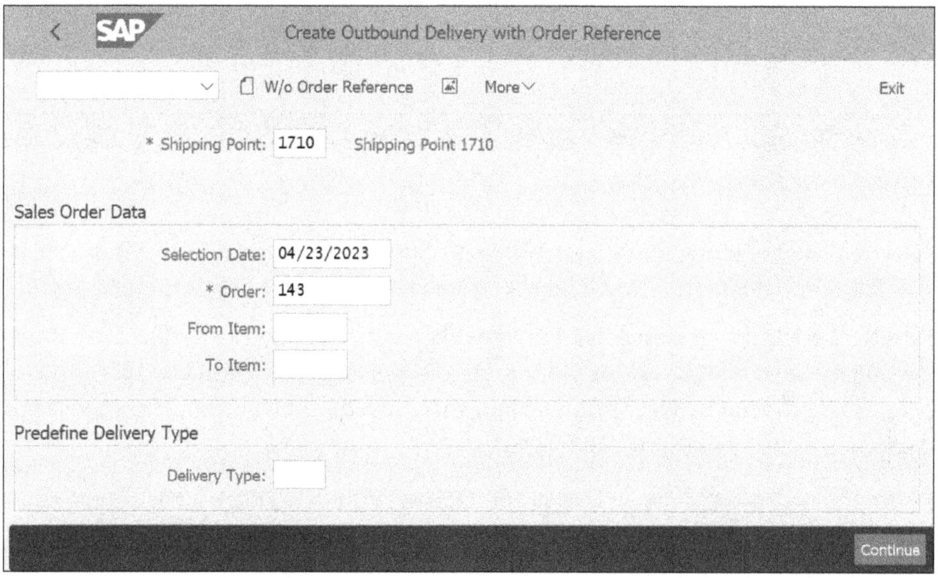

Figure 5.6 Create Outbound Delivery

Note

Shipping Point is a place or location where the goods and services are delivered to the customers. It's an independent organizational unit in SAP S/4HANA, and it's responsible for processing inbound and outbound deliveries. The shipping points are maintained with Transaction OVXD. We won't go deeper here as it would go far beyond the scope of financial accounting.

Click the **Continue** button, and the overview screen of the selected order appears (see Figure 5.7). In the **Picking** tab, enter the storage location, and enter other optional data in the other tabs, such as **Shipment**, **Loading**, **Status Overview**, and so on, depending on your company's requirements.

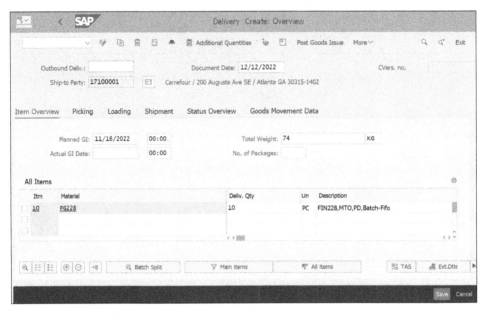

Figure 5.7 Create Delivery Fields

After you finish entering the necessary data, click the **Save** button, and a notification message with the outbound delivery number created is shown at the bottom of the screen.

Now to check what the outbound delivery that you just created looks like, click **More • Outbound Delivery • Display**. In the **Display Outbound Delivery** window that appears, enter the outbound delivery number, and click the **Continue** button. The overview is displayed as shown in Figure 5.8.

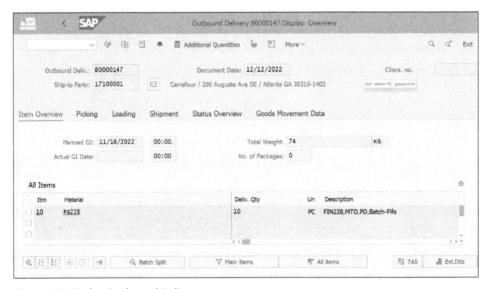

Figure 5.8 Display Outbound Delivery

SAP Fiori Apps

There are three available corresponding SAP Fiori apps that can be used to create an outbound delivery document. The following two are visually and functionally identical to the SAP GUI transaction:

- Create Outbound Delivery without Order Reference (Transaction VL01N)
- Create Outbound Delivery with Order Reference (Transaction VL01N)

The third corresponding SAP Fiori app is called Create Outbound Deliveries (Transaction F0869A).

In Figure 5.9, you can see that the mentioned app looks more modern in SAP Fiori, but the selection fields are the same. Using this app, it's possible to create an outbound delivery from a list of sales orders. Before you can create an outbound delivery, you must enter the **Ship-to Party**, **Shipping Point**, and **Priority** (if it's required). In the **Sales Document** field, you can select the items from the listed sales. If you have a sales order as a reference, you just select its checkbox and click on **Create Deliveries (1)**, as shown in Figure 5.9.

Figure 5.9 Create Outbound Deliveries App in SAP Fiori

Now that you've learned how to create an outbound delivery document, let's focus on the next step of the sales process: billing.

5.1.3   Billing Documents

The billing process takes place after the outbound delivery document has been generated. A *billing document* contains billing-relevant information for a specific transaction with the customer. A billing document can be created for credit memos, debit memos, invoices, canceled transactions, supplier invoices, and so on.

In SAP S/4HANA, you can create a billing document by following either the **Sales** path or the **Billing** path in the SAP tree menu (by executing Transaction VF01):

- Create a billing document in **Sales** by following menu path **Logistics • Sales and Distribution • Sales • Order • Subsequent function • Billing Document**.
- Create a billing document in **Billing** by following menu path **Logistics • Sales and Distribution • Billing • Billing Document • Create**.

Double-click **Create** to generate a billing document. In the **Create Billing Document** window that appears, the **Document** field shows the list of billing documents to be processed. Search for and select a billable transaction—either a sales order or an outbound delivery—in the **Docs to Be Processed** section, and press [Enter] or click the **Execute** button, as shown in Figure 5.10.

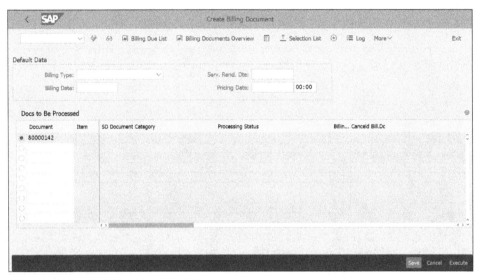

Figure 5.10 Create Billing Document Screen

In the next screen shown in Figure 5.11, you can see that the billing document consists of the header and items areas. The header contains data such as **Payer**, **Billing Date**, **Currency**, and so on, and the items area contains data such as **Material** number, **Item Description**, **Billed Quantity**, amount price (**Net Value**), and so on. After you've checked the billing document details, click the **Save** button, and you'll receive a notification message at the bottom of the screen with the saved document number.

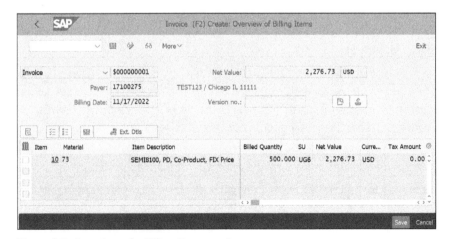

Figure 5.11 Overview of a Billing Document

A billing document isn't automatically reflected in accounting. You need to use Transaction VFO2 to transfer the billing document to the accounting records. After starting Transaction VFO2, choose **More • Billing Document • Release to Accounting**, as shown in Figure 5.12.

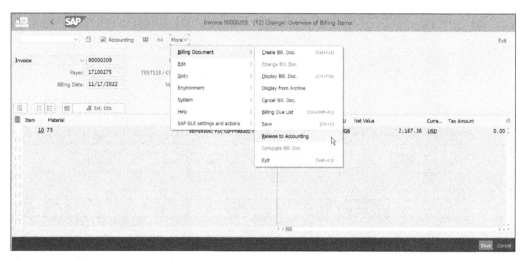

Figure 5.12 Billing Document Release to Accounting

SAP Fiori Apps

The corresponding SAP Fiori apps are called Create Billing Documents (VFO1) and Display Billing Documents (F2250). These apps are visually and functionally identical to the SAP GUI transaction.

In Figure 5.13, you can see how **Billing Document 90000209** is shown in SAP Fiori running the Display Billing Documents app. Enter the selection criteria for the billing document you've selected, and click the **Continue** button. In Figure 5.14, you can see the billing document overview.

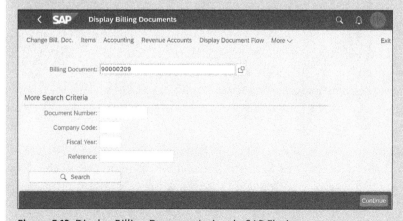

Figure 5.13 Display Billing Documents App in SAP Fiori

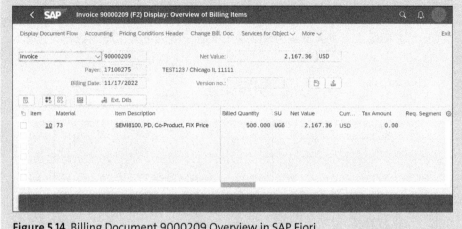

Figure 5.14 Billing Document 9000209 Overview in SAP Fiori

The next step after the billing document has been created is customer invoicing. From this moment, the final process steps take place in the accounts receivable ledger of financial accounting. To avoid repetition, we'll talk about customer invoicing in Section 5.3. After that, the order-to-cash process is completed by discussing the processing of incoming payments in Section 5.4.

Now that you know the basic steps of the order-to-cash process, we'll focus next on the customer accounts and their master data.

5.2   Customer Accounts

Customers are buyers of goods, products, and services offered by an organization. An SAP S/4HANA customer account is a master record that contains both accounting-relevant information for accounts receivable and logistics information maintained through sales and distribution. The customer master data contains all necessary information about the customer to receive orders, such as name, address, currency, payment conditions, contact person, and so on, as well as the accounting information, such as the reconciliation account in the general ledger. Accounts receivable is a subledger to the general ledger. The details of each individual transaction are maintained in the subledger customer accounts. The accumulative balance of all customer master records is reflected in a single general ledger account—the accounts receivable reconciliation account.

To create or maintain a customer master record, you can use Transaction FD01 (Create) or Transaction FD02 (Change), or you can follow application menu path **Accounting • Financial Accounting • Accounts Receivable • Master Records**. The customer master record is typically accessible and managed by the accounting and sales administration departments of the company.

Customer master data, like vendor master data, contains three segments:

- **General Data**
  In this segment, the general data of a customer account is maintained, such as customer name, shipping address, customer number, and so on.

- **Company Code Data**
  In this segment, the specific data of the company code is maintained. The most important field in this segment is the reconciliation account (**Reconciliation acct**) in the general ledger, which is synchronized with the customer subledger account, meaning that for every transaction posted on customer subledger accounts, the reconciliation account in the general ledger is updated at the same time. Other fields are related to the payment methods, specifications of interest calculations (if any), and withholding tax, if applicable.

- **Sales Area Data**
  In this segment, the terms of the payment billing document are maintained, showing the terms used for the sale process to the customer. Another field in this segment is **Taxes Billing Document**, which indicates whether a customer is tax exempt or responsible for taxes.

Let's walk through creating the data for the two main areas relevant for your financial accounting processes: **General Data** and **Company Code Data**.

5.2.1 Customer General Data

As we mentioned, master general data consists of data registered for each customer in your company (e.g., customer name, address, etc.). To create a customer master record, you need to double-click on **Create** from application menu path. The **Create Business Partner** screen appears, as shown in Figure 5.15. Select the business partner type (**Person**, **Organization**, or **Group**) that you're going to create. In this example, choose **Person** to create a customer master record as a person.

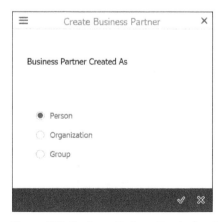

Figure 5.15 Business Partner Created as Person

You'll arrive at the **Create Person** screen, as shown in Figure 5.16. Fill in the required fields for the new record by going through the following tabs:

- **Address**
  You can fill in the most important fields, such as first name, last name, correspondence language, search term, and address (street number, postal code, and country). Optionally, you can fill in the remaining fields as well.

- **Address Overview**
  Information in this tab is automatically reflected after you've filled in the **Address** tab.

- **Identification**
  You can define some personal data of the customer, such as gender, marital status, nationality, identification number, tax number, and tax classification, if relevant.

- **Control**
  You can optionally define some control parameters, such as business partner type, authorization group, trading partner, print format, and some notes, if needed.

- **Payment Transactions**
  You can see the customer's bank details. This area of the screen provides the option of payment through credit card, and the credit card details can be entered in the respective fields.

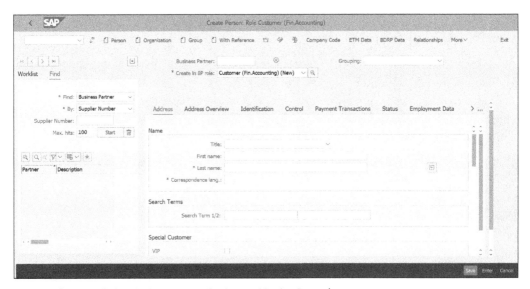

Figure 5.16 Create Person as a Customer Master Record

- **Status**
  You can enter other relevant information, such as profile status, end of business relationship, last date of customer contact, and so on.

- **Employment Data**

  You can enter information related to occupation data, such as monthly net income, currency, annual income, and so on.

- **Customer General Data**

  You can enter some general information about the customer, such as customer number, external customer number, and customer assignment to the account group. When it's created, a customer master record can be assigned to a customer account group through which the customer is classified into business partner functions. In SAP S/4HANA, there are different customer account groups, but the most frequently used are for sales, such as sold-to party, bill-to party, payer, ship-to party, and sales employee.

- **Customer Tax Data**

  This tab provides tax data and tax categories in case this information is relevant.

- **Customer Additional Data**

  This tab refers to some attributes and pricing condition groups as additional customer information.

After you've filled in all the required data, click the **Save** button.

To display a customer, you can double-click **Display** in the application menu path. You're redirected to Transaction BP (see note in the bottom of Figure 5.17).

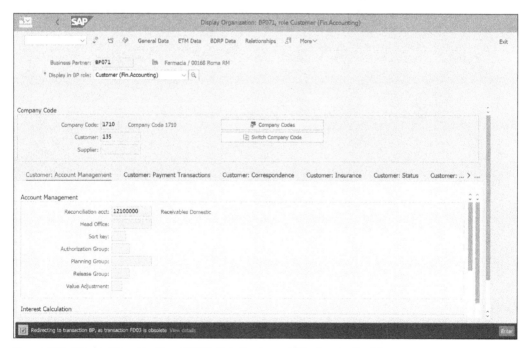

Figure 5.17 Display Organization: BP071, Role Customer (Fin.Accounting) Screen

If you then click on **General Data** in the menu bar at the top of the screen, you'll see details of the customer role of **Business Partner BP071**, shown in Figure 5.18 and Figure 5.19.

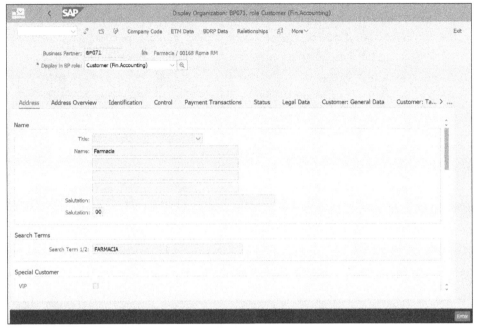

Figure 5.18 Customer Role of Business Partner BP071: General Data (1)

Figure 5.19 Customer Role of Business Partner BP071: General Data (2)

SAP Fiori App

The corresponding SAP Fiori app is called Manage Customer Master Data (F0850A), as shown in Figure 5.20. This screen lists all existing customers from which you can select to see all of their data. From this screen, you can click the **Create** button to set up new customer master data as **Person** or **Organization**. In Figure 5.21, you can see the fields you need to fill in while creating a new customer as a person.

Figure 5.20 Customer Master Data in SAP Fiori

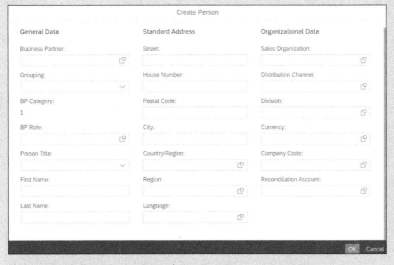

Figure 5.21 Create Master Record as a Person

In the next section, we'll explain the customer company code data, which refers to the accounting data of the customer.

5.2.2   Customer Company Code Data

You can use the same Transaction FDO3, Transaction BP, or the application menu path to display the general data or company code data of a specified customer. In the same screen that appears, as shown previously in Figure 5.17, you can toggle between general data or company code data by clicking on the menu items **Company Code** or **General Data**.

In Figure 5.22 and Figure 5.23, the **Customer: Account Management** tab shows the general data of **Customer 135 (Business Partner BP071)** for **Company Code 1710**. The reconciliation account in the general ledger is **Receivables Domestic** number **12100000**.

Let's take a closer look at each tab:

- **Customer: Account Management**
  You can see accounting data, such as interest calculations, reference data, withholding taxes, and the reconciliation account, which is the most important field of the customer master data. Every transaction posted in the customer subledger account, such as down payments, general ledger postings, and so on, is directly reflected in this reconciliation account.

- **Customer: Payment Transactions**
  You can see the payment data, such as payment method and payment terms, which defines and calculates the payment due date of the customer.

- **Customer: Correspondence**
  You can see the details for dunning and correspondence with the customer.

- **Customer: Insurance**
  You can see the customer's insurance information.

- **Customer: Status**
  You can see whether the customer is active or not. If the customer is inactive, then the customer file can be archived.

- **Customer: Withholding Tax**
  You can see the tax-relevant specifications for a customer, for example, the tax that is charged to the customer at the beginning of the payment flow.

- **Customer: Text**
  You can find other relevant details and a long text explanation for the customer.

The master data components need to be set up correctly from the beginning to process customer invoices and incoming customer payments properly. Now that you've learned about customer account master data, including general data and company code data, we'll now discuss customer invoice types and how to create them in the system.

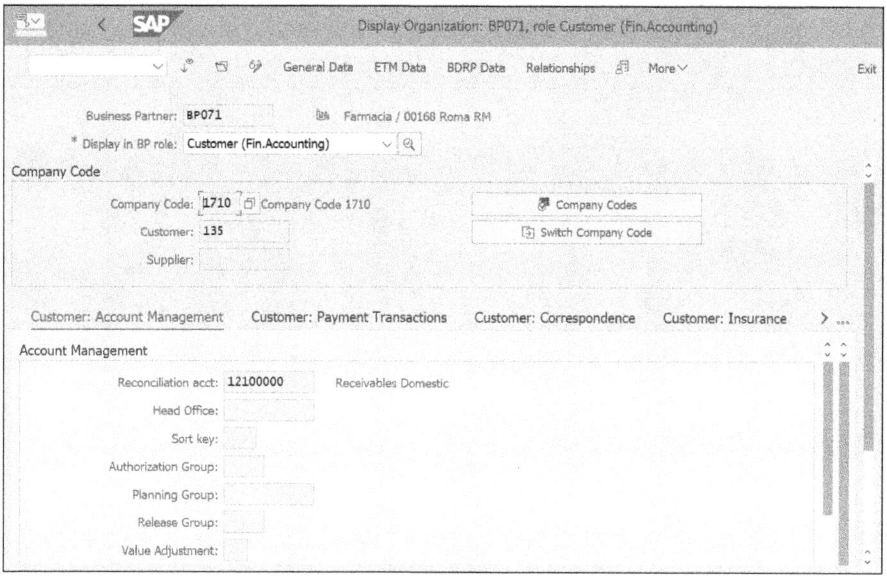

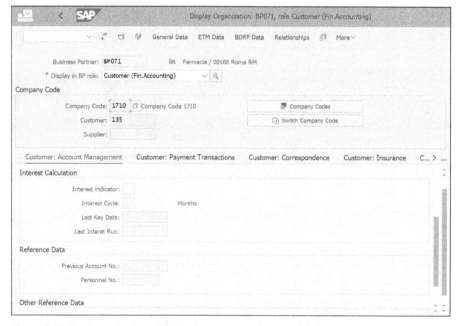

Figure 5.22 Business Partner BP071: Company Code Data (1)

Figure 5.23 Business Partner BP071: Company Code Data (2)

SAP Fiori App

To display the general data of a company, you can use the same Manage Customer Master app (F0850A).

In the main screen, enter the customer number in the **Business Partner** field, and click the **Go** button. You then have to click on the selected business partner. The result will appear as shown in Figure 5.24.

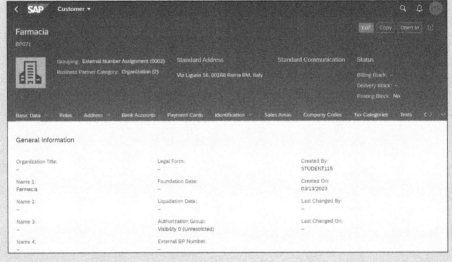

Figure 5.24 Display Company General Data

5.3   Customer Invoices

Each company needs to bill its customers for the goods and services shipped to them and must update its sales revenue accounting. Ideally, a customer invoice is created after receiving the confirmation that a service has been performed or that the goods have been shipped to the specified destination. The invoice contains information such as customer details, amount to be paid, payment terms, shipping address, and so on.

A customer invoice can be created directly in accounts receivable or in sales and distribution using the order-to-cash business process. Let's see now how both cases of customer invoice processing are treated in the system.

5.3.1   Automatic Creation of Customer Invoice (from Logistics)

Referring to our discussion of billing documents in Section 5.1.3, after the created billing is released to accounting, a respective accounts receivable invoice is automatically generated simultaneously. The billing document generated during this process creates two different documents:

- A sales and distribution invoice (the bill)
- An accounts receivable invoice

Let's follow an example to see how this process is performed in the system. To display a billing document, you can use Transaction VF03 or application menu path **Logistics • Sales and Distribution • Billing • Billing Document • Display**.

In the screen that appears, enter the billing document number, for example, "9000143", and press the ⌈Enter⌋ key. You'll arrive at the overview of the billing item, as shown in Figure 5.25.

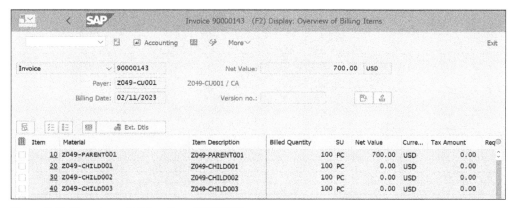

Figure 5.25 Overview of Billing Item 90000143

Now you can display the document flow to see the sales and distribution invoice and the accounting invoice. To do so, choose **More • Environment • Display Document Flow**. You'll arrive at the **Document Flow** screen shown in Figure 5.26.

Figure 5.26 Display Document Flow of Billing Document 90000143

To open the accounts receivable invoice document, select **Journal Entry 9400000003** in the listed document flow, and then click on the **Display Document** button. You'll arrive at the screen shown in Figure 5.27.

Here, you can see the accounting document invoice of the related billing document. In this example, this invoice isn't cleared, as you can see in the **Status** field in Figure 5.26.

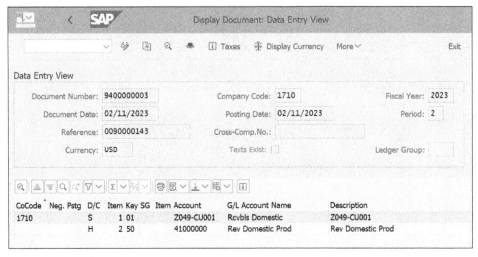

Figure 5.27 Display Accounting Document Invoice

Now, let's discuss how to create a "direct" invoice without connection to logistics in accounts receivable.

SAP Fiori App

The corresponding SAP Fiori app is called Display Billing Documents (F2250). It's visually and functionally the same as the SAP GUI transaction. However, there is a beautiful new app called Display Document Flow (F3665) for visualizing the document flow. It shows the same document flow as shown in Figure 5.26 but graphically presented, as shown in Figure 5.28. By clicking on **Display as T-Accounts**, you can see all relevant postings presented in t-accounts through the Display Journal Entries in T-Account View app (F3664), shown in Figure 5.29.

Figure 5.28 Display of Document Flow in SAP Fiori

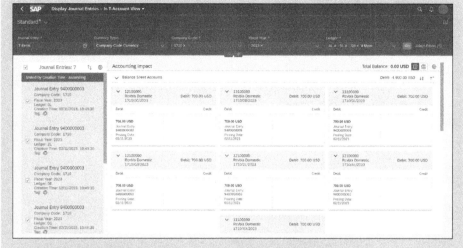

Figure 5.29 Display Journal Entries: T-Account View in SAP Fiori

> **Note**
>
> It's essential to know that accounting integration from sales and distribution to accounts receivable is a one-way direction, which means that updates to accounting documents are applied from sales and distribution to accounts receivable but not from accounts receivable to sales and distribution.

5.3.2   Direct Customer Invoices

There are some differences between automatic and direct invoicing. Direct invoices, unlike automatic invoices, don't refer to sales and distribution billing documents, which are created using Transaction VF01 as explained in the previous section. In addition, the standard document type for direct accounts receivable invoices is **DR – Customer Invoice**, whereas for the sales and distribution automatic invoices, it's **RV – Accounting Document for Billing**.

Direct invoices are created in accounts receivable using Transaction FB70 or application menu path **Accounting • Financial Accounting • Accounts Receivable • Document Entry • Invoice**.

Next, enter the **Company Code** you want to post the invoice in the screen that appears, as shown in Figure 5.30. Click the checkmark icon to continue or press the Enter key.

Figure 5.30 Enter Company Code Screen

The **Enter Customer Invoice** screen appears, as shown in Figure 5.31.

Figure 5.31 Enter Basic Data and the General Ledger Account Line Item

In the **Basic data** tab, specify the mandatory fields (e.g., **Customer** number, **Invoice date**, **Posting Date**, invoice **Amount**, and **Tax Amount**, if applicable), select the **Calculate Tax** checkbox if needed, and so on. **Paymt terms** and **Baseline Date** are automatically populated from the **Payment Terms** field in the **Payment** tab as explained later in this section. The other fields are optional and can be filled in if relevant. You can also enter the **G/L acct** as the revenue account in the **Items** area.

In the **Payment** tab, as shown in Figure 5.32, define the **Pyt Terms** (payment terms), which refer to the conditions settled for the invoice payment, and the **Bline Date** (short cut for baseline date), which refers to the date from which the payment applies. You can also fill in the other optional fields, such as **CD** (cash discount amount), **CD Base** (amount eligible for cash discount), **Payt Meth.** (payment method), **Inv. Ref.** (invoice reference), and so on.

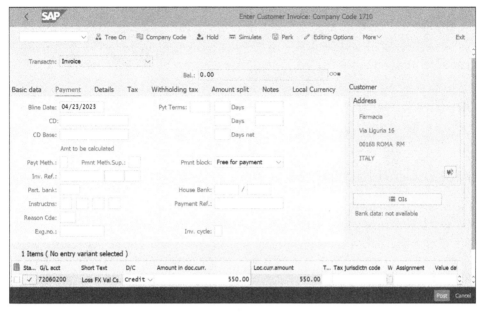

Figure 5.32 Defining the Payment Terms of the Invoice

The other tabs also refer to optional data that can be filled in depending on the specific case.

After you've entered the required data, you can click **More • Simulate** to check for errors before you post the invoice. If the simulation is successful, an overview screen will appear with overall information.

In the next step, you need to click on the **Post** button to post the customer invoice document. You'll receive a message with the new document number at the bottom of the screen.

You can display the document created by clicking **More • Document • Display** to arrive at your created invoice, as shown in Figure 5.33.

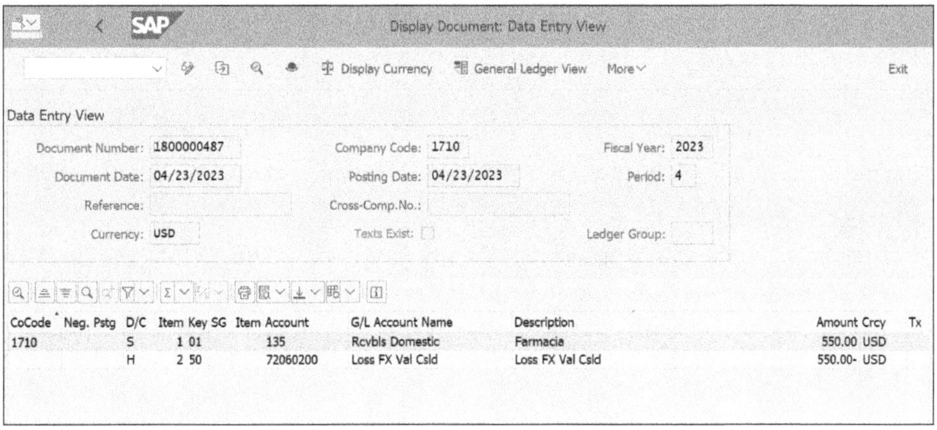

Figure 5.33 Display Document of the Customer Invoice

SAP Fiori App

The corresponding SAP Fiori app is called Create Outgoing Invoices (FB70). It's visually and functionally the same as the SAP GUI transaction.

Now that you know how to record customer invoices, we'll explain the customer payment process next.

5.4   Customer Payments

The incoming payments process is another important part of financial accounting in SAP S/4HANA. After the sale is performed and the customer invoice is recorded, the next step is to collect the revenues through the customer payment process. Before accepting the payment, it's necessary to know the payment method and advantages or disadvantages of different types of payment. An incoming payment document can be created in any payment form, including cash, credit card, mobile payments, bank transfer, bill of exchange, check, and so on.

In this section, you'll learn how to post incoming payments in SAP S/4HANA using the manual bank statement (MBS) and electronic bank statement (EBS). Usually, the automatic payment program, that is, EBS, clears the payment for most of the customer invoices. However, if payment isn't received via EBS, a manual payment (MBS) needs to be executed to clear the open items, for example, when the payment is needed before the next scheduled payment run to meet business requirements, such as down payments (covered later in this section). In these occasions, customer payment will be executed manually using Transaction F-28. In the following sections, we'll explain in detail each of the payment methods.

5.4.1   Manual Bank Statements

Incoming payments can be manually created in accounts receivable using both forms of the customer invoice document, that is, automatically from sales and distribution or manually in accounts receivable, as explained in the previous section. After creating the incoming payment, the next step is to collect the money from the customer.

The manual incoming payment can be performed in two variants, as with accounts payable:

- **Partial payment**
  This type of payment is used when you perform a partial payment for a certain open item. The system will keep both documents outstanding—the original open item (invoice) and the partial payment—until the full outstanding amount is settled.

- **Residual payment**
  This payment is related to partial payments, but the open invoice is cleared with the partial payment, and the system creates a new outstanding document.

Manual incoming payments are created using Transaction F-28 or by following application menu path **Accounting • Financial Accounting • Accounts Receivable • Document Entry • Incoming Payments**.

The **Post Incoming Payments: Header Data** screen appears, as shown in Figure 5.34. Enter the required data in the respective fields in the header data, such as **Document Date**, **Company Code**, **Posting Date**, **Currency/Rate**, document **Type** that classifies the accounting document, and so on. In the **Bank data** area, specify the **Account** that will be posted, the **Amount**, and any other important fields depending on your needs. In the **Open item selection** area, define the **Account** number from which the open items are to be selected for further processing, as well as the **Account type** from the following options:

- **D**: Customers
- **A**: Assets
- **K**: Vendors
- **M**: Materials
- **G**: General ledger accounts

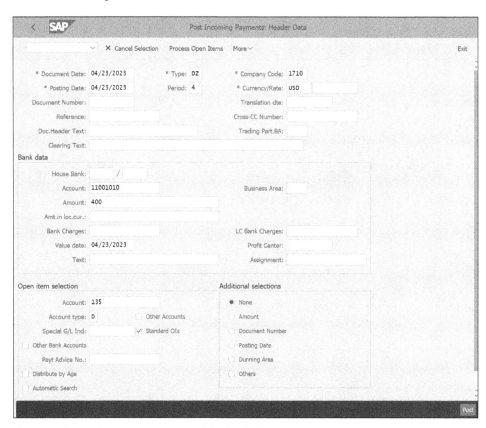

Figure 5.34 Post Incoming Payments: Header Data Screen

After you've entered all the required data, click **Process Open Items** at the top of the screen to arrive at the screen shown in Figure 5.35. In this screen, you see three listed open items, and one of them corresponds to the payment received, which was entered in the screen just shown in Figure 5.34 (**400.00** USD).

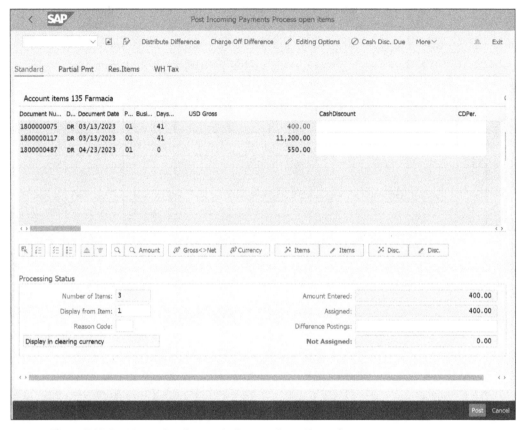

Figure 5.35 Post Incoming Payments Process Open Items Screen

Click the **Post** button. After the payment processing, you'll receive a message notification at the bottom of the screen with the new document number created. The documents posted with these manual transactions appear in the system with the DZ document type. When an incoming payment is posted, a clearing document is created, and the status of the accounts receivable invoice changes from **Open** (red) to **Cleared** (green).

To confirm that these items are successfully cleared, you execute Transaction FBL5N or follow application menu path **Accounting • Financial Accounting • Accounts Receivable • Account • Display/Change Line Items**.

In the **Customer Line Item Display** screen that appears, select the **Cleared Items** option, and click the **Execute** button. The results will be shown as in Figure 5.36.

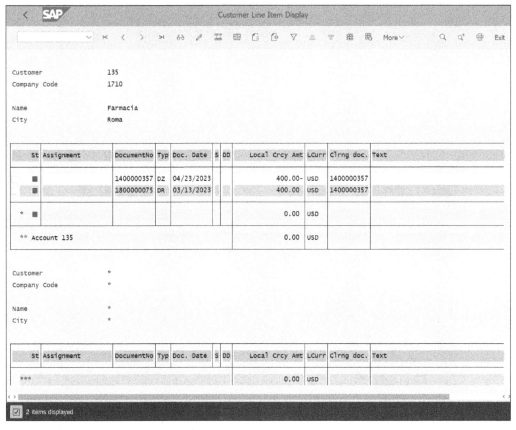

Figure 5.36 Customer Line Item Display Screen

You can also perform partial incoming payments using the same Transaction F-28. In the **Post Incoming Payments Process open items** screen (refer to Figure 5.35), go to the **Partial Pmt** tab, where you can define the partial amount you're going to post.

SAP Fiori Apps

The corresponding SAP Fiori app is called Post Incoming Payments (F1345). In Figure 5.37, you can see what this function looks like in SAP Fiori. After you've entered the required data (the same as the data entered for Transaction F-28), click the **Simulate** button. After a successful simulation, click the **Post** button.

Another available SAP Fiori app is called Clear Incoming Payments (F0773), as shown in Figure 5.38. Using this app, a receivable payment can be manually cleared. Although these payments are usually cleared automatically by the system, there are cases where the customer information isn't found, and it's difficult to find the open item that matches the specific payment.

In the listed entries, select and double-click on one of the items to go to the next screen, shown in Figure 5.39. After you click the **Clear** button, you can simulate and post this item as well.

Figure 5.37 Post Incoming Payments in SAP Fiori

Figure 5.38 Clear Incoming Payments App in SAP Fiori

Figure 5.39 Clear Items of Incoming Payment in SAP Fiori

Next, you'll see more detailed information about the EBS process.

5.4.2   Electronic Bank Statements

The EBS (part of bank accounting; see Chapter 3, Section 3.5.3) is another component in SAP S/4HANA that supports not only receivables and reliabilities management but also applications such as cash and liquidity management.

A lot of companies use the option to obtain bank statement data from the bank electronically. The bank statement file can be imported into SAP S/4HANA using the EBS, and the customer invoices are cleared automatically. During this process, SAP S/4HANA starts to match transactions included in the bank statement with the general ledger line items in bank clearing accounts.

The import of the EBSs is done using Transaction FF_5, which brings you to the screen shown in Figure 5.40.

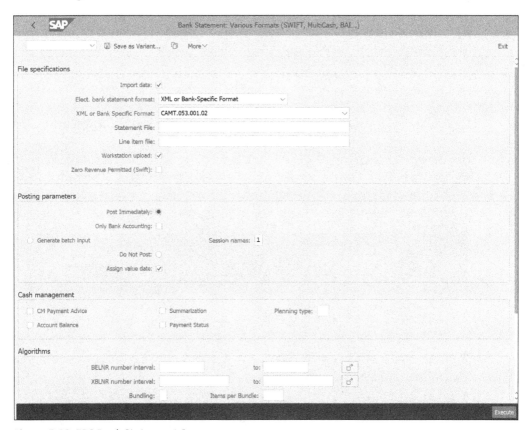

Figure 5.40 EBS Bank Statement Screen

In the **Statement File** field, enter the path name and file name of the file containing the statement data. In the **Line item file** field, enter the path name and file name for the file containing the line item data. You can also select the format of the EBS. In the **Posting**

parameters area, select one of the listed posting options, and also choose whether to select the **Only Bank Accounting** and **Assign value date** checkboxes. In the **Cash management** area, select one or more of the presented options. Go through the other areas, and check whether to select or enter any data, if necessary for your requirements.

> **Note**
>
> You can only use the import function if it's configured in the Customizing area of SAP S/4HANA. If this isn't done, you have to enter each line of the bank statement manually using Transaction FF67.

Assuming that you can import EBSs, the post-processing program is used to review the status of bank statements and to clear open items that didn't clear automatically. In SAP S/4HANA, you can run the post-processing program of an EBS using application menu path **Accounting • Financial Accounting • Banks • Input • Bank Statement • FEBA_ BANK_STATEMENT – Postprocess**.

The **Display Bank Statement Item** screen appears, where you can define several options and specifications, such as company code, house bank, account ID, statement number, statement date, and so on.

> **SAP Fiori App**
>
> A relevant SAP Fiori app is called Manage Bank Statements (F1564), as shown in Figure 5.41. With this app, you can create, edit, and post manual bank statements. Moreover, you can retrieve an overview of all bank statements for specific house bank accounts by filtering the selection criteria such as **House Bank Account**, **Bank Statement Date**, bank **Statement Status**, **Bank Statement No.**, and so on.

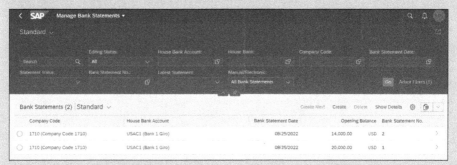

Figure 5.41 Manage Bank Statements App in SAP Fiori

> Now, you can create a manual bank statement by clicking the **Create** button in the menu. In the following **Bank Statement** screen, shown in Figure 5.42, fill out the required data in the **Bank Statement** area, such as **House Bank Account**, **House Bank**, **Company Code**, **Bank Statement No.**, **Bank Statement Date**, and **Opening Balance**. In addition, fill out the fields in the **Bank Statement Items** area, such as the **Manual Transaction** from the preconfigured list of manual transactions, **Value Date**, **Amount**, and **Description**.

Before you save this bank statement, note that in the **Bank Statement Items** area, you have the option to import an external bank statement by clicking the **Import** button or to generate a bank statement in Microsoft Excel format by clicking the **Generate Template** button.

After clicking the **Save** button, you'll arrive at an overview screen displaying the saved bank statement, as shown in Figure 5.43. On the top of the screen, you can click **Edit**, **Delete**, **Post**, or **Post in Background**, or you can create another bank statement (**Create Next**).

5

Figure 5.42 Create Manual Bank Statement

Figure 5.43 Bank Statement Overview

In the next section, we'll discuss process exceptions such as customer credit memos and down payments, which may occur during the daily operation of the order-to-cash process.

5.5 Process Exceptions

During daily business, activities can deviate from the standard process when any exception occurs and the process can't be followed in a straightforward way. For example, products sent to the customers may arrive damaged or not in the expected condition. In another scenario, a customer invoice may show incorrect data related to the amount, quantity, or product description due to mistakes in the material master data and/or wrong entries in the sales order. When these exceptions happen, you need to fix something to get the expected result.

In this section, we'll explain how to treat exceptions that may have occurred in the order-to-cash process related to accounts receivable. We start with creating customer credit memos (credit notes), and then we explain the treatment for down payments.

5.5.1 Credit Memos

As you've already learned in this chapter, for each good or service provided to the customer, the company expects an incoming payment from the customer. In some exceptions, the seller processes some adjustments regarding the amount paid from the customer in its account. Most of the time, customer claims end up in the release of a credit memo from the seller. A *credit memo*, also known as a credit memorandum or credit note, is a document representing a credit back to the customer account to correct the customer balance and offset incoming payment balances. It could be issued due to damaged goods, wrong quantity, wrong amount, wrong product, and so on. This document nets the balance in the customer account while netting the receivable amounts after the payment process.

In accounts receivable, you can generate a credit memo using Transaction FB75 or application menu path **Accounting • Financial Accounting • Accounts Receivable • Document Entry • Credit Memo**.

> **Note**
> This transaction is used to perform credit adjustments in general customer accounts and not for the sales operated in sales and distribution.

On the following screen, enter the **Company Code**, and press the ⌷Enter⌷ key or click the **Continue** button. You'll arrive at the **Enter Customer Credit Memo** screen, as shown in

Figure 5.44. Enter the required data in the **Basic data** tab, such as **Customer** number, **Document date**, **Amount**, **Posting Date**, **Reference** (contains the document number of the customer or any value), and so on. You can go through the other tabs as well, such as **Payment**, where you can define **Bline Date** (baseline date), which refers to the date from which the payment applies; **Payment terms**; and other tabs if necessary. In the **Details** tab, you can define the **G/L account** to which the transaction figures are updated, as well as the **Credit Area** that monitors a credit limit for customers. You can enter other fields in the remaining tabs if they are relevant to the transaction you're performing.

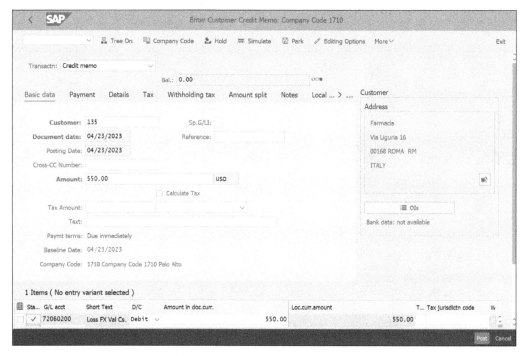

Figure 5.44 Enter Customer Credit Memo Screen

After you've entered the required data in the respective fields, go to the line items, and enter at least one general ledger line item (**G/L acct**, **D/C** [debit/credit indicator], **Amount in doc.curr.**, etc.). This line item corresponds to an offset of an incoming payment account.

In the next step, you can simulate the posting by clicking the **Simulate** button at the top of the screen. Based on the entered data in your example, you'll receive an unsuccessful result with an error message or a successful result showing how the document entries will be posted, as shown in Figure 5.45.

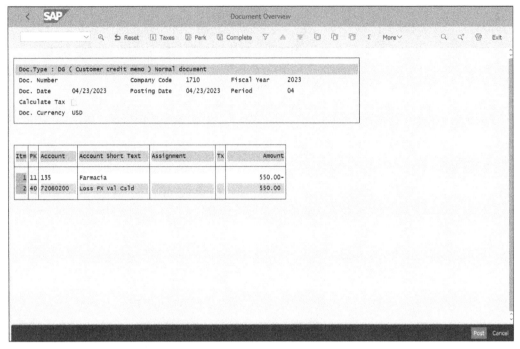

Figure 5.45 Credit Memo Document Overview/Simulation

After you've run the simulation, click the **Post** button, and a message with the new document number will appear. The customer credit memo that you just posted will appear as shown in Figure 5.46.

Figure 5.46 Display Document of Credit Memo

Click on each of the lines to display the document line items, as shown in Figure 5.47 and Figure 5.48.

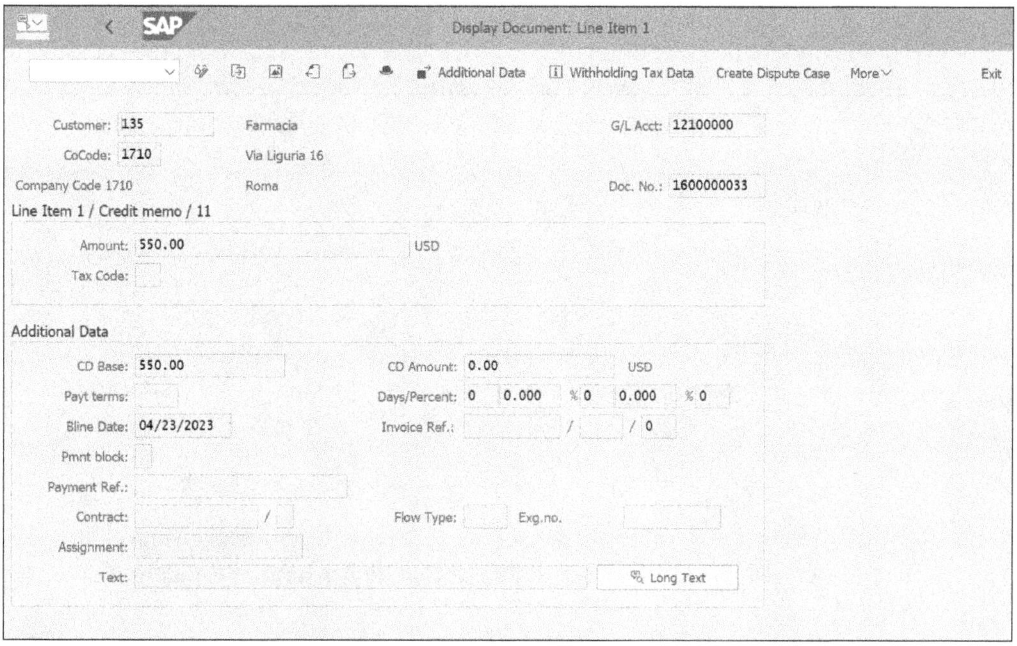

Figure 5.47 Display Document Line Item 1

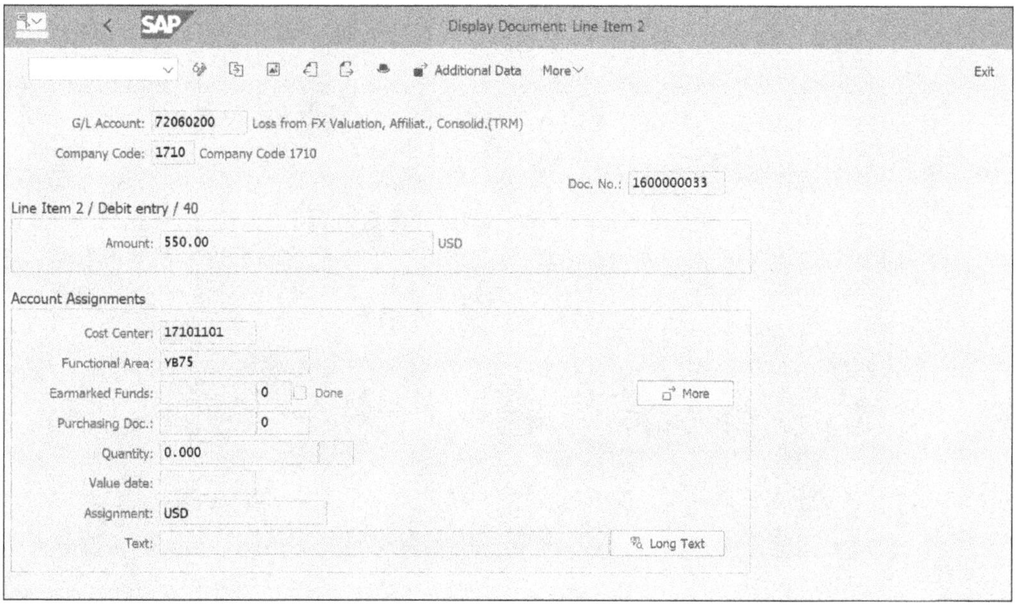

Figure 5.48 Display Document Line Item 2

Double-clicking on the first record, you can see the **Line Item 1** referring to the posting key **11** as a credit entry with the **Amount 550.00 USD**. There are also other details of the entry, such as **Customer** number, **CoCode** (company code), respective **G/L Acc**, **Doc. No.** (document number), **Bline Date** (baseline date), and so on.

In the second record, you can see the **Line Item 2** referring to the posting key **40** as a debit entry with the same **Amount 550.00 USD**. Here, you can also see similar fields as in the first line, such as respective **G/L Account**, **Company Code**, **Amount**, **Doc. No.** (document number), **Assignment** (used as an additional reference field), and so on.

SAP Fiori App

The corresponding SAP Fiori app is called Manage Credit Memo Request (F1989), as shown in Figure 5.49. Enter data based on the selection criteria, such as specific **Credit Memo Request**, **Sold-to Party**, **Customer Reference**, **Billing Date**, **Billing Status**, and **Document Date**, and then click the **Go** button to display the credit memo requests. For example, you can restrict your searching criteria by entering a specific customer in the **Sold-to Party** field, and the result will show the credit memo requests relevant to this customer. In Figure 5.49, the **Go** button has been clicked without defining any searching criteria.

To create a new credit memo request, click the **Create Credit Memo Request** button, which will lead you to the **Create Sales Documents** popup, from where you need to select the order type as a mandatory field. For this example, **CR Credit Memo Request** has been selected, as shown in Figure 5.50. The other available document types are as follows:

- **GA2**: Refers to credit memo request returning type.
- **RK**: Refers to the invoice correction request.

Then, optionally, you can define the other fields in the **Organizational Data** area and click the **Continue** button, which leads to the **Create Credit Memo Request: Overview** screen shown in Figure 5.51. In the header area, enter the required data, such as **Credit Memo Request** from the preconfigured values, **Sold-to Party** for the customer who makes the order, **Ship-to Party** for the party who receives the order, and **Cust. Reference**. You can also go through the **Sales**, **Item Overview**, **Item detail**, **Ordering party**, **Procurement**, and **Reason for rejection** tabs to define the required information, similar to the example in Section 5.1.

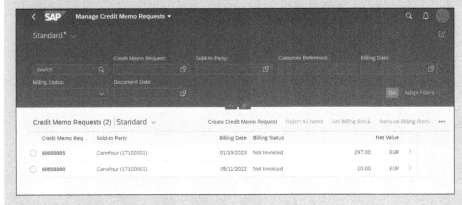

Figure 5.49 Manage Credit Memo Requests App in SAP Fiori

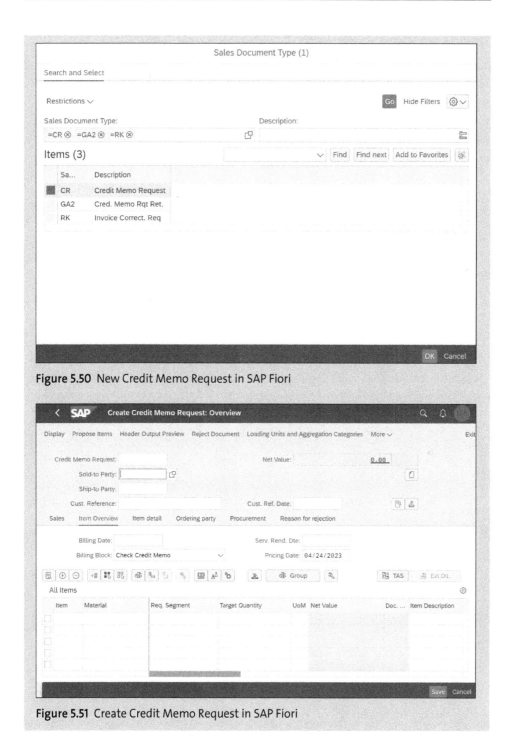

Figure 5.50 New Credit Memo Request in SAP Fiori

Figure 5.51 Create Credit Memo Request in SAP Fiori

5.5.2 Down Payments Received

Down payments received are very similar to received advance payments because they are payments made in advance from the customer before or while receiving goods or services. This may happen, for example, when the customer has a low rating on credit-worthiness. For that reason, the company asks for a prepayment from the customer by issuing a down payment request. That is also very common in long-term contracts, such as in the construction sector where the order fulfillment can take more than a year. A customer down payment request is entered in the system and then cleared against an incoming down payment.

Down payments are first initiated by a payment request, which is a note in financial accounting that doesn't impact the balance sheet at all. Therefore, the general ledger account balances remain unchanged. Only the incoming payment will impact the balance sheet but not income accounts. Upon goods/services delivery or receipt, the down payment starts the clearing process against the final invoice.

You can create a down payment request in accounts receivable using Transaction F-37 or following application menu path **Accounting • Financial Accounting • Accounts Receivable • Document Entry • Down Payment • Request**.

The **Customer Down Payment Request: Header Data** screen appears, as shown in Figure 5.52.

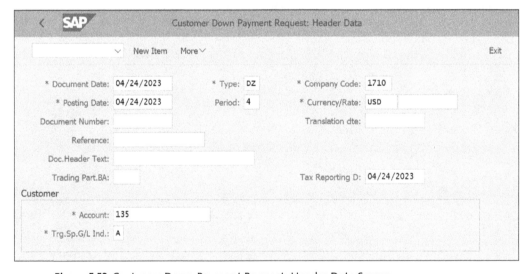

Figure 5.52 Customer Down Payment Request: Header Data Screen

Enter the required data in the document header area, such as **Document Date**, **Posting Date**, document **Type** (classifies the accounting document), **Company Code**, **Currency/Rate**, and **Tax Reporting D** (represents the date on which the tax on sales and purchases is due or the date on which the tax should be reported to the tax authority). Here you can also define other optional fields if necessary. In the **Customer** area, specify the **Account** and **Trg.Sp.G/L Ind.** as a special general ledger indicator for a down payment request with the possible values of **A** for down payment, **C** for rent deposit, **D** for doubtful receivables, and so on.

After you've completed the header data, click on the **New Item** button. In the **Customer Down Payment Request Add Customer item** screen that appears, enter the **Amount**, **Due on** (due date for the payment), and **Payt Method** indicator (direct debit, check, bank transfer, etc.), as shown in Figure 5.53. There are other optional fields, such as **Network**, **Cost Center**, **Profit Ctr**, **Assignment**, **Text** description, and so on, which, depending on the case, can be defined with a value.

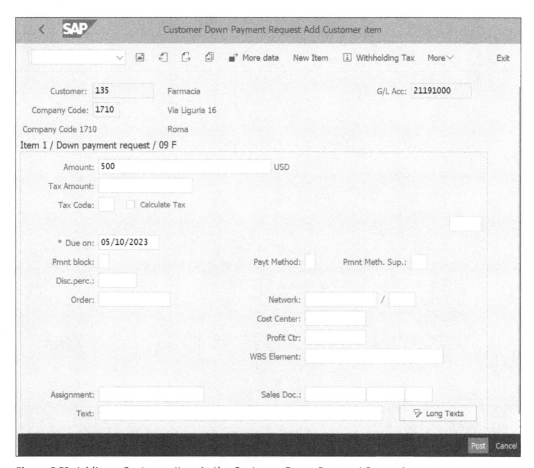

Figure 5.53 Adding a Customer Item in the Customer Down Payment Request

After you've entered the values in the header data, click the **Post** button, which posts the customer down payment request. At the bottom of the screen, you'll receive a message with the new document number created.

SAP Fiori Apps

The corresponding SAP Fiori app is called Manage Customer Down Payment Request (F1689). In Figure 5.54, you can see the screen for managing down payment requests for a specific customer in SAP Fiori. Click on the **Go** button after you've entered the search criteria in the relevant fields (e.g., **Customer**, **Company Code**, and **Posted By**) to show the list of the customer down payment requests.

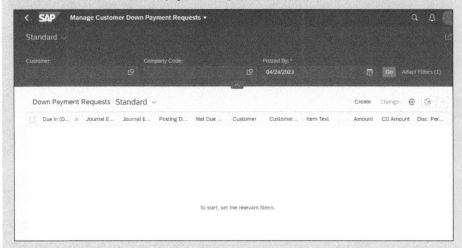

Figure 5.54 Manage Customer Down Payment Requests App in SAP Fiori

Click the **Create** button to create a new down payment request (see Figure 5.55). Enter the required data in the **Header** area (e.g., **Company Code**, **Journal Entry Date** referring to the document date, **Posting Date**, **Journal Entry Type** referring to the document type [e.g., **AA** asset posting, **AB** journal entry, **AD** accruals/deferrals, **DZ** customer payment], **Fiscal Year**, **Transaction Currency**, and other fields if necessary). In the **Items** area, enter data such as **Customer** and **Amount**, and then click the **Simulate** button. After a successful simulation, click the **Post** button to post the down payment request.

Figure 5.55 New Customer Down Payment Request in SAP Fiori

Another available SAP Fiori app is called Post Customer Down Payment Request (F-37). In this app, after you've filled in header data, you need to press [Enter], which leads to the next screen where you can add the customer item and click the **Post** button. The steps are similar to those explained for Transaction F-37 in SAP GUI.

Now that you've learned how to deal with the process exceptions, let's move on to the dunning process with the customer.

5.6   Dunning

Dunning is the process of sending letters to customers to remind them that they are late in paying. Dunning is an important communication activity that helps in collecting money from the customer faster. If there is no strict dunning process in place, the open items in accounts receivable may not be paid at all. The method of communicating with the customer depends on the overdue receivables and starts with friendly reminders that escalate up to official claiming letters and phone calls.

In SAP S/4HANA, to set up a dunning, you need to apply the necessary configurations and settings in the customer master data. However, because configuration isn't covered in this book, we'll only explain how you can execute a dunning program, assuming it's successfully configured and tested.

5.6.1   Automated Dunning Process

You can execute the dunning program using Transaction F150 or following application menu path **Accounting • Financial Accounting • Accounts Receivable • Periodic Processing • Dunning**. The **Dunning** screen will appear, as shown in Figure 5.56.

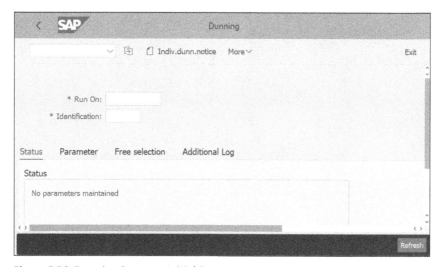

Figure 5.56 Dunning Program Initial Screen

On this screen, enter the date when the program is to be run in the **Run On** field, and use the **Identification** field to distinguish several runs with the same key date. The **Identification** field is automatically populated after you select the run date.

Click on the **Parameter** tab. In the **Dunning: Parameters** screen that appears, you can see that most of the fields such as **Dunning Date**, **Docmnts Posted up To**, **Company Code**, and values for **Customer** or **Supplier** in the **Account Restrictions** area are automatically updated, as shown in Figure 5.57, which you can also change per your case. **Dunning Date** refers to the issue date of the dunning notice and is also used as the basis for calculating the days in arrears. **Docmnts Posted up To** refers to the posting date up to which documents are included. Only items that have been posted up to this date can be processed. These two dates aren't meant to be the same value. After you've entered all parameters, you can save the dunning program by selecting **More • Dunning Notice Menu • Save**.

In the **Status** area, shown in Figure 5.58, there are three messages confirming that the parameters you've entered have been maintained, the dunning is scheduled for the indicated date, and the customer/vendor selection has been made.

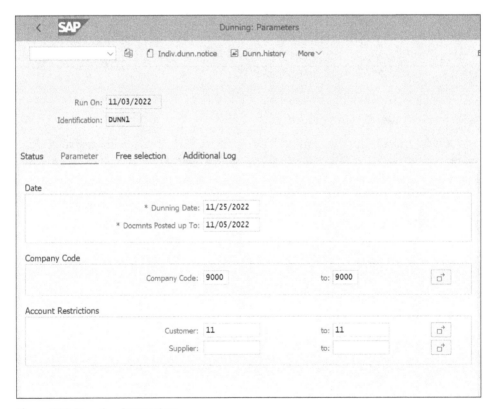

Figure 5.57 Dunning Parameters

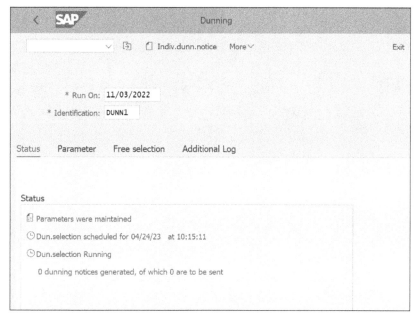

Figure 5.58 Dunning Program Status Messages

Now, after performing the dunning program, you can schedule the dunning run by choosing **More • Dunning Notice Menu • Schedule Sample dunn.printout**.

You'll arrive at the **Schedule Selection and Print** screen shown in Figure 5.59, where you can define the values for **Start Date** and **Start Time**, or you can schedule an immediate start by selecting the **Start Immediately** checkbox.

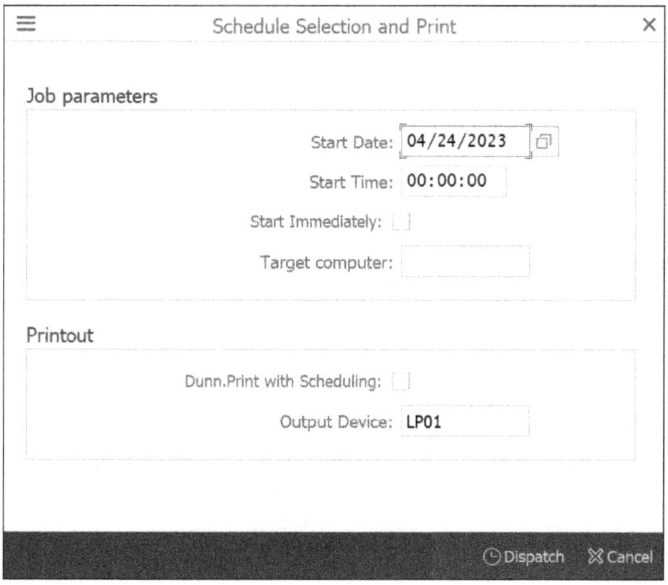

Figure 5.59 Dunning Program Schedule

You can also define the range of customers or vendors, and select the **Output Device** used for printing dunning messages generated during the process. After you've entered all the necessary values, click the **Dispatch** button in the dialog box.

> **SAP Fiori App**
>
> The corresponding SAP Fiori app is called Create Dunning Notices (F150). It's visually and functionally the same as the SAP GUI transaction.

Next, let's discuss how you can create an individual dunning notice letter.

5.6.2   Manual Dunning Letters

In the **Dunning** program screen that opens while executing Transaction F150, you also have the option to create an individual dunning notice. Click on **Indiv.dunn.notice** at the top of the window, and the **Output Parameters** screen will appear to allow you to select the output device. After you select the output device, click the **Continue** button to go to the **Individual Dunning Notice** screen, as shown in Figure 5.60.

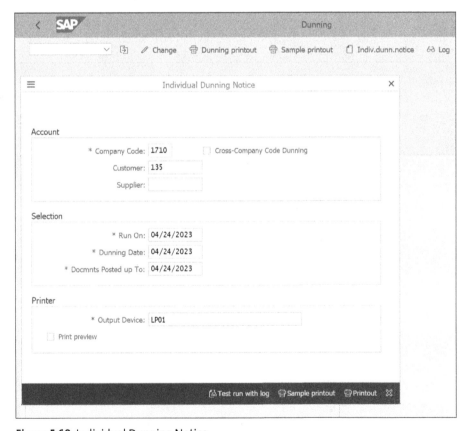

Figure 5.60 Individual Dunning Notice

Here, you can enter the required values in the following areas:

- **Account**
  Enter the **Company Code** and **Customer** account number to send the notice to.
- **Selection**
  Enter the **Run On** date showing the date on which the program is to be executed as planned, the **Dunning Date** on which you want to issue the notice, and **Docmnts Posted up To** date, which indicates that only documents posted up to this date are included in the process. You can enter the same value for each of these three fields.
- **Printer**
  Change the selected **Output Device** chosen from the initial step (**LP01** in this example).

Now you can click on the **Test run with log** button, and a message appears in a separate **Dunning Data** screen showing the dunning procedure final status. After that, you can print the dunning notice and send it to the respective customer.

In the next section, we'll explain the credit management process and the main credit management checks: simple and automated.

5.7 Credit Management

Credit management is another important subject in accounts receivable. As mentioned earlier, in business-to-business transactions, payments are due according to payment terms after goods have been delivered and services have been fulfilled. The threshold amount that a customer is allowed to order and receive without payment is maintained in the **Credit Limit** field as a part of the customer master data.

A *credit limit* is a credit facility—a temporary loan—granted to the customer by the company as a credit exposure allowance. Let's suppose you create a credit limit for one of your customers in the amount of 300,000 USD. The customer with this credit limit can purchase products and services to the amount of 300,000 USD without triggering any payments. The moment the order amount exceeds the credit limit amount, however, this order is automatically blocked by the system due to insufficient credit limit.

Credit limits can be different for each customer depending on the payment method, customer payment history, and the rating of creditworthiness provided by a credit inquiry agency. Credit management allows the company to monitor and mitigate the credit risk by setting up a credit limit for its customers. The responsible unit in the company receives warning alerts for a specific customer or group of customers. For example, customers with a good credit indicator can be assigned a grace period of a certain number of specified days according to the organization's standard rules. How credit management is configured changes from one organization to another based on different factors such as risk exposure, risk tolerance, customer risk categorization, customer payment behavior, customer history, and so on.

There are two types of credit management checks you can use:

- Simple credit limit check
- Automatic credit limit check

In the upcoming sections, we'll explain the credit master data and credit limits customization, as well as both types of simple and automatic credit limit checks.

5.7.1   Credit Master Data and Credit Limits

The credit master data is defined and updated in the master data record of the customer (or business partner, because vendors can also have credit limits). This credit master data of the business partner is the basis of the SAP S/4HANA credit management function, which is necessary for all credit ratings and evaluations of customers. The credit master data of a business partner can refer to the **Credit Profile** area, including scoring rules and credit limit calculations, external rating, risk classification, and so on, as well as the **Credit Segment Data** area, which includes credit segment, credit limit, credit exposure, payment behavior, and so on. In the business partner master data, you can define, for example, the rules to calculate the score, risk class, credit limit, customer credit group, special indicators, block reason records, and so on.

You can access the business partner master data using Transaction UKM_BP or application menu path **Accounting • Financial Supply Chain Management • Credit Management • Master Data • Business Partner Master Data**.

The **Maintain Business Partner** screen appears, as shown in Figure 5.61. You can create a new business partner as a **Person**, as an **Organization**, or as a **Group**. In this screen, you can also search for a specified business partner by its code number.

Let's create a new business partner as a person by clicking the **Person** button at the top of the screen. You'll arrive at the **Create Person** screen, as shown in Figure 5.62.

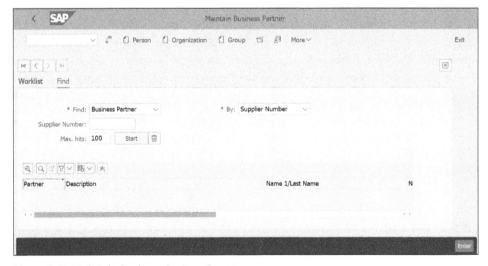

Figure 5.61 Maintain Business Partner Screen

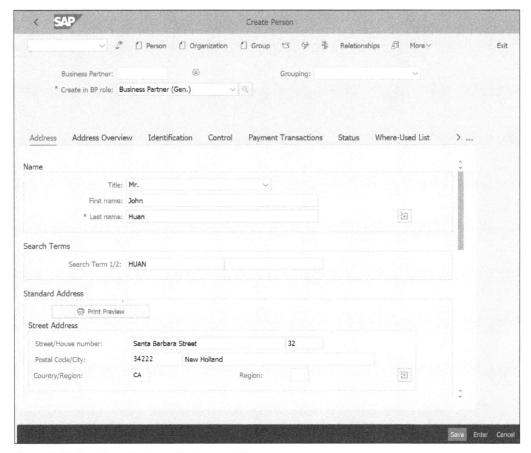

Figure 5.62 Creating a Business Partner as a Person

Enter the required data such as **Title**, **First name**, **Last name**, and **Search Term ½** to enter a searching term for this person being created. In addition, enter the address details such as house number, postal code, country, and communication (e.g., telephone, fax, email, etc.). In each of these areas, you can click the ⊞ icon to enter more information if necessary.

In the **Identification** tab, you can enter personal data (gender, nationality, marital status), **Identification** numbers (ID type, description, ID number, etc.), and tax numbers if relevant. In the **Control** tab, you can enter control parameters (business partner type, authorization group, printing format), notes, and so on. In the **Payment Transactions** tab, you can enter bank details and payment card dates. You can also go through the other tabs and enter the values in the fields if necessary.

After you've entered the values, click the **Save** button, and you'll receive a message with the business partner number created. You can display the business partner created by clicking the 🖉 icon (switches between display and change) or by choosing **More • Business Partner • Display – Change**. This leads to the **Change Person** screen, as shown in Figure 5.63.

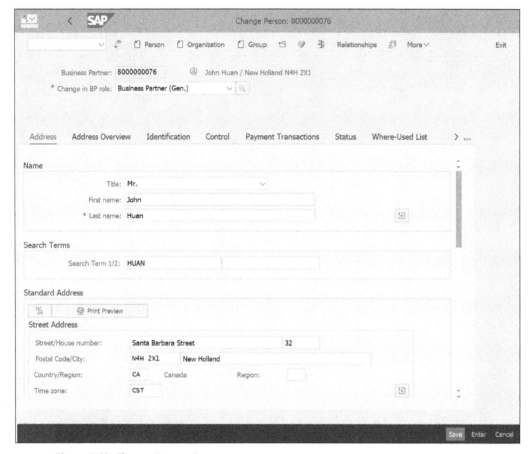

Figure 5.63 Change Person Screen

Now that you've created a general master data record for the business partner, you can customize settings for the scoring rule, credit limit calculations, check rules, risk classes, and so on. For that, in the screen shown in Figure 5.63, you need to change the business partner role to **SAP Credit Management (New)** in the **Change in BP role** dropdown. Then, you can define and customize the relevant credit limit settings in the following tabs:

- **Credit Profile**
  On the **Credit Profile** tab shown in Figure 5.64, enter a rule for calculating the score and credit limit of the business partner from the **Rules** checklist. For the system to calculate the score, choose the **Calculate with Formula** [icon] icon next to the **Score** level, which indicates the score calculated by SAP S/4HANA credit management for a business partner. This score can be automatically calculated, or you can overwrite it manually. **Risk Class** indicates the classification of the score, and this value can also be overwritten manually. If necessary, enter also a customer **Credit Group**, which is a selection criterion in the transactions for mass changes in the credit master data. If

necessary, you can enter **External Credit Information** or include the information using the **Import Data** button.

You can also enter a business partner relationship by choosing the **Relationships** button in the upper menu. This function is used to maintain the relationships of the business partner. The business partner can be an analyst or an analyst group. Using the **Relationships** functionality, you can restrict the relationship to one credit segment or allow it to be valid for all credit segments.

- **Creditworthiness Data**
  In the **Creditworthiness Data** tab shown in Figure 5.65, enter the values in **Credit Standing**, which indicates an internal, time-independent classification of the business partners; **Dt.Cred.Stndg** as the date on which credit standing information was provided; **Stat.Cred.Stndg**, which indicates the status of the credit standing information; **Cred.Stndg Text** for the additional text for the credit standing; and a **Rating** to store the business partner rating (**A**, **AA**, **AAA**, **B**, **BB**, **BBB**, etc.).

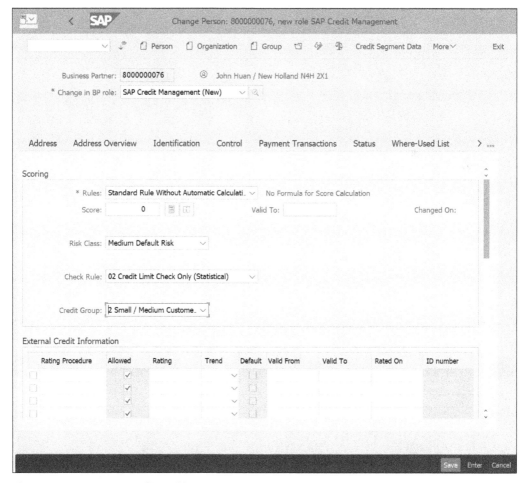

Figure 5.64 Customer Credit Profile

If necessary, mark the listed checkboxes **Affidavit**, which indicates that the business partner has made an affirmation of their assets; **Bankruptcy Proceed.**, which indicates that bankruptcy procedures have been initiated against the business partner; **Foreclosure**, which indicates that foreclosure procedures have been initiated against the business partner; and their respective dates on the right side. Selecting the **Status of Leg. Proc.** option shows the status of legal proceedings based on the national legal framework. Possible entries can be no legal actions taken; under judicial administration, receivership, or similar measures; bankruptcy/insolvency; and other legal measures. In the **Date of Legal Proc.** field, enter the date when legal proceedings were initiated.

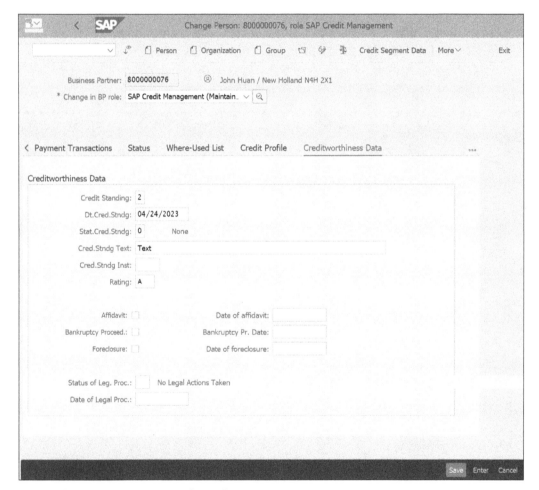

Figure 5.65 Customer Creditworthiness

After you've entered all the required data, click the **Save** button, and you'll receive the message that the changes you've performed have been saved.

SAP Fiori Apps

The corresponding SAP Fiori app for the business partner is called Manage Business Partner Master Data (F3163). It's visually and functionally the same as the SAP GUI transaction.

The corresponding SAP Fiori app to display credit master data is called Display Credit Master Data (UKM_BP_DISPLAY). It's visually and functionally the same as the SAP GUI transaction.

5.7.2 Simple Credit Check

The *simple credit check* compares the customer credit limit with the total number of open items and current sales order. If the total number of open items and current sales order exceed the credit limit value, then the system will send a warning message to the customer. The exposure of the customer always refers to the outstanding balance as a sum of open item values and current sales order values.

Note

To review, *open item values* refer to the sale orders that have been already delivered, billed, and reflected in financial accounting, but the payment isn't posted from the customer. *Current sales order* refers to the order that has been created but not delivered.

5.7.3 Automated Credit Check

The automated credit check is a configuration in the SAP S/4HANA system that provides additional credit facility to the customer even when his credit limit is exceeded. This can be applied to customers that have good purchase history. There are two types of automatic credit checks:

- **Static credit check**
  Checks the credit limit amount with the total value of open items, open delivery not invoiced, and billing values of open billing document not transferred to accounting.

- **Dynamic credit check**
  Checks the credit limit value with the total amount of open sales orders not yet delivered, open deliveries not invoiced, billing value of open billing document not transferred to accounting, and bill amounts that are transferred but not yet paid.

In the next section, we'll discuss the period-end closing of the accounts receivable subledger, referring to the most important topics such as the valuation of foreign currency, the billing due list, reclassification runs, and reconciliation.

5.8   Accounts Receivable Period-End Closing

We took our first look at period-end closing for the general ledger in Chapter 3, Section 3.6. Before continuing with the closing operations in general ledger accounting, you first need to perform the closing process in the subledger accounting you're using—in this case, accounts receivable. The period-end closing consists of two stages: First, a reconciliation process is required of accounts receivable general ledger accounts with the details in the accounts receivable application. Second, after this process is sorted out, you can update the record statuses and customer period statistics.

5.8.1   Foreign Currency Valuation

Foreign currency valuation refers to an accounting concept that defines the process by which the open items in foreign currency are valuated and translated into the company functional currency. This process can be applied for every accounting period.

The items and accounts included in the foreign currency valuation refer to the following:

- **Foreign currency balance sheet accounts, which are the general ledger account managed in foreign currency**
  The general ledger account balances, which aren't part of the open items, are valuated in foreign currency.

- **Open items posted in foreign currency**
  These items are open on the key date and are valuated in foreign currency.

In this section, we'll explain some configurations needed to set up and run the valuation process. Before a company creates financial statements, it has to perform foreign currency valuation for all the foreign currency transactions performed in accounts receivable.

To access the foreign currency valuation in accounts receivable, use Transaction FAGL_FCV, or follow application menu path **Accounting • Financial Accounting • Accounts Receivable • Periodic Processing • Closing • Valuate • Valuation of Open Items in Foreign Currency**.

You'll arrive at the **Foreign Currency Valuation** screen, as shown in Figure 5.66 and Figure 5.67, where several tabs and fields are available to be filled.

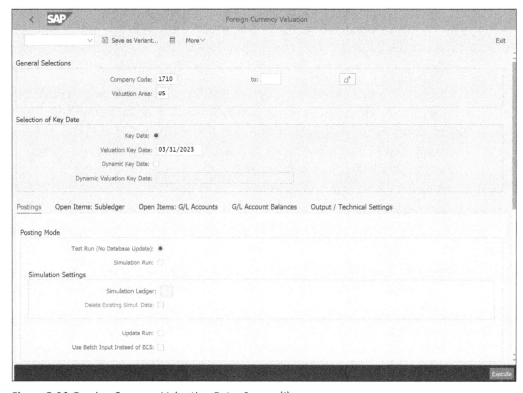

Figure 5.66 Foreign Currency Valuation Entry Screen (1)

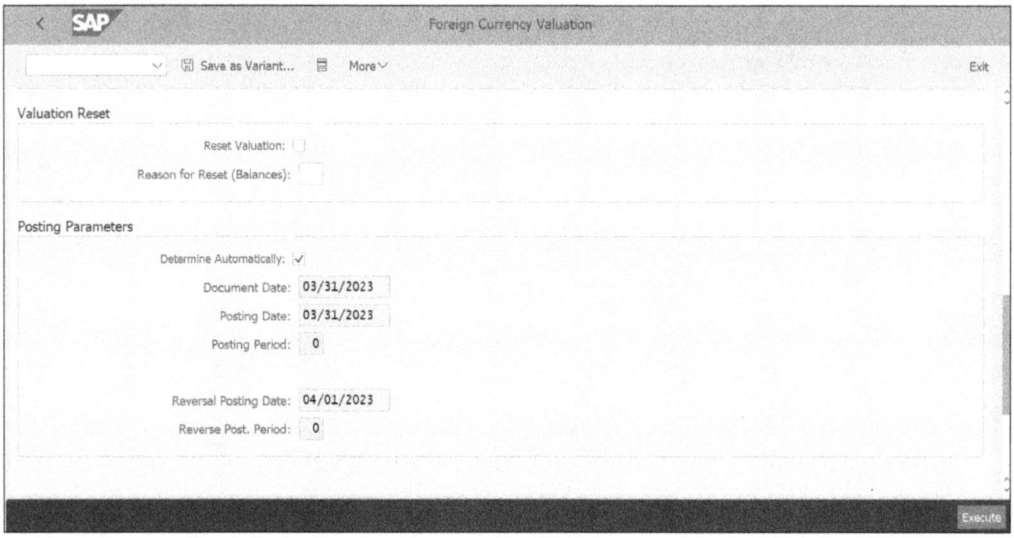

Figure 5.67 Foreign Currency Valuation Entry Screen (2)

Enter the required data in the **General Selections** area, such as **Company Code** and **Valuation Area**, as well as **Valuation Key Date** in the **Selection of Key Date** area. Then, go through the following tabs:

- **Postings**

  Under **Posting Mode**, choose one of the two options: **Test Run (No Database Update)**, which controls whether the test run takes place or not, or **Simulation Run**, which enables you to simulate a foreign currency valuation run in the same valuation area as the production run. Under **Simulation Settings**, define the **Simulation Ledger** in which the simulation run results are stored. Choose whether or not to delete the existing simulation data. You can enter the other fields as well if necessary.

- **Open Items: Subledger**

  Define the customer range to perform the valuation of open items for certain customer accounts.

- **Open Items: G/L Accounts**

  Define the selection criteria to valuate open items for certain general ledger accounts.

- **G/L Account Balances**

  Specify that the balances of the selected general ledger accounts will be evaluated.

- **Output / Technical Settings**

  Enter information about the log storage (if the logs are saved in the database or not), name the result list, and configure some other settings that are self-explanatory.

After you've entered and selected all necessary data, click on the **Execute** button to generate the valuation document.

SAP Fiori App

The corresponding SAP Fiori app is called Perform Foreign Currency Valuation (FAGL_FCV). This SAP Fiori app is visually and functionally the same as the SAP GUI transaction.

5.8.2   Billing Due Lists

The *billing due list* is considered a group or collection of transactions and deliveries that are already invoiced or billable. These documents are gathered and put together in the billing due list based on some predefined criteria. While processing the billing due list, it's not necessary to enter each document to be invoiced manually. The system lists the documents and makes the selection by considering certain criteria, which allows several deliveries to be combined and included together in one invoice document. When you save a transaction where at least one item is billing-relevant, data from this transaction is transferred to the billing component. In this step, this data is checked and supplemented with master data and then stored in a billing due list.

The criteria for how the system will select the worklist are defined before the billing document is created by considering some of the following conditions:

- Which transactions will be billed and how is based on options such as billing type, billing date, destination country, sold-to party, exchange agreement, and so on.
- How the selected document will be billed is based on characteristics such as order-related, delivery-related, and so on.

In SAP S/4HANA, you can process a billing document by running Transaction VF04 or following application menu path **Logistics • Sales and Distribution • Billing • Billing Document • Process Billing Due List**.

The **Maintain Billing Due List** screen appears, as shown in Figure 5.68. Enter the values in the **Billing Data** header section, such as **Billing Date From**, **Billing Type** (classifies types of billing documents that require different processing by the system), and **SD Document** range or a particular sales and distribution document.

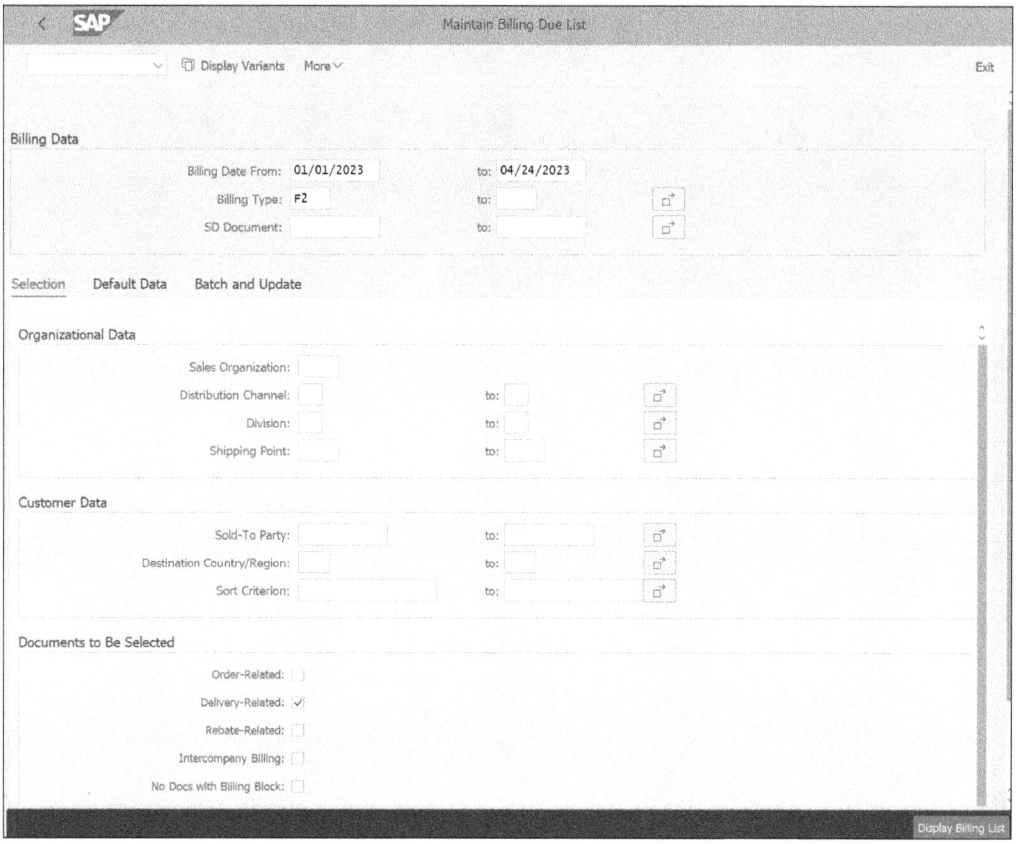

Figure 5.68 Maintain Billing Due List

Then, go through the following tabs:

- **Selection**

  In the **Selection** tab, you can enter **Organizational Data** (**Sales Organization** as a responsible unit for the sale of certain products), and **Distribution Channel**, which indicates how the order reaches the customer, for example, retail, wholesale, direct sales, and so on.

  In the **Customer Data** area, enter information for the **Sold-To Party** (the customer who orders the product), **Destination Country/Region**, and so on. In the **Documents to Be Selected** area, choose any of the options: documents that relate directly to sales documents, to deliveries, to intercompany billing documents, and so on.

- **Default Data**

  You can also go through the **Default Data** tab in which you can enter the billing type, billing date, date of service rendered (shows when the system calculates taxes), and pricing date.

- **Batch and Update**

  In this tab, you can select the output data form and the update process.

Then, click the **Display Billing List** button, and the billing list is presented as shown in Figure 5.69.

S	BlCat	SOrg.	Billing Date	Sold-to Party	BillT	Ctry/R	Document	DChl	Dv	Doc.Ca	Address	Sold-to Party Name	Sold-toLoc	ShPt	Net Value	Curr.	Typ	Name of Doc. Type
L	4900		03/24/2023	8000000055	F2	DE	80000378	01	01	J	28652	customer black	Frankfurt	4901	4.00	EUR	LF	Outbound Delivery
L	AG20		01/05/2023	67	F2	DE	80000162	10	00	J	25985	AG02 AG02	DE	1710	180.00	USD	LF	Outbound Delivery
L	AG20		03/01/2023	67	F2	DE	80000239	10	00	J	25985	AG02 AG02	DE	1710	1,600.00	USD	LF	Outbound Delivery
L	AG20		03/31/2023	67	F2	DE	80000402	10	00	J	25985	AG02 AG02	DE	1710	31,970.03	USD	LF	Outbound Delivery
L	DE00		04/04/2023	111	F2	DE	80000405	10	00	J	26738	Demo Customer 01	Nürtingen	DE0	50,000.00	EUR	LF	Outbound Delivery
L	DE00		04/19/2023	111	F2	DE	80000412	10	10	J	26738	Demo Customer 01	Nürtingen	DE0	500.00	EUR	LF	Outbound Delivery
L	ZDIB		03/28/2023	17100001	F2	US	80000379	ZD	ZD	J	23653	Carrefour	Atlanta	ZDIB	99.00	EUR	LF	Outbound Delivery

Figure 5.69 Billing Due List

In this screen, you can select/deselect the documents that you want to bill or not bill. Furthermore, you have several billing options, as you can see at the bottom of the screen:

- **Simulation**

  Billing documents are processed as a simulation. Therefore, the system simulates the selected documents from the preceding function, **Collective Billing Doc./Online**.

- **Individual Billing Document**

  A billing document can be processed for one selected document in the list. In this case, there isn't a combination of documents, and there is one preceding document for each selected document to the current billing document.

- **Collective Billing Document**
  All selected documents in the billing due list are combined and processed in background mode. After the processing, all these documents are returned in the billing due list where each of them has an indicator showing if the process was successful or not.

- **Collective Billing Doc./Online**
  With the selected documents, the system uses Transaction VF01, through which these documents are then collected following the selected criteria in the relevant function.

After displaying the billing lists and processing using one of the preceding options, you can click the **Simulation** button and then display the relevant processing log by selecting **More • Edit • Log** or directly by pressing ⌈Shift⌉+⌈1⌉ (see Figure 5.70).

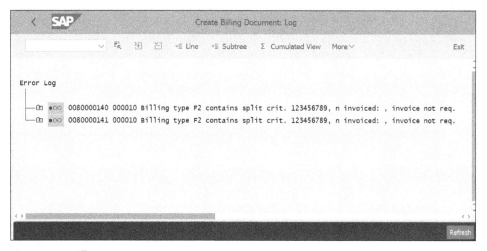

Figure 5.70 Billing Document Logs

In this log file, information regarding errors reported during the billing documents is displayed. In the log report, you can also see the billing documents that were successfully created.

SAP Fiori App

The corresponding SAP Fiori app to create and manage a billing due list is called Maintain Billing Due List, Create Billing Documents (VF04). This SAP Fiori app is visually and functionally the same as the SAP GUI transaction.

In the next section, we'll discuss the reclassification run procedure as part of the financial statement process.

5.8.3   Reclassification Run

The reclassification process in accounts receivable is an important closing step that is used to display receivables in the correct way. While preparing financial statements, there are two requirements to be fulfilled for accounts receivable:

- Display a credit balance on a customer account as payable and a debit balance on a vendor account as receivable in such cases.

- Sort items referring to the remaining terms for balance sheet reporting.

In this section, we'll walk through the reclassification run process, starting with the necessary configuration and ending with performing the run itself.

Configuration

In SAP S/4HANA, it's possible to fulfill both requirements using Transaction FAGL_CL_ REGROUP. For the reclassification process, or sometimes called the regrouping process, some basic configurations need to be customized. You must define a sort method interval in Customizing as well as accounts determination for the reclassification by following application menu path **Tools • Customizing • IMG • SPRO – Execute Project • SAP Reference IMG • Financial Accounting • General Ledger Accounting • Periodic Processing • Reclassify • Transfer and Sort Receivables and Payables • Define Sort Method and Adjustment Accts for Regrouping Receivables/Payables**.

In the **Change View "Sort Methods": Overview** screen that appears (see Figure 5.71), you can see the existing intervals by double-clicking the **Receivables** folder. The **Change View "Receivables": Overview** screen opens (see Figure 5.72), where you can see that the configuration contains two account determination keys for this sort method with the values **V00** and **V01**, respectively. These keys indicate time intervals of the sort method, which type of posting will be used, the managing method, and so on. These keys are also linked to the particular general ledger accounts that are taken into consideration during processing. The first key, **V00**, is determined for customer postings, or vendor postings in the case of payable sort methods, and general ledger account postings specified with a receivable due date less than or equal to a year. The other key, **V01**, is defined for the same posting types but for general ledger account postings with a receivable due date greater than a year.

Now you can click on the **Account** button of the first account determination key, **V00**, where you'll be asked to define the chart of accounts you're using. In this example, the standard chart of accounts (**YCOA**) has been entered, as shown in Figure 5.73.

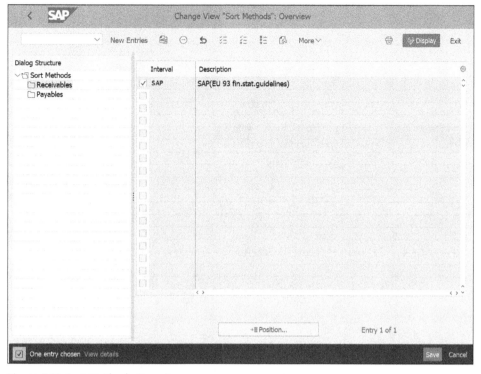

Figure 5.71 Sort Methods Overview

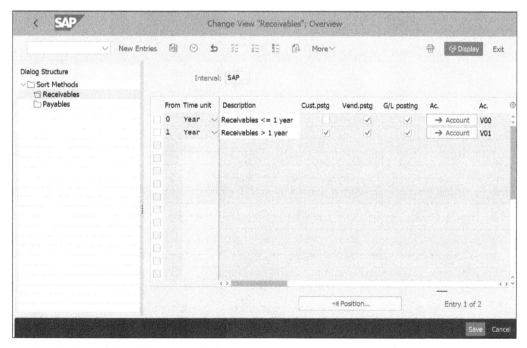

Figure 5.72 Change View "Receivables": Overview

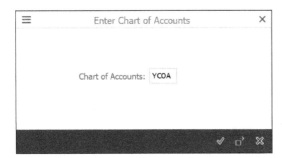

Figure 5.73 Enter Chart of Accounts Screen

After you've selected the chart of accounts, click the **Continue** (green checkmark) button, and the screen shown in Figure 5.74 appears, displaying the list of accounts defined to be used for the key. This list of accounts is a preconfigured list in the system belonging to the selected chart of accounts **YCOA**.

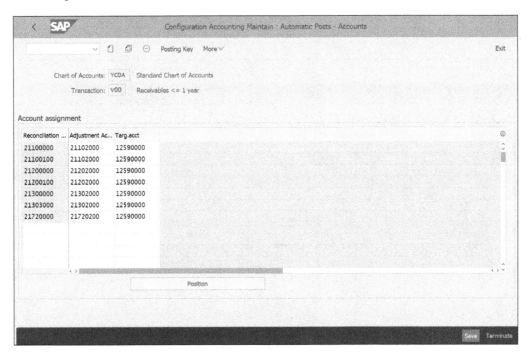

Figure 5.74 Configuration Accounting Maintain: Automatic Posts – Accounts Screen

The **Reconciliation account** column contains the preconfigured reconciliation accounts specified for the sorting and grouping program. The **Adjustment Account** column contains adjustment accounts that will be posted to. This account is presented in the balance sheet/profit and loss (P&L) statement together with the account to be adjusted. The **Targ.acct** column is for the target account that will be used for the offset postings. This is the account to which the amount is to be posted and by which the balance of the defined account is to be adjusted.

Process Open Items

Now that you've completed the configuration steps, let's focus on the processing of open items using the reclassification/regrouping report. You can run Transaction FAGLF101 or follow application menu path **Accounting • Financial Accounting • Accounts Receivable • Periodic Processing • Closing • Reclassify • Sorting/Reclassification (New)**.

The **Balance Sheet Supplement - OI - Analysis** screen appears, as shown in Figure 5.75. In the header area, enter the **Company Code**, **Balance Sheet Key Date**, **Sort Method** (as a unique key used for sorting open items according to a method), and **Valuation Area**.

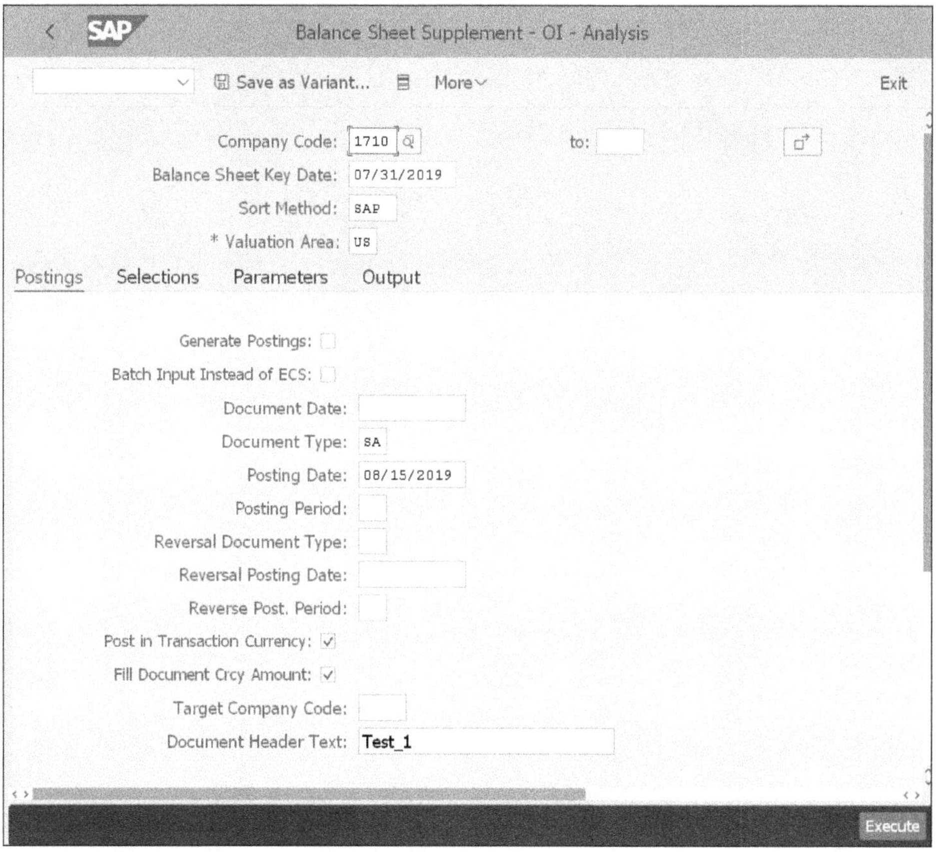

Figure 5.75 Balance Sheet Supplement Header Data

Then, in the **Selections** tab, enter the **Account Type** for customer (**D**) and **Customer** number, as shown in Figure 5.76. In the **Parameters** tab, you can select any options in the **Grouping** area, in **Other Parameters**, and **List Output** to define the layout for the list format. In the **Output** tab, you can define the log storage criteria, such as **Displaying Log**, **Saving Log**, and entering the **Name** under which the system stores the results list.

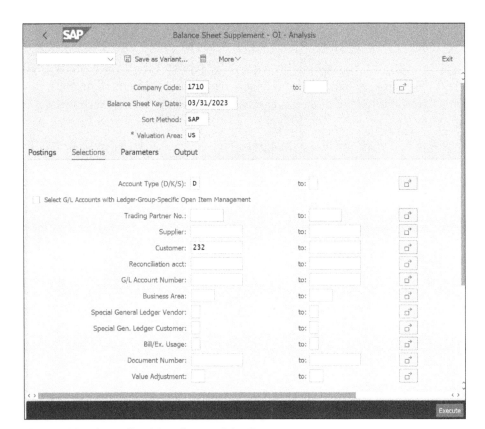

Figure 5.76 Balance Sheet Supplement Selections

After you've entered the necessary values, run the report by clicking the **Execute** button. The results will appear as in Figure 5.77. As you can see in the report in this example, items have been grouped by account and summed on the valuated amount.

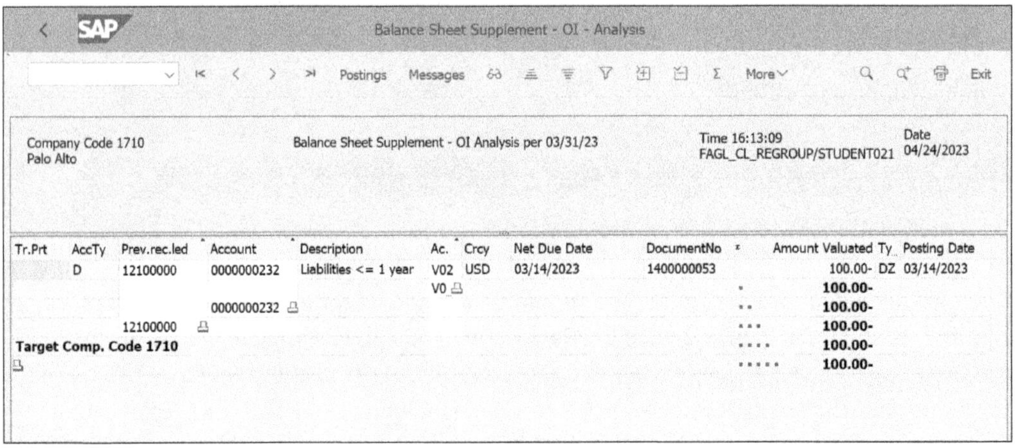

Figure 5.77 Balance Sheet Supplement Result

In this case, as only one customer account is selected, there is only one transaction of performed reclassification shown. If you click on **Postings**, you can see the postings the system has performed, as shown in Figure 5.78. Two postings for the one transaction are shown: one reclassification posting by the end of the period **03/31/2023** and the reversal of it by the beginning of the new period **04/01/2023**.

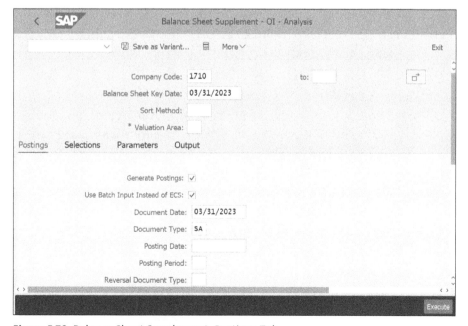

Ledger Gr	CoCd	DocumentNo	Document Header Text	Type	Posting Date	Text	Itm	PK	G/L Acct	Amount Crcy	Amnt in CC	LCurr	Amnt in GC	LCur2	AmntCrcy1	Free C
0L	1710	$000000001	B/S Adjustment FAGLF101	SA	03/31/2023			40	12102000	100.00 USD	100.00 USD		100.00 USD			
0L	1710		B/S Adjustment FAGLF101	SA	03/31/2023			50	21180000	100.00- USD	100.00- USD		100.00- USD			
0L	1710	$000000002	Reverse Posting FAGLF101	SA	04/01/2023			50	12102000	100.00- USD	100.00- USD		100.00- USD			
0L	1710		Reverse Posting FAGLF101	SA	04/01/2023			40	21180000	100.00 USD	100.00 USD		100.00 USD			

Figure 5.78 Postings for Reclassifications/Balance Sheet Supplement

Now, just like for accounts payable in Chapter 4, Section 4.6.5, in the **Postings** tab (refer to Figure 5.75), select the **Generate Postings** and **Use Batch Input Instead of ECS** checkboxes, as shown in Figure 5.79. In this way, you can view the posting records for the regrouped receivables. If you've selected the **Batch Input Instead ECS** checkbox, the system generates a batch input file, which later can be used for semimanual postings through batch-input processing by Transaction SM35.

Figure 5.79 Balance Sheet Supplement: Postings Tab

Click the **Execute** button, and the postings start to be generated. You can review the batch input session using Transaction SM35. There you can find the mentioned batch input file.

> **SAP Fiori App**
>
> The corresponding SAP Fiori app is called Regroup Receivables/Payables (FAGLF101). It's visually and functionally the same as the SAP GUI transaction.

Now that you've learned how to run resorting and reclassification of accounts receivable, let's continue with another important financial accounting process: accounts receivable reconciliation.

5.8.4 Accounts Receivable Reconciliations

As we also explained in Chapter 4, Section 4.6.6, for accounts payable, in SAP S/4HANA, the documents are stored in the main financial table ACDOCA. Unlike in SAP ERP, all financial-related information documents are stored in one single table instead of multiple tables. The reconciliation process is much simpler with table ACDOCA, which consolidates all separated tables into a single table, including accounts receivable, accounts payable, general ledger, asset accounting, controlling, and so on. So, the reconciliation between multiple tables or modules is now avoided.

In this section, we'll explain and perform an accounts receivable reconciliation. At the end of each reporting period, before closing the books, it must be verified that the total balances in the subledger accounts receivable match the accounts receivable reconciliation account in the general ledger. In this way, the financial accounting department ensures completeness and accuracy of the reported accounts receivable figures in the balance sheet.

For each customer, a separate account is created in the subledger that is linked to a certain SAP S/4HANA reconciliation account. At the moment you're creating a customer master record, the system will require you to enter the **Reconciliation account** field, as you saw in Section 5.2.2. The reconciliation account is considered a control account to perform the reconciliation between the subledgers and general ledger. You know that when you post an item to a customer subledger account, an entry in table ACDOCA is made, which populates the reconciliation account automatically in the same line. In this way, the accounts receivable and the general ledger are posted simultaneously.

In Chapter 3, Section 3.1.2, you've already learned how to create and display a reconciliation account in a master record. Here, we'll also explain how to perform the reconciliation process in accounts receivable.

During closing periods, no matter if it's month-end, quarter-end, or year-end, it's necessary to compare the transaction figures with the total balances of the posted items. The system will perform a comparative analysis as follows:

- The debit and credit balances in the customer accounts will be compared with the total balances of the debit/credit posted items.

- The debit/credit balances will be compared with the application indexes or the secondary indexes, which are used to manage accounts on an open items basis or line item display.

With reconciliation accounts for all subledgers, the subledger to general ledger reconciliation is guaranteed by SAP S/4HANA and its integration model. However, accountants want to be sure and have evidence by reconciling these balances. For this reason, there are a couple of reconciliation reports that show the accumulated values of the subledgers and compare these values (either balances of subledger accounts or the sum of subledger posting document amounts) with balances of the general ledger reconciliation accounts.

> **Note**
>
> You must close the posting period for which you're going to perform the reconciliation process/comparative analysis. This ensures that no adjustments are made to the transaction figures or items/documents during the reconciliation process. Changes performed during the reconciliation could cause problems.

Display Documents

Let's see how it looks when the reconciliation account is assigned to a customer after processing an incoming payment. Referring to Section 5.4.1, follow the same instructions to perform a manual payment using Transaction F-28 to clear the open items of a customer. This leads you to the screen shown in Figure 5.80. The example shown in Section 5.4.1 referred to customer **135** with the amount as 400.00 USD (see Figure 5.80).

After you've entered all the required data, click **Process Open Items** to arrive at the screen shown in Figure 5.81. In this screen, you see three listed open items and the amount entered (**30,010.40** USD) to be paid. So, we've selected all these open items to be cleared as shown with the total amount in the **Amount Entered** and **Assigned** fields.

Click the **Post** button. The document number created after posting the payment is **1400000357**. Now you can display this document using Transaction FB03 in accounts receivable or following application menu path **Accounting • Financial Accounting • Accounts Receivable • Document • Display**.

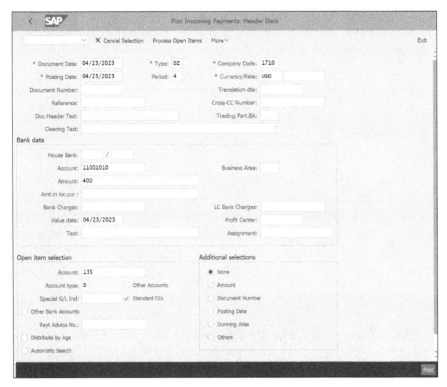

Figure 5.80 Post Incoming Payment for Customer 135

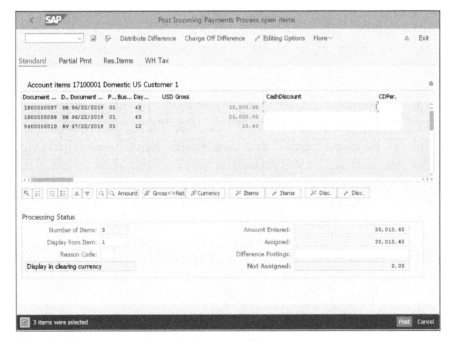

Figure 5.81 Process Open Items for Customer 135

The **Display Document: Initial Screen** appears, as shown in Figure 5.82. Enter the **Document Number** as "1400000357", **Company Code**, and **Fiscal Year**, and then click the **Continue** button.

Figure 5.82 Display Document 1400000357 Initial Screen

In the next screen, you can see the document created for the cleared items processed and posted (see Figure 5.83).

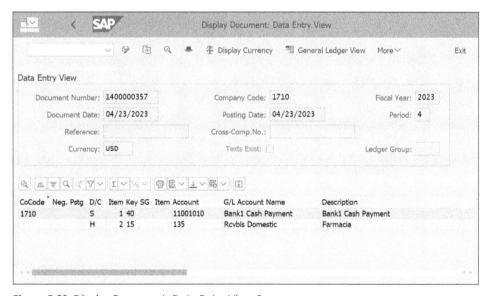

Figure 5.83 Display Document: Data Entry View Screen

The **Data Entry View** shows the financial entry posted with bank account **11001010** and customer account **135**. If you click on the **General Ledger View** button, the screen will appear showing the individual entries relevant to the open items, as well as the reconciliation account assigned to the customer master data, **Rcvbls Domestic** (see Figure 5.84). To switch to general ledger view, click **More • General Ledger View**, or, if the screen is opened in a wider mode, this option is automatically shown in the upper menu.

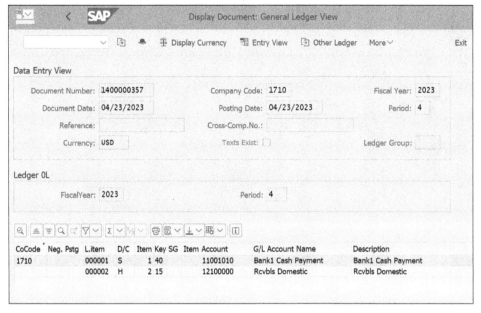

Figure 5.84 Display Document in General Ledger View

So, you can see that the posting entry performed to the customer account is automatically reflected to the reconciliation account as well. If you want to see the general ledger view for an item, just double-click, for example, in the first **L.item 000001**, and the display screen will appear as shown in Figure 5.85.

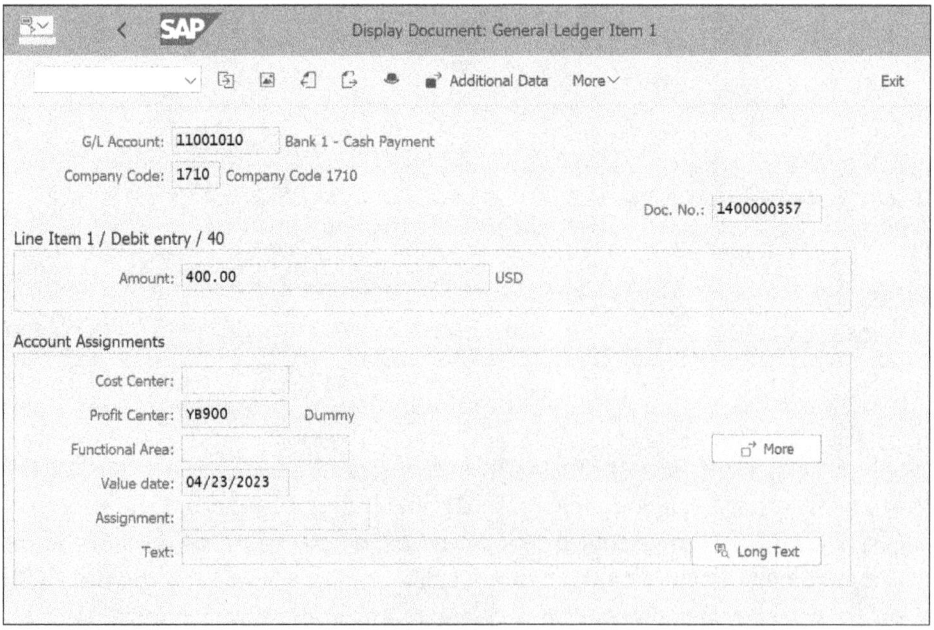

Figure 5.85 General Ledger View for Item 000001

Here, you can see that in the general ledger reconciliation account, the total amount of the incoming payment is reflected. These incoming payments cleared three open items.

Compare Balances and Open Items

At this point, an accountant would perform and check the accounts receivable reconciliation process. As in the accounts payable reconciliation process, it's recommended to compare general ledger account balances with accounts receivable balances and accounts receivable open items. To compare accounts receivable balances with general ledger balances, use Transaction FAGLB03, or follow menu path **Accounting • Financial Accounting • General Ledger • Account • Display Balances**.

Because you're very familiar with Transaction FAGLB03 as discussed for accounts payable in Chapter 4, Section 4.6.6, we'll show you an alternative way to show the general ledger account balances financial statement version. To do that, you can run Transaction S_ALR_87012284 or follow application menu path **Accounting • Financial Accounting • General Ledger • Information System • General Ledger Reports • Financial Statement/Cash Flow • General • Actual/Actual Comparisons • Financial Statements**. You'll arrive at the **Financial Statements** screen, as shown in Figure 5.86 and Figure 5.87.

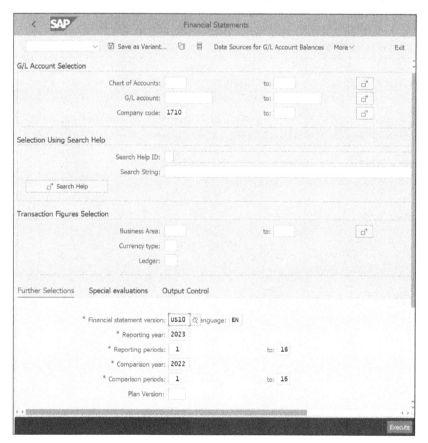

Figure 5.86 Financial Statement Entry Values (1)

Here, define the required values, such as the **Company code** for which you're executing the financial statement, the **Financial statement version** that specifies the key to identify the balance sheet and P&L statement version, the **Reporting year** for which the company is to establish its inventory and balance sheet, the **Reporting periods**, the **Comparison year**, and the **ALV Tree Control** option in the **List output** area to get a more structured overview. If required, you can also fill in the other option fields; depending on the situation, you may need to enter relevant information in them.

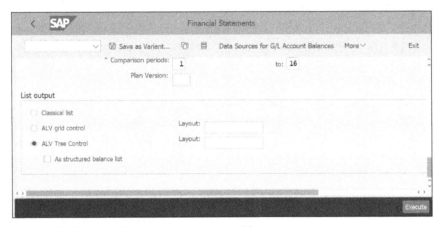

Figure 5.87 Financial Statement Entry Values (2)

Click the **Execute** button to execute the financial statement, and you'll arrive at the screen shown in Figure 5.88. Here, you can see the listed assets and liabilities items from which you can point out this example's **12100000 Receivables Domestic** account with the relevant balance of **1,116,420.45** USD.

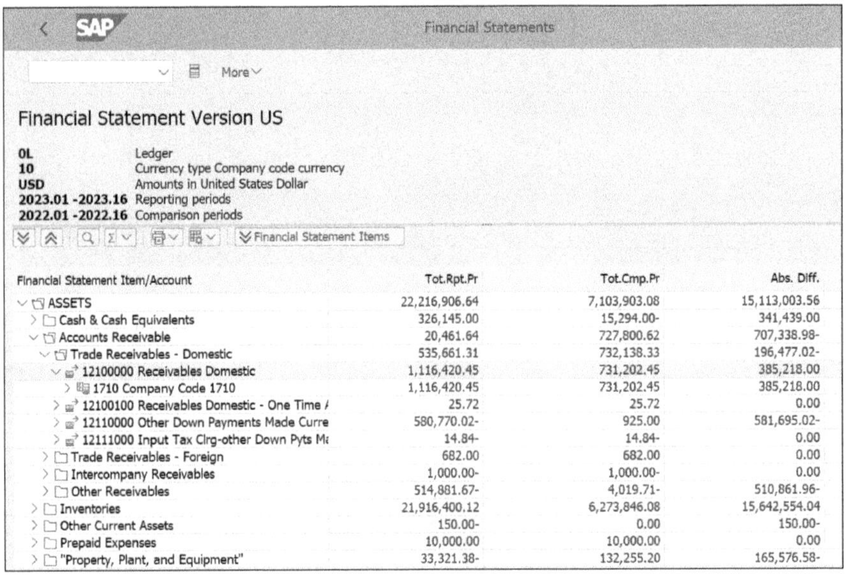

Figure 5.88 12100000 Receivables Domestic: Account Balance

To compare customer balances, use Transaction S_ALR_87012172 or follow menu path **Accounting • Financial Accounting • Accounts Receivable • Information System • Reports for Accounts Receivable Accounting • Customer Balances • Customer Balances in Local Currency.**

The **Customer Balances in Local Currency** screen appears after you double-click on the report name (see Figure 5.89). In this screen, define the selection criteria using the same values as in the general ledger account reconciliation report: **Company code**, **Fiscal Year**, and general ledger **Reconciliation Account 12100000**.

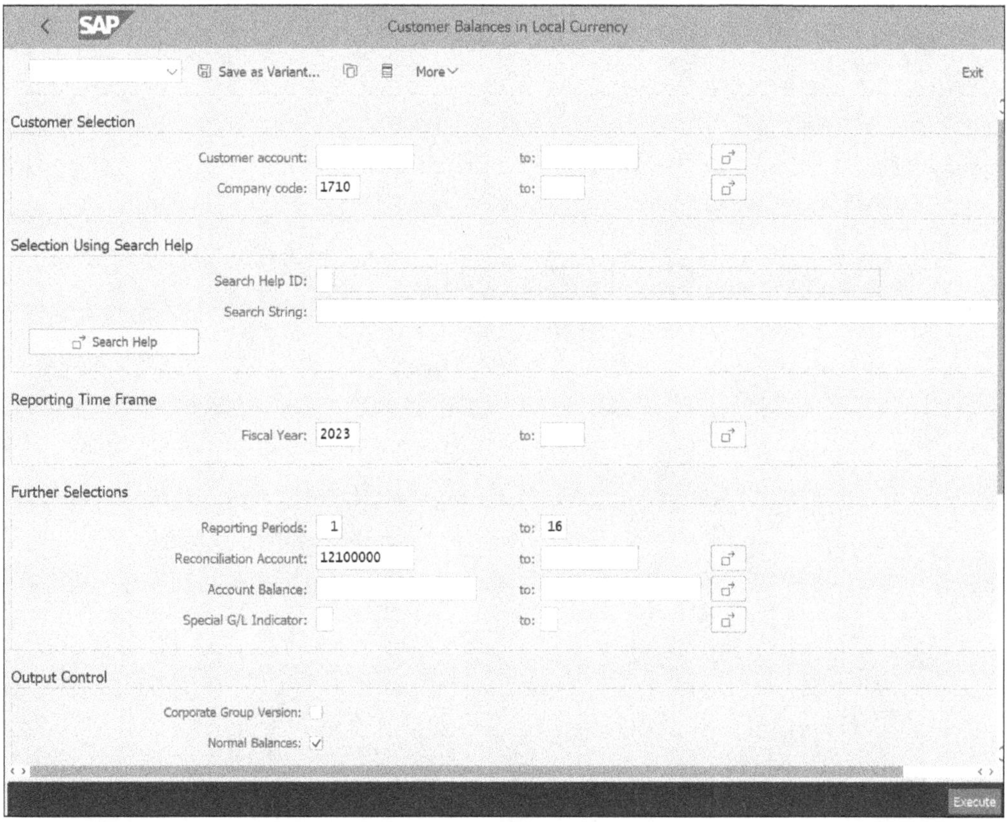

Figure 5.89 Customer Balances in Local Currency Screen

After the values have been entered, click the **Execute** button, and the overview report will show the result (see Figure 5.90 and Figure 5.91). You can see the balance for each customer in one line. This is a very clear report of the total of unpaid customer invoices per customer. At the bottom of the report, you can see the totals per reconciliation account and company code.

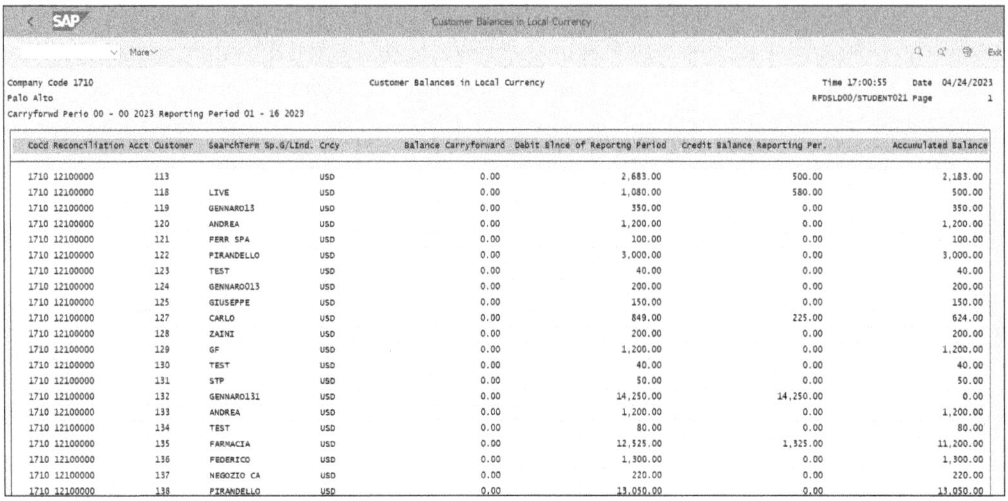

Company Code 1710 Customer Balances in Local Currency Time 17:00:55 Date 04/24/2023
Palo Alto RFDSLD00/STUDENT021 Page 1
Carryforwd Perio 00 - 00 2023 Reporting Period 01 - 16 2023

CoCd	Reconciliation Acct	Customer	SearchTerm	Sp.G/LInd.	Crcy	Balance Carryforward	Debit Blnce of Reportng Period	Credit Balance Reporting Per.	Accumulated Balance
1710	12100000	113			USD	0.00	2,683.00	500.00	2,183.00
1710	12100000	118	LIVE		USD	0.00	1,080.00	580.00	500.00
1710	12100000	119	GENNARO13		USD	0.00	350.00	0.00	350.00
1710	12100000	120	ANDREA		USD	0.00	1,200.00	0.00	1,200.00
1710	12100000	121	FERR SPA		USD	0.00	100.00	0.00	100.00
1710	12100000	122	PIRANDELLO		USD	0.00	3,000.00	0.00	3,000.00
1710	12100000	123	TEST		USD	0.00	40.00	0.00	40.00
1710	12100000	124	GENNARO013		USD	0.00	200.00	0.00	200.00
1710	12100000	125	GIUSEPPE		USD	0.00	150.00	0.00	150.00
1710	12100000	127	CARLO		USD	0.00	849.00	225.00	624.00
1710	12100000	128	ZAINI		USD	0.00	200.00	0.00	200.00
1710	12100000	129	GF		USD	0.00	1,200.00	0.00	1,200.00
1710	12100000	130	TEST		USD	0.00	40.00	0.00	40.00
1710	12100000	131	STP		USD	0.00	50.00	0.00	50.00
1710	12100000	132	GENNARO131		USD	0.00	14,250.00	14,250.00	0.00
1710	12100000	133	ANDREA		USD	0.00	1,200.00	0.00	1,200.00
1710	12100000	134	TEST		USD	0.00	80.00	0.00	80.00
1710	12100000	135	FARMACIA		USD	0.00	12,525.00	1,325.00	11,200.00
1710	12100000	136	FEDERICO		USD	0.00	1,300.00	0.00	1,300.00
1710	12100000	137	NEGOZIO CA		USD	0.00	220.00	0.00	220.00
1710	12100000	138	PIRANDELLO		USD	0.00	13,050.00	0.00	13,050.00

Figure 5.90 Customer Balances in Local Currency for General Ledger 12100000 (1)

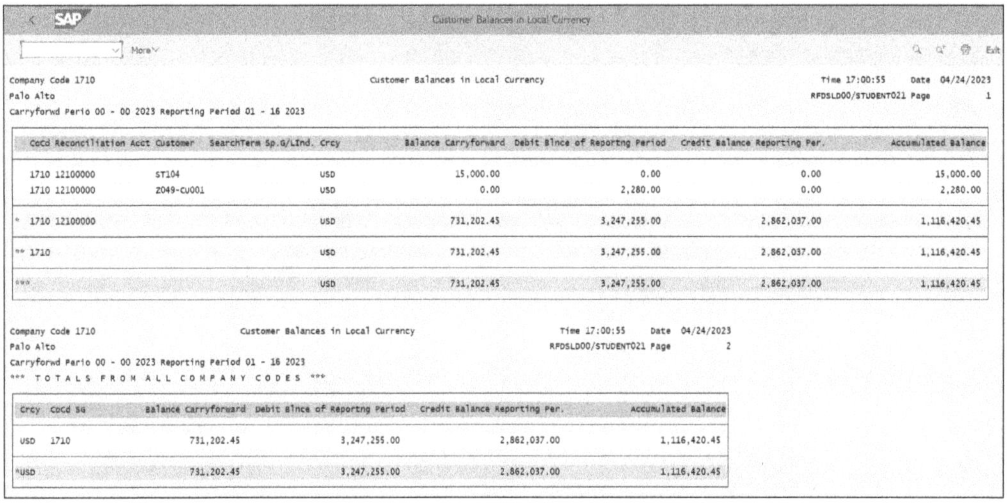

Company Code 1710 Customer Balances in Local Currency Time 17:00:55 Date 04/24/2023
Palo Alto RFDSLD00/STUDENT021 Page 1
Carryforwd Perio 00 - 00 2023 Reporting Period 01 - 16 2023

CoCd	Reconciliation Acct	Customer	SearchTerm	Sp.G/LInd.	Crcy	Balance Carryforward	Debit Blnce of Reportng Period	Credit Balance Reporting Per.	Accumulated Balance
1710	12100000	ST104			USD	15,000.00	0.00	0.00	15,000.00
1710	12100000	Z049-CU001			USD	0.00	2,280.00	0.00	2,280.00
* 1710	12100000				USD	731,202.45	3,247,255.00	2,862,037.00	1,116,420.45
** 1710					USD	731,202.45	3,247,255.00	2,862,037.00	1,116,420.45
***					USD	731,202.45	3,247,255.00	2,862,037.00	1,116,420.45

Company Code 1710 Customer Balances in Local Currency Time 17:00:55 Date 04/24/2023
Palo Alto RFDSLD00/STUDENT021 Page 2
Carryforwd Perio 00 - 00 2023 Reporting Period 01 - 16 2023
*** T O T A L S F R O M A L L C O M P A N Y C O D E S ***

Crcy	CoCd	SG	Balance Carryforward	Debit Blnce of Reportng Period	Credit Balance Reporting Per.	Accumulated Balance
USD	1710		731,202.45	3,247,255.00	2,862,037.00	1,116,420.45
*USD			731,202.45	3,247,255.00	2,862,037.00	1,116,420.45

Figure 5.91 Customer Balances in Local Currency for General Ledger 12100000 (2)

As you can see, the **Accumulated Balance** shown in the last column is the same amount as shown in the general ledger reconciliation account balance (**1,116,420.45 USD**).

Now let's see the last step of the comparison process to prove the amount reconciliation. To compare general ledger accounts with open accounts receivable items, access the customer open items report by using Transaction S_ALR_87012197 or by following menu path **Accounting • Financial Accounting • Accounts Receivable • Information System • Reports for Accounts Receivable Accounting • Customer Items • List of Customer Line items.**

You'll arrive at the **List of Customer Line Items** screen, as shown in Figure 5.92 and Figure 5.93. Select the same criteria as in the previous examples (**Customer account, Company code**). Under the **Line Item Selection/Status** area, choose whether you want to show only **Open Items**, **Cleared Items**, or **All Items** (open and cleared). Under the **Type** area, you can select any of the listed parameters, such as **Standard documents** (determines that only documents relevant to the accounting department will be evaluated), **Parked documents** (program also selects the documents from preliminary postings), and **Noted items** (noted items are to be evaluated). In the **Further Selections** area, define the line-item reconciliation account number in the **Master record recon. account** field.

Figure 5.92 Customer Line Items Entry Values (1)

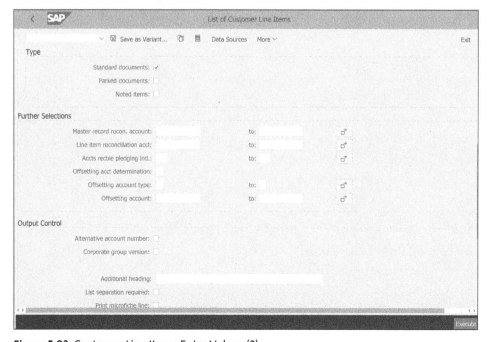

Figure 5.93 Customer Line Items Entry Values (2)

Click the **Execute** button, and in the next screen (see Figure 5.94 and Figure 5.95), the line items of the selected company and general ledger reconciliation account 12100000 are listed and grouped per customer account. In the last line in Figure 5.95, you can see the accumulated balance, which is the same amount as in the previous examples: **1,116,420.45 USD.**

Assignment	Pstng Date	Type	DocumentNo	Doc. Date	BusA	Itm	PK	NP	Dun	PM	Clearing	Clrng doc.	Cash Discount Amount	SG	Amount in Doc. Curr.
Customer 113 CoCode 1710Actg Clerk															
Name huhu															
Post.Code 80029															
City sant'antimo															
Region NA															
Ctry/Reg. IT															
	03/10/2023	DR	1800000002	03/10/2023		1	01				03/11/2023	1400000000	0.00		500.00
	03/10/2023	DR	1800000003	03/10/2023		1	01						0.00		800.00
	03/11/2023	DZ	1400000000	03/11/2023		2	15				03/11/2023	1400000000	0.00		500.00-
	03/12/2023	DR	1800000004	03/12/2023		1	01						0.00		966.00
	03/13/2023	DR	1800000069	03/13/2023		1	01						0.00		417.00
* Customer 113															2,183.00
Customer 118 CoCode 1710Actg Clerk															
Name Live															
Street via luigi pirandello 10															
Post.Code 80029															
City sant'antimo															
Region NA															
Ctry/Reg. IT															
	03/13/2023	DR	1800000005	03/13/2023		1	01				03/14/2023	1400000019	0.00		360.00
	03/13/2023	DR	1800000006	03/13/2023		1	01				03/14/2023	1400000005	0.00		220.00
	03/13/2023	DR	1800000047	03/13/2023		1	01						0.00		300.00

Figure 5.94 Customer Line Items Result (1)

Assignment	Pstng Date	Type	DocumentNo	Doc. Date	BusA	Itm	PK	NP	Dun	PM	Clearing	Clrng doc.	Cash Discount Amount	SG	Amount in Doc. Curr.
	11/23/2022	DR	1800000036	11/15/2022		1	01						0.00		10,000.00
	11/23/2022	DR	1800000037	11/17/2022		1	01						0.00		5,000.00
* Customer ST104															15,000.00
Customer Z049-CU001CoCode 1710Actg Clerk															
Name Z049-CU001															
Region CA															
Ctry/Reg. US															
	01/25/2023	RV	9400000000	01/25/2023		1	01						0.00		50.00
	01/27/2023	RV	9400000001	01/27/2023		1	01						0.00		100.00
	01/27/2023	RV	9400000002	01/27/2023		1	01						0.00		50.00
	02/11/2023	RV	9400000003	02/11/2023		1	01						0.00		700.00
	02/11/2023	RV	9400000004	02/11/2023		1	01						0.00		460.00
	02/12/2023	RV	9400000006	02/12/2023		1	01						0.00		460.00
	02/18/2023	RV	9400000007	02/18/2023		1	01						0.00		460.00
* Customer Z049-CU001															2,280.00
** G/L Account 12100000															1,116,420.45
*** Company Code 1710															1,116,420.45
****															1,116,420.45

Figure 5.95 Customer Line Items Result (2)

SAP Fiori Apps

The reconciliation between general ledger accounts, customer accounts, and customer line items can also be performed through SAP Fiori apps such as Financial Statement, Display Customer Accounts, and Manage Customer Line Items, in a similar manner.

However, in SAP Fiori, you can also shortcut the reconciliation process by executing the Display Line Item Entry report (F2218) or Display Line Item in General Ledger report (F2217). Here, you can define the **Company Code**, **G/L Account**, **Item Type**, **Status**, and **Open on Key Date** (showing all open items until this specified date). Then, click the **Go** button, which leads you to the list of items shown in Figure 5.96.

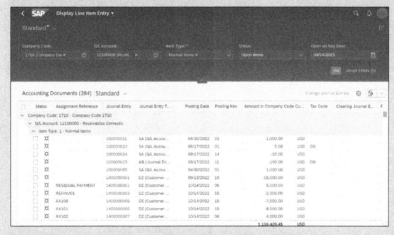

Figure 5.96 Display Line-Item Entry for 12100000 in SAP Fiori

Add the name of the customer column through the settings ⚙ icon. In the search box, enter "customer name" and put it in front using drag and drop. You'll get the view shown in Figure 5.97.

Figure 5.97 Display Line-Item Entry for 12100000: Customer Name

Then, right-click on the **Name of Customer** column title to group it. In this way, you get the customer balance report, as shown in Figure 5.98.

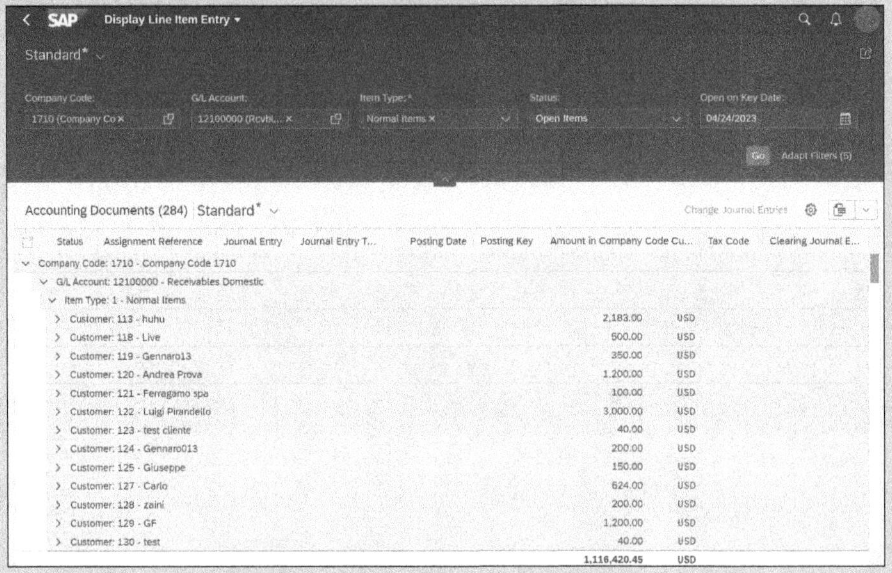

Figure 5.98 Customer Balance Report in SAP Fiori

In the next section, you'll learn how to perform an inquiry for a specific customer and how to show all the movements in this customer account.

5.9   Accounts Receivable Reporting

Accounts receivable reporting and analyzing features enable companies to verify and track revenues, incoming payments, uncollected account balances from customers, cash sales, credit sales, cash flow management, and so on.

Proper recording of accounts receivable entries facilitates the production of timely and accurate reports to ensure that customers have paid on time and the company credit rating isn't negatively affected. Comparing the company's accounts receivable lines over several years can help you understand how well the company is performing. You can see that although there is a high number of late-paying customers, there is also a huge increase in sales. You can use accounts receivable reporting and analyzing features in SAP S/4HANA to produce a variety of reports that give you up-to-date information with drilldown capabilities to investigate source documents and monitor company activity. Here, we'll explain some reports and transactions that are recommended for use in the accounts receivable ledger.

5.9.1   Accounts Inquiry

You can easily inquire about any customer accounts to check for customer invoices, transactions for a specific date, invoice payment status, open items and account clearing issues, balance confirmations, and several questions from the sales department or customers.

To inquire on customer accounts, you use Transaction FD1ON (Display Balances) and Transaction FBL5N (Display/Change Line Items). The difference between these two reports is that Transaction FBL5N shows the details per line item perspective so you can see all the information for a specific customer. Transaction FD1ON, on the other hand, shows the customer total balances per general ledger indicator category perspective. The connection between these two transactions is that you can get the details of Transaction FBL5N by drilling down to the total balance of a category in the **General Ledger Indicator** tab using Transaction FD1ON.

You can follow either of the following SAP S/4HANA application paths:

- **Accounting • Financial Accounting • Accounts Receivable • Account • Display Balances**
- **Accounting • Financial Accounting • Accounts Receivable • Account • Display/Change Line Items**

Let's start with using the customer account balances via **Display Balances**. In the **Customer Balance Display** screen that appears, enter the **Customer** number, **Company code**, and **Fiscal year**, as shown in Figure 5.99.

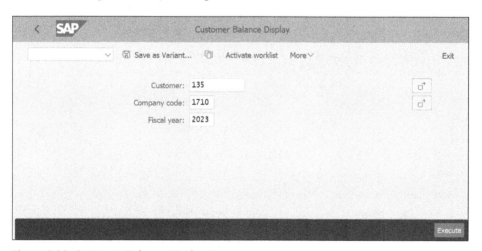

Figure 5.99 Customer Balance Display Screen

Click the **Execute** button, and the screen shown in Figure 5.100 shows the account balances for the selected customer **135**.

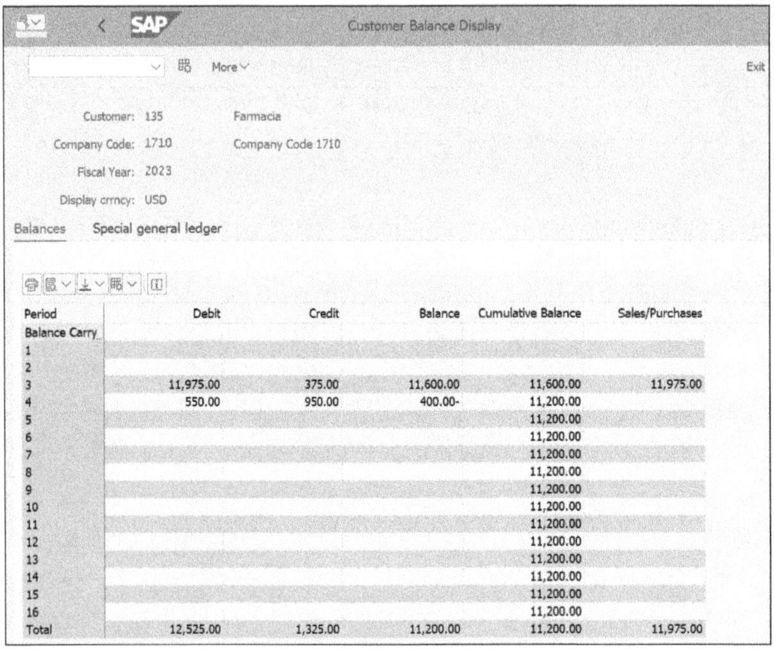

Period	Debit	Credit	Balance	Cumulative Balance	Sales/Purchases
Balance Carry					
1					
2					
3	11,975.00	375.00	11,600.00	11,600.00	11,975.00
4	550.00	950.00	400.00-	11,200.00	
5				11,200.00	
6				11,200.00	
7				11,200.00	
8				11,200.00	
9				11,200.00	
10				11,200.00	
11				11,200.00	
12				11,200.00	
13				11,200.00	
14				11,200.00	
15				11,200.00	
16				11,200.00	
Total	12,525.00	1,325.00	11,200.00	11,200.00	11,975.00

Figure 5.100 Display Balance for Customer 135

From there, you can easily drill down to transactions performed in any period. To see the details of all movements on a customer account, just click on the total in the **Balance** column. You'll see the complete list of line items processed in fiscal year 2023, as shown in Figure 5.101.

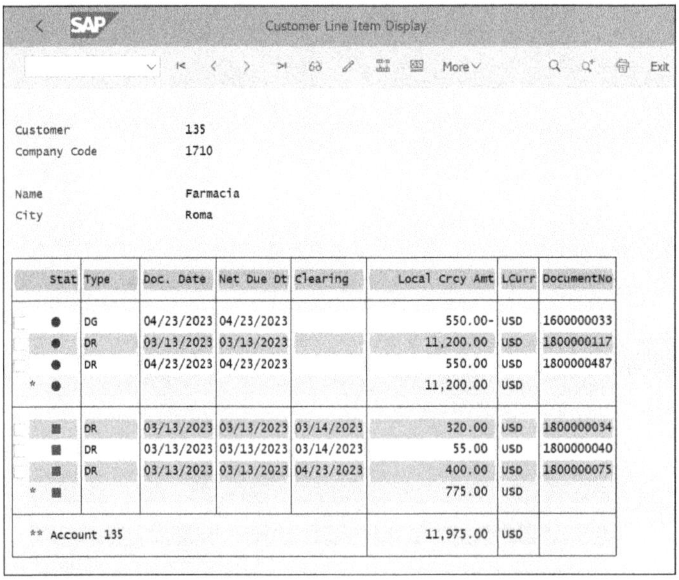

Stat	Type	Doc. Date	Net Due Dt	Clearing	Local Crcy Amt	LCurr	DocumentNo
●	DG	04/23/2023	04/23/2023		550.00-	USD	1600000033
●	DR	03/13/2023	03/13/2023		11,200.00	USD	1800000117
●	DR	04/23/2023	04/23/2023		550.00	USD	1800000487
* ●					11,200.00	USD	
■	DR	03/13/2023	03/13/2023	03/14/2023	320.00	USD	1800000034
■	DR	03/13/2023	03/13/2023	03/14/2023	55.00	USD	1800000040
■	DR	03/13/2023	03/13/2023	04/23/2023	400.00	USD	1800000075
* ■					775.00	USD	
** Account 135					11,975.00	USD	

Figure 5.101 Detail Transactions of Customer Account 135

If you would have clicked on **Cumulative Balance**, the system would generate a list of all transactions performed from the customer—regardless of the year.

The red **Stat** (status) flag means that the items aren't yet cleared. In this case, it means that the customer invoices of 135 aren't yet reflected as incoming payments. After the items are cleared, the status flag will turn green and won't be shown in this view.

You can also execute a similar transaction (Transaction FBL5H) or follow IMG menu path **Accounting • Financial Accounting • Accounts Receivable • Account • Line Item Browser**. Transaction FBL5H is a new transaction in SAP S/4HANA and has quite a similar selection screen compared with Transaction FBL5N; however, this new transaction can be executed faster. Once Transaction FBL5H is executed, the **Customer Line Item Browser** screen appears, as shown in Figure 5.102.

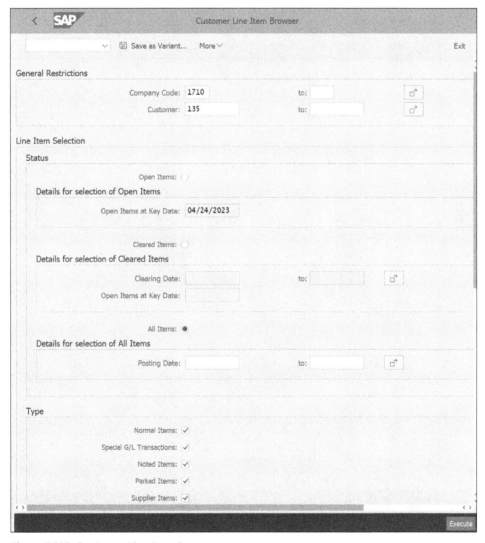

Figure 5.102 Customer Line Item Browser

On this screen, you can define the selection criteria such as **Company Code** and the **Customer** number. In the **Line Item Selection** area, choose one of the options (**Open Items**, **Cleared Items**, or **All Items**). In the **Type** area, you can select all listed types. Click the **Execute** button, and the line items of the selected customer are shown summarized by period, as depicted in Figure 5.103.

Click on the **Customer** column to redirect to the customer master data.

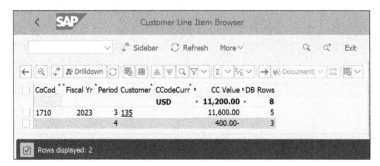

Figure 5.103 Customer Line Items Results

Another new feature of this report is that, if you want to show the line items, you need to select a particular line and then click on the **Call Line Item Report** icon ![icon] on the right of the screen. For example, let's click on the line in **Period 3**, which will take you to a similar screen to what would have appeared using Transaction FBL5N, as shown in Figure 5.104.

St	Assignment	DocumentNo	Typ	Doc. Date	S	DD	Local Crcy Amt	LCurr	Clrng doc.	Text
●		1800000117	DR	03/13/2023	🔲		11,200.00	USD		
* ●							11,200.00	USD		
■		1400000018	DZ	03/14/2023			375.00-	USD	1400000018	
■		1800000034	DR	03/13/2023			320.00	USD	1400000018	
■		1800000040	DR	03/13/2023			55.00	USD	1400000018	
■		1800000075	DR	03/13/2023			400.00	USD	1400000357	
* ■							400.00	USD		

Customer: 135
Company Code: 1710
Name: Farmacia
City: Roma

5 items displayed

Figure 5.104 Customer Line Items Display

SAP Fiori App

The corresponding SAP Fiori app is called Display Customer Balances (F0703). In Figure 5.105, you can see what the mentioned app looks like in SAP Fiori.

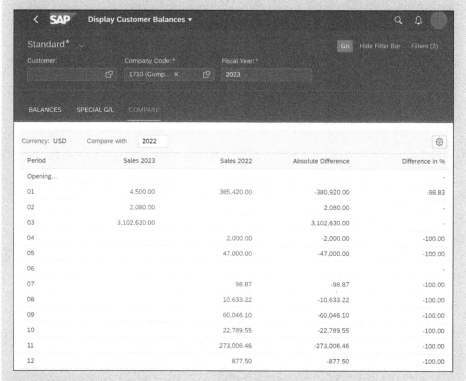

Figure 5.105 Display Customer Balances App in SAP Fiori

In the header section, enter the selection criteria, such as **Customer** (if you need to restrict for a particular customer), **Company Code**, and **Fiscal Year**, and then click the **Go** button to show the balances sorted by **Period 01** to **16**.

Using this app, you can display customer balances and compare sales as well. Debits balances, credit balances, and balances by company code, fiscal year, and particular customer are shown here. Moreover, you can drill down on a particular record of a period and further analyze the amounts by showing all related line items. For example, click on the balance for **Period 04**, and you'll be redirected to the Manage Customer Line Items app, as shown in Figure 5.106.

By clicking the **COMPARE** button, you can compare sales figures between two fiscal years, as shown in Figure 5.107.

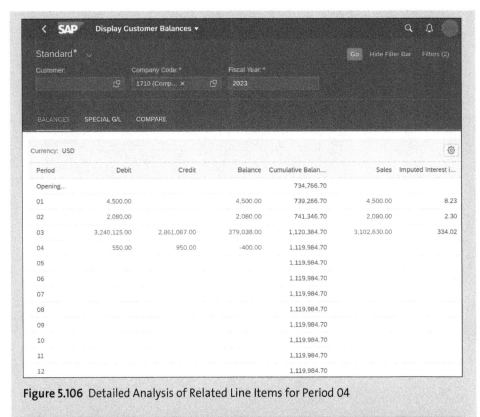

Figure 5.106 Detailed Analysis of Related Line Items for Period 04

Figure 5.107 Comparing Sales Balances

Sometimes, you need to verify beyond the account balances for a specific customer. You can analyze each customer account in more detail via line items. For this reason, in addition to the account balances, we'll also discuss how to manage the accounts receivable open item lists in SAP S/4HANA.

5.9.2   Account Balances Report

The customer account balances report is a helpful tool for accounts reconciliation in the context of preparing the financial statement. These reports help you track the outstanding balance amount of a customer or group of customers. They can also provide aging analysis such as the breakup of outstanding balances for the selected period.

In SAP S/4HANA, you can use Transaction S_ALR_87012172 or follow application menu path **Accounting • Financial Accounting • Accounts Receivable • Information System • Reports for Accounts Receivable Accounting • Customer Balances • Customer Balances in Local Currency**.

When you start the transaction, you reach the **Customer Balances in Local Currency** screen, as shown in Figure 5.108.

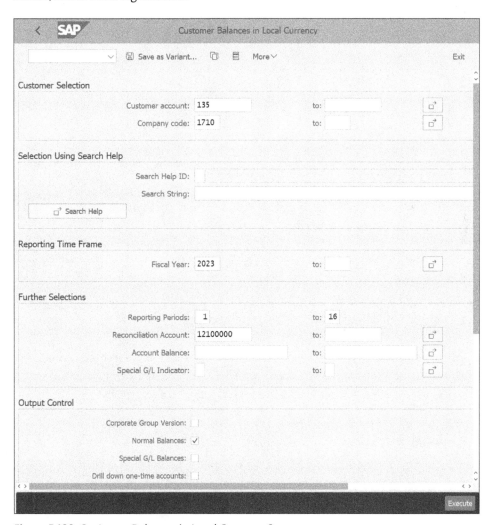

Figure 5.108 Customer Balances in Local Currency Screen

Here you can filter information referring to the **Customer account**, **Company code**, **Fiscal Year**, and **Reporting Periods**, as well as a **Reconciliation Account**, if you want to focus on a certain type of customer balances (e.g., domestic receivables).

After you've adjusted the mentioned filters, click the **Execute** button. The results screen shows you a list of all customer account balances line by line, starting with the balance carryforward, debit entries balance, credit entries balance, and accumulated balance. It sums up all the columns and gives you a total on the general ledger reconciliation account level. In Figure 5.109, you can see the results of the report of balances in local currency restricted only to a specific customer (**135**).

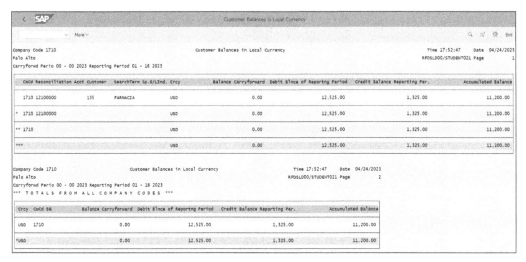

Figure 5.109 Customer Balances in Local Currency: Results

> **SAP Fiori App**
>
> The corresponding SAP Fiori app is called Display Customer Balances (F0703). You can refer to the instructions and explanation in the previous section for this app.

Sometimes, you need to verify beyond the account balances for a specific customer. You can analyze each customer account in more detail via line items. For this reason, we'll now discuss how to manage the accounts receivable open item lists in SAP S/4HANA.

5.9.3   Open Items List

The customer open items list in accounts receivable is a report with which you can display all unpaid or uncleared invoices of your customer. Using this report, you can track the status of the sales documents at your company. The report shows the documents and accounting line items posted to a customer account. You can easily find and manage the customers that still must pay for their orders.

Use Transaction S_ALR_87012197 to open the accounts receivable open items list screen. In the application menu, follow path **Accounting • Financial Accounting • Accounts Receivable • Information System • Reports for Accounts Receivable Accounting • Customers: Items • List of Customer Line Items**.

In the initial screen of the customer items line report, you can filter the information referring to **Customer account**, **Company code**, item **Status**, output **Type**, and so on, as shown in Figure 5.110.

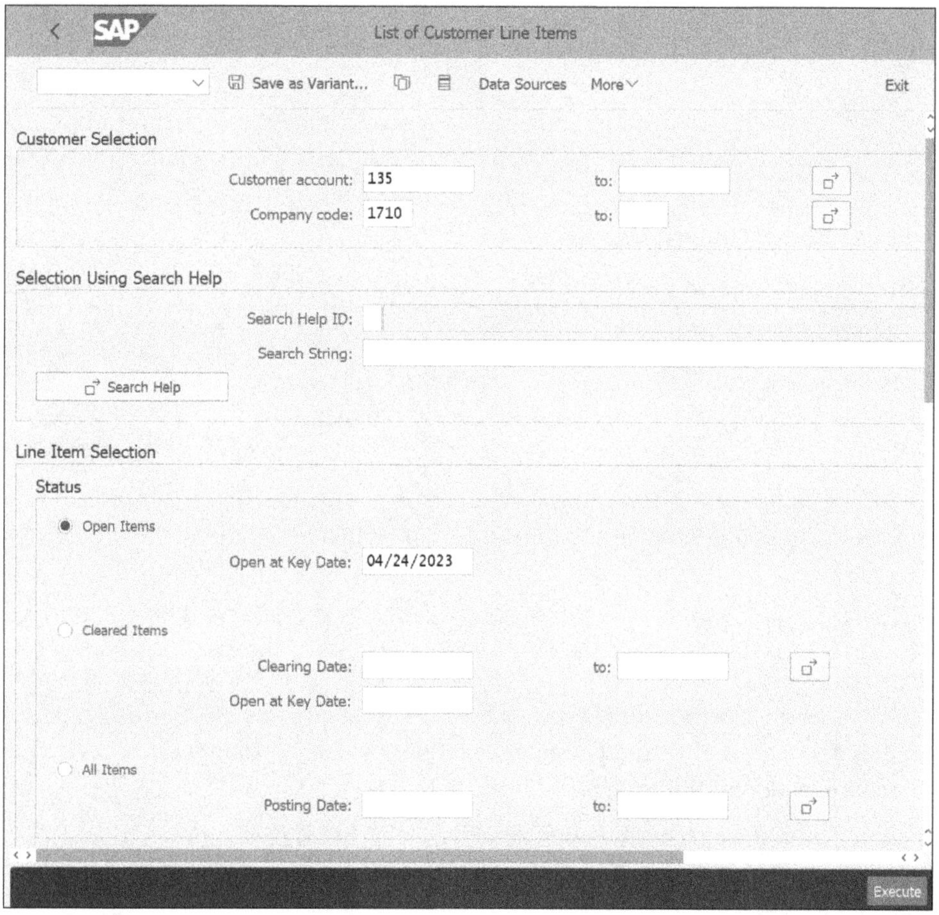

Figure 5.110 Entry View of Customer Line Items

If you want to display only open items, click on **Open Items** in the **Line Item Selection** area, and enter a reporting date (**Open at Key Date**). After execution of the report by clicking the **Execute** button, all open items of customer **135** for company code **1710** are listed, as shown in Figure 5.111. The listed open items are grouped by customers.

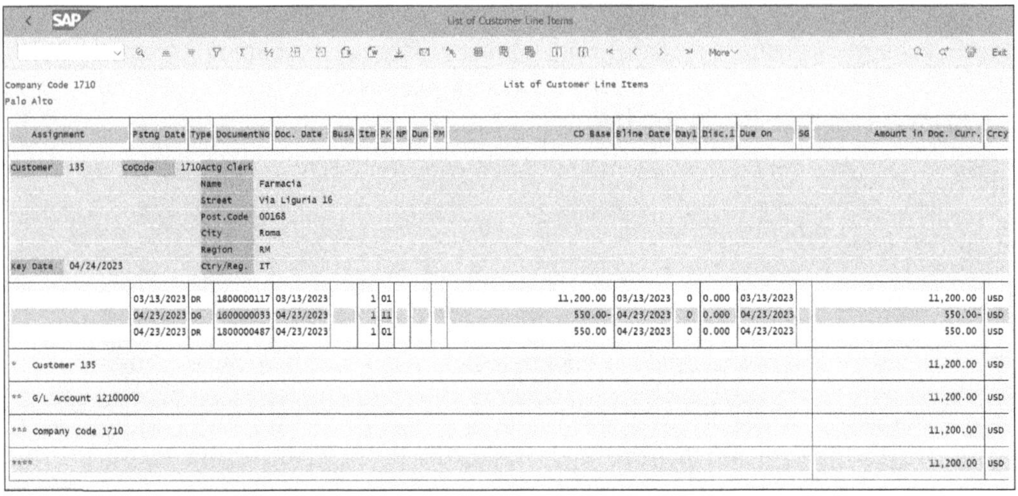

Figure 5.111 List of Customer Line Items

SAP Fiori App

The relevant SAP Fiori app to clear the open items is called Clear Open Items (F-13). It's visually and functionally the same as the SAP GUI transaction.

Now that you've learned how to display the customer's open item list, let's discuss how to generate the aging list report in the last section of this chapter.

5.9.4   Aging List

Another important report in accounts receivable is the aging list. Accounts receivable aging is a report that lists unpaid customer invoices by date ranges. The aging report is used as a tool for estimating potential bad debts, which are then used to revise the allowance for doubtful accounts.

To start the accounts receivable open item list screen, use Transaction S_ALR_87012178, or follow application menu path **Accounting • Financial Accounting • Accounts Receivable • Information System • Reports for Accounts Receivable Accounting • Customers: Items • Customer Open Item Analysis by Balance of Overdue Items**.

In the next screen (see Figure 5.112), define the selection criteria, such as **Company code**, **Fiscal Year**, **Open items at key date**, **Fiscal Period**, and **Line Item Reconciliation Acct**.

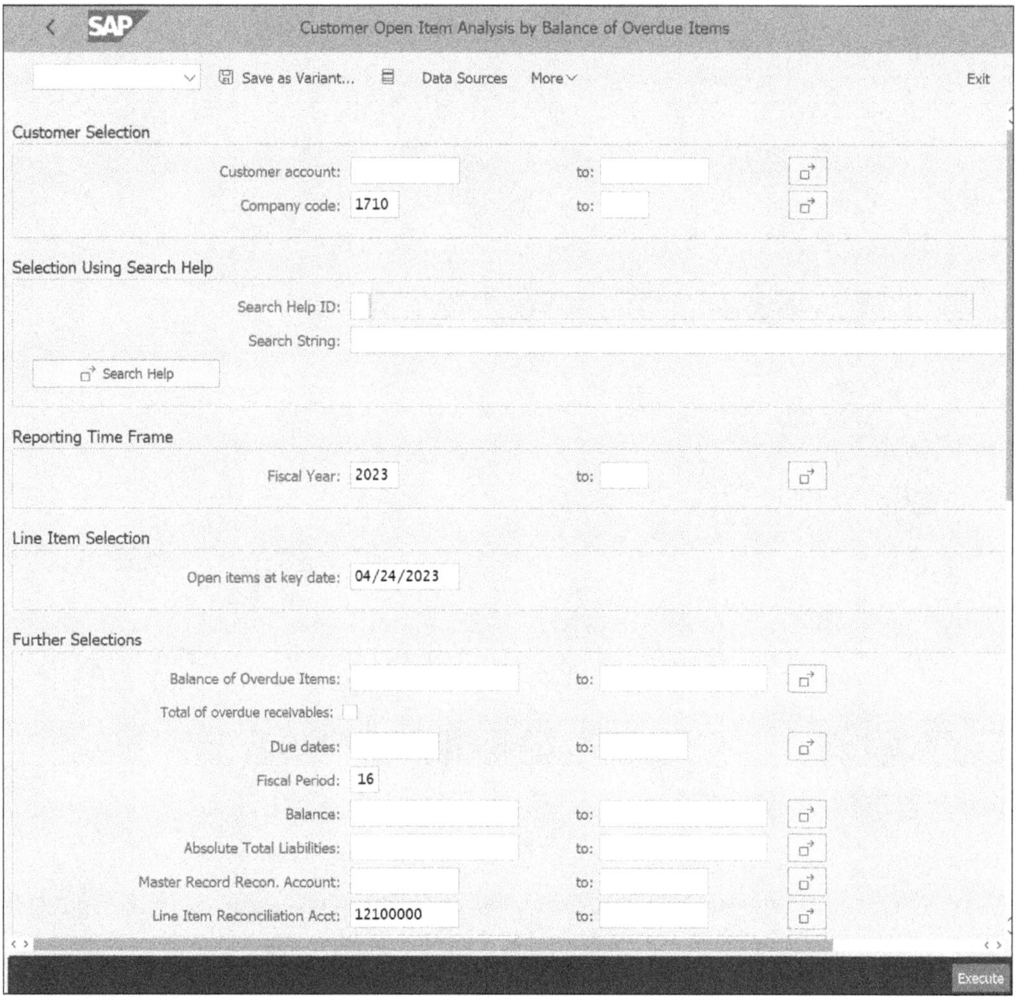

Figure 5.112 Aging Report Entry Values

The from/to ranges can be configured in the **Output Control** area before you run the report (see Figure 5.113). Other options to note include the following:

- **OI sorted list sorting (1,2)**
  This parameter monitors sorting within the open item list. It has two indicators: **1**, which refers to sorting by company code, accounting clerk, account number, and business area; and **2**, which sorts by all those attributes plus currency.

- **Summarization Level (0-6)**
  This parameter is used to limit the list output. The list spans from **0** to **6**, including the possible entries and their effects. For example, list **0** has address block, open item list, line items, total sheets per clerk, and overall total sheets. List **1** has address block, open item list, total sheets per clerk, and overall total sheets. In this way, the values are also set to be printed for other indicators. If you use **Summarization Level 6**, all invoices in a range are cumulated. This gives you the best overview.

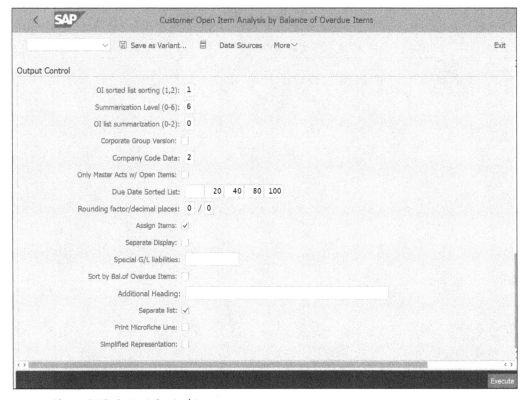

Figure 5.113 Output Control Area

- **OI list summarization (0-2)**
  This parameter is used to control the output of the open item list with their possible entries. In the list box to the right of each parameter, you can enter the indicator you're interested in. If you want to see each single invoice in the ranges, use **Summarization Level 1, 2**, or **3**.

- **Corporate Group Version**
  If this parameter is marked, it displays the selected company codes per account.

- **Company Code Data**
  This parameter controls whether the corresponding data per company code and account can also be output in addition to the master data and sorted list per account when the list is outputted as a group version.

- **Due Date Sorted List**
  This parameter is used to set the upper limit in days of a due date interval in the due date list.

- **Assign Items**
  This parameter sorts out the invoice-related items according to the same criteria as the invoice items to which they refer in the sorted item list.

Click the **Execute** button. The results will appear as shown in Figure 5.114.

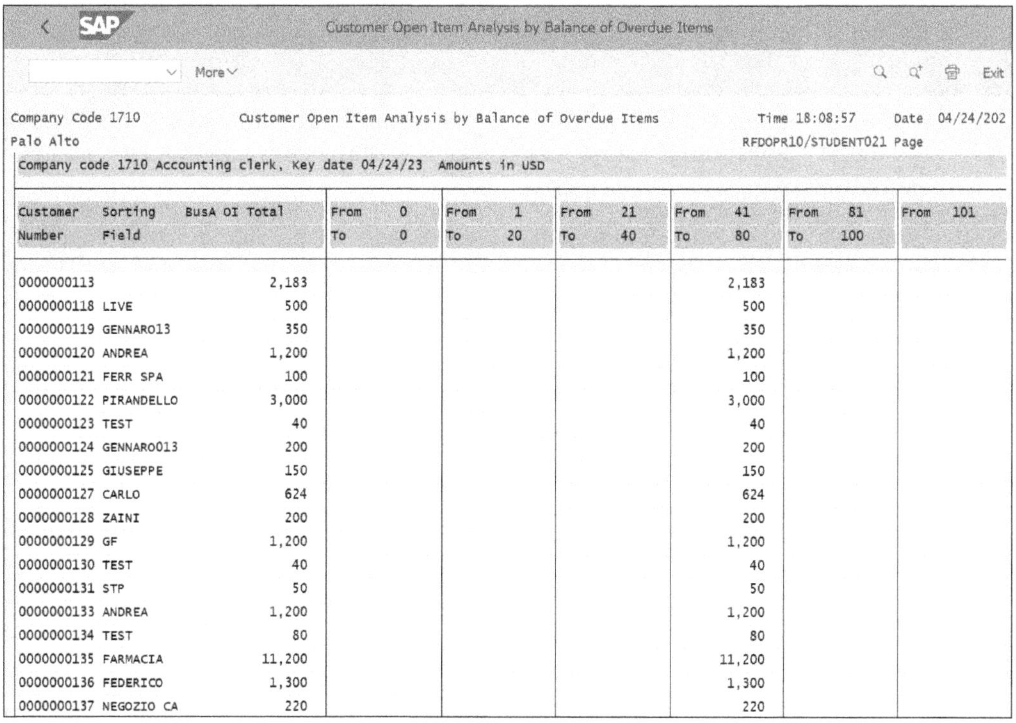
Customer Open Item Analysis by Balance of Overdue Items

More

Exit

Company Code 1710 Customer Open Item Analysis by Balance of Overdue Items Time 18:08:57 Date 04/24/202
Palo Alto RFDOPR10/STUDENT021 Page
Company code 1710 Accounting clerk, Key date 04/24/23 Amounts in USD

Customer Number	Sorting Field	BusA	OI Total	From 0 To 0	From 1 To 20	From 21 To 40	From 41 To 80	From 81 To 100	From 101
0000000113			2,183				2,183		
0000000118	LIVE		500				500		
0000000119	GENNARO13		350				350		
0000000120	ANDREA		1,200				1,200		
0000000121	FERR SPA		100				100		
0000000122	PIRANDELLO		3,000				3,000		
0000000123	TEST		40				40		
0000000124	GENNARO013		200				200		
0000000125	GIUSEPPE		150				150		
0000000127	CARLO		624				624		
0000000128	ZAINI		200				200		
0000000129	GF		1,200				1,200		
0000000130	TEST		40				40		
0000000131	STP		50				50		
0000000133	ANDREA		1,200				1,200		
0000000134	TEST		80				80		
0000000135	FARMACIA		11,200				11,200		
0000000136	FEDERICO		1,300				1,300		
0000000137	NEGOZIO CA		220				220		

Figure 5.114 Customer Open Items by Overdue Items

Here, you can see customer open items by balance of overdue items sorted by customer number. The report shows a list of the customer's open items that are past due and makes certain that the proper dunning level is being applied for these items.

5.10 Summary

In this chapter, we covered the main functions to manage the accounts receivable ledger and discussed how accounts receivable accounting works in SAP S/4HANA in terms of integration with the order-to-cash process, customer master data, and accounts receivable transactions, such as customer invoices and payment postings.

In the beginning of this chapter, you got an introduction to the order-to-cash process. In this context, you know now that the sales order is the starting point for all transactional accounting postings that follow.

You then learned about the customer account and its master data. You know how to set up a customer master account, and you understand the most important master data fields for accounting of a customer account.

Next to the customer accounts, you've learned how to post two types of customer invoices (automatic or direct), followed by the necessary configurations in the system. Further, we've shown how incoming payments can be processed manually or automatically.

In addition to the straightforward cases in accounts receivable, we also walked you through the deviating cases that need extra treatment, that is, the creation of a credit memo and down payment processing.

Later, you learned how dunning and credit management work and how important credit limits are in SAP S/4HANA. We finished this chapter with the period-end closing and reconciliation activities and discussed the most important reports from accounts receivable.

Overall, now that you understand the basic accounts receivable principles and use cases, you can manage your way through accounts receivable.

In the next chapter, we'll discuss fixed asset accounting.

Chapter 6
Fixed Asset Accounting

Fixed assets can be one of the largest asset groups within an organization, and it requires special accounting that differs from the accounting used for any other assets. This chapter covers all areas of the asset lifecycle: acquisition, capitalization, depreciation, impairment, and retirement. In addition, this chapter explains the closing and reporting capabilities of SAP S/4HANA for fixed asset accounting.

A *fixed asset*, sometimes referred to as a capital asset, in accounting is considered a long-term tangible asset, property, plant, or equipment that the organization owns and uses in its daily operations for revenues purposes. Fixed assets often cover a substantial portion of the total assets of a company and consequently play an essential role in the financial statement. Moreover, the determination of whether an expenditure denotes an asset or an expense can lead to a material effect on a company's reported results of its business activity.

Fixed assets can't be directly sold to the customers nor be easily converted into cash. Managing and monitoring fixed assets in SAP S/4HANA is done in fixed asset accounting, which is a subledger of financial accounting. The fixed asset subledger consists of fixed asset accounts, which are linked through a fixed asset class to the general ledger. Every transaction and every movement is done on each single fixed asset account. Some fixed asset transactions, such as a depreciation run, will touch many accounts at the same time. The general ledger account linked to the fixed asset class is known as the *asset reconciliation account*.

The fixed assets function in SAP S/4HANA enables you to have control in physical and financial aspects over the whole asset lifecycle, starting from acquisition and continuing to capitalization, depreciation, revaluation, and disposal.

In this chapter, we'll cover the most important areas of fixed asset accounting, such as the acquire-to-retire process, capitalization, depreciation, retirement, fixed assets master data, asset classes, depreciation areas, asset creation, accounts receivable period-end closing, and accounts payable reporting.

Let's start with the basic knowledge of the acquire-to-retire process and all of its related business processes.

6.1   Acquire-to-Retire Process

Acquire-to-retire is a core business process within SAP that refers to a collection of several processes a company has implemented, starting from asset requisition and the disposition of the assets at the end of their lifetime. Using this business process as the basis of our topic, we'll cover the whole asset lifecycle and some of its integration aspects into other subledgers. In this section, we'll discuss several involved business process steps in the acquire-to-retire process, such as asset acquisition, capitalization, depreciation, and retirement. Let's start with asset acquisition.

6.1.1   Acquisition of Long-Lived Assets

The initial phase in the acquire-to-retire business process is the asset acquisition. In this section, we'll talk about *long-lived assets*, which are the company's investments used over multiple operating cycles that provide an earning future contribution for many years. Long-lived assets are also termed long-term assets, fixed or noncurrent assets, or hard assets. Practically, it isn't easy and feasible to convert these kinds of assets into cash or cash equivalents. The long-term assets are recorded in the balance sheet as asset costs. Because the expenditure of the asset is expected to bring profits beyond the current operating year, these costs are usually capitalized. We'll discuss the capitalization process later in this chapter after you get to know the acquisition process.

The category of long-lived assets typically refers to assets such as the following:

- **Tangible long-lived assets**
  Property, plant, and equipment that can involve machinery, land, buildings, vehicles, computers, and so on.
- **Intangible long-lived assets**
  Trademarks, patents, copyrights, licenses, and so on.

The first topic in accounting faced during the initial phase of long-lived asset acquisition is how to define and control its cost. Having accomplished the acquisition and the asset creation process, the second step is to allocate the cost to expense over time. The main component of the acquisition cost of a long-lived asset is the *purchase price* or invoice, including import duties and other nonrefundable taxes. If the asset hasn't been acquired by a third party but produced by the company itself, the *production cost* is the basis for the valuation in the beginning. The production cost includes all the required expenditures to prepare the asset for its intended use.

In this section, you'll learn and understand how the asset acquisition types are practically managed within the organization and in the SAP S/4HANA system. We'll present you with three methods of long-lived assets acquisition:

- **External acquisition**
  Assets are bought from external companies or suppliers.

- **Internal acquisition**
  Assets are produced in-house.

- **Assets under construction (AuC)**
  Assets are in the building process and are generally presented as a separate balance sheet item, so a separate account determination is needed in their asset classes.

To perform an external acquisition transaction with a vendor in SAP S/4HANA, you can use Transaction F-90 or follow application menu path **Accounting • Financial Accounting • Fixed Assets • Posting • Acquisition • External Acquisition • With Vendor**. You'll see how this process works in Section 6.4.

6.1.2   Capitalization/Activation

As you learned in the previous section, the initial postings in asset accounting are asset acquisition and asset capitalization. Therefore, the lifecycle of an asset begins with its acquisition, which can be an external purchase or an in-house development or construction. In the case of AuC, costs are accumulated until the asset acquisition is completed. After that, it will be reclassified to the asset class where it belongs (e.g., buildings).

Thus, there are two stages in an asset's life that are relevant in financial accounting:

- Under construction (AuC asset)
- Productive life (final asset)

Posting the relevant amount to the AuC and settlement of this amount to a final asset is called the *asset capitalization* process. In other words, the capitalization process means recording a cost as an asset rather than an expense. This cost isn't projected to be immediately fully consumed, but it's distributed to be used over a long period of time. For example, production machinery with a useful life of eight years will be converted into an expense and completely consumed over eight years. So, every year, 1/8 of its purchase price will be expensed. In contrast, if there were no capitalization, the full purchase price would be expensed in the first year. The impact on the profitability of a company, if there is no capitalization, is obvious. Every acquisition would immediately affect the profit and loss (P&L) to the full amount of the purchase price.

As we mentioned in the previous section, the most common acquiring method is external acquisition, for which several transaction codes can be executed:

- **Transaction F-90 (Acquisition from Purchase with Vendor)**
  Generates a debit entry on the asset account and a credit entry on the vendor account. In this case, the asset capitalizing is done at the same time as the creation of the accounts payable invoice.

- **Transaction ABZON (Acquis. w/Autom. Offsetting Entry)**
  Capitalizes the asset value with an offsetting entry to the general ledger account. So, in this case, a debit entry is made in asset accounting, and a credit entry is made in the offset general ledger account. You can use this transaction in the cases of prepaid purchases, meaning that the vendor is prepaid, and it's not necessary to create an accounts payable invoice.

- **Transaction F-91 (Clearing Offsetting Entry)**
  Capitalizes the asset value with an offsetting entry to a general ledger clearing account generating a debit entry to the asset account and a credit entry to the offsetting general ledger clearing account.

In the previous section, we've already demonstrated the use of Transaction F-90 to acquire an asset from a vendor, which also capitalizes the asset value while creating the vendor invoice.

6.1.3 Depreciation

After the long-term asset has been acquired, its cost is regularly depreciated for the tangible assets or amortized for the intangible assets during the useful life of the asset. You can see this as a balancing process of the constant use of the asset and financial benefit resulting from its use, which calculates the asset's net book value. It may happen that the depreciation or amortization process is accelerated because of the higher frequent consumption of the asset during the early stage over its period of useful life. In accounting, a *depreciation* expense is used for the purpose of asset devaluation, meaning the reduction of an asset value over the usage time, and to allocate the cost of an asset over its expected useful life. Depreciation is an important stage during the month-end closing and year-end closing processes in financial accounting.

The main and most common types of depreciation methods are as follows:

- **Straight-line**
  This very common and simple method for expense calculating allocates the same expense amount every year.

- **Double declining-balance depreciation method**
  This method calculates the expense starting with a higher amount in the earlier years of the asset's useful life because the assets are more productive in their initial years than in the end of their life.

- **Units of production method**
  This method calculates the asset depreciation depending on the total number of produced units or used hours over its useful life.

- **Sum of years digits method**
  This accelerated method calculates a higher expense in the early years and a lower expense in the latter years of the useful life.

6.1.4   Retirement/Scrapping

Retirement/scrapping is also known as disposal of assets and refers to eliminating assets from the accounting records, removing all traces of an asset from the balance sheet (derecognition). Companies frequently take out an asset or part of an asset from the financial statements as soon as the asset becomes obsolete. They may become obsolete because of several existing circumstances:

- Consequence of physical depreciation
- Result of technological innovation
- Already been fully depreciated over its useful life
- Already reached the end of its useful life but has residual salvage or resale value
- Partially depreciated, with useful life and remaining resale value
- Partially depreciated, but with no remaining value to resale

> **Note**
>
> The term *residual salvage value* is often used as the expected estimated resale value at the end of the useful life of a fixed asset. This estimated amount is used as a component of depreciation expense calculation and is often assumed to be zero.

In this case, those assets can be sold or disposed of to another company, leading to retirement with the following types:

- An asset is sold, resulting in revenue as profit. The sale is posted with a customer.
- An asset is sold, resulting in revenue as profit. The sale is posted against a general ledger clearing account.
- An asset is scrapped. No revenue is earned from scrapping it.
- An asset is sold to another company using the manual posting function of intercompany asset transfer/retirement.

Regardless of the circumstances around why the fixed asset is retired, its purchase cost should be removed from the fixed assets account, including all information of historic accumulated depreciation value. Nevertheless, if the fixed asset is sold, scrapped/depreciated, or given away, the difference between its book value and any amount regained through disposal must be recorded, either as income or expense.

You can find several asset sales transactions that are executed for the asset retirement process. For example, you can refer to the sales Transaction F-92 if an asset is sold to an external customer. Through this transaction, it's created as a debit entry to accounts receivable, generating an accounts receivable invoice/document and credit entry to the asset. Alternatively, you can also use Transaction ABAON through which the retirement posting isn't made to the customer but through a general ledger clearing account. The difference is that Transaction ABAON creates a debit to a general ledger clearing account and a credit to the asset, whereas Transaction F-92 creates a debit entry to the receivable account and a credit entry to the asset account.

Another option, as you'll see in Section 6.4.5, is to scrap the asset using Transaction ABAVN. Through this transaction, no revenue is generated during the asset retirement process.

Now that you have a good overview of the acquire-to-retire process, let's dive deeper into the accounting activities, starting with setting up the fixed asset master account.

6.2   Fixed Asset Accounts and Master Data

Fixed asset accounting is an important part of SAP S/4HANA because almost all companies manage some types of fixed assets. From an accounting perspective, the most important accounting decision is made when setting up a fixed asset master record. The setup configuration affects the asset's life overall, its valuation, and its presentation in the financial statement. The major configuration elements in the asset master data refer to asset classes, account determination, depreciation areas and keys, and charts of depreciation. We'll discuss all of these elements in this section.

Fixed asset master data records contain essential information that directly affects the asset transaction, valuation, and presentation. In this section, we'll discuss the steps you need to know to create a new fixed asset master record. Through the master record, you can create, modify, and evaluate the master data, which is the basis for asset accounting. The asset master records consist of two data areas: general master data and master data for asset values calculation.

The general master data contains the specific information about the fixed assets, such as general information, posting information, account assignment information, information for plant maintenance, and so on.

In the master data for asset values calculation, you can define the depreciation terms for the depreciation area, such as depreciation key, depreciation starting period, useful life, scrapping value, and so on.

6.2.1   Asset Creation

Fixed asset accounting in SAP S/4HANA contains all the relevant transactions used for the asset master records, such as fixed asset creation, change, and display. Under this component, you can also select the function to lock or delete a fixed asset. The application menu path that leads to any of these tree nodes is as follows: **Accounting • Financial Accounting • Fixed Assets • Asset**.

Now, let's see how you can create a fixed asset by referring to a vendor invoice or using the standard manual procedure. You can create an asset using Transaction AS01 or application menu path **Accounting • Financial Accounting • Fixed Assets • Asset • Create •**

Asset. You'll arrive at **Create Asset: Initial screen**, as shown in Figure 6.1. Enter the values in the respective fields for **Asset Class**, **Company Code**, and **Number of Similar Assets**. The asset class can't be changed after the asset master record is created. If the wrong asset classes are assigned, then the asset should be transferred to a new asset by assigning a correct asset class. For asset transferring, you can get more information in Section 6.4.4. In the **Number of Similar Assets** option, you can define the number of similar assets that can be created in one master transaction.

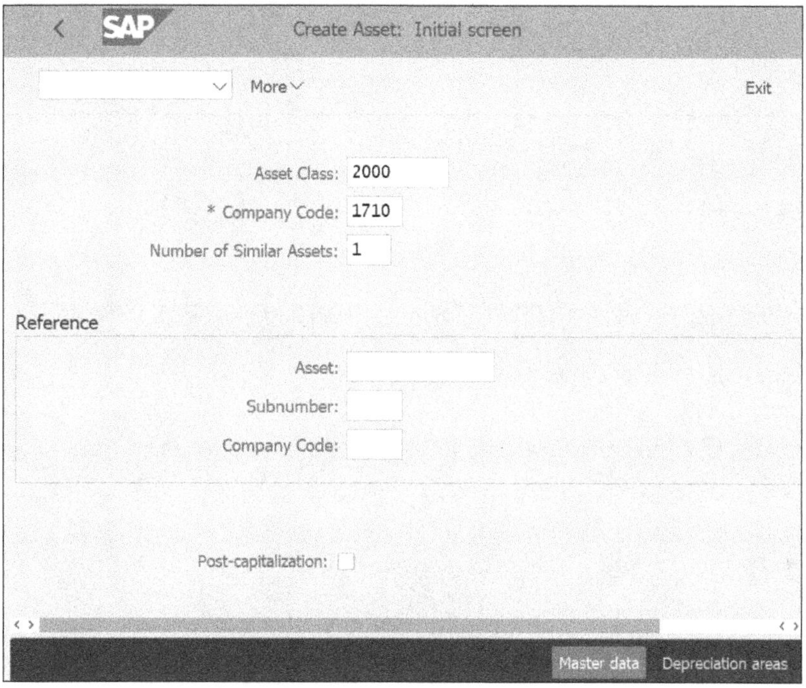

Figure 6.1 Create Asset Master Data Initial Screen

After you've entered the required data, click the **Master data** button, which leads to the **Create Asset: Master data** screen, as shown in Figure 6.2. Here, enter the required fields in the **General** tab such as an asset **Description**, which is a mandatory field; **Asset Main No. Text**, in which you can enter any desired name for the asset main number to be used in reporting; **Account Determ.**, which determines the reconciliation account in the general ledger as an attribute of the asset class; **Serial number**; **Inventory Number**; and **Quantity**.

After that, go to the **Time-dependent** tab, as shown in Figure 6.3, where you can optionally assign master data details, such as **Cost Center** and **Internal Order** to which depreciation and interest should be posted. You can also provide a **Plant** assignment to perform plant-specific analysis in asset accounting, **Location**, a specific **Room** for the asset, **Tax Jurisdiction** to define the tax authorities where you pay the taxes, and **Functional Area**.

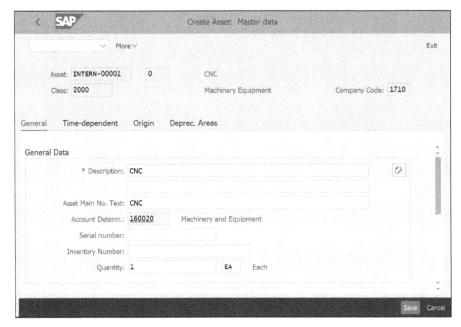

Figure 6.2 Create Asset: Master Data Screen

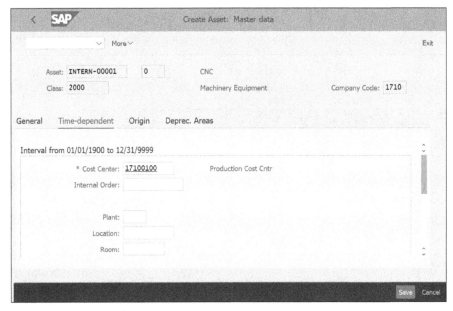

Figure 6.3 Create Asset Master Data: Time-Dependent Tab

In the **Origin** tab, you can define, if necessary, the vendor number, manufacturer, if the purchased asset was new or used, trading partner, country of origin, and so on. In the **Deprec. Areas** tab, as shown in Figure 6.4, you can see the listed depreciation areas that can be assigned to the asset classes and to the created master record.

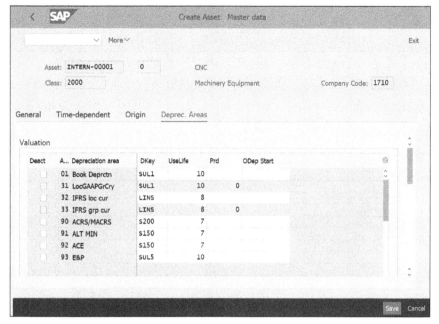

Figure 6.4 Depreciation Areas

As a final step, click the **Save** button, which will start to execute the creation procedure of the master record that concludes with a notification message at the bottom of the screen. You can display the master record by going to the display function and clicking on the **More** button, as shown in Figure 6.5.

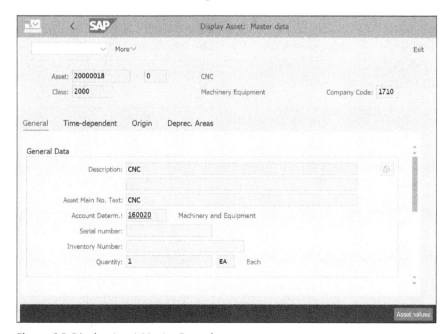

Figure 6.5 Display Asset Master Record

SAP Fiori App

The corresponding SAP Fiori app is called Create Asset (AS01). It's visually and functionally the same as the SAP GUI transaction.

In the next section, the asset classes and account determination process are explained.

6.2.2   Asset Classes

In this section, we'll describe some substantial configuration steps of the asset classes. Let's start by describing what an asset class is and identifying the main classes.

An *asset class* refers to a group of long-term assets with the same characteristics in terms of useful life and depreciation method. Some of the most common classes are as follows:

- Real estate/land
- Buildings
- Machinery and equipment
- Furniture and fixtures
- Leasing
- Intangible assets
- Investments

Asset classes are an important part of financial accounting that control account determinations, screen layouts, and the depreciation method for the depreciation expense calculation. They are configured in such a way to meet the financial reporting requirements on the financial statement. After an asset master record is created, it's assigned to one asset class.

Note

When creating the asset master record, it's important to ensure that it's assigned the accurate asset class. After an asset is created and linked to a specific asset class, you can't change the assigned asset class. If you make an incorrect assignment, you must create a new asset with the appropriate asset class and transfer the previous asset to the new one.

One of the available functions in SAP S/4HANA to access or modify the asset classes is through Transaction S_ALR_87009207 or via application menu path **Accounting • Financial Accounting • Fixed Assets • Environment • Current Settings • Change Asset Classes**.

After you run this report, the **Change View "Asset classes": Overview** screen appears. Here, you can switch to the display mode from the edit mode just by clicking the **Display** (or **Edit** when in display mode) button at the top right, accessing the screen shown in Figure 6.6.

Class	Short Text	Asset Class Description	Name of Account Determination	Name of screen layout rule
1000	Real Estate (Land)	Real Estate (Land)	Land and Land Improvements	Real estate
1100	Buildings	Buildings	Buildings	Buildings
1200	Land Improvements	Land Improvements	Land and Land Improvements	Real estate
1500	Leasehold Improvmnts	Leasehold Improvements	Leasehold Imrovements	Buildings
2000	Machinery Equipment	Machinery and Equipment	Machinery and Equipment	General machines
3000	Fixtures Fittings	Fixtures and Fittings	Furniture and Fixtures	Fixtures and fittings
3100	Vehicles	Vehicles	Vehicles	Vehicles
3200	Computer Hardware	Computer Hardware	Computer Hardware	Computers (Hardware/Software)
3210	Computer Software	Computer Software	Computer Software	Computers (Hardware/Software)
3300	Office Equipment	Office Equipment	Office Equipment	Fixtures and fittings
4000	AuC	Assets under Construction	Assets under Construction	Assets under construction
4001	Investment Measure	AuC as Investment Measure	Assets under Construction	Assets under construction
5000	LVA	Low-value Assets	Low Value Assets	Low value assets
6000	Leasing (oper.)	Leased assets (operating lease)	Leasing	Leasing
6100	Leasing (capital)	Leased assets (capital lease)	Leasing	Leasing
6210	FL Land	ROU Fin. Lease Land	Fixed Asset ROU RE Land - FL	Real estate
6220	FL Building	ROU Fin. Lease Building	Fixed Asset ROU RE Building - FL	Buildings
6230	FL Computer	ROU Fin. Lease Computer Hardware	Fixed Asset ROU Computer - FL	Computers (Hardware/Software)
6240	FL Fixture & Fitt.	ROU Fin. Lease Fixtures & Fittings	Fixed Asset ROU Fixtures - FL	Fixtures and fittings
6250	FL Machinery Fitt.	ROU Fin. Lease Machinery Equipment	Fixed Asset ROU Machine - FL	General machines
6260	FL Vehicles	ROU Fin. Lease Vehicles	Fixed Asset ROU Vehicle - FL	General machines
6270	FL Office Equipment	ROU Fin. Lease Office Equipment	Fixed Asset ROU Office Equipment - FL	Fixtures and fittings

Figure 6.6 Asset Classes Overview

Double-click on one of the listed asset classes, or click the **Display** button to show or change some details of that asset. For example, let's access the first asset class, **Real Estate (Land)**, whose details are shown in Figure 6.7.

In this screen, you can see the asset class details such as name, asset type referring to the account determination code, screen layout, base unit, and so on. As we mentioned earlier, the asset class controls the account determinations, screen layouts, and depreciation method determination. From the **Account Determ.** field, you can select a specific account from the listed accounts. This required field in the asset class defines the reconciliation accounts in the general ledger and their offsetting accounts affected while executing any business transactions. One account determination can be assigned in some asset classes with the condition to use the same chart of accounts and post in a similar way to the general ledger accounts. Referring to Chapter 3, Section 3.2.3, a chart of accounts determines all accounts in the general ledger in financial accounting. Each company has one (and only one) chart of accounts assigned. This assignment applies for asset accounting too.

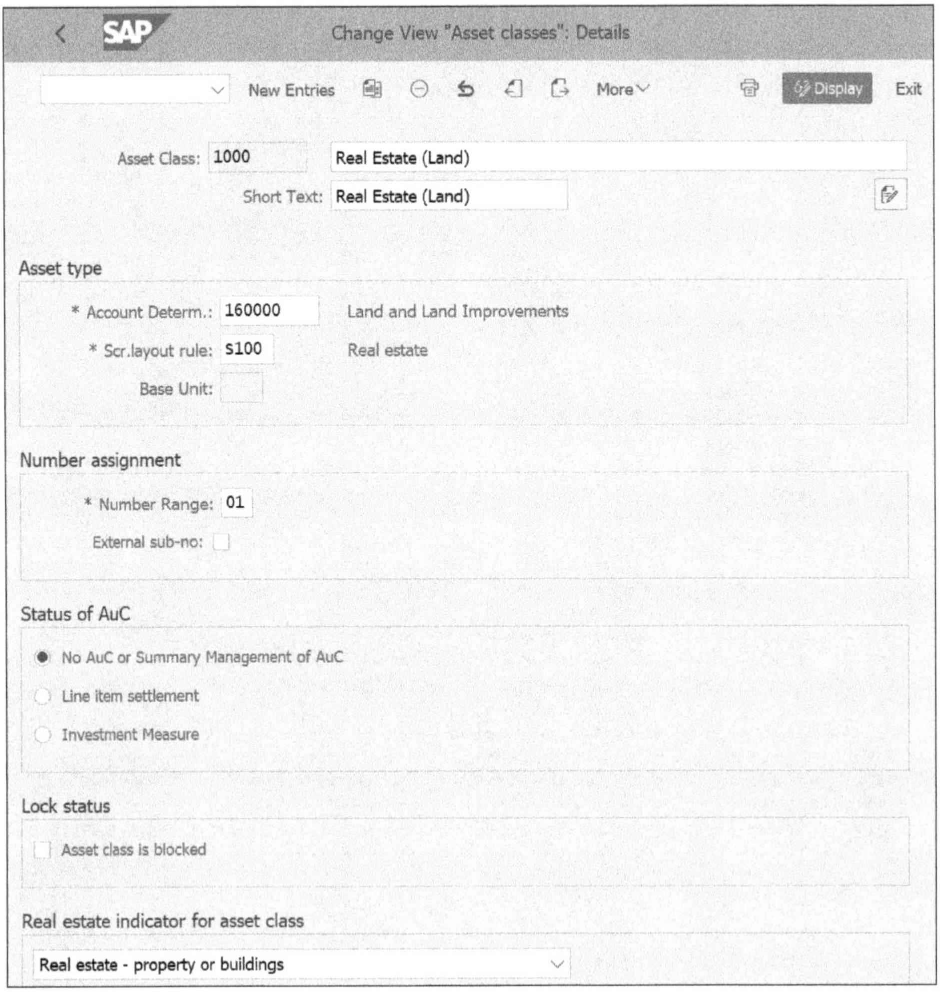

Figure 6.7 Real Estate (Land) Asset Class Details

> **SAP Fiori App**
>
> There is no corresponding Fiori app to change asset classes. However, to display the configuration, you can use the Directory of Asset Classes app (ANKA). It's visually and functionally the same as shown for SAP GUI (refer to Figure 6.6).

6.2.3   Account Determination

The next important element of financial accounting is *account determination*, which defines the general ledger accounts in financial accounting to be posted during any asset transactions for the depreciation area in the chart of depreciation. With so many different asset transaction types, it's clear that account determinations implementation is an important and sensitive process.

Account determination plays an important role in financial accounting because it automatically reflects any asset transaction to the general ledger accounts. When a posting is done with account assignment to an asset, the system defines the general ledger accounts that are automatically updated based on the selected company chart of accounts, the account determination key, and the depreciation area. Following are some of these asset transactions:

- Depreciation
- Down payments
- Transfer of reserves
- Profit/loss/revenue from sales activity
- Interest expenses
- Investment support
- Acquisition
- Retirements
- Revaluations

Setting up account determination for fixed assets in SAP involves several steps. Here's a general overview of the process:

1. **Define the asset classes**

   Asset classes group similar types of assets for accounting purposes. To define an asset class, you'll need to specify things such as depreciation areas, default values for depreciation, and general ledger account assignments.

2. **Define a chart of depreciation**

   A chart of depreciation defines the depreciation areas that apply to different asset classes. You'll need to specify the depreciation areas and the general ledger accounts to which depreciation is posted.

3. **Define the depreciation areas**

   Depreciation areas represent the different ways in which an asset can be depreciated, such as book depreciation, tax depreciation, or group depreciation. You'll need to specify the depreciation key, which determines how the asset is depreciated, and the general ledger accounts to which depreciation is posted.

4. **Assign asset classes to the chart of depreciation**

   Once you've defined your asset classes and chart of depreciation, you'll need to assign each asset class to the chart of depreciation.

5. **Define the asset transactions**

   Asset transactions are the different types of transactions that can be performed on an asset, such as acquisition, retirement, transfer, or write-off. For each asset transaction, you'll need to specify the general ledger accounts to which the transaction is posted.

6. **Define asset master data**

The asset master record contains all the information about a particular asset, including its acquisition date, acquisition value, and useful life. You'll need to specify the asset class and chart of depreciation for each asset, which determines the general ledger accounts to which transactions are posted.

7. **Test and validate the setup**

After you've completed the preceding steps, you should thoroughly test and validate the setup to ensure that everything is working as expected.

Note that these steps are a high-level overview, and the specific configuration steps may vary depending on your organization's specific requirements. It's important to work closely with your SAP consultant or IT department to ensure that the setup is configured correctly.

We won't go too deep into the configuration (IMG) in the system, but we want to explain how it principally works. To do so, we'll explain how depreciation keys and depreciation areas are set up.

> **SAP Fiori App**
>
> To date, no SAP Fiori apps have been created to configure asset accounting. However, to view the configuration, you can use the Display Asset Classes per Chart of Depreciation (ANKA) app. It's visually and functionally the same as shown for SAP GUI.

6.2.4   Depreciation Key

Depreciation keys contain the necessary settings to specify the methods of depreciation calculation and parameters that control the depreciation types, such as the following:

- **Ordinary depreciation**
  Represents the planned/calculated deduction during the normal life of an asset.
- **Special depreciation**
  Represents the deduction value of an asset from a tax-based perspective within a period defined by a tax authority.
- **Scrapping value**
  Represents the asset when it's completely depreciated by the end of its physical life.

Several calculation rule combinations are used for automatically calculating depreciation. Initially, the calculation method is defined, and then the depreciation key is defined and assigned to the calculation method.

Define Calculation Method

You can define the calculation method using the Customizing tools in the following application menu path: **Tools • Customizing • IMG • SPRO – Execute Project • SAP Reference**

IMG • Financial Accounting • Asset Accounting • Depreciation • Valuation Method • Depreciation Key • Calculation Methods.

Here, you can define a calculation method via the following options:

- **Define Base Methods**
  This method specifies the depreciation type (ordinary/special or scrapping depreciation type), depreciation method used (straight-line/write down value method), and treatment of the end of depreciation at the end of the planned asset's life.

- **Define Declining-Balance Methods**
  Known also as the reducing balance method, this accelerated depreciation method calculates a higher depreciation amount during the initial years of an asset life and a lower depreciation amount in the later years.

- **Define Maximum Amount Methods**
  Using this method, the depreciation amount is calculated by specifying the maximum amount to be charged as an expense in a particular year. In this way, depreciation can't be posted that exceeds this specified maximum amount.

- **Define Multi-Level Methods**
  Via this method, it's possible to specify different depreciation rates for different periods.

- **Maintain Period Control Methods**
  With this method, different rules can be set for periods in case of different asset scenarios.

Let's create the declining-balance methods. After selecting the **Define Declining-Balance Methods** option, the **Determine Work Area: Entry** screen appears, as shown in Figure 6.8. Select the chart of depreciation in the **Chart of Deprec.** field, and click the **Continue** (green checkmark) button.

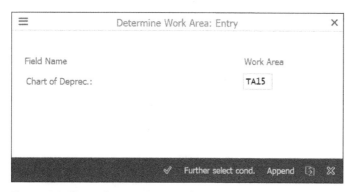

Figure 6.8 Chart of Depreciation Selection

In the **Change View "Declining-Balance Method": Overview** screen that appears, select one of the listed calculation methods or create a new declining-balance method record by filling in the following fields (see Figure 6.9):

- **Decl.-Bal.**
  The declining-balance method of the depreciation key for depreciation calculation.

- **Description of the Method**
  The formula used for the depreciation method.

- **Dec.Factor**
  Declining-balance multiplication factor used to determine the depreciation percentage rate for the declining-balance method.

- **Max.Perc.**
  Maximum percentage rate that represents the upper limit for the depreciation percentage rate.

- **Min.Perc.**
  Minimum percentage rate that represents the lower limit for the depreciation percentage rate.

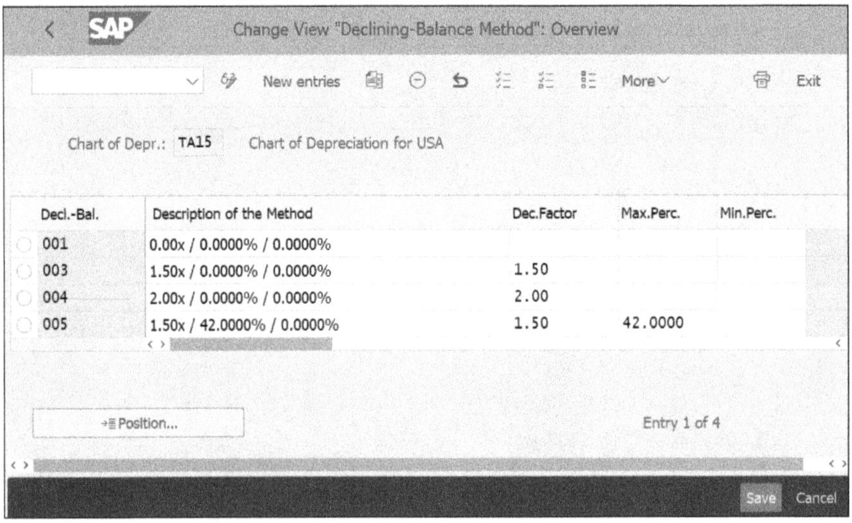

Figure 6.9 Declining-Balance Method

When you're done, click the **Save** button, which will then create a prompt request for Customizing, and a notification message will appear at the bottom of the screen that the data has been saved.

Maintain Depreciation Key

If you need to maintain the depreciation key, follow the original application menu path, and double-click on **Maintain Determination Key** to open the **Change View "Depreciation Key": Overview** screen, as shown in Figure 6.10.

Under the **Dialog Structure**, you can select the **Assignment of Calculation Methods** folder after you've selected the depreciation key. For example, select the depreciation key **LINS Str.-line over rem.life pro rata to zero**, and then double-click on **Assignment of Calculation Methods**, as shown in Figure 6.11.

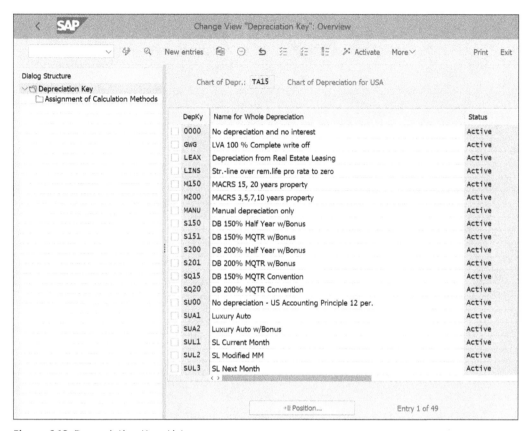

Figure 6.10 Depreciation Keys List

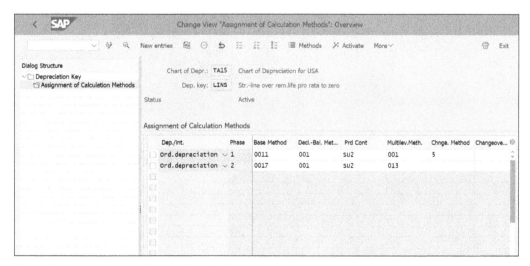

Figure 6.11 Assignment of Calculation Method

To create a new assignment calculation method, press F5 or select **More • Edit • New Entries** from the menu bar. You can fill in the following fields in the header area, as shown in Figure 6.12:

- **Chart of Depr./Dep. key**
  Defaulted and populated based on selections from the previous step.

- **DepType**
  Filled based on the reason for the depreciation as explained in the beginning of the section. These values are preconfigured values in the system.

- **Phase**
  The depreciation time can be divided into several phases, each using different calculation methods for calculating depreciation. Therefore, using the changeover method, it's specified that the system starts to use the respective calculation method for the next phase. These are also preconfigured values in the system.

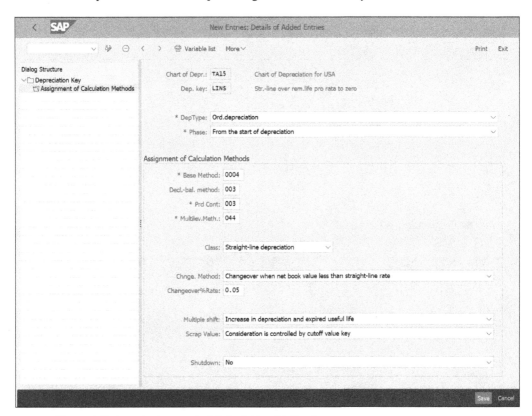

Figure 6.12 New Assignment of Calculation Method

In the **Assignment of Calculation Methods** area, you can define values for each listed method by selecting the preconfigured values in the system:

- **Class**

  This is an optional field with preconfigured values. You can use one of the preconfigured indicators to classify depreciation calculated with this depreciation key. This characteristic can also be used as a selection criterion in reporting.

- **Chnge. Method**

  This is an optional field with preconfigured values that specifies when the changeover to another phase of the depreciation key takes place.

- **Changeover%Rate**

  This field defines the net book value percentage rate for the depreciation changeover. It's the percentage of the acquisition value at which the system changes the calculation of depreciation.

- **Multiple shift**

  This is an optional field with preconfigured values to control the effects of multiple-shift depreciation.

- **Scrap Value**

  This is an optional field with preconfigured values used to specify the effect of scrap value on the base value.

- **Shutdown**

  This is an optional field with preconfigured values used to determine that depreciation will be reduced or stopped if there are specifications for shutdown periods in the asset master record.

After you've filled in your necessary fields, click the **Save** button, and the new calculation method assignment will be listed as you saw earlier in Figure 6.11.

SAP Fiori App

There is no corresponding SAP Fiori app available as of SAP S/4HANA 2022. However, the Depreciation Key: Display Details app (FAA_DEPRKEY_SHOW) is available, as shown in Figure 6.13 and Figure 6.14. It's visually a bit more modern but functionally the same as the SAP GUI transaction.

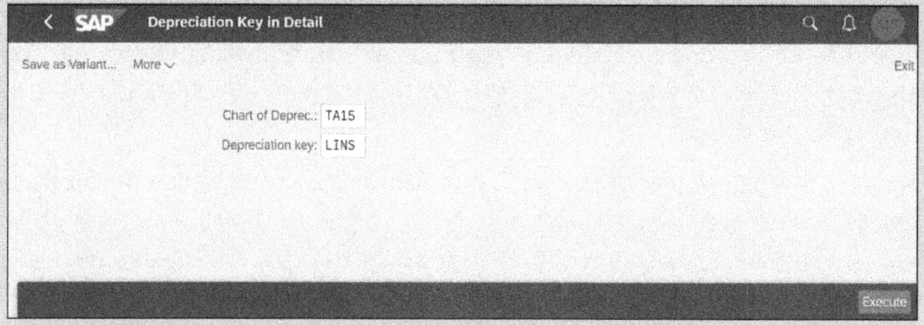

Figure 6.13 Entrance Screen of the Depreciation Key: Display Details App

---

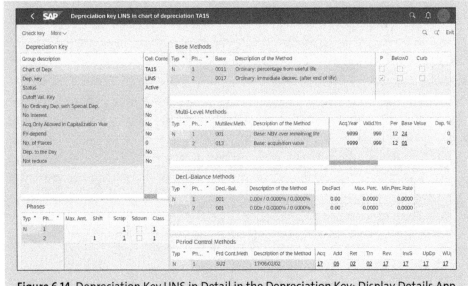

Figure 6.14 Depreciation Key LINS in Detail in the Depreciation Key: Display Details App

Now that you understand the depreciation key, let's discuss the depreciation area next.

6.2.5   Depreciation Area

Another important element during the asset configuration steps is to define the depreciation area and depreciation type. Specifically, you determine how to calculate the depreciation and how to post to the general ledger accounts. Depreciation calculation is an important stage in month-end closing and year-end closing processes in financial accounting and in the asset's net book value calculation.

After an asset master record is created, the capitalization process updates the asset subledger and the general ledger with the acquisition production cost. The asset's value is represented in the balance sheet. The depreciation amount is also posted regularly on the asset's life based on the defined method. The balance sheet reflects the accumulated depreciation amounts (e.g., applied on a monthly basis), and the P&L statement will reflect the depreciation expense postings. As mentioned previously, all these transaction entries in the general ledger are monitored and controlled from the account determination.

We defined the main depreciation methods in Section 6.1.3: straight-line, double declining balance, units of production, and sum of years digits. Now, we'll walk through how to add a depreciation area. Depreciation areas can be used to calculate different values simultaneously for each fixed asset and for different purposes. Let's say you need to have different types of values for the balance sheet, management accounting depreciation, book depreciation, tax depreciation purposes, and so on. In the depreciation area of each asset, you can manage the depreciation terms and needed values for this valuation using a specific depreciation method. Every depreciation area belongs to at least one chart of depreciation and is managed separately from other depreciation areas.

To add a depreciation area in SAP S/4HANA, you need to apply the relevant settings using the Customizing tool as follows: **Tools • Customizing • IMG • SPRO – Execute Project • SAP Reference IMG • Financial Accounting • Asset Accounting • General Valuation • Depreciation Areas • Define Depreciation Areas**. Alternatively, you can access this path using Transaction OADB or Transaction OADC.

After you run this transaction, in the **Select Activity** screen (see Figure 6.15), select the **Define Depreciation Areas** activity, and press `Enter`.

Figure 6.15 Select Activity Screen

You're then asked to define the chart of depreciation, as shown in Figure 6.16. In this example, enter chart of depreciation "TA15".

Figure 6.16 Chart of Depreciation Selection

This will lead to the **Change View "Define Depreciation Areas": Overview** screen, as shown in Figure 6.17.

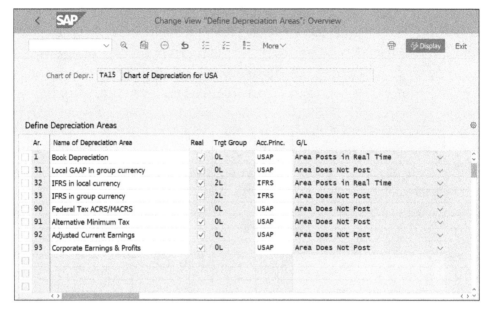

Figure 6.17 Define Depreciation Area

Now, if you want to create a new depreciation area, just click any of the existing ones, and click the **Copy As** 🔲 icon at the top of the screen. The **Change View "Define Depreciation Areas": Details of Selected Set** screen opens in which you need to define the values for the new depreciation area you're creating (see Figure 6.18).

Enter the following fields in the header area:

- **Chart of Depr.**
  A defaulted value is populated here because you've already chosen the chart of depreciation.

- **Deprec. Area**
  Define a number and a description for the depreciation area you're creating that will represent the valuation of the asset for a particular purpose.

In the **Define Depreciation Areas** area, mark the **Real Depreciation Area** indicator if you want the system to store the values of this depreciation area in the database. You can also enter your **Accounting Principle**, which is used to facilitate the depiction of parallel accounting in the system. These are preconfigured accounting principles designed for the legal regulations according to which financial statements are drawn up and rendered. Finally, define **Posting in the General Ledger** by selecting one of the listed options, depending on your requirements.

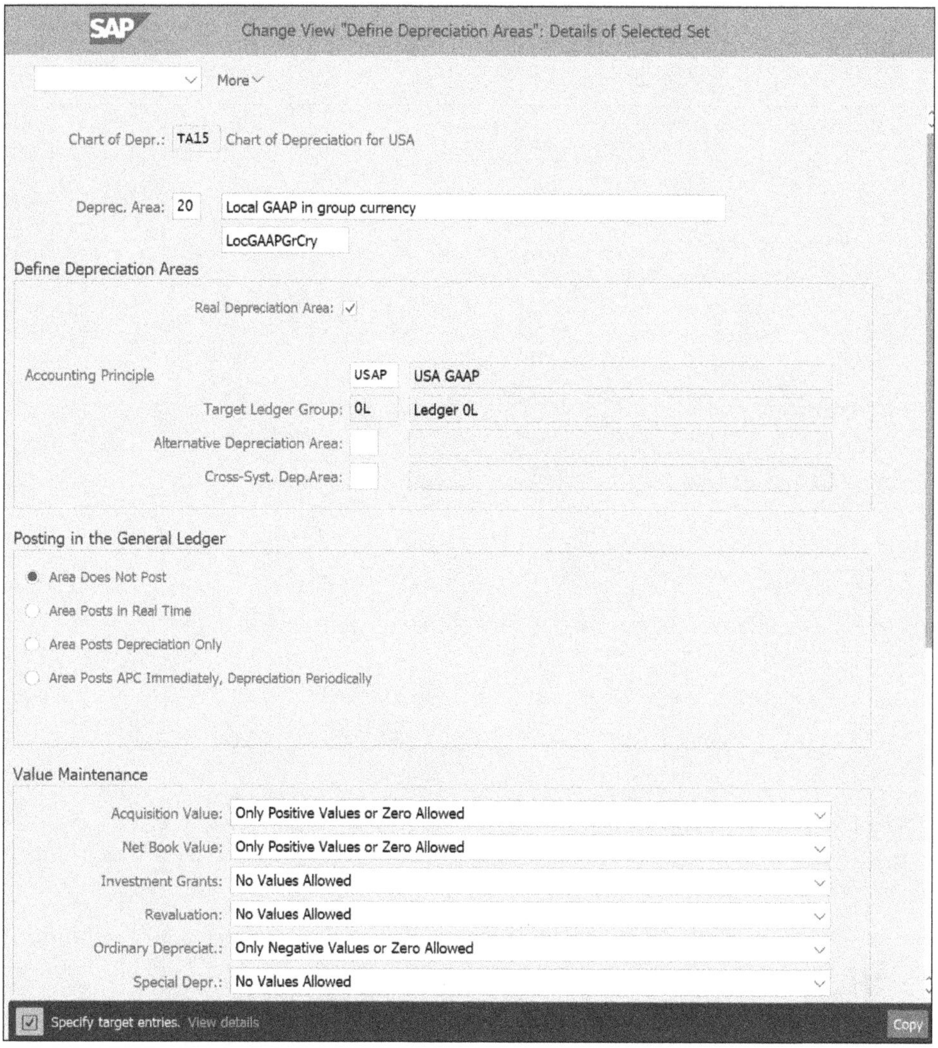

Figure 6.18 Define New Depreciation Area

Note

On each screen, to find out whether each field is mandatory or optional, you can select the desired field and press the ⌐F1⌐ key or right-click the **Help** function. A popup window will appear with the relevant explanation for each selected field.

Click the **Copy** button to apply all the changes entered, and the overview screen opens containing the recently created depreciation area (see Figure 6.19).

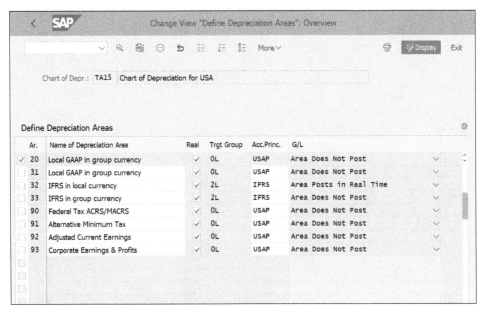

Figure 6.19 Newly Created Depreciation Area in the Overview Screen

Click the **Save** button to reflect the changes in the system.

> **SAP Fiori App**
>
> There is no corresponding SAP Fiori app available as of SAP S/4HANA 2022, which means that the configuration has to be done in SAP GUI.

In the next section, we'll explain the chart of depreciation and the ledger assignment process.

6.2.6   Chart of Depreciation and Ledger Assignment

A *chart of depreciation* functions as a directory of depreciation areas that is configured according to business requirements. Each chart of depreciation consists of an asset's evaluation rules that are relevant for a specific country. As mentioned, when configuring the account determination, a chart of depreciation must be created and assigned to the company code.

You can configure the chart of depreciation using the Customizing tools via Transaction OAOB or by following application menu path **Tools • Customizing • IMG • SPRO – Execute Project • SAP Reference IMG • Financial Accounting • Asset Accounting • Organizational Structure • Assign Chart of Depreciation to Company Code**. After you start this transaction, the **Change View "Maintain company code in Asset Accounting": Overview** screen appears, as shown in Figure 6.20.

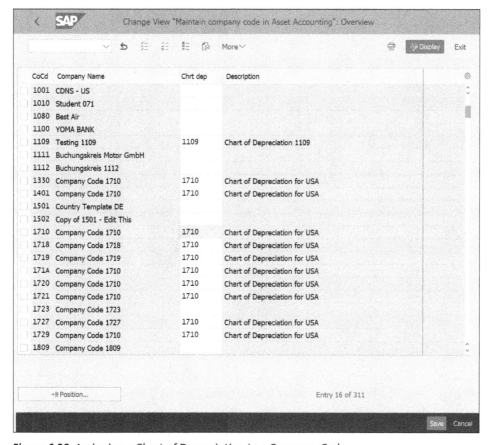

Figure 6.20 Assigning a Chart of Depreciation to a Company Code

Chart of depreciation **1710** is assigned to company code **1710**. Within chart of depreciation **1710**, there are several depreciation areas assigned (see Figure 6.21). With the help of multiple depreciation areas, you can value one and the same asset differently and post it in several ledgers simultaneously. For instance, you can depreciate a machine using the straight-line method for US Generally Accepted Accounting Principles (US-GAAP) reporting and using a declining-balance method for International Financial Reporting Standards (IFRS) if needed. Both methods lead to different book values for the same asset. In Figure 6.21, you see that the standard depreciation area **1 Book Depreciation** posts in ledger group **OL**, whereas the depreciation area **IFRS in local currency** posts **32** in ledger group **2L**. With this concept, you can realize an automatic parallel accounting for multiple accounting principles for fixed assets.

SAP Fiori App

There is no corresponding SAP Fiori app as of SAP S/4HANA 2022, which means that the configuration has to be done in SAP GUI.

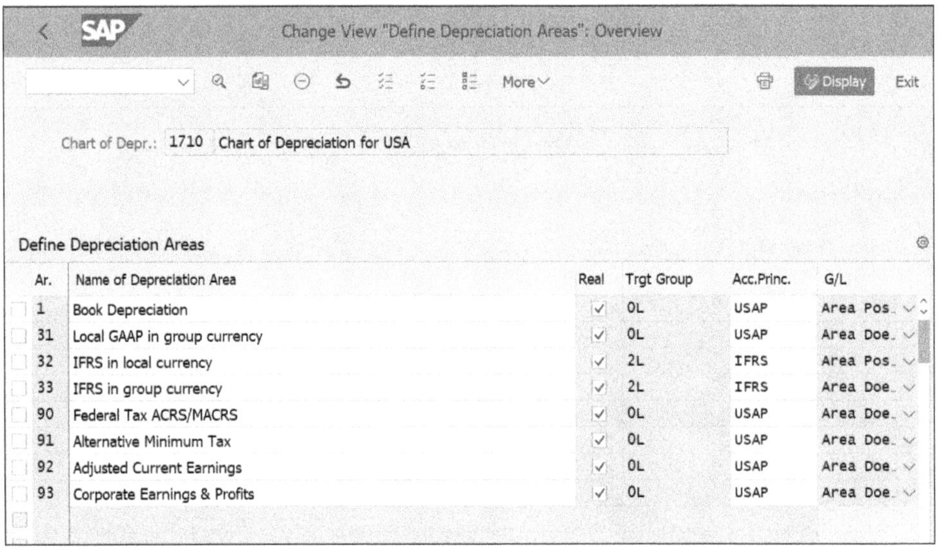

Figure 6.21 Depreciation Areas

6.3   Fixed Asset Explorer

Now that you understand how to create and maintain fixed assets, you need to know how to navigate and explore them. Asset quantities may vary from an easily manageable number up to thousands or more, which may cause lots of complications regarding how to keep control over them. For that reason, it's necessary to put practical tools in place to manage and monitor the fixed assets and their financial information.

In SAP S/4HANA, you can use the asset explorer functionality. This explorer is used to represent and analyze the comprehensive asset values that also contain the acquisition and production cost, depreciation values and parameters, planned and actual values, posted values, book values, master data records, and so on in various formats and accumulated levels.

To run the asset explorer function, you can use the corresponding Transaction AW01N or follow application menu path **Accounting • Financial Accounting • Fixed Assets • Assets • Asset Explorer**.

The **Asset Explorer** screen contains the header, in which you first select the **Company Code** and the **Asset** number; an outline tree to navigate among depreciation areas; an outline tree that shows objects related to the asset; and **Planned values**, **Posted values**, **Comparisons**, and **Parameters** tabs. You only have to select a company code and an asset, and then you can start to explore the asset transactions, which we'll do in this section.

SAP Fiori App

The corresponding SAP Fiori app for accounts determination is called Asset Values (AW01N). It's visually and functionally the same as the SAP GUI transaction.

6.3.1   Planning

On the **Planned values** tab, as shown in Figure 6.22, you can analyze planned values where you can see the acquisition and production cost transactions, acquisition values, unplanned depreciation values, and so on. To do so, select one of the listed **Depreciation Areas** in the left panel, which are categorized into two main groups per the accounting regulations: **USAP USA GAAP** and **IFRS International Financial Reporting Standards**.

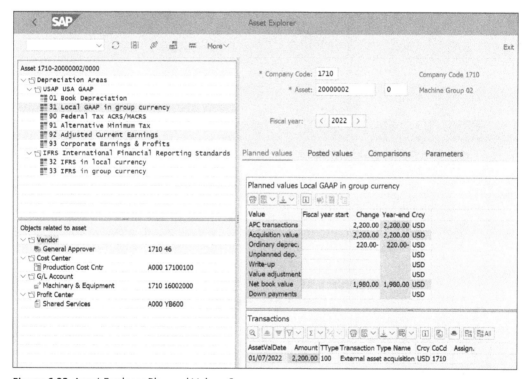

Figure 6.22 Asset Explorer Planned Values Screen

In this example, **01 Book Depreciation** is selected, and the fields in the right panel are updated accordingly with its planned values. If you double-click any of the listed planned values, another detailed screen will appear showing depreciation calculation methods on the period intervals. For example, click on the **Ordinary deprec.** planned value in the **Value** column to show the depreciation calculation for the period interval methods (see Figure 6.23). As you can see, the acquisition production cost is **2,200** USD, and the total ordinary depreciation value is **220** USD.

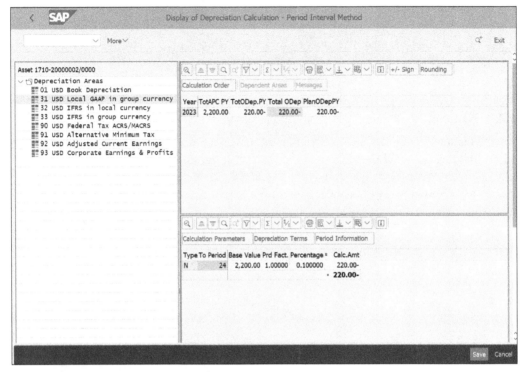

Figure 6.23 Depreciation Calculation

The depreciation calculation records displayed can be shown more analytically by clicking on the following tabs:

- **Calculation Parameters**
  You can see the calculation parameters for fiscal year 2022, such as the value **Type**, which, in this case, is **N** (ordinary depreciation); **Period** as a self-contained part of the fiscal year; **Base Value**, which is determined by the depreciation method; **Base Value Reduction; Calculation Method; Percentage Factor;** and so on.

- **Depreciation Terms**
  You can see the terms of depreciation, such as year, type, from period/to period as a self-contained part, fiscal year, depreciation key, useful life, asset class, depreciation phase, and so on.

- **Period Information**
  You can see information regarding the period, such as fiscal year, value type, period, useful life, and so on.

In the **Transactions** area at the bottom of the screen (refer to Figure 6.22), all the **Transactions** are displayed that affect the calculated depreciation, acquisition and production costs, net book value, and any calculated interest for the selected asset. You can double-click any of the listed transaction records to see the related entries. In this example, we've selected the transaction shown earlier in Figure 6.22 (under the **Transactions** area), and the result is shown in Figure 6.24.

Figure 6.24 Document Data Entry View

In this screen, you can see debit and credit generated entries and respective general ledger accounts regarding the selected asset transaction shown earlier in Figure 6.22.

Let's move on to the posted values and other configuration settings of the selected asset.

6.3.2   Actuals

On the **Posted values** tab, as shown in Figure 6.25, you can see all actual posted and planned depreciation values for the selected asset.

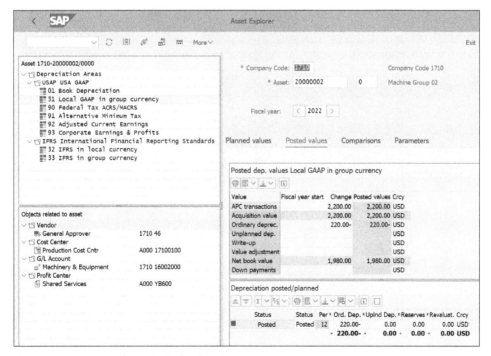

Figure 6.25 Asset Explorer Posted Values Screen

On the **Comparisons** tab, you can check and compare fiscal years and depreciation areas, and you can see the annual breakdown per the depreciation area and net book value (see Figure 6.26). The depreciation areas are vertically listed below the asset and the respective depreciation area relevant to the selected company code.

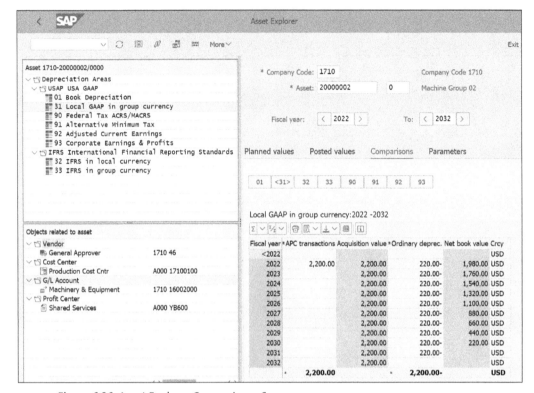

Figure 6.26 Asset Explorer Comparisons Screen

On the **Parameters** tab, specific settings of the asset depreciation are shown (see Figure 6.27), as follows:

- **Life**
  Contains the following key fields:
  - **Useful Life**: Represents the planned useful life in years over which the asset will be used and depreciated.
  - **Expired UL**: Shows the part of the useful life that has expired.
  - **Remaining life**: Shows the remaining useful life.
- **Start of calculation**
  Contains the following key fields:
  - **Dep. Start Date**: Shows the date when the depreciation calculation starts in the system.
  - **Spec.depreciation**: Shows the date when a special depreciation starts.
  - **Int.Calc. Start**: Shows the start date for interest calculation.

- ■ **Index specifications**

  Shows the **Index series** to calculate the replacement values based on the acquisition and production costs or the replacement value from the previous year. In the **Aging Index** field, you can enter an age-dependent index series for the calculation of special asset values (for example, insurance values).

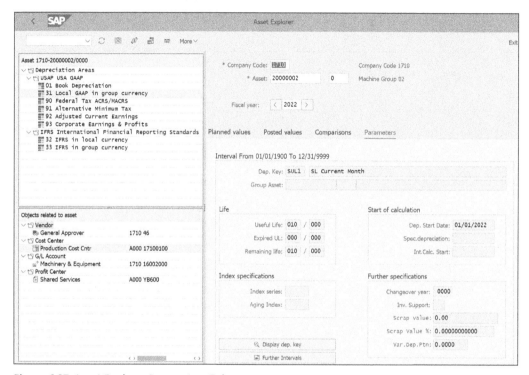

Figure 6.27 Asset Explorer Parameters Tab

In the **Dep. Key** field, you can explore the relevant depreciation key. In the **Parameters** tab, you can always check information related to an asset's depreciation calculation to validate the depreciation settings.

If you switch on the simulation mode ⊞ at the top of the screen or via the ⌐F6⌐ key, then certain fields of this screen became ready for input. These fields can be changed to simulate depreciation per different terms. This prompts a recalculation process of depreciation. The system then represents the simulated amount values directly in the **Asset Explorer** screen.

To show the depreciation key settings such as the methods used in the chart of depreciation, status, chart of depreciation, and so on, click on the **Display dep. key** button. You'll arrive at the screen shown in Figure 6.28, which represents four used methods: **Base Methods**, **Multi-Level Methods**, **Decl.-Balance Methods**, and **Period Control Methods**. Here, you can see what configurations are implemented for each depreciation method, which we've already explained in Section 6.2.4.

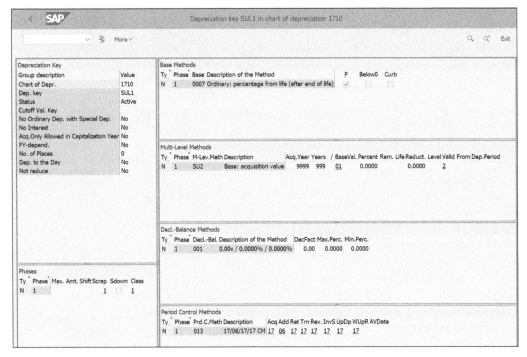

Figure 6.28 Depreciation Key Methods Settings

In the next section, you can see how easy it is to access the master record data of a specific asset from the asset explorer tool.

6.3.3   Master Data

In the **Asset Explorer** screen, you can directly jump to the master records without navigating in the SAP S/4HANA application menu path. For that, you can click the **Display Master Data** button at the top of the screen, which then opens the **Display Asset: Master data** screen, as shown in Figure 6.29.

By clicking the **Asset values** button, you can go back to the initial screen of the asset explorer.

Another available function provided by the asset explorer is to retrieve the reports relating to fixed assets by using the **Call Asset Reports** button at the top of the screen. The **Select Report** popup will appear, where you can select any of the listed asset reports (see Figure 6.30) and click the **Continue** button (checkmark). For example, let's call the **Asset History Sheet** report for the selected asset **200013**, as shown in Figure 6.31.

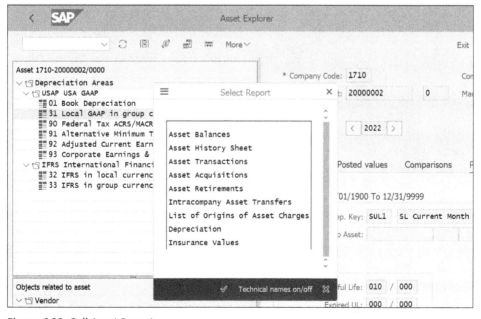

Figure 6.29 Asset Explorer Master Data

Figure 6.30 Call Asset Report

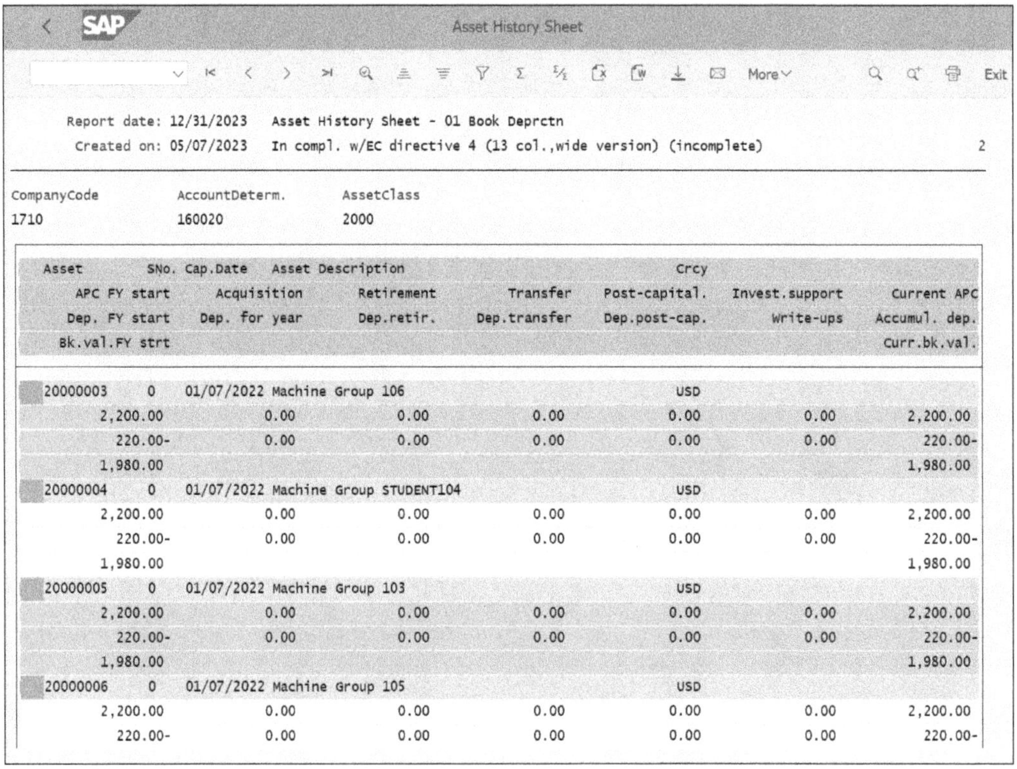

Report date: 12/31/2023 Asset History Sheet - 01 Book Deprctn
Created on: 05/07/2023 In compl. w/EC directive 4 (13 col.,wide version) (incomplete) 2

CompanyCode	AccountDeterm.	AssetClass
1710	160020	2000

Asset SNo. Cap.Date Asset Description				Crcy		
APC FY start	Acquisition	Retirement	Transfer	Post-capital.	Invest.support	Current APC
Dep. FY start	Dep. for year	Dep.retir.	Dep.transfer	Dep.post-cap.	Write-ups	Accumul. dep.
Bk.val.FY strt						Curr.bk.val.
20000003 0 01/07/2022 Machine Group 106				USD		
2,200.00	0.00	0.00	0.00	0.00	0.00	2,200.00
220.00-	0.00	0.00	0.00	0.00	0.00	220.00-
1,980.00						1,980.00
20000004 0 01/07/2022 Machine Group STUDENT104				USD		
2,200.00	0.00	0.00	0.00	0.00	0.00	2,200.00
220.00-	0.00	0.00	0.00	0.00	0.00	220.00-
1,980.00						1,980.00
20000005 0 01/07/2022 Machine Group 103				USD		
2,200.00	0.00	0.00	0.00	0.00	0.00	2,200.00
220.00-	0.00	0.00	0.00	0.00	0.00	220.00-
1,980.00						1,980.00
20000006 0 01/07/2022 Machine Group 105				USD		
2,200.00	0.00	0.00	0.00	0.00	0.00	2,200.00
220.00-	0.00	0.00	0.00	0.00	0.00	220.00-

Figure 6.31 Asset History Sheet through Call Asset Report

Here, you can see the asset history sheet that includes all relevant reports for each asset assigned to **CompanyCode 1710** and the **AssetClass 2000**. In this screen, each asset is represented by three lines. The current book value (**Curr.bk.val.**) for asset number **2000003** amounts to **1,980.00 USD**.

Now that you've learned how to navigate fixed assets through the asset explorer tool, let's discuss fixed asset transaction types in the next section.

6.4 Asset Transactions

In this section, we'll discuss the available transactions that can be performed on the asset's records, such as the acquisition process with the vendor invoice, standard depreciation, impairment process, transfers, and asset retirements. Let's start with the fixed asset acquisition with vendor invoice.

6.4.1 Acquisition/Integration to Vendor Invoice

In this section, we'll explain how to create a fixed asset vendor invoice entry in financial accounting. As you remember from Chapter 4, Section 4.3.2, we've used Transaction FB60 to post an invoice without a purchase order. We'll use the same transaction in this example to show you how to post an asset acquisition entry in the system. As a reminder, you can find this transaction by following application menu path **Accounting • Financial Accounting • Accounts Payable • Document Entry • Invoice**.

In the **Enter Vendor Invoice** screen (see Figure 6.32), fill in the required fields, such as your **Vendor** number, **Invoice date**, **Posting Date** (when the invoice is posted in financial accounting), **Amount**, and **Reference** number. In the **Items** area, enter the **G/L acct**, and indicate whether it's **Debit** or **Credit**.

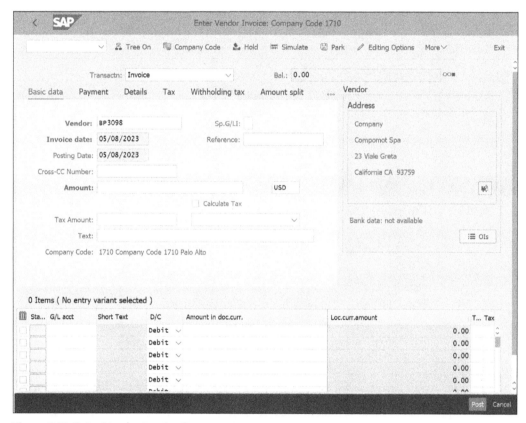

Figure 6.32 Enter Vendor Invoice Screen

After you've entered this data, select **More • Environment • Complex Posting** in the menu bar, which will lead you to the **Display Overview** screen (see Figure 6.33). In the **PstKy** field, select number **70** for asset debit, and in the **TType** field, select asset type **100**, which belongs to the external asset acquisition.

Next, to check for errors before posting, click the **Simulate** button, which you find either in the upper menu when the screen is expanded or under **More • Document • Simulate**. If the simulation of the document is successful, an overview screen will appear with overall information. Now you can click on the **Post** button to post the vendor invoice document, and you'll receive a message with the new document number at the bottom of the screen.

Figure 6.33 Display Overview: Asset Acquisition

SAP Fiori App

The corresponding SAP Fiori app is called Create Supplier Invoice (F0346A). In Figure 6.34 and Figure 6.35, you can see what the app looks like in SAP Fiori.

Like SAP GUI, you need to enter the required data in the header and at least one line item in the **Invoice Items** area. Then you can click the **Simulate** button to check if there are any errors before you post the document. If the simulation process is successful, click the **Post** button to post the vendor invoice.

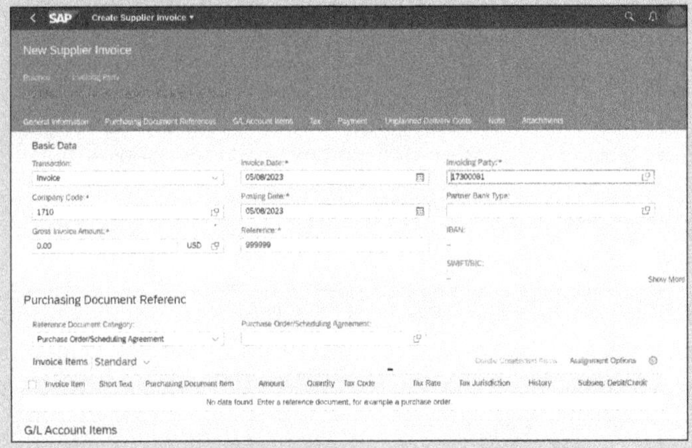

Figure 6.34 Create Supplier Invoice App in SAP Fiori (1)

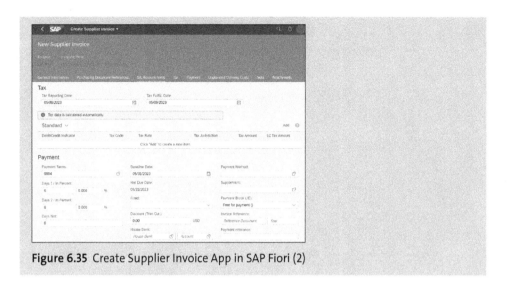

Figure 6.35 Create Supplier Invoice App in SAP Fiori (2)

In the next section, you'll see how the depreciation transaction is performed in the system.

6.4.2   Standard Depreciation

As we've discussed in this chapter, depreciation is a continuing loss of an asset's value over its lifetime. This value erosion is calculated and posted in the asset depreciation run.

To execute an asset depreciation in SAP S/4HANA, you can run Transaction AFAB or follow application menu path **Accounting • Financial Accounting • Fixed Assets • Periodic Processing • Depreciation Run • Execute**. You'll arrive at the **Depreciation Posting Run** screen, as shown in Figure 6.36.

Enter values in the following sections:

- **Posting Parameters**
  Enter the **Company Code** for which you want to run the depreciation, **Fiscal Year**, **Posting period**, and, optionally, an **Accounting Principle**, which can be the local GAAP or international IFRS.

- **Parallel Processing**
  Enter the **Server Group** for parallel processing (determines which application server will be used) and the **Number of Parallel Processes**.

- **Output Options**
  Select one of the listed options if you want to display a **Totals Log**, a **Detailed Log**, or **No Output Log**.

- **Test Run Parameters**
  Ensure that the **Test Run** checkbox is selected, which runs the depreciation in the test environment first.

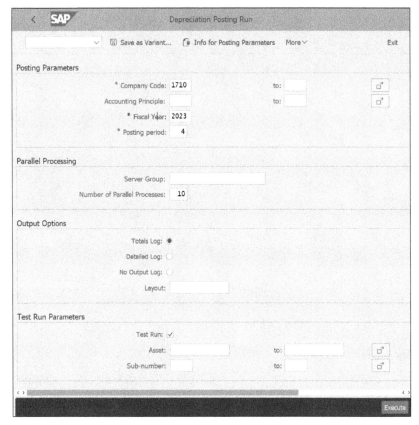

Figure 6.36 Depreciation Posting Run Entry Values Screen

The next step is to execute the process by clicking on the **Execute** button, which starts the run as a separate task in the background. The results will be shown as in Figure 6.37. (This topic is also discussed further in Section 6.5.4.)

Period	St	A	Ledg	Acc.P	Amount in Company Code Currency CompC	Amount in Global Currency Glob C	Profit Center	Segment		DocumentNo CoCo
TESTRUN										
Company Code:			1710							
Processed Fixed Assets:			3							
Fixed Assets Without Errors:			3							
Fixed Assets with Errors in at Least One Area:			0							
Run Date:			05/07/2023							
1	▣	1	0L	USAP	929.00- USD	929.00- USD	YB600	1000_C	0	$ 1 1710
2			0L	USAP	928.00- USD	928.00- USD	YB600	1000_C	0	
3			0L	USAP	1,071.00- USD	1,071.00- USD	YB600	1000_C	0	
4			0L	USAP	959.00- USD	959.00- USD	YB600	1000_C	0	
				•	3,887.00- USD	3,887.00- USD				
	△ 1			••	3,887.00- USD ••	3,887.00- USD				
1		32	2L	IFRS	928.00- USD	928.00- USD	YB600	1000_C	0	$ 2
2			2L	IFRS	929.00- USD	929.00- USD	YB600	1000_C	0	
3			2L	IFRS	1,047.00- USD	1,047.00- USD	YB600	1000_C	0	
4			2L	IFRS	947.00- USD	947.00- USD	YB600	1000_C	0	
				•	3,851.00- USD	3,851.00- USD				
	△3			••	3,851.00- USD ••	3,851.00- USD				
				•••	7,738.00- USD •••	7,738.00- USD				1710 △
				••••	7,738.00- USD ••••	7,738.00- USD				

Figure 6.37 Depreciation Posting Run Results

As you can see from the test run results, one fixed asset has been processed without error for **Company Code 1710**. When you run depreciation by executing Transaction AFAB, you'll see the errors and other details, but after posting is finalized, and any other user wants to view the logs, then you would use Transaction AFBP. This transaction can be accessed using menu path **Accounting • Financial Accounting • Fixed Assets • Periodic Processing • Depreciation Run • Display Log**.

You'll arrive at the screen shown in Figure 6.38, where you can enter the **Company Code** for which you want to check the report, **Fiscal Year** for which you want to check the postings, **Posting Period** for which you want to check the depreciation run, and **Accounting Principle** in case you need to restrict the report by this attribute.

Click the **Execute** button to arrive at the screen shown in Figure 6.39. This report shows if there are any errors in the depreciation run you've executed previously.

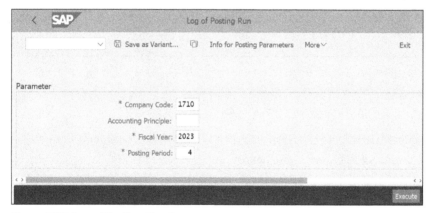

Figure 6.38 Log of Posting Run Screen

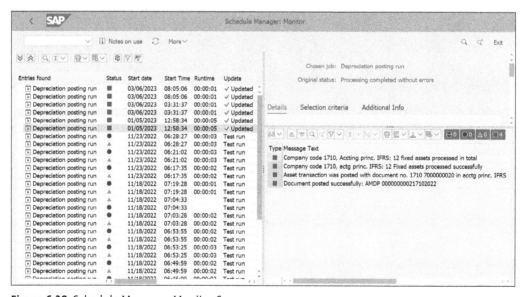

Figure 6.39 Schedule Manager: Monitor Screen

To get more depreciation log details, you can click on **Selection criteria** and **Additional Info**.

> **SAP Fiori App**
>
> The corresponding SAP Fiori app is called Schedule Asset Accounting Jobs (F1914). You'll learn how to use this app in Section 6.5.1.

6.4.3   Impairment (Value Adjustment)

Sometimes, for different reasons, it's necessary to make some adjustments on the value of fixed assets. For example, if a device (e.g., printer, laptop, etc.) is damaged, its value will drop instantly. Therefore, the value of this asset needs to be adjusted. On the other hand, there are also changes that positively affect the asset status, increasing its value. This change, which is called a *write-up*, increases the asset book value. This may happen when the carrying value is lower than the fair market value. When it's used in a depreciation method context, depending on the net book value, write-ups increase the planned and, later, the actual, depreciation amount.

The write-up is usually applied in the following scenarios:

- The company is being acquired, and its assets are restated to fair market value.
- The initial value of the asset wasn't appropriately registered.
- The asset wasn't capitalized in a fiscal year that is now closed, and this mistake must be adjusted in the subsequent year.
- An earlier write-down in the asset value was too high.

> **Note**
>
> An asset write-up procedure is the opposite of a write-down. They are both noncash items.

In SAP S/4HANA, you can use several available transactions to perform an asset value adjustment, which are available under **Manual Value Correction** in the **Fixed Asset** menu path:

- **Transaction ABZU (Write-Up)**
  With this transaction, you can post a write-up to any of the listed depreciation transaction types, such as ordinary and special depreciation, special tax depreciation, general unplanned depreciation, and so on (see Figure 6.40).

  Alternatively, you can also use application menu path **Accounting • Financial Accounting • Fixed Assets • Posting • Manual Value Correction • Write-Up**.

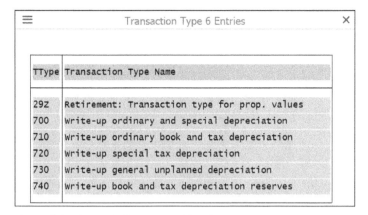

Figure 6.40 Depreciation Transaction Types

- **Transaction ABMA (Manual Depreciation)**
  With this transaction, you can post write-ups of manual depreciation.

  Alternatively, you can also follow application menu path **Accounting • Financial Accounting • Fixed Assets • Posting • Manual Value Correction • Manual Depreciation**.

- **Transaction ABAA (Unplanned Depreciation)**
  With this transaction, you can post manual depreciations of any assets besides the systematically performed depreciation run using, for instance, the useful life model.

  Alternatively, you can also follow application menu path **Accounting • Financial Accounting • Fixed Assets • Posting • Manual Value Correction • Unplanned Depreciation**.

- **Transaction ABMR (Transfer of Reserves)**
  With this transaction, you can post value transfers from one asset to another or from one account to another.

  Alternatively, you can also follow application menu path **Accounting • Financial Accounting • Fixed Assets • Posting • Manual Value Correction • Transfer of Reserves**.

- **Transaction ABNAN (Post Capitalization)**
  With this transaction, you can capitalize acquisition and production costs, which removes or reduces relevant acquisition and production costs from the P&L statement.

  Alternatively, you can also follow application menu path **Accounting • Financial Accounting • Fixed Assets • Posting • Post-Capitalization**.

Let's consider an example using Transaction ABZU. In the **Create General Header Data for Posting** screen, enter the values corresponding to the **Company Code**, **Asset** number, and **Trans. Type** ("700" for ordinary and special depreciation for this example), as shown in Figure 6.41. Click the **Continue** button (checkmark).

Figure 6.41 General Header Data for Write-Up Posting

In the next screen (see Figure 6.42) that appears, **Enter Asset Transaction: Writeup**, enter the required data in the **Transaction data** tab:

- **Area Selection**
  Define the **Accounting Principle** and **Depreciation Area**.

- **Basic Data**
  Fill in the **Document Date** and **Posting Date** as the date on which the transaction will be posted to the appropriate account. This field normally is defaulted with the current date, but it's also usually an editable field.

- **Write-Up Specifications**
  Enter some other details, such as ordinary depreciation, which represents the accumulated ordinary depreciation for part of an asset that is retired from the previous fiscal year; special depreciation amount, which represents accumulated special depreciation calculated from the previous fiscal year; unplanned depreciation amount from the previous year; and so on.

In the **Additional Details** tab, shown in Figure 6.43, you can define the **Posting period** and **Document Type**, which indicates to which group the document will be assigned. In the **Reference** field, enter a number that will be used as a search criterion when displaying or changing documents. Then, in the line items area, you can define the general ledger accounts, the amount that will be posted through this transaction, and so on.

As you're used to in SAP S/4HANA, you can first simulate the posting to check for possible errors by clicking the **Simulate** button. When finished, save the posting using the **Post** button, which will produce an informative message that the asset transaction has been posted with the new document number.

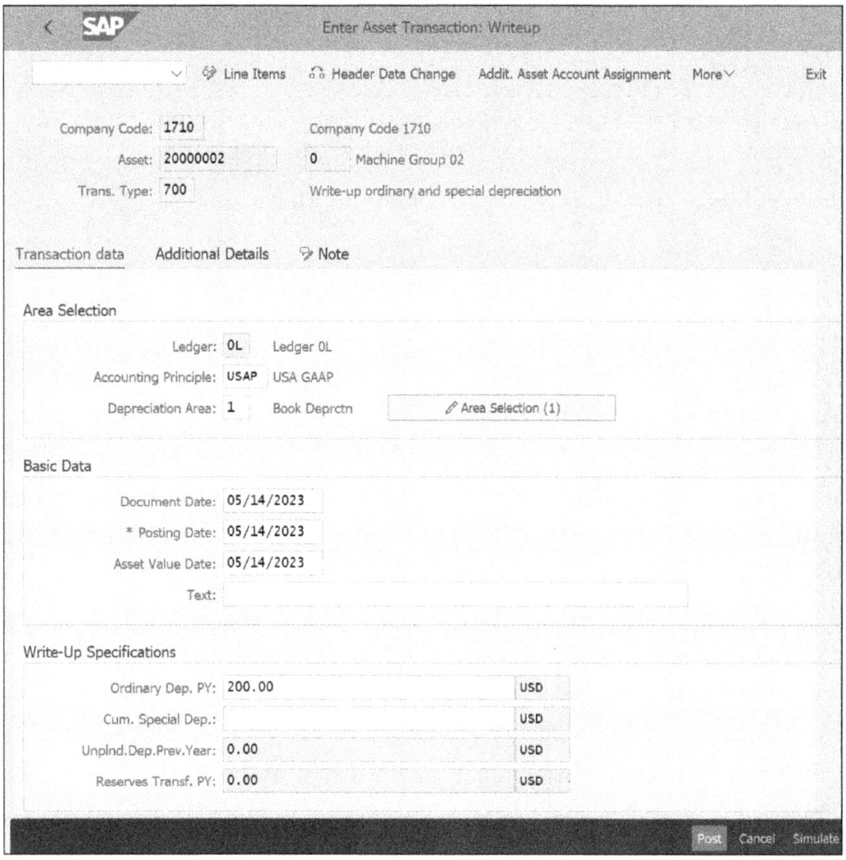

Figure 6.42 Enter Asset Transaction: Writeup Screen

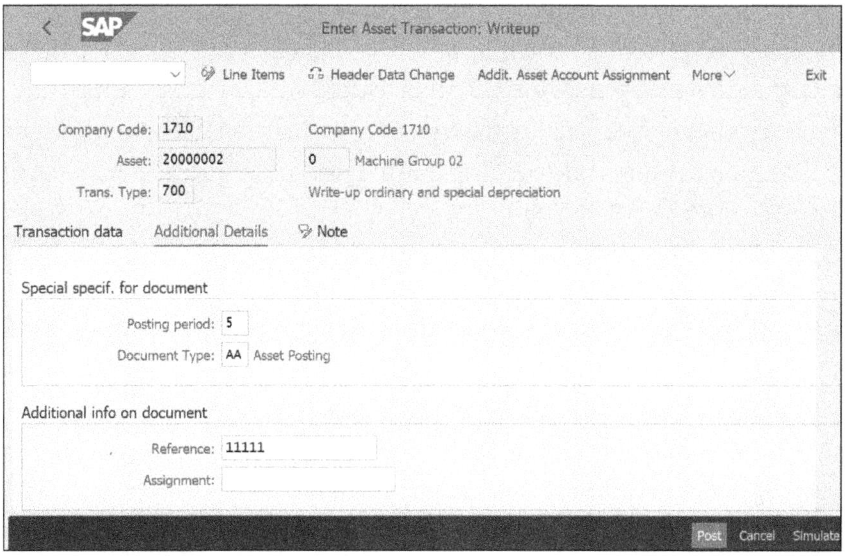

Figure 6.43 Additional Details

SAP Fiori App

The corresponding SAP Fiori app is called Post Writeup (ABZUL). It's visually and functionally the same as the SAP GUI transaction.

Let's move on to transferring an asset or parts of it to another asset.

6.4.4   Transfers

A *transfer* is considered a change of the asset from one part to another or a movement of assets/funds from one account to another. In asset accounting in SAP S/4HANA, two types of asset transfers are recognized:

- **Intracompany transfers**
  An asset or asset component is transferred to another asset master record. In this case, the target asset that is going to be transferred should be in the same company code as the sending asset.

  The intracompany transfer may happen due to the following reasons:
  - Rectifying an incorrect combination of asset and asset class (asset classes can't be changed, making a transfer to a new master record necessary)
  - Splitting up an asset or moving an asset component to another asset
  - Establishing an AuC and transferring it to a finished asset

- **Intercompany transfers**
  Unlike intracompany transfers, intercompany transfers allow asset transferring between different company codes. In this case, the asset is moved or disposed from one company code and acquired from another company code. If these companies belong to the same corporate group, the intercompany transfer has a zero-balance effect in the corporate history balance sheet. The intercompany transfer within a corporate group may happen for the following reasons:
  - Asset changes location, resulting in the asset transferring to another company code
  - Corporate group changes the organization structure, resulting again in the asset transferring to another company code

With this basic understanding of the assets transfer, let's focus on the available transactions that SAP S/4HANA offers to practically implement this procedure. There are two transactions you can execute for each transfer type—intracompany or intercompany—as follows:

- **Transaction ABUMN (Transfer within Company Code)**
  Used to transfer an asset from one department or unit within the company to another using the same company code.

  Alternatively, you can also follow application menu path **Accounting • Financial Accounting • Fixed Assets • Posting • Transfer • Transfer Within Company Code**.

- **Transaction ABT1N (Intercompany Asset Transfer)**
  Used to transfer an asset to a different company code within the corporate group.

  Alternatively, you can also follow application menu path **Accounting • Financial Accounting • Fixed Assets • Posting • Transfer • Intercompany Asset Transfer**.

When you access Transaction ABUMN, enter the company code you're going to process in the screen that appears, and click the **Continue** button. Then, you'll arrive at the **Enter Asset Transaction: Transfer Within Company Code** screen, as shown in Figure 6.44.

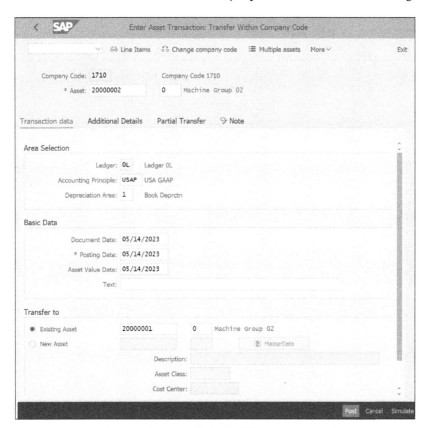

Figure 6.44 Intracompany Asset Transfer (within Company Code)

Fill in the required fields, such as **Asset** number, **Accounting Principle** (in this example, US GAAP [**USAP**]), **Depreciation Area**, **Document Date**, **Posting Date**, and the **Transfer to** area fields. Choose whether you want to transfer to an existing asset or to a new one that you need to create from the master data. In the **Partial Transfer** tab, you can specify relevant details for partial transfers, such as amount posted, quantity, and so on.

Alternatively, if you access Transaction ABT1N, you'll arrive at the **Enter Asset Transaction: Intercompany Asset Transfer** screen, as shown in Figure 6.45.

Figure 6.45 Intercompany Asset Transfer (to Another Company Code)

Enter the required details in the specified areas, such as **Document Date**, **Posting Date**, **Asset Value Date**, and the **Text** description for the transfer in the **Basic Data** area. Then, select the target company where you're going to transfer the asset or a part of the asset. Here you can either transfer to an existing asset by looking for it in the search loop or transfer to a new asset that you need to create directly from the master data by clicking the **New Asset** option. In the **Specifications for Revenue** area, you can select any of the available options to stipulate if the transfer will include revenue or not. If there is revenue assigned, you can choose the **Manual Revenue** option, where you can manually define the revenue amount, or choose **Rev. from NBV**, where you can refer to the net book value for the revenue exchange.

In both cases, after you've completed the required steps, click the **Simulate** button to precheck the entered data, and then finish the transaction using the **Post** button. You'll receive a notification message.

Now that you understand the asset transfer function, let's continue with the asset retirement process in the next section.

6.4.5 Retirements/Disposals

The term *retirement* is widely used in different fields with the meaning of removing of a person or object from one position, occupation, or current state. Retirement has the same meaning when referring to assets. When a company agrees to no longer use an asset, this asset is removed from the asset portfolio and therefore can be considered retired. It doesn't mean that the asset has no value, but the company won't receive any revenues from it at the moment when the asset is retired and derecognized from the asset ledger. In the system, there are a couple of fixed asset accounting transactions that apply to asset retirement.

As we've mentioned in Section 6.1.4, several asset sales transactions are executed for the asset retirement process. Now let's learn about some retirement transaction examples and see how to apply them in SAP S/4HANA.

Posting to Customer

When an asset is sold to a customer producing revenues, you can use Transaction F-92 or follow application menu path **Accounting • Financial Accounting • Fixed Assets • Posting • Retirement • Retirement w/Revenue • With Customer**.

Through this transaction, the entry is posted to accounts receivable where the revenue posting and asset retirement is done in one step. In other words, this transaction creates a debit entry to accounts receivable generating an accounts receivable invoice/document and creates a credit entry to the asset.

You'll arrive at the screen shown in Figure 6.46, where you can enter the required mandatory data, such as **Document Date**, **Posting Date**, **Company Code**, **Currency/Rate**, document **Type**, which classifies the accounting document (e.g., asset posting, journal entry, depreciation posting, etc.), and some other optional data (e.g., **Document Number**, **Reference**, **Doc.Header Text** as a note, and **Trading Part.BA**, which contains the business area of the trading partner).

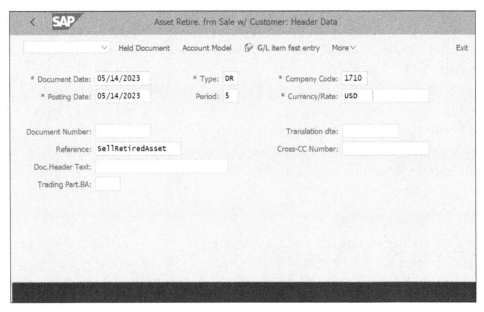

Figure 6.46 Entry Screen of Asset Retirement with Customer

Then, click the **G/L item fast entry** button to enter the general ledger account line items to be retired on the screen shown in Figure 6.47.

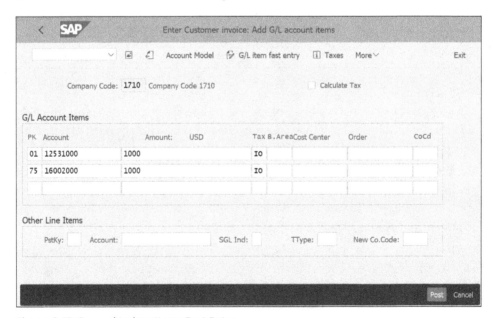

Figure 6.47 General Ledger Items Fast Entry

The key fields include the posting key (**PK**), which refers to the transaction type you're entering in the line item; the **Account** number to be posted; and the **Amount**. If relevant, enter the **Tax** code, which represents a tax category that is used during the tax return to authorities, business area, cost centers if relevant, and so on.

After you've entered the general ledger account line items, click the **Post** button, and a document number will be created.

SAP Fiori App

The corresponding SAP Fiori app is called Post Retirement (Integrated AR) – With Customer (F-92). It's visually and functionally the same as the SAP GUI transaction.

Posting to the General Ledger Clearing Account

Another option besides posting a retirement to a customer is also posting to a general ledger clearing account through Transaction ABAON or through application menu path **Accounting • Financial Accounting • Fixed Assets • Posting • Retirement • Retirement w/Revenue • Asset Sale without Customer**.

The steps followed for this transaction are similar to the steps explained in Transaction ABAVN in the next section. While executing Transaction ABAON, the process creates a debit entry to a general ledger clearing account and a credit entry to the asset.

SAP Fiori App

The corresponding SAP Fiori app is called Post Retirement (Non-Integrated) – With Customer (ABAON). It's visually and functionally the same as the SAP GUI transaction.

Asset Scrapping

Alternatively, you can also use the option to scrap an asset, which doesn't generate revenue from the asset retirement. To do that, you can execute Transaction ABAVN or follow application menu path **Accounting • Financial Accounting • Fixed Assets • Posting • Retirement • Retirement w/Revenue • Asset Retirement by Scrapping**.

Let's illustrate our example of asset retirement by scrapping. You'll arrive at the **Enter Asset Transaction: Asset Retirement by Scrapping** screen, as shown in Figure 6.48. Enter the **Asset** code, **Document Date** as a formal notice date, **Posting Date** as a default to today's date, **Asset Value Date** (takes the value from the posting date), and so on. In the **Additional Details** tab, you can enter some additional information, for example, the reason the asset is being retired.

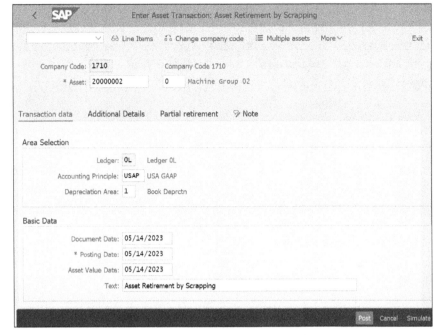

Figure 6.48 Enter Asset Transaction for Asset Retirement by Scrapping

In the **Partial retirement** tab (see Figure 6.49), you can fill in the **Amount Posted** if you're retiring an asset partially. If you want to retire the entire net book value, then leave it blank.

Figure 6.49 Partial Retirement Tab

Continue to fill in the **Percentage Rate** as part of the asset retirement in percentage and **Quantity**, which shows the portion of the costs that will be distributed to this account assignment item. In the **Reference** area, select the **Curr.-Year Acquisition** radio button if the asset is purchased during the current financial year, or select **Prior-Year Acquis.** if the asset was purchased in a year before the current one.

After that, click the **Simulate** button, which leads you to another screen showing the document header information and the created line items. Click the **Post** button, and you'll receive a message with the new document number created.

> **SAP Fiori App**
>
> The corresponding SAP Fiori app is called Post Retirement – By Scrapping (ABAVN). It's visually and functionally the same as the SAP GUI transaction.

Now that you know the steps involved in the fixed asset lifecycle, we can explain the financial closing activities for fixed asset accounting.

6.5   Fixed Assets Period-End Closing

Like the other topics we've covered in this book, in asset accounting, which is also a subledger to the general ledger, you need to follow some financial closing activities. In this section, we'll talk about the year-end closing process in asset accounting as a required step before closing the fiscal year in financial accounting. Serious issues can result if this step is omitted or not carried out in time, such as the following:

- Reconciliation issues coming from differences between asset accounting values and the general ledger, which results from the depreciation recalculation, data consistency, and difficulties in changing of master data because of issues such as incomplete assets.

- Period-end closing requires creating certain postings in the accounting system, implying that the posting period or the fiscal year has ended. You can transfer previous P&L general ledger account balances from one fiscal year or period to another.

Let's walk through the key steps to period-end closing for asset accounting, including setup, depreciation runs, closing periods, and reconciliation.

6.5.1   Change Fiscal Year

To perform the year-end closing, you need to change the fiscal year in fixed asset accounting to open a new fiscal year for the company. During this process, asset values are carried forward from the previous fiscal year into the new fiscal year. After the new fiscal year is open, it's possible to start posting to assets using value dates in the new fiscal year via Transaction AJAB or application menu path **Accounting • Financial Accounting • Fixed Assets • Periodic Processing • Year-End Closing • Execute (Cross-Company Code and Ledger)**.

In the **Year-End Closing Asset Accounting (Cross-Company Code and Ledger)** screen that appears (see Figure 6.50), enter the required values in the **Company Code**, **Ledger**, and **Fiscal Year to Be Closed** fields. You can close the fiscal year for one company code or more than one company code by entering a range. It's recommended to run the program in test mode first by marking the **Test Run** checkbox and then continue by clicking the **Execute** button. Transaction AJAB checks whether there are assets that aren't completely posted in the fiscal year (e.g., missing depreciation amounts). If there are such assets, they are detected while the program is running, and the transaction ends with an error log, as shown in Figure 6.51.

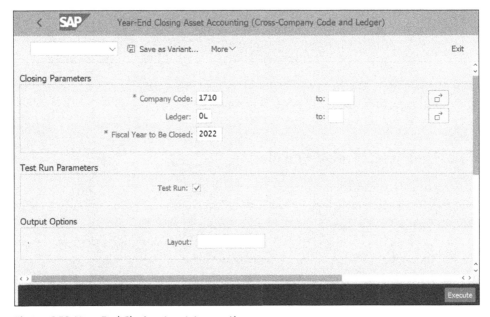

Figure 6.50 Year-End Closing Asset Accounting

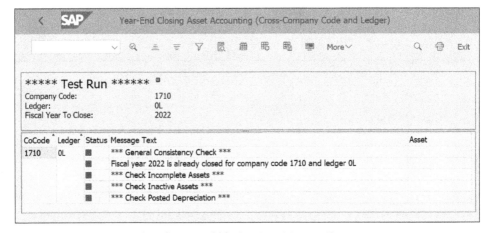

Figure 6.51 Test Run Results of Year-End Closing Asset Accounting

Now to run the program in the system, you need to execute it in the background. In the initial screen (refer to Figure 6.50), deselect the **Test Run** checkbox, and then select **More • Program • Execute in Background** (see Figure 6.52), or just press the ⌘F9⌘ key.

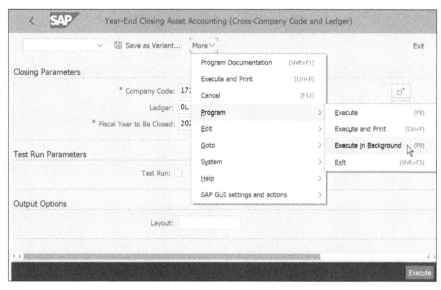

Figure 6.52 Run Program in Background

In the **Background Print Parameters** screen shown in Figure 6.53, enter the **Output Device** (printer or fax machine taken from master data), fill out the pages to be printed in **Page Area**, and select the **Print Time**. Then, click the checkmark icon and the **Save** button.

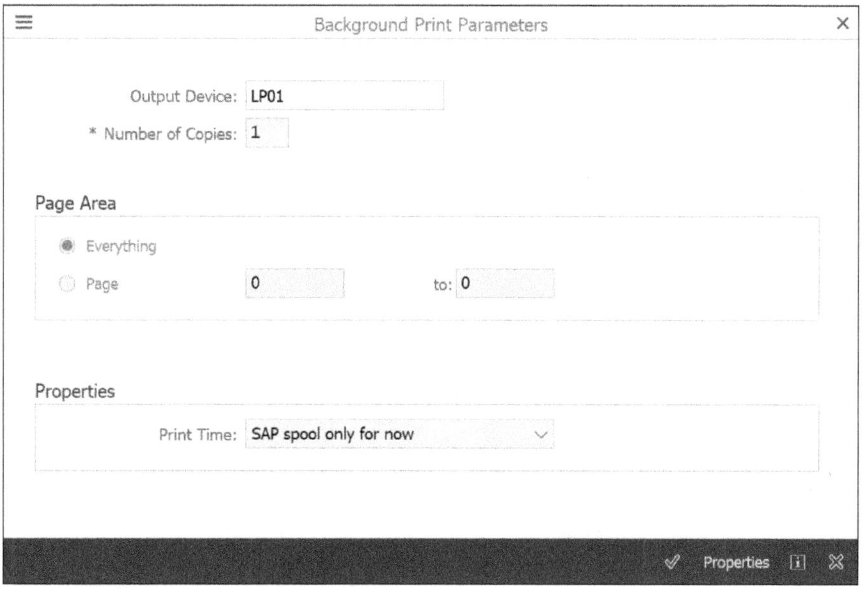

≡   Background Print Parameters   ✕

Output Device: **LP01**

* Number of Copies: **1**

Page Area

⦿ Everything

◯ Page   **0**   to: **0**

Properties

Print Time: **SAP spool only for now**   ▽

✓   Properties   🛈   ✕

Figure 6.53 Background Print Parameters

A new screen will appear where you have to schedule the job. Click **Immediate** if you want to run it now, as shown in Figure 6.54. If you want to run the report at a later time, for instance, overnight, you can schedule the time by clicking **Date/Time**.

Figure 6.54 Schedule Start Time for the Closing Job for Asset Accounting

After a successful run, you'll receive a message stating that the job with the specific assigned number has been successfully executed. You can view the job by choosing **More • System • Services • Jobs • Job Overview**.

In the **Simple Job Selection** screen, define the **Job Name** that was created after executing in the background, **User Name**, **Job Status**, and **Job Start Condition** to put the date and time range, and then click the **Execute** button, as shown in Figure 6.55.

After clicking **Execute**, you see all the job results produced by **STUDENT021**. You can see also the job results for the year-end asset closing activities, as shown in Figure 6.56.

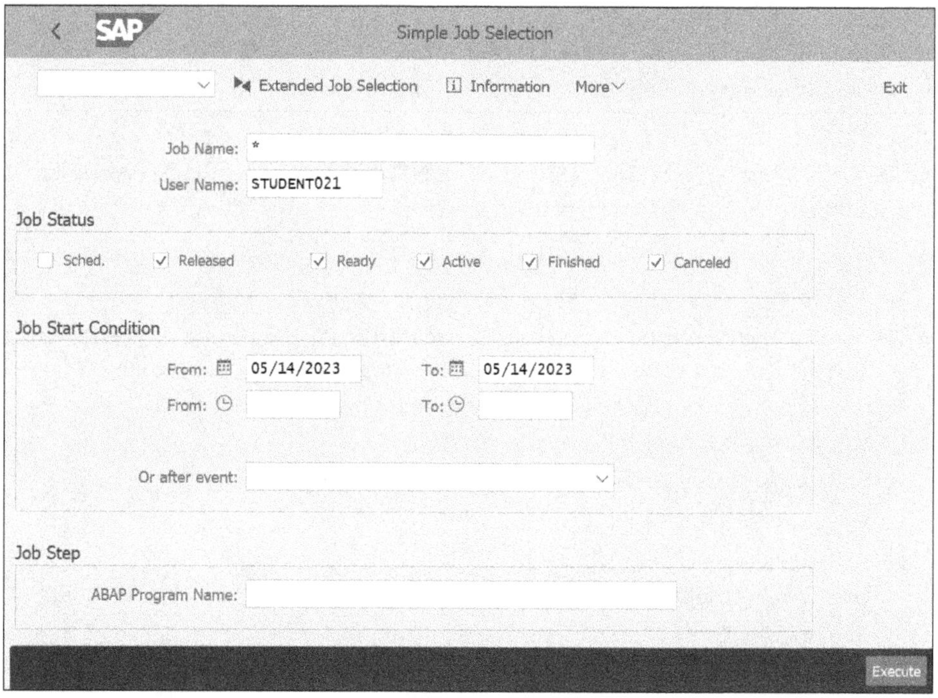

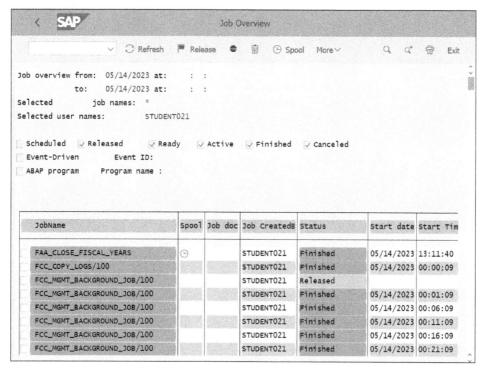

Figure 6.55 Simple Job Selection Screen

Figure 6.56 Job Results for the Year-End Closing Activities for Asset Accounting

Alternatively, you can also use Transaction AFAB in the dialog mode or follow application menu path **Accounting • Financial Accounting • Fixed Assets • Periodic Processing • Depreciation Run • Execute**. This transaction is nearly the same as Transaction AJAB.

To run in it in the live system, as mentioned earlier, it should be executed as a background job (refer to Figure 6.52). Enter the values in the respective fields, save as a variant, and then schedule the job to run automatically for the fiscal year to be closed.

SAP Fiori App

The corresponding SAP Fiori app is called Schedule Asset Accounting Jobs (F1914). Here you can define the selection criteria, such as **Job Status** (**Failed, Canceled, Finalized, In Process, Finished, Ready,** or **Scheduled**) and period time in the **Date From-To**. Click the **Go** button to get the results, as shown in Figure 6.57.

To create a new job schedule, click on **Create** in the initial screen. Define the specific criteria for the new job scheduling:

- **Template Selection**
  Select a **Job Template** (in this example, **Depreciation Posting Run**), and enter the **Job Name** (here, the same name as the template), as shown in Figure 6.58.

- **Scheduling Options**
  Check the **Start Immediately** checkbox to fill the date in the **Start** field.

- **Parameters**
  Define the **Accounting Principle** from the preconfigured list, **Depreciation Area** value, **Fiscal Year, Company Code**, and so on, as shown in Figure 6.59. To run in test mode, check the **Test Run** checkbox. Under the **Options** area, select one of the available options for how the logs will appear: **No Output Log, Totals Log,** or **Detailed Log**.

After you've defined the needed criteria, ensure that everything is fine using the **Check** button, and then continue with the **Schedule** button.

The scheduled job will be present in the job application list with the current status— **Finished**—as shown in Figure 6.60.

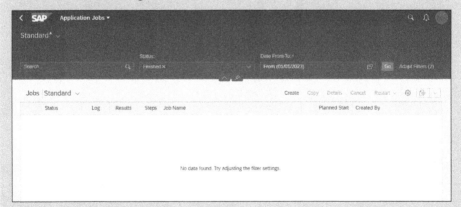

Figure 6.57 Application Jobs Screen

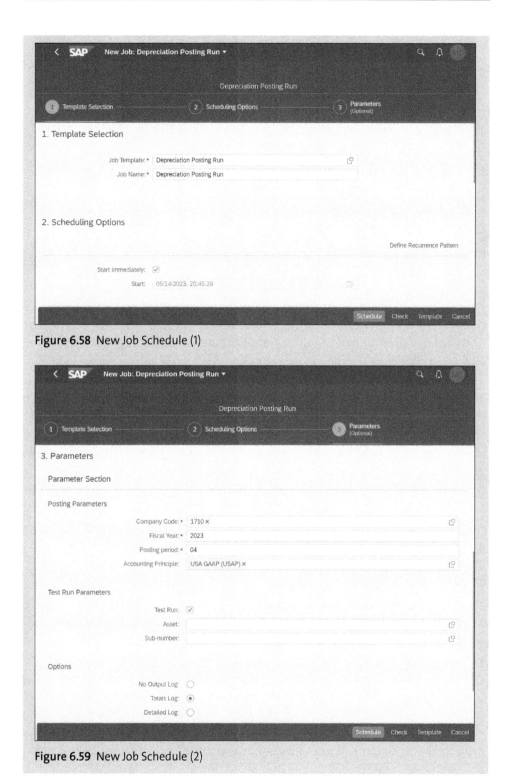

Figure 6.58 New Job Schedule (1)

Figure 6.59 New Job Schedule (2)

Figure 6.60 Scheduled Application Job

In the next section, we'll explain the asset depreciation run in the system.

6.5.2   Depreciation Run

Determining asset depreciation and posting asset depreciation expenses in the system may occur at different points in time. Practically, it's not possible to perform the year-end closing without first doing a successful depreciation posting run for the last period of the fiscal year. You can calculate the depreciation using Transaction AFAR, which determines the depreciation with each master record change on the asset and reflects these updates in the respective database accordingly. In addition, during the fiscal year change for the upcoming fiscal year, the determination of accrued depreciation is automatically processed and completed. When you start to execute the depreciation posting run, you're in the stage to begin with the preparation for the year-end closing. To post asset depreciation, you need to run Transaction AFAB, where the depreciation run takes up the planned asset values and posts them in financial accounting. The journal entry reflects the updated values in financial accounting at the asset level. The entry itself is recognized with the asset number. You must ensure that all assets are adjusted by the end of the year so that the depreciation posting run can be completely and successfully performed.

You can execute Transaction AFAB or use application menu path **Accounting • Financial Accounting • Fixed Assets • Period Processing • Depreciation Run • Execute**. You'll arrive at the **Depreciation Posting Run** screen, as shown in Figure 6.61. Enter the required data, such as **Company Code**, **Fiscal Year**, and **Posting period** as a self-contained part of the fiscal year, as well as **Accounting Principle** if needed, **Server Group** for parallel processing that determines which application server will be used, **Number of Parallel Processes**, and so on. In addition, define the **Output Options** by selecting one of the listed options based on how you'd like your results to appear. It's recommended to carry out the depreciation posting run in test mode beforehand by selecting the **Test Run** checkbox to detect possible errors.

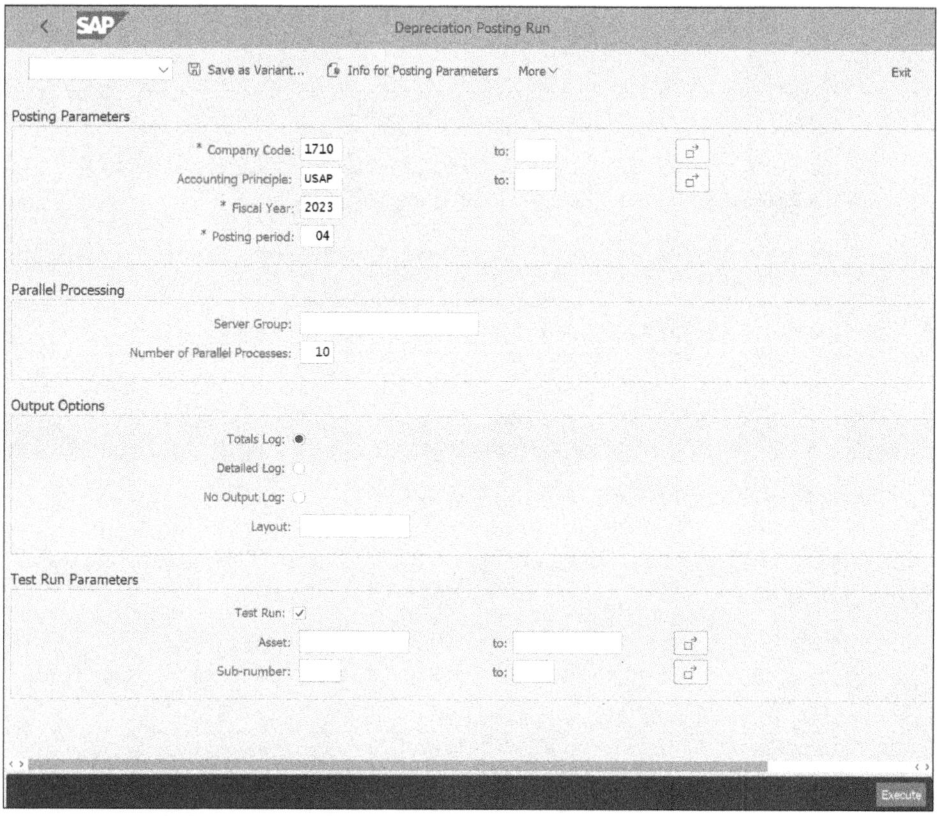

Figure 6.61 Depreciation Posting Run

Click the **Execute** button to continue, which will show another screen with the test run results (see Figure 6.62). Here, you can see the details of **Processed Fixed Assets, Fixed Assets Without Errors, Fixed Assets with Errors in at Least One Area**, and so on.

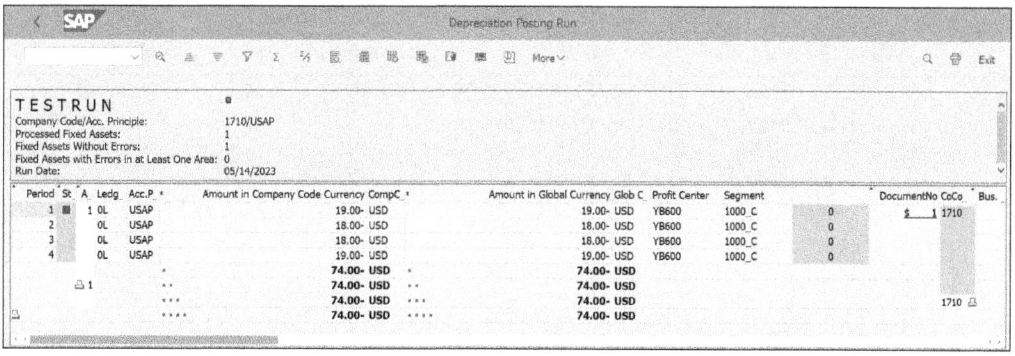

Figure 6.62 Depreciation Posting Run: Test Results

As you can see from the test run results, one fixed asset was processed without errors for **Company Code 1710**. If you click on the message log icon 📖, the **Document lines:**

Display messages screen appears to show the logs for the processed fixed assets in the selected company (see Figure 6.63).

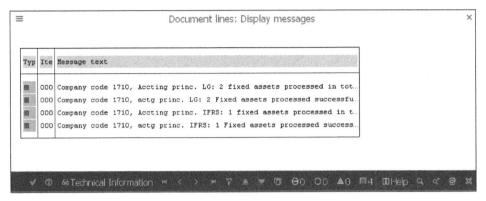

Figure 6.63 Display Messages Log

SAP Fiori App

The corresponding SAP Fiori app is called Schedule Asset Accounting Jobs (F1914). With this app, you can do all the fixed asset jobs you need: **Year-End Closing Asset Accounting**, **Depreciation Posting Run**, and **Recalculate Depreciation**. We've shown the use case for **Depreciation Posting Run** in the prior section.

Next, we'll show you how to disallow the posting to the previous period when you perform the year-end closing.

6.5.3   Closing Periods

In the time when you perform the month-end or year-end closing process, you need to apply some settings that stop users from posting to the previous period. You can define posting periods in the fiscal year variants and can open or close these posting periods for posting. Although you can open some periods during that same time, usually only the current posting period is open for posting.

To open and close periods in financial accounting in SAP S/4HANA, you can use Transaction FAGL_EHP4_T001B_COFI or follow application menu path **Accounting • Financial Accounting • General Ledger • Environment • Current Settings • Open and Close Posting Periods**.

Define the posting period variant in the **Determine Work Area** entry screen that pops up, and click the **Continue** button to arrive at the **Change View "Posting Periods": Specify Time Interval: Overview** screen. Click the **New Entries** button to arrive at the screen shown in Figure 6.64. Fill in the required fields as explained in Table 6.1.

Figure 6.64 New Entry Posting Period

#	Description
A	Enter the account type from several possible values (**+**: valid for all account types, **A**: assets, **D**: customer, **K**: vendors, **M**: materials, **S**: general ledger accounts, **V**: contract accounts).
From Acct	Enter the account number range for which you want to change the periods.
To Account	Define a range of account numbers starting with the from account number and ending with the to account number.
From Per.1	Enter a posting period from which you want to open the posting period.
Year	Enter the fiscal year for which you want to open the posting period.
To Period	Define a range of posting periods for which you want to enter posting periods.
Year	Define a range of years for which you want to open posting periods.

Table 6.1 Important Fields for Controlling Posting Periods

After you've saved all the entered data by clicking the **Save** button, the results will be shown as in Figure 6.65.

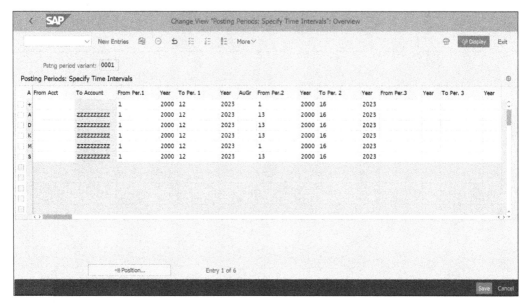

Figure 6.65 Controlling Posting Periods Results

In the **A** (account type) column, click the list box function next to the cell to see the relevant subledger account type (e.g., asset, customer, vendors, materials, etc.) (see Figure 6.66). For fixed assets accounting, **A** for **Assets** is the relevant **Account Type** parameter. Periods can easily be closed and opened by editing the period fields (refer to Table 6.1).

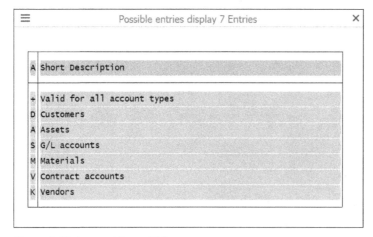

Figure 6.66 Account Types List

SAP Fiori App

The corresponding SAP Fiori app for accounts determination is called Open and Close Posting Periods (FAGL_EHP4_T001B_COFI). It's visually and functionally the same as the SAP GUI transaction.

6.5.4   Fixed Assets Reconciliations

As in the previous chapters where we explained the account reconciliation process, the fixed asset ledger also must be reconciled with the general ledger. Fixed assets reconciliation means that the accumulated ending balance should reconcile with the cost and accumulated depreciation amount on the general ledger balance for each asset class. Preparation of the financial statement is a very important process for the company. Therefore, the accuracy of asset figures is equally as important. At the beginning of the new fiscal year, the transaction data in asset accounting is compared with the corresponding entries in the general ledger accounts.

Performing consistent fixed assets reconciliation is one of the most important ways to control and ensure the accuracy and presence of fixed assets in the balance sheet. The reconciliation of fixed assets shows the summary of net book value, credits and debits to their accounts, and depreciation amounts.

In SAP S/4HANA, you can use several reports through which you can reconcile the fixed asset balances with the general ledger balances. For example, a reconciliation report will help you recognize discrepancies between asset accounting line items and the balances of the various asset reconciliation accounts for an explicit account. This report can be used if you stipulate differences between the general ledger balance and the amounts exposed in the asset history sheet. Inconsistencies can occur for many reasons, for example, when someone unintentionally changes the reconciliation account indicator in the general ledger master record. Usually, these changes happen when setting up SAP S/4HANA in the initial stages.

To avoid or to correct identified inconsistencies, dedicated analyses should be performed. We'll show you the classic way to perform the asset reconciliation process in this section.

You can reconcile the fixed asset sheet balances with the respective balances in the general ledger accounts records, such as the financial statement report. For that, you need to execute report S_ALR_87011990, which is relevant for the international asset balance sheet, or follow application menu path **Accounting • Financial Accounting • Fixed Assets • Information System • Reports on Asset Accounting • Notes to Financial Statements • International • Asset History Sheet**.

Next, in the **Asset History Sheet** screen, enter the required values for the **Company code**, **Report date**, **Depreciation area**, and **Sort Variant**, and then select one of the listed indicators: **List assets** (where every asset main number will be listed, including asset subnumbers if any), **or main numbers only** (to show main asset numbers only with cumulative values for all corresponding subnumbers), or **or group totals only** (where a cumulative list will be produced showing no other information on the individual assets). Moreover, in the **Display options** area, mark the **Use ALV grid** checkbox to get a more structured layout (see Figure 6.67).

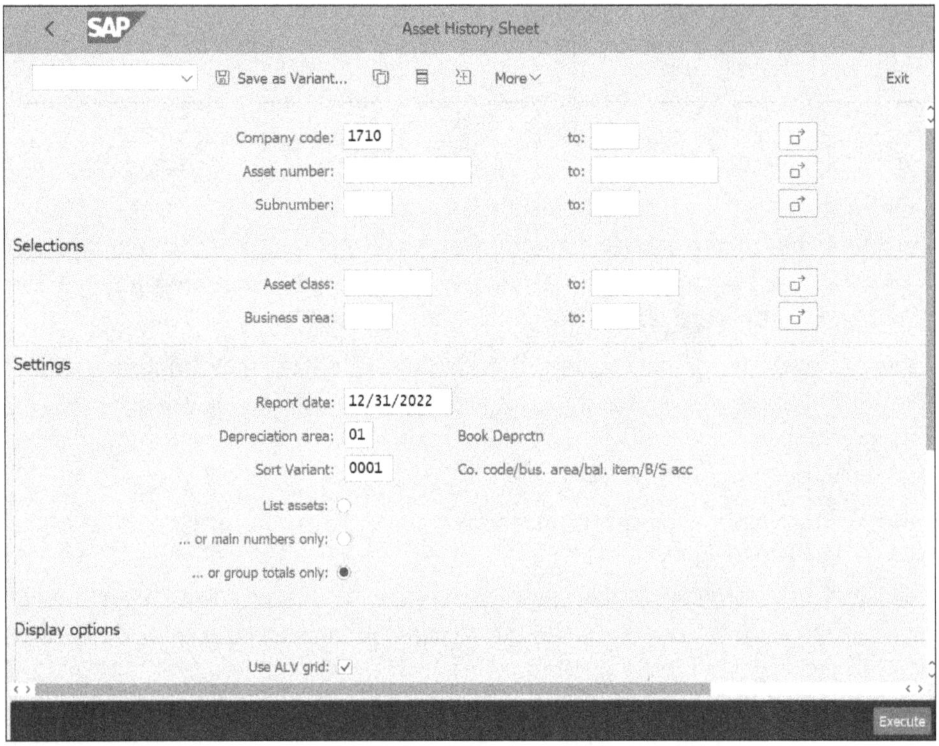

Figure 6.67 Asset History Sheet Entry Screen

Because you need to see all the assets, no filters are used in the **Asset number** field. If you leave any field empty, it means that you get all the information regarding that specific field. Click the **Execute** button, and the results will be shown as in Figure 6.68. You can find all the needed information for the assets here, such as the acquisition value, depreciation amount, retirement amount, current acquisition production cost, accumulative depreciation, and so on.

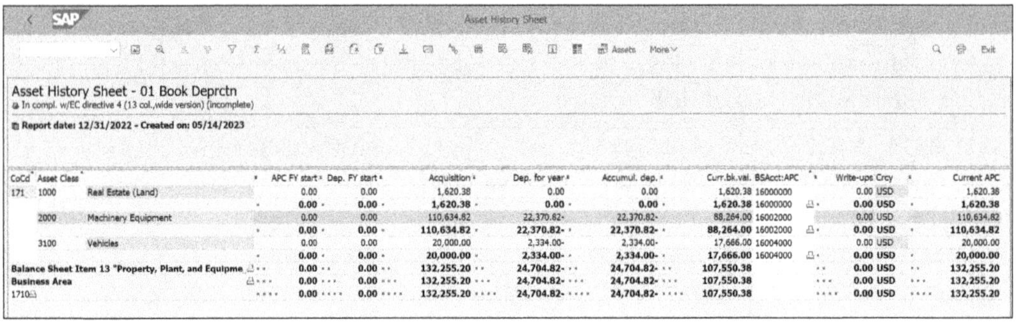

Figure 6.68 Asset History Sheet Report

The report shows year-to-date balances per asset class that can also be drilled down to the individual asset level. For example, double-click on the record of asset class **2000 -**

Machinery Equipment with the acquisition value **110,634.82** USD to arrive at the screen with a more detailed overview for the selected asset and different asset subcategories, as shown in Figure 6.69.

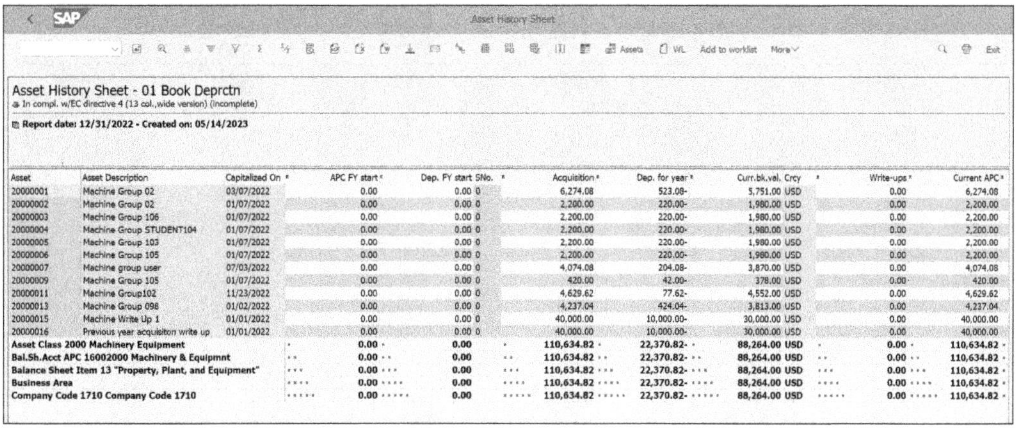

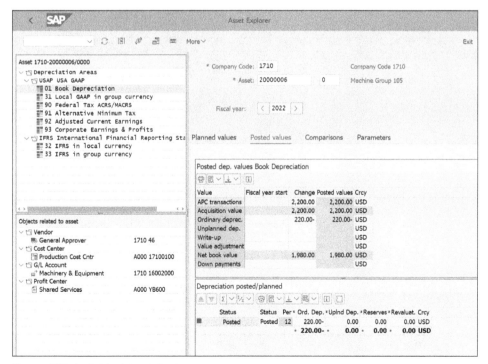

Figure 6.69 Machinery Equipment Asset Overview

Here, you can see the listed assets with their descriptions and their respective depreciation values, acquisition values, retirement values, and so on. If you double-click on one of the listed assets (e.g., **20000006**), it leads you to the asset explorer tool (refer to Section 6.3), as shown in Figure 6.70.

Figure 6.70 Individual Asset Explorer

With the report from Figure 6.68 opened, you can reconcile it with the respective general ledger accounts. A good report to see the general ledger accounts in a structured way is Transaction S_ALR_87012284, found under application menu path **Accounting • Financial Accounting • General Ledger • Information System • General Ledger Reports • Financial Statement/Cash Flow • General • Actual/Actual Comparisons**.

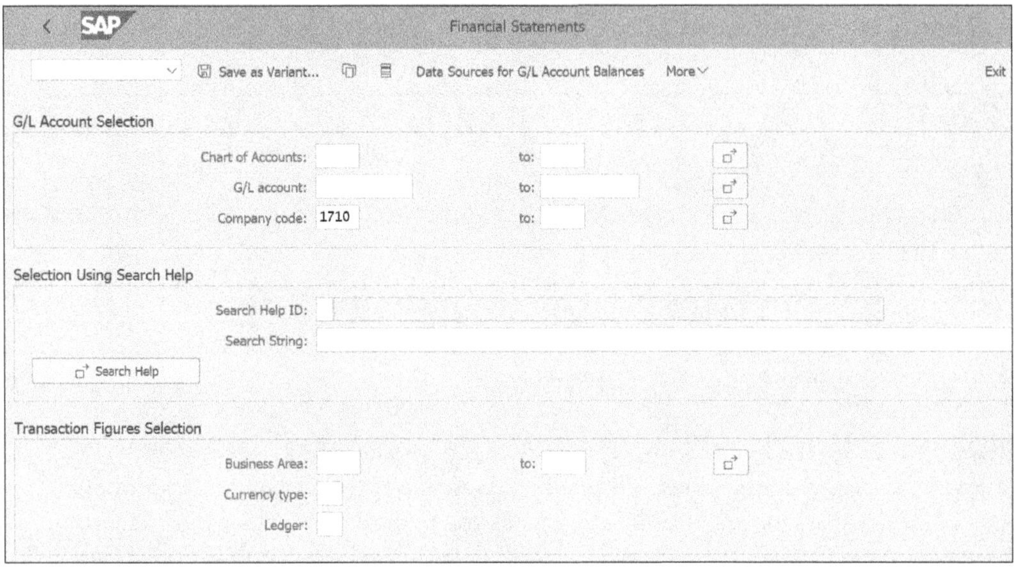

Figure 6.71 Financial Statement Entry Screen (1)

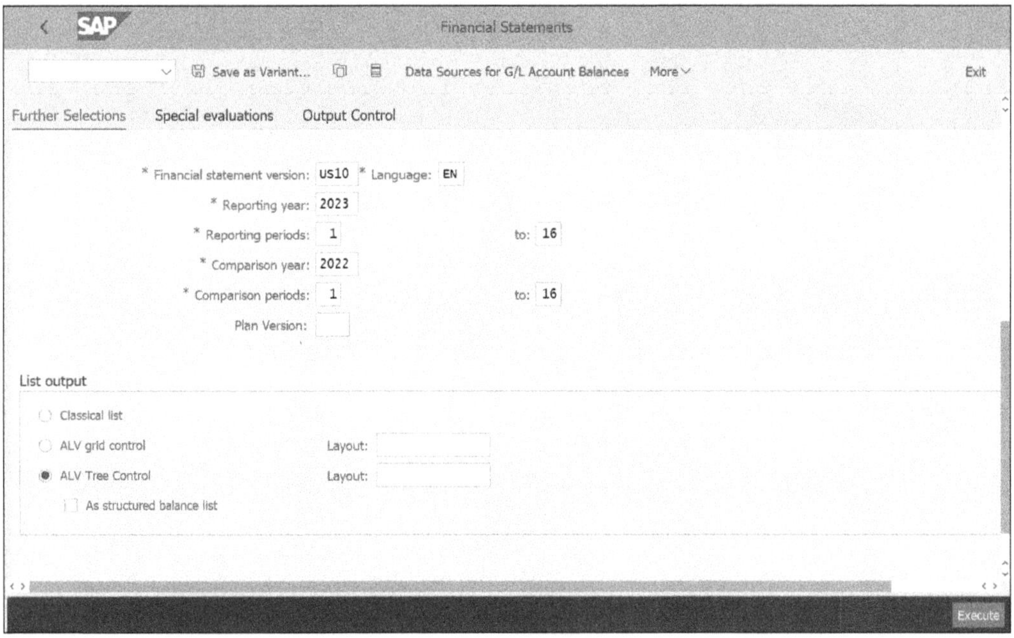

Figure 6.72 Financial Statement Entry Screen (2)

When you start this report, the **Financial Statements** screen appears, as shown in Figure 6.71 and Figure 6.72. Enter the required values, such as the **Company code** for which you're executing the financial statement, **Financial statement version** that specifies the key to identify the balance sheet and P&L statement version, **Reporting year** for which the company is to establish its inventory and balance sheet, **Reporting periods**, and **Comparison year**. To get a more structured overview, select the **ALV Tree Control** option in the **List output** area. The other fields aren't mandatory but can be adjusted per your business's requirements.

Click the **Execute** button, and in the results screen, as shown in Figure 6.73, you'll see the listed items with their respective balances. Now focus on the fixed asset section, where you're looking for **Property, Plant, and Equipment**.

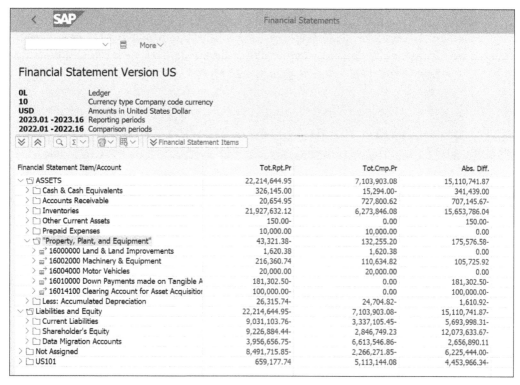

Figure 6.73 Financial Statement Result

Now, compare the general ledger account balances of the financial statement relating to the fixed assets with the current acquisition or production cost in the fixed asset history sheet. You see that the values in the fixed asset history sheet match with the financial statement: **Asset Class Real Estate (Land) 1000** matches with the balance of account **16000000** with **1,620.38** USD; **Asset Class 2000 Machinery Equipment** matches with the balance of account **16002000** with **110,634.82** USD; and **Asset Class 3100 Vehicles** matches with the balance of account **16004000** with **20,000** USD (refer to Figure 6.68).

Alternatively, instead of the financial statement report, you can also execute Transaction S_PL0_86000030 or follow application menu path **Accounting • Financial Accounting • General Ledger • Information System • General Ledger Reports • Account Balances • General • G/L Account Balances • G/L Account Balances (Detailed)**. However, we recommend using the asset history and financial statement reports.

SAP Fiori Apps

Following are the corresponding SAP Fiori apps:

- Asset History Sheet (F1615A)
- Balance Sheet/Income Statement (F0708)

For more details about the Asset History Sheet app, refer to Section 6.6.1.

Using the Balance Sheet/Income Statement app, you can define the selection criteria, such as the **Company Code**, **Ledger** as unique identification of a special ledger, **Statement Version** as a key that identifies the balance sheet and P&L statement version, **Statement Type** from the preconfigured options, **End Period**, **Comparison End Period**, and **Currency**. Click the **Go** button to show the result as in Figure 6.74.

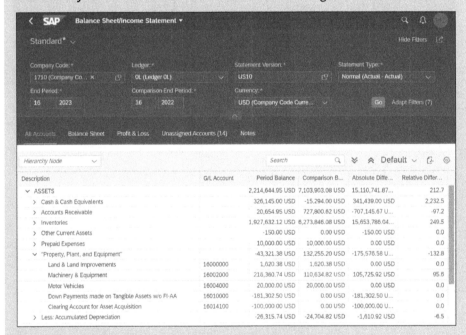

Figure 6.74 Balance Sheet/Income Statement App in SAP Fiori

Now that you know the reconciliation process of asset accounting, let's jump into the final section, where you'll learn how to report the activity of all fixed assets in your company.

6.6 Fixed Assets Reporting

In this section, as in the other chapters in this book, we'll also discuss the reporting period of fixed assets. Fixed assets reporting and analyzing features—as an integral part of all asset management processes—enable the company to verify and track assets' historical cost, depreciation values, capitalization amount, relevant transactions performed, and so on. The available SAP S/4HANA reports are used to generate accurate financial records for asset accounting, maintenance, and management objectives. Fixed asset transactions usually refer to the acquisition and disposal of assets and the distribution of related costs to reporting periods through depreciation expenses. Proper recording of fixed asset entries accelerates the production of timely and accurate reports, ensuring accurate financial reporting. Deficient fixed asset records can lead to incorrect financial reporting and consequently damage to management's credibility with shareholders, suppliers, customers, and so on.

Here, we'll explain some reports and transactions that are recommended to use for fixed assets reporting.

6.6.1 Fixed Assets History Sheet

The asset history sheet report, which we introduced in Section 6.5.4 for reconciliations, provides year-to-date balances per asset class and can be drilled down to the individual asset level. This report is one of the most powerful and comprehensive reports in SAP S/4HANA for fixed assets because its logic and layout can be configured according to a company's requirements. The report gives detailed information about the changes performed in the asset portfolio during the fiscal year and allows you to specify any particular transaction type to the relevant field in the report.

You can run this report using Transaction S_ALR_87011990 or following application menu path **Accounting • Financial Accounting • Fixed Assets • Information System • Reports on Asset Accounting • Notes to Financial Statements • International • Asset History Sheet**.

You can refer to Section 6.5.4 to see how the asset history sheet report works with asset balances.

SAP Fiori App

The corresponding SAP Fiori app is called Asset History Sheet (F1615A), as shown in Figure 6.75.

Here you can specify the searching criteria using the filters shown Figure 6.75. The preconfigured key figure groups contain key figure codes grouped in two categories: for posted values without hierarchy (AHS) and with hierarchy (AHS_HRY). The second category is for planned values without hierarchy (AHS_PLAN) and with hierarchy (AHS_HRY_PL). You can see these four key figures codes if you drill down on the right of this field. You can also specify the **Company Code**, **Ledger** as a unique identification of a special ledger, **Depreciation Area**, **Fiscal Year**, **To Period**, and **Currency Type**.

Execute this app by clicking **Go**, and you can show the asset history sheet that represents value changes to the fixed asset balances in a fiscal year for a specific depreciation area. In our example, shown in Figure 6.75, **Depreciation Area 01** (book depreciation) has been selected from the listed options. You can document and explain the balances on fixed assets for every accounting principle, any local regulation, and for management purposes.

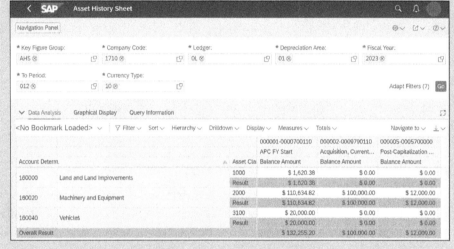

Figure 6.75 Asset History Sheet

6.6.2   Acquisitions List

Another important report that provides information for the asset acquisition is the asset acquisition report, which shows all purchasing documents in a fiscal year for the company's assets.

You can use Transaction S_ALR_87012050 or follow application menu path **Accounting • Financial Accounting • Fixed Assets • Information System • Reports on Asset Accounting • Day-to-Day Activities • International • Asset Acquisition**. You'll arrive at the **Asset Acquisitions** screen, as shown in Figure 6.76.

Here, define the selection criteria, such as **Asset class**, **Business area**, **Cost center**, and so on, if you need to generate the list for specific criteria. You can also specify some selections in the **Settings** area, such as **Report date** on which the evaluation should take place, **Sort Variant** to determine the sort levels and the summary for the displayed data records, and other selections optionally.

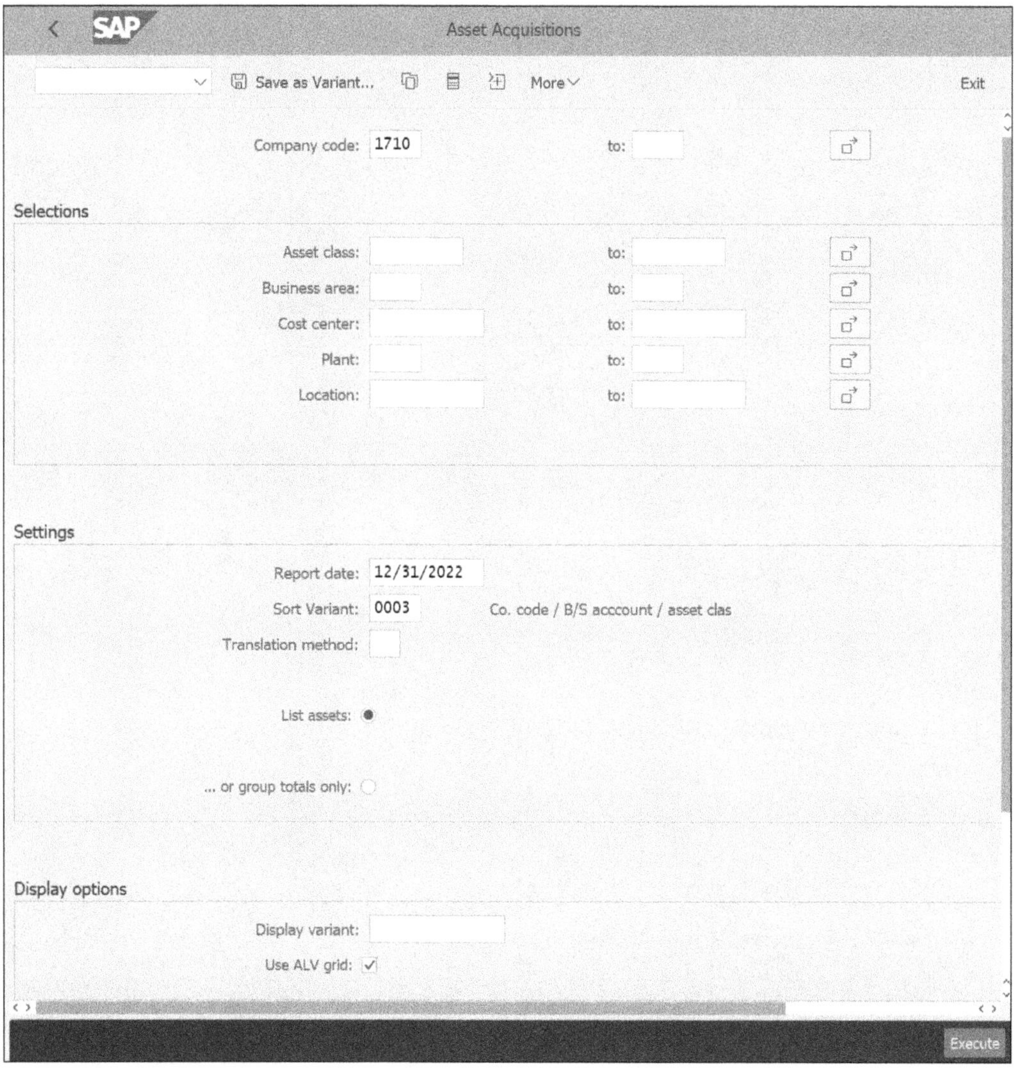

Figure 6.76 Asset Acquisition Entry Fields

There are two possible ways to present assets (see options in **Settings** area):

- **List assets**
  Show all assets.
- **or group totals only**
  Show assets grouped by asset classes.

Now click the **Execute** button, and the list of assets is displayed in another screen, as shown in Figure 6.77 and Figure 6.78.

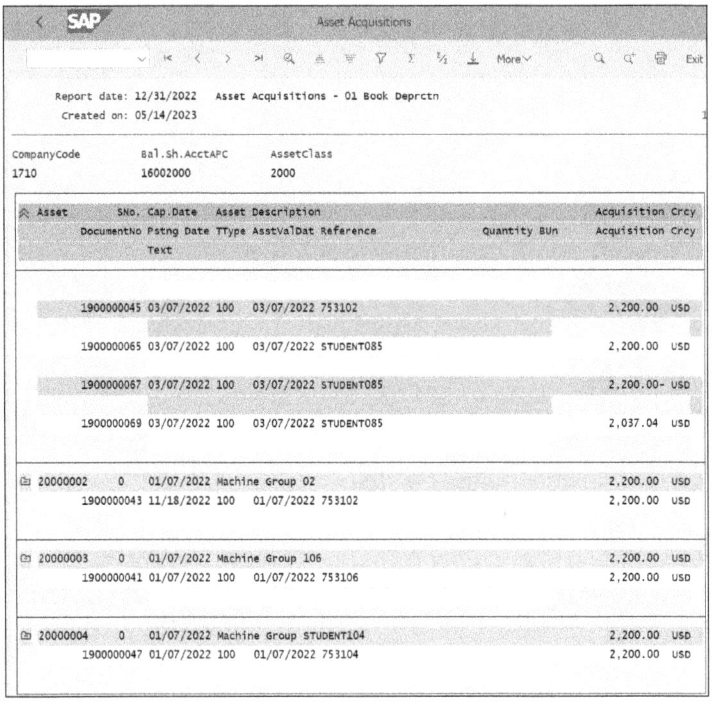

Figure 6.77 Asset Acquisition List (1)

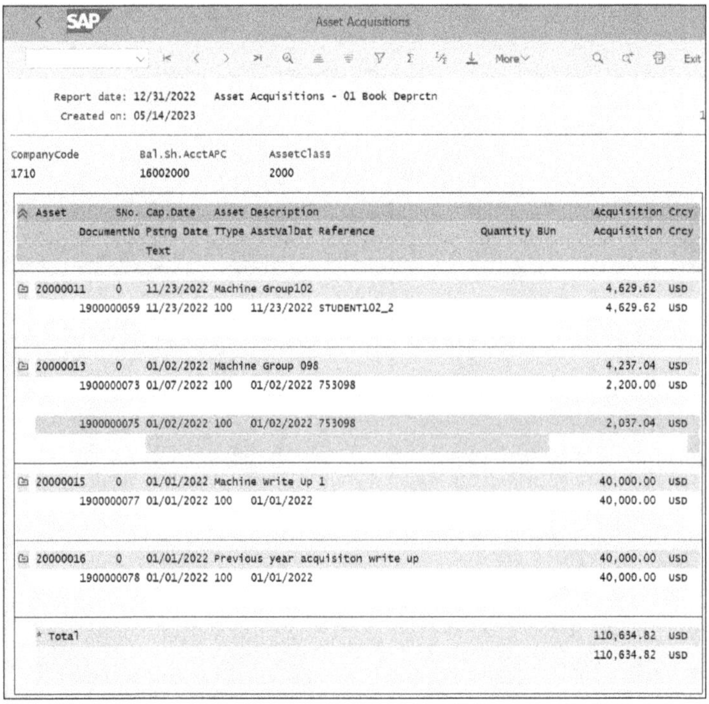

Figure 6.78 Asset Acquisition List (2)

In this report, you can easily distinguish all the assets that are included in each asset class. Scroll down the window to the bottom to see the other asset classes with their assigned assets.

If you select the **or group totals only** option, the list of assets is grouped per asset class, as shown in Figure 6.79. You can see the list of assets by double-clicking on the asset class record.

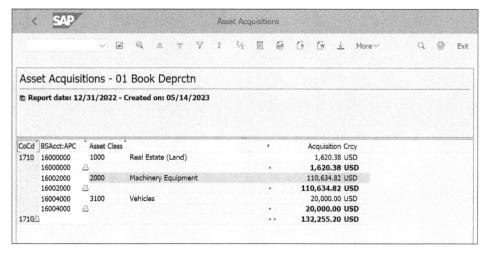

Figure 6.79 Asset Acquisitions Grouped per Asset Class

> **SAP Fiori App**
>
> The corresponding SAP Fiori app is called Asset Acquisition (S_ALR_87012050). It's visually and functionally the same as the SAP GUI transaction.

6.6.3   Depreciation Lists

The relevant report used to show the depreciation list, especially when you have to submit income taxes, is called the asset depreciation list report (S_P00_07000077). This report is designed for each country, and, in our example, we're referring to the report included in the folder belonging to Thailand.

In this case, the report can be accessed by using Transaction S_P00_07000077 or by following application menu path **Accounting • Financial Accounting • Fixed Assets • Information System • Reports on Asset Accounting • Preparation for Closing • Country Specifics • Thailand • Asset Depreciation List (TH)**.

The next step is to define some required mandatory data in the **Asset depreciation list (TH)** screen, as shown in Figure 6.80.

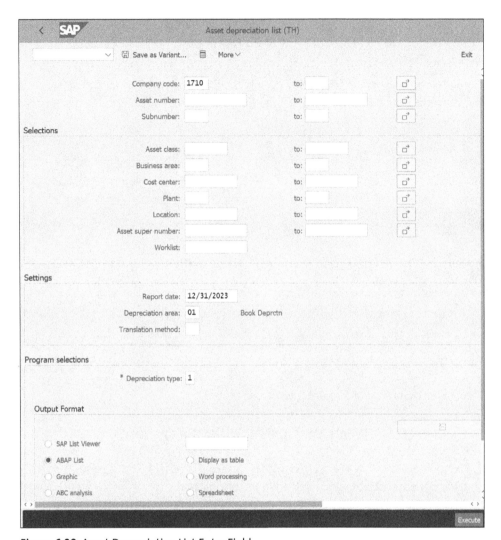

Figure 6.80 Asset Depreciation List Entry Field

This includes **Company code**, **Depreciation type** from the preconfigured list, **Report date** on which the evaluation should take place, **Depreciation area** from the preconfigured list, and so on.

In this example, the **ABAP List** format has been selected as an **Output Format** option. You can choose any of the listed formats. Click the **Execute** button, and the depreciation list will be displayed as shown in Figure 6.81 and Figure 6.82.

In this list, you can see all assets grouped by asset class, presenting the sum of the balance sheet account for current acquisition value, current booking value, capitalization date of assets, and so on.

<SAP> <   v   ▣ ⟲ ⟳ Σ ⊞ ⊞ ⊞ ALV ⅲ ↓ ♂ ⊞ ⊞ ⊞ ABC   Selections   More ∨   Q ∝ ⊕ Exit

Asset depreciation list (TH)

Report date: 12/31/2023   Asset depreciation list   Date create : 05/14/2023   Page : 1

Company code 1710

Business area

Asset	SNo.	Asset description	Cap.date	Current acq.val.		BV at FY begin		Acquisition this		Perce	Dep. year		Curr.bk.val.	

AM: Balance sheet pos. (debit)

Bal. sheet account: Acquisitio 16000000

Asset class 1000

| 10000001 | 0 | asset_re_user60 | 01/01/2022 | 1,620.38 | USD | 1,620.38 | USD | 0.00 | USD | 0.00 | 0.00 | USD | 1,620.38 | USD |

Sum of Asset class 1000   1,620.38 USD   1,620.38 USD   0.00 USD   1,620.38 USD

Sum of Bal. sheet account: Acquisition and production costs 16000000

Bal. sheet account: Acquisitio 16002000   1,620.38 USD   1,620.38 USD   0.00 USD   1,620.38 USD

Asset class 2000

20000001	0	Machine Group 02	03/07/2022	0.00	USD	5,751.00	USD	0.00	USD	10.00	523.08	USD	0.00	USD
20000002	0	Machine Group 02	01/07/2022	2,200.00	USD	1,980.00	USD	0.00	USD	10.00	200.00	USD	2,180.00	USD
20000003	0	Machine Group 106	01/07/2022	2,200.00	USD	1,980.00	USD	0.00	USD	10.00	0.00	USD	1,980.00	USD
20000004	0	Machine Group STUDENT104	01/07/2022	2,200.00	USD	1,980.00	USD	0.00	USD	10.00	0.00	USD	1,980.00	USD
20000005	0	Machine Group 103	01/07/2022	2,200.00	USD	1,980.00	USD	0.00	USD	10.00	0.00	USD	1,980.00	USD
20000006	0	Machine Group 105	01/07/2022	2,200.00	USD	1,980.00	USD	0.00	USD	10.00	0.00	USD	1,980.00	USD
20000007	0	Machine group user	07/03/2022	4,074.08	USD	3,870.00	USD	0.00	USD	10.00	0.00	USD	3,870.00	USD
20000009	0	Machine Group 105	01/07/2022	420.00	USD	378.00	USD	0.00	USD	10.00	0.00	USD	378.00	USD

Export   Cancel

Figure 6.81 Asset Depreciation List (1)

<SAP> <   v   ▣ ⟲ ⟳ Σ ⊞ ⊞ ⊞ ALV ⅲ ↓ ♂ ⊞ ⊞ ⊞ ABC   Selections   More ∨   Q ∝ ⊕ Exit

Asset depreciation list (TH)

Report date: 12/31/2023   Asset depreciation list   Date create : 05/14/2023   Page : 1

Asset	SNo.	Asset description	Cap.date	Current acq.val.		BV at FY begin		Acquisition this		Perce	Dep. year		Curr.bk.val.	
20000013	0	Machine Group 098	01/02/2022	4,237.04	USD	3,813.00	USD	0.00	USD	10.00	0.00	USD	3,813.00	USD
20000015	0	Machine write up 1	01/02/2022	48,000.00	USD	30,000.00	USD	8,000.00	USD	12.50	4,000.00	USD	34,000.00	USD
20000016	0	Previous year acquisition	01/01/2022	44,000.00	USD	30,000.00	USD	4,000.00	USD	12.50	1,666.00	USD	35,666.00	USD
20000019	0	TestOJ51	07/01/2022	100,000.00	USD	0.00	USD	100,000.00	USD	10.00	0.00	USD	100,000.00	USD

Sum of Asset class 2000   216,360.74 USD   88,264.00 USD   112,000.00 USD   1,610.92- USD   192,379.00 USD

Sum of Bal. sheet account: Acquisition and production costs 16002000

Bal. sheet account: Acquisitio 16004000   216,360.74 USD   88,264.00 USD   112,000.00 USD   1,610.92- USD   192,379.00 USD

Asset class 3100

| 50000002 | 0 | Vehicle Group 106 | 01/07/2022 | 10,000.00 | USD | 8,000.00 | USD | 0.00 | USD | 20.00 | 0.00 | USD | 8,000.00 | USD |
| 50000003 | 0 | Vehicles Group STUDENT104 | 11/15/2022 | 10,000.00 | USD | 9,666.00 | USD | 0.00 | USD | 20.00 | 0.00 | USD | 9,666.00 | USD |

Sum of Asset Class 3100   20,000.00 USD   17,666.00 USD   0.00 USD   17,666.00 USD

Sum of Bal. sheet account: Acquisition and production costs 16004000   20,000.00 USD   17,666.00 USD   0.00 USD   17,666.00 USD

Sum of AM: Balance sheet pos. (debit)   237,981.12 USD   107,550.38 USD   112,000.00 USD   1,610.92- USD   211,665.38 USD

Sum of Business area   237,981.12 USD   107,550.38 USD   112,000.00 USD   1,610.92- USD   211,665.38 USD

Sum of Company code 1710   237,981.12 USD   107,550.38 USD   112,000.00 USD   1,610.92- USD   211,665.38 USD

Overall total   237,981.12 USD   107,550.38 USD   112,000.00 USD   1,610.92- USD   211,665.38 USD

Export   Cancel

Figure 6.82 Asset Depreciation List (2)

SAP Fiori Apps

The corresponding SAP Fiori app is called Depreciation List (F1616). The result in this app screen helps you to analyze the interest and depreciation of fixed assets. Here, you can show depreciation values as a total or by depreciation type, such as ordinary depreciation, special depreciation, unplanned depreciation, write-ups, and transferred reserves. It's visually more modern but functionally the same as the SAP GUI transaction.

In Figure 6.83, you can see what the app looks like in SAP Fiori. Here you can define the searching filters of mandatory fields such as **Company Code**, **To Period**, **Depreciation Variant** (ordinary, special, unplanned, write-ups, or transferred reserves), **Ledger**, **Display Currency**, and **Depreciation Area** (select one of the listed options: **Book Depreciation**, **IFRS in local currency**, **Federal tax**, etc.).

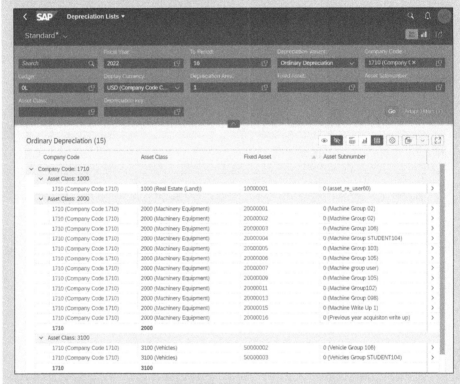

Figure 6.83 Depreciation List App in SAP Fiori

Now, we'll move on to the last fixed asset report in SAP S/4HANA for the disposal list.

6.6.4   Disposals

Similar to the depreciation list, when you have to submit income taxes, you must submit a list of asset disposals that contains revenue from disposals, net book value at the retirement time, gain or loss amount on disposal, and cost of retirement. This report is designed for each country, and, in this example, we're referring again to the report included in the folder belonging to Thailand.

In this case, the report can be accessed by using Transaction S_P00_07000078 or by following application menu path **Accounting • Financial Accounting • Fixed Assets • Information System • Reports on Asset Accounting • Preparation for Closing • Country Specifics • Thailand • Asset Disposal List (TH)**.

The next step is to define the required mandatory data in the **Asset disposal list (TH)** screen, as shown in Figure 6.84, which includes **Company code**, **Report date** on which the evaluation should take place, **Depreciation area** from the preconfigured list, **Transaction Type** from the listed transactions, **Gain/Loss on Asset Retirement**, and so on.

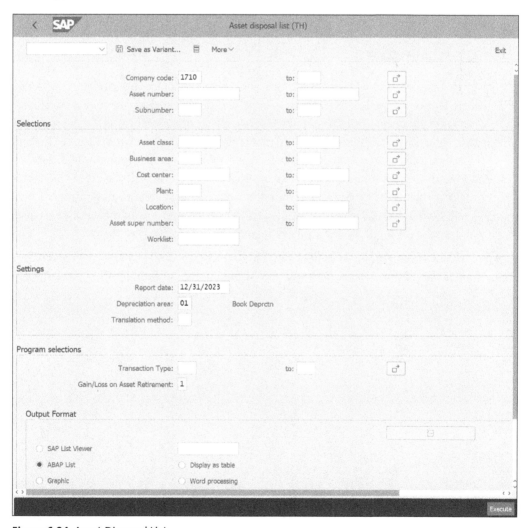

Figure 6.84 Asset Disposal List

In this example, the **ABAP List** format was selected as an **Output Format** option. You can choose any of the listed formats.

Click the **Execute** button, which starts the transaction and produces the list. The resulting list presents the asset disposals in case any disposals occurred in the selected period.

SAP Fiori App

The corresponding SAP Fiori app for Thailand is called Generate Asset Disposal List – Thailand (S_P00_07000078). It's visually and functionally the same as the SAP GUI transaction.

6.7   Summary

In this chapter, we started by walking through the acquire-to-retire process. While learning how to set up a fixed asset account, you also learned the most important master data and settings relevant for accounting, such as the account classes, depreciation key, depreciation area, and chart of depreciation. Later, we went step by step through different fixed asset transactions. You learned about the acquisition, transfer, depreciation, adjustment, and disposal of assets via transactions. Before we ended this chapter with the fixed asset reporting and the explanation of some important reports you may need, we discussed the reconciliation and the period-end closing process. These processes are very similar to what you've seen in the other subledger chapters.

In the next chapter, we'll discuss project accounting and event-based revenue recognition (EBRR) in SAP S/4HANA, which have been released in SAP S/4HANA Cloud and will be included in future on-premise SAP S/4HANA releases.

Chapter 7

Customer Project Accounting and Event-Based Revenue Recognition

In this chapter, we look at examples of how to leverage the potential of the Universal Journal. As an example, we take the customer project end-to-end scenario available in the public cloud, which integrates some of the applications we looked at in previous chapters. We also look at event-based revenue recognition, which is an important cornerstone of financials in SAP S/4HANA. The new direction in finance should become clear in this chapter.

In this chapter, we'll guide you through the project-based services scenario in SAP S/4HANA Cloud, public edition. In doing so, we'll demonstrate several innovations and benefits of the Universal Journal.

One innovation is the improved integration between applications that is provided in SAP S/4HANA Cloud for the customer project scenario. The correct customer contract setup is ensured, which benefits accounting because the data is available correctly, completely, and in real time—there is no manual additional journal entry needed. The system itself accounts the work in progress (WIP), recognizes the revenue, and derives the market segment information in real time.

If you look at relevant business processes, you'll see that they are all fully integrated into accounting. They automatically update the Universal Journal and the accounting applications. We've already dealt with the accounting integration of the time confirmation in Chapter 2, the supplier invoice in Chapter 4, and the customer invoice in Chapter 5. In addition, we'll apply manual accruals with a new revenue recognition application.

Based on the journal entries created by these business processes, we'll demonstrate Universal Journal reporting. You'll see how new reporting insights are enabled by SAP HANA and the Universal Journal.

You'll then learn about the new revenue recognition application mentioned earlier within project accounting called event-based revenue recognition (EBRR). In this context, SAP S/4HANA has implemented fully automated revenue recognition capabilities for the capitalization of services that aren't yet invoiced. EBRR is the development direction for revenue recognition in the cloud and on-premise, so in this edition, we'll be digging deeper into the topic. EBRR's functionality and the supported scenarios are growing continuously.

Finally, we'll provide an overview of the simplified accounting period-end close. By the end of this chapter, you'll have gained insights into the direction in which SAP is moving with SAP S/4HANA Finance.

7.1   Customer Project Scenario in SAP S/4HANA Cloud

The customer project scenario in SAP S/4HANA Cloud is tailored for professional service providers such as consulting, audit, tax, and accounting firms. Application integration and simplified end-to-end processes are available out of the box with the default content. The perfect integration of project operations, customer billing, accounting, and reporting is a major focus, and this integration ensures complete and accurate project data anytime and through all operational and accounting perspectives. Combined with the use of the Universal Journal, with its integrated profitability reporting and EBRR, the system simplifies the work of a general ledger accountant and allows out-of-the-box reporting in real time.

Although the processes are greatly simplified, the required functionality is still provided. In financial accounting, this applies above all through the enabling of automatic and intelligent processes and simplified period-end closing activities.

In this section, we'll explain how this all works through the following use case: Assume your consulting firm has a consulting project with which you implement SAP S/4HANA at a customer site. The consultants working for the customer record their time on the project. In addition, there are other expenses, such as travel expenses. The customer is billed based on the employee's time confirmation and expenses.

The scenario is also a good example of the SAP S/4HANA Cloud approach. You'll see how its guiding principles affect the business scenario as well.

Before we step into the scenario, we'll provide some motivation with first impressions and the underlying guiding principles of accounting.

7.1.1   Financial Accounting Innovations

Let's start with a look at an SAP Fiori app called Project Profitability Overview (F2794), which provides an aggregated view of all your customer projects. This app is assigned to the SAP_BR_Sales_Accountant business role. After opening the app's tile, the screen shown in Figure 7.1 appears.

In the selection criteria for this example, **Financial Statement Version YPS2**—needed for the determination of revenues and cost of sales general ledger accounts—has been defined. A reporting dashboard shows different key performance indicators (KPIs) of customer projects. For example, the top-left tile shows the top projects with the best margins; the next tile shows the aggregated margin across all projects with recognized revenue and costs; and other tiles show recognized margin, recognized revenue, and

WIP. You can select different dimensions for these KPIs, such as profit center and market segments (e.g., customer group, product group; refer to Chapter 2, Section 2.3).

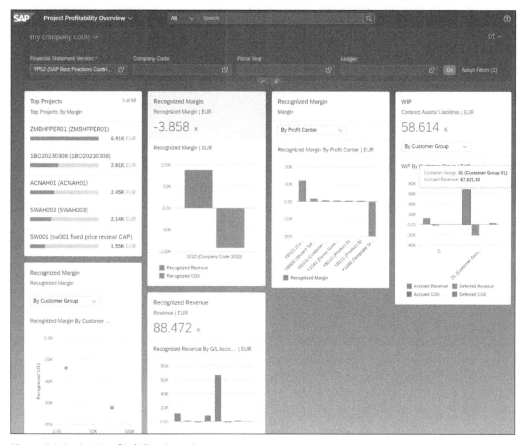

Figure 7.1 Project Profitability Overview App

You may be wondering what's new about this report. First, there are always current, unique, and expressive figures that are reconciled by design. There is only one margin and one KPI value provided across all financial applications based on the Universal Journal. Thanks to the SAP HANA database, all KPIs can be calculated by aggregation of the single journal entries. In SAP ERP, on the other hand, there are different data sources and structures in the general ledger, management accounting, results analysis, and profitability analysis (cost-based), which could show different values. The report from the Project Profitability Overview app is always up to date as soon as you start it because the matching principle for revenues and assigned cost of sales is supported inherently (explained later in this chapter). There is no need to run period-closing jobs such as revenue recognition or settlement first. Costs match revenue every time.

Second, management's decision-making is supported in a timely fashion. Up-to-date reporting—including margins—is available after every posting for every project and market segment, such as profit center, customer, customer group, sales organization, product, or product group. Furthermore, there are new reporting insights, including drilldowns for general ledger accounts (e.g., revenue and WIP) on project and profitability attributes (e.g., customer group or product group).

All of this provides benefits for several roles in SAP S/4HANA:

- **For the accountant**
  Accountants benefit from simplified period-end closing, which supports a fast close. They also can use new reporting insights, such as WIP drilldown by market segment and project (we'll discuss this further in Section 7.1.7).

  Accountants also benefit from enhanced analysis capabilities for revenue recognition values (e.g., drilldown to general ledger items and reference to source documents), which provides greater transparency of calculated revenue recognition postings and reduced auditing effort.

  No reconciliation between revenue recognition data and the general ledger is necessary.

- **For the cost accountant**
  Cost accountants benefit from real-time margin reporting per project and multiple market segment dimensions. They can use profitability views for multiple new available attributes, such as employee, resource, and service product.

  For customer project planning, revenues are calculated by revenue recognition, so plan revenues are calculated for exact periods and are available for forecast. We'll discuss these and further management accounting features in Section 7.1.7 and Section 7.2.4.

- **For the project manager**
  The project manager benefits from real-time project margin reporting. Always current WIP/unbilled revenue information on the project and employee levels is available, which is the basic information about items to be billed.

Next, we'll show you how to access these new financial accounting functionalities. One prerequisite is the simplified customer project contract setup.

7.1.2   Simplified Customer Project Contract Setup

In SAP S/4HANA Cloud, in the center of the project-based service scenario, there are SAP Fiori apps for maintaining customer project contracts. A guided procedure integrates all involved applications, such as sales/contract setup, project management, HR staffing, and especially financials. This allows simplified application integration and fulfills—by following clear rules—the prerequisite for the functionality gain in project accounting. In addition to this simplified customer project master data, dedicated best practice content enables all required subsequent business processes out of the box.

Within the SAP_BR_PROJ_MANAGER_PROF business role, you can access the Create Customer Project app (FO720) or the Plan Customer Projects app (FO719). Let's walk through the key tabs.

> **Note**
>
> The shown Customer Projects app isn't available in on-premise SAP S/4HANA. It's only available in SAP S/4HANA Cloud, public edition.

Project Header Information

You start with the maintenance of the customer project header in the **Information** tab, as shown in Figure 7.2.

Figure 7.2 Create Customer Projects App: Header Information

Let's look at the areas of the **Information** tab:

- **Customer Project**
  The **Customer** of this contract, the **Project Name** and **Project ID**, the **Duration** of the contract, and the contract **Currency** are assigned here. In addition, there are five different statuses enabled by the **Stage** field:
  - **In Planning**: Allows project work package set up and cost planning.
  - **Contract Preparation**: Allows billing plan maintenance and provides a view of the assigned sales order item.
  - **In Execution**: Allows you to post and confirm the time on the project. In addition, baseline planning is provided in the new plan database table ACDOCP (refer to Chapter 2, Section 2.3).

- **Completed**: Impacts revenue recognition. All posted costs and billed revenues are realized. All balance sheet values from revenue recognition are cleared, including manual accruals.

- **Closed**: Doesn't allow you to post on the project anymore, and the project isn't shown in some customer project–related apps. There are enhanced checks before you can close a project; for example, there must be no revenue recognition balance sheet values.

- **Accounting**
  The organizational data is defined in this area. The **Service Organization** is mapped 1:1 to the sales organization. It will later be transferred to the sales order, which is automatically created. The sales organization defines the company code (see Chapter 2). The **Profit Center** is maintained and stored as the default in all assigned work breakdown structure (WBS) elements.

Work Packages with Resource Planning

In the next step, in the **Work Packages** tab, you can structure the project work by creating work packages, as shown in Figure 7.3. In SAP S/4HANA Cloud, you can maintain all work packages of a customer project on only one level.

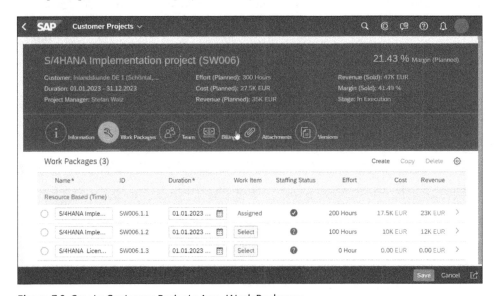

Figure 7.3 Create Customer Projects App: Work Packages

The available fields in this app screen are as follows:

- **Name**
  You can maintain a description of the work package.

- **ID**
  The work package ID is created automatically.

- **Duration**
  This is defaulted by the project header but can be shortened; however, it must be within the defined time frame of the header.
- **Work Item**
  This determines the kind of services, for example, training, documentation, and so on. You can define which work items can be used in the resource planning.
- **Effort/Cost/Revenue**
  These KPIs are the aggregated values of the resource planning for this work package.

For these work packages, you conduct the planning of time and expenses (T&E) by clicking the arrow on the right or by selecting the **Team** tab. The screen shown in Figure 7.4 appears.

Figure 7.4 Create Customer Projects App: Team

With this view, you can plan the roles and employees you need for the task. Each line reflects one resource requirement. First, you need to specify which **Role** you need for the task. With the definition of the **Role** (mapped in accounting to activity type) and the **Delivery Organization** (mapped to the sales organization for which the company code is derived; see Chapter 2, Section 2.2.2), a cost rate is derived. This rate is multiplied with the quantity maintained in the estimated **Effort** to calculate the **Cost (Planned)**.

> **Note**
>
> The cost rate can be maintained in the Manage Cost Rates Professional Services app (F3161) with the SAP_BR_Overhead_Accountant role. For more on this topic, including how the cost rates and the cost amount can be defined, check out the "Financial Accounting For Customer Projects In SAP S/4HANA Cloud" blog article (*http://s-prs.co/v569801*) or

read *Controlling with SAP S/4HANA: Business User Guide* (SAP PRESS, 2021), which is available at *www.sap-press.com/5282.*

In addition, the employee staffing application is integrated so that based on the selected **Delivery Organization** and the **Role**, you get proposals for employees. If there is an employee staffed and staffing is confirmed, this WBS element will appear in the employee's time sheet, which controls the time confirmation process. Further, the cost rate derivation is adapted. In the employee master data, a service cost level is maintained, which can be used for cost rate determination. Based on these plan values, financial plan data is stored in the new plan database table ACDOCP after the customer project **In Execution** status is set.

In the lower **Expenses** area, you can plan the expenses by distinguishing between the different expense types, such as **Accommodation**, **Airfare**, and **Ground Transportation**, as well as the required **Hardware** and **Licenses**. The expense types can be adapted by the customer within a self-service configuration task. In our example, we added 1,000 EUR for **Accommodation**, which will be visible in the project plan costs.

Sales Order Assignment and Billing Definition

By selecting the **Billing** tab, as shown in Figure 7.5, you can define the integration to billing and the sales order/contract. This step is only possible if you set the status to **Contract Preparation** or higher.

Figure 7.5 Create Customer Projects App: Billing and Sales Order View

In Figure 7.5, you define the **Contract Type**. Based on the contract types, the billing method and the revenue recognition method are derived for this contract item. With the delivered content, you ensure correct, process-driven revenue recognition. SAP S/4HANA Cloud best practice content provides four contract types to choose from in the **Contract Type** dropdown:

- **Time and Expenses**
This contract type enables billing based on the T&E confirmations on the assigned work packages. EBRR simulates T&E contract billing for every confirmation to determine the realized revenue.

- **Usage Based**
This contract type is similar to the T&E items. The billing is based on the confirmation of services. Additionally, there are nonbillable resource postings.

- **Fixed Price**
For these contract items, billing is based on the planned amounts and dates maintained in the billing plan. EBRR can calculate the matching revenues for every confirmation, for example, based on the cost-based percentage of completion (POC) method. The planned costs are taken from resource planning, and the planned revenue is taken out of the billing plan. The EBRR methods are explained in Section 7.2.2.

- **Periodic Service**
This item is used, for example, for licenses or other periodic services, which are valid for a time period. The billing is triggered based on the amount and date provided in the billing plan. You get access to the billing plan in Figure 7.6 by clicking the arrow on the far right for contract item **3**. For this contract type, a valid period is required for every billing plan item.

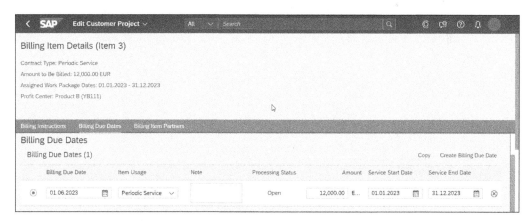

Figure 7.6 Create Customer Projects App: Periodic Billing Plan View

The **Product** in Figure 7.5 (for the **Time and Expenses** item in this example, it's product **P007**) is defaulted by contract type and can be overwritten. It's stored in the sales order item and will be derived as the **Product Sold** attribute in the Universal Journal item. The **Profit Center**—defaulted from the header entry—can be maintained on the billing item level as long there are no postings on the assigned WBS structure.

When you click the **Save** button, a sales order (here, ID **19668**) is created with sales order items per contract line item.

7.1.3   Customer Project Setup Overview

In this section, we'll provide orientation for how the logistic objects customer project and customer sales order play together, how revenue recognition is controlled, and how the market segment is determined.

First, let's get an overview of the object setup in an SAP S/4HANA Cloud customer project scenario. In Figure 7.7, you see the relationships between the sales order and project. There is always a 1:1 relationship between the sales order and project ID and the project billing element and sales order item enforced by the system. That is the prerequisite to allow a derivation of a unique profitability segment and to define a unique revenue recognition method on the billing element level.

The revenue recognition method is derived from the contract type, which defines the billing method. Self-service configuration is available (Section 7.2.7), which allows you to derive the technical revenue recognition key by contract type and—optionally—by the sales material defined in the sales order item. This recognition key is stored in the WBS billing element. (We'll discuss revenue recognition in Section 7.2.)

The market segment is defined by the sales order item, from which you get, for example, the customer and the product sold (refer to Chapter 2, Section 2.3.2). The project billing element is stored in the sales order item master. The sales order item profitability attributes are valid for all assigned project hierarchy elements below the billing element.

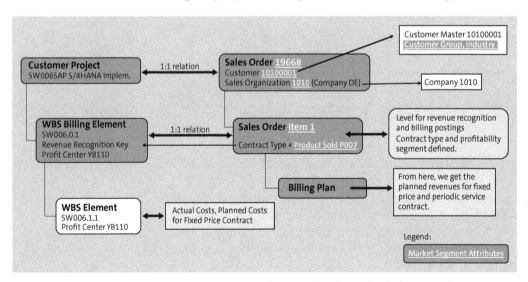

Figure 7.7 Customer Project Setup in SAP S/4HANA Cloud: Involved Objects and Project Accounting Impact

The following steps show the derivation of a market segment for a single posting:

1. With the confirmation to a work package in accounting, the superordinate project billing element is determined first.
2. With the project billing element, you get the link to the assigned sales order item.
3. The sales order item defines the profitability segment (e.g., product, customer).
4. As a result, the profitability segment attributes are determined, and you can enrich the accounting document line items, which are assigned to the work package with the market segment attributes.

To ensure the attributes of this profitability segment and the EBRR calculation, there must be a sales order item assigned to the billing element when the posting to the project occurs. You can't release the project as long as not all work packages are assigned to a sales order item.

> **Note**
>
> With the project billing element to sales order item assigned, there is a unique profitability segment and a unique profit center for these two objects and all assigned work packages. This ensures that the cost posting account assigned to the work packages and the billed revenue posting and revenue recognition posting account assigned to the billing element derive the same profit center and profitability segment.

This enforced object setup provides new insights into project accounting and reporting. We'll show you this in the next sections by posting several business transactions to a customer project.

Let's now move on to the business processes.

7.1.4   Customer Project Business Transactions

In the following sections, we present four typical processes for the professional service industry using SAP Fiori apps in SAP S/4HANA Cloud: employee time confirmation on the customer project, external (travel) expenses posted via a supplier invoice, project billing preparation, and invoicing to the customer. In Section 7.1.5, we'll show you how to analyze the revenue recognition data and manually accrue or defer revenues through the EBRR application.

These processes all have in common that revenue is recognized through a revenue recognition journal entry posted at the same time as the confirmation, which enables real-time margin reporting on the project. In addition, all projects assigned journal entry items are enriched with market segment information, enabling real-time market segment reporting.

Time Confirmation on a Customer Project

With the following business transaction, we'll demonstrate how a simple employee time confirmation on a customer project immediately affects SAP S/4HANA project accounting and management reporting. The process starts with a consultant's time recording on the example customer project named **SW006 SAP S/4HANA Implementation**.

To begin, consultant **John TESTER_01DE** needs to be assigned to the SAP_BR_Employee business role. He starts the Manage My Timesheet app (F1823) from the SAP Fiori launchpad. The screen shown in Figure 7.8 appears.

In the right pane, all the project tasks are provided for which the consultant is staffed. He searches the project by entering "S/4" under **My Tasks**. He marks the task from the project and captures one hour for January 16, 2023, by directly marking the time sheet. The height of the column determines the number of hours.

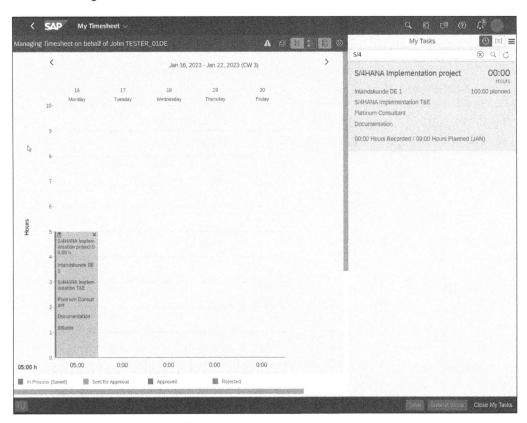

Figure 7.8 Time Sheet Confirmation to Customer Project

The consultant can apply a note about the work, which is provided (not shown). Then he can click the **Submit Week** button on the bottom right. Dependent on the configuration, the time is auto approved, or it's sent to the project's lead inbox for approval. This is the only required user interaction; all further process steps, including the accounting update, are done by the system.

In SAP S/4HANA Cloud, public edition, with approval, time recording is automatically transferred to financial accounting. In the accounting interface, several enrichment steps are processed. For example, a general ledger account is derived, the amount is calculated, the posting period is defined, and the profitability segment is derived.

The type of the provided service is defaulted by the project resource planning (refer to Figure 7.4). In the right side of Figure 7.8, you can see **Platinum Consultant** as a required service. This is mapped to the financial entity activity type. Based on the activity type and the consultant's service cost level, a cost rate is defined in the Manage Cost Rates app (not shown). In this example, a rate of 100 EUR per hour is defined. This rate is multiplied with the recorded time of one hour. Therefore, the system gets a cost amount of 500 EUR for this time confirmation.

Then, the market segment attributes are derived via the process explained in the previous section (refer to Figure 7.7). In Section 7.1.2, you see in the **Billing** view (refer to Figure 7.5) that the customer project is assigned to a sales order **19668** and therefore to the customer **10100001 Inlandskunde DE1**. In the contract item, additional **Product P007** is assigned, which is derived as profitability attribute **Product Sold**. These market segment attributes are now derived at the time of posting and applied to all general ledger line items posted to the WBS element. As explained in the previous section, these object assignments are ensured by design in SAP S/4HANA Cloud for customer projects.

The created two postings can be analyzed with the Display Line Items – Margin Analysis app (F4818) in Figure 7.9. In the selection, we apply the time sheet document number in the **Reference document** field, and then click **GO**.

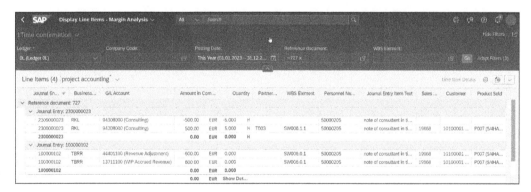

Figure 7.9 Journal Entries Created by the Time Sheet Entry

> **Note**
>
> For the different roles—general ledger accountant, cost accountant, and sales accountant—there are specific line item reports available: Display Line Items in General Ledger (F2217), Display Line Items – Cost Accounting (F4023), and Display Line Items – Margin Analysis (F4818).

The first journal entry, **23000000023**, including two line items, reflects the management accounting posting for the time confirmation. It leads to a cost allocation between cost center and project (discussed in Chapter 2, Section 2.3). The two line items are as follows:

- **Item 1**
  The cost center of the employee is credited with 5 hours and 500 EUR costs.

- **Item 2**
  The customer project is debited with the quantity of 5 hours and 500 EUR costs.

The second journal entry (**100000102**) is created by EBRR (Section 7.2) with its own **Business Transaction Type TBRR** (second column). It contains the following two line items:

- **Item 3**
  The calculated recognized revenue is posted on the billing element by using the income statement general ledger account **Revenue Adjustment**.

- **Item 4**
  The activation of accrued revenue/WIP is posted with reference to the billing element using the balance sheet general ledger account **WIP Accrued Revenue**.

Note that both journal entries refer to the time sheet document. We use the **Reference document** as grouping criteria in this report. There is a link from the revenue recognition posting to the time sheet source document and vice versa. This simplifies tracing and reviewing.

Let's now walk through the key columns shown for these journal entries:

- **WBS Element**
  You can see that the management accounting document and the revenue recognition document post on the project with different WBS elements. The time confirmation posts on work package **SW006.1.1**, on which the employee is planned. The revenue recognition postings are accounts assigned to billing element **SW006.0.1**, on which the billed revenue is posted later in the process too.

- **Personnel Number** and **Journal Entry Item Text**
  The information about the consultant who performed the time and the note that the consultant provided in the time confirmation is stored in all journal entries. One usage for this information is in project billing, which you'll see later.

- **Sales Document/Customer/Product Sold**
  The three columns on the right reflect the market segment attributes derived from assigned sales order **19668** and stored in journal entry items, which are account assigned to the project.

Now let's discuss how we get the value of 600 EUR for the realized revenue. In this example, the assigned accounting principle allows that revenues can already be recognized with the confirmation. The method for determining the realized revenue for this confirmation is defined by the contract type in the assigned sales order item (refer to Figure 7.5). In contract **Item 1**, the **Contract Type** of **Time and Expenses** is assigned. In this case, the billable amount is defined by the expenses and time confirmations posted to the project and persisted in the Universal Journal. With the confirmation line item, the **Time and Expenses** type is simulated by the revenue recognition application. In this case, the provided service—activity type T003 **Platinum Consulting**—is mapped to billing material T003. For this billing material, a sales price is defined; in our example, you get a sales price of 120 EUR per hour. As five hours were recorded, you get a billable amount of 600 EUR, which is posted as recognized revenue. Therefore, it's ensured that you get the same billing amount as later will be billed, which we'll discuss further in this section.

The sales price is determined in the Manage Prices – Sales app (F4111), as shown in Figure 7.10.

Figure 7.10 Maintenance of Sales Price with the Manage Prices – Sales App

With this app, you can define time-dependent sales prices with several dimensions. We select the prices for **Sales Organization** as **1010** and **Distribution Channel** as **10**. Clicking **Go** brings up a list for product-dependent prices. For our **Product T003**, there are two prices maintained for different time frames. The current price—on January 16, 2023—is 120 EUR (see second line).

This new creation and enrichment of accounting documents provides new fascinating insights for the accountant and the project manager. We'll look at this in Section 7.1.7, but first, let's look at the other business transaction postings on the customer project.

Supplier Invoice Posting to a Customer Project

In this example, you receive an invoice for travel expenses, which has been incurred for the employee within the scope of the project. Following the discussion of accounts payable in Chapter 4, we'll show you now the expense posting on the customer project by a supplier invoice.

Within the SAP_BR_AP_ACCOUNTANT business role, you can access the Create Supplier Invoice app (FO859), as shown in Figure 7.11.

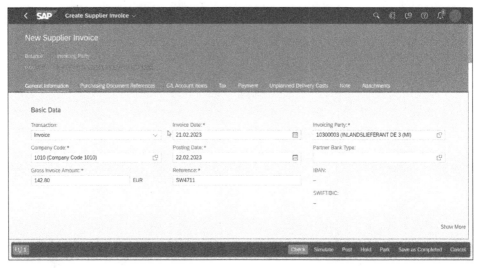

Figure 7.11 Supplier Invoice: Heading Information

The **Invoice** option is already defaulted in the **Transaction** field, but you need to select the supplier in the **Invoicing Party** field, enter the **Company Code** (here, enter "1010"), and enter the **Invoice Date**. The **Posting Date** is defaulted with the current day. The **Gross Invoice Amount** is the complete amount, including input taxes, which will need to be paid to the supplier. You can add some more invoice information in the **Reference** field, for example, the document number of the supplier.

In this business scenario, the travel expenses will be posted without a purchase order reference, so you can directly navigate to the **G/L Account Items** tab, which opens the screen shown in Figure 7.12.

Add the expense **G/L Account** and the related debit **Amount**. You can apply additional information in the **Item Text** field (here, "Workshop Expenses"). This information will be visible later in the project billing to the customer. In the **Tax Code** field, entering "V1" causes the system to calculate the value-added tax (VAT). Because the expense general ledger account is a cost element (refer to Chapter 2, Section 2.3.3), you must assign a cost object in the **WBS Element** field in the **Account Assignment** area (here, enter the customer project work package "SW006.1.1"). **Profit Center** and **Functional Area** get derived by the work package master (refer to Section 7.1.2). Because the travel expenses were incurred by the consultant, you add the consultant's ID in the **Personnel Number** field.

Click the **Post** button at the bottom. You'll get a success notification, which includes the ID of the created supplier invoice (5105601657/2023) and the related accounting document/journal entry (5100000030).

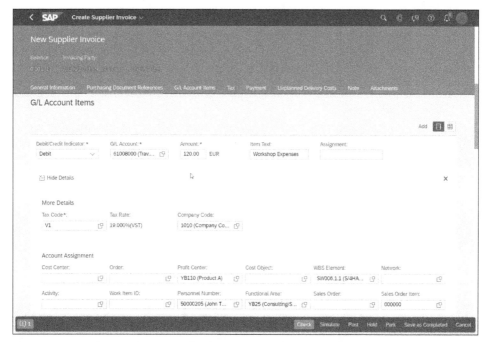

Figure 7.12 Supplier Invoice General Ledger Account Item Information

The created journal entries can be analyzed with the Display Line Items – Margin Analysis app. As selection criteria, use **Reference document,** which is equal to the supplier invoice document in the success notification, **5105601657.** In Figure 7.13, you see two journal entries created by the supplier invoice.

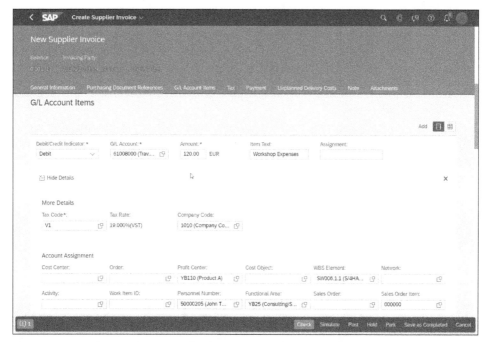

Figure 7.13 General Ledger Journal Entries of the Supplier Invoice

The first line item of journal entry **510000030** is the accounts payable item. The second line item of this journal entry—posted with the **Travel Expenses Miscellaneous** general ledger account—is account assigned to work package **SW006.1.1.**

The second journal entry **100000195** is created by EBRR, which you can see from the **Business Transaction Type TBRR** (second column). In this case, in the contract with the customer, it's defined that the expenses are charged with the same amount as they arise, so revenue of **120 EUR** is realized. The revenue recognition postings are accounts assigned to the billing element **SW006.0.1**, on which the billed revenue is posted later in the process too.

With the first revenue recognition journal entry item, the calculated realized revenue is posted by using the **Revenue Adjustment** income statement general ledger account. With the second item, the accrued revenue is posted with the **WIP Accrued Revenue** balance sheet general ledger account.

The same as for the time confirmation, the profitability segment of the assigned sales order item is derived, and the profitability attributes of the Universal Journal are updated. For example, see the far-right **Customer** and **Product Sold** columns.

You can check the created accounts payable open item with the Manage Supplier Line Items app (F0712), as shown in Figure 7.14.

Figure 7.14 Accounts Payable Open Item

Select **Supplier 10300003** of our created invoice, and click the **Go** button to get the list of the open items for this supplier, which will be cleared by an upcoming payment (see Chapter 4).

Billing Preparation: WIP Management

In the next step, we want to bill the consultant's T&E confirmation to the customer. The billing document is carried out by a resource-related billing method. In other words, billing proposals are created based on the expenses and time confirmations posted to the project and persisted in the Universal Journal. Billing materials are determined for the different resource types (e.g., senior consulting or platinum consulting), for which prices—also project-specific—can then be defined (refer to Figure 7.10).

Within the SAP_BR_BILLG_SPCLST business role, the project manager can check the due billing items on customer projects with the Manage Project Billing app (F4374). First, the project manager gets an overview of all their projects with due items (see Figure 7.15).

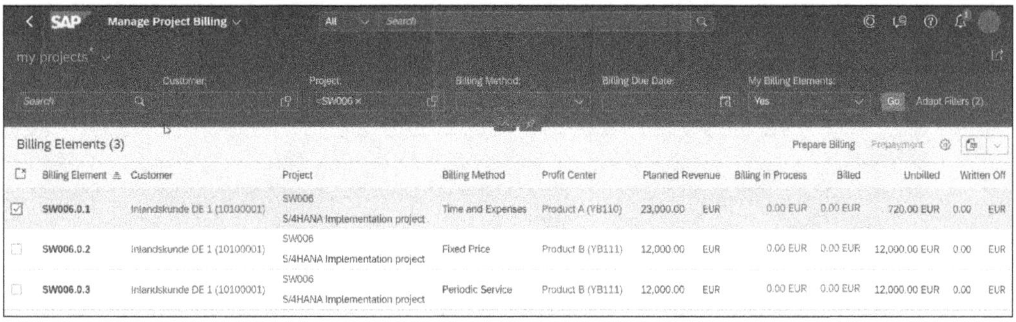

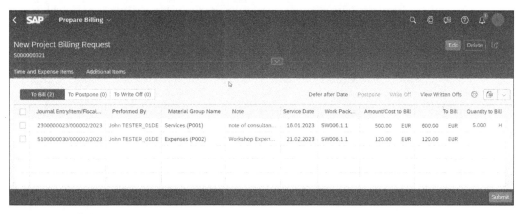

Figure 7.15 Manage Project Billing App

In this screen, you get a billing overview for your customer projects. KPIs are provided, such as the already **Billed** amount and the **Unbilled** amount. In the first line, you see the **Billing Element** on which we assigned the time confirmation and supplier invoice previously. There is an unbilled amount of 720 EUR, resulting from the time confirmation and expense posting. Select this item, and click **Prepare Billing** to see the single confirmation items on the screen that appears, as shown in Figure 7.16.

Figure 7.16 Billable Customer Project Items

In the far-left column, you can see that all billing item proposals are based on **Journal Entry**. The first item reflects the five hours of time confirmation of the consultant, and the second line reflects the expense posting. Select the time confirmation for billing (checkbox for the first line item) and postpone the expense posting by not selecting its checkbox.

Now, to bill a one-hour time confirmation to the customer, you need to write off one hour and defer three hours and the expense. For this, select the first item, and click the **Edit** button at the top-right area of the screen. The screen in Figure 7.17 appears.

Figure 7.17 Billable Item Maintenance

Enter "3" hours in the **Quantity to Postpone** column, and enter "1" hour in the **Quantity to Write Off** column. The result is a **Quantity to Bill** of 1 hour. Click **Save** to save and postpone the travel item too. This leads to the billing proposal result in Figure 7.18.

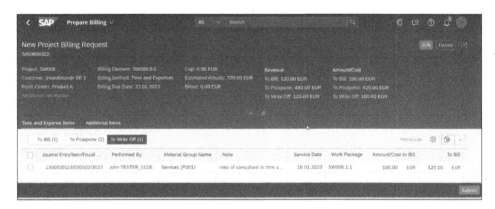

Figure 7.18 Final Billing Proposal

You see that the **To Bill** tab shows **(1)** item, **To Postpone** shows **(2)** items, and **To Write Off** shows **(1)** item. The details of the one item to write off are shown below the tabs.

Click the **Submit** button at the bottom of the screen to create the billing document request (BDR). The **Success** box appears to inform you of the successful creation and to provide the BDR ID (see Figure 7.19).

Figure 7.19 Success Box Noting the Billing Document Request Was Created

With this, two subsequent processes are triggered:

- The billing request is created, which will lead to a billing document and finally to billed revenues on the project.
- The write-off of one hour impacts revenue recognition, of course. This write-off must reduce the WIP/accrued revenue.

Let's first look at the write-off. With the save of the BDR, EBRR is triggered and the journal entry in Figure 7.20 is created.

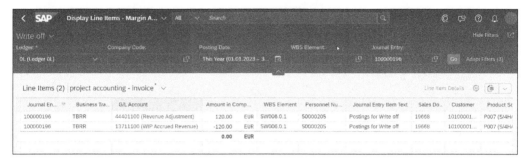

Figure 7.20 EBRR Journal Entry for Write-Off

The one hour had originally been activated with 120 EUR. As you write off this one hour, the WIP is reduced with this amount. For transparency, **Postings for Write off** is stored in **Journal Entry Item Text.**

Now, let's bill the created BDR.

Billing a Customer Project

Within the SAP_BR_Billing_clerk business role, the subsequent billing processes can be performed with the Create Preliminary Billing Documents app (F2876), as shown in Figure 7.21. You can get directly to this app with the link in the BDR **Success** box.

Figure 7.21 Create Preliminary Billing Documents App

In the selection screen, the BDR ID is entered in the **SD Document** field.

Select the item, and click **Create Preliminary Billing Documents** to automatically create a customer invoice and its related accounting documents. You can analyze the invoice with the Manage Billing Documents app (FO797).

In Figure 7.22, you can see the created billing document with one billing item for one hour (**1 H**) and a **Net Value** of **120 EUR** assigned to WBS billing element **SW006.0.1**.

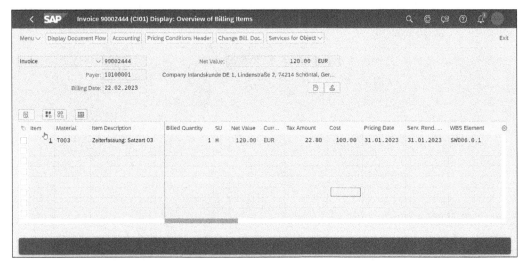

Figure 7.22 Billing Document

You can analyze the created journal entries again with the Display Line Items – Margin Analysis app, as shown in Figure 7.23, by selecting the **Reference document** equal to the billing document.

Figure 7.23 Journal Entries Created by the Billing Document

There are two journal entries posted by the customer invoice. Just as with the time confirmation and supplier invoice, the customer invoice is accompanied by the matching revenue recognition document. The grouping criterion for both journal entries is the original billing document as the **Reference document**.

The first journal entry **9400000045** reflects the accounts receivable posting. The first line item is the debit of the accounts receivable. The second line item—posted with the **Billed Revenue Domestic** profit and loss (P&L) general ledger account—is an account assigned to project billing element **SW006.0.1**.

The second journal entry **100000203** is the matching revenue recognition document: the first line item is the debit of the realized revenue posted on the billing element. The second line item posts on the **Deferrals Revenue** balance sheet account. As in this example, the International Financial Reporting Standards (IFRS) accounting principle is applied, and revenues are recognized already with the time confirmation and the expense posting. Billing must not again lead to additional revenues; the billed revenues must be deferred (Section 7.2.1).

The same as for the time confirmation and the supplier invoice, the profitability segment of the assigned sales order item is derived, and the profitability attributes of the Universal Journal are updated for all line items that are account assigned to the project billing element. For example, the **Customer** and **Product Sold** columns are selected on the far right.

You can check the created open item with the SAP_BR_AR_Accountant business role in the Manage Customer Line Items app (F0711). Enter **Customer** "10100001" to whom the invoice was billed, click the **Go** button, and you'll get the list shown in Figure 7.24.

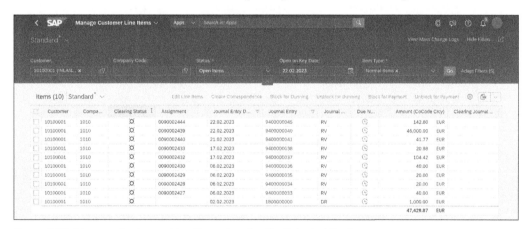

Figure 7.24 Manage Customer Line Items App for the Selected Customer

All open items for this customer are listed. The key columns to note are as follows:

- **Clearing Status**
  Shows that all the items aren't cleared.

- **Assignment**
  Shows the reference to the billing document. Our created document, **90002444**, is shown in the first line.

- **Due Net**
  Shows the **Due Net** symbol. Green symbols aren't yet overdue.

For follow-up processes, you can mark a line item on the left and click an activity button in the table header bar, such as **Block for Dunning** and **Unblock for Dunning** (refer to Chapter 5, Section 5.6).

7.1.5   Customer Project Period-End Close

In the customer project scenario, period-end close can be limited to revenue recognition activities. A settlement to the market segment isn't required due to the Universal Journal's integrated profitability. The following sections describe two EBRR activities:

- Optionally entering manual accruals
- Required netting of balance sheet accounts (accrued and deferred revenues)

Manual Accrual Posting for a Customer Project

Now let's discuss the use case in the system when you know that the customer will get a volume discount in the final billing. You need to consider this at the period-end close. With an already realized revenue of 600 EUR, this is 25 EUR for the project. The revenue already realized is reduced by the amount, and a provision for the expected revenue reduction is recognized in the balance sheet.

For entering the manual accruals for single projects, you start within the SAP_BR_SALES_ Accountant business role and access the Event-Based Revenue Recognition – Projects app (F4767).

In the selection screen, you can further restrict the selected project billing elements by project definition, by project manager, or by revenue recognition key. Enter "SW006" in the **Project Definition** field, click the **Go** button, and get the billing elements of the project, as shown in Figure 7.25.

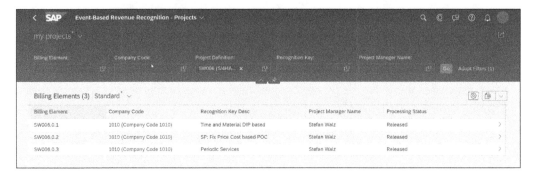

Figure 7.25 Event-Based Revenue Recognition – Projects App: Selection Screen

Select the first line, and click the arrow on the far right of the line item to see the details for the project, as shown in Figure 7.26.

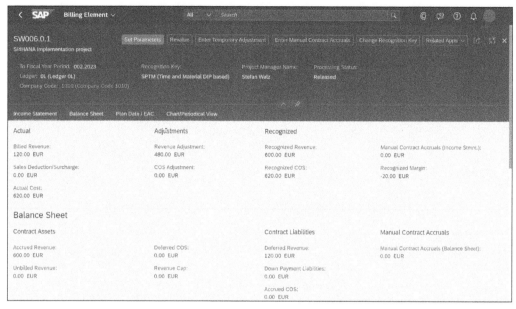

Figure 7.26 EBRR Detail Screen for One Project Billing Element

In the header of the detail screen in Figure 7.26, you see the selected project billing element **SW006.0.1 S/4HANA Implementation project** and master data information for it: the used revenue recognition key that defines the revenue recognition method, the assigned project manager, and the status of the project. On the left, you get information about the **To Fiscal Year Period** (here, February 2023) and the **Ledger** (here, ledger OL). You can change these two parameters by selecting **Set Parameters**. We'll discuss the other activities on this activity bar in Section 7.2.5.

Let's now go to the revenue recognition data. In the upper section, you see the **Income Statement** information, which was created by the business activities you performed in the preceding sections:

- Billed revenue of 120 EUR
- Actual costs of 620 EUR created by the time confirmation and the travel expense posting
- The revenue adjustment of 480 EUR, reflecting the realized revenues for the expenses and the hours, for which no billing has yet happened
- The recognized revenue of 600 EUR, reflecting the sum of the billed revenue for the time confirmation (120 EUR) and the revenue adjustment (480 EUR)
- The recognized costs of 620 EUR and the recognized revenue of 600 EUR, resulting in an actual negative margin of 20 EUR

In the lower section, you can see the **Balance Sheet** values:

- The accrued revenues of 600 EUR created by the cost postings
- The deferred revenues of 120 EUR posted by the billing

Selecting the **Enter Manual Contract Accruals** activity at the top, you'll arrive at the screen shown in Figure 7.27.

Figure 7.27 Manual Accruals Entry for the Customer Project

You can enter a manual accrual entry for the current period "002.2023". To allow simplified tracking and classifying of the accruals, you can add a note, which will be transferred in **Journal Entry Item Text**. In Customizing, you can predefine general ledger account pairs for the balance sheet and income statement. For this example, add **25 EUR** in one line for one general ledger account pair, enter the text "expected volume discount" in **Journal Entry Item Text**, and click **Post**.

A revenue recognition document is created, as shown in Figure 7.28.

Figure 7.28 Revenue Recognition Box for Successful Posting

The revenue recognition document is persisted as a journal entry in the Universal Journal, so you can analyze it with the Display Line Items in Margin Analysis app (see Figure 7.29). Select the posted revenue recognition document number in the **Reference document** field.

As expected, you get two journal entry items, posted with the general ledger accounts selected in the **manual accrual** screen. With the second line, the realized revenue is decreased by 25 EUR, and reserves for anticipated sales deductions are built with the first item. The note entered in the manual accruals popup is persisted in the **Journal Entry Item Text** column.

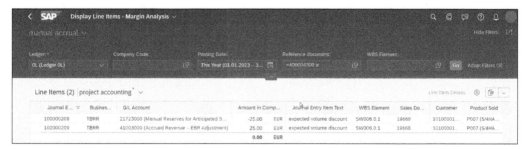

Figure 7.29 Journal Entry Created by the Manual Accruals Posting

Both journal entry items are account assigned to the project billing element **SW006.0.1**. This enables the enhanced reporting insights you'll see in the next section. Note that the same profitability attributes are derived as for the business transactions posted previously. On the right, you can see the sales order, the derived customer, and the product sold.

Balance Sheet Netting for a Customer Project

As shown previously in Figure 7.26, for the project, we have created contract assets (balance sheet debit) of 600 EUR as a result of the confirmations and contract liabilities of 120 EUR (balance sheet credit) as a result of the billing. This must be balanced. To do so, select the **Revalue** button (shown previously in Figure 7.26) to get the view shown in Figure 7.30.

Figure 7.30 EBRR Revaluation

Select the **Simulate** button to get the new results in the right column. You see the deferred revenue cleared to zero, and the accrued revenue is reduced from 600 EUR to 480 EUR. Click **Post** to get the success box shown in Figure 7.31.

Figure 7.31 Revaluation Posting Success Box

There is again a revenue recognition document **400004400** posted, which we'll analyze in Figure 7.32.

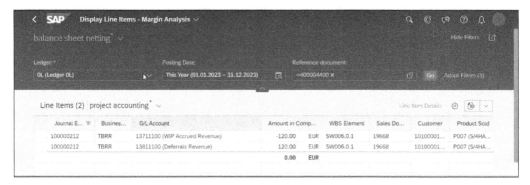

Figure 7.32 EBRR Journal Entry for Balance Sheet Netting

The first journal entry item reflects the credit of the **WIP Accrued Revenue**, and the second reflects the debit of **Deferrals Revenue**. As for all project-related transactions, the WBS element is assigned, and the market segment attributes are derived.

So far, our example project has used the **Time and Expense** contract type. Next, we'll take a look at two more customer project contract types.

7.1.6   Fixed-Price and Periodic Service Contracts

Let's start with the **Fixed Price** contract type, the second item in our project's **Billing** tab (refer to Figure 7.5). We'll work with a cost-based POC method in EBRR (for an explanation of this method, see Section 7.2.2). So, we need planned costs and revenues: the amount to be billed of 12,000 EUR is the revenue, and the cost calculation of the work package is the planned costs (refer to Figure 7.3, the second item with 10,000 EUR). We post a time confirmation, which leads to the journal entries shown in Figure 7.33.

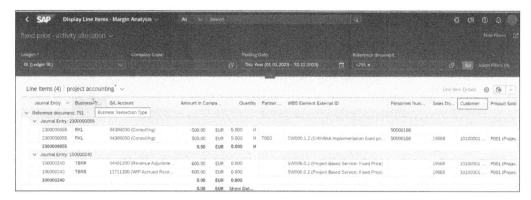

Figure 7.33 Time Confirmation on a Fixed-Price Contract Type

The two journal entries look quite similar to the time confirmation on the T&E project in Figure 7.9 earlier: one prima nota creates two journal entries. However, the EBRR values are calculated differently: the realized revenues are calculated based on a cost-based POC. You can get an overview of the values in the Event-Based Revenue Recognition – Projects app in Figure 7.34. Same as in the T&E scenario before, we realize revenue already with the cost posting.

Figure 7.34 Event-Based Revenue Recognition – Projects App for the Fixed-Price Project

Let's analyze how the values are calculated. At the top of the monitor, you see the fixed-price billing element **SW006.0.2** and the revenue recognition key **SPFC** (fixed-price, cost-based POC). At the bottom, you see the plan data described earlier.

As the **Actual Cost** is 500 EUR, the POC is 500 EUR ÷ 10,000 EUR = 5%. The 5% costs are multiplied with the **Planned Revenue** of 12,000 EUR, which leads to 600 EUR recognized revenue.

Now we look at the **Periodic Service** contract type, reflected by billing element **SW006.0.3**—the third item in the **Billing** tab shown previously in Figure 7.5. The periodic billing plan was also shown in Figure 7.6. There is a billing amount of 12,000 EUR planned, which is due on June 1. The contract is valid for all of 2023. This is defined with the service start date of January 1, 2023, and the service end date of December 31, 2023.

As the contract is valid for 12 months, we need to realize revenue for every month, although the billing is done in June only. This will be done via period revenue recognition. Start the Event-Based Revenue Recognition – Projects app for this billing element for January 2023 and revalue to get the calculated amount shown in Figure 7.35.

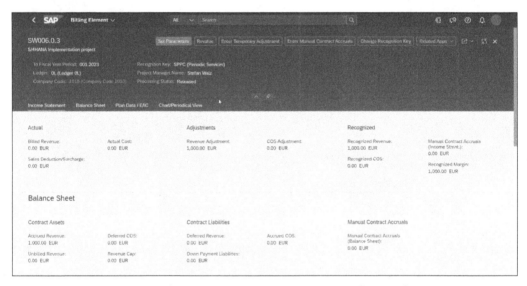

Figure 7.35 Event-Based Revenue Recognition – Projects App for Periodic Service

At the top, you see the selected period **001.2023** and the **Recognition Key** for period services, **SPPC**. As expected, there is revenue realized. The billing amount of 12,000 EUR is divided by 12 months, which leads to a realized revenue of 1,000 EUR per month.

After we've booked some accounting documents based on project-related business transactions, let's look at how this is reflected in accounting reporting.

7.1.7   Financial Reporting Insights

In this section, you'll gain some insight into which new reporting functionalities are possible based on the Universal Journal architecture. Bringing the financials applications together leads, as you've seen, to a journal entry enrichment with profitability attributes. EBRR ensures a real-time margin. SAP HANA allows reporting on journal entry items, which enables you to drill down to all Universal Journal dimensions. In this section, we've put together some use cases for you to consider.

Real-Time Project and Market Segment Information

Enabled by EBRR (refer to Section 7.2) and the derived market segment attributes, you always get a current project margin and all project-related KPIs on the market segment. With the SAP_BR_SALES_Accountant role, you can start the Project Profitability app (F2764). Select project **SW006** to see the report in Figure 7.36.

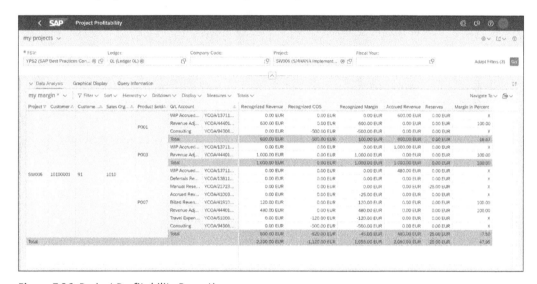

Figure 7.36 Project Profitability Reporting

Based on the journal entries of the business processes we discussed before, you can report KPIs for our project such as the **Recognized Margin** of **1055 EUR**, the **Accrued Revenue** of **2080 EUR**, and a **Margin in Percent** of **47.95**. Additionally, the market segment attributes are updated. For our customer project, the market segment attributes **Customer 10100001**, **Sales Organization 1010**, and **Customer Industry 91**. For the three products sold, **P001** (fixed price), **P003** (periodic service), and **P007** (T&E contract type), you can, for example, report a margin.

These KPIs are all based on journal entry line items of the Universal Journal, so many additional reporting dimensions are available to add for drilldown. By clicking on the arrow on the far left in the middle of the screen, you can see additional dimensions, which you can add in the report via drag and drop (see Figure 7.37).

Figure 7.37 Project Profitability Reporting Dimensions

> **Note**
>
> If you add customer-specific extensibility attributes—for example, in your market segment—they will be available in the dimension list.

Another option is to navigate to further reports by marking a line item—here, **Project SW006**—and clicking **Navigate To**. You'll get several navigations targets, as shown in Figure 7.38.

As all reports are based on the Universal Journal, the typical general ledger reports are available for further analysis. You can see some of the offered reports here.

> **Note**
>
> These analysis and navigation options are available for all accounting and controlling reports, such as for the Project Profitability Overview app shown previously in Figure 7.1. You can verify all the KPIs via single journal entries, which provides total transparency and increases confidence in the KPIs shown.

As mentioned in Chapter 1, extensibility tools are in place to enhance the Universal Journal (the complete details are beyond the scope of this book). Tools are also available for defining customer-specific market segment attributes. You can add your own specific market segment fields, which will enhance the Universal Journal, and you can define derivation logic to get the values for these fields. The applied extensibility fields are automatically integrated in the standard reports, such as the Project Profitability report.

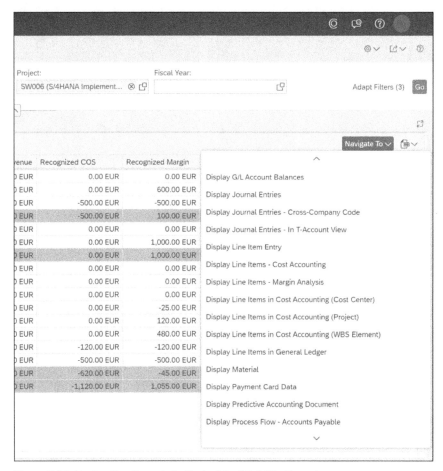

Figure 7.38 Navigation Targets in Project Profitability Report

Enhanced General Ledger and WIP Reporting

With the integration of market segment reporting and revenue recognition in the Universal Journal, there are now enhanced reporting and tracing options available for accountants. For example, drilling down the WIP value by WBS element and market segment (product sold, customer, etc.) is possible, as the revenue recognition postings stored in the Universal Journal and their line items include the market segment.

Within the SAP_BR_GL_Accountant role, you can start the Balance Sheet/Income Statement app (F0708), as shown in Figure 7.39. You select the **Company Code**, **Ledger**, financial **Statement Version**, and reporting **Periods**. Click **Go** in the header bar to get the data.

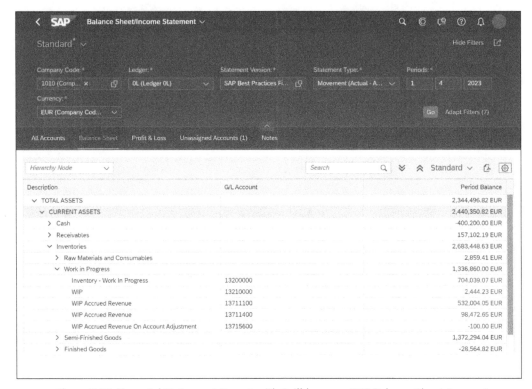

Figure 7.39 Financial Statement Report with Drilldown on WIP Balance Sheet Accounts

You can drill down on the arrows reflecting the financial statement version nodes to **Inventories** and **Work in Progress**. For example, you get the WIP value on **G/L Account 13711100** of **532,004,05 EUR**. If you now want to get more information about the origin of this amount, you can analyze it by clicking on this value. You'll get a popup with navigation target **Display GL Line Items**. When you click on this link, you're taken to the Display Line Items in General Ledger app.

The parameters are defaulted by the selection in the financial statement: **Ledger OL**, **Company Code 1010**, **G/L Account 13711100**, **Fiscal Period**, and **Fiscal Year of Ledger**. In Figure 7.40, you get the single journal entries whose aggregation results in **532.004,05 EUR** for **G/L Account 13711100**.

In these reports, you can create and save your own layout by selecting the column fields according to the Universal Journal fields. Based on these fields, you can define a grouping and a sorting (here, grouping by **Product Sold** and **Project**).

The entire WIP amount can be assigned to market segment attributes (here, **Product Sold** and **Customer**). Select product sold **P007**, which has a value of **480 EUR**. Drill down on the projects with product sold **SW006** only. For project **SW006**, you can show every single journal entry item, which add up to the 480 EUR. You get the same drilldown for the periodic service example with product sold **P003**. The same is possible for P&L accounts, which are used for customer project postings.

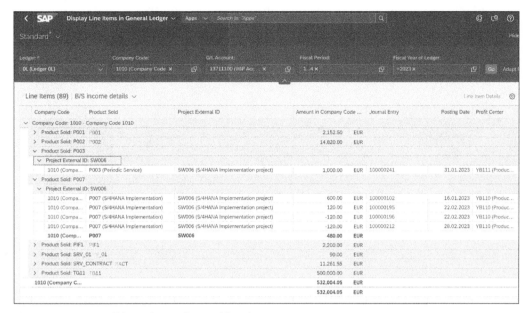

Figure 7.40 WIP Drilldown by Product Sold and Project

Now, let's look at the billed revenue accounts. Select the **Profit & Loss** header tab, and drill down to the **Gross Sales Revenue** financial statement node by clicking the node arrows on the left to get the view shown in Figure 7.41.

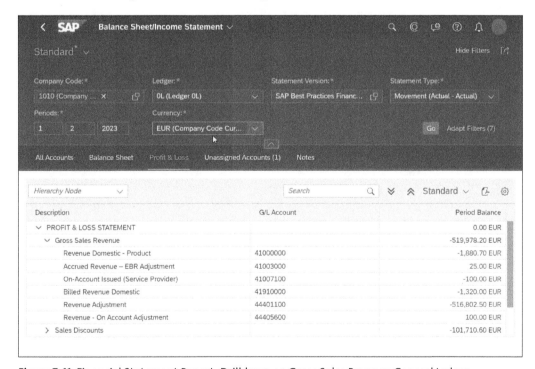

Figure 7.41 Financial Statement Report: Drilldown on Gross Sales Revenue General Ledger Accounts

G/L Account 41910000 (Billed Revenue Domestic) shows an amount of **1,320.00 EUR**. Click on this amount to open the popup with the **Display GL Line Items** navigation target. Select it, and the report shown in Figure 7.42 appears.

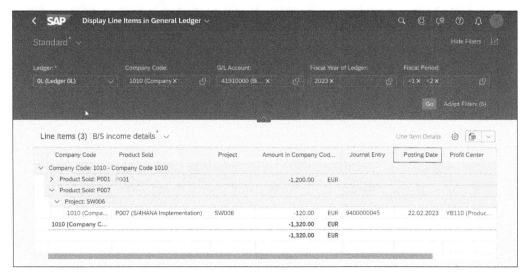

Figure 7.42 Billed Revenue Domestic Drilldown by Product Sold and Project

Just as for the WIP account before, let's group by product sold and project. You can assign the complete amount to these attributes. For **Project SW006**, drill down to the single journal entry item.

For the T&E project billing scenario we showed previously, enhanced WIP details reporting is available. Start the Display Project WIP Details app (F4766), which is part of the SAP_BR_SALES_ACCOUNTANT role, and select project **SW006**. After clicking **Go**, you'll get the view shown in Figure 7.43.

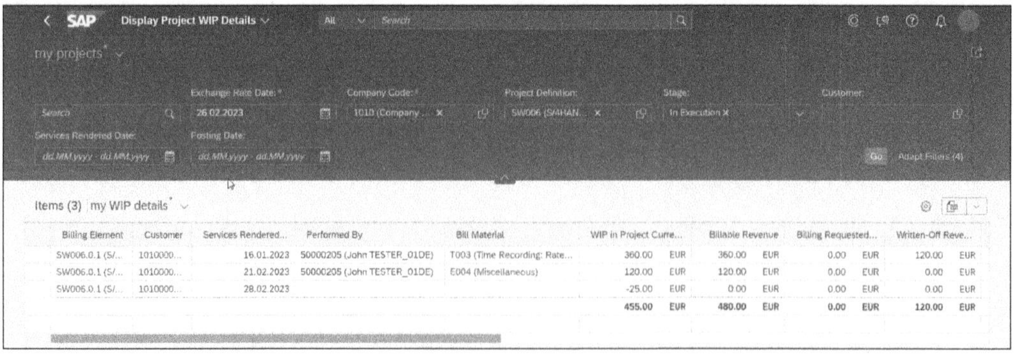

Figure 7.43 Display Project WIP Details

You get detailed information about the business transactions posted to the project. This data is only available for projects with a T&E contract, not for a fixed-price scenario.

In the first row, you see the time confirmation: there is still WIP (**WIP in Project Curre**) available of **360 EUR**. You can also see the **Written-Off Revenue** of **120 EUR**. The second row is the time expense, which has a **WIP in Project Curre** value of **120 EUR**.

To allow reconciliation with the WIP balance sheet accounts in the general ledger in this report, you include the manual accruals—here, 25 EUR posted on the reserves balance sheet account (refer to Figure 7.29)—which you see in the last row.

> **Note**
>
> These examples demonstrate that there are entirely new reporting insights possible through the integration of revenue recognition and profitability into the Universal Journal. Thanks to the SAP HANA database, aggregated reporting is based on single journal entry items. In principle, this allows aggregated reporting on all Universal Journal fields.

Now that you've seen the EBRR functionalities and their significance for the service solution, let's take a closer look at the details of EBRR.

7.2   Event-Based Revenue Recognition

EBRR is the most comprehensive revenue recognition solution in the SAP S/4HANA portfolio. Started as a public cloud solution for the professional service scenario, it now covers additional business processes and is also available in on-premise SAP S/4HANA. EBRR not only covers the requirements of revenue recognition, but it's also an essential component for the new profitability solution, margin analysis.

In SAP S/4HANA Cloud, public edition, EBRR is *the* revenue recognition solution. In on-premise SAP S/4HANA, EBRR is seen as the successor to the results analysis solution for single controlling objects such as customer projects or service orders. In addition to these scenarios, EBRR offers revenue recognition for the sell-from-stock scenario.

In this section, we'll start with an overview of the principles and characteristics of EBRR (e.g., the posting logic) based on the business processes of the previous section. We'll explain the advantages we get with the integration into Universal Journal, how EBRR supports the cloud principles, why it's so simple to use, and how it increases transparency. We'll give more insights into the available functionalities in the customer project scenario and first insights into the sell-from-stock and service management scenarios. EBRR covers IFRS 15 functionality, so we'll share some features and show a system example for revenue allocation. Many management accounting features are incorporated into EBRR, for which we give you an overview. Then, we'll provide insight into the configuration of EBRR. Finally, we'll discuss its availability in both on-premise SAP S/4HANA and SAP S/4HANA Cloud.

7.2.1 Principles of Event-Based Revenue Recognition

EBRR has its origins in the public cloud and thus naturally follows cloud principles. Thus, SAP has ensured easy setup, simplified period-end closing, and a high level of transparency and traceability through integration into the Universal Journal. These properties are applied in all business scenarios and are available on-premise too.

Real-Time Matching Principle for Cost of Sales and Revenues

Revenue recognition postings are generated simultaneously with the source documents account assigned to the customer project and directly stored in the Universal Journal. In this way, a real-time matching principle is provided for cost of sales and revenues. This allows you to always have up-to-date margin reporting for revenue-generating cost objects such as customer projects or sales orders. Because market segment attributes are derived and stored in the journal entry too, you also get market segment margin reporting that is always current.

Figure 7.44 illustrates the general posting logic of EBRR with the example of the time confirmation on customer project. A pretty similar example was shown in Section 7.1.4 with the journal entries in Figure 7.9. The source document—here, a time confirmation—creates two separate journal entries: one journal entry for the initial source document (here, the time confirmation posted as the management accounting document), and a second for the matching revenue recognition journal entry.

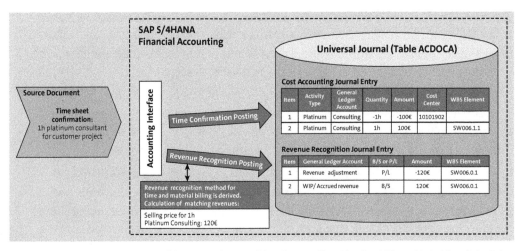

Figure 7.44 Event-Based Revenue Recognition Supporting the Real-Time Matching Principle

The revenue recognition method is derived depending on the contract type. Here, the revenue is calculated based on the selling price of the provided service—Platinum Consulting (refer to our T&E billing example in Section 7.1.4).

The calculated realized revenue is posted to the **Revenue Adjustment** P&L account and activated on the **Accrued Revenue** balance sheet account.

A posting overview based on a graphical t-accounts representation for the single process steps on a customer project is shown in Figure 7.45. The general ledger accounts that are account assigned to the project are tagged with "PRO".

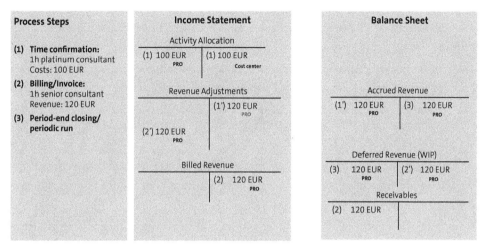

Figure 7.45 General Posting Logic of EBRR with Cost-Based Revenue Recognition

This posting logic is the same for a cost-based POC method in a fixed-price contract type (refer to Section 7.1.6) and time and material billing when revenues are recognized already with the confirmation.

Now, let's discuss each of the three steps:

1. With time confirmation, revenues are realized on the **Revenue Adjustment** income statement account and capitalized in the balance sheet with the **Accrued Revenue** general ledger account (refer to the posting examples in Figure 7.9 and Figure 7.33).

2. The customer invoice posts billed revenue on the income statement account. In this case, the revenue needs to be event-based deferred because revenue realization already took place with the confirmation. The **Deferrals Revenue** balance sheet general ledger account is credited (refer to Figure 7.23). Debiting the **Revenue Adjustment** general ledger account with 120 EUR takes its balance to zero on the customer project. The realized revenue of the project is now shown on the **Billed Revenue** account.

3. The accrued and deferred revenue will be balanced at period-end (refer to the journal entry shown in Figure 7.32). Because balance sheet corrections don't influence profitability reporting, they are only made with the period-end run and are not event based.

The revenue adjustment is a P&L general ledger account on which recognized revenues are shown temporarily. When the project is completed, this general ledger account will be balanced to zero—just like the balance sheet accounts for accrued and deferred revenue.

Now let's turn to the next principle of EBRR.

Universal Journal Integration

As you've already seen in the posting examples in Section 7.1.4, EBRR is fully integrated with the general ledger, and the revenue recognition data is stored in the Universal Journal, just as cost and revenue data is. Thanks to this integration, you're free of the limitations imposed by periodic processes and different table structures for the applications.

This principle avoids the need for any reconciliation between revenue recognition data and the general ledger. Regardless of which day of the month it is, cost and revenue information are reconciled and up to date. The same entities and semantics are used, such as the general ledger account, the ledger, or the currency fields. This also greatly simplifies the period-end close process.

As revenue recognition data is stored in the general ledger, the data inherits its functionality and its line item attributes (e.g., ledger, currency, and profitability segment), enabling new reporting insights.

Now let's look at Figure 7.46, which shows some of the revenue recognition postings created in the example earlier in Section 7.1.4 on the T&E contract type. The first journal entry is the manual accrual, the second is the reaction of the write-off, and the third is the EBRR journal entry for the time confirmation.

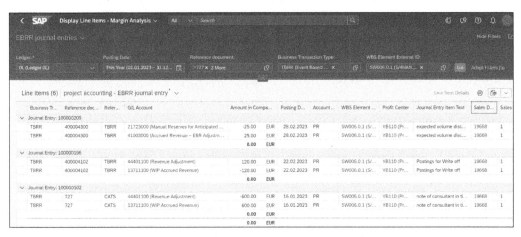

Figure 7.46 EBRR Journal Entries for Customer Project SW006

Let's direct our attention to some key **Line Items** attributes:

- **Business Transaction Type**
  As already mentioned, there is a separate business transaction type used for event-driven revenue recognition to identify these documents easily (**TBRR**).

- **Reference document/Ref. Doc type**
  For every revenue recognition journal entry, you get the reference document and the reference document type. This provides a link from the revenue recognition

journal entry to the source document, and vice versa, which simplifies tracing and reviewing.

- **Posting Date**
  The posting date is the same as the posting date of the referenced business transaction. For manual accruals—first journal entry—and period-end postings, the posting date is the last day of the period.

- **Account Assignment Type**
  This field in the Universal Journal qualifies the real account assignment. It's needed because the system now provides multiple account assignments in parallel in one journal entry item for some scenarios. The real account assigned cost object is only relevant for follow-up processes such as revenue recognition, overheads, and settlement. Here, **PR** indicates assignment to a project/WBS element.

- **WBS Element/Sales Order Item**
  In this example, these are both provided in one journal entry. The real account assignment in all revenue recognition lines is defined with **PR**, the project WBS element. Therefore, the revenue recognition postings—including the balance sheet journal item—are real accounts assigned to the WBS element. The assigned sales order item is just an additional attribute, which you need to derive the additional profitability attributes and to determine the contract data (see the posting examples and reporting in Section 7.1).

- **Profit Center**
  The profit center is derived from the project billing element master and applied to all assigned postings, including the revenue recognition balance sheet accounts.

- **Journal Entry Item Text**
  This text can be filled with a note for the manual accruals (refer to Section 7.1.4). In the T&E scenario, it covers the note of the employee or the information of the write-off.

> **Note**
>
> Controlling account assignments relevant for EBRR are, for example, WBS element, sales order item, and market segment. Controlling account assignments are mandatory for P&L accounts, for which a cost element has been defined. For EBRR balance sheet journal entry items, we also set a controlling account assignment, which, in this example, is the WBS element. The account assignment to a controlling object is the prerequisite for margin reporting on this object.
>
> In addition to the controlling account assignment, there can be additional (attributed) controlling objects in parallel added in a journal entry. In this example, the sales order item and the market segment are attributed.

In our example, margin analysis is activated, thus market segment attribution is applied for the EBRR journal entry items, causing the EBRR journal entries to be part of the margin reporting (refer to Figure 7.36).

Parallel Valuation

By being integrated into the general ledger, EBRR inherits another capability to update parallel ledgers with the option of different calculated values based on the ledger's assigned accounting principle.

We inherited parallel valuation in our fixed-price example in Section 7.1.6. Let's apply different EBRR revenue recognition methods per ledger:

- In ledger OL (as discussed), we applied the cost-based POC revenue recognition method.
- In ledger 2L, we'll apply the revenue-based POC method.

When we now post, for example, a time sheet entry on the project, both ledgers are updated with the journal entries, but with different values in EBRR:

- When you refer to Figure 7.33, you see that in ledger OL, we realized revenue of 600 EUR based on the cost-based POC.
- In ledger 2L, where revenue-based POC is applied, the EBRR journal entry items are different (see Figure 7.47).

Figure 7.47 Time Sheet Journal Entries in a Parallel Ledger with Revenue-Based POC

In the revenue-based POC method, revenues are first realized with billing. Thus, the 500 EUR costs posted from the time sheet needs to be deferred and posted on a WIP general ledger account instead of accrued revenue. EBRR uses a different P&L general ledger account too: instead of revenue adjustment, now **Adjustment to Reserves for Unrealized Costs** is used.

There is an IMG activity available to activate the parallel valuation. You get to the configuration shown in Figure 7.48 via menu path **Controlling • Product Cost Controlling • Cost Object Controlling • Product Cost by Sales Order • Period-End Closing • Event-Based Revenue Recognition • Define Replacement Rules of Recognition Keys**.

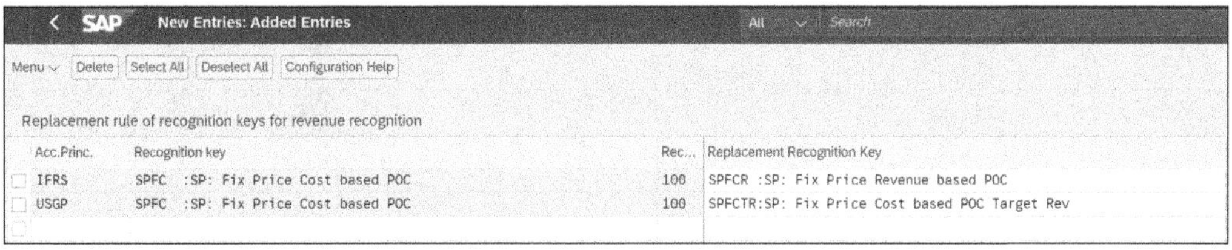

Figure 7.48 EBRR Configuration for Parallel Valuation

The replacement rules are defined per accounting principle. In Chapter 2, you learned that for each ledger, an accounting principle is assigned. In our example, the following rules apply:

- Ledger OL is the local ledger with German GAAP applied.
- For ledger 2L, the IFRS accounting principle is applied.

For the accounting principle IFRS, the revenue recognition method cost-based POC—reflected with key SPFC—is replaced with key SPFCR, revenue-based POC.

Another example for ledger-dependent valuation of EBRR was shown in our example in Section 7.1.5 where we created the manual accruals. The manual accruals we created with the Event-Based Revenue Recognition – Projects app (refer to Figure 7.27). In the app, **Ledger OL** was selected. The created journal entry was only valid for ledger OL (refer to Figure 7.29). There was no update of parallel ledger 2L. Thus, you can apply manual accruals per ledger/accounting principle.

These two examples show that EBRR supports different valuations in parallel by using parallel ledgers.

> **Note**
>
> Additionally, EBRR supports universal parallel accounting (refer to Chapter 2, Section 2.3.3 and Chapter 3, Section 3.3.7). Universal parallel accounting enables end-to-end parallel value flows, including EBRR.

Multiple Currencies

A further advantage of the integration into the general ledger is the support for parallel currencies. In Figure 7.49, we analyze the time confirmation on the project with its EBRR journal entry.

You see five columns for amounts in different currencies for the revenue recognition postings: the company code currency, global currency, object currency (defined in the customer project header; refer to Figure 7.2), transaction currency, and a freely defined currency, which needs to be activated in configuration (see Chapter 2).

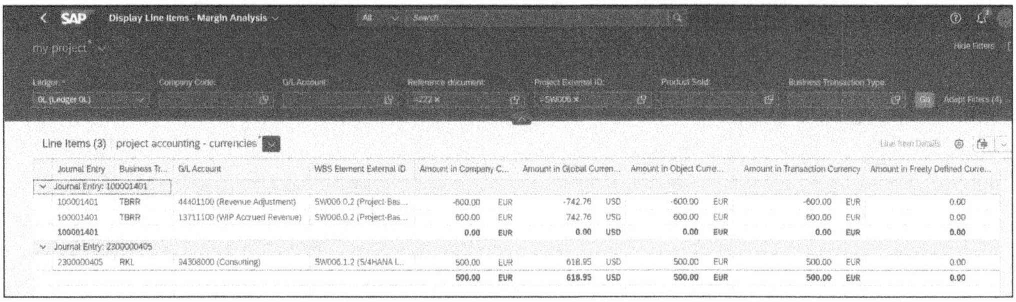

Figure 7.49 EBRR Supports Parallel Currencies

Now let's move on to the next principle, where you'll see that EBRR is highly integrated into logistics processes.

Integration into Logistics

We always take the contract data from the corresponding logistics object: the sales order item, service order item, or service contract item. There is no separate EBRR persistence. This is especially valid for the billing data:

- For the customer project scenario, as shown already in this section, the billing method, planned revenues, and billing plan details with its time frames are defined in the **Billing** tab.

- In the sell-from-stock scenario, the product sold and the selling price are stored in the sales order item (refer to Section 7.2.6).

- In the service order, the billing method is defined as fixed price or confirmation based. This influences the EBRR methods. The planned revenue values can be found in service order item pricing (refer to Section 7.2.6).

- The service contract contains a detailed billing plan with time frame, which is relevant for EBRR revenue realization. Although this isn't shown here, you can get more information at *http://s-prs.co/v569802*.

We've already seen how logistics integration plays out in the public cloud customer project scenario in Section 7.1. Let's review the most important points:

- First, the logistics object setup provided (refer to Figure 7.7) is optimized to support simple and transparent revenue recognition and margin analysis. A sales order is assigned to every customer project, and a sales order item is assigned to every WBS billing element. The sales order item defines the customer contract, where the billing method, billing plan, pricing, and revenue recognition key are defined. Thus, all contract-related information is stored in the sales order. There is no separate contract data persistency for revenue recognition purposes, which avoids redundancy and thus reconciliation issues. The required data for revenue recognition is provided already when the sales order item or contract is created.

- The **Billing** tab reflects the view of the assigned sales order items (here, **Sales Order 19668**; refer to Figure 7.5 for the customer project **Billing** tab). There are three items with different **Contract Type**s assigned, which reflect the sales order items. The **Contract Type** is identical to the sales order item category and determines the billing method. **Contract Type** and **Product** derive the revenue recognition key (discussed later in Section 7.2.7).

- The values in a billing plan are the basis for revenue recognition in a fixed-price scenario and periodic service scenario (refer to our example of a periodic service billing plan in Section 7.1.2 and Section 7.1.6).

- The sales pricing conditions, including project-specific prices, are the basis for the realized revenue related to T&E.

- For a fixed-price contract type, the planned costs are taken from the resource planning on the customer project work package, and the planned revenues are taken from the billing plan (refer to Figure 7.3).

- For the customer project, there is only one status available (in the **Stage** field), which you maintain on the customer project header (refer to Figure 7.2). No additional statuses in parallel are maintainable in other applications, especially not in accounting. This customer project status is relevant for revenue recognition. With the **Completed** status, all posted costs and revenues of assigned project elements are realized, and all balance sheet values are cleared.

- On the other hand, the logistics application (here, sales and project management) needs to ensure correct financial data and especially revenue recognition. As mentioned, SAP S/4HANA Cloud provides clear guidance and subsequent checks for completeness in the customer project setup to allow complete financial data and especially real-time revenue recognition postings and profitability segment enablement. Note the following:

  - A customer project can only be released when all work packages are assigned to a project billing element. This guarantees that all data is available for revenue recognition when a posting is done on the work package.

  - Another important aspect is the 1:1 relationship between a sales order item and a WBS billing element. This allows a clear definition of the revenue recognition key and method based on the sales order item (refer to Figure 7.7). This can't be changed.

- In SAP S/4HANA Cloud, public edition, four contract types are delivered to which unique business functionality is assigned by default. This ensures that, for these contract types, correct end-to-end processing is available out of the box by all involved applications. In particular, the correct revenue recognition methods are assigned.

7.2.2   Event-Based Revenue Recognition for Customer Projects

EBRR covers the extensive requirements of the project-based services industry for revenue recognition in the form of an easy-to-use application with a simplified period-end closing. In this industry, revenue recognition is an important component for legal accounting but also an indispensable basis for management reporting. A proportional revenue share is calculated and posted for expenses and time confirmations that have already been posted but for which no revenue has yet been invoiced. This provides the project manager with real-time information about confirmations that still need to be invoiced. The integrated margin analysis enables the controller not only to perform real-time margin reporting for the project but also for market segments such as customers, products, or lines of service. All these allow impressive new reporting insights.

In addition to the insights gained so far in this chapter, we show more features of EBRR for customer projects. Let's start with the available contract types and their realization methods. We'll then take a look at how EBRR covers some special business transactions in the customer project scenario. We'll discuss the handling of down payments and the special scenario in which there is a billing limit (known as a *cap*) agreed to with the customer in a T&E contract type.

Supported Contract Types and Realization Methods

As mentioned, revenue recognition needs to follow the sales order item contract type because it defines the billing method. Of course, the billing method has an impact on the required revenue recognition methods. With the revenue recognition method, you define when revenues and matching costs are realized. In this section, we'll look at these contract types and how revenue recognition supports them.

There are two supported contract types, T&E and fixed-price billing. The T&E contract type (similar to the usage-based billing contract type) was shown in Section 7.1.4. For revenue recognition calculation, T&E billing is simulated for each cost posting (e.g., confirmation of consulting time) on a customer project. Billing material gets mapped to the single confirmation, and the sales price is picked up in the sales pricing application (refer to Figure 7.10). Therefore, you can even get project-specific prices for revenue calculation (if maintained). You'll get the same result for revenue recognition valuation later in the billing process. The revenue recognition posting logic is similar to the cost-based POC method in the fixed-price scenario.

In the fixed-price billing scenario, the invoicing values are defined in the billing plan and fixed. There are three different revenue recognition methods, which we'll describe with t-accounts based on an example.

Example

In the customer project, planned costs of the work packages are 10,000 EUR, and the planned revenues from the billing plan are 12,000 EUR, just like our example shown previously in Figure 7.3, in the second line.

In this example, we'll post a time confirmation with costs of 500 EUR with the corresponding EBRR journal entry to the work package. Then, we'll bill 400 EUR according to the billing plan. The last step is the periodic EBRR run.

Following are the associated revenue recognition methods:

- **Cost-based POC method**

  In fixed-price contract type scenarios, EBRR calculates the POC for every single confirmation item based on the actual costs of the confirmation and the aggregated plan costs. This POC is multiplied by the planned revenues of the contract item to get the matching realized revenue for this confirmation. The planned cost comes from customer project resource planning, and planned revenues are taken out of the billing plan (refer to the example shown earlier in Figure 7.34).

  Revenues are already realized with the cost posting. For every single posting, a POC is calculated, and the matching revenues are posted by EBRR. The billing is deferred because the revenue realization happened already with the cost posting. The periodic EBRR just nets the balance sheet accounts. A complete posting logic example is shown in Figure 7.50.

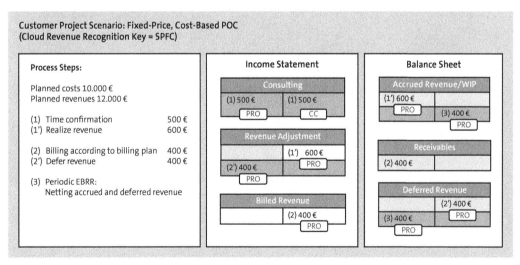

Figure 7.50 Posting Logic for Cost-Based POC Method

Revenues are already realized with the cost posting. For every single posting, a POC is calculated, and the matching revenues are posted by EBRR. The billing is deferred as the revenue realization happened already with the cost posting. The periodic EBRR just nets the balance sheet accounts.

- **Completed contract**

  In the completed contract scenario, all costs and revenues posted on the project are deferred. With the completed status, all posted costs and revenues are realized with the clearing of the balance sheet accounts (see Figure 7.51).

  During the lifetime of a project, all costs and revenues are deferred. When the completed status is set for the project, all billed revenues and posted costs are realized. In the fixed-price case, the status is also defined as completed, if no billing plan item is open.

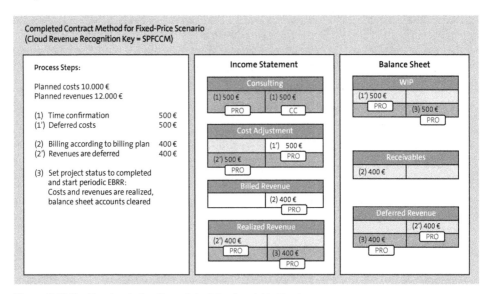

Figure 7.51 Posting Logic for Completed Contract Method

- **Revenue-based POC**

  In the revenue-based POC scenario, the costs are deferred as WIP as they occur. Realized revenues are equal to the billed revenues. With billing, revenues and the matching cost of sales are realized. If WIP exists, then it will be reduced by the realized COGS amount. If the WIP value is less than the realized cost of sales—only possible in a fixed-price scenario—reserves for missing costs are accrued for the difference.

  In the example shown in Figure 7.52, with the billing of 480 EUR, a POC of 4% is realized. The realized costs are calculated with 4% multiplied with 10,000 EUR = 400 EUR.

  There is an additional revenue recognition method available: no revenue recognition posting. If this method is applied, costs and revenues are realized as they occur. No accruals or deferrals get posted. In this case, the matching principle for costs and revenues isn't ensured.

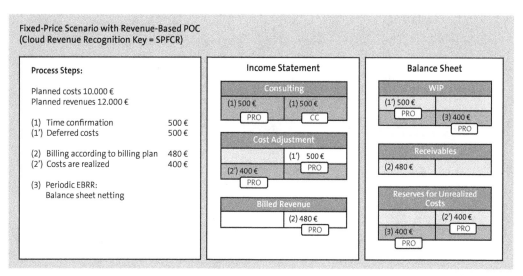

Figure 7.52 Posting Logic for Revenue-Based POC

- **Periodic service**

  We discussed this scenario in Section 7.1.6. For the periodic service contract type, revenues are realized based on the time-based billing plan (refer to Figure 7.6). In this scenario, for every billing plan item, a valid time frame needs to be maintained. Based on this time frame, EBRR distributes the realized revenues to the periods. Revenue is only realized with the periodic run (refer to the monitor in Figure 7.35). Therefore, the billed revenue is completely deferred.

  A posting logic example is shown in Figure 7.53. Because the service time starts already in January, EBRR realizes a 12th of the planned billing amount = 1,000 EUR. The billing amount in February is completely deferred because the revenue realization is done with the periodic EBRR run.

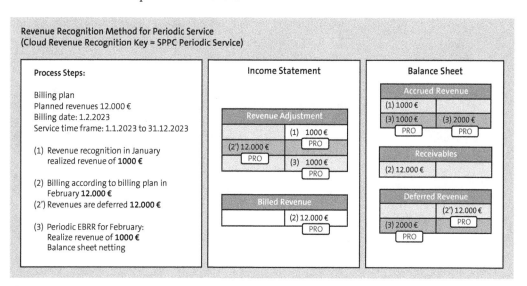

Figure 7.53 Revenue Recognition Posting Logic for Periodic Service

Down Payments

With IFRS 15, you must net received down payments with the accrued revenues. We'll show how this is done with EBRR via an example. Let's request a down payment from the customer for our customer project. For this, we add a down payment request in the billing plan of a T&E contract item, as shown in Figure 7.54.

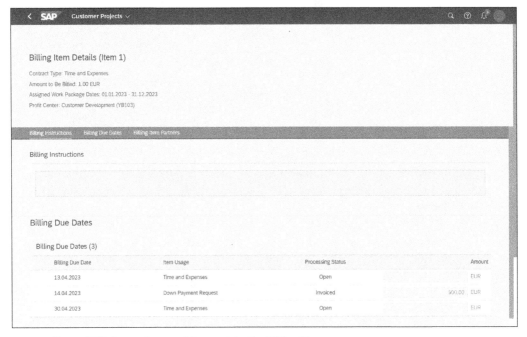

Figure 7.54 Down Payment Request in the Billing Plan

The second billing plan item is the **Down Payment Request** of 500 EUR. Let's issue the down payment request to the customer with the Manage Project Billing app (refer to Figure 7.15). As shown in Figure 7.55, select customer project **SW010**, and click on **Prepayment**. A popup appears with the **Down Payment** of **500 EUR**, which was planned in the billing plan.

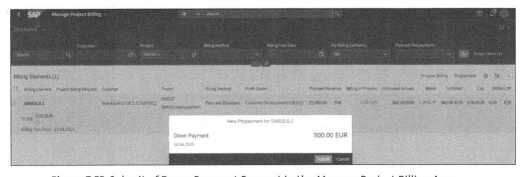

Figure 7.55 Submit of Down Payment Request in the Manage Project Billing App

As the next step, enter the time confirmation of a consultant of 8 hours on the project. Both created journal entries are shown in Figure 7.56.

Figure 7.56 Created Journal Entries for the Project, Including the Down Payment Request

The time confirmation has led to an accrued revenue of 960 EUR as the second journal entry item. The down payment request is reflected with the journal entry on the bottom. It's posted as a contract liability from the down payment request and the account assigned to the project. This down payment request of 500 EUR is visible in reporting.

As the next step, we post the incoming payment of 500 EUR from the customer with the Post Incoming Payment app (F1345; see Chapter 5, Section 5.4). With this, a down payment received is posted to the project, which is recognized in EBRR.

Start the Event-Based Revenue Recognition – Projects app, and select project **SW010** to get the values shown in Figure 7.57.

In the **Balance Sheet** section, you'll see the **Accrued Revenue** of 960 EUR and the **Down Payment Liabilities**, updated with the received payment from the customer of 500 EUR.

Select the **Revalue** button, and then click the **Simulate** button in the popup, and you'll get the results shown in Figure 7.58.

Note that EBRR nets the accrued revenue with the down payment received; the **Accrued Revenue** is decreased by 500 EUR from 960 EUR to 460 EUR, and **Down Payment Liabilities** is cleared. The posted journal entry is shown in Figure 7.59.

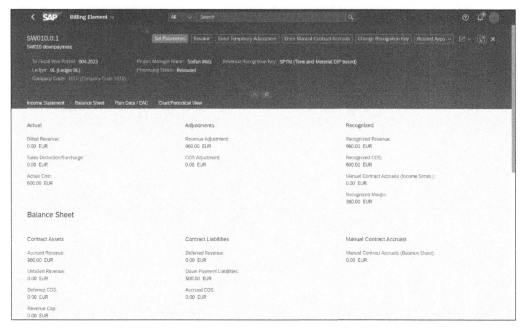

Figure 7.57 Event-Based Revenue Recognition – Projects App with Down Payment

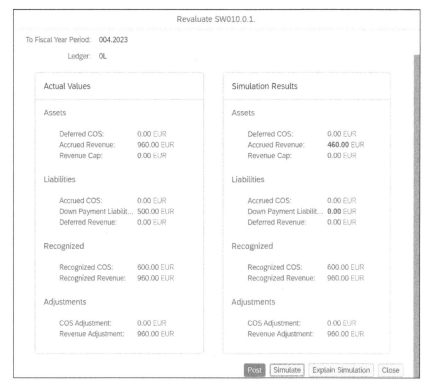

Figure 7.58 EBRR Simulation with Down Payment Netting

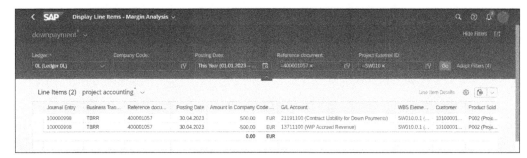

Figure 7.59 EBRR Journal Entry for Down Payment Netting

> **Note**
>
> The netting of down payment received and accrued revenue in EBRR can be controlled by configuration. Because it's an IFRS 15 requirement in SAP S/4HANA Cloud, public edition, it's active by default.

Caps

In this business scenario, there is a T&E agreement with the contract, but only until a limit. Let's look at an example to see how this is reflected in EBRR. First, a cap needs to be maintained in the **Billing** tab of the Customer Projects app, as shown in Figure 7.60.

Figure 7.60 Contract Item with a Cap Assigned

For the third contract item, a T&E contract item, an **Amount Cap** of 1000 EUR is maintained. As the next step, two employees confirm time to the project. The journal entries are shown in Figure 7.61:

- Employee 1, personnel number **50000635**, confirmed 8 hours, which leads to an accrued revenue of 960 EUR
- Employee 2, personnel number **50001077**, confirmed 8 hours, which leads to an accrued revenue of 800 EUR

Overall, this leads to an accrued revenue of 1,760 EUR, which is higher than our maintained cap of 1,000 EUR.

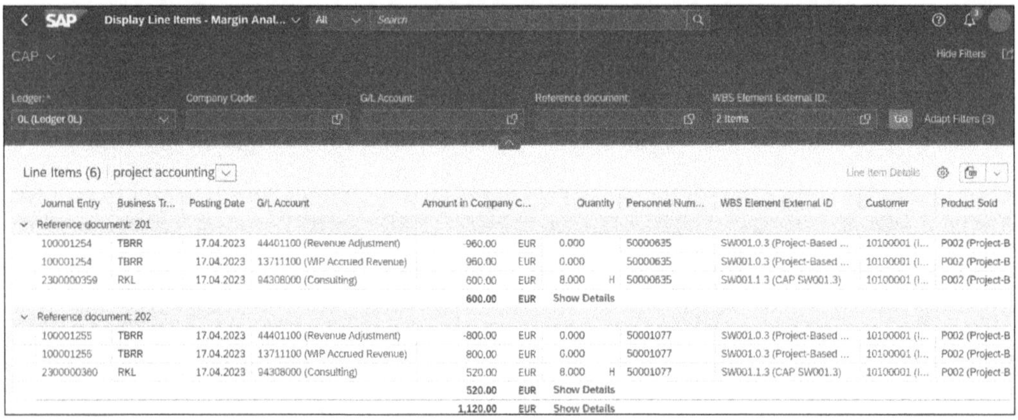

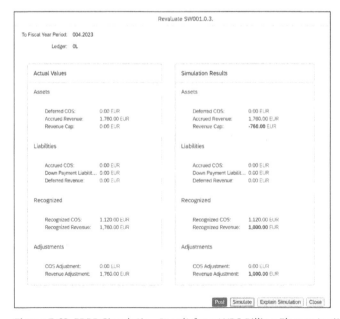

Figure 7.61 Confirmations of Two Employees on a Cap Billing Item

Start the Event-Based Revenue Recognition – Projects app to check how EBRR reacts. Select our project, click the **Revalue** button in the popup, and click **Simulate** to get the result shown in Figure 7.62.

Figure 7.62 EBRR Simulation Result for a WBS Billing Element with Active Cap

On the top-right part of the screen, you see in the **Simulation Results** a **Revenue Cap** adjustment of –760 EUR. Like the asset, the recognized revenue is decreased from 1,760 EUR to 1,000 EUR.

Click the **Post** button to get the overview of all EBRR data, as shown in Figure 7.63.

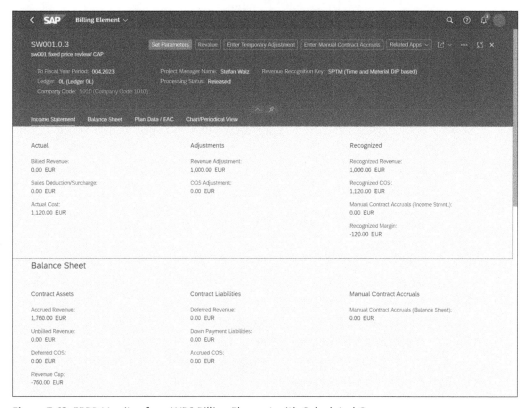

Figure 7.63 EBRR Monitor for a WBS Billing Element with Calculated Cap

The **Recognized Revenue** is now reduced to 1,000 EUR. On the bottom of the screen, a **Revenue Cap** of -760 EUR is shown. Let's take a look at the posted journal entry in Figure 7.64.

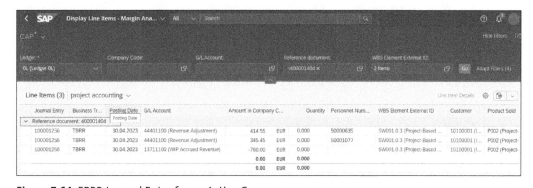

Figure 7.64 EBRR Journal Entry for an Active Cap

With the third journal entry item, the balance sheet WIP accrued revenue is reduced; with the first two journal entry items, the realized revenue is reduced. To allow the enhanced reporting of revenue follows employee (Section 7.2.4), the reduced amount is distributed on the employee level. The share per employee is determined on the basis of the originally realized revenues per employee (refer to Figure 7.61). Thus, the reduced share of employee 50000635 is 960 EUR ÷ 1,760 EUR × 760 EUR = 414.55 EUR.

7.2.3   IFRS 15 Capabilities

With IFRS 15, new requirements have been placed on revenue recognition. We'll explain how EBRR supports the main requirements in this section.

EBRR covers the common IFRS 15 requirements in a customer project and sell-from-stock scenario:

- Supports the five-step model defined for IFRS 15, which we'll explore in this section
- Provides an option for a multielement arrangement within one sales order
- Differentiates accrued revenue/contract assets and deferred revenue/contract liabilities
- Differentiates accrued revenue by contract asset and unbilled revenue

The following provides some insight into the functionality. Although we won't cover all the details, the basic principles should become clear:

- The IFRS 15 functionality is highly integrated into the logistic processes. Therefore, you define which items you bundle in the contract item, and the transaction prices and standalone selling prices (SSPs) are part of the sales order pricing scheme.
- The matching principle of cost and revenues is provided and is now based on allocated revenues.
- The calculation results are posted in the Universal Journal. Therefore, IFRS 15 functionality is integrated in the Universal Journal; there is no custom persistence for the IFRS 15 functionality.

Let's consider an example where revenue needs to be allocated between contract (sales order) items, that is, a *multielement arrangement*.

Five-Step Approach

With IFRS 15, revenue recognition needs to follow the five-step model:

1. Identify the contracts with the customers.
2. Identify the separate performance obligations in the contract.
3. Determine the transaction price.
4. Allocate the transaction price to the different performance obligations in the contract.
5. Recognize revenue when the performance obligation is satisfied.

We'll show these steps in the following example. Say you've concluded a contract with a customer that consists of a bundle of two items: a fixed-price service for the software implementation and a software license valid for eight months.

The contract price for the license and the implementation is 10,000 EUR each. If you sell the implementation standalone, the price would be 15,000 EUR. For this contract item, you're giving a discount of 5,000 EUR. Because you only give this discount in combination with the license, you must also take it into account in the revenue recognition of the license item.

Let's see how this example looks in the system:

1. **Create the customer project**
   We'll create a new customer project for this example. In Figure 7.65, you see the **Billing** tab for the two sales order items.

Figure 7.65 Billing Tab with Bundled Sales Order Items and SSPs

2. **Define the performance obligation**
   This is done with the creation of the sales order items. The performance obligation is equal to the sales order item. In this example, the fixed-price item for project implementation is one performance obligation (equal to the sales order item), and a second performance obligation comes with the license.

3. **Determine the transactions prices and SSP**
   For revenue allocation purposes, there is an additional pricing condition available—the standalone selling price (SSP). This reflects the price that you usually realize when you sell it standalone. This price can be flexibly defined for each sales order item.

   In contract item 1, software **License**, the **Amount to Be Billed** and the **SSP** are the same: **10,000 EUR**. For item 2, **Fixed price Consulting**, you define an **Amount to Be Billed** of **10,000 EUR**. The SSP is **15,000 EUR**.

4. **Allocate revenues**

   With the sales order creation, the system automatically calculates the allocated revenues for the two items based on the **SSP** and the **Amount to Be Billed**. In IFRS 15 terms, the sales order corresponds to the revenue contract, and one sales order item corresponds to one performance obligation.

   The revenues to be generated from the two items, that is, **Amount to Be Billed**, are added together to get 20,000 EUR. This amount is divided among the positions in the ratio of the **SSP**—here, 2:3 (license to fixed-price item). This leads to the result shown in Figure 7.66 in the Allocated Revenue app within the SAP_BR_SALES_Accountant role.

   In this app, all sales order items are listed that are bundled and for which subsequent revenue is allocated.

Figure 7.66 Allocated Revenue Calculation for a Sales Order Bundle

   The **Standalone Selling Price** and **Transaction Price** (taken from **Amount to Be Billed**) are taken from the sales and distribution pricing conditions (refer to Figure 7.65). The **Allocated Revenue** column on the far right shows the calculated revenue per sales order item.

   For the fixed-price item, the allocated revenue is calculated as follows: 3/5 of the aggregated amount to be billed—20,000 EUR—leads to an allocated revenue of **12,000 EUR**.

   For the license item, the allocated revenue is calculated as follows: 2/5 of the aggregated amount to be billed—20,000 EUR—leads to an allocated revenue of **8,000 EUR**.

   – Item 1: 20,000 EUR ÷ 25,000 EUR × 15,000 EUR = 12,000 EUR

   – Item 2: 20,000 EUR ÷ 25,000 EUR × 10,000 EUR = 8,000 EUR

5. **Recognize revenue when performance obligation is satisfied**

   For revenue recognition, the allocated revenue is taken as plan revenue.

Let's look at how this revenue allocation impacts the license and the periodic service. We check the billing plan item in Figure 7.67.

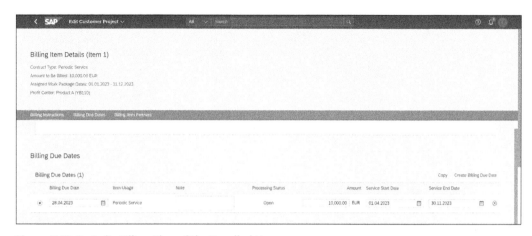

Figure 7.67 Periodic Billing Plan of the Bundled License

The planned billing amount of **10,000 EUR** is valid for the eight-month period from April to November 2023.

Let's start the revenue recognition calculation with the Event-Based Revenue Recognition – Projects app (see Figure 7.68). Select **Ledger 2L**, the IFRS ledger, and the period **004.2023**, the first period the billing plan item is valid.

Figure 7.68 Revenue Recognition for the Bundled License Item

The system calculates for April 2023, the first valid month of the license period, 1/8 of the allocated revenue of 8,000 EUR. You can see the **Planned Revenue** of **8,000 EUR** on the bottom of the screen with a **Recognized Revenue** of **1,000 EUR**.

The fixed-price scenario will also take the allocated revenue as base, so 12,000 EUR is taken as planned revenue. If a confirmation is now posted on the fixed-price project, then the POC is multiplied with the allocated revenue of 12,000 EUR and not with the planned billing amount of 10,000 EUR to get the recognized revenue.

> **Note**
>
> The multielement arrangement functionality we've seen here is only available in SAP S/4HANA Cloud, public edition, and is only possible within one sales order in the sell-from-stock and the customer project scenarios.
>
> The functionality can be activated per ledger. In SAP S/4HANA Cloud, public edition, it's enabled per default for the IFRS ledger. Additionally, the SSP functionality can be controlled on the sales order item category.

Treatment of Balance Sheet Values

EBRR covers the IFRS 15 requirements regarding the presentation of balance sheet accounts in the financial statement. IFRS 15 differentiates between contract liability, contract asset, and receivables. In this context, EBRR distinguishes between deferred revenue and accrued revenue:

- EBRR *accrues* revenue once a good or service is provided to the customer; one of several examples was shown previously in Figure 7.9.
- EBRR *defers* the billed revenue from the customer invoice; you saw an example earlier in Figure 7.23.

Additionally, accrued revenue and unbilled revenue for the contract assets must be distinguished. Confirmations that haven't yet been billed are generally treated as contract assets. You can now also distinguish between accrued revenue and unbilled revenue. If the asset can't be billed to the customer, you handle it as accrued revenue. If it's just not billed but it's principally billable, you can qualify the contract assets as unbilled revenue.

> **Note**
>
> You can get additional information regarding the multielement arrangement functionality covered by EBRR at the following links:
> - *http://s-prs.co/v493803*
> - *http://s-prs.co/v493804*

7.2.4   Supported Management Accounting Features

As you've seen in the examples, EBRR covers more than balance sheet valuation. Several management accounting features are also incorporated as summarized in the following list:

- **Real-time margin and WIP reporting**
  EBRR supports the real-time matching principle for revenue and cost of sales. With this principle, you get real-time margin for cost objects such as projects and market segments, but also real-time WIP information. For example, this covers the request of project managers to get an up-to-date view of the margin and the unbilled revenue of the project. You've seen this event-based approach before, in which we post the EBRR journal entry with the prima nota, in the several project scenarios, and you'll see it in Section 7.2.6 for sell-from-stock and service scenarios.

- **Provisioning of market segment attributes**
  Market segment attributes are derived and applied for all revenue recognition journal entry items. When EBRR creates a journal entry, it uses the Universal Journal integrated market segment functionality to get the market segment attributes derived and stored in the journal entry. You've seen this in the preceding project scenarios—for example, refer to Figure 7.36—and you'll see it for sales and service scenarios as well. The derived market segment attributes are persisted in the revenue recognition P&L and balance sheet items. With this functionality and the support of the matching principle for cost of sales and revenues, EBRR is a prerequisite for the new margin analysis application.

- **Consulting margin** reporting
  In the professional service business, it's a key reporting requirement to trace the realized revenue per consultant: the revenue needs to follow the employee. The margin by consultant can be calculated based on the consultant's confirmation on customer projects and the recognized revenue. Margin is recognized revenue (regardless of whether billing has already been done) minus the consultant's confirmation costs. With the T&E contract type, employee information is applied in all journal entry items end to end from the consultant's confirmation over EBRR to billing. You can follow this with the time confirmation shown earlier in Figure 7.61 and the billing document shown earlier in Figure 7.23. Thus, revenue follows employee reporting is enabled.

  The consultant's realized margin is visible in the Project Profitability app. Select entries under **Full Name** (employee name) and **Project** to get the margin reporting shown in Figure 7.69. In this report, you get information about the realized margin by single consultants based on all customer projects.

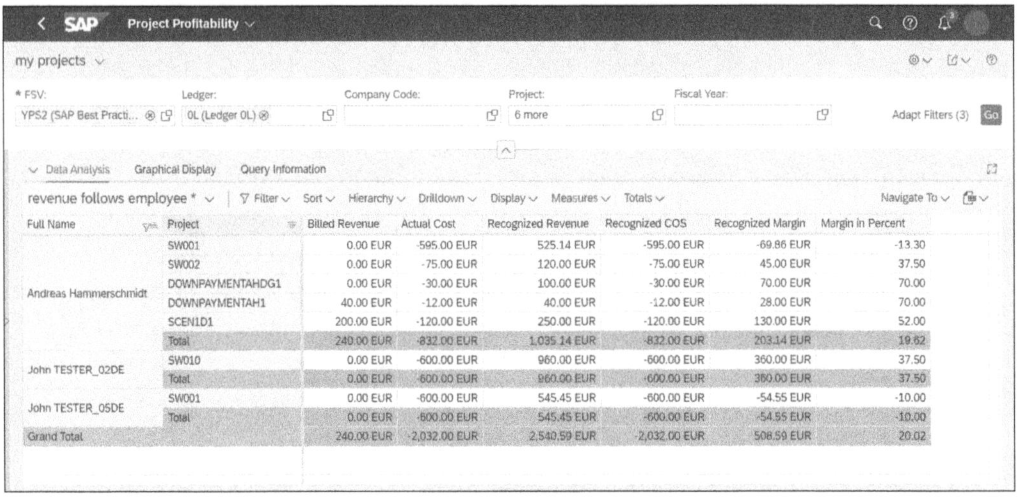

Figure 7.69 Realized Margin per Employee in Customer Project Scenario

- **Margin per contributing profit center/origin profit center**

  In professional service businesses, it's common for employees from different profit centers to contribute to a customer project. The customer project has one responsible profit center, for which revenues are realized and invoiced to the customer. The supporting profit centers want to get a share of the realized margin.

  To support the requirement to show the project margin not only for the responsible project profit center but also for the contributing profit centers, there is a new field in the Universal Journal: **Origin Profit Center**. This is derived from the employee. As you've seen previously in the T&E scenario, the employee is available for each journal entry item. Thus, you write the origin profit center for all journal entry items, including WIP and realized revenue. An example for a posting is shown in Figure 7.70.

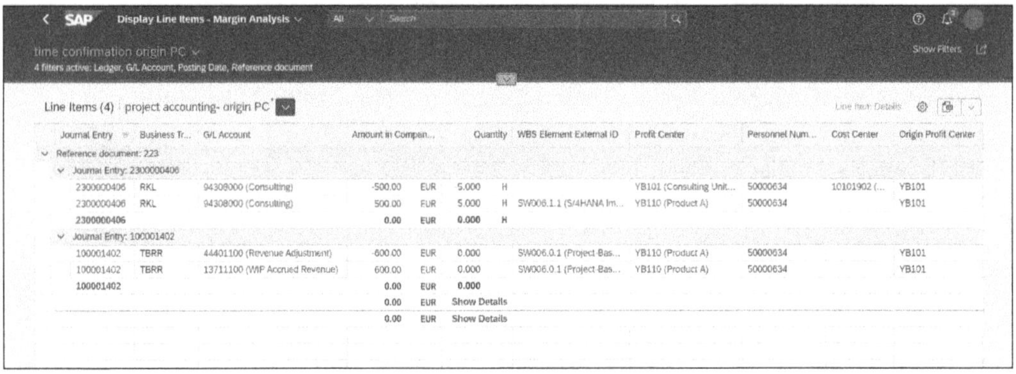

Figure 7.70 Journal Entry with Origin Profit Center

Profit Center YB110 is taken from the project master (refer to Figure 7.5). The **Origin Profit Center YB101** is taken from the employee master. When you look at the project with an origin profit center view, then you get costs and realized revenues for the supporting origin profit center **YB101**.

An example for such reporting is available with the Project Profitability app, as shown in Figure 7.71. For project **SW006**, the responsible profit center **YB110** realized a margin of 1,875 EUR with a margin of 22.06%. In this case, this margin was realized by three employees of origin profit center **YB101**.

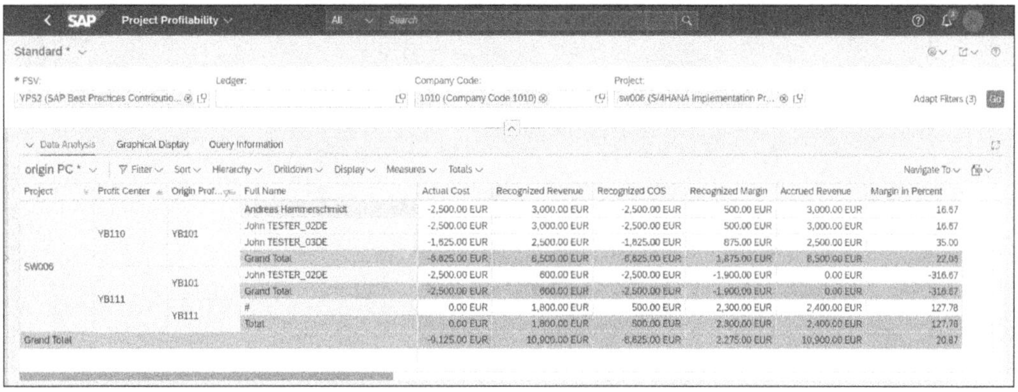

Project	Profit Center	Origin Prof...	Full Name	Actual Cost	Recognized Revenue	Recognized COS	Recognized Margin	Accrued Revenue	Margin in Percent
	YB110	YB101	Andreas Hammerschmidt	-2,500.00 EUR	3,000.00 EUR	-2,500.00 EUR	500.00 EUR	3,000.00 EUR	16.67
			John TESTER_02DE	-2,500.00 EUR	3,000.00 EUR	-2,500.00 EUR	500.00 EUR	3,000.00 EUR	16.67
			John TESTER_03DE	-1,625.00 EUR	2,500.00 EUR	-1,625.00 EUR	875.00 EUR	2,500.00 EUR	35.00
SW006			Grand Total	-6,625.00 EUR	6,500.00 EUR	-6,625.00 EUR	1,875.00 EUR	8,500.00 EUR	22.06
	YB111	YB101	John TESTER_02DE	-2,500.00 EUR	600.00 EUR	-2,500.00 EUR	-1,900.00 EUR	0.00 EUR	-316.67
			Grand Total	-2,500.00 EUR	600.00 EUR	-2,500.00 EUR	-1,900.00 EUR	0.00 EUR	-316.67
		YB111	#	0.00 EUR	1,800.00 EUR	500.00 EUR	2,300.00 EUR	2,400.00 EUR	127.78
			Total	0.00 EUR	1,800.00 EUR	500.00 EUR	2,300.00 EUR	2,400.00 EUR	127.78
Grand Total				-9,125.00 EUR	10,900.00 EUR	-6,625.00 EUR	2,275.00 EUR	10,900.00 EUR	20.87

Figure 7.71 Origin Profit Center Profitability

The additional analysis for employee and origin profit center you've seen so far is available for T&E scenarios as you get the billed revenue and the EBRR journal entry items per employee. To have such reporting for the fixed-price scenario too, a revenue recognition method is provided for EBRR.

- **Calculating target revenue in fixed-price scenarios**
  In a fixed-price scenario, to provide information about the revenue, an employee would generate whether they worked for a T&E contract. You calculate this value during revenue recognition too and post it as target revenue. This has no impact on legal reporting; it's just for management accounting purposes.

  This EBRR scenario is controlled with a revenue recognition key, which we applied for ledger 3L (refer to Figure 7.48 for the replacement topic) when using the target revenue method for accounting principle USGB. The time sheet confirmation on the fixed-price project we showed previously in Figure 7.33 gets two additional journal entries for target revenue with this method, as shown in Figure 7.72.

  The third and fourth journal entry items of the EBRR journal entry reflect the target revenue and are posted with the general ledger account **49999900 (Clearing Target Revenue Reallocation)**. Journal entry item 3 is posted with the employee **500000634** and the derived **Origin Profit Center** of **YB101**. The profit center of the fixed-price item is **YB111**. With this journal entry item, the **Origin Profit Center YB101** gets a recognized revenue of 600 EUR assigned.

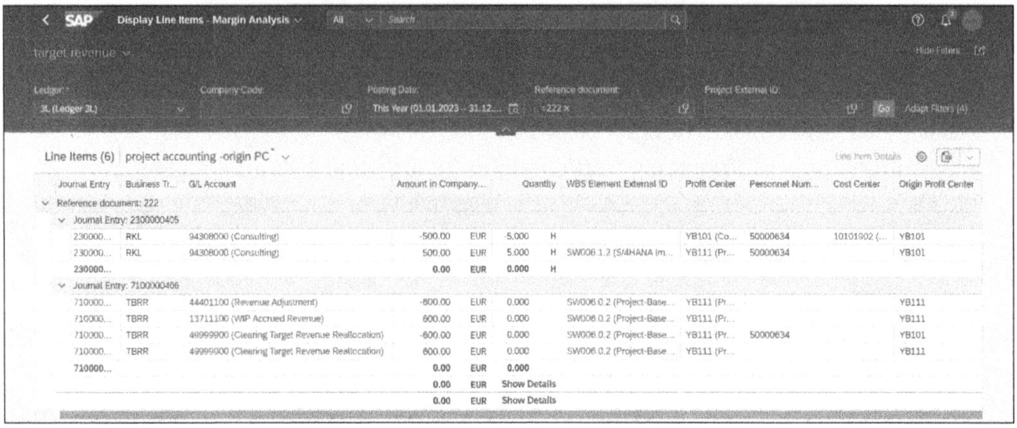

Figure 7.72 Target Revenue Provided by EBRR

> **Note**
>
> Origin profit center and the EBRR target revenue method are only available in SAP S/4HANA Cloud, public edition. These topics are described in detail at *http://s-prs.co/v493805*.

- **Prediction and periodic plan data**

  In the professional services scenario we discussed previously (refer to Figure 7.4), the resource planning can be distributed across periods. This provides you with cost planning for the project on exact periods. Based on the costs by period, the matching plan revenues per period are calculated by EBRR. The transferred costs and calculated revenues are stored in plan table ACDOCP, which has the same structure as the Universal Journal. Therefore, plan margins for the project are available in the exact periods and become available for forecast reporting. The revenue recognition method is the same as for actuals.

  In the service contract scenario, a periodic billing plan is provided, as in the customer project scenario shown previously in Figure 7.6. For such service contracts, prediction data is calculated based on the EBRR functionality and stored in a prediction extension ledger (refer to Chapter 2, Section 2.2.3).

7.2.5   Revenue Recognition Apps

For EBRR, several apps are available to analyze data and provide periodic valuation. We'll take a closer look at them in the following sections.

Event-Based Revenue Recognition – Projects

The Event-Based Revenue Recognition – Projects app (F4767) has already been discussed extensively in this chapter. As a quick recap, it's used for manual revenue recognition and analysis for single billing element items. You get it within the SAP_BR_SALES_Accountant business role. Figure 7.73 shows the revenue recognition data and, in the header, further possible activities.

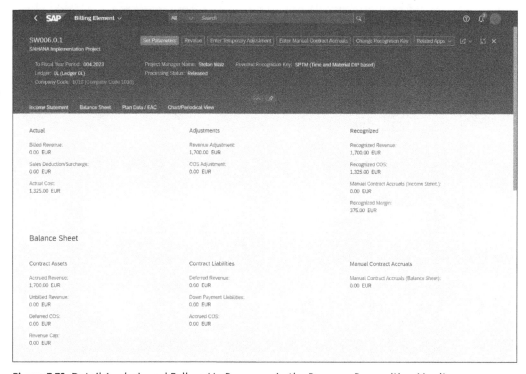

Figure 7.73 Detail Analysis and Follow-Up Processes in the Revenue Recognition Monitor

Let's walk through your options:

- **Set Parameters**
  Here you can define the period and the ledger for which you want to analyze or enter the EBRR data.

- **Revalue**
  Here you can revalue the EBRR data based on current information. When you click this button, a popup appears, as shown earlier in Figure 7.30.

- **Enter Temporary Adjustment**
  As with manual accruals, you can also enter temporary adjustments; however, these are only valid for the selected period—here **004.2023**—and are automatically cleared with the next period-end run.

- **Enter Manual Contract Accruals**
  You can enter manual contract accruals, as shown earlier in Section 7.1.5. Manual accruals are automatically cleared with project completion.

- **Change Recognition Key**

  You can change the recognition key and thus the revenue recognition method. For example, you may no longer want to do revenue recognition with this project. You can set the corresponding **No Revenue Recognition** key and start a revaluation. Then, all balance sheet values are cleared, and the posted costs and revenues are recognized.

- **Related Apps**

  You can navigate to three reporting apps: **G/L Account Line Items**, **Project – Actuals**, and **Project Profitability**.

A monitor app is available for each business scenario. In the next section, we'll see the monitor apps for service documents and sales orders. Additionally, there is a monitor for provider contracts that is only available in SAP S/4HANA Cloud, public edition.

Inspect Revenue Recognition Postings

Figure 7.74 shows the Inspect Revenue Recognition Postings app (F4008), which allows you to analyze the postings on projects—including the EBRR postings—based on a t-account presentation.

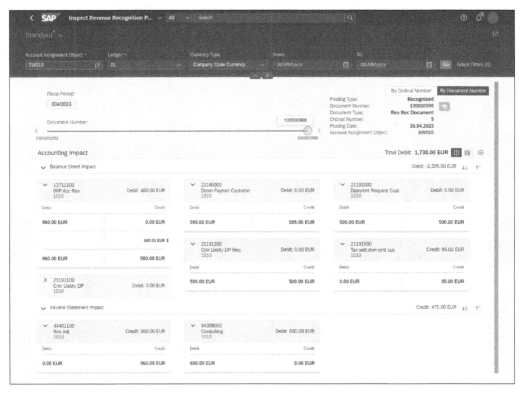

Figure 7.74 Inspect Revenue Recognition Postings App

You can select an account assignment object. Here, we've selected project **SW010**, on which we posted the down payment example. You get the amounts posted on the general ledger accounts used during the process. It's possible to trace to single documents.

Manage Event-Based Revenue Recognition Issues

In some cases, if data is missing, EBRR journal entries can't be posted in real time together with the prima nota or at the period-end run. In these cases, a log is written, which can be analyzed with the Manage Revenue Recognition Issues – Projects app (F100), as shown in Figure 7.75.

Figure 7.75 Manage Revenue Recognition Issues – Projects App

All the relevant issues are shown for the selected **Fiscal Year Period**, **Company Code**, and **Ledger**, in which the EBRR document could not be posted. In this example, there is one issue. By clicking on the **Error (1)** in the **Status** column, you get detailed information, as shown in Figure 7.76. For the WBS billing element **TESTNOCOST01.0.1**, the plan costs are missing, so the POC can't be calculated.

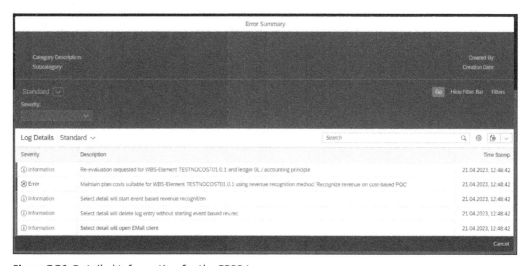

Figure 7.76 Detailed Information for the EBRR Issue

Now you can apply the plan data and click the **Reprocess** button, as shown earlier in Figure 7.75. With this the prima nota is reprocessed and the EBRR posting is created. With this the log entry will be cleared.

Such an app is available for sales orders, service documents, and provider contracts too. Additionally, the Manage Real-Time Revenue Recognition Issues app (F4101) is available, which shows the real-time issues per period and company code for all account assignment objects.

Solving all real-time issues is a prerequisite to running the periodic revenue recognition job, which we'll describe next.

Periodic Event-Based Revenue Recognition Run

You still need to run a periodic revenue recognition at period end. During the period, EBRR-relevant data can be changed in the following ways:

- The POC or project planning was adjusted by the project manager in a fixed-price contract.
- The sales price conditions have been adjusted in a time and material scenario.
- The billing plan was changed in a fixed-price or periodic service contract type.
- The status of the project changed.

In addition, the balance sheet corrections by netting accrued and deferred revenue are only done with the EBRR periodic run (refer to Figure 7.32 to see such a posting). These nettings aren't posted in real time because these postings aren't relevant for margin reporting and project control.

There is an app available for every accounting object. Let's discuss the Run Revenue Recognition Projects app (F4277), which is part of the SAP_BR_SALES_Accountant business role. Starting the app, you get the selection screen shown in Figure 7.77 for the periodic run.

To use the app, follow these steps:

1. Select the template. In our example, we selected the template for projects.
2. Decide if you want to schedule the job for a specific date or start it immediately. The job will be processed in the background.
3. Define the job parameters. The fiscal period, the company code, and the ledger are mandatory.

On the bottom bar, you have the option to use **Check** to determine if the job can be executed or if there are still some real-time issues. With **Schedule**, you start the job.

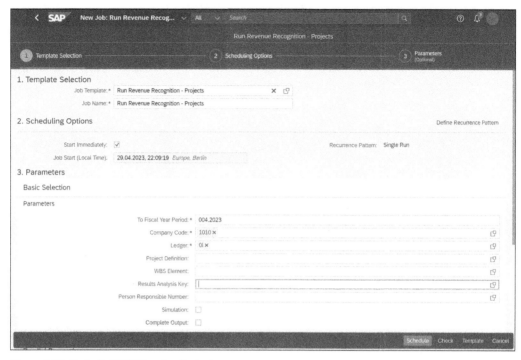

Figure 7.77 Periodic EBRR Run for Projects

Analyze Revenue Allocation Results

If you allocate revenue between performance obligations in an IFRS 15 scenario, you can analyze the allocation results with the Display Allocated Revenue app (F3039), which we showed previously in Figure 7.66. The app is part of the SAP_BR_SALES_Accountant role.

Analyze WIP Details in a T&E Scenario

In the T&E project billing scenario, enhanced WIP reporting is available via the Display Project WIP Details app (F4766), as shown earlier in Figure 7.43. With this report, you can explain the WIP based on business processes posted to the project. You'll see the single time confirmations and expense postings that haven't yet been invoiced.

On-Premise Testing and Analyzing Tools

In on-premise SAP S/4HANA, additional transactions are available, which we'll discuss in this section. Transaction REV_REC_SUP, as shown in Figure 7.78, offers a central entry to multiple analysis possibilities and to the simulation of the EBRR closing for a single account assignment object such as a billing WBS element.

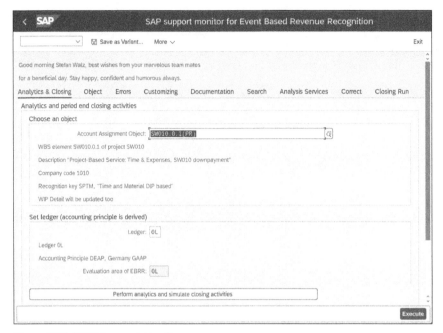

Figure 7.78 EBRR Support Monitor

On the top bar, there are several navigation options:

- **Object**
  This tab offers information about account assignment objects in your system that are relevant for EBRR.

- **Errors**
  This tab provides information about EBRR issues and includes options to resolve them.

- **Customizing**
  On this tab, you can check EBRR configuration settings.

- **Documentation**
  On this tab, you have access to links for multiple information sources.

- **Search**
  This tab provides options to analyze EBRR postings and EBRR-relevant account assignment objects.

- **Analysis Services**
  On this tab, you can simulate EBRR calculations such as the apportionment per period in a periodic service scenario or the realized revenue calculation in a T&E scenario.

- **Closing Run**
  On this tab, you can start and test the closing run for projects, services, sales orders, and provider contracts. You can also check the issue log.

By clicking the **Execute** button or the **Perform analytics and simulate closing activities** button, you can access the detailed information for the selected account assignment object (here, **SW01.0.1**), as shown in Figure 7.79.

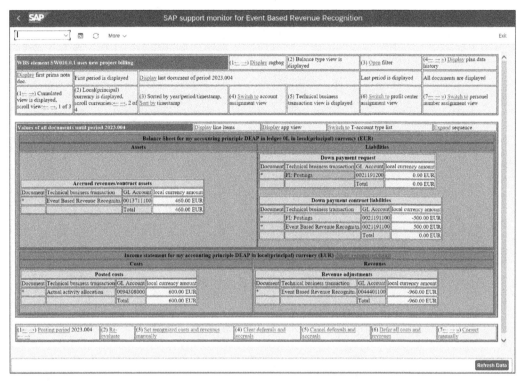

Figure 7.79 EBRR Support Monitor Detailed Information for One Account Assignment Object

Based on t-accounts, you can analyze all postings that are account assigned to the selected billing element SW010.0.1, which was our down payment example. On the top bar, you'll see links for various analysis options.

> **Note**
>
> Because EBRR is integrated into the Universal Journal, a special EBRR reporting app isn't necessary. As you've seen, revenue recognition can be analyzed via general ledger reporting.

7.2.6 Supported Business Scenarios

We'll first cover the sell-from-stock scenario, which is available in on-premise SAP S/4HANA with limitations. In addition, we'll take a quick look at the new service management, which is available in SAP S/4HANA Cloud, public edition and with a small initial scope in on-premise release 2022.

> **Note**
>
> We can't discuss these scenarios in detail in this book, so you can find more informa-
> tion in the following E-Bite and book:
>
> - For EBRR functionality, check out the E-Bite *Introducing Event-Based Revenue Recog-
>   nition (EBRR) with SAP S/4HANA* (SAP PRESS, 2023), which is available at *www.sap-
>   press.com/5679*).
>
> - For illustrations of the controlling aspects for these scenarios, refer to *Controlling
>   with SAP S/4HANA: Business User Guide* (SAP PRESS, 2021), which is available at
>   *www.sap-press.com/5282*).

Sell from Stock

This business scenario deals with the selling of inventory-managed products, including
manufactured goods. The product is planned in a sales order item, delivered by outbound delivery to the customer, and then billed. These process steps create journal
entries for COGS and billed revenue with matching EBRR journal entries. Same as in the
customer project scenario, the Universal Journal incorporated margin analysis is
updated. The market segment (technical account assignment type **EO**) is used as the
account assignment object.

Let's look at an example in the system. First, a sales order is created with Transaction
VA01, as shown in Figure 7.80.

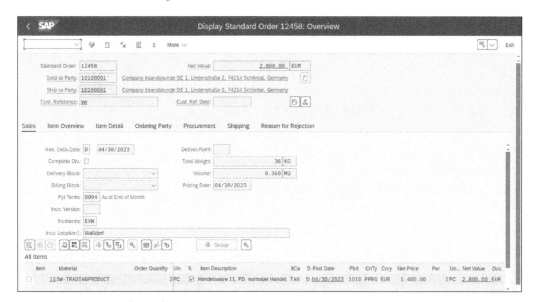

Figure 7.80 Sales Order Master

In sales order **12458**, customer (**Sold-to Party**) **10100001** is assigned. In **Item 10**, product **SW-TRADINGPRODUCT** is planned with an **Order Quantity** of **2** pcs. A price of 1,400 EUR per piece has been determined.

Next, you create a delivery for the sales order with Transaction VL01N of the planned two pieces—shown in Figure 7.81—and post goods issue.

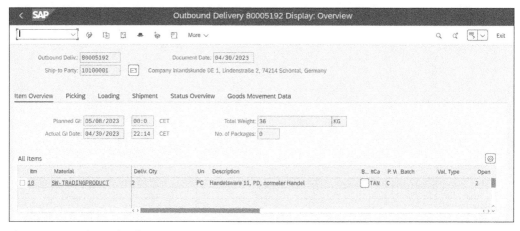

Figure 7.81 Outbound Delivery

The goods issue document is reflected in financials. You can analyze it with the Display Line Item – Margin Analysis app, as shown in Figure 7.82.

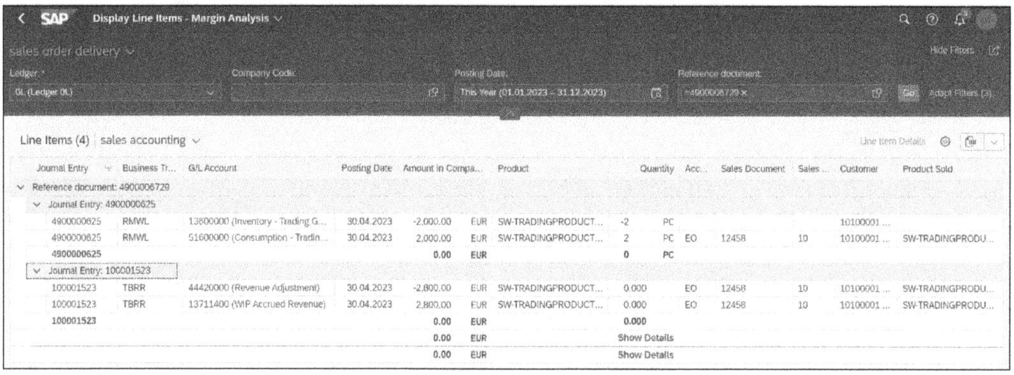

Figure 7.82 Journal Entries for Delivery

The first journal entry reflects the delivery: the **Inventory** is credited, and the **Consumption Trading** goods general ledger account is debited with the cost of sales.

At the same time, with reference to the goods issue document, the EBRR journal entry is created. The planned billing amount of 2,800 EUR for the two pieces is recognized as revenue and accrued on the **WIP Accrued Revenue** general ledger account.

Note that the COGS journal entry item and the EBRR journal entry items are account assigned to the market segment (account assignment type is **EO**). The four columns on the right show the attributes of the market segment: **Sales Document**, **Sales Item**, **Customer**, and **Product Sold**.

With this goods issue posting a margin is already realized, which you can report per sales order and market segment. You can analyze this in EBRR with the Event-Based Revenue Recognition – Sales Order app (F2441A), as shown in Figure 7.83.

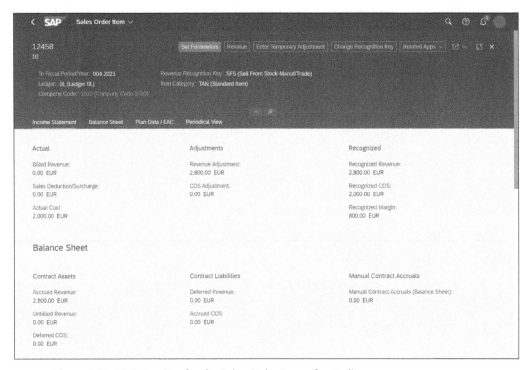

Figure 7.83 EBRR Monitor for the Sales Order Item after Delivery

In the **Income Statement** tab, the **Actual Cost** of the delivery of **2,000 EUR** and the **Recognized Revenue** of **2,800 EUR** are shown for period **004.2023**, which leads to a **Recognized Margin** of 800 EUR. In the **Balance Sheet** area, you can see the **Accrued Revenue** of **2,800 EUR**.

Now we bill in the next period with Transaction VF01. In Figure 7.84, you see the billing date **05/01/2023** and the two pieces billed for **Net Value 2,800 EUR** plus tax.

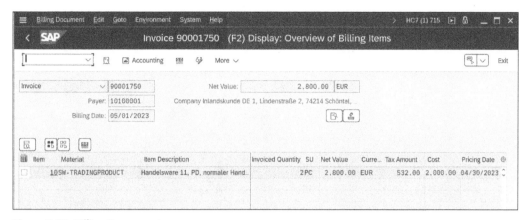

Figure 7.84 Billing Document

This leads to the financial postings shown in Figure 7.85. The first document is the accounts receivable document; the second document is the matching EBRR document. The billed revenue is deferred as we realized the revenue already with the delivery.

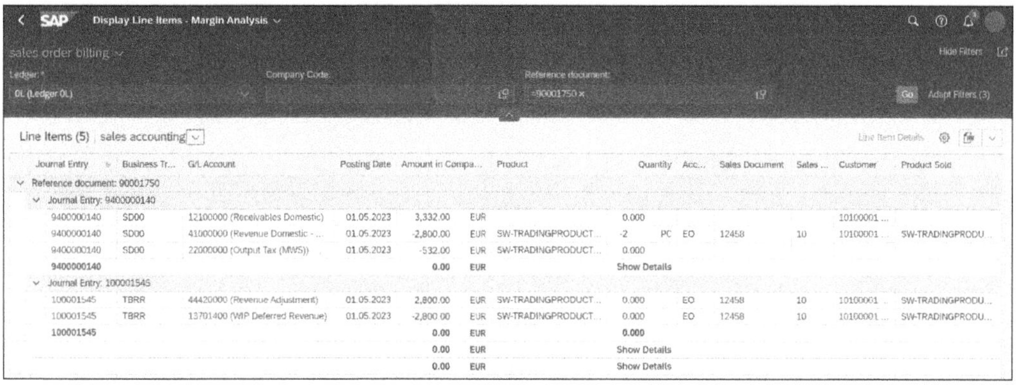

Figure 7.85 Billing Document Journal Entries

Similar to the goods issue journal entries, the **Revenue Domestic** journal entry item and the EBRR journal entry items are account assigned to the market segment (account assignment type **EO**). The attributes of the market segment are again shown in the four columns on the right: **Sales Document**, **Sales Item**, **Customer**, and **Product Sold**.

Now start the Event-Based Revenue Recognition – Sales Order app for period 05/2023, click **Revalue** and **Simulate** to get the simulation results shown in Figure 7.86.

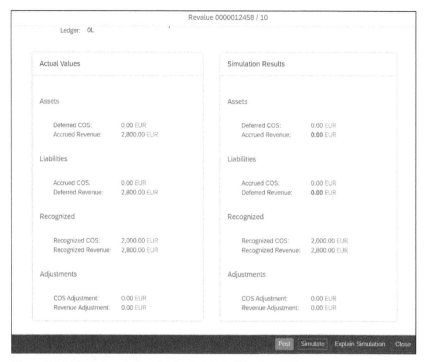

Figure 7.86 EBRR Simulation for Period 05/2023 after Billing

The simulation results on the right side show that the **Accrued Revenue** and the **Deferred Revenue** would be netted and balanced to zero. A summarization of these postings is illustrated via t-accounts in Figure 7.87.

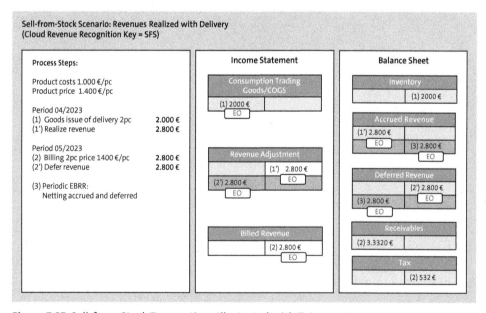

Figure 7.87 Sell-from-Stock Transactions Illustrated with T-Accounts

This example shows the delivery with the cost of sales posting in period 04/2023 and the billing with the billed revenue in period 05/2023. So, you need to accrue the revenue in period 04/2023 to get the correct financial statement and reasonable margin analysis reporting.

Depending on accounting principles and valid Incoterms, the revenue recognition method can be different. The following methods are supported:

- **Completed contract**
  Revenue and costs are realized when orders are finally billed and delivered. Cost of sales and billed revenue will be deferred in real time.

- **Revenue realization already with delivery**
  This is the same as shown in the preceding example, except that the billed revenue isn't deferred, but accrued revenue is direct netted.

- **Revenue-based POC based on plan costs and revenues**
  Cost of sales will be deferred. Revenues will be recognized with billing according to a revenue-based POC.

Service Management

Service businesses deal with service contracts and service orders. *Service contracts* can be used to close service agreements with customers. As an example, a maintenance contract can be signed for one year with the customer, for which an annual fee is due at the point in time of contract creation. EBRR uses a periodic revenue recognition like that used in the customer project scenario earlier in Section 7.1.6.

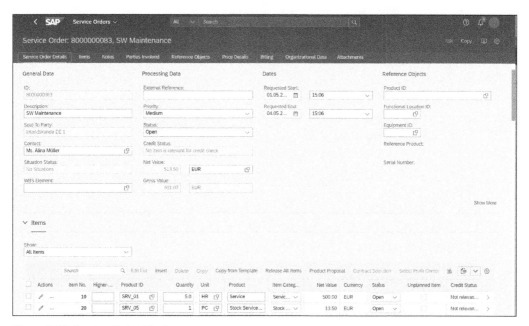

Figure 7.88 Service Order Master

The *service order* enables the provisioning and billing of services to a customer, such as a repair at the customer site, spending technician hours and spare parts. Let's briefly walk through this example to get a better understanding.

First, you create a service order and start the Manage Service Orders app (F3571A), which is part of the SAP_BR_Customer_SRVC_MGR role. In Figure 7.88, you see service order **8000000083** with two items: one with 5 hours of time planned and one for one piece of a stock service part.

You create the confirmation for the time, as well as the stock material and release for billing. The created journal entry for item **10**, the time entry, is shown in Figure 7.89.

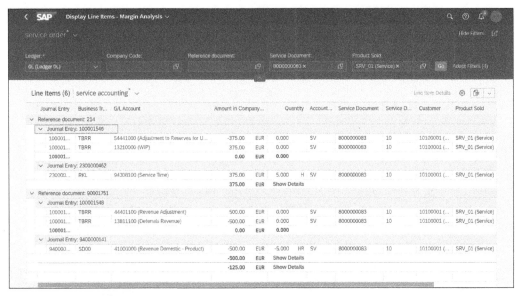

Figure 7.89 Service Order Journal Entries for the Service Time Item

The first reference document reflects the time confirmation and the EBRR journal entry. A completed contract method is applied here. Thus, the **Service Time** cost of **375 EUR** is just deferred as **WIP**. The same is valid for the second reference document, which is the billing document. The billed **Revenue Domestic - Product** of **500 EUR** is deferred with the general ledger account **Deferrals Revenue**.

Note the account assignment type **SV**; this reflects the new controlling object for service. It's assigned for the costs, billed revenue, and EBRR journal entry items together with **Service Document 8000000083** and **Service Document Item 10**. As in the customer project and sell-from-stock scenario, the market segment attributes are derived and stored in the journal entry. Here, in the two far-right columns, we show the **Customer**, which is derived from the service order, and the **Product Sold**, which is derived from the service order item.

Now start the EBRR monitor with the Event-Based Revenue Recognition – Service Documents app (F6007) for this service order item. In Figure 7.90, in the **Balance Sheet** section, you see the **Deferred COS** of **375 EUR** and the **Deferred Revenue** of **500 EUR**.

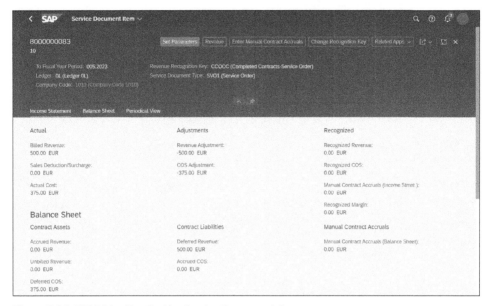

Figure 7.90 EBRR Monitor for the Service Document Item

As the service order is now finally confirmed and billed, the status completed contract is achieved. Click the **Revalue** button and then select **Simulate** to get the simulation results in Figure 7.91.

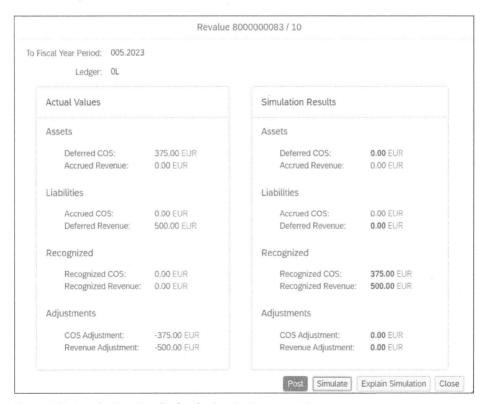

Figure 7.91 Revaluation Results for the Service Document Item

In the simulation results on the right, the deferred balance sheet values are cleared to zero, and there are now **Recognized COS** of **375 EUR** and **Recognized Revenue** of **500 EUR**.

The following additional methods are supported:

- *Cost-based POC method*, which is based on the cost and revenue plan of the service order
- *Confirmation-based revenue recognition*, where with the cost postings, revenue is realized based on the expected billing value for the service order item

> **Note**
>
> Service order and service contracts are available in the public cloud together with the EBRR functionality. With on-premise SAP S/4HANA release 2022, only very limited functionality is available. For current information about availability and restrictions, check SAP Note 2581947.

7.2.7   Activation and Configuration

In SAP S/4HANA Cloud, public edition, the business scenario defines the valuation of the processes and the revenue recognition method. This is provided by out-of-the-box best practice content. Thus, very few Customizing activities are open to the user—mainly for derivation of customer-preferred general ledger accounts. In this section, we'll walk through the configuration based on the SAP S/4HANA Cloud configuration UIs. The configuration we'll show is valid for on-premise too.

With the BCP_EXPERT business role, you can access the Manage Your Solution app and then click the **Configure Your Solution** activity to get a list of Customizing activities.

Select **event-based revenue** to see the EBRR entry, as shown in Figure 7.92.

Figure 7.92 SAP S/4HANA Cloud, Public Edition: Configuration Activity for EBRR

Click the arrow on the far right to access the configuration steps shown in Figure 7.93:

- Behind step **1**, **Maintain Settings for Event-Based Revenue Recognition**, you find the heart of EBRR. Here you define the revenue recognition methods; you can define the functionality and the general ledger accounts used for revenue recognition postings.

- In step **2** to step **5**, the derivation rules for the revenue recognition keys are defined. There are separate steps for customer projects, service documents, sell from stock, and provider contract.

- Step **6**, **Define Replacement Rules of Recognition Keys**, is used if you want to use a ledger/accounting principle-dependent valuation. We explained the use case earlier in Section 7.2.1 with the configuration UI shown previously in Figure 7.48.

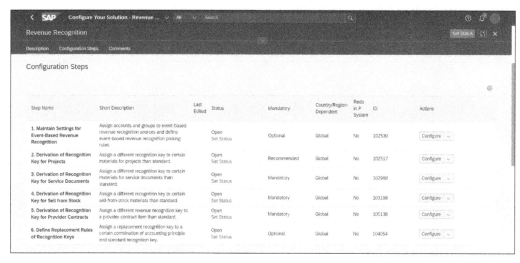

Figure 7.93 EBRR Configuration Steps

Now let's take a look into the heart of the configuration. In the first row, click the **Configure** button to arrive at the screen shown in Figure 7.94.

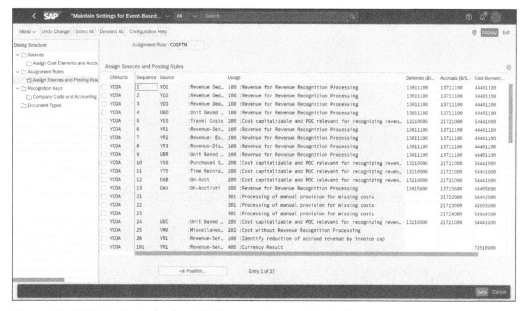

Figure 7.94 EBRR Posting Rules for a T&E Revenue Recognition Method

In the pane on the left, the **Dialog Structure** provides the main activities for EBRR control:

- **Sources**
  You can define which general ledger accounts of the prima nota postings are recognized in EBRR. For example, you can define whether a special expense account should not be included in the POC calculation.

- **Assignment Rules**
  You define the steps that are executed during EBRR calculation, as well as which general ledger accounts EBRR uses for posting.

- **Recognition Keys**
  These are assigned in the contract master as in the customer project. With the key, you define the recognition method and the assignment rule.

- **Document Types**
  You can define with which document type EBRR posts per company code and ledger, among others.

Figure 7.94 shows the execution steps of the assignment rule **COSPTM**, which is the rule we used for T&E projects. For each step, you can define general ledger accounts that you want to use for revenue recognition postings. Therefore, the three columns on the far right are available for maintenance of the balance sheet accounts for **Deferrals (B/S)**, **Accruals (B/S)**, and the P&L account (**Cost Element**) for the adjustment posting. In SAP S/4HANA Cloud, the processes are supported by best practice content, so there is no need to change the method and the revenue recognition processes, which is why the left side is grayed out and can't be changed.

As an example, let's look at line **21** to line **23**, where the **Usage 301 Processing of manual provision for missing costs** is applied. With these lines, manual accruals are enabled. You saw the three pairs of general ledger accounts in the far-right column when we applied manual accruals that were offered while applying the manual accruals for the customer project (refer to Figure 7.27).

Let's look at the recognition key shown in Figure 7.95. Select the revenue recognition key **SPTM** that we used in our T&E scenario. You see that the revenue recognition method for one key can derive different revenue recognition methods dependent on the company code and most notably the accounting principle. This allows a ledger-dependent valuation.

The **Revenue Recognition Method** column defines how the revenue recognition is calculated. For example, based on calculation methods such as the POC method or T&E billing, which is shown here, you can realize revenues already with the cost posting, with the billing, or first when the **Completed** status is activated. The option for different revenue and cost realization points in time is important above all else for covering the different accounting principle requirements.

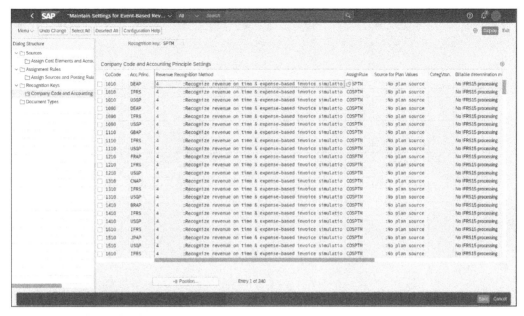

Figure 7.95 EBRR Settings per Accounting Principle

> **Note**
>
> Some Generally Accepted Accounting Principles (GAAPs) allow recognition of revenues and matching costs first with the completed contract; meanwhile, IFRS already recognizes revenues in a customer project scenario with the confirmation. You can use both valuation methods in parallel by using two parallel ledgers: one with the local GAAP assigned, and the other with IFRS. Depending on the accounting principles, you can control revenue recognition.

Now let's come back to step 2 shown earlier in Figure 7.93, the **Derivation of Recognition Key for Projects**. Select this configuration activity to arrive at the screen shown in Figure 7.96.

With the derivation of **Recognition Key**, you activate revenue recognition. Parameters for the derivation are **Contract Type** (mapped to sales order item category) and **Material** (product sold) (refer to Figure 7.7). Per default in SAP S/4HANA Cloud, revenue recognition keys and subsequent revenue recognition methods are already assigned. Therefore, revenue recognition is active and works out of the box by default. On the far right, you see the **Bundling** column: this flag controls the IFRS 15 case for revenue allocation we discussed before. If it's flagged, you can enter an SSP, and revenue allocation is calculated.

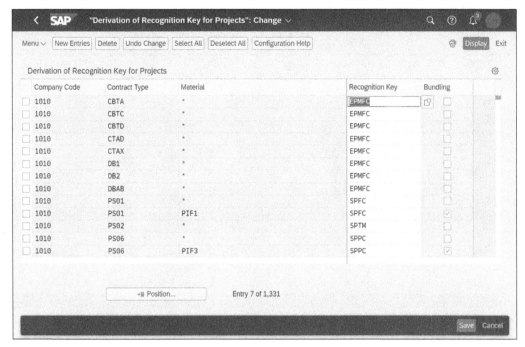

Figure 7.96 Configuration for EBRR Key Derivation

> **Note**
>
> Now let's take a quick look into on-premise SAP S/4HANA, where you have access to the EBRR Customizing tables and can change various controls. You can access the views shown previously and more by following IMG menu path **Controlling • Product Cost Controlling • Cost Object Controlling • Product Cost by Sales Order • Period-End Closing • Event-Based Revenue Recognition**.
>
> We can't discuss all the functionality in detail, but we hope that the configuration we've shown in this section gives you an impression of how flexibly you can control the EBRR functionality.

7.2.8 Positioning and Availability in SAP S/4HANA

EBRR is the most comprehensive revenue recognition solution in the SAP S/4HANA portfolio. In addition to covering the legal revenue recognition requirements, it's also an important part of other financials functionalities such as margin analysis, universal parallel accounting, and predictive analytics.

In SAP S/4HANA Cloud, public edition, EBRR supports—as the only solution—customer project, service order and service contracts, sell-from-stock scenarios, and provider contract scenarios.

In on-premise SAP S/4HANA and SAP S/4HANA Cloud, private edition, EBRR is offered for customer projects and sell-from-stock scenarios. With releases 2022 and 2023, the new service management solution is available, which offers EBRR functionality.

> **Further Resources**
>
> You can get current information about availability and restrictions in SAP Note 2581947.
>
> For more information about EBRR, read *Introducing Event-Based Revenue Recognition (EBRR) with SAP S/4HANA* (SAP PRESS, 2021), which is available at *www.sap-press.com/5679*.

Nevertheless, EBRR is positioned as *the* revenue recognition solution in SAP S/4HANA and as the future successor for results analysis. It's planned to be continuously enhanced on SAP's roadmap.

When we look at on-premise SAP S/4HANA, the EBRR functionality for customer projects looks different because the customer project scenario described in Section 7.1 isn't available. To achieve EBRR functionality in on-premise, several tasks need to be organized by the customer, such as assignment of the sales order item to the billing element, completeness of the billing plan on the sales order item, derivation and storage of the revenue recognition key on the billing element, and complete planned costs on the project for the fixed-price scenario. However, you get all the advantages of the Universal Journal integration, simplified period-end close, and enhanced reporting insights.

7.3   Simplified Period-End Close

To close the chapter, we'll discuss how the period-end close has been heavily simplified. First, let's look at how a period-end schedule could look in SAP ERP to see current project margin reporting.

As you can see in Figure 7.97, traditional customer project analysis could require multiple period-end steps, including user interaction and batch jobs. The steps depend, of course, on the system setup and applied processes. For example, it was necessary to transfer the data between the accounting applications by settlement (revenue recognition data to general ledger and profitability analysis) or to transfer data to the business warehouse for flexible high-performance reporting.

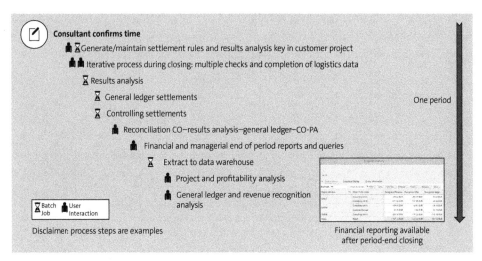

Figure 7.97 Traditional Period-End Close in SAP ERP

In SAP S/4HANA Cloud, these steps are obsolete. As shown earlier in Section 7.1.4, the time confirmation—and every other posting on the customer project—leads immediately to enriched reporting, as shown in Figure 7.98.

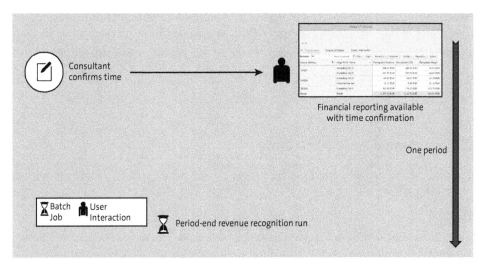

Figure 7.98 Simplified Period-End Close in SAP S/4HANA Cloud

The realized revenue is posted based on the cost posting transaction on the customer project, which enables real-time margin reporting for the customer project. In addition, the market segment attributes incorporated in the Universal Journal provides immediate margin reporting for the market segment. Real-time profitability reporting is possible independent of period-end closing activities.

As mentioned, only one step is necessary at period-end: a revenue recognition run takes events into account that didn't lead to postings during the period (e.g., manual maintenance of estimation to complete/POC, project status change, and sales price condition change).

Let's walk through what has been simplified:

- A settlement in the sense of providing market segment reporting is obsolete because the general ledger line item already includes profitability attributes.
- A settlement of revenue recognition data to the general ledger is obsolete because EBRR already posts in the Universal Journal.
- Because all data is stored in the Universal Journal, there is no reconciliation effort between different data sources, such as P&L, revenue recognition data, and profitability reporting.
- Thanks to SAP HANA, reporting on the general ledger line items is possible, so you can also get reports on all the provided attributes stored in the Universal Journal. Therefore, there is no need to transfer data to a data warehouse or build any aggregated data.
- Traceability has been increased, especially for revenue recognition postings, which helps speed up auditing.
- Additional information can be provided in the financials statement for the general ledger account, which simplifies follow-up activities.

7.4 Summary

In this chapter, you've seen which new approaches are possible in financial accounting based on SAP HANA and the Universal Journal. Bringing together the accounting applications, such as the general ledger, management accounting, profitability, and EBRR into one database creates the potential for completely new reporting insights. The power of the SAP HANA database enables reporting on all Universal Journal dimensions. This and EBRR also simplify period-end closing.

EBRR follows this approach. It's incorporated into the Universal Journal and enables simplified processes with more functionality (real-time matching principle, parallel ledgers, and currencies) and greater transparency (WIP by market segment and links to the original document). It supports up-to-date P&L, profitability reporting, and WIP. In addition to covering legal requirements, EBRR also provides a wide range of management accounting features.

Coordination with the logistical components is a prerequisite for correct, complete, transparent, and timely accounting data. The accountant must focus on the direction of codetermination of the logistical processes. Then, process simplifications and completely new insights are also possible in accounting.

You've now completed your journey through financial accounting in SAP S/4HANA with insight into the direction in which SAP S/4HANA accounting is moving.

The Authors

Jonas Tritschler is a managing director at an IT consulting firm. As a certified accountant and holder of a PhD in accounting, he trains CPAs in SAP for performing financial audits and internal control tests over the preparation of financial statements. In 2020, he became a professor of accounting at the University of Victoria, Berlin.

Jonas is responsible for the audit and evaluation of IT systems and applications, and ensures the security and compliance of applications, especially in the sensitive areas of accounting and finance. In this role, he benefits from his experience as an SAP user, which he gained over many years as interim manager and CFO.

Stefan Walz is chief business process architect for SAP S/4HANA financials at SAP. He has more than 30 years of SAP financials experience through his work in consulting and financials development. He is co-inventor of the Universal Journal-based management accounting and event-based revenue recognition. Today, Stefan is responsible for the process integration of customer projects, service management, and sales into SAP S/4HANA financial accounting.

Reinhard Rupp is a professor of controlling, finance, and accounting. With many years of experience as an auditor and 18 years of experience as a top executive/CFO in various companies, including responsibility for IT/SAP systems, he has a profound understanding of the practical requirements and an eye for the strategic possibilities of the new architecture.

Nertila Mucka is a senior IT auditor at ING, holding a master's degree in information technology and finance and accounting systems. She has six years of experience in reviewing accounting and ERP systems, especially finance and Basis components in SAP for compliance and security purposes. She is a co-teacher for SAP for certified accountants in Germany, and develops automated tools for reviewing settings for the SAP S/4HANA environment.

Index

- Master your core controlling tasks in SAP S/4HANA

- Assess overhead, manufacturing, sales, project, and investment costs

- Streamline your operations with both the new and classic user interfaces

Janet Salmon, Stefan Walz

Controlling with SAP S/4HANA

Business User Guide

SAP S/4HANA brings change to your routine controlling activities. Perform your key tasks in the new environment with this user guide! Get click-by-click instructions for your daily and monthly overhead controlling tasks, and then dive deeper into processes such as make-to-stock/make-to-order scenarios, margin analysis, and investment management. Finally, instructions for inter-company transactions and reporting make this your all-in-one resource!

593 pages, pub. 05/2021
E-Book: $74.99 | **Print:** $79.95 | **Bundle:** $89.99

www.sap-press.com/5282

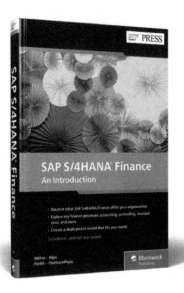

- Discover what SAP S/4HANA Finance offers your organization

- Explore key finance processes: accounting, controlling, financial close, and more

- Choose a deployment model that fits your needs

Mehta, Aijaz, Parikh, Chattopadhyay

SAP S/4HANA Finance

An Introduction

Beginning your finance transformation? Looking to learn what SAP S/4HANA has to offer? This book is your starting point for SAP S/4HANA Finance! Learn about the suite's architecture and explore its capabilities for your core finance processes: financial accounting, management accounting, treasury and risk management, planning, consolidation, and close. Unlock enterprise-wide finance reporting, assess your deployment options, and design your finance project with this introductory guide!

394 pages, 2nd edition, pub. 01/2023
E-Book: $74.99 | **Print:** $79.95 | **Bundle:** $89.99

www.sap-press.com/5606

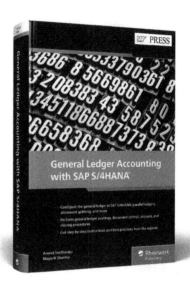

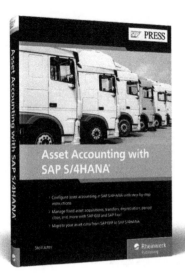

- Configure asset accounting in SAP S/4HANA with step-by-step instructions

- Manage fixed asset acquisitions, transfers, depreciation, period close, and more

- Migrate your asset data from SAP ERP to SAP S/4HANA

Stoil Jotev

Asset Accounting with SAP S/4HANA

Get the details you need to get asset accounting up and running in SAP S/4HANA! Walk through the configuration that underpins all of asset accounting, starting with organizational structures and master data. From there, master key tasks for asset acquisition and retirement, depreciation, year-end close, reporting, and more. Finally, see how to migrate your legacy asset data from SAP ERP to SAP S/4HANA. Covering both user interfaces, this guide has it all!

337 pages, pub. 04/2020
E-Book: $84.99 | **Print:** $89.95 | **Bundle:** $99.99

www.sap-press.com/5028